Science, Money, and Politics

Science, Money, and Politics

Political Triumph and Ethical Erosion

DANIEL S. GREENBERG

The University of Chicago Press
Chicago and London

DANIEL S. GREENBERG is a Washington-based journalist specializing in the politics of science. He has published extensively in professional journals, newspapers, and popular magazines and is the author of a classic work, *The Politics of Pure Science*, published in a new edition in 1999 by the University of Chicago Press. While conducting research for *Science, Money, and Politics*, he held an appointment at Johns Hopkins University as a visiting scholar in the Department of History of Science, Medicine, and Technology.

The University of Chicago Press, Chicago 60637
The University of Chicago Press, Ltd., London
© 2001 by Daniel S. Greenberg
All rights reserved. Published 2001
Printed in the United States of America

10 09 08 07 06 05 04 03 02 01   1 2 3 4 5
ISBN (cloth) 0-226-30634-8

Library of Congress Cataloging-in-Publication Data
Greenberg, Daniel S., 1931–
    Science, money, and politics : political triumph and ethical erosion / Daniel S. Greenberg.
        p. cm.
Includes bibliographical references and index.
    ISBN 0-226-30634-8 (hardcover)
    1. Federal aid to research—United States.   2. Science and state—United States.   I. Title.
    Q180.55.G6 G74 2001
    338.973'06—dc21

                                                      00-013226

For Wanda

Contents

Acknowledgments and a Note on Sources and Methods

COUNT AMONG the wonders and advantages of journalism the willingness of many people to help an inquiring reporter.

Interviews with a long succession of presidential science advisers and many others in science politics and policy were indispensable for writing this book, as is evident from their frequent appearances in the pages that follow. In lengthy interviews, we spoke literally on the record, with my running tape recorder visible nearby. These interviews are identified as such in the text; shorter conversations, recorded in notes, are identified as conversations. On all substantive matters, sources are identified, thus eliminating the deservedly suspect practice of anonymous assertion.

Invaluable guidance on the numerical facts of money and science were patiently provided by John E. Jankowski Jr., head of the research and development statistics program at the National Science Foundation. Staff members and officials in many federal research agencies, the White House and Congress, and scientific societies helped, too, providing me with personal recollections and documents. For examining the interminable controversies over the adequacy of Ph.D. production, Charlotte Kuh, Executive Director of the Office of Scientific and Engineering Personnel at the National Academy of Sciences, was an especially helpful guide. Access to historical materials was provided by the National Archives and Records Administration and the Manuscript Division of the Library of Congress.

The book manuscript, in whole or part, benefited from readings by several knowledgeable observers of science politics, among them, Philip Boffey, former science editor and deputy editorial page editor of the *New York Times*; Skip Stiles, an alumnus of long service on the House Science Committee; and Greg Zachary, a *Wall Street Journal* reporter and biographer of Vannevar Bush.

I am grateful to the Alfred P. Sloan Foundation for a grant that enabled me to concentrate on the book project. In the best tradition of philanthropy, the foundation provided help without hindrance.

I also benefited from the scholarly and friendly atmosphere of the Department of History of Science, Medicine, and Technology at Johns Hopkins University, where I held an appointment as a visiting scholar while researching and writing.

Though all of the above, and others, too, provided valuable assistance, I alone am responsible for any errors, omissions, or other shortcomings in this book.

Introduction

I [dream] that I am Oliver Twist and I tremble as I shuffle down the aisle of the NSF [National Science Foundation] orphanage, my empty soup bowl uplifted. The youngest orphans stare at me. They have no bowls, for they have never received NSF support. . . . Among the throng I spy the shocked and bewildered faces of scientific luminaries, prizewinners, even Nobel laureates. I raise my bowl to the Director and in a trembling voice ask, "Please, sir, one little laser."

"What," he thunders, "You have already had more than your share. Out!"

—Daniel Kleppner, professor of physics, MIT,
"Night Thoughts on the NSF" (*Physics Today*, April 1990)

THIS BOOK is about the politics and finance of science in America from the end of World War II to the turn of the century. It examines and seeks to explain a great and unusual success: the prosperity and autonomy of science, a deliberately nonpolitical enterprise embedded in a political system of rewards for vote gathering and campaign fund-raising. Science prospers on government money, though aloof from these activities. Success, however, came at serious costs to science. Long ago it left the cloistered laboratory to make its claims on resources in the clamor of competitive America. In the process, the veneration and pursuit of growth spawned a supportive, inventive bureaucracy that has eroded the right values of science and transformed it into a clever, well-financed claimant for money, in its own nonpolitical fashion. Without lobbying or manipulative tactics, science would have fared well in post–World War II high-tech America, which recognized the value of science, and provided generous support, even before the evangelists came on duty. However, with persistent lobbying and overwrought alarms of dangerous neglect, science fared even better, though leaving behind shreds of integrity.

The methods of success matter because the American people and their political representatives have trustfully endowed science with generous resources and considerable independence in their use. This book is in large part concerned with misuse of that confidence: in acquiring support and in the conduct of research, from the quest for medical knowledge to the deepest depths of the atom. Far-fetched claims of cures and industrial "spin-offs" that never arrive, baseless warnings of foreign scientific supremacy, contrived allegations of public hostility to science—these are matters we will study.

We will devote considerable attention to money, because the politics of science is registered in money awarded or denied. Statistics about money infest the politics of science, and, though tiresome to the outsiders of science, cannot be ignored. (The financial details are provided in an appendix of tables.) Money will serve as a diagnostic tool for our study. The *apparatchiks* of science policy dote on research statistics. Expensive conferences, artful publications, and long, rewarding careers are devoted to tracking and parsing the percentage of gross domestic product, the share of discretionary federal spending expended on this or that kind of science, in comparison to the practices of other nations and prior years. These matters may be important; our interest, however, is not in the arithmetic of support for science but in the political use that is made of the numbers.

This is not a work of reverence, as are many books about science, even in this age of irreverence. Rather, after forty years of reporting and writing about science politics, my aim is to share what I have seen, like a traveler returned from a strange land, which is how I still regard the scientific enterprise. In a narrow but important respect, the enterprise can be likened to another institution, religion—in the sense that true believers are fervent in their faith, and uncomfortable with or even hostile to external scrutiny; outsiders, at least in tolerant lands, politely refrain from critical inquiry and commentary that might be regarded as disrespectful. The central theme of this book is that science in the American polity is well supported and respected, despite its habitual assertions of neglect and hostility, but its most influential institutions are underscrutinized by other sectors of society. In a ghetto of its own, science is voluntarily, safely walled off, thriving aloof from conventional politics, with little critical press observation or effective public accountability. The reigning institutions of science have eluded scrutiny by successfully arguing the necessity of self-governance if science is to produce the benefits that it alone can furnish to society. We will follow the historical path to this unusual status.

Since World War II, America's scientists have received a great deal of money, public and private, and have used it to build the world's greatest enterprise for scientific discovery. They have successfully pleaded the cause of support, autonomy, and minimal, if any, accountability in science. The position they occupy in politics and society is privileged and unique. And they have used it well to produce knowledge.

ETHICAL CONCERNS

However, success in the politics of science has been accompanied by ethical doubts and contention. Failings in openness, collegiality, respect for human and animal experimental subjects, and scientific and financial integrity are common topics in scientific journals and on a thriving conference circuit. The hand-wringing, arguments, and recriminations go on, within and beyond the boundaries of science. But ethical concerns are a sideshow of science, providing grist for the press and moralizing politicians, though with little actual effect on the conduct of the research enterprise. Within science, the ethical issues are overshadowed by material concerns. These concerns consume more energy than any attempts to rectify ethical shortcomings. More money for more science is the commanding passion of the politics of science. More is deemed better, including the production of more scientists from a university system that is well supported by, but ingeniously decoupled from, the general economy. Even in these prosperous times, young Ph.D. graduates, once hopeful but now often embittered, stack up in low-wage postdoctoral holding patterns. The growing corporate presence in science arouses unease—as did the military presence, huge and pervasive during the Cold War but now receded, and, strangely enough, mourned in academic quarters for the loss of its money. Nonetheless, the courtship between university-based science and industry persistently intensifies, with academe often the suitor, in single-minded pursuit of more money for science.

Some findings here differ from prevalent beliefs, popular and scholarly, about relations between science and society. Despite its ethical angst and shortcomings, science today is only a short way down the path to becoming a toady of corporate power. Disturbing evidence is plentiful for concern about the ethical costs of science's single-minded pursuit of money. But reasons for hope exist in the writhings of conscience much in evidence in scientific circles. In making this point, it is not my intent to glorify the scientific enterprise or its cast of leaders as exemplars of independence and social responsibility. Rather, it is necessary to recognize that, as relations between science and society evolved over the postwar years, government, military, and corporate power found it beneficial to accommodate the sciences' strong desire for intellectual liberty. Politicians, generals, and CEOs by and large proceed—though not always—from the belief that science unfettered works better for them. This belief is receding as corporate financiers of research, and scientists themselves, fence off and seek to profit from types of basic knowledge previously regarded as in the public domain. The situation has always been different in technology, where purpose and defined goals reign in the government's civilian and military laboratories and their profit-seeking corporate counterparts.[1]

In academic science, despite rhetoric to the contrary, laissez-faire remains strong, even as scientists become more entangled with corporate money and restrictions. In return for public money for research, politicians demand "strategic plans" from science. In response, federal accountability rules of one sort or another are intermittently proposed, and sometimes implemented, in endless but vain efforts—akin to trying to capture and weigh a fog—to quantify value from government spending on research. Science, however, continues remarkably free to pick its goals and methods, though its ceaseless grousing about government intrusions and neglect and societal hostility and ignorance creates a counterimpression.

SCIENTISTS AND POLITICS

We will also search for the power and influence of scientists in national politics and policymaking. Events have not confirmed the often-repeated, ominous prophecies of scientists illicitly worming their way into political power by dominating crucial technical decisions. Curiously, scientists today are largely missing in action from American politics and public affairs beyond the clear boundaries of science. On the national political landscape, science has settled into its own territory, a scientific ghetto that we will examine in detail. On those rare occasions when scientists attempt to expand their influence into political affairs, they encounter strong, effective resistance from conventional politics. The impression of a scientific pres-

---

1. The similarities and differences between science and technology, and their relationship, have spawned long-running definitional disputes, with the current fashion favoring a blurring or rejection of a distinction between basic and applied research. The late Donald E. Stokes made a persuasive case for the holistic approach in *Pasteur's Quadrant: Basic Science and Technological Innovation* (Washington, D.C.: Brookings Institution Press, 1997). Here, we proceed from the recognition that science and technology differ at their extremes: the former seeks knowledge, the latter seeks to incorporate knowledge into an object or process. But often, too, they overlap, invigorate each other, and in many instances, as Stokes demonstrates, cannot be separated.

ence in politics is a leftover from Cold War days when scientists were summoned to the high councils of government to provide advice on the creation and control of new weapons. From that privileged base, their influence spread for a time, and then receded. Scientists in public office, or exerting influence offstage in matters beyond their direct professional cares, are actually rare. Scientists interested in attaining political goals generally find themselves frustrated by Washington. Advanced scientific training is astonishingly rare among elected officials at all levels of government; few professional scientists move on to appointive positions outside the government agencies that manage and support scientific work.

BEYOND THE SCIENCE ESTABLISHMENT

In a previous book, *The Politics of Pure Science* (New American Library, 1967; published in a new edition by the University of Chicago Press, 1999), I described the World War II beginnings and early postwar development of the relationship between science and government in the United States and the role played by what was then an easily delineated scientific "establishment." The establishment initially consisted of a handful of institutions and scientists who became "political scientists" through their World War II accomplishments. By the 1970s, "establishment" still referred to a fairly small cast of scientists who could influence the money tap in Washington or at least easily deliver their messages to the reigning politicians. At the institutional core, count among them the elite National Academy of Sciences, chartered by Congress in 1863 as an honorary body and adviser to the government;[2] the American Association for the Advancement of Science, open to all comers, and noted mainly as the publisher of the weekly *Science* (an eminent journal of original scientific papers and science-policy news and discussion); the White House Office of Science and Technology Policy, home base of the president's science adviser; and the House Science Committee (the latter two under varying titles over the years). Add in the Defense Science Board, the senior science and technology advisory body in the Pentagon, and a few budding lobbies for academic science, and there was the "establishment." But that was long ago, in the early days of creation. Since that time, research expenditures and activities have grown

---

2. At the end of the twentieth century, the venerable NAS rechristened itself as the National Academies, a simplified title that conveniently accommodates the other organizations under its umbrella: the National Academy of Engineering, the Institute of Medicine, and the National Research Council. As most of the events discussed in this book occurred prior to the name change, we will abide by the old titles.

manyfold, the institutional and individual casts have expanded greatly, and a sprawling, dense network of relationships has evolved among universities, government agencies, Congress and the White House, scientific and professional societies, and industry and business. The institutions of the original establishment survive and retain influence, but now share it with others who hold, or claim, stakes in science. Because of these changes in the topography and economics of science, the term "establishment" has lost its cogency. A different term is needed for what we will explore: let's call it the scientific *enterprise,* a large and amorphous collection of activities and interests bound by many common characteristics, but not among them a tightknit, small group that decisively governs its important affairs.

SELLING SCIENCE

Several themes run through this book. One is that the politics of science is not laden with the dispassionate objectivity traditionally associated with the conduct of scientific research. Like generals pleading for new weapons, or highway contractors pining to pour concrete, many of the politicians of science employ the hard sell and a stretched tale or two to make their way in the competition for money, public and private. Another of this book's themes is the durability of self-serving political myths and fables of science, each usually containing a trace of reality sufficient to suggest plausibility. Among the sophisticates of science, we will encounter examples of the "magical thinking" characteristic of primitive societies: belief in nonexistent cause-and-effect relationships in politics, and reveries for a paradisiacal "golden age" in government support for science and the volume of money for research.

The 1990s—the first post–Cold War decade—were particularly trying for the sector of the scientific enterprise dependent on government money. In their anxiety-filled understanding of politics, the leaders of science saw fear of the Soviet Union as the principal motivation for Washington's spending on research. Suddenly, the USSR was gone, and they were convinced that financial disaster loomed. It did not occur. Little actually changed in the financial fortunes of science, which continued on an upward path. Nonetheless, the alleged retreat of the U.S. government from the financing of science came to be accepted, among scientists and in the popular press, as an established matter of fact. In reality, in the final decade of the last century a record volume of government money surged into science—to the accompaniment of intensified lobbying by science, in its own special fashion for influencing politics. Did the campaign for money, with its warnings of national peril in trimming science budgets, turn the tide? Undoubtedly, it had some effect, thus encouraging science to even more muscular efforts in Washington. But the proclamations of budget-cutting intentions were of questionable power against the great government-financed scientific enterprise that had risen on the American landscape over the preceding half century. The political and financial triumph of science confounded the antideficit crusade and the antigovernment Republican Revolution. By virtually every relevant measure, the United States leads the world in the financing, quality, and volume of research; it has held this lead since the end of World War II, and appears bound to maintain, and increase, its supremacy far into the new century.

SCIENCE WITHOUT THE COLD WAR

The Cold War's influence on science funding declined substantially a decade or more before the end of the Cold War; it was replaced by other motivations, principally faith in research for industrial competitiveness, good health, a clean environment, and other important, widely endorsed social and economic purposes. Government support of science has increased substantially since the demise of the Soviet Union; in recent years, the increase in some sectors, especially medical research, has accelerated. But overall, the rise is insufficient to underwrite all the aspirations of our scientists and the institutions that employ them. The system possesses a metabolism that assures that more is never enough.

The existence of a pervasive public hostility to science is another fabricated demon of the scientific enterprise, though an abundance of evidence indicates that the public is very favorably disposed toward science, and is committed to its support—otherwise, how could it be so well supported? Closely related to the hostility alarms is the contention that mass ignorance of science threatens public support of research. Such ignorance should be corrected, but not for the specious reason that it undermines support of science. In fact, no relationship is evident between public understanding of science and government spending on science. Nonetheless, from contrived alarms about the political menace of ignorance, the scientific enterprise has developed a thriving offshoot devoted to improving the public understanding of science. Like the race-track rabbit, however, the goal remains forever ahead, thus inspiring, from the public-understanding bureaucracy, earnest pleas for even greater support of its vital work.

But Does It Matter?

Finally, we must consider why these matters deserve our attention; after all, the scientific enterprise is productive, irrespective of its detachment from conventional politics, ahistorical beliefs, cultural mythologies, and undainty tactics in pursuit of money. Attention is warranted because science has effectively insulated itself against independent scrutiny by its political paymasters and, in turn, the public. A gullible press routinely proclaims the success stories of science—principally lay-language "translations" of reports from leading research journals, which, by the nature of scientific publication, ensure that the majority of science news is good news: news of cures; clues to the origin or prevention of disease; new products, processes, and gadgets; and fascinating views from deep space. Scientists rarely write papers about their failures in the laboratory or the clinic, especially when testing pills for the pharmaceutical industry. The less-welcome consequences of scientific and technical developments, typically a drug side effect or an environmental hazard, are also extensively reported when public danger is attributed to them; the press is receptive to nasty news about science-related matters, from nuclear accidents to fraud in the laboratory. But little or no attention is given to the genesis of scientific and technical developments or the detachment and avoidance of responsibility of their creators in politics and science. In its style of fecundity, science leaves the baby on the public doorstep and returns to the laboratory. It may be countered that the scientific enterprise acknowledges this behavior, and in response, for example, the government's Human Genome Project allocates up to 5 percent of its funds for ethical, legal, and social studies. Thus is provided a bonanza for financially parched fields of academic scholarship. But the Genome Project, and associated clinical trials in gene therapy, vigorously proceeds on a wild-west frontier of science that has already killed a few trusting patients in experimental pursuit of scientific glory and biotech profits.

The Illusion of Scrutiny

Researchers and the managers of government-financed research periodically appear before congressional committees to report accomplishments and aspirations. In prior times, they encountered some skepticism, sometimes uninformed skepticism but nonetheless enough to establish that popular and political approval was not a given for science. Thus, the legislation that created the National Science Foundation after World War II was the product of five years of deep inquiry and ideological strife over the appropriate role of government in the support of science. In the late 1960s and early 1970s, proposals to declare the so-called war on cancer evoked a serious debate that exposed the faulty wisdom of the proposed Manhattan Project assault on the disease. But as science grew and acquired political sophistication and economic importance, its relations with Congress evolved, or deteriorated, into exchanges of affection. In a stylized political format that has prevailed for at least the past two decades, scientists praise the leadership of the legislators who provide them with money; the legislators declare their reverence for science, the sole beneficiary of federal support that costs no votes. Very rarely a convulsion of congressional resistance occurs, such as the abrupt termination of the multibillion-dollar Superconducting Super Collider in 1993, a turnabout inspired by brazen misrepresentation of soaring costs in a period of government retrenchment. The norm of congressional surveillance, however, is the International Space Station: repeatedly condemned over a decade of congressional hearings as an extravagance of marginal scientific and technical value, it nonetheless survives on the political strength of its aerospace industrial backers.

Science is a vote winner, not only because it advances knowledge and benefits humanity, as supportive legislators regularly proclaim. Science also wins votes because it brings large sums of federal money to research facilities and programs throughout the country. Legislators from districts heavy with federal grants and research facilities are primarily concerned with at least preserving, but better yet, expanding, the good fortune of their constituents. Those whose areas have been left out either support science spending as a means of eventually getting a share or devote little attention to research issues. Overall, the politics of science is governed by an autonomic acceptance of the value of science, by Democrats and Republicans alike, a bipartisan abdication of responsibility accorded to no other activity, not even defense.

The infrequency of searching questions about scientific programs is often attributed to the paucity of scientific training among politicians. A poor grasp of science does account for some of the cringing, the genuflecting timidity, and inflated expressions of reverence that legislators bestow upon the scientists who come before them. But the commonly offered expressions of respect for science are not solely a product of legislators' sparse academic credits in college science courses. Ignore the stereotypes. Members of Congress are by and large intelligent high-achievers. Moreover, they can, and do, command any professional expertise they desire, in their full-time staff assistants, Congress's own research agencies, specialists on loan from federal agencies, and consultants from academe, professional socie-ties, and industry. The difficulty in the way of legislative inquiry is that those who ask inconvenient questions about scientific programs or the fi-nancing of research risk the shame of being branded enemies of scientific enlightenment. Senator William Proxmire's "Golden Fleece Awards" gained national attention for the otherwise drab Wisconsin legislator by ridiculing seemingly wasteful government projects, including several sponsored by federal research agencies. However, by the time Proxmire retired from the Senate in 1989, his scientific awards had deservedly acquired the stigma of boorish taste. Science was tacitly declared out-of-bounds for ridicule by legislative buffoons. But along with that desirable turn of events, science was also tacitly declared out-of-bounds for serious scrutiny of its objectives, values, and goals.

Outside inquiry was not welcome, though like other minorities that feel beleaguered, science relishes internal deprecations that would be con-sidered blasphemous from outsiders. For nearly half a century, scientists have ridiculed their foibles in the *Journal of Irreproducible Results* and more recently in the annual award of "Ig Nobel Prizes" by the publisher of the *Annals of Improbable Research*. This is in-group humor—in friendly hands, safely under control. It is not lack of scientific understanding that forestalls fruitful inquiry into science. Rather, except on rare occasions, and we will examine several, the will for such inquiry has been neutralized by a combi-nation of scientific browbeating and suave assurances that all is well—ex-cept, of course, for insufficient public finance. When Congress or the press wishes to penetrate the fog, the task can be accomplished, to the benefit of science, society, and politics.

This book does not attempt to assess research strategies, or to rate the scientific value of particular projects and their findings. Rather, the ap-proach is to illuminate the constricted processes of review and evaluation that politics applies to science, in large part because of the extensive success of the scientific leadership in repelling closer examination. Could science serve us better? Does it ignore important opportunities for the advancement of knowledge and the betterment of humankind? Probably so on both points. But, in general, we don't know, the reason being that the questions are unwelcome and close examinations have not taken place.

So much for a broad explanation of why these topics rate scrutiny. Now to an amorphous topic that's difficult to explore, but extremely impor-tant—namely, the soul of science. The retreat from politics, the aging into caution-bound institutional maturity, the competition for survival and growth, and the ensuing ravenous quests for money have left their marks on modern science. These money-seeking tactics have raised doubts and alarms within the ranks of science itself. In a world increasingly dependent upon knowledge beyond the comprehension of all but a few, can the few be trusted when the pursuit of money increasingly takes precedence in their working lives? In the interlocking realms of public science and profit-seeking private science, who represents the public? These are the issues roiling the politics of science at the beginning of the new millennium.

A Personal Background Note

This book is the product of two years of focused research and writing appended to nearly forty years of journalistic immersion in the politics of science. In 1961, I joined the newborn News and Comment section of *Science,* the journal of the American Association for the Advancement of Science, following three years as a reporter on the *Washington Post* and a year on Capitol Hill as a congressional fellow of the American Political Science Association. As the first news editor of *Science,* I presided over a rapid expansion of the reporting staff and the coverage of science-policy news. After a decade of reporting science politics for *Science,* including two years based in London as the journal's European correspondent, I cast off and founded my own publication, *Science & Government Report* (*SGR*), a twice-monthly newsletter that I wrote and published from 1971 to 1997 (when it was acquired by John Wiley & Sons). Situated outside the scientific enterprise, *SGR* provided me with an independent perch to observe and write freely about science politics. *SGR* quickly developed a devoted readership in the United States and abroad. Along the way, I have also written about science policy and politics for other publications, including the *Washington Post,* the *New York Times,* the *New England Journal of Medicine, The Lancet, Nature,* and *New Scientist;* my prior book, *The Politics of Pure Science,* was initially published in 1967 and reissued several times, most recently in 1999 by the University of Chicago Press. The background for the present book is those many years of reporting and innumerable conversations, ranging from long tape-recorded interviews to brief telephone chats, with the political leaders of American science and government administrators and elected officials concerned with research.

How We Will Proceed

This rendition of science politics does not employ a chronological format, nor does it concentrate on legislative battles or the evolution of particular research programs. These are worthy approaches, successfully employed in the literature of science politics. There is no need, however, for another step-by-step account of the origin, development, benefits, and difficulties of the extensive relationship between the federal government and the research enterprise. Our approach is thematic—we will explore the politics of science by examining beliefs, vulnerabilities, social and political characteristics, goals, and revealing episodes in the relationship between science and politics. The road map is as follows:

Chapter 1, "The Metropolis of Science," delineates the scientific enterprise, establishing its whereabouts on the American landscape, in its various institutional settings, in academe, government, and industry. Chapter 2, "The Ossified Enterprise," examines an important but generally overlooked characteristic of the enterprise: the institutional rigidity of American science in its maturity and aversion to risk and change.

Chapter 3, "Vannevar Bush and the Myth of Creation," demonstrates the prevalence of myth in the belief systems of science, as manifested in the worship of Vannevar Bush as the architect of the postwar relationship between science and government. Chapter 4, "The Glorious Past," records another myth, in the nostalgic lamentations by leaders of science for a "golden age" of science, of doubtful reality.

Chapter 5, "The Whimpering Giant," explores the sciences' persistent allegations of public neglect and hostility, in the face of public beneficence and approval. Chapter 6, "Money, More Money, Statistics, and Science," traces the postwar record of money for research, as the billions mounted, amid complaints that more was never enough.

Chapter 7, "The Malthusian Imperative and the Politics of Trust," examines the reproductive impulse in science and its contribution to disequilibrium in the economy of science through the relentless production of doctoral degrees without regard to their employability. Chapter 8, "Ph.D. Production: Shortfall, Scarcity, and Shortage," relates the embarrassing tale of an effort by the National Science Foundation to manufacture a shortage of doctoral degrees. Chapter 9, "The Congressional Griddle," describes the skeptical congressional inquiry into the Ph.D.-production ploy and a host of revealing memoranda disgorged by Congress's investigative authority.

Chapter 10, "Detour into Politics," tells of a nearly forgotten episode in the political life of American science: a large-scale, organized scientific participation in a presidential campaign, and the morning-after regrets by scientists who took part. Chapter 11, "Nixon Banishes the Scientists," relates the repeated collisions between Richard Nixon and scientists who served in his White House, and beyond, and his abrupt abolition of the central scientific presence in Washington, the White House Office of Science and Technology. Chapter 12, "The Sciences' Way of Politicking," describes the many well-financed lobbying organizations that are based in Washington for acquiring public money for research, and chronicles the tactics they employ.

Chapter 13, "The Public Understanding of Science," is concerned with publicly financed efforts that sustain a bureaucracy that thrives on alarming reports of public ignorance of science. Chapter 14, "The TV Solution," tells of a proposed TV science dramatic series that, fortunately for science, never aired.

Chapter 15, "Science and the Illusion of Political Power," charts a rarely commented-on fact of American political life: the virtual absence of scientists from elective office and politics, contrary to early postwar prophecies of a coming age of scientists in political power. Chapter 16, "The Political Few," traces the political odysseys of the very small number of scientists in contemporary politics and examines the factors that deter scientists from pursuing political participation. And chapter 17, "The Scientific Ghetto," goes beyond the dearth of scientists in politics to demonstrate the actual withdrawal of science from public affairs and political participation.

Chapter 18, "Connecting to Politics," tells of the loyalist style of relations with politics adopted by science after the trauma of Richard Nixon's abolition of their high place in government. Chapter 19, "Politicking by Report," describes the apolitical techniques developed by the scientific leadership for promoting government support of science, without risking the perils of elective politics. Chapter 20, "Science to the State Department: You Need Us," presents the woeful tale of efforts, over four decades, to implant scientific advice in the State Department.

Chapter 21, "From Social and Political Passion to Grubbing for Money," correlates the decline of external concerns and the accompanying rise and dominance of the quest for money as a preoccupation of the politics of science. Chapter 22, "The Ethical Erosion of Science," provides a survey of scientific misbehavior in the gold rush on the endless frontier.

Chapter 23, "Post–Cold War Chills," describes fright that spread through the scientific enterprise when the Cold War ended and seemed to take with it the major motivation for government support of science. Chapter 24, "What Future for the National Science Foundation?" offers a case study demonstrating how the champions of basic research, in science and in politics, triumphed over demands for a utilitarian strategy in government support of science.

Chapter 25, "Clinton, Atom Smashing, and Space" describes the sciences' fears of financial catastrophe under the newly inaugurated Clinton administration. Chapter 26, "Caught between Clinton and Congress," extends the tale of financial fright, particularly as it affected the National Institutes of Health. Chapter 27, "Science versus the Budget Cutters," details the confrontation between the research enterprise and the Republican Revolution.

Chapter 28, "The Political Triumph of Science," brings our tale of science and politics to its new millennium conclusion. And finally, the epilogue presents a case for prodding science into the rough waters of the political mainstream.

CHAPTER 1

The Metropolis of Science

> There is something like a Parkinson's Law that scientific activity will
> grow to meet any set budget and find it to be grossly inadequate.
> It is in the very nature of science that new discoveries open new
> fields of further activity. It is like climbing a mountain peak and
> seeing new landscapes not visible in the valley.
>
> —I. I. Rabi, Nobel laureate in physics,
> address to the Israel Institute of Technology, 1963

THE WORKPLACES and practitioners of research
are now so abundant and so widely dispersed throughout modern America that the familiar terms "scientific community" and "establishment,"
though convenient and widely used, reflect the cohesion, isolation and
smaller scale of a bygone era. Moreover, during the postwar decades, the
entanglements between basic and other types of research, and relations
among the institutions in which they are performed, have become so extensive that it would be incorrect to assume the existence of a clearly definable
community. Basic research once existed as a distinct entity, situated almost
wholly in universities, freestanding philanthropically financed research institutes, and a few elite corporate and government laboratories. But in recent years, government has used its financial and regulatory powers to encourage, often with strong incentives, collaborative relations among basic
researchers in universities, the government's own laboratories, and industrial organizations. Under the Bayh-Dole Act of 1980, universities, small
businesses, and some contractors running government laboratories received the right to patent the results of federally financed research; the lure
of government money was thus enhanced by the possibility of postproject
royalties. In 1987, President Reagan extended the provision to large business firms. The National Science Foundation makes money available to universities for collaborations with industry, an enticement for universities to
search for corporate partners. Industry, aiming to find profit in research

distant from immediate commercial application, has on its own initiative expanded its relations with universities and federal laboratories. Between 1992 and 1997, industrial support for research in universities rose from $1.3 billion to $1.71 billion—7.1 percent of all research spending in university facilities.[1] The industrial money is a small percentage of the total expenditures for academic research, and the growth of industrial funding for universities has tapered off in recent years. But industrial money is a particularly enticing kind of money for universities. As a relatively unexploited source of support in the harshly competitive business of academic fund-raising, it inspires high hopes and aggressive tactics to get some, or more. Many universities, desiring new sources of revenue, chase industrial research partnerships without prompting from Washington. In conjunction with this quest, they are increasingly attentive to the potential of royalties from discoveries in campus laboratories. This pursuit has broadened a career path for lawyers, as university patent attorneys; it has spawned its own professional society, the Association of University Technology Managers. In 1997, according to the association, gross income for universities from licenses and options reached a record high of $591 million, an increase of nearly 20 percent since 1995.[2] That's a minor amount when measured against the $25 billion expended on university research of all types in 1998 by the federal and state governments, private foundations, and the universities themselves.[3] But large shares of the royalty income were concentrated in a small number of universities, where they often exceeded 10 or 15 percent of total expenditures for research. In 1996, for example, Stanford University spent $395.4 million on research and received $43.7 million in gross licensing income. The comparable figures for Columbia University were $231.6 million in expenditures and $40.6 million in gross income, and for Michigan State University, $139.8 million and $17.2 million. Licensing income, however, lagged far behind these plump figures in other well-known universities. Harvard University, for example, reported $347 million in research and only $7.6 million in licensing income, and Ohio State University $207.7 million for research and $1 million in income. For many financially hard-pressed university administrators, the large licensing fees collected by a few institutions are an inspiration to get in on the game of wringing revenues from science through commercial transactions with industry.

1. *Industrial Research and Development Facts* (Washington, D.C.: Industrial Research Institute, 1997).
2. *AUTM Licensing Survey: Fiscal 1996*, p. 2.
3. *National Patterns of R&D Resources, 1998* (NSF-99-335), p. 8.

The boundaries between academic science and commerce are also blurred by the money-making opportunities created by the dynamic pace of modern research. In biotechnology, electronics, materials, and other fields, the intervals between discovery and commercial application have greatly diminished, thus drawing universities and industry into closer relationships. Academe, however, writhes with ethical concerns about the propriety of its expanding links with industrial mammon, which can be accompanied by restrictions on publication of scientific findings and skewing of academic programs toward industrial interests.

Pained assessments, while increasingly heard, are disputed by many university administrators, researchers, and industrial managers. They insist that academic-industrial collaboration can be structured for the benefit of both parties, without endangering traditional educational values and the principles of scientific collaboration and openness. Perhaps. But during the 1990s, ethical agonizing about the growing presence of commercial values in university laboratories rose from a distant whisper to an unavoidable din in the scientific enterprise. In May 2000, Harvard University, following a two-year study, reaffirmed its limitations on commercial involvements by its faculty members, limiting outside employment to 20 percent of work time and prohibiting stock holdings of more than $20,000 in firms financing research in their laboratories. Though similar rules exist at other universities, they are often winked at; while at some institutions, it's open season on outside financial ties.

THE WORKFORCE AND ITS LOCALES

For the nearly 3.2 million people with bachelor's or advanced degrees employed in 1995 in occupations categorized by the National Science Foundation as "science or engineering," there is no single community.[4] Rather, the nation's scientific and technical enterprises are akin to a major metro-

---

4. Accurate data on science and engineering (S&E) employment in the complex American economy are elusive. In addition to reporting nearly 3.2 million S&E degree holders employed in 1995 in "a science or engineering occupation," NSF also notes that another 4.7 million S&E degree holders were employed in "non-S&E occupations." In the latter group, however, NSF found that four-fifths of those whose highest degrees were a master or doctorate and three-fifths with only bachelor degrees "reported that their job was closely related to their degree." The official occupational count lists 1.2 million engineers, 446,000 computer and mathematical scientists, 297,000 life scientists, 312,000 physical scientists, 384,000 social scientists, and 550,800 in "non-S&E fields." *Data Brief, 1998* (NSF 98-325).

politan area that sprawls beyond the irregular boundaries of its core city. At the center are the traditional institutions of science: some two hundred Ph.D.-granting universities, of which perhaps fifty are major-league science centers, and about seven hundred laboratories of the federal government, ranging from small research units of the National Forest Service to the great research centers of the Department of Energy and the National Institutes of Health, with thousands of staff scientists and budgets each of a billion dollars or more. At the core, too, are elite corporate laboratories that bridge basic science and advanced technology, few in number but professionally close to academe and increasingly so. The core of the metropolis of science includes the money-dispensing federal research agencies and the advisory bodies that link science and government; the professional societies that foster individual scientific disciplines; the multidisciplinary organizations, such as the elite National Academy of Sciences and the open-to-all American Association for the Advancement of Science; and the professional journals that publish research and news of science.

Beyond the core are federal, state, and local agencies, in public health, environmental safety, law enforcement, transportation, and other public-sector functions, that rely on sophisticated technology for fulfilling their responsibilities; and, increasingly, research universities function as the centerpieces of state and regional undertakings to promote innovation and the creation of high-tech employment. The dream is to emulate the productive academic-industrial couplings of Stanford University and Silicon Valley, MIT-Harvard and Route 128 (in its boom period), and North Carolina's Research Triangle Park and the surrounding universities.

In ways that are not yet clearly defined, many of these institutions are melding with the new information economy and the associated software and dot-com industries. But a kind of self-segregation still prevails in science politics, with the pre-Internet veterans of Washington committee rooms, and the system in which they politick, showing remarkable durability, while the Silicon Valley elite and their professional brethren concentrate on making money. Until recently, the cyber chieftains deliberately avoided politics and its Washington manifestations. However, the Microsoft antitrust case demonstrated that Washington cannot be ignored. The corporate wizards of the new economy have responded by signing up old-fashioned Washington lobbyists and contributing heavily to both political parties, rather than by knocking on the doors of old-fashioned science politics. Little changed in style over many decades, those politics still dispose of billions of dollars of government money for research.

The Cast of Science Politics

Thousands of scientists perform the housekeeping chores of the research enterprise, serving, for example, on committees that evaluate grant applications and that advise Washington on emerging fields of research; others assist regulatory agencies with technical advice concerning pharmaceutical drugs and environmental issues. Thousands more stick to their work in the laboratory, aloof from the inner sanctums of policy, politics, and decision making in the capital city. At the interface of science and politics, the cast is small, perhaps two hundred in all. Participatory roles in science politics come ex officio with particular jobs in the federal research hierarchy, Congress, and in the nongovernmental infrastructure of the scientific enterprise. Certain positions come with preordained political roles. Thus, the senior science official in the U.S. government, the president's science adviser, serves as a link between science, especially university-based science, and real politics. The academic emphasis in that role comes by default: industry mainly looks after itself in scientific matters, though it often deals with the president's assistant for science and technology on issues of industrial-government cooperation in research; the government's own science agencies cultivate congressional ties for their political well-being. For academic science, the scientist in the White House is a special friend—and, with rare exception throughout the postwar decades, the scientist in the service of the president is a career academic. The directors of the two federal mainstays of academic science, the National Institutes of Health and the National Science Foundation, customarily feign political chastity. But in annually presiding over the distribution of billions of congressionally appropriated dollars, while always seeking more, they must be attentive to power and influence in Washington and its extensions nationally. The director of NIH prudently refrains from battles over right-wing restrictions on fetal research, and the director of NSF wisely supports special programs to assist backward states in raising their capacity to compete for research funds from the elitist agency. The administrator of NASA, whatever his professional background, is necessarily and primarily a politician, managing the warring tribes of aerospace in doling out shares for the space station, planetary exploration, commercial technology, aeronautics, and academic programs.

The president of the National Academy of Sciences, an organization close to but officially separate from the federal government, occupies an assured place in the politics of science, whether or not he (since its founding in 1863, it has always been a he in the overwhelmingly male Academy) is suited by temperament and experience for science politics at the national level. The Academy looms large in government scientific and technical affairs principally because of its cultivated reputation as a provider of untainted, expert scientific and technical advice for federal agencies and Congress. From 1981 to 1993, the Academy presidency was filled by Frank Press, a distinguished geophysicist, long steeped in Washington affairs as a part-time White House adviser and, from 1977 to 1981, as President Carter's special assistant for science and technology. Press knew his way around Washington, and, notably, virtually alone among the science mandarins, cautioned against demanding a blank check for science—not because he felt it was undeserved but because it wouldn't sell politically, he warned his clamoring colleagues. In 1993, when Press completed the two-term maximum for an Academy president, the elders of the institution opted for a political virgin, choosing as his successor an outstanding molecular biologist, Bruce Alberts, of the University of California, San Francisco. After repeatedly declining, Alberts was ultimately persuaded to accept nomination for the presidency, with his election assured by the Academy's Stalinist tradition of one-candidate ballots. Upon taking office, Alberts boasted that he knew nothing about Washington or politics; his consuming interest, he declared, was the improvement of precollege science education. Nevertheless, Academy President Alberts, by virtue of his office, was unavoidably drawn into the politics of science.

Mixed in with the ex officio participants are volunteers from the scientific enterprise who appear to relish science politics, often from a taste of it in a prior official capacity. Their motivations may vary, from personal glory-seeking to the performance of good works in the public interest. These volunteer politicians of science, joined by similarly inclined engineers, educators, and high-tech corporate executives, stimulate one another by voicing and endorsing arguments for politics to pay more attention to science and scientists. Count among them H. Guyford Stever, renowned as a work-horse committeeman in the decades following his service as director of the National Science Foundation under Richard Nixon and then as President Ford's special assistant for science and technology; Richard Garwin, a career-long IBM physicist, esteemed by peers as stunningly brilliant and recognized as a tireless arms-control advocate and White House adviser through many presidential administrations; Leon Lederman, Nobel laureate in physics, irrepressible evangelist of science education and the public understanding of science, and advocate of open-ended federal financial support for science; D. Allan Bromley, White House science adviser under

George Bush, and before and after, professor of physics at Yale, and president, post–White House, of several leading national scientific societies; Edward E. David Jr., a durable figure in science politics for decades after emerging unscathed from thankless service as science adviser to President Richard Nixon; David Hamburg, a psychiatrist who headed the Institute of Medicine, the health-policy arm of the National Academy of Sciences, before becoming the president of the philanthropic, bountifully endowed Carnegie Corporation; Maxine Singer, president of the Carnegie Institution of Washington, one of the very few women prominent in the politics of science; Robert M. White, who, as president of the National Academy of Engineering from 1983 to 1995, publicly chastised his scientific colleagues for their unceasing demands for more government money; John A. Young, cochair of the President's Committee of Advisors for Science and Technology under President Clinton, former president of Hewlett-Packard, and founding chair of the Council on Competitiveness, a creation of high-tech industries and big-league academe united in support of government research spending; Erich Bloch, former IBM computer engineer and research executive, who, after six years as director of the National Science Foundation under President Reagan, proselytized for science as a distinguished fellow of the Council on Competitiveness; Roland W. Schmitt, a GE research executive, university president and ubiquitous committeeman; Lewis Branscomb, who went from director of the National Bureau of Standards to chief scientist of IBM and then to head of the Science, Technology, and Public Policy Program at Harvard's Kennedy School of Government.

The aforementioned were among the relatively few eminent citizens and allied neighbors of the scientific community active to greater or lesser degrees in the politics of science for decades in the last century and, in most instances, into the new millennium. Aloof from conventional political tactics, such as collectively raising campaign money to buy access to politicians, they approached their goals confidently, with unalloyed shared faith in the worth of science for prosperity, national security, health, and many other desirable goals. At hearings on Capitol Hill, these and other politicians of science regularly convened with the elected politicians who, by choice or the workings of congressional seniority, occupied important roles in the affairs of science. Always prominent among them was the chairship of the House Science Committee, which, over three decades, served as a forum for the leaders of science to express their anxieties and hopes concerning federal dealings with science. The committee, as we shall see, possessed little legislative power; no matter, it provided a guest pulpit for science. Of a different order were Congress's thirteen appropriations subcommittees, key junctures for getting money from the U.S. Treasury. In the politics of science, none came to be so important, or revered, as the subcommittee responsible for the National Institutes of Health. Not merely by the luck of congressional seniority, but as a reflection of American cultural values, the chairs of the NIH subcommittees have invariably performed as enthusiastic boosters of health research. In grateful response, the biomedical-research enterprise has bestowed upon them innumerable medals, plaques, certificates of appreciation, and all other honors within its reach. In the politics of science, gratitude is expressed to legislators who provide money, but for financing research against dreaded diseases, sainthood is the reward.

Having made a reconnaissance of the metropolis of science, we will now move closer to examine a little-recognized characteristic of major sectors of American science: they creak with age and are bound by conservatism. The geriatric condition merits notice for the strong effects it radiates on the politics of science.

The Ossified Enterprise

. . . the community of federally funded researchers shares many
attributes with other interest groups that receive federal support:
it resists change; it seeks additional resources as a cure for internal
stress; it develops political (i.e., subjective and partisan) strategies to
promote its agenda and demonstrate the need for special treatment;
it unselfconsciously gives its own values primacy; and, in particular,
it strives to show that it is an essential contributor to the national
interest.

—Report of the Task Force on the Health of Research,
Science, Space, and Technology Committee,
U.S. House of Representatives, 1992

OVER FIVE postwar decades, the institutional structure
for research in universities and government laboratories evolved from vigorous growth to maturity to calcification. The transition led to a politics
based on assuring survival in an enterprise that is intrinsically restless, worshipful of growth, and very expensive. The institutions of science have dug
in, and, with increasing recognition of their local economic significance,
have formed political alliances to improve their survivability. The insatiability of science, the opportunities forever beckoning on the horizon, generally assure a sense of deprivation and difficulty. Whatever the merits of proposed changes in the distribution of money, resistance is assured from
established institutions if they glimpse a possibility that they stand to lose
or will not share in the gains.

By historical measures, and in comparison with other nations,
American science is unparalleled in its scale, scope, and volume of money.
Nevertheless, in the publicly financed sector it exists in a scarcity economy
of too many people, too many institutions, too many promising ideas
pursuing too little money. The paradox of financial scarcity amid record
amounts of money arises in part from the antigovernment, antitaxation

politics of our time. But it is also due to the inherent insatiability of research, which can always use more money to expand an existing activity or to open a new line of inquiry. Science today operates in an environment of competitive harshness and professional difficulty and disappointment for many of its practitioners, particularly the beginners, who must quickly demonstrate productivity to survive in the system. It is difficult to create or terminate a federal research institution; births occasionally occur, and a few obsolete or politically friendless institutions pass away, but not many of either these days.

Universities, though heavily dependent on federal money for scientific research, obtain some relief from state and industrial sources; in recent years, a lucky few schools have received huge gifts from alumni who hit the jackpot in business or industry. To hold or expand their lead in high-tech industrial competition, states rich in science-based facilities periodically muster special funds to create new research centers. Building on success, these are usually appended to existing institutions, as was the case in 2000 when the State of California provided $300 million to establish new institutes for research in nanotechnology, biotechnology, and telecommunications and computing. The winners, in a statewide competition for the money, were alliances of campuses in the University of California system. Double the amount of the state money was pledged by corporate sponsors, including, as the *New York Times* described it, "some of the biggest names in high technology."[1] But financial anxieties pervade even affluent centers of academic research: the rich require more money. University humanities departments are accustomed by necessity to frugality, living almost wholly on funds provided by the university and several small philanthropies, because government money for their needs is scarce. The National Endowment for the Humanities, the principal government benefactor in that region of scholarship, teaspooned $150 million in 1999 to hundreds of universities and other beneficiaries.[2]

In 2000, the National Science Foundation, one of several government sources of research support, poured out over $3 billion to its university clients, as well as another billion or so for precollege science programs and

---

1. "California Sets Up Centers for Basic Scientific Research," *New York Times,* December 8, 2000.

2. It can be argued that a library and a laptop suffice for research in the humanities, whereas progress in contemporary science requires extraordinarily expensive equipment. True, but the humanists too would prefer to travel and confer at government expense and employ graduate assistants, and no doubt would extend their use of computerized research if additional funds were available.

other activities designed to nourish deep roots for scientific endeavor. University science departments are intrinsically expensive to run; they regard large-scale federal support as the natural order, and they are appropriately nerve-racked by fears of financial reverses. "When I find myself in the company of scientists," W. H. Auden wrote in 1963, "I feel like a shabby curate who has strayed by mistake into a drawing room full of dukes." In science, even in the relatively good times at the turn of the twentieth century, many of the dukes felt shabby—their high expectations having outrun resources that appear miraculously bountiful to other fields of scholarship.

VETOING CHANGE

The prospect of even small shifts in government science allocations agitates the system. In 1999, for example, a proposal to establish a highly specialized Ph.D. program for fifteen students at the federal government's superbly staffed and equipped National Institutes of Health was quietly abandoned by the NIH management following strong expressions of opposition by university representatives. It's not needed, argued Shirley Tilghman, professor of life sciences at Princeton University, who had recently chaired a National Academy of Sciences study of the workforce in the biological sciences. The Academy study had confirmed that the biomedical-research enterprise was burdened with thousands of postdoctoral scientists in low-paying jobs. NIH director Harold Varmus argued that the proposed program was designed to relieve a shortage of researchers trained in both basic science and clinical research—scarce specialists for moving science from the laboratory to the bedside—and that the need was not being satisfied under existing programs. Varmus added a sweetener, promising emphasis on attracting minority recruits to the program. But the academic opponents were adamant: if the program is needed, give us money and we'll run it. Off and on over the previous twenty-five years, proposals for establishing doctoral programs at NIH had been inconclusively discussed. This time the university reaction was direct and emphatic, and NIH quickly retreated. Following withdrawal of the training proposal, Michael Gottesman, a senior NIH official explained, "There was enough negative reaction to make us believe that this would be an irritant in relations with our academic colleagues."[3]

In 1999, a proposed reorganization of the NIH peer review system—

3. "NIH Abandons Proposal to Create a Ph.D. Program in Biomedical Research," *Chronicle of Higher Education*, October 1, 1999.

often disparaged as scientifically obtuse and creaky in its operations—quickly evoked expressions of concern from university chemists who feared the changes would hinder their quest for NIH money. The proposed changes came from a source that was both knowledgeable and devoted to the progress of science, the NIH-sponsored Panel on Scientific Boundaries for Review, chaired by the president of the National Academy of Sciences, Bruce Alberts, a molecular biologist. Nonetheless, opposition flared. As reported in *Chemical & Engineering News:*

> Kenneth N. Raymond, vice chairman of the department of chemistry at the University of California, Berkeley, sent a heated e-mail to colleagues when he got wind of the changes. He says a concern he shares with many in the chemistry community is that there appears to be an absence of molecular sciences in what the boundaries panel has proposed, just when this discipline is increasing in importance. . . . "I'm going to be looking for a crisp, concise statement about the importance of medicinal chemistry" in health-related research, says Columbia University professor of chemistry Ronald Breslow. He says he is not aware of any chemist who believes that what the boundaries panel has proposed so far will lead to increased support for chemistry.

The news report concluded: "Perhaps the primary issue [Chairman] Alberts and other panel members have had to confront is the conservative sentiment, 'If it ain't broke, don't fix it.'"[4]

THE PARENTAGE OF THE GENOME PROJECT

The Human Genome Project is widely regarded as the crowning achievement of twentieth-century biology, and a credit to its principal financier, the National Institutes of Health. Initially, however, NIH, managed by an elephantine, unadventurous bureaucracy, obtusely resisted involvement in the project. The genesis of the NIH role in what became a great endeavor was derisively described to me by Bernadine Healy, who inherited the fledgling project when she became director of NIH in 1991:

---

4. "NIH Peer Review System under Scrutiny: Impenetrable Report Proposing Overhaul of System Raises Chemists' Alarms; Institute Backpedals Furiously to Contain Damage," *Chemical & Engineering News,* October 11, 1999.

It was the fear that DOE [Department of Energy] was going to take it. If DOE would go away quietly, and forget about the idea, that would have been fine, and we would not have a Human Genome Project here [at NIH]. It was purely defense that led NIH to embarking—primarily defense; I shouldn't say purely—because there were some who championed it.[5]

Among the champions and innovative practitioners of genome research was a veteran scientist at NIH, J. Craig Venter. Exasperated by his dealings with the NIH bureaucracy, Venter jumped ship in 1992, founding a nonprofit organization, TIGR [The Institute for Genomic Research] and teaming up with Hamilton O. Smith, who shared the 1978 Nobel Prize for medicine or physiology. Venter later became the founding head of Celera Genomics, Inc. His technique for accelerating the mapping of the genome, so-called shotgun sequencing, was rejected by NIH as impractical, but it proved to be the major tool for completing the mapping of the human genome—several years before the target date set by NIH.

As for DOE's initial interest, and continuing involvement, in the Human Genome project, credit that to an institutional instinct for survival. With the cessation of the Cold War, the bomb-building DOE sought new work for its decades-old laboratories for radiological studies. The genome beckoned and DOE leaped, thus inspiring the torpid NIH to bestir itself and take the leadership.

A Decline into Senescence?

Addressing the difficulties of change in the modern university, Donald Kennedy, a former president of Stanford University who first made his reputation as a neurobiologist, declared, with a seeming sense of hopelessness:

> . . . at every hand, universities display their devotion to programs and physical plants that endure. Most buildings are constructed as monuments for the ages, not as flexible, inexpensive, modular facilities that invite changes in function. Appointments are made at senior levels in preference to junior ones whenever the opportunity presents itself. Programs are designed and launched with elaborate care, and longevity is often cited as the primary criterion on which their success is to be judged.

5. Interview with author, May 27, 1993, in *Science & Government Report* [hereafter abbreviated as *SGR*], June 1, 1993.

Perhaps as cause and perhaps as consequence, universities seek to endow nearly everything. Endowment is an attractive form of fund-raising, because it can attach a program or a building to a donor's name and because it has such a reassuring ring of permanence. But it inevitably builds in longevity, often causing programs to outlive their usefulness and to resist change.[6]

Kennedy related that during his long academic career, he had received advice from and served on many university visiting committees. These consisted of outside consultants, presumably unentangled in politics on the host campus, called in to provide objective evaluations and advice on administrative and academic matters, often of a contentious nature. However, he wrote, over forty years, "I never heard one propose significant reductions in the department it visited. Instead, the committee members usually become advocates for their [academic] area—one of unique potential—or, in the words of one overly enthusiastic colleague, 'a virgin field, pregnant with possibilities.'" Summing up, Kennedy declared that academe is bound by "a set of policies and practices that favor the present state of affairs over any possible future. It is a portrait of conservatism, perhaps even of senescence."

Conservatism and resistance to change are intertwined, ancient characteristics of the academic world, well chronicled by frustrated professors. Skeptics can properly point to the academic environment's inclination to grousing: the professoriate is articulate, finds time on its hands, especially in the off season, and, in its squabblings, justifies the ancient quip that academic politics are so vicious because so little is at stake. Nonetheless, resistance to change is a remarkably persistent attribute of the academic world and its scientific sectors. In 1992, for example, a report issued by the Association of American Medical Colleges, the Washington-based lobby for mainstream medical schools, proclaimed "a disturbing reality: over the last 60 years, most medical schools have done little to correct the major shortcomings in the ways they educate their students, even though these deficiencies have been documented repeatedly."[7] Cited were eleven major reform proposals for medical education issued between 1932 and 1986. Has receptiveness to change improved since then? In 2000, after surveying the progress of medical-curriculum reform in ten schools deemed representa-

6. Donald Kennedy, *Academic Duty* (Cambridge: Harvard University Press, 1997), p. 272.
7. *Educating Medical Students* (Washington, D.C.: Association of American Medical Colleges, 1992).

tive of medical education nationwide, the AAMC reported progress in the first two years of study, but dourly concluded:

> The ten schools . . . found it difficult, and in some cases, almost impossible, to make fundamental changes in the last two years of the curriculum, when most clinical education occurs. . . . The lack of innovation in the last two years is almost certainly due to the fact that many members of the clinical faculty do not believe that changes are needed.
>
> The attitude that change is not needed in the design and organization of the last two years of the curriculum ignores certain current realities. It is contradicted by published reports indicating that, at the time of graduation, medical students too often lack fundamental clinical skills that they should have acquired during their clinical education.[8]

ANTI-INNOVATION

In the era of institutional calcification, it is difficult to terminate an existing research institution, even one that has long survived its original purpose and found no new one; it is equally difficult to create an institution. Starting in 1990, a large and diverse group, eventually including over two hundred heads of universities, proposed the creation of a government-financed, research-oriented National Institute for the Environment that would be independent of the many other federal agencies concerned in one way or another with environmental issues. Among the advocates was Rita Colwell, president of the University of Maryland Biology Institute, who was appointed director of the National Science Foundation in 1998. The proposal for the environmental institute drew congressional interest, leading to a request for the National Science Foundation to present its views. In April 1998, the National Science Board, the policymaking body of the Foundation, hurled a batch of territorial-protective arguments against the proposal:

> Establishing a stand-alone entity or agency is not an effective means of achieving the proposed intellectual goals of an environmental institute. Such an entity would almost certainly introduce unnecessary costs, and would duplicate management structures, scientific staffs, and programs already in place at NSF and other agencies. In addition, it would likely

8. "The Education of Medical Students: Ten Stories of Curriculum Change," Association of American Medical Colleges and Milbank Memorial Fund, 2000, p. 1.

have the undesirable side-effects of isolating environmental research
from the disciplinary science bases and the mission agencies, and possibly distancing agency decision-makers from research results. A centralized approach is inimical to sustaining diversities of viewpoint, research
direction and competition.[9]

NSF thus provided "a predictable bureaucratic response to a new proposal," said Stephen P. Hubbell, professor of ecology and evolutionary biology at Princeton University and board chair of the Committee for the
National Institute for the Environment.[10] The merits of the proposal are
arguable. Regardless, the era of institutional maturity virtually assured a
cold reception by existing institutions and bolstering of their defenses
against intruders. Three months after dismissing the proposal for an independent National Institute for the Environment, the National Science
Board recommended an expanded role for NSF in environmental studies.
The report, produced by a task force established by the board a year earlier—
as the proposal for an independent environmental institute gained momentum on Capitol Hill—said NSF should commit $1 billion over five years for
environmental research.[11] An accompanying press release stated the task
force report "maintains that NSF is uniquely positioned to provide leadership in basic environmental research in the future." Absent, without explanation, was the National Science Board's previously expressed fear of isolating environmental research from the mission agencies, i.e., the regulatory
agencies on the frontlines of environmental issues. As a bastion of basic
research, NSF takes pride in its safe distance from the political urgencies of
the mission agencies.

The new politics of science is built on strong survival instincts and mili-
tant resistance to change in established institutions, despite commencement platforms that resonate with paeans to change. Along with academic
conservatism and the will to survive, conventional politics provides support
for maintaining the status quo. During the 1996 presidential campaign, Bob
Dole, the Republican candidate, assured voters in New Mexico that the
state's two great federal research installations, the Los Alamos National Laboratory and the Sandia National Laboratories, are "going to remain open"—

---

9. "NSF Response to Congressional Language on the Creation of a National Institute for
   the Environment" (National Science Board, April 1998).
10. "NSF Resists Congressional Proposal to Create a National Institute for the Environ-
    ment," *Chronicle of Higher Education,* April 17, 1998.
11. *Environmental Science and Engineering for the 21st Century: The Role of the National Science
    Foundation* (NSB 99-140).

contrary to numerous official findings that these Cold War relics had outlived their usefulness. Meanwhile, President Clinton and Vice President Gore, campaigning in Tennessee, declared their support for the big federal science facility in that state, the Oak Ridge National Laboratory, but warned that a Dole victory would bring its demise. Behind the traditional campaign rhetoric was the potent political reality of jobs, votes, and mutually protective congressional alliances with politicians in states that also feared for the survival of their federal laboratories. An awakened scientific version of Rip van Winkle would navigate easily in the government-supported sector of research.

THE RIGID FEDERAL ESTABLISHMENT

Despite the Clinton administration's commitment to "reinvent" government, and similar goals under other slogans in prior presidencies, the federal government's organization and procedures for the conduct and support of research have remained virtually unchanged for more than forty years. Given the wealth and dynamism of the national research enterprise, it may be surprising to recall that the creation of NASA in 1958 essentially completed the organizational structure for the federal government's role in research. Several changes did occur through the amalgamation of small federal agencies, resulting, for example, in the creation in 1970 of the National Oceanographic and Atmospheric Administration and the Environmental Protection Agency; and some new functions were appended to old agencies. An especially horrifying change for the politicians of science occurred in 1973, when President Nixon, distrustful of his science advisers, petulantly abolished the White House Office of Science and Technology, the scientific community's valued connection to political power. Three years later, however, the connection was reestablished through a collaboration between the Ford administration and congressional friends of science. In the restored version, the White House office was rooted in an act of Congress rather than presidential preference, and its title was expanded to the Office of Science and Technology Policy. In substance, no change there.

Seeking greater commercial dividends from the government's expenditures on military research, the Clinton administration embraced the concept of "dual use" and dropped "Defense" from the title of a legendary research agency in the Pentagon, the Defense Advanced Research Projects Agency, thus turning DARPA into ARPA. In Congress and in the Pentagon, resistance to change swiftly ensued: ARPA reverted to DARPA.

Starting in 1981 with the Reagan administration, "downsizing" was en-

shrined as a managerial goal in the federal government, but the number of
government laboratories has actually changed very little over the long span
of years before and after the Reagan presidency. In 1969, according to the
National Science Foundation, the federal government owned 723 "R&D installations."[12] In 1996, the General Accounting Office, which conducts studies for Congress, reported that the roster had expanded to 736 "laboratories," a figure that included "satellites" of other laboratories.[13] There is no
certainty that the "R&D installations" of 1969 and "laboratories" of 1996
were equivalent, an NSF analyst cautioned me, but they appear to be, he
said. The telling point is the undeviating number of laboratories over nearly
three decades.

DEPARTMENT OF SCIENCE

The system's stability, or rigidity, is also visible in the repeated failure
of proposals to establish a cabinet-level federal Department of Science that
would incorporate many far-flung science agencies of government. An
amalgamation of that kind is probably a poor idea, simply on procompeti-
tive, antimonopolistic principles, though some merging would make sense,
such as removing support for physics from the ineptly managed Department of Energy and relocating it in the well-managed National Science
Foundation. But the pros and cons have never been seriously examined.
The recurring departmental proposals invariably founder on territorial objections from the managers and beneficiaries of the existing, fragmented
system. In 1995, the opening year of the so-called Republican Revolution,
Representative Robert Walker (R-Pa.), newly installed as chair of the House
Science Committee, revived the departmental proposal. Recognizing political reality, Walker's plan—though never introduced as a legislative bill—
focused on the various research agencies already under the jurisdiction of
the Science Committee: the National Science Foundation, NASA, the science programs of the Department of Energy, the Environmental Protection
Agency, and the National Institute of Standards and Technology, in the
Department of Commerce. Beyond Walker's political reach, and therefore
not included, were the science programs of the two largest federal research
sponsors: the Pentagon and the National Institutes of Health, each responsi-

12. *Directory of Federal Research and Development Installations for the Year Ending June 30,
    1969* (NSF 70-23).
13. General Accounting Office, *Federal R&D Laboratories,* letter report to Representative
    John Kasich, Chair, House Budget Committee, February 29, 1996 (GAO/RCED/NSIAD-
    96-78R).

ble to House and Senate legislative committees that would never willingly yield their prized jurisdictions to Walker's Science Committee or any other. But it never came to a struggle among congressional barons. From within the existing organization for science, opposition to the Walker proposal was instantaneous and widespread. John Gibbons, President Clinton's science and technology adviser, observed that the departmental concept "was first proposed in 1884, and again over 100 times over the past three decades." Pluralism and the "'mosaic' of science support and performance by federal agencies, universities, and industry" are America's secret of success in science and technology, Gibbons declared.[14] Probably so, but another factor was involved, too: the flaring distrust between the science wing of the Clinton White House and Chairman Walker's Science Committee. Gibbons saw himself as a builder of federal research programs, from basic science to the industrial technology programs especially favored by Clinton and his economic advisers. Walker, too, backed basic science, declaring it a special federal responsibility because of its value to the nation and limited means of finance. But otherwise, Walker was committed to the Republican Revolution's goal of a reduced federal presence in domestic matters; in particular, he and his Republican colleagues were deeply opposed to Clinton's ambitious plans to spend heavily on the development of industrial technology, viewing the White House design as a political gambit to win favor for Clinton and company. As a longtime personal friend and ideological comrade in arms of House Speaker Newt Gingrich, Walker was high in the House leadership, serving as chair of the Science Committee and as vice chair of the House Budget Committee. Whatever its merits, a Department of Science would consolidate a great deal of science power in Walker's hands. The Clinton administration was firmly opposed, and so was the scientific enterprise.

Walker was advised of the hopelessness of the departmental plan by W. Henson Moore, a former Louisiana congressman, who had experienced science's resistance to change while serving as deputy secretary in the Department of Energy. "I tried to initiate a system for the prioritization of science projects within the considerable DOE science budget," Moore testified when Walker chaired an exploratory hearing on his department proposal. "I soon learned that prioritization threatened laboratories, research jobs, appropriations, and projects themselves which in turn caused concern in members [of Congress] representing those installations. I ran into most

---

14. John H. Gibbons, remarks, to American Association for the Advancement of Science, Policy Colloquium, April 12, 1995.

of the reasons which will be given in opposition to broader effort at centralization. If one cannot do it internally, imagine the difficulty of trying to do it across multiple agencies." Concluding his pessimistic observations, Moore told Walker: "I wish you luck in this good government endeavor as I believe you will find the opponents many and the supporters few."[15] Testifying at the same congressional hearing, George A. Keyworth II, White House science adviser in the Reagan administration, declared that "American science has become a bureaucracy. As with all bureaucracies," he said, "preserving the status quo has become the overarching goal, replacing the pursuit of excellence."

Excellence, however, is still achieved, because even under the weight of institutional conservatism and obsolescence, the scientific enterprise is rich and robust, nurturing outstanding scientists from American youth and drawing high-ranking science students and accomplished researchers from abroad. By many measures, the American system of science is nimble, competitive, and innovative in comparison to foreign counterparts. Would better performance be achieved under conditions less encumbered by the grandfathered institutional structure of American science? Though introspective about many of its internal operations, the scientific enterprise has not delved into that potentially disruptive question; and managerial issues in research are generally below the threshold of notice of conventional politics. Walker recognized that an attempt to change the federal science structure would send the science agencies and their congressional representatives to the political barricades. He quietly dropped his proposal for establishing a U.S. Department of Science.

On even simple matters, sensible proposals for change perish in the cobwebs of the established order. Attempts have been made in Congress to rechristen the National Science Foundation as the National Science and Engineering (or Technology) Foundation to reflect the agency's expanded role in applied research. Invariably, these proposals have been easily defeated, at the anxious insistence of the science clan, which fears the name change would diminish its prestige and budget share. In 1996, a proposal to change the name from the National Science Foundation to the National Science and Engineering Foundation slipped through the House Science Committee on a 23-22 vote. The NSF managers, egged on by their science constituents, obtained help from one of the few science Ph.D. holders in the House, Representative Roscoe Bartlett (R-Md.), a physiologist. Introducing a

15. House Committee on Science, *Restructuring the Federal Science Establishment: Hearings before the House Science Committee,* 104th Cong., 1st sess., June 28, 1995.

blocking amendment, Bartlett warned: "We need to be careful when chang-ing names because we may do more than change the name." The name change was defeated, 339-58.[16]

However, when financial and institutional insecurities are not present to animate the defensive instincts of the scientific enterprise, the symbol-ism in names counts for naught. In 1988, congressional Democrats, seeking to enlarge the government role in industrial research, legislated new, com-mercially focused programs for one of the oldest federal research agencies, the National Bureau of Standards. Founded in 1901, it is known to the pub-lic as the nation's official keeper of weights and measures and time. To re-flect its new industrial programs, the old Bureau was rechristened as the National Institute of Standards and Technology (NIST). The name change raised nostalgic concerns among old-timers in the Bureau, but did not be-come a cause célèbre there, in the wider research community, or in Con-gress. Unlike NSF, the Bureau of Standards did not give away money to out-side supplicants, who might have felt threatened by the change in title. Its external dealings were predominantly with industrial firms that shared the costs for specialized technical studies and standards setting. Nothing but sentiment was at stake in the change of name from the National Bureau of Standards to the National Institute of Standards and Technology.

During the Cold War, and especially after, many proposals have been made to abolish or scale down the great nuclear-weapons laboratories born during or soon after the World War II Manhattan Project. Years later, they were still operating, under the Department of Energy, the descendant of the Manhattan Project via the postwar Atomic Energy Commission. Substantial staffing reductions have been made, but the weapons laboratories them-selves are as resistant as ever to change and politically armored against ter-mination. In 1997, the General Accounting Office reported to Congress that "Although the nation has changed considerably during the decades since the War [i.e., World War II], DOE's contracting practices for its manage-ment and operating contracts have remained much the same as they were in the 1940s."[17] Plumbing the mystery of DOE's apparent immunity to post–Cold War reductions in its budget, the GAO found that "budget cuts did not result in commensurate reductions in spending. DOE spent almost the same in 1996 as it did in 1994. While Congressional funding decreased from $19.5 billion to $17.4 billion (or 11 percent) between those years,

16. "In Brief," SGR, June 15, 1996.
17. *Department of Energy: Contract Reform Is Progressing, But Full Implementation Will Take Years* (GAO/RCED-97-18, 1997).

spending only decreased from $20.4 billion to $19.9 billion (or slightly over 2 percent)."[18] Explanation: DOE has a mountain of taxpayer money stashed away for uncertain times. After taking another look at the Department of Energy, the GAO concluded in 1998 that "fundamental change remains an elusive goal."[19]

IMMORTAL WEAPONS LABORATORIES

The U.S. commitment to a nuclear test ban once seemed to pose a bleak future for the Lawrence Livermore National Laboratory. That is, until the Clinton administration designated Livermore, located in vote-rich California, as the manager of nuclear stockpile stewardship; to do the job, a laser device, the National Ignition Facility, initially estimated at $1.5 billion, would be constructed at Livermore to test minuscule quantities of nuclear explosives without violating the ban on explosive tests. The costs inevitably tripled, as is the custom with these things. "We don't need three weapons laboratories," D. Allan Bromley, the elder President Bush's science adviser, assured me, referring to Livermore, the Los Alamos National Laboratory, and the Sandia National Laboratories. Each of the three laboratories consumes over $1 billion per year. Sandia, Bromley explained, had reoriented itself toward research on industrial manufacturing methods—a politically trendy activity, in response to the nation's economic difficulties. "So, they were okay," Bromley said, recalling his assessment of Sandia's prospects during his tour as science and technology adviser in the Bush White House. "I figured that Livermore was finished," he explained, "but Clinton realized he needed the full California [congressional] delegation, and one way to really help that was to announce, as he did, we're going to build the National Ignition Facility. Well, once that was stated, Livermore was home free."[20] It should be noted that the survival of the superfluous weapons laboratories under Clinton merely extended their immunity under Bush and Reagan and their predecessors. Military bases have finally been deprived of immortality by the grinding processes of deficit reduction in the post–Cold War peacetime. Science establishments have taken their place.

18. *Department of Energy: Funding and Workforce Reduced, but Spending Remains Stable* (GAO/ RCED-97-96, 1997).
19. *Department of Energy: Uncertain Progress in Implementing National Laboratory Reforms* (GAO/RCED-98-197, 1998).
20. Interview with author, October 7, 1998.

The Pentagon's Own Medical School

None is better protected against termination than an institution that is both military and academic. Such is the Uniformed Services University of the Health Sciences (USUHS), the Pentagon's own medical school in Bethesda, Md., across the road from the National Institutes of Health. Unusual in this age of institutional clamoring for attention, the school keeps its head down to avoid public notice that might lead to wonderment about its existence. USUHS was the eccentric creation of the late congressman F. Edward Hébert of Louisiana, for whom a military medical school was an idée fixe for many years. Hébert's congressional colleagues ignored his obsession. But Hébert turned his dream into a reality following his automatic ascent via seniority in 1972 to chair of the House Armed Services Committee, a site of genuflection by the military. While Hébert was a mere congressman, the Pentagon dismissed his enchantment with military medical education as an unneeded diversion of money from weapons and troops. But when Chairman Hébert insisted on founding the school, the Pentagon complied, though reluctantly. Prior to startup of the new school, however, Hébert was deposed from his Armed Services chairmanship in a rare coup against the congressional seniority system, whereupon the Pentagon sought to strangle the fledgling medical institution before the first class was admitted. But Hébert's House colleagues, feeling he had suffered sufficient humiliation at their hands, insisted on fulfilling his dream, later christened, and known to this day, as the F. Edward Hébert School of Medicine. With ample, guaranteed federal funding in a prime location, it has evolved into an excellent institution, by many accounts. But among 125 allopathic medical schools, plus 19 osteopathic schools, the Hébert School of Medicine is superfluous in a nation so glutted with physicians that immigration restrictions for foreign-trained physicians are strongly advocated by the Association of American Medical Colleges; as the lobby for domestic medical schools, the AAMC is merely performing a predictable service of territorial protection by proposing to shift the burden of retrenchment elsewhere.[21]

---

21. Like a sausage factory set on automatic, the medical-education industry has annually graduated virtually the same number of graduates for two decades. In academic year 1980–81, 126 medical schools enrolled 65,497 students and graduated 15,667 (*JAMA*, December 25, 1981); in academic year 1998–99, 125 medical schools enrolled 66,489 students and graduated 16,143 (*JAMA*, September 1, 1999). While the number of students was essentially unchanged, the size of the full-time faculty nearly doubled during the two decades, from 50,536 to 98,202. The faculty growth was partially due to the increasing complexity of medical education, but staffs were also drawn by the surge of NIH research money into medical schools and a slice of Medicare reimbursements for faculty performing clinical duties in teaching hospitals. Numerous studies

Over the past quarter century, the Pentagon itself has repeatedly attempted to terminate its own medical school, arguing that military scholarships at civilian institutions can satisfy the armed services' needs for physicians, at far lower cost. Data cited by the chair of the House Defense Appropriations Subcommittee in 1990 put the cost of medical training at the Hébert School of Medicine at $527,000 per graduate, compared to $125,000 per military scholarship at civilian institutions. Moreover, the military medical school awarded a mere 162 M.D.s that year, compared to 4,100 under the Pentagon's scholarship program in civilian medical schools. The adverse numbers were disputed by the military school's authorities with conflicting statistics and assertions that the lengthier service requirements for military graduates translated into lower costs per physician for the services; also that medical education in civilian schools receives hidden subsidies that were not figured into the cost comparisons. In the practical world of policymaking, the facts matter little in this matter, as in so many others concerning the wisdom of specific government expenditures. Despite several close calls, the Pentagon's own, though unwanted, medical school survives under the watchful care of the Maryland congressional delegation, a growing body of alumni and assorted allies for preservation of the status quo.

THE ETERNAL ACADEMIC ELITE

Over decades, only small shifts have occurred in the lineup of top university recipients of federal research funds. In 1980, the top ten consisted of Johns Hopkins, MIT, Stanford, the University of Washington, the University of California at San Diego, the University of California at Los Angeles, Harvard, Columbia, the University of Wisconsin at Madison, and Cornell University. By 1995, five remained in the top ten (Hopkins, Wisconsin, Washington, MIT, UC San Diego), while the others were still in the top twenty.[22] The system oscillates in a narrow band between sensible reward of scientific excellence and pragmatic response to political pressures for sharing the wealth. The rich universities do get richer, in line with St. Matthew's dictum—"Unto everyone that hath shall be given."[23]

---

have concluded that medical-school enrollments are far in excess of the need for physicians (especially under the spartan regime of managed care), but—except for a few mergers of financially sinking schools—the system remains unchanged.

22. National Science Foundation, *Survey of Federal Science and Engineering Support to Universities, Colleges, and Non-Profit Institutions, Fiscal Year 1995* and *Fiscal Year 1980*.

23. Or, as was unsurprisingly concluded from an elaborate analysis of grants awarded by the National Institutes of Health: "Research funded by NIH is becoming more concen-

But in an egalitarian departure from the original biblical dictum, the modern-day adaptation does not penalize the poor. As the lower-tier universities intensify their competition for government research money, the number of dollars going to the top universities has increased but their share of the pie has declined, though not by much. Thus, in 1979–80, the top ten universities received 20.2 percent of federal R&D money in academe; by 1989–90, their share had slipped to 17.9 percent; in the same period, the share of the top one hundred declined from 83.7 percent of the total to 81.7 percent, as even lower-ranked universities aspired to research money.[24] The federal system of university-research support employs peer-reviewed competition, insulated against political interference, for awarding money. But in response to political reality, appended to the system are special programs to mollify the have-nots by nurturing their capacity to compete for peer-reviewed money. These efforts to expand the roster of universities receiving federal research money are understandably resented by the haves. In 1999, the National Science Foundation devoted $48.4 million to its helping-hand effort, the Experimental Program for the Stimulation of Competitive Research (EPSCoR), which aims to strengthen the have-nots for the rigors of competing for federal research money. Reporting misgivings about this venture into scientific welfare, the *Chronicle of Higher Education* observed, "Some view it as an unjustified set-aside within the NSF's $3.6 billion budget. 'It always seemed strange to us, when NSF talked about funding the very best research, that there was this program,' said Allen J. Sinisgalli, associate provost for research at Princeton University. 'This is kind of an unnecessary propping up of individual institutions in regional areas.'"[25]

Calls for change in the structure and workings of the scientific research system remain plentiful, but there is little agreement on why change is needed, or what should change, in a system that, after all, remains successful at producing scientific knowledge. It could be better, the critics say. But consensus on change remains elusive. In 1997, House Speaker Gingrich, a self-described "techno-nut," assigned a rare Ph.D. physicist in the House, Representative Vernon Ehlers (R-Michigan), to conduct a study of federal

---

trated in the medical schools that are most active in research." Ernest Moy et al., "Distribution of Research Awards from the National Institutes of Health among Medical Schools," *New England Journal of Medicine*, January 27, 2000.

24. Roger Geiger and Irwin Feller, "The Dispersion of Academic Research in the 1980s," *Journal of Higher Education*, May/June 1995.

25. "Reassessing an NSF Program for Research Have-Nots," *Chronicle of Higher Education*, October 15, 1999.

science policy and propose recommendations for improvement. Titled *Unlocking Our Future: Toward a New National Science Policy,* delivered September 24, 1998, the Ehlers report concluded that the federal system of science support is essentially sound. "The fact that we advocate not a major overhaul but rather a fine-tuning and rejuvenation is indicative of its present strength."[26] Gingrich thanked him warmly, but evidently unsatisfied, said that further study is needed. Gingrich was soon gone from politics. Minus its patron, the expected next stage of the Ehlers study inconspicuously dwindled away. Nothing changed.

Having examined the institutional durability of the scientific enterprise, we will now take an unconventional, roundabout route deeper into the politics of science. The purpose is to examine two persistent and influential myths in science, one depicting the origins of the postwar relationship between science and government, the other alleging the existence and then the loss of a golden age in that relationship. In science politics, as in all politics, the realities of the past are often reshaped to suit the needs of the present.

---

26. House Committee on Science, *Unlocking Our Future: Toward a New National Science Policy,* September 24, 1998.

CHAPTER 3

Vannevar Bush and the Myth of Creation

In lapidary inscriptions, a man is not upon oath.

—Samuel Johnson

GREAT RELIGIONS worship a messiah and a sacred text.

For a wide swath of science in America, the messiah is Vannevar Bush: engineer, inventor, industrial entrepreneur, educator, impresario of the nation's military research in World War II, and visionary politician of science. For physicists, chemists, and mathematicians in academe, and their benefactors in government, Bush, who died in 1974, is revered as the political founder of the modern American scientific enterprise, celebrated in their ceremonials as the creator. However, in the biomedical- and defense-research communities—the largest sectors of the enterprise—Bush is totally ignored, like a prophet from another religion; the same is true of the social and behavioral sciences. These different perspectives provide us with further insights into the politics of science.

Vannevar Bush's seminal text is *Science, The Endless Frontier*,[1] his proposal in 1945 for the federal government to assume financial responsibility for the postwar support of science. During the war, Bush headed the Office of Scientific Research and Development, the civilian agency created, at his recommendation, for the management of much of the nation's wartime research. In that role, Bush was a paragon of leadership and foresight at the frictional interface of the military's technological conservatism and the civilian scientists' and engineers' enthusiasm for radical innovation, sometimes assisted by military mavericks.[2]

---

1. Vannevar Bush, *Science, The Endless Frontier*, NSF 40th anniversary edition (Washington, D.C.: National Science Foundation, 1990).
2. In a postwar book, *Modern Arms and Free Men* (New York: Simon & Schuster, 1949), Bush cited numerous wartime encounters with military opposition to unorthodox technology. He noted, for example, that the tracked amphibious vehicle, which proved in-

He was proclaimed "Vannevar Bush: General of Physics" in a 1944 *Time* cover story. But Bush himself acknowledged falling far short, if not failing, in achieving his grand design for the peacetime support of science. The Bush design, in fact, was not implemented. No matter. The legend of Bush as the architect of America's postwar rise to world leadership in science flourishes to this day, though it has wilted a bit under the unsentimental scrutiny of a new generation of scholars. Nonetheless, for exploring the abundance and function of myth (occasionally rising to delusion) in the politics of science, it is rewarding to visit the still-thriving legend of Vannevar Bush the creator, as initially spun and maintained by the old scientific establishment and reverentially embraced by its descendants in our own time. The purpose is not to depreciate Bush, whose honored place in history is assured, despite the rejection of his postwar plans for science. Rather, it is to observe the flourishing presence and function of political fantasy deep in the soul of science.

POSTWAR PLANNING FOR SCIENCE

President Franklin Roosevelt commissioned *Science, The Endless Frontier* in November 1944, five months before his death. Bush delivered the report to President Truman in July 1945, a little over a month before the surrender of Japan ended World War II. Bush, a seasoned science politician, had asked Roosevelt to assign him to prepare a proposal for the postwar support of science. For science, Bush thus initiated a postwar genre, politicking and persuading by report, the most potent weapon available for a community unconnected to elective politics. For carrying out his presidential assignment, Bush commissioned advisory reports from four panels of scientists and educators that he appointed, but he freely exercised the chair's prerogative of adoption, modification, or rejection from among their many recommendations. The ensuing Bush tract proposed a radical innovation in peacetime relations between science and government: creation of a government-financed, but largely autonomous agency, the National Research Foundation, to support basic research in universities. In the nineteenth century, science and government joined in agricultural research and in the geological sciences, both valuable for development of the virgin American continent; early in the twentieth century, the aeronautical

---

valuable for landing troops on Japanese-held islands, "came into existence because of the vision of a small group of civilian engineers, plus the encouragement of unconventional generals with a flair for pioneering. In fact, there was probably more obtuse resistance to this device than to any other in the war."

sciences received attention in Washington. Otherwise, with special and rare exceptions, science and government kept a mutually wary distance—especially so in the conduct of basic research. This was an elite activity, largely financed by private philanthropy and concentrated in a handful of universities and independent research institutes. For fighting the war, Bush and his colleagues called science to arms and organized the massive and diverse research enterprise that extended from the atomic-bomb project, radar, and the proximity fuse to the development of antibiotics, malaria drugs, and tracked amphibious vehicles. Much of the work they sponsored was conducted in universities, the peacetime workplace for many of the civilian managers, scientists, and engineers summoned to wartime research.

Bush spent much of his career at MIT, where he joined the faculty in 1919 and was appointed vice president and dean of engineering in 1932. In 1938, he moved to Washington as president of the Carnegie Institution of Washington, a prestigious, multidisciplinary complex of private research institutes. In 1945, on the eve of the war's end, Bush urged the U.S. government to commit itself to the financing of basic research in universities as a necessary ingredient of postwar military strength, economic prosperity, and national well-being. Prior to the war, recommendations for broad government support of science failed because of indifference in Washington and fear among scientists that government money would encumber science with foolish regulations and contaminate it with political interference. But by war's end, with the potency of science inscribed on public and political consciousness, the necessity for government support was broadly accepted in politics and science. For simply raising the issue of postwar support of basic science, the Bush report performed valuable missionary work in the Congress and among the public, both untutored in the financial needs of research. In that important respect, Bush's endeavors in behalf of postwar science were educationally valuable, though it can be argued that they were superfluous for selling science to politics and the public. Hiroshima and Nagasaki, penicillin and radar had spectacularly demonstrated the powers of research and created a new consciousness of the value of science, in politics, as well as among the general public. Bush stressed the importance of linking basic research and higher education, leading to his recommendation for government support of science in universities, where graduate students serve apprenticeships in science. But with or without the Bush report, government was destined to become the chief patron of science in universities. After the war, America's triumphant scientists returned to their universities. Private philanthropy, even if willing, lacked the needed scale of finance for their ambitions, while industry was not inclined to lavish big money on university professors. The inevitability of large-scale government support for university science is not a presumptuous hindsight: in fact, government was moving into the role of academic-science patron even as the Bush report arrived and then languished for years in Harry Truman's White House.

Though the general principle of government finance of civilian research was widely accepted as a necessity of the postwar era, the organizational and managerial specifics of Bush's proposal aroused serious opposition within both politics and science.[3] As a direct result, a prolonged stalemate ensued. The plan that was finally adopted, after a five-year impasse, bore only a faint resemblance to his proposals in *Science, The Endless Frontier.* During those years, however, financial relations between science and government flourished, without Bush's participation. Meanwhile, functional channels for the support of academic research were established by legislation or through administrative arrangements within military agencies and in the newly created Atomic Energy Commission. These channels were initially regarded as interim devices for supporting science, pending creation of the foundation proposed by Bush. But they achieved immortality, as sometimes happens with interim arrangements in government.

THE VETOED DESIGN

With his prewar inclinations reinforced by wartime experience, Bush was distrustful of government as he contemplated the future of science in peacetime. But the need for government money for science necessitated a link to the U.S. Treasury. To achieve the holy grail of money without interference, Bush recommended the creation of a federally financed, but virtually independent foundation. As described in *Science, The Endless Frontier,* it would be a scientific philanthropy dedicated to the support of a broad spectrum of research—the natural and physical, military and medical sciences—in accompaniment to the training of scientists for these fields and the publication and international distribution of scientific information. Predictably, the military services would have none of Bush's scheme for "civilian-initiated and civilian-controlled military research." The social sci-

3. The politics of postwar science support was complicated by ideological conflict over patent rights, the controls and goals of scientific research, and residual resentment of Bush's autocratic management of research during the war. The most revealing examination of the postwar controversy and related matters is in David M. Hart's *Forged Consensus: Science, Technology, and Economic Policy in the United States, 1921–1953* (Princeton, N.J.: Princeton University Press, 1998).

ences were offended by their omission from the list of disciplines to be supported, a precursor of the neglect they were to experience in later years. The National Institutes of Health was then a small agency within the staid U.S. Public Health Service, with no apparent sign that NIH would blossom into the postwar colossus of medical-research finance. But the medical men, like other scientists, were ambitious. Peering into the uncertain postwar future, Bush's advisory panel for the medical sciences did not favor the inclusion of medical research in his multidisciplinary National Research Foundation. Instead, the medical panel, with nine of ten members drawn from medical schools, called for the establishment of the medical sciences' own financial stronghold in Washington, an independent National Foundation for Medical Research. With clear political foresight, they saw no merit in being relegated to a medical division within a catchall government agency designed by an engineer from MIT, an institution without a medical school. Bush also proposed the creation of a "permanent Science Advisory Board" to advise the White House and Congress "as to the policies and budgets of Government agencies engaged in scientific research." The proposal for the board was initially ignored by Truman and company, though it can be regarded as the kernel of what many years later evolved into the science-advisory apparatus at the White House. In summary, the specifics of Bush's proposal for postwar science did not resonate with the politics of the time. Even so, it had a didactic value for politics and the attentive public, but an unfortunate one, in important respects.

BASIC VERSUS APPLIED RESEARCH

In arguing for government support of basic research, Bush adopted what has since come to be known as the "linear model," which holds that technology is the offspring of scientific understanding developed through basic research. In contrast to this model, the history of technology reveals a complex, interactive relationship between science and technology. For example, the steam engine, innovated by engineer-craftsmen, gained efficiency through increased theoretical understanding of thermodynamics. In other instances, such as explorations of radioactivity and uranium fission, basic science provided the foundation for applications, which then led to instrumentation for further exploration of basic scientific phenomena. Bush, however, opted for selectivity and simplicity: "The scientist doing basic research," his report stated, "may not be at all interested in the practical applications of his work, yet the further progress of industrial development would eventually stagnate if basic scientific research were long neglected. . . . The simplest and most effective way in which the Government can strengthen industrial research is to support basic research and develop scientific talent." Bush, the science politician, thus articulated a utilitarian rationale for spending government dollars on activities outside the understanding of the scientific illiterates who populated Congress and other sites of power and influence. For this, he has been praised by latter-day strategists of science and government for political wisdom and also criticized for creating a conceptual wall between pure and applied science.[4]

Though Bush pinned his argument on the ultimate practicality of basic research, he only gestured toward specific steps for assisting the transition from basic knowledge to industrial value. In the report, he referred to the creation of "research clinics" to bring the benefits of science to small business enterprises, tepidly describing the concept as "certainly worthy of further study."[5]

However, the underlying concept of "research clinics" for small firms, mirroring the well-established system of agricultural extension stations that provided technical assistance to farmers, was so at odds with American business culture and political sentiment that it took nearly forty years to achieve a modest implementation. Bush's detached treatment of the subject did not nudge it forward.

But even without the resistance and objections evoked by the details of design for the postwar support of science, the Bush proposal was politically doomed. While diplomatically stating that the proposed foundation "must be responsible to the President and the Congress," Bush also recommended "complete independence and freedom" in operating the foundation. Under the Bush formula, the link to government would be through a presidentially

4. In discussing inventors and inventiveness in his memoir, *Pieces of the Action* (New York: William Morrow & Co., 1970), Bush introduced a lyrical dimension absent from his dry-prose presidential report: "An invention has some of the characteristics of a poem. . . . It is said that a poet may derive real joy out of making a poem, even if it is never published, even if he does not recite it to his friends, even if it is not a very good poem. No doubt one has to be a poet to understand this. . . . An inventor invents because he cannot help it. . . . One has to be an inventor to understand this" (p. 150).

5. Richard R. Nelson, a Columbia University economist, and others, fault Bush with encouraging a pernicious dichotomy between basic research and technological applications: "Bush went out of his way to define basic research not only in terms of the search for fundamental knowledge that is involved in the activity, but also in terms of a lack of conscious targeting to specific areas of human need." Richard R. Nelson, "Why Bush's 'Science, The Endless Frontier' Has Been a Hinderance to the Development of an Effective Civilian Technology Policy," in *Science for the 21st Century: The Bush Report Revisited* (Washington, D.C.: AEI Press, 1997).

appointed board of private citizens "not otherwise connected with government." The foundation's director would be appointed by, and exclusively
answerable to, the nongovernmental board. Political factors may have been
complicated by contrasting personal characteristics: Truman, the folksy,
midwestern, dyed-in-the-wool Democrat never warmed to the autocratic
Yankee conservative Vannevar Bush. Truman rejected the autonomous organizational formula as a violation of the principles of accountability for
government funds. With his foundation plan derailed, and his advice no
longer sought by the White House, Bush was distanced and eventually disconnected from political power. He remained in Washington as president
of the Carnegie Institution of Washington, a post he had retained throughout the war; he also chaired the Pentagon's newly established Joint Research
and Development Board, an unsuccessful effort to curtail interservice rivalry for postwar weaponry. And he politicked on Capitol Hill in behalf of
the National Research Foundation.[6]

Though Bush was out of national science policy making, science policy
remained a concern of the White House. While the Bush proposal remained
motionless on Capitol Hill, Truman assigned a trusted aide on the White
House staff, academic economist John R. Steelman, to study the federal role
in research as chair of a presidential scientific research board. Bush took no
part in the Steelman proceedings, which resulted in a five-volume survey
of the nation's scientific resources and needs. *Science and Public Policy* was
delivered to the president in 1947. Addressing the lingering proposal for a
National Research Foundation, the Steelman report stressed the importance
of positioning it under direct presidential authority. Bush clearly was offended by the content of the Steelman report and the manner of its preparation. Responding to a request for his views from Secretary of the Navy James
Forrestal, the normally reserved patrician engineer poured out his distress:

6. "Dr. Bush is now on the outside so far as Government scientific matters are concerned,
a position of which he is very conscious and to which he referred time and time
again," William T. Golden observed in a "Memorandum for the File" after meeting
with Bush on October 24, 1950. Golden, a New York financier commissioned by Truman to study the organization of presidential science advice, added, "Though President Truman is very cordial to him, he does not call upon him for advice, though
Dr. Bush has pointed this out to him on several occasions. He feels this is not because
of any personal dislike but rather because President Truman just doesn't operate in this
way—the contrast between President Truman and President Roosevelt is very strong in
this respect. It is evident that Dr. Bush, who had a very close working relationship
with President Roosevelt, does not approve of the present state of affairs." *Impacts of
the Early Cold War on the Formulation of U.S. Science Policy: Selected Memoranda of William T. Golden, October 1950–April 1951* (Washington, D.C.: American Association for
the Advancement of Science, 1995), p. 9.

You realize that on matters concerning science and our government, Mr. Steelman and I frequently hold diverse views. . . . The President has made it clear that it is Mr. Steelman's report, not that of the board that was set up to advise him. Unfortunately, it does not summarize scientific thought in this country; it expresses the opinions of a small group within government. Very few scientists were consulted during the preparation of the report and the report itself shows this. . . . I am convinced that a more sound approach would have been to include scientists of the highest caliber in planning and issuing the report.[7]

In that same year, 1947, Congress adopted a modified version of the Bush proposal, which Truman vetoed on the familiar grounds of lack of accountability to the president. In the meantime, the general acceptance of postwar government responsibility for science in universities was manifested in the flow of money from the U.S. Navy and later from the Atomic Energy Commission to hundreds of basic research projects in universities. As noted by science historian Daniel J. Kevles, a newly established navy research office was offering universities money for basic research in 1945, the debut year of *Science, The Endless Frontier.* By August 1946, when the navy office was formally established by Congress as the Office of Naval Research, it "already had in force 177 contracts, totaling $24,000,000, with eighty-one universities or private and industrial laboratories. ONR was supporting more than 602 academic research projects, which together involved some 2,000 scientists and an equal number of graduate students."[8]

The issue of quality control in the distribution of military money for academic science was raised by James Conant, president of Harvard, Bush's partner in the leadership of wartime research. In a letter to Bush in 1946, Conant wrote:

The gossip I pick up in academic circles, both here and in other colleges (through the respective presidents) is that there is a great deal of concern about the way the Navy is pouring out money for so-called fundamental research. The recipients are glad to get it, of course, but are wondering why it is flowing in that particular channel, and rather suspect

7. Vannevar Bush papers, Manuscript Division, Library of Congress, Box 73, September 10, 1947.
8. Daniel J. Kevles, *The Physicists: The History of a Scientific Community in Modern America* (New York: Alfred A. Knopf, 1978), p. 355.

there is a joker somewhere. I have also heard that some of the grants are
to very second-rate people in third-rate institutions.[9]

Bush responded that "I had quite a bit to do with starting of the Navy
program, intending it as a 'stop-gap,' " he noted, pending creation of his
proposed foundation. To which he added, "Certainly they support second-
rate people in third-rate institutions. I'm not sure that OSRD [the wartime
Office of Scientific Research and Development] did not do it. The same
thing may be true of any large program, but it seems to me on balance they
have a pretty good record so far."[10]

In the folklore of science, the ONR of early postwar days is wistfully
remembered as an ideal benefactor of university science, notable for its ab-
horrence of red tape and its faith in the trustworthiness and talents of American scientists. The congenial postwar union of science and the military did
not surprise Bush, who observed in his memoirs, "It was inevitable . . . that
the armed services would themselves continue to support research in civilian hands along the lines of their special interests."[11] After the wartime accomplishments of science, and with rapidly worsening relations with the
Soviet Union instigating the Cold War, government could not revert to its
prewar aloofness from university-based science, the principal locale for basic research and training of scientists and engineers in America. Observing
the growing stream of money for academic science from the navy and the
Atomic Energy Commission, Bush asserted "there would still remain a serious lack if the program included no more than this, for basic research, fundamental research, would hardly be supported adequately by those with
special interests." Bush continued to lobby for a civilian-run foundation
dedicated exclusively to academic basic research. But it was the Steelman
report, embraced by politicians but long forgotten by the mythologists of
the scientific establishment, that actually shaped events. Bush chafed under
his neglect by Truman, attributing it to the White House " 'palace guard,'
meaning John R. Steelman, Truman's vigorous and scienceminded special
assistant and the linchpin of his staff," according to an official history of
the conception and early years of the National Science Foundation.[12] In
1950, more than five years after Bush delivered *Science, The Endless Frontier*

9. Vannevar Bush papers, James Conant to Bush, Manuscript Division, Library of Congress, Box 27, October 31, 1946.
10. Ibid., Bush to Conant, November 4, 1946.
11. Vannevar Bush, *Pieces of the Action,* p. 65.
12. Milton Lomask, *A Minor Miracle: An Informal History of the National Science Foundation*
(Washington, D.C.: National Science Foundation, 1976), p. 62.

to the White House, a shrunken, presidentially controlled version of Bush's formula for the support of research was enacted into law as the National Science Foundation. To assuage scientific sensitivities, the legal authority for the foundation was vested in a twenty-four-member National Science Board, which, by the founding statute, was to be afforded an opportunity to suggest candidates for the director of the foundation. Both the board members and the director would receive six-year appointments, a duration that provided detachment from the four-year presidential term, since hold-overs would normally remain into the next administration. But both the board and the director were presidential appointees, subject to approval by the Senate. And, as stated in the founding legislation, the president held ultimate authority over the director, "who shall serve for a term of six years unless sooner removed by the president." On the crucial political issue of ultimate presidential control, Vannevar Bush was rejected, as was his design for incorporating defense and medical research into the foundation. As Truman considered appointees for the first National Science Board, Bush removed himself from the running, telling Truman, "I know my name is on the list, but I wish you would leave me off." He cautioned the president, "If you put me on the board, they will elect me chairman, and I do not think the body of scientists are going to like this continuation of one man in the top post."[13] Steelman corroborated Bush's frank assessment of the likely reaction to his board appointment, telling an interviewer, "Quite frankly, I thought it unwise to put his name on the list for the reason that a number of scientists whom we had approached about sitting on the Board said they wouldn't serve if Bush were a member. Their reasons were that he was 'overbearing,' that if he were on the Board, he'd take charge of everything."[14]

Half a century after the difficult birth of the National Science Foundation, it remains a comparatively small source of government research support, managing some $4 billion of a federal research and development budget that exceeds $75 billion; within that larger sum, of about $18 billion devoted to basic research, only $2.5 billion comes from the National Science Foundation. About half of the government's $75 billion for R&D belongs to the Pentagon. Defense research, which was to be a major function in the foundation contemplated by Bush, is not specifically undertaken by NSF, though in the natural flow of scientific knowledge, NSF-supported research is available to the Pentagon. Ironically, in a turnabout from Bush's

13. Ibid., p. 62.
14. Ibid., p. 64.

plan for civilian management of money for military research, the Pentagon provides over $1 billion a year for university-based, unclassified research indistinguishable from projects supported by the nonmilitary NSF. Medical research (another significant, but ignored, part of the Bush concept) is politically fueled by its own special advantages—cures promised and achieved and public hopes for even more cures—and possesses an independent bastion in Washington, the National Institutes of Health. Though NSF supports molecular biology, biochemistry, and other life-sciences research, the medical sciences are overwhelmingly dominated by NIH, with funds in 2000 totaling nearly $18 billion, over four times NSF's budget. Civilian space research belongs to NASA, whose 2000 budget of $13.6 billion also dwarfs NSF. The Department of Energy, descended from the Manhattan Project, provides over $2 billion annually for physics, the nuclear sciences, and other disciplines in science and engineering. Rather than being the central agency for government support of basic research, as envisaged by Bush, the National Science Foundation is a small part of the total.

Small as it is, however, NSF is regarded by many university scientists as their own agency in Washington, the only one specifically responsible for university-based pure science, in close association with the training of Ph.D. scientists and engineers. In this respect, NSF differs from the so-called mission agencies of government—for example, the Department of Energy and NASA, which are dedicated to tangible goals. But despite the esteem of its beneficiaries and the rationale for its creation, NSF even lags behind the mission agencies in the volume of support it provides for basic science, which was to be the prime responsibility, the raison d'être, of Bush's foundation. In 1996, all federal agencies together provided a total of $14 billion for basic research; of this amount, NSF provided $2.1 billion, the balance of its budget going to science education and engineering;[15] in the Clinton proposal for 2000, the combined basic research funding of all federal agencies was set at $18.1 billion—with $2.5 billion, or 14 percent, designated for NSF.[16]

THE PROPAGATION OF MYTH

Nevertheless, within the scientific enterprise, and particularly in NSF circles, the celebration of Vannevar Bush as the postwar architect of Ameri-

---

15. *National Patterns of R&D Resources, 1996* (NSF 96-333), pp. 121–22.
16. Committee on Science, Engineering, and Public Policy, *Observations on the President's Fiscal Year 2000 Federal Science and Technology Budget* (Washington, D.C.: National Academy Press, 1999), p. 5.

can science policy flourishes to this day, even as critical reappraisals conflict with decades of hagiolatry. Since 1980, the National Science Board, NSF's governing body, has annually presented the Vannevar Bush Award to a leading figure in science, with a tilt toward those who are also accomplished in the politics and administration of science.[17]

The adulation of Vannevar Bush extends beyond NSF. As noted in the previous chapter, Representative Vernon Ehlers (R-Michigan), who has a Ph.D. in physics, produced a 1998 science-policy study commissioned by House Speaker Newt Gingrich. "The policies that Vannevar Bush outlined in his 1945 report *Science, The Endless Frontier,*" Ehlers declared, "still, to a large extent, guide the research enterprise."[18] Congressman Ehlers merely restated the fable of creation, a familiar exercise in the science community throughout the postwar years. In 1990, the Bush report as genesis was hailed in a special anniversary edition published by the National Science Foundation.[19] Even those who should have known better joined in the hosannas with introductory remarks. "*Science, The Endless Frontier,*" wrote science historian Daniel J. Kevles, "insisted upon the principle of federal patronage for the advancement of knowledge in the United States, a departure that came to govern federal science policy after World War II." Quoting from Bush's report, Kevles hailed its insistence on "'freedom of inquiry,'" and the "'free play of free intellects, working on subjects of their own choice, in the manner dictated by their own curiosity for the explanation of the unknown.' These principles," Kevles reverentially declared, "have become so much a touchstone for the federal government's relationship to science that they have taken on a life of their own, achieved a kind of timeless, abstract quality." With its sweeping, unwarranted assumptions of a connection between the Bush report and the postwar evolution of relations between science and government, Kevles's sacramental appraisal merely reiterated the clichés of science politics. In a foreword to the anniversary edition of the report, rejected though it was by Harry Truman, NSF Director Erich Bloch stated: "Bush's vision of the role of science and engineering in a modern society has served as the blueprint for our long term national investment of research and education." At Bush's funeral, in 1974, MIT President Jerome B. Wiesner declared, "No American has had greater influ-

---

17. Six of the nineteen recipients through 1999 were former presidential science advisers: James Killian, Lee DuBridge, I. I. Rabi, Jerome Wiesner, Frank Press, and H. Guyford Stever.

18. Vernon J. Ehlers, "The Future of U.S. Science Policy," *Science,* January 16, 1998, p. 302.

19. One of several editions in the postwar decades.

ence in the growth of science and technology than Vannevar Bush, and the 20th century may not yet produce his equal."[20]

The encomiums to Bush as the architect of the postwar relationship between science and government are countless. In 1991, the centenary of Bush's birth, NSF and the Carnegie Institution of Washington, where Bush served as president from 1939 to 1955, held a symposium in his memory. "Through 'Van' Bush's foresight and lobbying," said Carnegie President Maxine F. Singer, "the National Science Foundation was born"—a striking reconstruction of events, in view of Truman's veto of Bush's plan and the disparity between Bush's prescription and the ultimate creation of Steelman, Truman and Congress. In 1999, under the title "100 or So Books That Shaped a Century of Science," *The Scientist* coupled C. P. Snow's *The Two Cultures* with Bush's *Science, The Endless Frontier*, explaining: "Snow shows science as a major element of the culture for our century, and Bush explains what a democracy might do about that."[21]

Bush evidenced no pride of authorship in the outcome of his proposal for government support of science. Given the absence of political independence in its structure, and military and medical research among its responsibilities—features he deemed essential for the foundation—"Bush felt he had given birth to an orphan and had little to do with it," writes G. Pascal Zachary, author of the only book-length biography of Bush.[22] Looking beyond Bush's proposed foundation, David M. Hart, a Harvard political scientist, observes that

> science and technology policy was not spun from a master design. Vannevar Bush was brilliant and effective in mobilizing the nation's scientific and technological resources for World War II, but *Science, The Endless Frontier* is better seen as a political tactic than as an original blueprint. Bush himself tacitly acknowledged as much, nearly passing over the report in his memoirs.[23]

Hart's study of the transition from prewar to postwar science policy is the most penetrating yet of a subject befogged by scientific sentimentality

---

20. Quoted in G. Pascal Zachary, *Endless Frontier: Vannevar Bush, Engineer of the American Century* (New York: The Free Press, 1997), p. 407.
21. Philip and Phylis Morrison, "100 or So Books That Shaped a Century of Science," *The Scientist*, November-December 1999.
22. G. Pascal Zachary, op. cit., p. 369.
23. David M. Hart, *Forged Consensus: Science, Technology, and Economic Policy in the United States, 1921–1953* (Princeton: Princeton University Press, 1998), p. 206.

and indifference to facts. In assessing the "blueprint" analogy, Hart concludes: "The institutions of American government and the style of American politics precluded the dominance of any single vision of the state, even
in an area of public life apparently so esoteric as science and technology
policy."

Other recent analyses, generally from outside the temples of science,
have also tended toward nonhagiographic depictions of Bush as the grand
architect of American science policy. "As an institutional blueprint for the
fifty years of federal policy that followed its release, the Bush Report was
largely a failure," asserts David C. Mowery, Professor of Business and Public
Policy at the University of California, Berkeley. "The bulk of its specific recommendations for a National Research Foundation, as well as its recommendations for mechanisms to finance university basic research and the
training of undergraduate and graduate students, were not implemented.
Nor were the report's less specific but no less insightful and promising comments concerning the relationship between basic research in universities
and industrial innovation ever followed up."[24]

Science, The Endless Frontier was "something of a failure in its own time,"
according to William A. Blanpied, a physicist and senior analyst at NSF,
who, in 1998, observed, "In truth, the recent salutes to Vannevar Bush and
his report have tended to distort both past and present realities." Recalling
Bush's design for a single federal agency encompassing virtually all fields
of basic research, Blanpied points out another irony of Bush worship:

> By the mid-1950s, it had become conventional wisdom to extol the ge-
> nius of the pluralistic U.S. research system, which permitted academic
> scientists to receive grants from more than one government agency—
> a majority of them mission agencies. Yet the greatly revered Bush report
> had taken precisely the opposite line, emphasizing the need for a single
> agency to support all nongovernment research and explicitly rejecting
> the claim that any mission agency had the capacity to do so. Indeed, for
> at least a year after the NSF was established, it was widely assumed by

24. David C. Mowery, "The Bush Report after Fifty Years—Blueprint or Relic?" in Claude
E. Barfield, ed., *Science for the 21st Century: The Bush Report Revisited* (Washington, D.C.:
AEI Press, 1997). Nonetheless, after decades of reverential repetition, the myth of Bush
as creator remains ensconced in the folklore of science. In a book on the sociology of
science, published in 1999, a passing reference states: "Enabling legislation for a National Science Foundation—funded meagerly *but organized as Bush had envisioned* [ital-
ics supplied]—passed Congress and was signed into law by Truman in 1950." Thomas
F. Gieryn, *Cultural Boundaries of Science: Credibility on the Line* (Chicago: University of
Chicago Press, 1999), p. 67.

scientists that other agencies would willingly transfer their basic research portfolios—along with their associated budgets—to the new agency on the block.[25]

In recent years, the mythology-based Bush worship has continued to yield to historical fact, slowly, but significantly, even at a leading fount of reverence: the National Academy of Sciences. In an observation concerning Bush that would have been considered blasphemous in earlier times, an Academy report in 1999 observed, "Although several of his specific policy recommendations were never enacted"—a rare concession—"the model in the plan, picturing innovation as a linear process moving from basic research to applied research to development to production and operations, achieved pervasive and lasting influence." The report goes on to concede that since the end of the Cold War, "the linear model has come to be seen as less descriptive of real-world relationships, and therefore less useful."[26]

As a "political tactic," Bush's design invited attention to the issue of postwar financial support of research and strongly influenced the scope of debate by prejudging universities as its appropriate venue. The record shows, however, that Bush was not alone in recognizing both the importance of postwar support for science and the advantages of supporting it in universities: the navy and other government agencies moved quickly to maintain the flow of money to academic science during and beyond the transition from wartime to peacetime. From that shared conceptual beginning, the federal research system that evolved over the postwar period diverged on its own path and became only distantly related to the Bush design.

MYTH IN THE SERVICE OF POLITICS

Nonetheless, the dual myth of Bush as messiah and *Science, The Endless Frontier* as sacred text persists to this day in political dialogue in and around the scientific enterprise. Like many old myths, it is useful for present purposes. For the postwar managers of science in its relations with government, the ahistorical reformulation of the Bush story was not a deliberate attempt at misrepresentation. The tale as told contained enough elements of truth to make it recognizable, impressive, and attractive: the masterful wartime

---

25. William A. Blanpied, "Inventing US Science Policy," *Physics Today,* February 1998.

26. *Harnessing Science and Technology for America's Economic Future: National and Regional Priorities* (Washington, D.C.: National Academy Press, 1999), p. 11.

president seeking the counsel of the sage wartime leader of science, who gave his benediction to science financed by government, ruled by scientists, and conducted in universities. The legatees of Bush could proudly claim a noble ancestry, and in their relations with politics and pursuit of expansion, could assert faithfulness to principles of the founder. And they frequently did. In 1995, Sigma Xi, a major national scientific society, observed the golden anniversary of *Science, The Endless Frontier* with a two-day forum titled "Vannevar Bush II—Science for the 21st Century: Why Should Federal Dollars Be Spent to Support Scientific Research?" Laments for financial hard times for the sciences were a common theme throughout the proceedings, which were paid for by a bevy of federal research agencies and private foundations, including NASA, the National Institutes of Health, the Department of Energy, the Environmental Protection Agency, the William and Flora Hewlett Foundation, the Lucille P. Markey Charitable Trust, the David and Lucille Packard Foundation, the Alfred P. Sloan Foundation, and Carolina Power and Light. Frank Press, former president of the National Academy of Sciences, tireless, politically astute champion of government money for basic research conducted in universities, opened the proceedings by asking: "Why are we thinking about a new epoch, Vannevar Bush II, rather than keeping a steady course charted by Vannevar Bush I?" The reason, he explained, is that "Without a new and credible Vannevar Bush II to shape the views of decision makers, the days may be behind us when presidents of the United States equated a strong science with a strong America."[27] The disconnect from reality was striking.

In 1997, the National Science Board issued a "working paper" on science-policy issues, *Government Funding of Scientific Research,* a characteristically opaque, inconclusive discussion of the difficulties of setting priorities within and among scientific disciplines.[28] Priority-setting means winners and losers, and therefore makes slow, if any, progress within most fields of science, and none in allocating shares among the various fields seeking federal funds.[29]

Under a heading in the paper titled "Justification for Government Sup-

---

27. *Vannevar Bush II—Science for the 21st Century: Why Should Federal Dollars Be Spent to Support Scientific Research?* proceedings, Sigma Xi forum, March 2–3, 1995 (Sigma Xi, 1995), p. 3.

28. *Government Funding of Scientific Research, A Working Paper of the National Science Board* (NSB 97-186, 1997).

29. Astronomy, virtually alone among the scientific disciplines, draws up a list of desired facilities and programs every ten years—usually a long list. Other disciplines shun the political perils of wish-list rankings.

port of Scientific Research," the board of the National Science Foundation looked back fifty-two years to the Bush report, noting that it linked scientific research to "health, our jobs, and our national security." The board proceeded to speculate, "Were Bush writing today, he would probably add others, including 'the environment,' 'green manufacturing,' and 'clean energy sources.'" Whether or not Bush would have added that trio is neither knowable nor relevant to policy choices today, though it seems likely that he would include them among the beneficiaries of his single-minded devotion to undirected basic research in universities. But it should be noted that the board's working paper on government funding coincided with the rising prominence of environment, green manufacturing and clean energy sources among the post–Cold War programs of the National Science Foundation. The sainted founder would approve, according to the board, which also observed that "As a result of implementing the Bush vision, our research universities have become the envy of the world."

Some effusive commentaries on *Science, The Endless Frontier* are remarkably disconnected from its contents. "The Bush paradigm of 'science for science's sake' seems to be moving to 'science for society's sake,'" states an introductory section in a collection of science-policy papers published in 1997 by the American Association for the Advancement of Science.[30] Science for science's sake? Not in *Science, The Endless Frontier*, which states:

> Advances in science when put to practical use mean more jobs, higher
> wages, shorter hours, more abundant crops, more leisure for recreation,
> for study, for learning how to live without the deadening drudgery
> which has been the burden of the common man for ages past. Advances
> in science will bring higher standards of living, will lead to the preven-
> tion or cure of diseases, will promote conservation of our limited na-
> tional resources, and will assure means of defense against aggression.[31]

Sentiment and hunger for a hero account for some of the declarations of reverence for Bush. He was indeed a great figure, without the hallucinatory invention of his postwar role as architect of American science policy. But another factor was at work, too: competition among ideological sectors in the politics of science, each asserting that time and events had, at last,

---

30. Albert H. Teich, Stephen D. Nelson, and Celia McEnaney, eds., *AAAS Science and Technology Policy Yearbook* (Washington, D.C.: American Association for the Advancement of Science, 1997), p. 19.
31. Bush, op. cit., p. 10.

overtaken the Bush blueprint and brought on the need for a successor to *Science, The Endless Frontier.* The plan that was never put into effect—that, in fact, was rejected—thus became the starting point, nearly fifty years later, for a new series of science-policy polemics.

For the Clinton administration's economic-policy strategists, the desired goal was deeper government involvement in industrial technology, and—to the horror of the science establishment—a *lessened* emphasis on basic research. "At the end of World War II," declared a 1992 Clinton-Gore election-campaign paper, "Vannevar Bush defined the framework for U.S. science policy in his report, *Science—The Endless Frontier.* It made the United States a world leader in science. . . . For several decades after the war, we did not perceive the need for a technology policy to complement this science policy." Consequently, other nations reaped the commercial benefits of America's prowess in science because "science policy alone does not address these issues." Proposed solution: a package of federal dollars and policies to "restore America's technological leadership."[32] Once in office, the specific Clinton proposals for supplanting the Bush design came quickly, with an ambitious plan to assist high-tech innovators and entrepreneurs with hundreds of millions of dollars in venture capital through the little-known Advanced Technology Program in the Department of Commerce. Vannevar Bush, though his design for postwar science failed, proved to be a man for all seasons, through the second half of the twentieth century and into the new millennium.

Thriving with the myth of Bush the creator were inspiring recollections of a lost Eden in the collaboration between science and government. That it never existed is of no consequence. Like the Bush fable, it exerted influence. We will now examine tales of the golden age.

---

32. "Technology: The Engine of Economic Growth—A National Technology Policy for America," issued September 21, 1992, by Clinton-Gore National Campaign Headquarters, Little Rock, Arkansas.

CHAPTER 4

The Glorious Past

Golden Age: 1. an imaginary early age in which mankind was ideally
happy, prosperous, and innocent   2. a period of great progress,
prosperity, or cultural achievement
　　　　　—*Webster's New World Dictionary of the American Language,*
　　　　　　　　　　　　　　　　　　Second College Edition

IN THEIR internal discussions, and in their appeals to the
public and politics, the leaders and publicists of science, and the attending
chorus in the press, occasionally refer nostalgically to a bygone "golden
age" of science which, they say, stands in contrast to the leaden deficiencies of the moment. Nostalgia for golden ages, real or imagined, occurs in
other professions, too, for example, painting, film, sports, exploration.
These other golden ages, however, tend to be concerned with substantive
achievements. Not so science.

In science, the golden age dialogue is overwhelmingly keyed to
the gross volume of government money spent on research, particularly
university-based research, rather than the qualitative, or even the quantitative, matter of knowledge. Money is indispensable for the professional conduct of research; even pencil-and-paper work requires salaries and desk
space. But the direct relationship between the quantity of money and
achievement in science is unknown and perhaps unknowable. Great Britain
has accomplished a great deal scientifically on relatively modest science
budgets; the Soviet Union had relatively little to show for its enormous
spending on research. A one-to-one relationship between money going in
and science coming out has never been established. The volume of money,
however, is countable, and comprehensible to scientists, politicians, and
the public. Understood by all is the necessity of money for the training and
well-being of scientists and the nurturing and advance of science. In the
politics of science, the golden ages of science are thus usually equated with

money, not with discovery, though the underlying assumption is that more money will produce more science.[1]

In rare outbreaks of candor, or exuberance, the golden age of science is hailed as here and now. However, in science, as in other sectors of governmental dependency, there can be no profit in acknowledging financial sufficiency; better to complain of neglect or remain silent than invite envy from less-fortunate sectors or, worse, the attention of economizers.

Little agreement exists on the temporal whereabouts of the golden age of science, but a number of commentators are fixed on the late 1960s or the end of that decade. By a very wide margin, however, the majority agrees that it is not now, though scattered reports indicate it is making a return. The golden age topology is complex: some reports of its whereabouts suggest periods in which all scientific disciplines feasted on ample support; others are specific to particular disciplines. Also to be noted is a paradox in some recollections of golden ages: During the various periods in the past in which, in retrospect, one or another golden age is said to have occurred, leaders of science in those prior times also denounced conditions of the moment and reminisced to even earlier times as the golden age. Like sonar signals pinging back to reveal submerged objects, these projections of nostalgia reveal the political and financial insecurities of the scientific enterprise and its capacity for believing it is the victim of neglect and hostility.

THE ROLLING GOLDEN AGE

In 1987, the National Science Foundation reported that "a charting of all the R&D expenditures of universities and colleges made since 1964 clearly shows an end of the so-called 'Golden Age' of academic funding at the close of the decade of the Sixties."[2] It's not clear whether the "close of the decade" literally means the last day of the 1960s or is to be taken as an approximation. In any case, it is to be noted that, around that time, specifically in 1968, the New York Academy of Sciences, discontent with the level of support for research, convened a national meeting on "The Crisis Facing

---

1. A provocative variation on the golden-age theme is expressed in *The Coming of the Golden Age: A View of the End of Progress* (Natural History Press, 1969), by Gunther S. Stent, a noted molecular biologist. In his fearful formulation, science will eventually create a golden age of human well-being, to an extent where "further scientific research appears to have arrived at the point of ever-decreasing utility. Thus, it seems possible," he speculates, "that there could occur a waning of the present high social interest in supporting the sciences" (p. 110).

2. NSF, Division of Policy Research and Analysis, *Infrastructure: The Capital Requirements for Academic Research*, PRA Report 87-3, May 1987.

American Science."[3] A background paper for attendees stated that "Young scientists often find it virtually impossible to obtain funds for their work. New research ventures, in a broad spectrum of activities from basic physics research to clinical medicine are also having severe difficulties attracting support." By that account, at least, 1968 was a difficult time in the finances of science; it was no golden age. In 1991, however, Nobel physicist Leon Lederman (then president of the American Association for the Advancement of Science) deplored the level of government support for research in 1991. Looking back to 1968, the year of the New York Academy's crisis meeting, Lederman described it as "the peak year of what we call the Golden Age" in government support of research. Since then, he said, support had declined, creating "a depth of despair and discouragement that I have not experienced in my 40 years in science."[4]

Responding a short time later to Lederman's dour assessment, Roland W. Schmitt, an experienced participant in the Washington science-advisory system and, at the time, president of Rensselaer Polytechnic Institute, agreed that the "golden era," as it is sometimes referred to, had indeed faded away with the 1960s. But, in contrast to Lederman's gloomy assessment of conditions in 1991, Schmitt reported that a financial revival had actually occurred: "We are back to per capita expenditures near those of the Golden Era of the late 1960s." But Schmitt then acknowledged that complaints about the adequacy of federal support are "at a fever pitch." Drawing upon surveys of morale among physicists—systematic emotional introspection is part of modern science—Schmitt observed that "young physics faculty felt best in 1977, after several years of diminishing support and felt worst after the sustained growth in per capita support during the 1980s."[5] Moving past his colleagues' monofixation on the volume of money, Schmitt offered a diagnosis: the golden age had spawned so many new science departments in the universities that in turn produced swarms of new students and researchers, that all were competing for funds in the face of the rising costs of research.[6] More money had not bought happiness, because, even with

---

3. *The Crisis Facing American Science: A Preliminary Report on the Effect of Decreased Federal Support of Scientific Research and Education*, edited proceedings, New York Academy of Sciences, 1968.
4. "AAAS Head Toots Tin Trumpet for Science Funding," *SGR*, January 15, 1991.
5. Schmitt's observation was derived from a report, "Their Most Productive Years," published in 1990 by the American Physical Society, comparing surveys of morale in samplings of physicists in 1977 and 1990.
6. "Tracking the Remedies for the 'Crisis' in Science," *SGR*, June 1, 1991 (report on testimony to House Science, Space and Technology Committee, March 20, 1991).

more financial support coming from Washington, there was not enough to satisfy the increase in demand, Schmitt concluded.

In 1990, a few months before Lederman and Schmitt delivered their reports, Nobel biologist David Baltimore offered a somewhat different time-table for nirvana in his field of research, though without employing the term "golden age": "For years, research money seemed limitless. In the 1960s and 1970s, the ratio of funds to practitioners in biomedical research was so high that research addicts like me experienced their pleasure unalloyed with concerns about how to pay." By 1990, he laments, "The money seems to be drying up."[7] Thus, for Baltimore, the golden age encompassed 1968—the year of the New York Academy's crisis meeting—and extended into the 1970s.

If the golden age withered around the end of the 1960s, as many contend, it apparently experienced a resurrection at an unspecified date, only to sink again, in the perception of an especially well-qualified observer. Kenneth Brown, the former head of research-related statistics at the National Science Foundation, reported in his 1998 book *Downsizing Science: Will the United States Pay a Price?*[8] "strong evidence that the golden age of U.S. science is over, that there is a decline—or at best a leveling out—in practically every statistic that describes scientific activity." In a chapter titled "The End of the Golden Age," Brown wrote, "Most conspicuous is the expected downsizing of federal funding for R&D. . . . Financial support for science is not anywhere near the top of the political agenda, except within the scientific community"—true, but neither new nor surprising in the grand context of national politics.[9] Brown's pessimistic financial forecast, based on the 1995–97 competition in budget-cutting vows between the Clinton White House and the Republican-controlled Congress, reflected the sciences' anxieties at the time he set it in writing. But in the interval between writing and publication, the melancholy expectations were overridden by events in the form of a monsoon of federal dollars. Research, woven into the essence of American society, again mocked political rhetoric. The downsizing prediction by Brown arrived in the very year of a record-breaking $2 billion (14.6 percent) increase for the National Institutes of Health and a $215 million (6.3 percent) increase in research funds for the National Science Foundation. The increase for medical research was so large that Senator Pete Domenici (R-New Mexico), chair of the Senate Budget Committee, was re-

7. David Baltimore, "Research Endangered," *Technology Review,* May/June 1990.
8. Washington, D.C., AEI Press.
9. Ibid, p. 4.

ported to be concerned about "overwhelming" NIH with money.[10] In 1999, the gusher of funds for NIH reached such great proportions that a new anxiety arose: "Research institutions are pleased by the largesse," the *Chronicle of Higher Education* reported after Congress approved a record NIH budget of $17.9 billion, "but it has also raised some problems and questions for them—chiefly, how to absorb all that money, given limited laboratory facilities."[11]

FURTHER SIGHTINGS

Yet another sighting of the golden age was reported by the recipient of the 1998 Priestley Medal of the American Chemical Society, Professor F. Albert Cotton of Texas A&M University. In an acceptance address titled "Science Today—What Follows the Golden Age," Cotton observed that the golden age extended "from the mid-50s to the mid-80s"—a unique time spread among golden age spotters. In mourning its end, Cotton scornfully identified a culprit, the benighted masses, declaring that "the public seems to shun science in many aspects of daily life, preferring totally unscientific, medieval, and even premedieval practices."[12] This hint at strange, perhaps satanic, preferences after a golden age of three decades was not enlarged upon.

On the other hand, Frank Press, in his 1988 presidential address to the National Academy of Sciences, adopted a bold and lonely stance: in contrast to the negative expressions of many of his colleagues, Press declared that "this can indeed be called the 'Golden Age of Science'—a time of unprecedented progress in scientific discovery and its applications." For this Press credited "the high level of financial support by governments and industries." Though he referred to financial matters on that occasion, Press is unusual among golden-age spotters for his emphasis on the substance, the output, of scientific activity. In "Growing Up in the Golden Age of Science," an article he published in 1995, Press looked back over the previous forty-five years and observed, "This period has been described as a 'Golden Age of Science' because of the wealth of discoveries in science and engineering."[13]

However, in 1994, just one year before Press published that favorable

10. *Washington Fax*, December 3, 1998.

11. "A Downside to Federal Largesse?" *Chronicle of Higher Education*, November 5, 1999.

12. "Science Today—What Follows the Golden Age," *C&E News*, March 30, 1998.

13. Frank Press, "Growing Up in the Golden Age of Science," *Annual Review of Earth and Planetary Sciences* 23 (1995): 1–9.

golden-age assessment, the *Washington Post* had declared otherwise under the headline "Golden Age Ends." The *Post* reported, "Until recently, American science was living in what many call a golden age that began shortly after the end of World War II."[14] Now, the *Post* explained, though government money for research had substantially increased, it had not increased sufficiently to provide for all qualified contenders and the rising costs of scientific equipment.

MATHEMATICS' OWN GOLDEN AGE

In 1998, the American Mathematical Society attested to a different life span for the golden age, as far as that discipline was concerned, concluding in an analysis of the president's proposed budget for fiscal 1999: "For thirty years we have been in the midst of a golden age of mathematics research." However, referring to an NSF study of the financing of mathematics research, it added that "Although American mathematics is the envy of the rest of the world, our leadership is in jeopardy." The danger was attributed to "inadequate support."[15] The mathematicians' report of a golden age of thirty years' duration presents some difficulty. Counting back from 1998, the golden age of mathematics research would extend to 1968, the year in which the New York Academy of Sciences declared the scientific enterprise sunk in crisis; 1968 was also around "the close of the decade of the sixties," which is when the golden age of academic research funding ended, according to the previously mentioned study by the National Science Foundation. However, it was then, by the count of the mathematicians, that their discipline entered a golden age of thirty years' duration. However, at least fifteen of those thirty years were cited as a dreadful period for mathematics by Edward E. David Jr., who chaired a study of the discipline for the National Academy of Sciences. Writing in *Scientific American,* David called November 19, 1969, "a black Wednesday for basic research in mathematics." On that date, Congress adopted an appropriations measure, the Mansfield amendment, that limited the Pentagon's research money to projects directly related to defense purposes, thus reducing military support in academe. "Although Federal support for fundamental mathematics had begun to wane as early as 1968," David observed, "the budget politics articulated

14. *Washington Post,* December 25, 1994.
15. *Notices of the AMS,* September 1998.

by the Mansfield Amendment helped to bring about a fifteen-year period of neglect of the field."[16]

But assistance for all the sciences is imminent, declared Richard Zare, chair of the National Science Board, in hailing the nomination in February 1998 of NSF Director Neal Lane to be President Clinton's assistant for science and technology. In a congratulatory message, Zare stated: "We're on the threshold of what Neal Lane and others call 'a golden era of science.'"

Having looked into the topography of the research enterprise, the myth of genesis, and legends of bygone riches, we will now examine an important characteristic within science: a well-exercised capacity for self-pity and allegations of mistreatment, in the face of abundant evidence of public and political appreciation of science and generous financial support.

16. Edward E. David Jr., "The Federal Support of Mathematics," *Scientific American,* May 1985.

CHAPTER **5**

The Whimpering Giant

> But support for science, as the saying goes, is a mile wide and an inch deep.
>
> —Representative George E. Brown Jr., of California,
> ranking Democrat and former chair, House Science Committee,
> interview with author, January 24, 1996

> The process of applying for grants is cumbersome and time consuming. It takes very significant bundles of time away from research and teaching. Scientists, young and old, beginning and distinguished, feel like beggars.
>
> —Maxine F. Singer, president,
> Carnegie Institution of Washington,
> at the Vannevar Bush Centenary Symposium, March 20, 1991

EDWARD E. DAVID JR., who served as President Nixon's special assistant for science and technology, relates that in 1972, the president summoned him to the Oval Office during a time when disruptive demonstrations against the Vietnam War raged on university campuses. David swam into strange waters when he moved to the White House staff from the elite Bell Labs, where his accomplishments in research brought him election to both the National Academy of Sciences and the National Academy of Engineering by age forty-five—rare dual honors. David was a nonpolitical scientist-technocrat, not even an onlooker to politics. But he was intrigued by the offer to serve as the senior science official in the U.S. government. Recalling that summons to the president's office years later, David told me, "He wanted to know, 'Ed, how much money does the federal government put into MIT every year?'" The Massachusetts Institute of Technology was of special interest to Nixon and his political coterie. Not only was it the site of uproarious antiwar activities, but the president of

MIT, Jerome Wiesner, was an outspoken Democrat who had conspicuously worked for John F. Kennedy's election victory over Nixon in 1960, and then served in the White House as Kennedy's special assistant for science and technology. In the 1964 presidential election, while dean of science at MIT, Wiesner was at the political ramparts again, as a leader of Scientists & Engineers for Johnson-Humphrey, a mobilization against Barry Goldwater's presidential campaign. Holding a doctorate in electrical engineering, Jerry Wiesner was a prototypical practitioner of the postwar politics of science, oscillating between campus and Washington, more knowledgeable about science than any politician, more knowledgeable about politics than most scientists.

Offhand, David didn't know the precise amount that Washington sent to MIT. But, as the top science official in Washington, as well as an alumnus of MIT, he knew that MIT received scores of millions from Washington for academic programs and major defense projects—actually $104.8 million in 1972, making it number one that year among academic recipients of federal R&D money.[1] "Nobody had warned me that this was coming along," David said in looking back to that episode, "but I made a guess at it which wasn't too far off, and the president said, 'Well, considering what Jerry Wiesner and others out there are doing to me, I want that cut off.'"[2]

"I said," David related, "'Mr. President, you've got to recognize that MIT is one of the most important contributors to the defense of this country. I mean, all of the inertial guidance for our missiles comes out of MIT. You don't really want to do that, do you?'"

"'I want it all cut off,'" Nixon commanded.

"I quoted a number of other things MIT had done," David recalled, "and said, 'With all of that, you can't stop all of that work, first of all. And,

---

1. *Federal Support to Universities, Colleges, and Selected Non-Profit Institutions, Fiscal Year 1978* (NSF 80-312), p. 28.

2. Wiesner was included in Nixon's anti-Semitic rantings, according to an account attributed to the late John Ehrlichman by Seymour Hersh, a Pulitzer Prize–winning investigative journalist. Hersh reports that in 1969, after Wiesner publicly criticized Nixon's decision to deploy a limited antiballistic missile system, "Nixon angrily denounced Wiesner in front of Kissinger as 'another one of those Jews.'" Seymour Hersh, *The Price of Power: Kissinger in the Nixon White House* (New York: Summit Books, 1983), p. 85. In a secret White House recording from 1971, released by the National Archives in 1999, Nixon says, "Most Jews are disloyal," and remarks to his chief of staff, H. R. Haldeman, "But, Bob, generally speaking, you can't trust the bastards. They turn on you. Am I right or wrong?" Haldeman agreed, and added, "And they are smart. They have the ability to do what they want to do—which is to hurt us." *Washington Post*, October 6, 1999.

secondly, it wouldn't be good for the country.' But he insisted." David told me that he left the Oval Office with John Ehrlichman, assistant to the president for domestic affairs, and others, "in a great state of confusion."

"And I went back to my office and sat there for a few minutes and thought about it," he said. "So, I got Ehrlichman on the phone and I said, 'What do you do about this?'"

"He said, 'Don't do anything. A week from now he will have forgotten that he said it.' So, I didn't do anything. He was just mad about something. It was just a way of venting his spleen to make himself feel better."[3]

INTERDEPENDENCE

Was this a near collision with catastrophe—reminiscent of the French Revolutionary Tribunal declaring that "the Republic has no need of men of science," in sentencing Antoine Lavoisier, the "father" of modern chemistry, to the guillotine? So it might appear. But the reality was different. Even if the paranoically simmering Nixon had persisted, he could not have undone the nation's dependence on science and technology to accomplish its ends, in matters of weaponry, as in many others. Nor would the political system tolerate serious injury to an institution renowned for serving the nation's needs in science and technology. Washington had many years earlier reached the point where it needed MIT as much as MIT needed Washington. Despite Nixon's dour dealings with the scientific community and several of its prominent leaders, federal R&D spending during his presidency rose from $14.9 billion to $18 billion.[4] Long before Nixon became president, science and technology, research and development, had become essential ingredients of modernism, national power, and public and personal well-being. And the combined growth of federal and state government and industrial financing of these activities assumed an astonishingly robust pace, increasing nearly tenfold, from $26 billion in 1969, when Nixon entered the White House, to an estimated $227 billion in 1998.[5] The

---

3. David, interview with author, July 1, 1998. MIT was much on the mind of the beleaguered Nixon. Hugh Loweth, who was managing science budgets in the Office of Management and Budget at that time, recalled that "the [OMB] branch chief and I were both called in and told, 'You got to figure out how to cut federal support to MIT by 50 percent.'" Loweth, as amazed and resistant to that proposal as Science Adviser Edward David, says that "we were able to pull some budget legerdemain to show that [the cuts were made, though, in fact, they were not]." Interview with author, March 15, 1999.

4. *Science Indicators: The 1985 Report* (National Science Board, NSB 85-1), p. 217.

5. *Science and Engineering Indicators 2000,* vol. 2, appendix tables (National Science Board, NSB-00-1), p. A-17.

numbers and trends will be examined in fine detail in the next chapter. The important point here is that the United States was on a research spending spree. Nonetheless, under the management of the scientific leadership and its attendant staffs, the public dialogue concerning research consistently and stridently promoted the impression of science as an indifferently cared-for, financially deprived ward of government. In 1990, for example, Leon E. Rosenberg, dean of the Yale University School of Medicine, wrote a *New York Times* op-ed article whose lugubrious message was accurately reflected in its headline: "Medical Research Is in Ruins."[6] Accusing the federal government of indefensible neglect of the National Institutes of Health, Rosenberg stated, "Today our nation's health research program is burning, and the conflagration is spreading."

In this, as in many expressions of distress from scientific leaders, rhetoric and reality were distinctly different. From 1980 to 1990, appropriations for NIH rose from $2 billion to $4.7 billion. The gain was "real" in purchasing power calculated at 1992 levels: NIH was $1.7 billion richer in 1990 than in 1980. In 1989, the year preceding the reported conflagration, 26,541 biomedical-research articles were tabulated for the United States; for 1992, the article count rose to 27,782.[7] The paper count is a revealing measure of scientific activity: papers are the work product of science. Perhaps money was being burned at NIH, as skeptics suggested, but health research prospered then, as it does today, with the annual NIH budget ascending to over $20 billion in 2001, amid urgings from scientists and their supporters for additional growth, and congressional assurances that, somehow, it will be provided. Throughout the 1990s, a decade in which science budgets fared relatively well despite the difficulties of deficit-reduction politics, the cries of neglect from the scientific establishment were gullibly accepted at face value by the popular press and, in turn, by the public. Thus, in 1998, a wealthy private donor to medical research explained his beneficence in the *Wall Street Journal* as follows: "Money is drying up in Washington, and new approaches are needed."[8] In fact, in "constant" dollars, calibrated to 1992, annual federal support for basic research remained steady throughout the 1990s, at about $15.5 billion. In "current" dollars, the currency of Congressional deliberations, the appropriations for basic research rose from $14 billion in 1990 to $17.6 billion in 1997—despite repeated political

6. *New York Times*, September 2, 1990.
7. *Science & Engineering Indicators, 1998*, p. A-293.
8. "Brushes with Death Turn the Very Wealthy into Medical Medicis," *Wall Street Journal*, January 6, 1998.

commitments to cap or cut federal spending, eliminate the deficit, and balance the federal budget. Nonetheless, expressions of insecurity persisted.[9] When plump appropriations confounded the forecasts of savage reductions, a leading apostle of budget gloom, Albert H. Teich, head of the Science and Policy Programs Directorate of the American Association for the Advancement of Science (AAAS), warned against complacency: "While some in the scientific community may feel they can breathe a sigh of relief on seeing the latest [budget] figures," Teich told an AAAS-sponsored budget conference, "it is important to remember that these numbers don't mean that things are getting better for R&D—they're just projected to decline more slowly."[10]

FISCAL DOOM MONGERING

In biomedical research, the most generously favored scientific ward of American politics, anxiety has repeatedly obscured reality: "Today we are fortunate to be experiencing unprecedented public support, at least for some of our science," Richard D. Klausner, director of the National Cancer Institute, conceded as the medical-research budget for 1999 moved toward a historic high in Congress. But, he cautioned, "I worry how deep that support is . . . I worry that support exists in a metastable state of grace in a society not truly scientifically literate."[11] Government support of science created dependency and expectations, and understandably so, as was clearly acknowledged by a scientist testifying at one of Congress's customarily superficial inquiries into the state of American science:

> Well, I think that when people go into research or devote their lives to a
> research career, they more or less assume that the Federal Government is
> going to be their source of support. They make a commitment. I think
> the Government has to make a commitment back to them. . . . I think
> that when funds suddenly disappear and people are displaced . . . you
> owe something more to them than that. . . . It is like somebody trained

9. For navigating through the budgetary thickets, keep in mind that appropriations are the amounts voted annually by Congress; obligations, the sums often stated in NSF's reports on R&D, represent financial transactions anytime in the future, regardless of when the money was appropriated. Because of these differing budget categories, numbers used here may not match up with the financial tables in the appendix, but they are usually fairly close.
10. Quoted in *Campaign Update*, AAAS Center for Science and Engineering, spring 1997.
11. Richard D. Klausner, "Telling Our Stories of Science," address to the Albert and Mary Lasker Foundation Medical Research Awards Foundation, September 25, 1998.

to be a violinist for 30 years, and then somebody steps on his violin and says you can't play any more.[12]

Bizarre theories of political causation, intellectually on a par with reports of alien abductions and communication with the dead, easily flourished in respectable scientific ranks. In the late 1980s, Congressman John Dingell (D-Michigan), renowned for his bullying manner, held contentious hearings concerning misconduct charges against a scientific collaborator of Nobelist David Baltimore; Baltimore, who was not charged with any offense, came to the aid of his accused colleague, and thus was created "the Baltimore case." Analyzing the congressional proceedings in the *MIT Faculty Newsletter*, Professor Jonathan King wrote:

> The investigation of Baltimore can be most readily understood as the
> first salvo in the effort by some in Congress to shrink the NIH and re-
> lated programs, in order to protect other sectors from cuts, the largest of
> which is the DOD [Department of Defense] budget. One traditional tac-
> tic in efforts to cut popular programs has been to discredit the program:
> First one charges fraud; if there is fraud, clearly there is waste in the bud-
> get; if there is waste, cuts are in order.[13]

In contrast to that Machiavellian analysis, the record shows Congressman Dingell as a strong, consistent supporter of increased budgets for NIH, and as a persistent critic of waste in defense spending. It was Dingell who exposed the Pentagon's $640 toilet seat, which became a vivid metaphor for military wastefulness. Dingell noted with pride that his brother, Jim Dingell, was a public health physician on the staff of NIH, and that their late father, a member of the House from 1933 to 1955, was a legislative founder of the modern NIH.

THE REAGAN REVERSE

The rhetoric of frugality long standard in elective politics quite rightly evoked fear in science and other dependencies of government that could look only to Washington for their support. The defensive reaction, though

---

12. Ronald Otto Rahm, a researcher at the Oak Ridge National Laboratory, testimony to the Task Force on Science Policy, House Committee on Science and Technology, 99th Cong., 1st sess., July 9, 1985.
13. Jonathan King, "The Loss of David Baltimore and the Role of the Dingell Hearings," *MIT Faculty Newsletter*, November 1989.

overwrought, was natural, expectable. Ronald Reagan began his presidency with announced plans to reduce the government's civilian budget, including research, by substantial amounts. Accustomed to growth, rather than reductions, the institutions of science reacted to what they regarded as an impending disaster, showering Congress and the press with pleas and warnings. However, even if the budget-cutting plans were put into effect, they could not have endured. Reagan, like Nixon, could not disentangle modern America from its reliance on science and technology and the need for generous support inherent in that reliance. Tending to the liberal side of the political spectrum, scientists withheld their cheers for Ronald Reagan. But by 1989, when his second term ended, substantial gains in government support for science and technology were plain to see in Washington's basic research spending: up from $7.1 billion at the beginning of the first Reagan administration to $11.7 billion at the close of the second. Reagan was primarily a megaproject enthusiast, giving political birth to the most grandiose high-tech endeavors of the late twentieth century: the Strategic Defense Initiative, the space station, the Superconducting Super Collider, and the Human Genome Project. But under Reagan "little science" prospered too. Frank Press, who served as President Jimmy Carter's science adviser, amply credits Reagan as a benefactor of research: "Reagan looks very good in his support of science. At first he was terrible, then he came up nicely."[14] All too nicely, according to David Stockman, whom Reagan installed as director of the Office of Management and Budget, with orders to gut federal civilian spending. Stockman ruefully recalled that his reduction plan for the NASA budget evoked a powerful protest from astronaut-turned-senator Jack Schmitt (R-N.Mex.), who walked on the moon in 1972 as a member of the sixth and final Apollo lunar landing. The senator-spaceman, Stockman wrote, "was always trying to show that he was more conservative than thou, but when it came to his moon complex there was no limit to what he wanted to spend." Schmitt prevailed. "We would end up adding billions to our original five-year space budget," Stockman sourly noted.[15]

The cycle of threat and salvation was repeated in 1995, when Republicans took control of the House. We will later examine in fine detail the so-called Republican Revolution and its impact on science. But at this point, it is pertinent to recall the blitzkrieg arrival of Republican chieftain Gingrich and company on the national political scene. Brandishing their government-shrinking Contract with America, the Republican victors

14. Interview with author, May 14, 1998.
15. David A. Stockman, *The Triumph of Politics* (New York: Harper & Row, 1986), pp. 151–52.

called for a 30 percent reduction over seven years in domestic discretionary spending, the budget sector that finances federal support of science—a horrific prospect for an enterprise long attuned to budget increases. However, as in Reagan's presidency, the spartan budget plan evaporated in the heat of politics and was succeeded by emphatic bipartisan commitments to large and rapid increases in science spending. "As little as a year ago, forecasts of break-even for the current fiscal year seemed to be little more than wishful thinking," the newspaper of the American Physical Society reported in late 1998. The dismal prospects, however, were reversed, it continued, "when President Clinton delivered a blockbuster of a science budget in February," followed by House Speaker Gingrich "calling for doubling funds for science over eight years."[16]

The Gingrich-led Republican Revolution was already collapsing from its own political folly. But its demise was helped along—and science spending was salvaged—by hard lobbying by scientific organizations, in the politically antiseptic fashion of science. The scientific message was apolitical and strictly economic, unembellished by lyrical appeals to the cultural importance of science or antiquated recitations about the value of knowledge for the sake of knowledge. In money-minded America of the last decade of the twentieth century, politics and the public worshipped the commercial successes produced by science, deifying Bill Gates—an entrepreneurial college dropout—but displaying scant interest in comprehending the scientific and technical knowledge that produced his wealth. Appropriately, scientists confronted by the politics of budget austerity warned that failure to spare science would inevitably create a cascade of economic misfortunes and ultimate American decline. The message was an artful contrivance by politicians of science, protecting their profession's stake in the federal budget by resurrecting the discredited linear model of science as the precursor of technology. Confessions of unwarranted panic-rousing are virtually nonexistent in science politics, as in other sectors of public affairs, but now and then a bit of candor can be detected. In 1999, the Board on Science, Technology and Economic Policy (STEP) of the National Academy of Sciences concluded in a report on the technological condition and competitiveness of American industry:

> The STEP Board's inquiry about U.S. industrial performance was
> prompted by the contrast between the diagnosis of the 1980s of secu-

---

16. Michael S. Lubell, APS Director of Public Affairs, "Inside the Beltway," *APS News*, August/September 1998.

lar economic decline and permanent loss of competitiveness and the experience in the late 1990s of growth, profitability, and stock market acceleration. In part, the earlier pessimism was a function of the narrow focus on manufacturing industries and overestimation of their foreign competition. But it is also true that underlying U.S. strengths in innovation were masked by adverse macroeconomic conditions, especially high interest rates and the high valuation of the dollar.[17]

In fact, since World War II, science has been deeply absorbed into the nation's economy and culture. Apart from heady interludes of antispending bombast, science is indisputably regarded, at times uncritically, as essential to prosperity, national security, environmental protection, and fulfillment of our hopes for healthful longevity. The processes and findings of research also engage millions of laypersons as an enjoyable, fascinating spectacle, as evidenced, for example, by public excitement over photos transmitted from Venus and Mars. John Glenn's return to space in November 1998 was a NASA extravaganza propelled by nostalgia and circus-barker claims of research on the processes of aging. But it, too, excited the public. Press reports of advances in biomedical research regularly produce floods of inquiries from an anxious, hopeful public. From expectations of utility, and strong public interest, research and development—including basic science—are generously supported by the federal government, industrial corporations, private philanthropies, and the universities of this richest of nations. Their previously cited combined annual expenditure of $227 billion in 1998 is about $80 billion above the comparable figure in 1989, when the Berlin Wall came down and the Cold War rapidly flickered out.

The National Science Foundation reported in 1997 that "the United States accounts for roughly 44 percent of the industrial world's R&D investment total and continues to outdistance, by more than 2 to 1, the total research investments made by Japan, the second largest performer."[18] Given the size and wealth of the United States, it is not surprising that American R&D spending exceeds that of any other country. But the total also exceeds the combined R&D spending of Japan, Germany, France, the U.K., Italy, and Canada. Science in Russia and the other descendants of the USSR barely survives, relying heavily on foreign charity, and no longer enters the list.

17. *Securing America's Industrial Strength* (Washington, D.C.: National Academy Press, 1999), p. 49.
18. *Science & Engineering Indicators, 1998,* pp. 4–5.

Those who are concerned about the adequacy of support for nonmilitary research in the United States correctly point out that the U.S. total is swollen by uniquely large spending on defense R&D—about half of the $78 billion that the president proposed for R&D in fiscal 2000, and a considerably larger share in prior years. But despite many doubts and ideological reservations, the huge sums apportioned to defense research do indeed benefit important sectors of scientific research and "downstream" activities in the civilian economy. Pentagon money underwrote the development of computer science and contributed to the creation of the Internet. Nonetheless, deduct the defense money and the American research enterprise still leads any other nation in nonmilitary research by a wide margin.

In 1998, NSF reported that "federal R&D support to academia has been increasing continuously since 1982, even after adjustment for inflation."[19] The numbers do not address the question of how much is enough, but they do establish that nostalgia for the presumed golden ages of scientific finance is poorly, if at all, related to the easily verifiable amounts of money provided for science in bygone times. Stated simply, the amount of money for research, and the purchasing power of that money, grew substantially between 1968 and 1991—years of financial decline, according to Nobelist Leon Lederman, and others.[20]

Whether measured in current dollars or in purchasing power compared to prior years, the gloom-filled modern times were far better financed than the long-ago golden age for which many scientists pined. Nonetheless, in 1991, Lederman, then president of the American Association for the Advancement of Science, wrote that "our current capability for research is only about one-third what it was in the late 1960s—a golden age whose achievements the nation is still profiting from."[21] The statement invites examination.

19. Ibid., pp. 4–8.
20. In 1968, described by Lederman as "the peak year in what we call the Golden Age," federal support for research performed in universities totaled $1.5 billion in current dollars and $5 billion in dollars adjusted for the purchasing power of 1987. In 1991, when Lederman and others wistfully looked back to what they recollected as the golden age, the current dollar total of federal support for university-based research stood at $10.2 billion and the inflation-adjusted total (in 1987 dollars) was $8.7 billion. From 1970 to 1993, support of basic research, from government, industry, and other sources, rose from $3.5 billion to $26 billion, in current dollars, and from $10 billion to $21 billion, in constant 1987 dollars. *Science & Engineering Indicators 1993* (NSB 93-1), pp. 331–32, 334.
21. Leon Lederman, "The Privilege and Obligation of Being a Scientist," *Physics Today*, April 1991.

DOLLARS AND PAPERS

As noted previously, the primary product of science comprises papers published in journals, whether in print or electronically, as is increasingly the case. Other products come out of science, too, important ones, such as trained graduates and patents. But, in the culture of science, published papers are the primary goal and the measure of achievement for recognition and personal advancement. Papers are what scientists produce, just as auto workers produce cars and apple growers produce apples. Gross production numbers reveal nothing about the quality or value of any of them. But they do tell something about the capability for producing them. Nonetheless, it is worth noting that science operates on the assumption that quality control is built into the research system through peer-review screening of applications for grants to conduct research and peer review of the ensuing papers submitted for publication. After papers are published, their worth is presumably subjected to scrutiny and criticism by knowledgeable researchers in the discipline. Accepting the dogma of scientific quality assurance at face value, let us assume, though perhaps naively, that banality in scientific literature is no greater today than in the past.

We will look only at the gross numbers of research papers produced by American scientists and published in any of the thousands of journals that are regarded as the primary literature of modern science. In 1973, American-produced articles in all the major fields of science and medicine totaled 103,778.[22] In 1991, the year in which Lederman lamented the reduced "capability for research," the number of publications stood at 142,334.[23] In Lederman's discipline, physics, the number of papers attributed to American researchers rose from 14,474 in 1981 to 22,670 in 1995, falling only slightly to 22,159 in 1998.[24]

The assertions of a *decline* over many years in the government's support of science are often repeated as straight matters of universally accepted fact, as incontestable as cents in a dollar or feet in a yard. Thus, in 1999, an op-ed column contributor, identified as "a senior research physicist at Yale University," tells readers of the *New York Times* that Congress "has cut the

22. *Science & Engineering Indicators* [hereafter *Indicators*] *1991*, p. A-388.
23. *Indicators 1998*, p. A-263.
24. The census of papers, conducted by the Institute for Scientific Information, refers to original research articles, notes, reviews and proceedings, a mix that remains fairly constant over time. The totals cited here for physics differ somewhat from the counts reported by the National Science Foundation, which derives its count from analyses of ISI data performed by a contracting firm. In both counts, the physics papers rise from the early 1980s to the mid-1990s and then level off.

budget for basic research every year since the 1970s, and especially in the 1990s, sending a message to potential physicists."[25] But the federal budget for basic research rose from $2.4 billion in 1970[26] to $19.5 billion in 1998,[27] and over $20 billion voted by Congress for 2000—data easily found in reliable, publicly available documents.

In a profession built on numeracy and dedicated to accuracy, what accounts for these topsy-turvy misstatements of fact? The complaints and the mangling of financial data without doubt reflected actual distress, principally of a localized nature: the number of money-seeking scientists was growing faster than the money. Lacking any real political power—a topic we will explore in greater detail later—science employed desperate appeals, in which precision took second place to propaganda. The interesting questions are why and how that happened and why it was permitted to happen. We will explore that matter next, armed with the understanding that leaders of science and their assistants are not the most reliable commentators on the historical, political, and financial realities of their profession. We will now proceed to a close examination of the quantity of money and, in particular, the often-made claims that the end of the Cold War terminated the principal rationale for government support of science and reduced the flow of money.

25. Alan Chodos, "Wanted: American Physicists," *New York Times,* op-ed, July 23, 1999.
26. *Indicators 1998,* p. A-127.
27. *National Patterns of R&D Resources 1998* (NSF 99-335), p. 37.

CHAPTER 6

Money, More Money, Statistics, and Science

The Government are very keen on amassing statistics—they collect them, add them, raise them to the nth power, take the cube root, and prepare wonderful diagrams. But what you must never forget is that every one of these figures comes in the first instance from the *chowty dar* [the village watchman], who just puts down what he damn pleases.

—Josiah Stamp, *Some Economic Factors in Modern Life,*
1929, quoting an unnamed English judge in India

IN PLUMBING science's sentimental recollections of its presumed golden ages, whatever the diverse datings of the various moon-struck commentators, it is useful, first, to document the amount of money provided for research by the federal and state governments, industry, and other sources during the past half-century. This can be a wearisome exercise, as we must tread through thickets of numbers to catalog the funds and trends of the numerous categories of research. The official compilations from which these numbers are taken are booby-trapped with footnotes declaring definitional shifts from past series of numbers, warnings of noncomparability, ex–post facto amendments to previously declared final data, cautions against misinterpretation, and other mystifications of the statistics trade, including confessions of errant billions.[1]

---

1. For instance: In *Science & Engineering Indicators,* the doomsday book of R&D statistics published by the National Science Board, page A-122 of the 1998 edition presents the following footnote to a table titled "U.S. R&D Expenditures, by Performing Sector and Source of Funds: 1970-97": "Expenditure levels for academic and Federal Government performers are . . . in reference to calendar years, which represents a change from previous reporting in *National Patterns of R&D Resources* [also published by NSF]. These levels are approximations based on fiscal year data. For 1977 and later years, the calendar year approximation is equal to 75 percent of the amount reported in the same fiscal year plus 25 percent of the amount reported in the subsequent fiscal year. For years prior to 1977, the respective percentages are 50 and 50, since earlier fiscal years began on July 1 instead of October 1."

Among the lacuna of research statistics are many billions of dollars. "For 1995," the NSF counters state,

> federal agencies reported $30.5 billion in total R&D obligations *provided* [original italics] to industrial performers, compared with an estimated $21.7 billion in federal funding *reported* by industrial performers. . . . Overall, governmentwide estimates equate to a "loss" of 31 percent of federally reported R&D support.[2]

Since the specialists have not sorted this out, and appear unperturbed by $8.8 billion gone astray, I will not try. Allowing a margin of error of a few billions, the essence of the story is rapid growth of money for research through most of the postwar years, with a leveling off and a few minor dips in the early 1990s, followed by a resumption of robust growth. In broad-brush fashion, we will note several financial fundamentals of the American system of R&D at the start of the twenty-first century:

- Contrary to a widely held impression, industry—not government—is the biggest spender on R&D, providing over 68 percent of the national total, mostly for development, i.e., design and engineering of hardware, machines, and other tangible products.
- Though the federal government is a junior partner in the financing of R&D, it dominates basic research, which is conducted mainly in universities and in the government's own laboratories. Because government is political, the politics of science focuses on the government portion of science.
- As the rate of growth for government support of academic research tapered off in the 1990s, universities and industry expanded their collaborations in research. Overall, however, industrial spending on university-based research remains relatively small, at about 7 percent of total academic research spending.
- State governments and universities, from their own resources, spend several billion dollars a year on university-based research, a financial fact that tends to be overlooked in the Washington-oriented fascination with the politics of science.

2. *Indicators 1998*, pp. 4–44.

In sum, the financing of research resembles a complex irrigation system, with the money flow originating at many points and flowing along diverse channels to many recipients.

The long-term record shows ever-greater amounts of government money pouring into the academic research system, accompanied by ever-greater choruses of complaints of inadequate support, warnings of the urgent need for even more money to avert serious damage to national well-being, and edgy expressions of anxiety about the fate that awaits science in distant fiscal years. Thus, in 1999, when the Clinton administration, responding to the political popularity of science, proposed substantial increases for academic research, budget analysts at the National Academy of Sciences nonetheless found reason to quibble and fret. Under the president's budget proposal, they acknowledged, "In constant dollars, support for R&D at colleges and universities would be up 16.6 percent from FY 1997 to FY 2000"—a notable increase, given the antideficit restraints mandated for federal spending. But, they pointed out, the growth in federal science spending in academe came largely from the soaring budget of the National Institutes of Health: when NIH funding "is excluded, support for R&D at colleges would increase only slightly. The increase in support from FY 1997 to FY 2000 without NIH is only 6.6 percent, and in constant dollars it is only 1.9 percent." The Academy's analysis also cautioned that "current projections of the FS&T [federal science and technology] budget indicate a 7.0 percent decline in constant dollars from FY 1999 to FY 2000, according to the AAAS [American Association for the Advancement of Science] analysis of the outyear projections of the FY 2000 budget. . . . If the projections hold, they pose serious problems for the overall health of the nation's research enterprise."[3] Unmentioned was the historical fact that up to that time, the projections had never held, and this instance was no exception. Plump though the president's budget was, Congress exceeded it by over $1 billion. The dialogue was unengaged to reality (as is much else in science politics), but as an instrument for getting the money sought by science, largely on its own terms, it worked. Readers who are satisfied with that financial synopsis may wish at this point to move on to the next chapter. To the others: slog along with me.

We will look at the gross numbers of money for research both in so-

3. Committee on Science, Engineering, and Public Policy, National Academy of Sciences, "Observations on the President's FY 2000 Federal Science and Technology Budget," in *Research & Development FY 2000* (Washington, D.C.: American Association for the Advancement of Science, 1999).

called current (everyday) dollars and constant dollars (dollar amounts reflecting purchasing power). The data are from *Science and Engineering Indicators 2000,* and the relevant tables from that publication are reproduced in the appendix to this book.

In current dollars, total spending for research in universities increased annually, without exception, in good and bad economic times, starting at $273 million in 1953 and rising to $26.3 billion in 1998. The federal portion rose from $149 million to $15.5 billion.[4] Again, in current dollars, there was no backsliding by federal and state governments, the major sources of external support for university-based research. In the early years, industry lagged a bit; but after a seven-year plateau of around $40 million per year beginning in the 1960s, industry entered a period of uninterrupted growth in support of academic research, raising its share to nearly $1.9 billion in 1998. The initial surge of industrial money created expectations of more to come among university researchers and in academe's burgeoning ranks of front-office drumbeaters and deal makers. But industry, attentive to return on expenditures, has actually been frugal in support of university science. Generally overlooked, in contrast, is the steady rise in their own funds—from tuition, endowment, gifts, etc.—that universities devote to research. Collectively, in current dollars, these expenditures increased from $37 million in 1953 to nearly $5 billion in 1998. Why is this home-based finance—which is far above industry's research spending in universities—virtually absent from public discussions of money and academic science? Because federal support of scientific research in universities has become a well-established practice—in contrast to financing the English department or library services, for which support from the federal government is scarce.

OVERHEAD AND UNDERHAND

To pay for scientific research, universities understandably prefer money from outside sources and spend their own funds reluctantly, usually only when other money is unavailable. In addition to its abundance, federal money for work in the laboratory is made even more attractive by the additional funds that accompany it for "overhead" costs. Also known as indirect costs, these are payments for ancillary expenses incurred in the course of performing research, including administration, library facilities, utilities, depreciation of buildings and research instruments, student services, and

---

4. *Indicators 2000,* p. A-311.

a host of activities that are remote from the actual conduct of research. University administrators correctly point out that the research activities financed by the government raise the costs of running academic institutions; also, that their pursuit of even more research dovetails with the nation's commitment to a flourishing research enterprise. But even though large sums are provided for indirect costs, the recipients ceaselessly complain that the amounts are inadequate for covering the overhead burdens generated by government-financed research. In 1999, indirect-cost payments constituted approximately 23 percent of the $14 billion in government science money for universities, according to Milton Goldberg of the Council on Government Relations, an association of some 145 research universities.[5] By that reckoning, about $3 billion never reached a laboratory. Shortly after taking office in 1993, the Clinton administration declared that overhead was taking an excessive bite from research funding:

> In 1972, each dollar of direct research funding paid to universities cost an additional 30 cents for the overhead allocated to Federal research. By 1990, 46 cents in overhead was paid for each dollar spent on direct research.[6]

The White House said the payments would be reduced and the savings redeployed to research. Loud protests followed, leading to only minor reductions. It should be noted that overhead payments in grants to academe by private foundations are generally capped by the donors at comparatively low levels; 15 percent is not unusual.

Many academic scientists chafe at the indirect-cost system, charging that it diverts precious research money into a bottomless pit of university bureaucracy. In 1982, James B. Wyngaarden left his position as chair of the research-oriented Department of Medicine at Duke University to become the director of NIH. Disturbed by the large proportion of NIH "research" money going into overhead payments, Wyngaarden called for revamping indirect-cost accountancy—downward. Applause came from the leading Washington lobby for the scientists who depended on NIH grants: the Federation of American Societies for Experimental Biology. Indignant hoots came from the organizations that represented central academic management: the Association of American Universities, the National Association

---

5. Conversation with author, January 19, 2000.
6. *A Vision of Change for America,* the White House (U.S. Government Printing Office, 1993), p. 90.

of State Universities and Land Grant Colleges, the American Council on Education, and others. Responding to an "options paper" presented to them by Wyngaarden for revising the criteria for indirect costs, they declared:

> The source of our difference is quite clear. It is your inference, repeated
> in the paper you have supplied, that indirect costs are not parts of
> grants and hence are not research costs but are a separate and less impor-
> tant class of costs; and by the proposition that those less important,
> non-research costs have risen "disproportionately." It is precisely the
> truth of those two propositions that is an issue.[7]

Minor adjustments followed in calculating indirect costs, but the system remained essentially unchanged—and unchangeable, like so much else in the ossified scientific enterprise.

The rate of overhead payments for any given institution varied, however, in reflection of their actual costs, which differed by region, level of academic grandeur, and the inventiveness of their business offices in billing Washington for segments of their activities. In 1989, researchers at Stanford University protested the university's soaring indirect-cost rates, charging it put their grant applications at a disadvantage. Under the heading "Faculty in Revolt Over High Costs of Research; Stanford Takes Steps to Hold Down Costs," the Stanford University News Service explained: "The faculty, fearing the rising rate will inhibit their ability to get grants from a diminishing federal pot, have anecdotal evidence that it is happening already." The dispensers of federal research money, meanwhile, insist that grants are awarded on scientific merit, not on price.

The invocation of "anecdotal evidence," usually scoffed at by scientists as untrustworthy, reflects the high-strung anxieties of the grant economy. Administrators contend that the overhead allowances are unrealistically low, and that official overhead rates, set in negotiations with government auditors, create a misleading impression of the amounts involved. The average official rate is around 50 percent; for elite private universities, it's usually far higher—for example, 79.9 percent at Harvard Medical School in 1998. The rates are widely thought to indicate the actual share for indirect costs sliced from a research grant before the balance is made available to the researcher. But with various caps and disallowances, the effective rate

---

7. "The Cost Options on Which Academe Gagged," *SGR,* April 1, 1983.

for indirect costs is approximately 30 percent, and the dollars for indirect costs are added to, rather than extracted from, the payment of direct costs for research—salaries, equipment, supplies, travel, and other items closely connected with the actual conduct of research. Thus, a scientist who receives a $100,000 grant for research does not yield any part of it to grooming the campus shrubbery or running the library. Nonetheless, money for indirect costs comes out of the pool of government money appropriated for science; it is not a separate item in the federal budget.

With large sums at stake, the intricacies of indirect-cost computation have spawned a subdivision of micro-accountancy with two branches: one, on the administrative side of universities, seeks to get as much as it can from the federal research agencies that support university science; the other, on the government side, is dedicated to minimizing the expenditures. Looking on, and aggrieved, are the scientists, convinced that "their" money is being squandered for nonscientific purposes.

As with science politics in general, the overhead controversies that chronically simmer in academe rarely rate public notice. But occasionally, they boil over into public view. In 1991, Stanford University President Donald Kennedy was pilloried by the sulfurous Congressman John Dingell after a government auditor accused the university of rapacious billing tactics in claims of overhead costs that Stanford submitted as reimbursable by federal research agencies. Cited were a variety of pricey antiques for Kennedy's presidential residence at the university, among them a $1,200 nineteenth-century Italian fruitwood commode and expenditures of $17,730 for catering, liquor, heated tents, "rental of champagne flutes and silver trays," and other items for Kennedy's wedding reception.[8] Widely hailed up to that time as an exemplar of academic leadership, Kennedy resigned soon afterward. Several years later, in a reflective book on the modern university, he lamely attributed the overhead debacle to the financial intricacies of academic-federal relations:

> The problem, of course, lay in the concept of pool accounting. Under
> that principle, expenses that most citizens would quickly conclude
> should be eligible for full government reimbursement as research costs
> are treated the same as ones that sound outrageously irrelevant to re-
> search. Certainly, the government shouldn't pay 23 percent of the cost

---

8. Subcommittee on Oversight and Investigations, *Financial Responsibility at Universities: Hearings before the House Committee on Energy and Commerce,* 102d Cong., 1st sess., March 13 and May 9, 1991, p. 184.

of flowers for university entertainment. But 100 percent of the salary of the staff member serving the Human [Research] Subjects Committee would sound quite legitimate. The pool includes both research-related and unrelated items; on average, 23 percent of all the expenditures were shown by statistical studies to be research-related, and as a matter of auditing simplification they all carry the same reimbursement. The revelations were damaging, and made more so by the way in which the "sensitive items" were represented. For example, there was no $1,600 shower curtain and no $7,000 bed sheets. The government's auditors failed to recognize that vendors often lump purchases. The shower curtain was one minor bill for a large amount of upholstery and drapery work, and the sheets item was actually an extensive one-time replacement of all the house's table linens. . . . As for the fruitwood commode—actually a cherry chest of drawers—the chairman [Congressman Dingell] could not resist a wry reminder of the costly toilet seat made famous in his earlier hearings on defense contractors. By innuendo and creative imprecision, he made his contempt for the university clear.[9]

Extensively publicized, and deeply embarrassing to the university as well as to the carefully guarded reputation of academic science, the Stanford episode sent shivers throughout the university research system. Representative Dingell was on the warpath, demanding that the major recipients of federal science money explain and justify their claims for indirect-cost reimbursement. Several major universities hurriedly revised their government billings, among them MIT, which announced in April 1991 that it had voluntarily withdrawn $731,000 claimed in indirect costs for the years 1986–90. MIT's accompanying statement provided another window on the mysteries of science finance, as explained by James J. Culliton, MIT's vice president for financial operations, who cited "the desire to avoid any risk of continued damage to the long-standing government-university partnership so vital to national research":

Reimbursement for the costs of official functions—dinners, dinner meetings and receptions—at the president's house was withdrawn. The savings average $24,000 a year, a total of $120,500. Costs withdrawn from the President's House involved catering, food, flowers, alcohol, rental of chairs and printing of programs for official functions. The total included

9. Donald Kennedy, *Academic Duty* (Harvard University Press, 1997), p. 171.

an average of $2,700 a year—about $13,600 over five years—for flowers for the public meeting and reception areas downstairs in the President's House.[10]

The MIT announcement made it clear that the relinquished sum was a minuscule portion of MIT's research money: "The $731,000 withdrawn over a five-year period represents significantly less than one percent of the $482,000,000 in indirect costs of MIT and Lincoln Laboratory [a defense facility managed by MIT for the federal government] research during that time. MIT on-campus research for those five years totaled $1.36 billion, including $978 million in direct costs and $383 million in indirect costs."

UPWARD IN PURCHASING POWER

Calculated in constant dollars adjusted to 1992, the record of support for academic research, from all sources, is also strongly upward, though with slight—but far from ruinous—dips in several years. From 1960 to 1998, the constant-dollar total rose from $3 billion to $23.3 billion.[11] The first year that didn't bring greater purchasing power was 1969, when total support declined by less than one percent, to $7.8 billion—about $35 million below the previous year. In 1970, growth resumed, bringing the total to a record high of $7.9 billion. In summarizing the financial history of federal support of academic science, NSF reports that 1998 "was the 24th consecutive year in which constant dollar spending increased from the previous year."[12]

Within these grand totals, relative levels of support for the disciplines varied over the years in response to changing national priorities, political influence, and, especially, scientific advances that created further opportunities for research. Hence, as the totals rose, some elements would, nonetheless, experience losses or an absence of growth, while others gained. For example, following the OPEC oil embargo of 1973, the Nixon and later the Ford and Carter administrations favored research on energy conservation and development of renewable energy sources. Accordingly, money from the Department of Energy (and its variously named predecessors) flowed into academic science, rising from $94 million in 1971, under Nixon, to

10. "Indirect Costs: MIT Announces On-Going Audit Review; Withdraws $146K Per Year for FY 86-90," MIT News Office, April 23, 1991.
11. *Indicators 2000,* p. A-312.
12. *Indicators 2000,* vol. 1, pp. 6–7.

$300 million when Carter left office in 1981. Over that decade, the financial growth produced real gains in purchasing power (calculated in 1987 dollars), from $259 million in 1971 to $386 million in 1981.[13]

The financial fortunes of academe contrasted greatly with horrendous economic declines and disruptions in other sectors of the great metropolis of science and technology as the Cold War waned and budget-balancing passions gripped American politics. Between 1989 and 1994, the workforce of the aerospace industry declined by 32 percent, or 471,000 jobs.[14] In contrast, the university-centered Ph.D. workforce rode out that economic storm essentially intact. In 1989, the year the Berlin Wall came down, academic institutions employed 206,000 doctorates in science and engineering, including the social sciences. By 1995, the number had risen to 217,000.[15] From 1973 to 1996, the medical sciences, mainly financed by the National Institutes of Health, were the biggest gainers in shares of federal funds, with their proportion rising from 22.4 to 27.6 percent of federal academic support.[16] Between 1990 and 1998, the NIH budget rose by 80 percent, while the overall federal budget for civilian purposes went up by 48 percent.[17] Yet, until NIH was awarded an unprecedented $2 billion budget increase for 1999, the medical sciences exceeded all other branches of science in alleging neglect by the federal government. And, immediately upon receiving that increase, the medical-research lobbies issued strong public warnings against backsliding of support.

Before they tapered off into modest increases in the early 1990s, the growth rates for federal finance of the major scientific disciplines were extraordinarily robust, far above the nation's economic growth or the federal tax collections that pay the bills for research. In the life sciences, for example, federal obligations for basic research increased, with only minor fluctuations, from $372 million in 1963 to $4.2 billion in 1988, and then rose to over $15 billion in 1999. In the physical sciences (primarily astronomy, chemistry, and physics) federal support increased from $228 million in 1963 to $1.8 billion in 1988 and $2 billion in 1995.[18] By the reckoning of

13. *Indicators 1996*, p. A-176.

14. Aerospace Industries Association, *1993 Aerospace Industry Employment Survey*, press release, March 14, 1994.

15. *Indicators 1998*, p. A-229

16. Alan I. Rapoport, "How Has the Field Mix of Academic R&D Changed?" *Issue Brief* (Washington, D.C.: National Science Foundation, December 2, 1998).

17. *Scientific Opportunities and Public Needs: Improving Priority Setting and Public Input at the National Institutes of Health* (Washington, D.C.: National Academy Press, 1998).

18. Budget data compiled from *Science & Engineering Indicators* editions for 1982 and onward.

the National Academy of Sciences, federal obligations for research and development at colleges and universities rose from $12.7 billion in 1997 to $15.4 billion proposed by the president for the year 2000—a gain of 16.6 percent in purchasing power.[19] The dollars and percentage gain turned out to be even higher when Congress exceeded the sums requested by the president.

Minor declines, from one year to the next, occasionally occurred before growth resumed. The National Institutes of Health would sometimes respond to these declines by "negotiating"—i.e., unilaterally decreeing—reductions of 5 to 15 percent in the phased payment of previously awarded multiyear grants. The managers of NIH said the grants must be trimmed to accommodate a disappointing budget. But to scientists on the losing end of this process, the government appeared to be reneging on promised grants, though the recipients had been warned about possible reductions. Publicly, the outcome was yet another din alleging neglect of science, though over the long stretch, the growth in federal support of basic research can be described only as phenomenal. Along the way, changes in priorities were frequently dictated by the interplay of politics and economics. Even so, the federal commitment to academic research remained intact, providing the finances for a system in which annual increases came to be regarded as the natural order of things, equilibrium as a setback, and decline as catastrophic.

The sums, as we have seen, are colossal in their scale and continually upward. We now turn to the strange circumstances that assure that more is never enough.

---

19. Committee on Science, Engineering, and Public Policy, *Observations on the President's Fiscal Year 2000 Federal Science and Technology Budget* (Washington, D.C., National Academy Press), April 13, 1999.

CHAPTER 7

The Malthusian Imperative
and the Politics of Trust

Scientists and engineers are now a couple of percent of the labor force of the United States, and the annual expenditure on research and development is about the same fraction of the Gross National Product. It is clear that we cannot go up another two orders of magnitude as we have climbed the last five. If we did, we should have two scientists for every man, woman, child, and dog in the population, and we should spend on them twice as much money as we had. Scientific doomsday is therefore less than a century away.

—Derek J. de Solla Price,
Little Science, Big Science (1963)

FOR DECADES, the reproductive urge in science and engineering was abetted by policies that sanctified and subsidized the training of doctoral students, with little or no regard to their employability, except as cheap labor in the academic research system. A confident belief in infinite demand for science and scientists and commensurate public benefits from their propagation extended back at least to Vannevar Bush's 1945 proposals concerning the postwar relationship of science and government. Prior to World War II, the proportion of young Americans attending college was far lower than it is today, and fewer could afford, or even aspire to, graduate education. The war, approaching an end when the Bush report was conceived, was fought with wondrous technologies that raised expectations of even greater achievements to come for military and civilian purposes. That more scientists and engineers would be needed was self-evident. Reporting to Bush, the Committee on Discovery and Development of Scientific Talent, chaired by Henry Allen Moe (secretary-general of the John Simon Guggenheim Foundation), endorsed expansionism—without reservation:

> We are convinced that there is no possibility that too much ability of
> the highest order can be discovered and developed: the needs of our
> complex social organization for brains and character at the highest level
> can never be surfeited.[1]

That faith, in tandem with the labor requirements of an expanding
research system, inevitably produced that recurring paradox of the postwar
years: bigger budgets for research and training leading to greater financial
crises in the community of science. More money for science was deified as
indispensable to national well-being by the National Academy of Sciences,
the National Science Foundation, and the lobbying associations working
in Washington for the universities that awarded the bulk of the graduate
degrees. More federal money for science education at all levels, but especially for graduate training, was a basic part of their prescription for assuring
American leadership and safety. With access to the congressional and executive agencies that ultimately controlled the money they sought, these organizations—disputed by few if any dissenting voices—sketched the reality
that guided the politics of science. In the congressional witness chair, "crisis" was a key word in their testimony on the closely linked topics of money
for research and the need to produce more scientists and engineers.

In the late 1980s and in the 1990s, when the predicted demand did not
materialize, and, to the contrary, unemployment and underemployment
became the fate of many postgraduates, an inexorable *future* need for more
was confidently, and aggressively, forecast. As credibility drained out of the
shortage warnings, a new rationale was fielded to justify the maintenance,
and even the expansion, of the education system: the science and engineering degree should be regarded as a ticket to "alternative careers," just
as the law degree has traditionally opened doors for well-paid employment
apart from the practice of law. In 1995, the prestigious Committee on Science, Engineering, and Public Policy of the National Academy of Sciences,
replete with tenured, well-paid professors, expressed opposition to any reduction in Ph.D. output. The graduate education system, it said, should
carry on as before, with traditional research-based training, but should also
adopt measures to "meet the expanding need for advanced scientists and
engineers in careers outside research."[2] When the job market failed to co-

---

1. Vannevar Bush, *Science, The Endless Frontier,* 40th anniversary edition (Washington,
   D.C.: National Science Foundation, 1990), p. 147.
2. *Reshaping the Graduate Education of Scientists and Engineers* (Washington, D.C.: National
   Academy Press, 1995), pp. 5–16.

operate with this hopeful vocational scenario, realism belatedly won out, many years into the contrived shortage saga. Noting that the annual production of doctorates in the life sciences exceeded job openings in the universities by two and a half times and was also in excess of the needs of industry and government, another committee of the National Academy of Sciences diplomatically, but clearly, stated:

> In response to the increasing difficulty of finding employment in traditional sectors, trainees and their mentors have looked to alternative careers, such as law, science writing, science policy and secondary-school teaching. Our analysis suggests that opportunities in these fields might not be as numerous or as attractive as advocates of alternative careers imply.[3]

THE SCIENTIFIC WORKFORCE

In examining supply and demand for doctorates, the ultimate educational product of the research system, we must first recognize that census-taking in this area, as with much else in the statistics of research, is enmeshed in uncertainties. The doctoral degree as a "ticket" of admission or "union card" matters greatly in academe, which almost invariably insists on it as a prerequisite for professorial and research appointments; greater flexibility exists in the nonacademic sectors of serious scientific work. As careers evolve and circumstances change, scientists without Ph.D.'s succeed as researchers and research managers in industry and government, while some with Ph.D.'s in science move to non-scientific fields. Foreigners, who constitute a large proportion of the doctoral population, remain in the United States in numbers that change with economic and political conditions in their homelands and domestic immigration policies and quotas.

The tracking systems lose sight of many people. The fast-growing computer and software industries are less interested in educational achievement than in potential and on-the-job performance. The academic sector keeps good numbers on employment within its own institutions and on its production of degree holders. However, industry and business are less attentive to the credentials of their employees, and increasingly so as booming commercial technologies diverge from traditional academic course work. As often noted, Bill Gates is a Harvard dropout; other billionaire barons of the

---

3. *Trends in the Early Careers of Life Scientists* (Washington, D.C.: National Academy Press, 1998), p. 3.

new industries are similarly short on academic credits. However, the politics of science, anchored in major research universities, still revolves around academic research and the closely associated training of researchers to the Ph.D. level, though they represent a minuscule splinter of the American labor force. Nonetheless, graduate students and employed postdoctoral fellows are important for the conduct of academic research and they are numerically accounted for—allowing for the quantification on which science politics feasts, even if the numbers are detached from the real workings of the overall research enterprise.

The rarity of Ph.D. scientists in the American workforce makes economic sense, since their extensive, specialized training is directly applicable only to narrow slices of the work economy. They are exotics—rare species in the job market. In 1995, when employment of all occupational categories in the U.S. totaled nearly 125 million, merely 305,300 postdoctorates were employed in what some of the practitioners haughtily refer to as the "hard sciences": the natural and physical sciences, mathematics, computer science, and engineering. Another 143,000 held Ph.D.'s in psychology, sociology, education, and other fields sometimes derided as the "soft sciences." The total annual conferral of Ph.D.'s in the so-called hard-science fields has always been small relative to many other job categories, totaling 19,219 graduates in 1995, about 10,000 above the annual output thirty years earlier.[4] Universities are the main workplace of postdoctorates in the "hard" sciences and engineering, employing 154,150 in 1995; industry and business were second, with 126,870; the federal government was a distant third, with 26,310.[5]

Despite the relatively small size of the nation's cast of scientists, the politics of science has frequently resounded during the postwar years with deliberations and controversy over Ph.D. production. One reason is that ever since the end of World War II, the federal government has paid a substantial share of the cost of Ph.D. training in science and engineering (and, until the physician glut became too big and troublesome to ignore, also in medicine), in contrast to providing loans and a limited number of fellow-

---

4. *Science & Engineering Degrees, 1966–95* (NSF 97-335), p. 43.

5. The comparatively low number of government-employed doctorates does not reflect the powerful presence of Washington in the national science economy; a major portion of the salaries and costs of research performed in universities and industry is financed with grants and contracts from government agencies. NIH, for example, spends only about 10 percent of its budget on research in its own laboratories, with virtually all the rest of its billions flowing to "extramural" researchers and the indirect costs of their employers.

ships in the arts and humanities and the various fields of professional training. With science initially thriving as a component of national security on
the Cold War front, federal assistance for training scientists and engineers
easily followed; it persisted, even after the end of the Cold War, when international economic competition was pushed (even by political conservatives) as the rationale for heavy federal involvement in basic research.

The "Stoop Labor" of Science

The provision of federal money inevitably inspired a clamor for more
money as universities comfortably adjusted to Washington as a fount of
support. As John E. Jankowski, director of NSF's R&D statistics program,
observed in 1998, "In the past, many in academia simply got used to a good
thing."[6] An accompanying reason for the prominence of Ph.D. issues in
science politics is that doctoral candidates are an essential part of the research enterprise, deeply integrated into the primary task of producing research papers. Ph.D. candidates qualify for the degree by serving their laboratory chiefs as the scientific equivalent of the stoop labor of agriculture.
And with jobs appropriate to their training and preferences in short supply
after they receive the degree, thousands survive as low-paid postdoctoral
fellows. In a 1999 *Science* (the weekly journal of the American Association
for the Advancement of Science) news report titled "Cheap Labor Is Key to
U.S. Research Productivity," a scientist asked, "What's the most economical
way to finance high-quality research? There's no question," he answered,
"that you get the biggest bang for your buck by using postdocs"—scientists
who have completed their training and can apply advanced skills to a research project. Wages for scientists are relatively low, an economist explained, because "young scientists are more committed to their work than
to financial rewards. They refuse to bail out, even when the job market
tightens, creating an excess supply that holds down wages. And postdocs
are on the bottom of that heap."[7] The low status, low pay, and uncertain futures of the postdoc population evoke sympathy from their better-
situated superiors, but little else. Addressing a meeting of the President's
Committee of Advisors for Science and Technology in December 1999,

6. John E. Jankowski, "Statistical Data and Their Impact on University Research Efforts:
   Trends and Patterns of Academic R&D Expenditures," paper delivered at the Confer-
   ence on Performance Measurements for Research and Development in Universities and
   Colleges, sponsored by the International Quality and Productivity Center, Washington,
   D.C., May 18–19, 1998.
7. *Science*, September 3, 1999, p. 1519.

Frank Press, former president of the National Academy of Sciences, expressed dismay about the plight of the postdocs. "It depresses me to see
these sad sacks in their third or fourth postdoc appointment," Press said.
But, he noted, too, that postdocs—young and strongly motivated—were
in the forefront of scientific accomplishment.

By century's end, abuse of postdocs had become so common and blatant that the prestige-laden National Academy of Sciences—previously indifferent to their well-known plight—proclaimed the need for humanitarian relief. The concept of postdoc appointments is sound in principle, an
academy committee stated, but, it continued:

> Postdocs often receive no clear statement of the terms of their appoint-
> ment and have no place to go to determine appropriate expectations or
> redress grievances. Often the sole person to whom they can turn for as-
> sistance is the Principle Investigator (PI) who hired them and upon
> whom they depend not only for support in their current position but
> also for help in advancing their careers. . . . At the lower end of the
> [post-doc] salary range—which is typical of the life sciences in aca-
> demia—the pay is embarrassingly low. . . . There is no standard health
> benefit for postdocs. . . . [W]e also learned about postdocs who are ne-
> glected, even exploited inappropriately, while making creative and fun-
> damental contributions to the research projects on which they worked.
> The need to improve the postdoctoral experience has led some institu-
> tions to formulate policies to govern their employment. . . . In other in-
> stances, postdocs themselves have formed organizations to promote com-
> mon interests. Other indications of serious dissatisfaction are the
> occasional discussions of unionization and even litigation; though rare,
> these more confrontational calls for action are at least a sign that reform
> is needed.[8]

With Ph.D. training and thesis writing in the sciences rarely taking less
than five years, the job market that awaits an entering candidate is hidden
in the distant mists of the proudly unplanned, vigorous American economy. And it has remained so despite numerous scholarly attempts to divine
the job markets of the future. The Congressional Office of Technology Assessment (OTA) emphasized that uncertainty in its 1985 review of scientific

---

8. Maxine Singer, preface to *Enhancing the Postdoctoral Experience for Scientists and Engineers: A Guide for Postdoctoral Scholars, Advisers, Institutions, Funding Organizations, and
Disciplinary Societies* (Washington, D.C.: National Academy Press, 2000).

staffing studies: "Given the problems with forecasting supply and demand for scientists and engineers, predictions of shortages based on such forecasts should be treated with skepticism."[9] Citing a retrospective study of the 10–15 year forecasts of the demand for engineers that the Bureau of Labor Statistics (BLS) made in 1960 and 1965, OTA noted that the BLS "overprojected" by 20 to 55 percent: "The errors were caused by the understandable failure of the BLS to anticipate the cutbacks in Federal R&D expenditures in the early 1970s and the recession in the mid-1970s." On the supply side, the OTA analysis continued, NSF was far off in the past in estimating future Ph.D. awards in science and engineering, forecasting in 1967 that they would number 30,500 in 1975. The actual number in that year: 17,784.[10] But the mid-1980s cautions against crystal-ball gazing failed to quell ostensibly authoritative warnings of a coming, crippling shortage of Ph.D.'s in science and engineering.

THE SPECTER OF SOVIET SCIENCE

The Cold War provided fertile ground for American doctoral expansionism, right up to the unforeseen disintegration of the Soviet Union. The West was aware of Marxism's reverence for science, the privileged place of science in the spartan Soviet economy, and the prowess of the Soviets in space and nuclear weaponry. The evidence seemed to substantiate the scientific leadership's warnings that an accelerating red tide of Soviet science threatened American security. Presented dispassionately, decade after decade, by distinguished scholars and leaders of science in the United States and Europe, the drumbeat of warnings raised serious concern. In 1963, C. P. Snow praised the rigor, scale and pervasiveness of scientific and technical education in the Soviet Union:

> With some qualifications, I believe the Russians have judged the situation sensibly. They have a deeper insight into the scientific revolution than we have, or the Americans have. . . . As the scientific revolution goes on, the call for these [scientifically and technically] trained men will be something we haven't imagined, though the Russians have.[11]

9. Office of Technology Assessment, *Demographic Trends and the Scientific and Engineering Work Force: A Technical Memorandum*, 1985.

10. Ibid., p. 24.

11. C. P. Snow, *The Two Cultures and a Second Look* (New York: Mentor Books, 1963), p. 39.

In 1985, Frank Press, president of the National Academy of Sciences, stated that "the USSR has the largest science and engineering manpower pool of any nation, and in many areas of science and technology Soviet accomplishments are at the forefront."[12] Warnings of this nature were amply backed by the numbers collectors of the National Science Foundation and their statistical counterparts in the Organization for Economic Cooperation and Development (OECD), the Paris-based association of industrialized nations. In a frequently cited measure, percentage of gross national product devoted to research and development, the USSR led the world by far throughout the 1970s and 1980s, spending 3.9 percent of its wealth on R&D in 1984, compared to 2.6 percent by the United States. Even if accurate, the comparison was chimerically meaningless, given the far larger size of the American economy, the decrepitude in the USSR of the industrial infrastructure on which modern science depends, and the near-isolation of Soviet scientists from the stimulus of world-leading Western scientific research. But the comparative standings in share of gross national product expended on research and development carried the ring of statistical authority, and menace to American security. By a wide, and alarming, margin, the Soviets also led in claimed numbers of scientists and engineers engaged in research and development. The NSF-OECD statisticians were appropriately modest in their workforce reports for the secretive Soviets, merely estimating the R&D ranks at between 1,399,000 and 1,603,000 in 1982. But, in relation to either level, the United States was a laggard, with only 722,000.[13] Testifying in support of Soviet-American scientific exchanges, Academy President Press not only emphasized the massive scale of the Soviet research enterprise, but stressed that "in many areas of science and technology Soviet accomplishments are at the forefront," citing "impressive achievements in astronomy, geology, oceanography, electrochemistry, fluid dynamics, and material sciences, and their capabilities in molecular biology are increasing."[14] The message was clear, and in harmony with prevailing assessments of the USSR's overall might: the American scientific enterprise faced challenges from its well-supported counterpart in the world's other superpower. Though much of the chill had gone out of the Cold War by the late 1980s, the two nations still faced each other on hair-trigger nuclear

12. Frank Press, testimony, Subcommittee on Europe and the Middle East, House Committee on Foreign Affairs, 99th Cong., 2d sess., July 31, 1986.

13. *International Science and Technology Data Update 1986* (NSF 86-307), pp. 4, 24.

14. Press, op. cit.

alert, and official relations remained prickly. Up to the end of the Cold War, invocation of worrisome comparisons with the USSR, sinking though it was, remained a durable tactic in American science politics. Buttressed with numbers, the arguments for more money, more research, and more scientists were tinged with warnings of danger.

In 1988—three years before the collapse of the Soviet Union—a typical warning concerning the educational underpinnings of Soviet scientific strength emanated from the American Chemical Society, a leading professional organization spanning industry and academe. Following an educational tour of the Soviet Union, cosponsored by the science academies of the two nations, the director of the Lawrence Hall of Science at the University of California, Berkeley, gushed with admiration for elementary and secondary science education in the USSR and expressed fears for its American counterparts. "Our talented students will still achieve success, but we are losing our scientific and technological edge to other nations," she reported to ACS members.[15]

Paradoxically, American visitors to Soviet laboratories usually returned with puzzled, if not disparaging, reports of dowdy buildings, obsolete equipment, and backward methods. In 1987, James B. Wyngaarden, director of the National Institutes of Health, toured Soviet medical-research facilities. It is a reasonable assumption that the Soviets wished to make a favorable impression on the head of NIH, the world's greatest biomedical research institution. Yet Wyngaarden reported: "We were shown laboratories that were even more primitive than the ones that I saw when I was a medical student at the University of Michigan in the early 1940s. They've not even advanced to that stage," he concluded.[16]

The widely offered explanation for the disparity between the warnings about Soviet scientific strength and foreign visitors' firsthand observations of dilapidation was that Soviet science existed in two separate realms: an antiquated, neglected civilian sector and a well-supported, hidden military sector that was said to compare favorably with modern Western facilities. Firsthand accounts of the presumed world-class facilities were virtually nonexistent. In their penchant for secrecy, the Soviets even concealed the names of the senior administrators of their space program. However, the paucity of reliable information about the Soviet research system aided

15. Marjorie Gardner, "How Does Ivan's and Yelena's Education Compare with Johnny's and Helen's?" *CHEMTECH*, August 1988.
16. Interview with author, January 2, 1987, in "Q&A: NIH Director Ranges Over Budget, Fraud, Soviet Ties," *SGR*, February 1, 1987.

rather than impeded the alarmists. When they said Soviet science was ten feet tall, who could prove otherwise? After all, the Soviets had opened the space age in 1957 by launching Sputnik into orbit, thus humiliating America and loosening a fear-driven surge of government support for catching up in science, technology, and related graduate training. But after the triumphant Apollo moon journey in 1969, the fright level in the United States declined, and with it, the sense of urgency for bolstering American strength in science and technology. Was another American humiliation needed to counter the return of complacency? The United States obviously needed more science. More science would require more scientists, and, because of the organizational structure of science, they would produce more scientists.

Soviet Science: Postcollapse Assessment

Following the disintegration of the USSR, a seasoned American scholar of Soviet science, Loren R. Graham, concluded that it had performed well under extraordinarily difficult circumstances. But he also noted that "the Soviet Union was underachieving, not receiving as much outstanding science and technology as it should have in return for its enormous expenditures on research and development."[17] While noting high-level Soviet achievements in space, nuclear power, theoretical physics, and mathematics, and a strong presence in other fields, Graham added: "When one considers that the mature Soviet Union possessed the world's largest scientific establishment, one has to conclude that the output of that system was disappointingly meager. No matter what criterion of excellence one chooses—number of Nobel Prizes awarded, frequency of citation of Soviet research, number of inventions registered abroad, or honorary membership in foreign scientific societies—the achievements of Soviet scientists were disproportionately small."[18]

The Cold War's quasi-mobilization against the Communist threat provided an easily comprehensible rationale for producing more scientists and engineers. Medical research, distant from national security, thrived by addressing and nurturing America's fears of disease and rising hopes for preventive measures and cures. An unarguable rationale held that more scientists would produce more research, which would lead to treatments and

17. Loren R. Graham, *What Have We Learned about Science and Technology from the Russian Experience?* (Stanford, Calif.: Stanford University Press, 1998), p. 133.
18. Ibid., p. 85.

cures for the health afflictions of the American people. Who could quibble with that obviously sensible, alluring proposition?

As federal funds for research and development in universities increased, so did federal money for graduate training, either as supplements linked to research projects or as direct grants to students. And, as the federal money for research increased, the demand for laboratory workers propelled universities into allocating more of their own resources for graduate-student support. Academic pride played an important part. A presence in big-league science was a mark of distinction for a university, its status-conscious professors and administrators, and proud alumni. Community boosters also relished the glow of scientific recognition for the hometown university, as did state legislatures for public institutions.

The capacity to perform research is essential in attracting projects and financial support. In 1999, the University of Florida, at Gainesville, ambitious and climbing in national academic rankings, was completing construction of a $100 million-plus cluster of research buildings: the Brain Institute, the Physics Building, and the Particle Science and Technology Building. The Physics Building, which cost $32 million, was already credited with drawing new projects. "We're finding that the university gets called into leadership roles in a way it didn't used to," the chair of the physics department proudly explained, adding that "a second-class physics department at a university of our size and prestige was totally unacceptable."[19] With its knack for statistics, science joined intercollegiate sports as a quantifiable symbol of academic standing, citing scientific counterparts of yards gained rushing, games won and lost, and trophies collected. Thus, in 1999, the president of Yale University, Richard Levin, announced a $500 million construction plan for science and engineering facilities on campus. As reported in the *New York Times:*

> Aided by its medical school, Yale is stronger scientifically than its reputation might suggest, Mr. Levin contends. He said it was among the top four universities in grants from the National Institutes of Health and among the top four in scientific articles cited by others. Most of its science and engineering departments are ranked among the top 12 nationally, he said, and two—physiology and pharmacology—are number one in graduate department ratings. Sixty-three Yale professors are members of the National Academy of Sciences, placing it fifth after Harvard (158),

19. "Scientific Super Structure," in *Explore: Research at the University of Florida,* spring 1999.

the University of California at Berkeley (115), Stanford (111) and the Massachusetts Institute of Technology (100). But the Yale faculty includes only one Nobel laureate in the sciences: Sidney Altman, who won the Nobel Prize in chemistry in 1989 for research on RNA.[20]

COMPETING FOR SCIENCE

Starting early in the postwar period, and rapidly accelerating as Washington opened the treasury to science, the status conferred by research fueled competition in which the top institutions experienced a new threat: pressure from below. Between 1975 and 1995, the number of universities receiving federal research money rose from 555 to 882.[21] In the years following 1965, 39 medical schools were founded, bringing the national total to 126, thus enlarging the constituency for the financial mainstay of medical research, the grant-giving National Institutes of Health. Like airlines for third-world nations, or major-league sports teams for cities seeking to rise from Podunk status, science served as a confirmation of accomplishment for diverse interests bound together by ambitions for recognition, glory, growth, and the performance of good works.

Colleges and universities that were late arrivals in the science business writhed under a system that rewarded scientific competence with government grants that further strengthened the recipients for the next round of competition. This was indeed a system that, left to the scientists who ran it, guaranteed that the rich got richer. Of the 3,600 institutions of higher education in the United States, 200 accounted for 94 percent of all academic research spending in 1995.[22] Six states—California, Michigan, New York, Massachusetts, New Jersey, and Texas—received half of the $177 billion that government and industry spent on R&D in 1995.[23] Within that grand total, thirteen states received nearly two-thirds of all federal funds for research in universities—particularly choice money, since academic research support, most of it awarded competitively, signified quality and was a magnet for high-tech industry and its clean, high-paying jobs. For getting research done, the lopsided distribution of money was unassailable, as relatively few schools among the mass of institutions were capable of performing high-grade research. The situation, however, was politically unten-

---

20. "At Yale, a $500 Million Investment in Science," *New York Times,* January 19, 2000.
21. *Indicators 1998,* pp. 5–14.
22. Ibid., pp. 5–10.
23. Ibid., pp. 4–30.

able because of its vulnerability to populist denunciation as elitist and unfair. State and local politics resonated with dreams of science-based prosperity anchored in university science departments buoyed by federal grants. Fear of a backlash from the have-nots was recognized as a political danger by the managers of the National Science Foundation. In 1978 they began their special effort to nurture research-poor universities into the charmed circle of grant recipients: the Experimental Program to Stimulate Competitive Research (EPSCoR), designed "to improve the quality of science and increase the ability of scientists in eligible states to compete successfully for Federal funds."[24] The departure from scientific competition served the dual purpose of placating the aggrieved and, when successful (as it has been in some instances), increasing the number of customers for grants—a strong selling point for NSF and other government research agencies when they pleaded that funds were inadequate for good science waiting to be done. As noted earlier (see chapter 2), from an NSF budget that totaled over $3.5 billion in 1999, EPSCoR was allotted merely $48.4 million for the task of uplifting scientifically backward institutions, but at this relatively minor cost, it helped stifle the cries of the have-nots. EPSCoR-style programs were soon emulated by other federal agencies, even as scientists in universities that had long ago made the grade were complaining of inadequate support for first-class research. The EPSCoR concept soothed the irritations created by a quality-based, competitive scientific enterprise embedded in an egalitarian political system.

With federally supported training programs annually graduating more grant-seeking doctorates into the system, the process defied an equilibrium between financial supply and demand. Regardless of the heights attained in the money accounts, the bygone days looked golden. In the hydraulics of the grant system, "proposal pressure" went up and down with the money supply—naturally so, since applying for a government research grant is an onerous task, often requiring months of diligent labor, for an uncertain outcome. More money generated more applications. More money for research also underwrote the training of more graduate students, many of whom would seek grants themselves. In 1990, in one of the few examinations ever made of the phenomenon of proposal pressure, the Congressional Office of Technology Assessment found sharp increases in the number of proposals reviewed by federal research agencies between 1977 and 1988—a period of rapidly rising government support for research: from 14,499 to 26,802 at

---

24. U.S. House, *Authorization for NSF*, Report No. 95-993, 95th Cong., 2d sess., June 1, 1978, pp. 23–24.

the National Science Foundation; from 13,304 to 19,205 at the National Institutes of Health. During that time, OTA observed, "17,000 to 20,000 new Ph.D.s in science and engineering were awarded annually. . . . Add to these the number of non-Ph.D.s who apply for Federal funds for the first time in any given year and the roster of potential investigators is growing (despite increases in retirements)."[25] The OTA report concluded that the rapid growth of the federally financed scientific enterprise was accompanied by a liability—one rarely mentioned by the leaders of science clamoring for more:

> in the transformation of funding that began in the 1960s, perhaps the sheer number of researchers and the academic reward system—operating within universities and without—overwhelmed proposal review. A kind of lottery mentality appears to have taken hold in the 1980s: the more grant proposals submitted, the greater the probability that one would be funded. As competition grows, resources for rewarding quality *seem* [original italics] to shrink. In addition, some researchers, both those who often succeed in winning Federal funds and those who do not, argue that agency decisions tend to grow conservative and the chief attribute of basic research—risk taking—declines.[26]

Guy Stever, presidential science adviser in the Ford administration (among other senior posts), once told me, "I guarantee you, if somebody really had complete control of the quality of our system, and could cut out everything at the low level, we could survive beautifully on less money."[27] However, nobody had control of the system or its impetus for expansion.

25. In the mid-1990s, however, the number of grant applicants at NSF mysteriously leveled off, despite brisk budget growth. Noting a decline in grant applications from young scientists, NSF reported a six-year-long virtual plateau—30,700 in 1995; 29,420 in 2000. The unexpected phenomenon may be linked to the relative stinginess of NSF grants, which averaged $92,788 in 1999 (*FY1999 Report on the NSF Merit Review System*). That's small change for most modern science, leading to speculation that applicants were shifting their hopes to the more bountifully budgeted NIH. Sluggish demand is an embarrassment for a philanthropic enterprise that routinely appeals to Congress for more funds. Citing their record-breaking budget for fiscal 2001, NSF officials said they hoped "that the prospect of work in new fields like information technology and nanotechnology will encourage more researchers to submit proposals" ("NSF Officials Worry as Number of New Grant Applications Falls, *Chronicle of Higher Education,* June 9, 2000). NIH grants averaged $294,000 in 1999.

26. Office of Technology Assessment, *Proposal Pressure in the 1980s: An Indicator of Stress on the Federal Research System,* staff paper (Daryl E. Chubin, senior analyst), 1990.

27. Interview with author, February 16, 1996; "In the Words of the Wise," in *SGR,* March 1, 1996.

Within the scientific community, authority was diffused among the disciplines and institutions seeking government money, and among the half-dozen or so federal agencies that provided virtually all the money. Fearful of any single interest running the system, the leaders of science preferred having no one in charge. And starting in the 1960s, as the big machines of science, such as particle accelerators, assumed pork-barrel significance, real politics began to overlap with science politics, and even more new Ph.D.'s poured out of academe. In 1954, the number of full-time graduate students in doctorate-granting university departments totaled 67,136; of these, 6,751 received federal support. In 1983, the number of students had risen to 243,646, of whom 47,402 were federally supported. Between 1966 and 1985, the annual number of doctorates awarded in science and engineering rose from 11,570 to 18,935, and then to 26,515 in 1995.[28]

THE HIDDEN LABOR SURPLUS

Viewed in relation to the ever-growing role of science and technology in the American economy, and especially in the rapid defense buildup of the Reagan years, were these relatively small numbers sufficient? Even in the worst of times, the reported unemployment rate among Ph.D. scientists and engineers was negligible in most fields, thus suggesting a tight labor market that could quickly tip into disruptive shortages. In the recession year of 1993, when the national unemployment rate stood at 6.8 percent, unemployment of Ph.D. scientists and engineers was gauged at a trifling 1.2 percent.[29] However, the numbers are misleading. The actual unemployment rate for this group is considerably higher when the category "involuntarily out of field" (IOF) is taken into consideration. The overall IOF rate persisted at 4.2 percent in 1993 and 1995, NSF reported, with a low of 3.3 percent in the life sciences and 6.3 percent in the physical sciences.[30] The real employment picture is even dimmer if the growing practice of serial postdoctoral appointments is recognized as a form of underemployment and stockpiling of surplus labor.

As job opportunities failed to keep up with Ph.D. output, the postdoctoral system became a "holding pattern" for otherwise unemployed young scientists. In 1998, a study of biomedical-research staffing by the National Research Council reported "an ever-growing pool of post-doctoral fellows—

---

28. *Science and Engineering Degrees, 1966–95* (NSF 97-335).
29. National Science Foundation, *Data Brief, 1997*, no. 3, March 13, 1997 (NSF 97-305).
30. Ibid.

now estimated to number about 20,000—who engage in research while obtaining further training and waiting to obtain permanent positions. . . . The frustration of young scientists caught in the holding pattern is understandable," the report acknowledged, noting that "these people, most of whom are 35–40 years old, typically receive low salaries and have little job security or status within the university."[31] In its 2000 report on the plight of postdocs, the National Academy of Sciences estimated that, across all disciplines, their numbers in universities rose from 18,000 in 1981 to 39,000 in 1998. Adding in the postdocs working in government and industrial laboratories, the estimated count stood at 52,000. Slightly more than half were non–U.S. citizens, a particularly vulnerable status in the master-apprentice relationship of the laboratory.[32] It could be argued that these frustrated scientists entered Ph.D. training as presumably aware young adults and had themselves to blame for aspiring to careers in what were visibly overcrowded fields. America, however, has a soft spot for scientists out of work—relatively few as they are. Periodically the popular and professional press relates mournful tales of disappointed young scientists. Although the plight of the jobless in nonscientific fields is also reported, the tales of unemployed and underemployed Ph.D. graduates often convey the moral of an unfair fate, a violation of America's faith in the elevating power of education. Typical of this selective reportage is a 1993 *Wall Street Journal* article titled "Black Hole Opens in Scientist Job Rolls," which describes a young physicist "at a nearby community college earning $300 a week with no fringe benefits. He says he can't find a better job. 'I've had people say to me: Rewrite your resume, leave out your Ph.D., and you might get a job,' he adds."[33] There was another difference between the unemployed in the sciences and the jobless in other fields: the question of shortage or surplus of scientists became a political issue because Washington paid for training many of them.

THE SHORTAGE DEBATE

As a knowledgeable, disinterested participant in the staffing debates of the mid-1980s, the Congressional Office of Technology Assessment (OTA) expressed skepticism toward the mounting warnings of Ph.D. shortages in

31. *Trends in the Early Careers of Life Scientists* (Washington, D.C.: National Academy Press, 1998), p. 2.

32. Op. cit., *Enhancing the Postdoctoral Experience for Scientists and Engineers*, p. 8.

33. *Wall Street Journal*, April 14, 1993.

science and engineering. OTA, which performed research for congressional committees, reported that the extensive scholarly literature on Ph.D. supply and demand showed a redeeming elasticity in supply and nothing worse than brief periods of so-called spot shortages in demand—that is, limited numbers of specialized job openings for which suitable workers were not readily available. The OTA concluded:

> Occupational mobility from related fields is the short-term response to shortages. The Manhattan Project in World War II, the Apollo program in the 1960s, the environmental and energy programs of the 1970s, and the rapid buildup of the semiconductor and computer industries all relied successfully on the importation of scientific and technical talent from related fields. Many analysts consider the mobility and adaptability of the Nation's scientific and engineering work force to be one of its greatest strengths.[34]

When the market beckoned, OTA argued, demand was satisfied from the large pool of scientists and engineers who shifted from less rewarding or less interesting jobs. Nonetheless, the danger warnings continued. "I don't want to project a crisis," Daniel Kleppner, professor of physics at MIT, told a congressional hearing in July 1985, as he proceeded to do so. Referring to an employment study by the American Institute of Physics, Kleppner cautioned that "it is foreseeable that one could occur." Physics faculty might be in short supply, he warned, and "this could signal a deterioration of universities."[35] Others, however, candidly confessed to an inability to foresee the nation's longterm needs for scientists and engineers. Alan Fechter, the head of staffing studies at the National Research Council, cautiously advised Congress that the supply of research personnel appeared to be adequate for the next five to ten years. But, he added, "The situation expected beyond ten years from now is less clear. . . . Unfortunately, we are unable currently to forecast supply and demand that far ahead with sufficient precision to draw strong policy inferences."[36] Did the computer- and software-led boom of the 1990s vindicate the shortage warnings? No,

---

34. OTA, op. cit., *Demographic Trends*, p. 6.
35. House Task Force on Science Policy, *Scientists and Engineers: Supply and Demand: Hearings before the Committee on Science and Technology*, House of Representatives, 99th Cong., 1st sess., July 9, 1985, p. 73.
36. Ibid., p. 43.

according to a report produced in 2000 under the auspices of the National Academy of Sciences, at the request of NSF and the Sloan Foundation:

> By the early 1990s, a growing share of new Ph.D.s was experiencing difficulty in obtaining permanent employment upon graduation. Government demand for new Ph.D.s has been declining. Academic hiring has remained flat because state contributions to public colleges and universities have declined, and academia, both public and private, has come under increasing pressure to slow the growth of tuition and costs. Industry demand, which is cyclically sensitive, has been growing slightly, but many of the large industrial laboratories have been drastically downsized in the past decade. These forecasts of undersupply that did not materialize have led policymakers for graduate training and research to be highly skeptical of any forecasts and to worry about the self-interest of the forecasters.[37]

However, during the 1980s, and into the early 1990s, in the conflict between the candidly humble agnostics and the shortage-shouting evangelists of crisis and national decline, science's reproductive urge was not to be throttled by frank admissions of inability to read the future. In the mid-1980s, the tireless push to expand Ph.D. production was intensified in a brazen campaign orchestrated by the traditionally chaste National Science Foundation. We will look at this episode, and the political ripples it created beyond NSF, in some detail, because it provides instruction on the inner workings of the venerable NSF and its relations with the surrounding political structure.

---

37. Office of Scientific and Engineering Personnel, National Research Council, *Forecasting Demand and Supply of Doctoral Scientists and Engineers: Report of a Workshop on Methodology* (Washington, D.C.: National Academy Press, 2000), p. 11. The assertion that "state contributions to public colleges and universities have declined" is puzzling, given NSF reports that annual state and local support for academic R&D increased from $1.1 billion to $2 billion between 1988 and 1998 (*Indicators 2000*, p. A-311).

Ph.D. Production: Shortfall, Scarcity, and Shortage

Do we have too many scientists? No, we don't. I believe that science is providing important discoveries and a societal payback that more than justify growing support.

—Frank Press, president of the National Academy of Sciences,
"Talking Our Way into Scientific Decline,"
address to the annual meeting of the Academy,
April 30, 1991

The unemployment situation facing young people in mathematics is far worse than the dismal unemployment statistics for any single year's class suggest. Consider the invisible "unemployed." There is already the equivalent of several years' annual Ph.D. production embedded in the woodwork of U.S. colleges and universities as post-docs, part-time faculty, adjunct faculty, and, of course, the actively unemployed. . . . At current hiring levels, it would take several years to absorb this backlog, even if *all* Ph.D. production suddenly ceased. . . .

—"Myths in Math,"
Notices of the American Mathematical Society,
August 1995

IN 1984, Erich Bloch, newly installed as director of the National Science Foundation, ordered NSF's internal think tank, the Division of Policy Research and Analysis (PRA), to undertake a review of scientific and engineering employment, research facilities, and other major responsibilities of the foundation. Directives for grand-sweep studies of this type are routine in the debuts of new agency heads, in the research agencies, and elsewhere in government. If such studies are actually carried out after they are announced—not always the case—the ensuing reports are often shelved upon completion without disturbing organizational tranquility.[1]

However, in temperament and experience, Bloch was a bureaucracy-rattling manager, unusual for NSF. His arrival at the foundation coincided with a new surge of political interest, and therefore money, in Cold War weaponry, following the slack years of the Carter administration. In March 1983, President Reagan announced the Strategic Defense Initiative, a technological enterprise that potentially dwarfed the Manhattan Project and the Apollo moon landing. Star Wars, as it became known, was budgeted to spend about $15 billion on research between 1985 and 1989.[2] Beyond that, unknowable but immense sums loomed for procurement and deployment, with estimates running from $400 billion to $800 billion. As a purely civilian agency, NSF was not directly in line for the coming monsoon of military wealth. But, recall the structure of research finance as an irrigation network: in high-tech, science-oriented America, big government research projects in one sector could bring benefits to faraway regions of the science system. NSF's responsibility for training scientists and engineers and tracking their numbers was thus timely for Bloch's directorship, because the president's ambitious missile-defense program created uncertainties about the adequacy of the science and engineering workforce. Bloch's own experience qualified him to address this issue. A computer engineer, he had spent thirty-two years at IBM, rising through a series of major research and administrative assignments to Vice President for Technical Personnel Development at the time of his NSF appointment. As a member of the National Academy of Engineering, he was awarded the National Medal of Technology for leading the development of IBM's 360 computer system. In a directly relevant prelude to serving at NSF, Bloch chaired one of the many new links between high-tech industry and academe, the Semiconductor Research Cooperative, a consortium of computer and electronics firms that provided funds for research in universities.

---

1. Such was the outcome, for example, in the reign of Bernadine Healy as director of the National Institutes of Health from 1991 to 1993. At her command, the NIH management sullenly devoted thousands of hours, including a series of weekend retreats, spread over nearly two years, to preparation of a comprehensive "strategic plan" for biomedical research in general and NIH in particular. The plan, completed near the end of Healy's tenure, was ignored immediately upon her departure. Several senior post-Healy officials at NIH acknowledged to me that they had not read the strategic plan bequeathed to them by the previous director, nor did they intend to. In Orwellian fashion, it was down the memory hole.

2. Council on Economic Priorities, *The Strategic Defense Initiative: Costs, Contractors and Consequences* (1985), p. 53.

Breaking with NSF Tradition

Bloch's appointment to the NSF directorship departed from tradition in two respects, and might not have occurred, except for an unusual circumstance. First, since NSF's creation in 1950, his seven predecessors at the head of the agency had roots in academic research, all coming to NSF directly from university science or engineering departments or from research agencies of the federal government that financed research in academe; recruitment from those backgrounds followed naturally from NSF's role as *the* federal agency primarily responsible for financing nonmedical science in universities. And, second, unlike all previous heads of NSF, Bloch did not possess a doctoral degree. He was a mere bachelor of science, in electrical engineering, from an institution of no great renown, the University of Buffalo, which he attended after studying at the Federal Polytechnic Institute in Zurich, Switzerland (where he spent his youth as a refugee from Nazi Germany). The new director's lack of the Ph.D. was noted in the upper echelons of academic lobbying, which regarded NSF as its own bastion in Washington. "I think most of us from universities will want to look at him as an individual and judge him on his performance, not his pedigree," remarked Robert M. Rosenzweig, president of the elite Association of American Universities.[3]

In 1984, en route to retirement from IBM at age fifty-nine, Bloch was awaiting appointment as deputy director of the foundation, its number two position, when Director Edward Knapp unexpectedly resigned to return to research, just eighteen months into his statutory six-year appointment. Obtaining a replacement might easily extend for months or more in the federal government's sluggish appointment process. The NSF director is appointed by the president—a matter that was settled in the five-year-long postwar fight over the degree of autonomy to be given the foundation. But, in a minimal concession to the sensitivities of the early postwar science establishment, the National Science Foundation Act specifies, "Before any person is appointed as Director, the President shall afford the [National Science] Board an opportunity to make recommendations to him with respect to such an appointment."[4] When a director was sought, custom called for the board—NSF's policymaking body—to appoint a search committee to undertake deliberations of unknowable duration to identify a suitable, willing,

3. "NSF Director Resigns in a Surprise Move; IBM Engineer to Be Named as Successor," *Chronicle of Higher Education,* June 13, 1984.
4. *National Science Foundation Act of 1950,* 42 U.S.C. Public Law 1864, Sec. 5(a).

and promptly available candidate, whom the president might or might not find acceptable. Recruitment at that level of work can be difficult, given that desirable candidates are likely to be deeply involved in their current responsibilities. Furthermore, government pay and perks are poor in comparison to the offerings of major-league academe and high-tech industry, the favored recruiting grounds for seeking outsiders for senior research posts in Washington. If an available candidate is acceptable to the White House, the mandatory next step is deep background checks, usually taking many months, to assure that the president does not endorse a candidate who later might be embarrassingly exposed as a miscreant. Finally, the candidate for NSF director must transit the Senate confirmation process. For the carefully apolitical NSF, confirmation is customarily a smooth, bipartisan ritual. But scheduling difficulties on the Senate calendar can put off the committee hearing and floor vote for months, or the nomination might become innocently entangled in senatorial stalling tactics arising from unrelated matters. Given these uncertainties, the White House, with a nod from the National Science Board, chose to fill the NSF directorship quickly by upgrading Erich Bloch's nomination from deputy director to director. Bloch possessed a great advantage: He was there.

SHAKE UP THE FOUNDATION

Confident, witty, often impatient and caustic with subordinates, Bloch received orders to shake the foundation from its tradition-bound, cautious role as a passive patron of university-based research and education. Despite four postwar decades of heavy federal investment in science and technology, the United States was either losing ground or threatened by rising competition in international high-tech markets. The Reagan administration demanded a response from all sectors of American society, including science—which, increasingly, claimed contributions to economic growth as yet another reason for government support. Tracing his arrival at NSF directly to his acquaintanceship with George A. Keyworth II, President Reagan's science adviser, Bloch told me, "Yeah, I got marching orders, very clearly, from Keyworth: 'Go do something with the National Science Foundation. It needs rejuvenation. It doesn't pull its weight. It's not what it's supposed to be. It's not helping the country. It's not helping industry.'"[5]

For NSF, with its mission to promote science and engineering, the num-

---

5. Interview with author, June 8, 1998.

bers, types, and quality of scientists and engineers were crucial for "helping the country." Bloch's marching orders thus meshed with workforce studies already under way in the foundation's Division of Policy Research and Analysis, under the direction of its chief, Peter W. House, who had formerly practiced the craft of policy analysis at the Environmental Protection Agency and the Department of Energy. House attributes his appointment to NSF to a suggestion from the longtime specialist for research-related affairs at the Office of Management and Budget, Hugh F. Loweth. "We became colleagues," House recalls, through a policy analysis of the National Energy Plan that House produced while at EPA.[6] "I wanted a change and Loweth mentioned PRA"—NSF's policy shop, which had responded unsatisfactorily to the Reagan administration's interest in identifying the economic benefits of government research expenditures. Trust us, the scientific leadership regularly pleaded, when we assert that the public investment in science returns a wondrously large dividend. But for politicians, and for OMB's Loweth (who was sympathetic to science), the trust argument, unaccompanied by firm data, was insufficient.

For its central task of funding academic research, NSF was organized into directorates based on scientific and engineering disciplines—for example, a directorate for biological sciences, one for the mathematical and physical sciences, another for engineering. The catchall for many other activities at the foundation was the directorate for Scientific, Technological, and International Affairs. STIA, in abbreviationese, housed the offices that administered NSF's collaboration with other countries, collected data about money and staffing for science, and conducted policy-related studies of various sorts. Within STIA, House's Division of Policy and Research Analysis ranked as an administrative equal of the Division of Science Resources Studies (SRS). Prior to House's arrival, the two divisions coexisted peacefully. Not so afterward, as House adopted a broad view of policy research and analysis and expanded into territory that the SRS division considered its own.

SRS was responsible for collecting and publishing statistical data about research and development, scientific employment, and related matters—a task assigned to NSF in its founding statute. The number gathering was intrinsically factual and neutral, though in facile hands, statistics become weapons. In the hands of Washington's science lobbies, the SRS numbers served as the raw data for discussing government support of science, with an

---

6. Interview with author, March 4, 1999.

emphasis on statistically demonstrating governmental neglect of science—irrespective of ups or downs in appropriations. Even if the money was up, it might be argued that the percentage of gross national product devoted to research and development was higher in other nations; if the slice of GNP for R&D compared favorably on the international scale, it might be argued that the share of federal discretionary spending was down, or, even if it was up, that the rate of growth was down.[7]

The NSF Division of Science Resources Studies produced raw numbers, without political flavoring. Initially issued in a variety of specialized, separate reports, the data were eventually combined into a single volume published usually every two years. Launched as *Science Indicators 1972,* the title was expanded, starting with the delayed 1987 edition, to *Science & Engineering Indicators,* plus the year, to reflect NSF's growing support for engineering, and to appease the recognition-hungry engineers. Reflecting the utility of statistical data in the politics of science, and the infinity of numbers to be collected (if only you look hard enough), the *Indicator* series was of ever-growing girth, expanding from 145 pages in the debut 1972 edition to 710 pages in *Science & Engineering Indicators 1998* and to more than 900 pages in *Indicators 2000.* As it expanded, *Indicators* provided more details concerning the federal, state, and industrial sources of money for R&D, and the universities, industries, and other sectors that received it. SRS also collected and published large blocks of data on college and university enrollments in science and engineering studies, degrees awarded, employment, research papers published, patents issued, and, on most of these matters, comparisons with other nations. The series reported the findings of surveys commissioned by NSF to measure public understanding of and attitudes toward science. These efforts to read the public mind arose from the scientific leadership's voodoo conviction that public ignorance and hostility impeded their progress to bigger budgets. With hard statistical data, NSF's

---

7. A typical example of polemical juggling of research data appears in a 1999 report by the Council on Competitiveness, a Washington-based, science-boosting lobby: "As a percentage of GNP, the value of total U.S. R&D expenditures is still lower today than it was during the 1980s. Moreover, even recent increases in R&D lag behind the rate of growth that occurred in the economic expansions of the late-1970s and 1980s. . . . Furthermore, total spending on basic research (typically university-based) has been declining even more steeply as a percentage of GNP than overall R&D. . . . Indeed, Federal R&D as a percentage of GNP fell 26 percent between 1990 and 1997" (*The New Challenge to America's Prosperity: Findings from the Innovation Index* [Council on Competitiveness, 1999], p. 41). As we have seen, in dollar amounts, and purchasing power, U.S. R&D expenditures have soared since the 1980s, rising, in current dollars, from $63 billion in 1980 to $205 billion in 1997 (*Indicators 1998,* p. A-121), and to over $227 billion in 2000.

leaders and supporters believed, science could assert a stronger case for government support. Reflecting the importance that NSF attached to the *Indicator* series, the big book, virtually alone among hundreds of publications issued by the foundation, bore the imprint of the presidentially appointed National Science Board, NSF's governing body, and was addressed to the president of the United States as the annual report of the board, in fulfillment of a 1968 amendment to the National Science Foundation Act. The role of SRS was thus straightforward: collect and publish statistics. Other sections of NSF and outside organizations were enlisted in this effort, but SRS was the orchestrator. Interpretative text crept into *Indicators,* but it was invariably bland and brief. The *Indicators* series was criticized for some shortcomings, for example, for failure to match financial inputs into science with beneficial results that could reliably be attributed to the inputs. The first edition of *Indicators* anticipated that criticism, candidly explaining that "relatively few output measures of either an intrinsic or extrinsic nature are presented, because of the limited data available and methodological problems of separating the distinct contributions of science and technology from those of other factors."[8] Over the years, some progress was achieved in that area. But, in the early days, SRS was heavily engaged in collecting and organizing the widely scattered data and publishing it in timely fashion (though it was often quite late).

POLICY STUDIES

The jurisdiction of the Division of Policy Research and Analysis—SRS's separate but equal stablemate within the directorate for NSF's Scientific, Technological, and International Affairs—was less clear. House, taking charge of PRA in 1983 (one year prior to the arrival of Director Erich Bloch), inherited a staff of about forty professionals and a series of ongoing studies related to political concerns about the rationale for government spending on science and technology. Starting with Lyndon Johnson's presidency, the White House periodically demanded to know what the taxpayers were getting for their continuously rising, though never sufficient, spending on research, particularly in the strange grantland of academic basic science, and why they weren't getting more. Members of Congress would sporadically play on this theme, too. These were threatening questions for the policy champions and performers of academic basic research and their financial

8. *Indicators 1972* (NSB 73-1), p. vii.

providers at the foundation. PRA looked for answers, through its own research and in studies that it financed in universities. At the Executive Office
of the President, the Office of Management and Budget continued asking
hard questions, for which firm answers were chronically absent in the ever-
growing volumes of data collected and published by SRS in the ever-heftier
Indicators series. Disappointment and the quest for enlightenment raised
questions about PRA. Myles G. Boylan, an economist who joined the PRA
division in 1977, recalled that at OMB, "Hugh Loweth was getting disgusted
with NSF. He wanted his man in there, someone he could trust."[9] That's
how Peter House came to take over the NSF Division of Policy Research
and Analysis. Hugh Loweth, a frustrated friend of science in the Office of
Management and Budget, steered him there in the hope that House would
produce data that would help Loweth help science when the budget pie
was divided at the White House. Energetic, confident, disdainful of disagreement, and bound by faith in what he regarded as the unique revelatory
powers of policy analysis, House chose to reach unusually far for the head
of a small office deep inside a minor government agency. "I built PRA to
serve three audiences," House explained to me years later. These were the
Office of Management and Budget, where House was collegially linked to
Hugh Loweth (appropriately anonymous as a civil servant, but well-known
in science-policy circles as a critically important and supportive figure in
budget making); the White House Office of Science and Technology Policy,
headed by the president's special assistant for science and technology; and
House's place of employment, the National Science Foundation. "I would
talk to each group, and we'd bring back problems and we'd produce issue
papers and distribute them—scores of papers," House said. The government
paid for his division's research, he said, and he saw no reason to keep the
results cooped up at NSF.

Myles Boylan, long in government service, recalled that Bloch brought
a "private-sector mindset" to the foundation when he arrived as director
in 1984. Like a profit-minded corporate executive, Bloch sought to identify
each component's contribution to the bottom line, Boylan said. The new
director became known for his persistent curiosity concerning why things
were the way they were at the foundation. "Bloch would come up to our
offices and ask, 'What do you do?' He listened carefully for several months,"
Boylan told me, "and said little in response." House, describing his early
contacts with the new director, said he and his staff briefed Bloch about

9. Interview with author, March 8, 1999.

PRA's activities and were asked to provide answers to several questions—
one of them concerning the development of a promising scientific instrument, the electron tunneling microscope, for which the Nobel Prize in
physics was awarded in 1986. "He knew about it," House said, "but he was
testing us. We passed. He liked the answer he got, but he didn't like the
organization of PRA." Bloch expressed disapproval of House's self-initiated
connections to the Office of Management and Budget and the Office of
Science and Technology Policy, lofty White House appendages normally
dealt with only by the director of NSF or NSF staff members designated to
respond to special requests. Suddenly, PRA faced doom. Boylan related that
in 1984, "on Christmas Eve, Bloch told Peter [House] that he had decided
to get rid of PRA. He said, 'You do good work, but I don't need you.' Peter
protested, and said the office could serve Bloch, if Bloch would tell us what
he wanted." Bloch granted a reprieve—but with a staff reduction at PRA
from forty to ten or twelve professionals. Bloch told House to cut his connections to the White House agencies. Starting in 1985, PRA worked exclusively for Bloch, in an ever-closer relationship, Boylan said. "Bloch wanted
information. He would tell us, 'I don't want to know how the watch works.
I just want to know what time it is.'" But, Boylan recalled, "Bloch also
wanted to know how the watch worked." House's division was now restricted to providing information to the director of NSF. But Bloch also
soaked up information from the NSF budget office and from the statistics-
gathering Science Resources Studies division. "The competition wasn't too
bad at first," Boylan said. But later it became intense and bitter. After that
happened, he said, "SRS had two agendas: To supply good numbers and get
rid of House."

Though Bloch's edict reduced PRA's size and reach, House described
the ensuing relationship with the NSF director as "a policy analyst's dream.
Erich [Bloch] had an insatiable appetite for information," House admiringly
recalled, "and no patience for a bad piece of analysis. He was very rigorous."
The director wanted reliable numbers concerning the scientific community's claimed needs for new laboratories and equipment, and on the effects
of NSF's politically popular Experimental Program to Stimulate Competitive
Research (EPSCoR), designed to help universities in "have-not" states compete for federal research money. Bloch "wanted analysis without interpretation," House said. "He felt that the policy and political side of it did not
belong to my office. . . . Erich didn't come from an academic background—
he approached the job differently. It was a very satisfying time." Bloch declared himself pleased by the scaled-down policy office. Testifying in Congress in 1987, the NSF director described Peter House's operation "as a very

important function of the Foundation, and it's doing good work." Bloch added, "And I would say that by reducing the budget, PRA was able to concentrate on things more in depth than being all over the place, and that was the object of the game."[10]

Resentment in the Ranks

The NSF director and his policy-research expert were conspicuously satisfied with their working partnership; others at the foundation were distressed by their relationship. Some old-timers at NSF looked upon House's policy research with disquieted puzzlement. NSF considered itself the spiritual, even if not the structural, embodiment of Vannevar Bush's postwar design for science, a special apolitical creation in the politically driven, practical-minded U.S. government. Regardless of which party was up or down in politics, NSF existed to advance pure science by financing the work of the best scientists and the training of the most promising students. NSF kept close to its academic clients by bringing university scientists on board at NSF headquarters to help administer the awards of research money; known as "rotators," hundreds of them were serving at any one time, usually for periods of two years. Behind the grumbling common to government agencies, a high sense of mission permeated the staff, which generally exuded pride in NSF's objectives and performance. House's earnest advocacy of his professional specialty—he was the author or coauthor of fifteen books on policy research and analysis—was viewed with suspicion by NSF's stalwarts. Some looked upon his craft as computerized nonsense. In a book coauthored by House, *The Practice of Policy Analysis: Forty Years of Art and Technology*, the introduction was headed by an epigraph that might ordinarily be regarded as merely ironic wit from the bureaucratic battlefield: "*Some* numbers beat *no* numbers every time. Anonymous."[11] For the manpower studies that House produced for Director Bloch, the quip proved prophetic, until the political roof caved in on NSF on Capitol Hill. The collapse followed a struggle between the politically cautious old-line civil servants at NSF and allied organizations and the new hard-sell tacticians who were gaining influence in science politics.

10. House Subcommittee on Science, Research and Technology, *1988 National Science Foundation Authorization: Hearings before the Committee on Science, Space and Technology*, 100th Cong., 1st sess., March 11, 1987 [no. 13], p. 337.
11. Peter W. House and Roger D. Shull, *The Practice of Policy Analysis: Forty Years of Art and Technology* (Washington, D.C.: The Compass Press, 1991).

The "Pipeline" Studies

With Star Wars money about to gush into the research economy in the mid-1980s, discussions flourished about how civilian activities might be affected by a suddenly expanded military demand for engineers and other specialists. PRA's Myles Boylan recalled that "in that atmosphere, we were asked to study the 'pipeline'"—the term used in science- and education-policy ranks for the flow of humanity from birth to conferral of the doctoral degree. In the ensuing studies, and political blowup, the arcane arithmetic of doctoral-degree production dominated center stage. Holders of master's degrees in science and engineering were, as might be expected, far more plentiful; in 1985, master's degrees outnumbered Ph.D.'s by 261,585 to 24,962.[12] But Ph.D.'s are the knights of the scientific and technical enterprise; the holders of master's degrees are mere foot soldiers, though some would go on to the Ph.D.; the bachelor's degree ranks in science and engineering are raw recruits for the higher degrees. The key age group in the Ph.D. calculations was twenty-two, the median age for receiving the bachelor's degree, and, for a tiny portion of those graduates, the age for commencing the long process of acquiring the Ph.D. Drawing upon population statistics, Boylan and colleagues calculated that because of the "baby bust" that began in the early 1960s, the United States faced what they termed a "shortfall" of 675,000 bachelor of science and engineering graduates between 1986 and 2010. (In some renditions, the latter date varied.) Keyed to domestic birth statistics, the pipeline controversy virtually ignored the continuing abundance of foreign-born personnel in the American research enterprise. The immigrant population, trained abroad or in the U.S., has durably accounted for a sizable portion of the nation's working scientists and engineers since World War II, and has demonstrated high "stay rates," contrary to alarmist warnings of an impending exodus to the homelands. This balance for the baby bust was scarcely mentioned by the shortfall theorists; skeptics of their ominous forecasts were reluctant to hinge their doubts on the availability of foreign scientists and engineers.

The shortfall arithmetic was lucidly simple, if demography is destiny: fewer newborns would translate into fewer bachelor's degrees, leading to a decline in master's and doctoral degrees. House, however, introduced even more confusion into this debate by insisting that "demography certainly is not destiny, as witnessed by the fact that the *total* [original italics] number

---

12. *Science & Engineering Degrees, 1966–95* (NSF 97-335), pp. 36, 43; deducted from my figures are degrees awarded in psychology and the social sciences.

of bachelors' degrees conferred has continued to grow even after the demographic falloff began."[13] Thus, his warnings about the baby bust were accompanied by his observation that—so far, at least—it had not resulted in fewer bachelor's degrees. In any case, the demographic record showed that, starting in 1980, the population of twenty-two-year-olds went into a long-term decline, falling from 4.3 million in that year to 4.1 million in 1986. In projections for 1990, the number declined to 3.6 million—a confident forecast derived from birth statistics. Then, the forecast continued, after a few, small upward moves, the annual numbers of twenty-two-year-olds over the 1995–2000 range would be between 3.4 million and 3.5 million. Academic records dating back to 1970 showed that between 4.1 percent and 5.2 percent of twenty-two-year-olds received "technical degrees"—bachelor's degrees in science or engineering.[14] Of these bachelor's degree holders, about 5 percent went on to receive the Ph.D. In the ensuing debate, the distillation of those few doctorates from the great mass of bachelor's degrees in science and technology was simplified to "5 percent of 5 percent," in the educational process that stretched "from grade school to grad school." Those percentages had not varied significantly for many years, but the underlying numbers were about to go into a nosedive, raising anew the shortage alarms and arousing interest in raising the percentages of students pursuing studies in science and engineering. The most worrisome number in the calculations was 675,000, the anticipated "shortfall" in bachelor's degrees in science and engineering. "I was the one who started it all," Myles Boylan said fifteen years later, referring to a PRA "issue paper" in which his sole aim, he explained, was simply to review the pipeline data. The main finding, he recalled, was that the labor force in science and technology was "stable"—and at that time, consisted overwhelmingly of white males. "The only thing arguable," Boylan maintained, "was how movable was the percentage. I argued it was movable," he said, referring to the potential for raising the low percentage of women and minority-group members awarded bachelor's degrees in science and engineering, "but you had to move it." Boylan also noted a truism of policymaking and statistics: "When you create a number, that number takes on a life of its own."

The 675,000 shortfall was prominently displayed in a series of "pipeline" reports issued by House's PRA division starting in 1987, and in a

13. House Subcommittee on Investigations and Oversight, *Projecting Science and Engineering Personnel Requirements for the 1990s: How Good Are the Numbers? Hearing before the Subcommittee on Investigations and Oversight of the Committee on Science, Space, and Technology* (no. 173), 102d Cong., 2d sess., April 8, 1992, p. 307.

14. *Monthly Labor Review*, February 1992, reproduced in ibid., p. 193.

widely distributed "working draft" of a provocatively titled paper produced
by PRA in 1989, "Future Scarcity of Scientists and Engineers: Problems and
Solutions." Report by report, the PRA inquiry transited from unflavored
arithmetic description to the sighting of a problem and the provision of a
solution. The "scarcity" paper, as it came to be known, stated that "because
of demographic trends, the United States faces a much reduced production
of NS&E [natural science and engineering] bachelors and Ph.D. graduates
over the next two decades. . . . This situation is likely to increase a scarcity of
NS&E graduates for the NS&E labor force. The extent of the scarcity depends
critically on the rate of increase in research and development activity." The
record indicated, the paper pointed out, that "the combination of increased
federal support of graduate education and market forces" had in the past
increased Ph.D. production, while reductions in federal support and market demand had negative effects.[15] Strongly recommended throughout the
debate, and ever since, were greater efforts to enlarge the relatively small
proportion of women and minority-group members in science and engineering. In 1988, women received only 8 percent of the doctorates awarded
in engineering and 17 percent in the physical sciences; blacks received
fewer than 100 of the 14,352 doctorates awarded that year in the natural
sciences and engineering.[16] In discussions within scientific circles, the primary motive for enlarging female and minority participation was not social
policy or equity. Rather, it was argued that with a bigger intake from these
underrepresented groups, the depleted flow into the "pipeline" could yield
more graduates, thus overcoming the looming shortfall and scarcity.

Praise from Bloch

Following the distribution of a series of drafts, the workforce data and
policy proposals were incorporated into a 405-page book, published in 1989
by House's PRA division under the NSF imprint: *The State of Academic Science
and Engineering*.[17] In a foreword, Erich Bloch, the demanding director of NSF,
strongly endorsed the publication, expressing "thanks to an excellent staff
for an excellent piece of work" and certifying the importance of the data
and analyses produced by House and his division: "Much of their work is

15. Reproduced in *Projecting Science and Engineering Personnel Requirements for the 1990s*, op.
cit., p. 1058.

16. NSF, *Science and Engineering Doctorate Awards: 1997* (NSF 99-323), p. 32.

17. National Science Foundation, Directorate for Scientific, Technological, and International Affairs, Division of Policy Research and Analysis, *The State of Academic Science
and Engineering* (NSF 90-35, 1989).

used in the day to day activities of the Foundation, and serves as a basis of policy decisions by the National Science Board [NSF's policymaking body]. It is also used extensively in Congressional testimony and in discussions with the scientific and engineering communities as well as in international discussions." In NSF's internal politics, such praise from the chief was both rare and useful.

A preface signed by House was not modest about the work of his division and the publication it had produced in response to Director Bloch's "demand for quantitative, factual descriptions of current and past performance of the academic science and engineering community." House wrote, "the staff sought out, evaluated, and calibrated the largest collection of consistent data on U.S. higher education ever assembled." With "the Director's encouragement," he continued, the division developed "a user-friendly, quick-response microcomputer database system . . . using state-of-the-art technology." The system "provides answers to complex factual questions in a matter of seconds when previously they required several days"—a slighting reference to the paper-shuffling Division of Science Resources Studies, where computerization was slow to catch on and reports were often embarrassingly late. Citing the book's "breadth, depth, and vigor," House offered "special thanks to the Director, Erich Bloch, and his staff. Mr. Bloch," he stated, "cajoled and bullied us to produce analyses and briefings that others would have deemed impossible"—"others" being the technologically backward drudges in the Division of Science Resources Studies and other offices of the foundation. House's laudatory assessment of his own work ended with an Aesopian passage that, for the bureaucratic cognoscenti, acknowledged the controversy surrounding his activities at NSF: Praising his senior staff as "a consistently productive, multidisciplinary group dedicated to thorough analysis," House concluded with: "We were supportive of each other, without losing sight of the necessary criticism which permitted us, instead of professional colleagues and senior executives, to discover fallacies and problems before publication."

The convoluted language meant that the work of House and colleagues had not been subjected to NSF's sacred screening for quality: independent peer review. House triumphantly declared that he and his colleagues had utilized do-it-yourself peer review. It was not odd, then, that the volume opened with an obfuscatory disclaimer: "This manuscript is the collective work of the staff of the NSF Division of Policy Research and Analysis. However, the report does not represent the official policy of the Foundation, nor necessarily the judgment of any particular staff member." The necessity for the disclaimer later became clear.

In propounding the shortfall thesis, House and his policy crew echoed the central theme of postwar science policy: more is better, less is dangerous. The thesis was not uncongenial at the upper levels of science politics. No one in authority, at NSF or in the White House, contested the shortfall warnings. Within NSF, however, House's findings and claims of superior methods of data collection and analysis created doubts and resentment. House's aggressive style of operation and close relationship with Director Bloch grated on his colleagues. For them to reveal personal pique about House would be unseemly; rather, their concerns were manifested in fears for the integrity of NSF, the apolitical bastion of basic science in a highly political city. In a memo dated February 2, 1990, House requested clearance for publication of his tome of data, analysis, and shortfall warnings, *The State of Academic Science and Engineering,* as an official NSF document, as he had for various drafts of "shortfall" reports and the "scarcity" paper. In this instance, as in all cases, clearance was refused by the chief of NSF's relations with the political realm, Ray Bye, head of NSF's Office of Legislative and Public Affairs. Undeterred, House published anyway, identifying the source for each publication as "The National Science Foundation, Directorate for Science, Technological, and International Affairs, Division of Policy Research and Analysis." Thus the publications appeared to bear the imprint of the respected National Science Foundation. Director Bloch, legendary for his fine-detailed knowledge of the foundation's activities, did not object.

WORD GAMES

The documents from the policy division were semantically cautious in characterizing the arithmetical forecasts. "Shortfall" was the favored term, with "scarcity" a late arrival in a series of drafts. House generally stuck to "shortfall," which he described as a noncommittal statistical term that simply reflected the indisputable decline in the population of twenty-two-year-olds. "Shortage" was not proclaimed in the various PRA publications, nor was "crisis." *The State of Academic Science and Engineering,* produced by House and colleagues, plainly explained that "The 'shortfall' is not necessarily a 'shortage' unless the demand . . . exceeds the declining supply." Listeners might be puzzled, on the basis of colloquial usage and dictionary definitions that usually couple "shortfall" with "shortage" (as in *Webster's New World Dictionary,* Second College edition: "The act or an instance of falling short, or the amount of the shortage"). Not surprisingly, "shortage," sometimes coupled with "crisis," was the chosen word elsewhere as alarm over what appeared to be a looming and dangerous scientific manpower deficiency was reiterated in many forums. The dour statistics emanating from NSF were embraced by a former director of the National Science Foundation, Richard C. Atkinson. As chancellor of the University of California at San Diego, he addressed its regents on February 12, 1989, with a speech titled "Supply and Demand for Science and Engineering Ph.D.s: A National Crisis in the Making." Atkinson warned that "by the early years of the next century, the annual supply of [science and engineering] Ph.D.s available to the nation's workforce will be about 10,500 versus a demand for about 18,000. . . . This *imbalance* [italics supplied] will have devastating consequences for colleges and universities and for business and industry." In 1990, Atkinson delivered the same message, under the same title but in slightly modified form, in his inaugural address as president of the American Association for the Advancement of Science.[18] He predicted that "the shortage of Ph.D.s will become evident in about six years."[19]

SOME NUMBERS BEAT NO NUMBERS

Shortages, scarcities, and shortfalls of anything desirable—gasoline, affordable mortgages, transplantable body organs—are anathema to the wealthy United States. The alarms emanating from the respected National Science Foundation proceeded to ascend the food chain of news, initially ingested by publications that serve the scientific community, from whence they were swallowed by the popular press. "Wanted: 675,000 Future Scientists and Engineers" headlined a news article in *Science:* "The crisis that is being widely predicted over the next decade is rooted in an incontrovertible demographic fact: because of the low birth rates in the 1960s and 1970s, the college-age population—the raw material for tomorrow's educated workforce—is shrinking." Among the solutions proposed, *Science* reported, was expanded recruitment of women and minority-group members into science and engineering fields.[20] Citing NSF's forecasts, the *Christian Science Monitor* reported that "by the year 2006, the U.S. will have a cumulative shortfall of 675,000 persons with bachelor's degrees in natural science and

18. *Science*, April 27, 1990, p. 425.

19. In 1996, 19,740 doctorates were awarded in the natural sciences and engineering. Unemployment was rare among them, but lack of suitable jobs, underemployment, and prolonged postdoctoral appointments confronted many of these graduates. (*Science and Engineering Doctorate Awards: 1997* [NSF 99-323], pp. 3–6). As noted before, the soft market for many types of science and engineering doctorates persisted during the economic boom of the late 1990s and into the new century.

20. *Science*, June 30, 1989, p. 1536.

engineering."[21] Doing its own reckoning, the *Los Angeles Times* trimmed the deficit but extended the time horizon, reporting, "In all, the NSF predicts a shortfall of 560,000 scientists and engineers by 2010."[22] From 675,000 in 2006 to 560,000 in 2010? The varying numbers may indeed have been rooted in demographic projections. However, throughout the shortfall episode, as in other public controversies, seemingly authoritative numbers were introduced and accepted into public dialogue without critical examination of their validity or explanation for deviations from previously cited numbers—substantiating the line cited in House's book: "*Some* numbers beat *no* numbers every time." And then another menace was reported to portend even worse consequences from the reduced flow through the pipeline: a decline in science enrollments within the declining pool of undergraduates, as reported by the *Wall Street Journal* under the headline "Shortage of Scientists Approaches a Crisis as More Students Drop Out of the Field."[23]

Further regurgitations of the shortfall statistics were delivered by Robert C. Rosenzweig, president of the Association of American Universities, and John C. Vaughn, the AAU's director of federal relations. Writing in the winter 1990–91 *Issues in Science and Technology,* the quarterly policy journal of the National Academy of Sciences, they recycled the numerical data and alarms that had migrated from House at NSF to Chancellor Atkinson in the presidency of the American Association for the Advancement of Science, and beyond. As stated by the AAU authors, "the nation could face an average annual shortfall of 9,600 Ph.D.s between 1995 and 2010, according to projections made by Richard Atkinson . . . based on recent analyses by the National Science Foundation. He anticipates shortfalls rising from about 3,000 in 1995 to approximately 14,000 in 2010." Rosenzweig and Vaughn then introduced additional grist for anxiety: If Ph.D. production was not increased, they predicted, "industry, government, and universities will be pitted against each other in a battle for this critical human resource, and the entire nation will pay the price—diminished leadership and competitive strength"—boilerplate bombast in the prose productions of the leaders of science. They recommended doubling the number of federal fellowships and traineeships and an increase in student stipends and associated payments to universities. The total cost of their proposals, they wrote, would

21. *Christian Science Monitor,* June 18, 1991.
22. *Los Angeles Times,* February 1, 1990.
23. *Wall Street Journal,* September 17, 1990.

be $403 million per year, "less than three-tenths of one percent of the estimated $150 billion the United States will spend on R&D in 1990."[24]

The prospect of intersectorial competition over an inadequate supply of science and engineering doctorates inspired a new argument for additional federal funds to produce them: restrained wages. Introducing a barrage of seemingly authoritative numbers, House and colleagues stated, "The effect of expanded fellowship support of doctoral students in NS&E fields is expected to be highly favorable in terms of expanded supply of new doctorates and reduced salary inflation." By spending an annual average of $612 million on student support from 1989 to 2006, they asserted, the "program would generate average annual salary savings estimated at $1.81 billion during the same period."[25] Again, any numbers beat no numbers. If the government would spend a bit more, academe and industry would save a great amount on payroll, they argued.

THE SKEPTICS STIR

The shortfall thesis evoked doubts and hostility, particularly among engineers, historically subordinate to their often-supercilious scientific colleagues in the pecking order of the technical professions. As it evolved after its difficult birth as a patron of basic science, the National Science Foundation also provided funds for research and training in engineering, mainly in response to pressures from the White House and Congress to do something visibly useful for the economy. Nonetheless, the foundation remained the National *Science* Foundation; efforts to add engineering or technology to the title were invariably defeated, upon the insistence of the scientists, who deemed NSF *their* philanthropy in government. Fearful for the durability of government support for basic research, the scientists were sensitively protective of their symbolic standing in Washington. The venerable National Academy of *Sciences,* founded in 1863, held the congressional charter under which the latecomer National Academy of Engineering came into existence, in 1964. The science academy was the engineers' landlord in their joint Washington headquarters building, and was far richer and more influential than the engineering academy. The founding engineers had initially toyed with establishing a freestanding academy of engineering, but were coaxed

---

24. John C. Vaughn and Robert C. Rosenzweig, "Heading Off a Ph.D. Shortage," *Issues in Science and Technology,* winter 1990–91.

25. *The State of Academic Science and Engineering,* op. cit., p. 226.

into accepting a separate, though unequal, relationship with the scientists, who offered housekeeping support and a going operation. But beneath the congeniality, resentment about their status seethed among the engineers.[26]

The Defense *Science* Board is the senior science and technology advisory body in the Department of Defense, though the Pentagon is far more concerned with technology than with science—and spends its research money accordingly. Most engineers work for industry, where employment levels mercilessly move with the ups and downs of defense contracting and the general economy. Science doctorates are thickest in universities, where the many fortunate among them are shielded from the marketplace by tenure. While many engineers chafed at the shortfall thesis and denounced it as out of touch with the job market, NSF Director Bloch, an engineer by training and practice, was not among them. Myles Boylan, with a front-row seat in the NSF Division of Policy Research and Analysis, told me, "Bloch listened carefully but did not make his position clear."

In 1990, as the "shortfall" warnings continued at NSF, Robert M. White, the president the National Academy of Engineering, issued a somber, detailed rejoinder in his annual presidential address to the academy. White was steeped in the science-government relationship from years of service in old-line government science, rather than in the gold-rush setting of postwar research in universities. Trained as a meteorologist, he served as an atmospheric researcher for the Air Force during World War II, later became chief of the U.S. Weather Bureau, and was founding head of the U.S. National Oceanic and Atmospheric Administration, serving in that post from 1971 to 1977. In 1998, the National Science Board honored him with its highest prize, the Vannevar Bush Award; of seventeen prior recipients, White was the first who had spent a major portion of his career in government service.

26. Science hijacked the Nobel Prize, excluding engineers, though they fell within Alfred Nobel's criterion of benefits for humankind as the basis for selection, declared Professor Henry Petroski, a member of the National Academy of Engineering. In "Engineering Is Noble Too," Petroski deemed October—when the Nobel Prizes are announced—"the cruelest month," adding: "For engineers, it is a month of honors that might have been theirs, of lost ground and lost respect, of political realities that exclude them from sharing that ultimate symbol of brilliance and beneficence—the Nobel Prize." He noted that, in a competitive reaction, the Academy of Engineering established the $500,000 Draper Prize in 1988, awarded every other year, to honor the contemporary greats of engineering (*Wall Street Journal*, October 19, 1999). In 2001, the engineers upped the prize ante, making the Draper an annual award and adding another $500,000 award, the Russ Prize, to their roster. "We will now award three $500,000 prizes every two years," announced the president of the National Academy of Engineering, William A. Wulf (*The Bridge*, National Academy of Engineering, winter 1999).

Noting that "increases in total R&D expenditures, generous by any standards, have not been able to sustain the resulting increases in R&D population," White scoffed at the contention "that the United States will face a mounting 'shortfall' of gargantuan proportions—400,000 to 700,000 scientists and engineers cumulatively by the year 2011, based on estimates made by the National Science Foundation," White said, thus putting his own set of numbers into the discussion. "This 'shortfall' has been interpreted as presaging a massive shortage of scientists and engineers for whose services there is and will be a demand. Care must be taken in equating the word *shortfall* with *shortages* [original italics]. The one implies a reduction in production rates, the other a demand that cannot be satisfied." The latter is nowhere evident or foreseeable in the American economy, White pointed out, except for short-lived spot shortages.

Asserting that "we need to acknowledge the amazing fecundity of American higher education," White described the growth from 1977 to 1987 in the ranks of Ph.D. scientists and engineers in academic R&D as "nothing short of phenomenal, increasing 65 percent in the decade, from 94,000 to 155,000." During those years, he continued, money for academic R&D had risen from $8 billion to $14 billion, a 75 percent increase in dollars adjusted for inflation. Nevertheless, White continued, scientists across a wide span of disciplines feel deprived: "The biomedical research community, favored with federal largesse in recent decades above all other fields of civil science and engineering research, has recently convened a major national symposium on the biomedical funding crisis. This is a field that accounts for over half the federal basic science budget with annual expenditures in excess of $5 billion . . . by almost any measure, we have been supported munificently"—an acknowledgement of financial reality never heard from the mandarins of science. For them, science policymaking consisted of demands for more money, accompanied by warnings of dreadful consequences for the nation if they were not heeded.

A Voice in the Wilderness

Would still more money solve the problems? Perhaps for a brief period, White suggested, but then the rising costs and expansion of research and the inevitable, accompanying Malthusian increase in the number of grant-seeking doctorates would generate a new round of crises. As Peter House at NSF continued to spread the "shortfall" alarm, White and others argued that expanding the workforce was not the solution. "The fact is," White declared, "that there are just too many science and engineering investigators chasing too few dollars."[27] From the perspective of the sciences' enthusiasm for growth, as regularly enunciated in pleas on Capitol Hill and elsewhere, White's analysis was both sacrilegious and defeatist and politically misguided. If too many scientists were chasing too few dollars, the solution was obvious and urgently required: increase the number of dollars. The plain truth of White's analysis was not welcome in the management of American science. Financial restraints on research were senseless, Nobelist Leon Lederman argued, because "it is one of the best investments the nation can make." To provide additional funds for scientific research, Lederman blithely suggested, consideration should be given to taxing "high-technology consumer goods." Lederman thus demonstrated his tin ear for the antitax fervor in America and the public opprobrium that would descend on science for raising the price of VCRs and microwave ovens. Seasoned in Washington politics, which Lederman was not, Frank Press, president of the National Academy of Sciences, responded that "No nation can afford to write a blank check for science."[28]

Even as House's "shortfall" prophecies echoed in the professional and popular press and in grave congressional testimony by respected scientists, reports of unemployment and a scarcity of research funds in science and engineering circulated widely. In 1992, under the headline "Amid 'Shortage,' Young Physicists See Few Jobs," the *New York Times* reported, "Permanent research jobs for young physicists have virtually dried up, partly because the recession has drastically undercut the resources of universities and commercial research institutions." The article noted that the chair of the Amherst College physics department had received 813 applications for a single opening.[29] *Science* magazine published an account headlined "Young Investigators at Risk": "Starting out in any career is tough, but in the current bleak funding environment, even the best and the brightest young scientists are struggling to make it in academic science."[30]

The articles reflected the here and now, and therefore did not conflict head-on with the distant harsh future depicted in the "shortfall" liturgy. Even so, the warnings of shortages amid an already depressed market aroused resentment among doctorates, young and old, who knew the difficulties of finding work appropriate to their lengthy training, which they

27. Robert M. White, "Science, Engineering, and the Sorcerer's Apprentice," address to the annual meeting of the National Academy of Engineering, October 2, 1990.
28. "AAAS Head Toots Tin Trumpet for Science Funding," *SGR*, January 15, 1991.
29. *New York Times*, March 3, 1992.
30. *Science*, July 27, 1990, p. 351.

had usually endured on modest graduate-student stipends. Suffering in silence, the customary decorum for jobless scientists, was no longer stylish. For years, the leaders of science and their political supporters had urged scientists to team up and take the case for science directly to the public. In 1990, a postdoctoral fellow in physics at the Naval Research Laboratory, Kevin Aylesworth, adapted that advice to the job situation, setting up an e-mail alliance, the Young Scientists' Network, to swap information, and dismay, about job prospects. "I have conducted an informal poll of 25 postdocs and recent recipients of Ph.D.s in physics," Aylesworth wrote in *Physics Today,* the monthly magazine of the American Institute of Physics. "I have found that all of them have been seriously hunting for permanent positions for the last three to six months with absolutely no success."[31] Aylesworth doggedly telephoned, wrote to, e-mailed, and visited reporters and congressional staff members in Washington, supplying them with details of the bleak job market and urging skepticism toward the shortfall-shortage alarms. Engineers, particularly afflicted by the poor job situation, lashed the "shortfall" forecasts in their professional publications. "Annual Surplus of 10–15k EEs Predicted" headlined an article in the July 30, 1990, *Electronic Engineering Times.* The engineers also took their grievances to Congress. The result was a rare event, a probing, skeptical congressional hearing into the shortfall issue and the internal workings of the NSF and its allies in academe and in the bastions of science in Washington.

---

31. *Physics Today,* October 1990, p. 13.

The Congressional Griddle

"It's the same argument every year, about losing the lead."
—Representative Edward P. Boland (D-Mass.),
chair of the House Appropriations Subcommittee for NSF,
Feb. 26, 1985

"THE ENGINEERS blew the whistle," said Edith Holleman, a congressional staff counsel and a central figure in investigating the shortfall saga.[1] Holleman found the engineers credible and the shortfall warnings doubtful: "I knew you didn't calculate a labor shortage with demographics"—meaning that fluctuations in the population of various age groups revealed nothing about supply and demand for particular skills. Holleman confirmed her doubts with workforce specialists at the Bureau of Labor Statistics, the National Academy of Sciences, and within NSF, where the officially designated specialists were unhappily relegated to the sidelines of the debate. House had direct access to Director Bloch, Holleman found, "and no one went up against House."

BLOCH DEPARTS NSF

In August 1990, Bloch completed the statutory six-year term as director of NSF; the Bush administration, which inherited him from the Reagan administration, chose not to reappoint him.[2] During the next six

---

1. Interview with author, February 12, 1999.
2. As Bloch's NSF termed neared its end, I asked him whether he would take a post with the Bush administration. Bloch said he was uncertain whether he wanted one, and added, "I'm not so sure there would be a willingness to keep me on" (interview with author, May 1, 1990). There wasn't. When I asked D. Allan Bromley, President Bush's science adviser—and top science recruiter—about lack of a post-NSF offer for Bloch, Bromley replied, "It was just that Erich is abrasive. He had not really been all that successful in dealing with Congress. So, our hope was that we were going to get somebody that was going to improve relations with Congress" (interview with author, October 7, 1998). After leaving NSF, Bloch was appointed a distinguished fellow at the

months, while NSF was headed on an acting basis by the deputy director, Frederick M. Bernthal, the shortfall thesis was disavowed in cautious steps by NSF, and it finally crumbled under congressional battering. Addressing the workforce issue in a December 1990 speech, Bernthal said, "The question of what our needs will be in the future and whether we will meet them is complex, and lately has generated some controversy. At present, the supply of scientists and engineers, at both the B.S. and Ph.D. levels is, for the most part, keeping up with demand. However, we face an uncertain future."[3]

The squelching of shortfall alarms accelerated with a Jan. 2, 1991, e-mail sent to NSF executives by Jim Hays, senior science adviser in Acting Director Bernthal's office. Titled, with a touch of post-Bloch irreverence, "Shortfall or Not," Hays's message said, "Although it is not clear that there is, or ever has been, an 'NSF position' on the many separate issues making up this subject, it has become desirable to develop a brief statement on the subject that we can all stand behind—whether or not it qualifies, amplifies, or contradicts prior statements that may be attributable to NSF sources." For this purpose, Hays advised his colleagues, Acting Director Bernthal wanted a "mini–task force" established to review the shortfall controversy, including any "statements, reports, projections, analyses, etc., from NSF speakers or bearing NSF imprints [that] have been issued in the recent past on this subject." The "Shortfall or Not" message initiated a massive search of NSF's files for statements that Bloch and other senior NSF officials had made on workforce issues. Joel Widder, the chief congressional lobbyist for NSF, reiterated the necessity of a thorough search: "We think we have not used the word 'shortages' but we need to make absolutely certain," he wrote to a task force member, requesting a review of the "last three or four years" of NSF's congressional hearings. The search team responded with a memo four days later: "While the concept of a 'shortfall' may be inferred from Erich Bloch's speeches," he "avoided using the term or citing any specific numbers because the history of NSF's scientific manpower projections has

---

Council on Competitiveness, a Washington outpost, heavy with high-tech industry, that lobbied for tax credits for research and government support of academic science and engineering.

3. The text of Bernthal's talk, "The Role of Science and Engineering in the 21st Century," is included in House Subcommittee on Investigations and Oversight, *Projecting Science and Engineering Personnel Requirements for the 1990s: How Good Are the Numbers? Hearing before the Subcommittee on Investigations and Oversight of the Committee on Science, Space, and Technology,* 102d Cong., 2d sess., April 8, 1992. Unless otherwise specified, direct quotes and documentary material concerning the shortfall controversy are taken from this hearing volume, which comprises 1,332 pages of testimony and documents.

been fraught with failures. . . . Routinely, Erich Bloch's speeches laid out the rationale for expecting shortages without making specific predictions."

In March 1991, as the shortfall inquiry continued at NSF under Bernthal, Walter E. Massey, formerly vice president for research at the University of Chicago, came aboard as Bloch's successor. Massey understandably had no liking for the rising concerns about NSF's integrity generated by the nasty "shortfall" versus "shortage" controversy. Meanwhile, Peter House, without his NSF link to the top, lost status in a reorganization that moved his Division of Policy Research and Analysis into a newly created Office of Planning and Assessment, in which House held the subordinate title of deputy director. Looking back on PRA's duties in its reorganized state, Myles Boylan, the veteran of policy analysis at NSF, told me, "There was nothing going on. We went to the [NSF research and education] directorates, seeking work. The intent was that we would never embarrass NSF again." House remained at the foundation until December 1994, when he moved to the Smithsonian Institution. No one in senior management at the foundation fended off the criticism directed at the "shortfall" thesis and its leading proponent, Peter House. Old-timers at NSF who had suffered from House's special access to Director Erich Bloch had grievances to avenge—six years' worth.

A WELL-SITUATED CONGRESSMAN

Representative Howard Wolpe, a seven-term Democratic congressman from rural southern Michigan, was politically secure for conducting an inquiry that inevitably would embarrass the prim NSF, a small, obscure agency on the Washington landscape, but one with a good name in Congress. "There was no research and development in my district," Wolpe explained to me. He was thus spared the risk of a constituent backlash by NSF beneficiaries and others concerned for the reputation and political fortunes of NSF.[4] Reflecting an interest that he developed in energy policy while serving in the Michigan legislature, Wolpe was a member of the House Science, Space, and Technology Committee. Established in 1959 in response to Sputnik, the committee held law-writing authority over an imposing roster of federal research agencies and activities: NASA, NSF, the National Institute of Standards and Technology, the White House Office of Science and Technology Policy, environmental and energy research, and various other items

4. Interview with author, March 22, 1999.

in the federal science portfolio. However, the jurisdictional list was not accompanied by commensurate legislative power or influence in the workings
of the House. The Science Committee, as it was known, was an authorizing,
not an appropriations, committee, which meant it wrote laws specifying
that this or that shall or shall not be done and stating the maximum to be
spent doing it. The committee, however, lacked direct authority to provide
the money for the activities it deemed desirable. The effective congressional
power over science, meaning the ability to start, stop, or alter federal spending, was held not by the Science Committee but by the money-voting appropriations subcommittees for the research agencies. In this two-part process of authorization and appropriation, the economizing spirit on Capitol
Hill dictated that NSF and many other agencies routinely received less than
the sums stated in their generous-sounding authorization bills. Moreover,
in the distribution of congressional authority, the Science Committee was
fenced off, even for law writing, from the largest and most politically potent
sectors of government-supported research, defense and health, which have
consistently accounted for at least two-thirds of all government R&D
throughout the postwar years.[5] The political guardians and beneficiaries of
defense and health research were satisfied with their familiar and supportive locations elsewhere in the House committee structure and had no desire
for those activities to be folded into the Science, Space, and Technology
Committee (renamed the Science Committee in 1995).

   Though esteemed by the science establishment as its political haven on
Capitol Hill, for lack of a better choice, the Science Committee functioned
mainly as a debating society focused on the obscurities of science policy.
On this topic, it regularly held hearings and sponsored lengthy staff studies,
for which the leaders of science cooperatively furnished testimony and specially prepared reports.[6] In line with the Science Committee's lack of money

5. Chairman Robert Walker of the House Committee on Science put the figure at 67.8 percent in 1995. *Background Brief,* the Committee on Science, June 27, 1995.
6. The grandest of all such studies, conducted from 1985 to 1987 by the specially created
   Task Force on Science Policy of the Science Committee, resulted in the publication of
   twenty-four volumes of testimony and associated documents from hundreds of witnesses, plus twelve volumes of commissioned studies and background papers. The volumes ranged from a few hundred pages to an 1,886-page blockbuster, *Science in the Mission Agencies and Federal Laboratories.* The marathon exercise was abruptly terminated
   when its creator, Committee Chairman Don Fuqua (D-Fla.), resigned to become an
   aerospace lobbyist. The task force proceedings may have had a cathartic effect on its
   many participants, but the ensuing product left no evident effects on legislation or on
   congressional dealings with science and technology. The Senate has never manifested
   a similar passion for science policy and has no full-scale committee version of the
   House Science Committee. Within the Senate Committee on Commerce, Science, and

power and limited jurisdiction, it ranked low in the House pecking order, a status that allowed members to hold seats on the Science Committee while also serving on major committees, such as Foreign Affairs and Judiciary. (Wolpe, who held a Ph.D. in political science from MIT, where he had specialized in African studies, also chaired the subcommittee on Africa of the House Foreign Affairs Committee.) Such double seating was necessary to attract enough members to fill the Science Committee roster.

In 1990, Representative George E. Brown Jr. (D-California) became the new chair for the Science, Space, and Technology Committee. Representative Wolpe didn't know it, but he was marked for an important role in Brown's plans to increase the power and influence of the Science Committee. The shortfall controversy was to be a stepping stone.

WOLPE'S NEW ROLE

George E. Brown Jr. represented San Bernadino, California, another area bypassed by the torrents of federal R&D money. First elected to Congress in 1962, Brown stepped up to the chairship of the Science Committee at age seventy with broad-gauged, long-range plans for the committee and his role as chair. Brown was a science enthusiast, and though a career politician, proudly claimed scientific roots, noting in his biographical entry in the *Congressional Directory* that he possessed a "B.A. in industrial physics." Brown manifested an avuncular mock-gruff manner toward the leaders of science, frequently chastising them for not performing better at selling science to the masses and their political leaders; science wasn't doing enough for society, he often told them. Lacking other such devoted critics on Capitol Hill, the chieftains of research applauded and showered awards on Congressman Brown. Brown and the scientists who flocked to Capitol Hill made a happy match. With shared faith in the beneficial powers of science, and convinced that it was underfinanced, they symbiotically lavished attention on each other. Chairman Brown was dubbed "Mr. Science" on Capitol Hill.[7]

The Science, Space, and Technology Committee, like many committees on Capitol Hill, was a partner and promoter—rather than an independent

---

Transportation, a subcommittee holds jurisdiction over the research agencies that constitute the full jurisdiction of the House Science Committee.

7. "I can't say this award is entirely undeserved," Brown wisecracked upon receiving the Award for the Support of Science from the Council of Scientific Society Presidents in 1991 ("In Brief," *SGR*, December 15, 1991). The audience of scientists and science lobbyists laughed appreciatively at George (a name that, in science-policy circles, represented none other than Science Committee Chairman George Brown).

overseer—of the agencies and interests under its jurisdiction. Though the committee's restricted powers provided only limited opportunities for serving the folks back home, every bit counted, especially for members from university towns and areas housing federal research facilities. As Congressman Wolpe saw it, "Most members on the committee were there to provide maximum protection for their constituent interests." In the 1989–90 Congress, the committee's subcommittee on space was chaired by the congressman whose district included the NASA launch facility at Cape Canaveral, Florida; in the chair of the subcommittee on energy was the congresswoman who represented Oak Ridge, Tenn., site of the Department of Energy's Oak Ridge National Laboratory.

Chairman Brown sought to gain credibility for his committee by shaking off its docile reputation and making the Science Committee a power center in science politics. One way to do this was to unleash its subcommittee on investigations and oversight. I&O, as it was known, held virtually unlimited authority to look into any aspect of the National Science Foundation and the other federal agencies within the full committee's jurisdiction. The I&O subcommittee, however, maintained a long tradition of inactivity. But Brown presented a surprising invitation to Wolpe: give up the chairmanship of the subcommittee on Africa and take the I&O chairmanship. Brown promised Wolpe a free hand in staff selection and investigative targets, and assured him of strong backing if he ventured into politically hostile territory. To the surprise of congressional power trackers, who knew the relative standing and prestige ratings of the Science Committee and the Foreign Affairs Committee, Wolpe accepted. "It was a new challenge, a chance to do investigative work," Wolpe explained to me, adding that the offer excited him. The African affairs specialist was soon deeply involved in two of the bitterest episodes in post–World War II science politics—the "shortfall" controversy and the demise of the Superconducting Super Collider, the big atom smasher sponsored by the Department of Energy.

As a boost for Brown's buildup plans for the Science, Space, and Technology Committee, the top Republican seat on the investigations and oversight subcommittee went to Representative Sherwood Boehlert, from the Utica-Rome region of upstate New York, a cheerfully independent, politically moderate legislator who frequently voted against his own party. The Democratic majority controlled the committee agenda, but the minority party could be an impediment, if it so chose. Boehlert was another legislator without science interests to protect. In addition, Boehlert held a grievance about the government's management of science, dating from the rejection of a proposal he backed in the nationwide competition to provide a site for the colossal Superconducting Super Collider. Boehlert supported a proposal to build the SSC near his congressional district, on a site spanning the U.S.-Canadian border. He noted with amused disdain that the sponsoring Department of Energy described the multibillion-dollar SSC as an "international project" in its attempts to placate Congress with assurances that American seed money would be followed by foreign contributions, thus lessening the burden on American taxpayers. The site he supported was truly international, the only one of its kind, he reminded DOE officials, who brushed him off as just another pork-seeking congressman.

Safely unbeholden to their investigative targets, Democratic Chairman Wolpe and Ranking Republican Boehlert were comrades in arms in taking up their role as overseers and investigators of science. Together, they announced that a public hearing would be held on April 9, 1992, titled "Projecting Science and Engineering Personnel Requirements for the 1990s: How Good Are the Numbers?"[8] The question mark in the hearing title signaled skepticism, as did the witness list, heavy with workforce specialists who had been shunted aside by the House-Bloch alliance at the National Science Foundation.

House was on the witness list, but not Bloch, though he was within reach of a congressional invitation. "He was gone from the agency," explained subcommittee counsel Edith Holleman. "And he wasn't going to help my case. He was aggressive and would attack my boss," she added, noting that the mild-mannered Wolpe "did not like being mean." But before Wolpe opened the congressional hearing, he told me, he encountered a strong, home-state appeal to call it off. It came, he said, from James J. Duderstadt, in the dual roles of president of the University of Michigan and chair of the National Science Board, NSF's governing body. By Wolpe's and Holleman's accounts, Duderstadt expressed fear that the hearings would tarnish NSF and diminish public and political support for science. "Jim Duderstadt was upset by the investigation," Wolpe said. "We met for lunch, and he was absolutely offensive. He said the staff [of Wolpe's subcommittee] was demagogic, and that the hearing was being held for political reasons.

8. As it turned out, the science hearings came near the end of Wolpe's fourteen years in Congress. As a result of Michigan's population decline in the 1990 census, his congressional district was dissolved and its population distributed among adjacent districts. As of the end of 1992, at the conclusion of the second session of the 102d Congress, Representative Howard Wolpe would be an ex-congressman. He subsequently made a failed run for the Democratic nomination for governor in Michigan and then served in the State Department as President Clinton's special envoy to the Great Lakes Region of Africa.

I was stunned," Wolpe said, adding, "It was a hard-edged conversation, and inappropriate." Wolpe was unmoved.[9]

NSF in the Dock

In preparation for the hearing, Wolpe's staff, exercising his subcommittee's investigations and oversight authority, commandeered cartons of files from NSF and interviewed members of Peter House's staff, including Myles Boylan, who recalled to me: "I met with Holleman. It was like being deposed. She was just trying to see how she could trap me." Prepped by his staff, Wolpe commenced the hearing with caustic references to the "shortfall" thesis and its alarming offshoots in public dialogue. Citing warnings of the 1950s that "the Russians are coming," later alarms that "the Japanese are coming," and the "shortfall" predictions of 675,000 bachelor's degrees in science and engineering, Wolpe accused NSF of faking a crisis to boost its budget: "In 1986 the then Director of the Foundation [Bloch] took that number to Congress and started the shortfall ball rolling in his fiscal year 1987 budget." Wolpe noted the "confusing and interchangeable use of the words 'shortfall,' 'shortage,' and 'scarcity,'" charging they were employed as scare words to panic the public and politicians into believing that "a real shortage of workers was looming, and government intervention in the form of increased financial support for science and engineering education was necessary." The shortfall reports, he continued, contained "no statement of methodology, data points, lists of assumptions, or bibliography." Within the foundation staff, criticism of the report was "ignored and even suppressed," Wolpe charged.

In a public display of animosity—unusual for the staid policy-research community—acrimonious, personal conflict between NSF's shortfall advocates and the doubting Congressional Office of Technology Assessment spilled out at the hearing. John Andelin, a senior official at OTA, accused House's policy-research division of what "appears to be an off-the-record attempt to silence dissent and intimidate dissenters—even those in another

---

9. Duderstadt assailed the hearing in an opinion column published in the *Washington Post* (June 2, 1992) under the title "Too Many Scientists? Don't Believe It." Rejecting warnings of an impending "glut of scientists and engineers in America," he recalled similar past warnings and asserted, "But those projecting an oversupply were wrong then, and they are wrong now." As it turned out, however, the warnings of oversupply were unfortunately correct. Asked about Wolpe's and Holleman's allegations that he attempted to stifle the hearings, Duderstadt told me he had no recollection of ever discussing the hearings or the shortfall issue with them. (Conversation with author, April 13, 1999.)

Federal agency." Entered into the record was a 1988 letter from NSF Director Bloch to OTA Director John Gibbons, in which Bloch chastised OTA for "subjective opinions, inaccuracies and inconsistencies" in OTA's critique of the shortfall argument. The barbed language was uncharacteristic of the scholarly, temperate NSF. As such things are done inside bureaucracies, the letter was probably drafted by the combative Peter House for Director Bloch's signature. OTA's Andelin assailed the chieftains of science who had echoed the shortfall alarms: "The imprimatur of the Foundation has been used repeatedly by leaders of the academic research community," he declared, "to argue that shortages of scientists and engineers are a certainty, and that graduate fellowships and traineeships are the only short-term remedy for the 'imminent crisis.'"

From inside NSF came an account of harsh treatment of critics of the shortfall thesis, provided in a statement by Joel L. Barrie, head of a workforce study group from 1980 to 1990 in the foundation's often-slighted Division of Science Resources Studies (SRS). In contrast to House's policy division, SRS was old-line NSF—slow, cautious, and, as deemed essential in the NSF culture, careful to pave its path to publication with approving reviews of its work by presumably objective specialists. Barrie related that in 1989—during the Bloch reign, when shortfall was the official line at NSF—he supervised the preparation of a report that "did not project any significant personnel shortages." Barrie's heretical document disappeared into NSF's internal review process, never to appear again, he reported. His division chief then "arranged a meeting with Peter House to see what the problem was. At the meeting," Barrie continued, "Dr. House said the problem was that the report did not support the director's [Bloch's] position that there would be serious personnel shortages in the 1990s."

Barrie related another "shortfall" confrontation. This one arose from a dissection he coauthored of "Future Scarcities of Scientists and Engineers: Problems and Solutions," one of a series of basically similar publications in the long "pipeline" sequence produced by House's Division of Policy Research and Analysis. Barrie stated that "A vitriolic response was received from Dr. House" accusing the Science Resources Division of "'a sloppy critical review'" that "'reduced the effectiveness of NSF management by creating uncertainty about the information provided to them.'" House, he concluded, "ignored and tried to suppress all critiques of his work . . . that questioned his methodology or conclusions, as they interfered with the scenario put forward to the Director of the Foundation by Dr. House's office."

As Congressman Wolpe's hearing continued, an official of the General Accounting Office (GAO), Congress's investigative agency, contested

House's claim that the shortfall publications had undergone peer review. "NSF identified nine specific individuals who, according to NSF's recollection, were asked to review the thesis," the GAO witness stated. "However, we contacted these individuals and found that no formal review had occurred." Wolpe's hearing showed that the accumulating criticism had generated considerable unease within NSF, where a Boy Scout spirit of untarnished probity was deemed essential to assuring political support for a continuing flow of money for research. In an e-mail to several colleagues in 1991, Marta Cehelsky, a senior staff member at NSF, brushed off the criticism from Congress's Office of Technology Assessment. However, she noted with concern that Alan Fechter, on the staff of the National Academy of Sciences, was persisting in his severe critiques of House's workforce projections. OTA and the Academy occupied far different positions in the politics of science: OTA was many layers down in the legislative process, conducting research for congressional committees, and held no direct or even spiritual connection to NSF. The Academy, on the other hand, was the prestigious high temple of science; its members, supposedly the most accomplished researchers in the nation, personified the scientific excellence financed by NSF, and many of them held influential positions in the linkage of science and government. "NSF needs to look responsible and responsive," Cehelsky wrote. "Disagreement with OTA is one thing. But open warfare with the Academy is another."

The Defiant Witness

The *pièce de resistance* for Wolpe's congressional production, Peter W. House, conceded nothing in his turn in the witness chair. He appeared without counsel or supportive colleagues; his patron, Erich Bloch, had long ago left NSF. The hearing occurred, he later told me, while his father was terminally ill. Referring at the outset to his office's demographically based forecasts of bachelor's degrees in science and engineering, House curtly stated, "The degrees have fallen approximately as were projected. There remains debate about the significance of the downturn." Jousting then began between Chairman Wolpe and Peter House, champion of policy research and the "shortfall."

Wolpe sought an explanation of the epigraphic line in House's book "that some numbers beat no numbers every time," inquiring whether it meant "that in a political debate the side that can buttress his case with numbers will prevail, that has more potency, if you will. Is that your view?"

No, House responded, explaining that "numbers are a valuable contribution to the policy process and are probably more useful than pure rhetoric or opinions. They're an attempt to get dimensions, to get boundaries, etc., into a political discussion, rather than draw opinion." The "pipeline" studies, House continued, provided a base for NSF to proceed beyond demographic analysis to an examination of why students did or didn't choose science or engineering courses, "and begin to try to understand the complex phenomenon." One aspect of the study, he said, is "Why do they drop out?"

Wolpe: But again. How did your study affect policy as you see it?
House: That was just another input. It's an information input.
Wolpe: Did it have any impact on policy?
House: I can't answer that in an evidential—I mean, I have no way to demonstrate that.
Wolpe: You don't think it had any impact on policy?
House: I don't know, sir.

Wolpe brought up the projection of a 675,000 shortfall in bachelor's science and engineering degrees. Pointing to a graph set up in the hearing room that depicted the "baby bust," Wolpe said, "You arrived at your shortfall figure of 675,000 by just drawing a line from historically high degree years and comparing them to the demographic dip in the number of twenty-two-year-old students. Those are your proxies for supply and demand," Wolpe declared. "Aren't they?"

House replied that "proxy demand" was "not a demand in the sense of a market demand."

Seemingly puzzled, Wolpe asked, "Well, what do you mean by demand?"

House replied, "This was our best estimate of the number of degrees that would have been produced if you kept the level at this 1984 to 1986 level." Expanding that explanation under questioning by Wolpe, he added, "I'm saying that study states very clearly that all we did was produce a projection which told you that the number of degrees in natural science and engineering was going to fall between 1986 and 2006. . . . we did not do a market analysis to relate it to jobs because we didn't know."

Wolpe: Can I ask you then why do you use the word scarcity in the title?
House: The paper goes on to talk about the effect of this shortfall in bachelor of science degrees on Ph.D.s in natural science and engineering. It was a generic—

Wolpe   [interrupting]: Fine. But the title of this book, "Future Scarcities of Scientists and Engineers: Problems and Solutions." Now are you telling me that the notion of scarcity as reflected in this title has nothing to do with your notion of whether or not the fact that you're going to have a fall off from degrees was relevant to anything?

House: No, the reason that title is picked is that the last part of the report talks, as the OTA report did, about attraction-retention strategies that one might want to put in place if one thought that you needed those degrees. . . .

Wolpe: I'm sorry. I'm absolutely stunned. . . . I mean, I find this extraordinary that you're telling us that.

BLOCH'S ROLE

Wolpe then turned to the transformation in public dialogue of "shortfall" into "shortage." "Mr. Bloch frequently mentioned shortage, supply and demand, and the press picked up his terms and your numbers. Did you ever remind Mr. Bloch, or the press, or anyone else for that matter that you were addressing only one part of this equation, only one part of supply, and that you did not have anything really to say about demand and that you did not know anything about shortage, which I take it was your testimony a few minutes ago?"

House replied, "I briefed the Director often on this subject. I'm aware of the fact that he knew what the shortfall concept was."[10]

Accusing Bloch of an alarmist campaign based on House's shortfall calculations, Wolpe asked: "Did you ever go to him knowing that this was the

---

10. In public dialogue, Bloch actually avoided "shortage," though a listener could easily get the impression that he was warning of one. In a prepared statement for the Senate Labor and Human Resources Committee in 1986, Bloch asserted: "We are not attracting enough young people to science and engineering to assure an adequate supply in the future." In 1987, in testimony before a subcommittee of the House Science, Space, and Technology Committee, Bloch stated, "we are not attracting enough Americans into graduate schools, especially into the Ph.D. track." The numerous public utterances by Bloch compiled in the voluminous appendixes to the Wolpe hearing do not include the use of "shortage" by the NSF director. At a hearing in 1990 before a subcommittee of the Senate Committee on Commerce, Science, and Transportation, Senator Gore, noting erroneous past predictions of shortages, asked Bloch, "if you were a betting man, what kind of odds would you give that there will in fact be, without changes in current policy, a serious shortage of well-qualified scientists and engineers by the year 2000?" Bloch replied, "Two to one," adding that because of demographics, and assuming no change in enrollments, "a shortfall would exist to the tune of roughly 675,000 people by the year 2000 or 2005."

manner in which your numbers were being used and say to him that he is misrepresenting the meaning of your study?"

House: I neither wrote the Director's speeches nor reviewed them.

Wolpe: Were you aware of them?

House: Not—I would have to say, I just don't know. No, in general, I didn't pay attention to them.

Wolpe: You don't know whether you were aware of them?

House: In general, I didn't pay attention to Erich's speeches.

Noting House's insistence that the data produced by his division did not justify the transformation of "shortfall" into "shortage," Wolpe repeated his prior inquiry, asking, "Did you ever go to him and say that's a misuse of my data, a misuse of my study?"

House sidestepped the question: "What I said was my study was one of the inputs into the Office of the Director. If indeed he heard from professional societies, from his directorates, from his advisory committees, that indeed they were going to need more scientists and engineers across the disciplines, then it was perfectly within his purview to be able to call [t]his dip in degrees and translate it into a shortage."

In response to questions by Wolpe, House denied that he had attempted to suppress internal criticism of the shortfall projections, noting, however, that his division of Policy Research and Analysis and its sister division at NSF, Science Resources Studies, "were in a contentious mode." Wolpe introduced a memo House wrote in 1989 to the NSF official who supervised both divisions, in which House complained that "a sloppy critical review by SRS caused PRA to spend a couple of person-months on unnecessary research and analysis." Repeating the assertion that "a shortfall is not synonymous with a shortage," House's memo to his superior stated, "It represents a target variable for future analysis of behavioral, institutional and public policy factors influencing supply and demand outcomes for natural scientists and engineers." House concluded the memo with a jab at his critics: "The tradition of in-house collegial review of research or analysis is worthwhile only if the critic honestly seeks to help to improve the outcome. Conscientious review of in-house analytical reports requires serious thought and careful attention to facts and analysis. Sloppy critical review is damaging to NSF." The disparaging remarks in his memo, House testified, reflected his concerns that friction between the two divisions "confuses the issue and does the Science Foundation no good, nor does it do us any good as an organization. And that's what I was aiming at. It was a memo to my organization."

Wolpe confronted House with several critical internal NSF assessments of the shortfall reports. Wolpe read from one: " 'There is so much wrong with this report that I simply can't give a brief wrap up.' The reviewer finds that the report is, and I quote, 'Based on dubious research methods, unsupported statements of fact, data aggregation which obscure the real reviewability of participation in NS&E [natural science and engineering] education, which denies that the labor market affects such participation, and ignores future demand in the process of supply adjustment.' " Wolpe noted that the reviewer concludes, " 'Can cost us our credibility with the public.' "

House smoothly fielded the allegations, saying that, in response to the criticisms, he and his staff reviewed and revised the shortfall report "to make clearer, to add footnotes, to describe the model in more detail—." Wolpe continued the pursuit, introducing an analysis of the "scarcity" report conducted at NSF's request by Robert R. Trumble, dean of the School of Business at Virginia Commonwealth University. Solicitation of assessments by outside specialists was a standard management tool at NSF. Trumble criticized House's demographic approach, noting in a letter report to NSF dated July 26, 1989—while Bloch was still director—that "the emphasis on twenty-two-year-olds is overplayed because it ignores the large stock and the high number of persons already trained in the natural sciences and engineering. A substantial number of these people are not working in science and engineering and could be attracted into that portion of the labor force with higher salaries, etc." The analysis by Trumble thus matched the earlier criticisms from the workforce specialists at the National Academy of Sciences and the Office of Technology Assessment. Trumble terminated his letter of findings with: "Now that I have concluded with my reports and meetings with you and others at NSF, I would appreciate receiving the amount that we agreed upon prior to my entering into this effort. The amount is $3,000 and should be sent to me at . . ."

Describing Trumble's assessment as "a pretty devastating kind of critique," Wolpe asked House how he had responded to it at the time. House at first said he did not recall seeing Trumble's report, but added, "No, actually, I did. I thumbed through it, and I just put it, you know, in the file." Asked about Acting Director Bernthal's assertion that, at present, the supply of scientists was adequate, House said, "I've never seen the speech." Wolpe pressed on with a recitation of events at NSF following Bloch's departure in August 1990: "Now, in fact, a purge of your own study, in reference to the shortfall numbers, from NSF's lexicon was about to begin." Confronting

House with other internal NSF memos that documented mounting concern with the skepticism generated by the shortfall scenarios, Wolpe declared: "you were warned repeatedly by people inside and outside the Foundation that your study said very little about either the supply or the demand of personnel, and that it would eventually get the Foundation in some difficulty." Chairman Wolpe asked House whether he ever attempted to "correct any misunderstandings about the meaning of your studies" among journalists, members of Congress or congressional staff. No, he had not, House replied. "One has a sense," Wolpe concluded, "that the goal was to create the impression of a crisis to lend urgency to the effort to double NSF's budget." At the end of a long battering in the witness chair, House did not reply. As the chief of policy research and analysis for the National Science Foundation, he had received bravos from Director Erich Bloch. But Bloch was gone, and House was left alone to defend a thesis that grossly embarrassed the foundation.

Wolpe was respectful and brief with the final witness of a hard day on Capitol Hill for NSF, Walter E. Massey, who had been sworn in as NSF's director in March 1991, a little over a year earlier. Referring to the shortfall controversy, Wolpe asked, "Do you think this was a question simply of misperception or do you think there may have actually been something wrong happening with the agency as it related to this report?" Massey replied diplomatically, "I've tried not to go back and reconstruct other people's motives . . . I've made a number of reorganizations within the Foundation to better suit the way I would like to manage and review materials, both internally and externally."

Two days after the hearing, former director Bloch protested his exclusion from the proceedings in a letter to Chairman Wolpe that denounced the hearing as "a low point in Congressional fairness." Bloch denied that the manpower statistics were manipulated and broadcast to increase the NSF budget. His letter to the congressman ended with a disdainful jibe that would have been unthinkable if he were still director of the foundation: "Members of Congress, lawyers and MBAs are not going to improve our competitive standing in the world. Scientists and engineers just might." In reply, Wolpe dismissed the irate ex-director without apology. "None of the persons who cited the [House] study as projecting 'shortages,' 'shortfalls,' or imbalances in 'supply' and 'demand' over the past several years were asked to testify, as there was abundant written material available to document the study's use." Wolpe did not refrain from adding a grating observation: "I'm also sure that you agree that the integrity of the National Science Foundation should not be eroded by the release of poorly done,

non-peer-reviewed draft studies." Referring to testimony by Bloch's successor as director of NSF, Wolpe stated, "I was very encouraged by Dr. Walter
Massey's commitment to the Subcommittee to put procedures in place that
would prevent such an incident in the future." As staff aide Edith Holleman
preferred, a face-to-face confrontation did not occur between her boss and
NSF's combative former director.

Director Massey came away from the hearing disturbed by the allegation that NSF had invented a Ph.D. shortage to prod Congress into raising
its budget. A month later, Massey took his concerns to the National Science
Board. The minutes for that meeting state:

> Dr. Massey reported also on the recent hearings by Congressman How-
> ard Wolpe . . . which focused on an analysis by NSF staff showing a
> "shortfall" in the number of BS degrees under certain assumptions.
> Dr. Massey summarized the Committee's findings and expressed his
> deep concern over the adverse publicity that was generated against NSF
> as a result of the hearings. Dr. Massey indicated that he planned to de-
> velop points that could be used as the basis of communications with the
> press that would acknowledge the seriousness of the issue and assure the
> agency's rigid standards of excellence for all of its activities.[11]

FINDINGS OF GLUT

Following the Wolpe hearing, learned inquiries into Ph.D. supply and
demand continued to flourish—the specialists for that function remained
in place and funds for studies were available from NSF and private foundations. The findings were now strikingly different from the shortfall data
that dominated the discussions during the 1984–90 Bloch regime at NSF.
Warnings of scarcity, present or future, were no longer credible after a dozen
or so uninterrupted years of reports in professional and general publications
of unemployment and underemployment among doctorates in science and
engineering. In 1995, a study derived from a survey of 344 faculty members
at nineteen institutions, including nine that award Ph.D.'s in science and
engineering, concluded that doctoral production is detached from and
oblivious of the job market. Reporting that "perhaps twenty-five percent of
newly-minted doctorates end up unemployed," the study concluded that

11. National Science Board, minutes, May 1, 1992.

the natural production rate of doctorates is driven by departmental needs [in universities] for research and teaching assistants, and that departmental doctoral-student intake is limited by financial constraints rather than output market considerations. . . . Faculty tend to believe that more scientifically-trained manpower is better than less, and that job opportunities will materialize somehow. . . . In any case, the department's shortrun requirements for inexpensive research and teaching labor, and the desire of faculty to replicate their own skills, is of stronger relevance to admissions decisions than the more abstract and distant concept of labor market balance.[12]

The study possessed an impeccable pedigree: the authors were Professor William F. Massy, of the Stanford University School of Education, and Charles A. Goldman, of the RAND Institute for Education and Training; support for the study was provided by the Alfred P. Sloan Foundation, RAND, and the U.S. Department of Education's Office of Education Research and Improvement.[13]

Systematic studies of the Massy-Goldman type were complemented by individual accounts of the crowded and harshly competitive culture of science produced by the inflexible output of the nation's Ph.D. industry. Speaking at a 1996 conference—"Science in Crisis at the Millennium"— Robert Pollack, a biologist and former dean of the College at Columbia University, delivered a morose assessment of contemporary science. Collegiality has vanished, Pollack said, replaced "by a Hobbesian world of each against all." Unlike many of his colleagues, Pollack did not blame the level of finance. The number of NIH grants, he correctly observed, had gone up in recent years, as had the amount per grant, while the quality of scientific leadership at NIH had also risen under Director Harold Varmus, the first Nobel laureate to head the organization. Nevertheless, Pollack asserted, a brutish, competitive spirit pervades the scientific enterprise. "Why help a post-doc to get started as an independent scientist, if you are going to be competing with that person a few months after he or she leaves your lab?

12. William F. Massy and Charles A. Goldman, *The Production and Utilization of Science and Engineering Doctorates in the United States* (Stanford Institute for Higher Education Research, Discussion Paper, 1995).
13. In his ruminations on the "Golden Age of Science" (see chapter 4), Frank Press, former president of the National Academy of Sciences, parenthetically observed, "An unwritten story is the role of graduate students functioning as working scientists to the extent that in many of the best [university] departments half the papers were coauthored by them" ("Growing Up in the Golden Age of Science," *Annual Review of Earth and Planetary Sciences* 23 [1995]: 1–9).

Why share data or material? Why let someone 'clone by phone,' as the saying goes, if your stuff has a chance of being patented?" Science professors and basketball coaches lure the young with suggestions of fabulous career opportunities, "with a tenured job at a major university being the equivalent of an NBA [National Basketball Association] offer," Pollack asserted. "The low to vanishing probability of either the professorship or the starting [basketball] position are known to both college coaches and directors of training grants alike. And both manage to avoid telling the quantitative truth to the young people from whose work they and their senior colleagues maintain their productivity and reputation. It is exceedingly rare to find an example of a mid-career, tenured university scientist who gives any students, undergraduate, graduate, post-doc, a reasonable estimate of the chance they have to become a tenured university scientist in turn."[14]

However, the Malthusian Imperative continued to thrive. In 1998, the National Research Council, the working arm of the National Academy of Sciences and its various components, published a study inspired by concerns over prolonged job shortages in the life sciences.[15] Doctoral awards in these fields, it reported, had risen from 2,700 in 1965 to 5,000 in the mid-1980s, to 7,696 in 1996. Foreign students accounted for a majority of the increase since 1987, the study found, but whatever the cause, "the increase was not accompanied by a parallel increase in employment opportunities." More scientists were spending more time in low-paying, professionally limited postdoctoral "holding patterns," the study found. In 1973, only 11 percent of doctorates held such postdoctoral jobs five to six years after receiving their degrees. By 1995, the figure had reached 38 percent. "What may be most alarming about the 1995 figure," the academy report stated, "is that it reflects the situations of those earning Ph.D.s in 1989 and 1990, at the beginning of the sharp rise in Ph.D. production." Noting that continuation of the pace of increase in awards of doctorates in the life sciences would double the ranks in fourteen years, the report plaintively observed: "Life science faculties need teaching assistants and research assistants, and limiting the number of entering graduate students will be resisted." The hope for self-restraint on the part of laboratory chiefs was also dismissed: "Some might argue that this solution is expecting unreasonably altruistic behavior on the part of established investigators." In a futile gesture for

14. Robert Pollak, comments to conference on "Science in Crisis at the Millennium," sponsored by the George Washington University Center for the History of Recent Science, Washington, D.C., September 19, 1996.

15. *Trends in the Early Careers of Life Scientists* (Washington, D.C.: National Academy Press, 1998).

slowing the system, the academy report recommended "no further expansion" of existing training programs and a moratorium on the creation of new programs, except "under rare and special circumstances."

In the following months, however, the financial wherewithal for taking on additional graduate students in the life sciences was assured when Congress raised the budget for the National Institutes of Health by $2 billion, followed, in 1999, by a $2.2 billion increase for NIH. The additional money enabled NIH to expand its research program by several thousand new projects, each carrying funds for Ph.D. graduate assistants.

At about the same time, the National Science Foundation quietly retreated still further from the wreckage of Ph.D. prophecy. Noting a "mixed situation" of surpluses of job seekers in some fields and shortages in others, NSF safely observed: "Identifying current and future supplies of scientists and engineers is extremely difficult: predictions of an oversupply in the 1970s did not come true, and predictions of shortages in the late 1980s also failed to occur. What is clear is that S&E [science and engineering] positions are in a state of flux."[16]

GROWTH, TRUST, AND ELECTIVE POLITICS

The shortfall episode revealed the tension between science's powerful impulse to enlarge its ranks and its sensitivity to the trust and goodwill of the national political system on which it relies for money. Once exposed as flimsy and misleading, the House-Bloch formulation was promptly abandoned by the scientific leadership. However, science did not give up or soften its pleas for growth. Leaving behind the shortfall episode as an unwholesome aberration, NSF's managers, supporters, and clients relied on the traditional arguments of national security, health, prosperity, and, increasingly, international high-tech competition—durable selling points for science, never out of fashion, even during the ill-fated run of the shortfall thesis. With perhaps more of a damper than usual on outrageous assertions, warnings of danger and promises of benefits continued as the weapons of science in its relations with politics. We must recognize, however, that a further step was possible: collective participation in elective politics, through money raising and vote gathering for candidates and parties favorable to science. Politicking of that kind is firmly established in major professions. Physicians, lawyers, and teachers long ago plunged into elective

---

16. *Retention of the Best Science and Engineering Graduates in Science and Engineering* (NSF 99-321), p. 1.

politics to protect and advance their interests. Science, however, deliberately rejected that choice, with one narrowly focused, long-ago exception that was inspired by unusual political circumstances. Exceptions can be illuminating; therefore, we will look at science's sole large-scale postwar departure from ballot-box political aloofness.

CHAPTER 10

Detour into Politics

Science can be the basis of an objective criticism of political
power because it claims no power itself. Politics can afford the
independence of science because science does not attempt to dictate
its purposes.

—Don K. Price, *The Scientific Estate*

THE ONLY large-scale involvement of scientists in na-
tional politics took place in the presidential campaign of 1964, under the
banner of Scientists and Engineers for Johnson-Humphrey. When the scientists successfully completed their political work in that campaign, many
of them feared they had damaged the sanctity of science. Never again in
significant numbers did science return to ballot-box politics.

The genesis and motivating force of the 1964 mobilization of
scientists was revealed at the time in the open acknowledgment that
the organization should realistically be titled Scientists and Engineers
Against Goldwater. Barry Goldwater, the Republican nominee, was a self-
proclaimed hard-liner at a perilous period in Cold War relations with the
Soviets. In his postcandidate years, Goldwater acquired the persona of a
benign, likable curmudgeon, basking in the respect that America usually
bestows on the runner-ups for its highest office. But Goldwater's presidential run evoked serious fears. In his memorable acceptance speech for the
nomination, he belligerently proclaimed that "extremism in the defense of
liberty is no vice. And let me remind you also that moderation in the pursuit
of liberty is no virtue." He wisecracked about lobbing a missile into the
men's room at the Kremlin, thus reinforcing his trigger-happy reputation.
Goldwater's truculence, nuclear bravado, and well-publicized status as a
major general in the air force reserve alarmed many Americans, especially
the influential arms-control wing of the scientific community. Consisting
mainly of veterans of the World War II weapons laboratories, these scientists were linked to Washington by a network of full- and part-time advisory

positions interwoven with personal and professional associations. Their political concerns rose as the 1964 election approached. In prior presidential
campaigns, small numbers of scientists and other academics had joined
with various professionals in letterhead listings for one or another candidate—showcase activities, distant from the political battlefront. Scientists
were sometimes included in so-called brain trusts that produced position
papers and analyses for the candidates—again, politically low-impact activities. In the 1960 election, Kennedy versus Nixon, the Democrats fielded a
National Committee of Arts, Letters and Sciences, including a contingent
of Nobel and Pulitzer prize recipients. On the Republican side, support of
the learned classes was symbolized by Scholars for Nixon-Lodge. The Kennedy brain trust in the 1960 campaign included Jerome B. Wiesner, an MIT
professor who had developed close ties to Kennedy. However, for Wiesner
and many other scientists, the Goldwater candidacy was too frightening to
be met with a superficial response.

MOBILIZATION FOR POLITICS

Many scientists wanted to do more than cast their votes against Goldwater. In the summer of 1964, following Goldwater's nomination, a spark
was touched to these sentiments by Donald MacArthur, an ambitious
thirty-three-year-old engineer working for a high-tech defense company.
Born in Detroit but raised and educated in Scotland, MacArthur received a
Ph.D. in chemistry at Edinburgh University. MacArthur returned to the
United States at age twenty-six, taught for a year at the University of Con-
necticut, and then became head of the chemistry and life sciences division
of Melpar, Inc., a Westinghouse defense subsidiary on the outskirts of
Washington, D.C. Since the anti-Goldwater spirit was already flourishing
within the scientific community in the summer of 1964, there is no way
of knowing whether the events that ensued would have occurred without
MacArthur's involvement. Clearly, the tinder was present and might have
been kindled in some other fashion. But ignition was needed and MacArthur supplied it. The charming young fellow with the Scottish brogue was
inexperienced in the political arts, but he was personally well-situated for
skipping the freshman level. Great encouragement for political involvement was provided by his wife, the former Diana Taylor, a niece of Lady
Bird Johnson. Diana Taylor MacArthur worked in Washington for the Peace
Corps, and she and her husband were regulars at family gatherings and social events in the White House of Uncle Lyndon and Aunt Lady Bird John-

son. As the 1964 election approached, Diana recalled to me, she and Donald pondered how they might contribute something special to Johnson's election campaign. "I suggested to Donald that he try to do something with the scientists. And we went from there."[1]

Through family and social connections, Donald MacArthur possessed access to the president, senior administration officials, and the political professionals organizing Johnson's election campaign. MacArthur moved confidently in networking his way through official Washington. He also knew a few key scientists and how to gain access to others, including Jerome Wiesner, who had served as Kennedy's science adviser and, after Kennedy's death, briefly as Johnson's before returning to MIT. Diana MacArthur recalled that she and her politically energized husband concluded that, for their purpose, Jerry Wiesner, a prototype political scientist, held the key to the American scientific community. Wiesner expressed enthusiasm for a political mobilization of scientists, and doors to the senior suites of the scientific community smoothly opened. One week after Goldwater's nomination, MacArthur enlisted a close colleague at Melpar, Rodney Nichols, a Ph.D. physicist who tested nose cone materials for missiles. MacArthur and Nichols met with Harold Brown, the Pentagon's director of research and engineering, to discuss the potential for organizing a scientists' campaign against Goldwater. Brown was supportive and optimistic. The prospect was raised with Donald Hornig, the Princeton University chemist who had succeeded Wiesner as Johnson's science adviser. Hornig reported inquiries from scientists and engineers who wanted to join the campaign. Among them were two nationally prominent scientists with Republican affiliations, both alarmed by the Goldwater candidacy: George B. Kistiakowsky, who had served as Eisenhower's science adviser, and Detlev Bronk, the ultimate establishment insider. Bronk was president of the Rockefeller Institute (later called Rockefeller University), former president of the National Academy of Sciences, former president of Johns Hopkins University, and longtime chair of the National Science Board.

1. Donald MacArthur died of a heart attack at the airport in Austin, Texas, in 1988, while returning to Washington from a family Thanksgiving weekend at the LBJ ranch. I am indebted to Diana MacArthur for sharing her recollections of the 1964 scientists' campaign (interview with author, June 21, 1999) and providing me access to correspondence and campaign literature. Mrs. MacArthur succeeded her late husband as chief executive officer and president of the Dynamac Corp., an environmental services and research firm; during the Clinton administration, she served on the President's Committee of Advisors for Science and Technology. The account here builds on my reporting of the 1964 scientists' campaign, "Venture into Politics: Scientists and Engineers in the Election Campaign," parts 1 and 2, *Science*, December 11 and 18, 1964.

THE WHITE HOUSE SCIENCE SET

The cast of science advisers serving the White House was an inbred group, brought into government service, full-time or as advisers commuting from academe, without regard to Republican or Democratic party affiliations or the lack thereof. They were naturally drawn from the broad ideological center, thus excluding peaceniks from the left, such as Leo Szilard, and hard-liners from the right, such as Edward Teller. Otherwise, the senior mandarins of science easily fit into the White House advisory system under Eisenhower, Kennedy, and Johnson without concern, on their part or the politicians', for matching their party affiliations with that of the presidents they served. During Kistiakowsky's service as Republican Eisenhower's science adviser, Democrat Wiesner served on the President's Science Advisory Committee, the federal government's highest body of scientific counselors. PSAC assembled at least monthly in Washington to commune with Kistiakowsky and occasionally with the president. Also serving on PSAC during Eisenhower's presidency was Princeton chemistry professor Donald Hornig. After Kennedy's election in 1960, Wiesner moved from MIT to the position of full-time science adviser to the Democratic president, while Kistiakowsky, returning to his professorship in chemistry at Harvard, served part-time as a member of PSAC. When Wiesner returned to MIT, early in the Johnson administration, Hornig came down from Princeton as his successor.

Presidents had reached across party lines on prior occasions, though usually to broaden their political base in difficult circumstances, as FDR did in appointing a venerable Republican, Henry Stimson, secretary of war in World War II. In bringing scientists into the high councils of government, the presidential indifference to their politics and party affiliations reflected the belief that science and scientists were above politics. FDR appointed Vannevar Bush to head research during the war because Bush was a famously capable administrator and researcher with excellent connections throughout the scientific enterprise—not because he was an anti–New Deal conservative. Scientists might consider themselves Republicans or Democrats, but, as politicians saw it, science was their true party affiliation—and scientists saw it that way, too. The Goldwater candidacy inspired a change. The misgivings came later.

The science establishment, as it then existed, was overwhelmingly in the anti-Goldwater camp, and, departing from tradition, many of its members were restless to get into the campaign. Confident that they could enlist the prestige of science in behalf of the Johnson election campaign, Donald MacArthur and his colleague Rodney Nichols rented office space in downtown Washington, a short walk from the White House, laying out $2,250 of their own money for a second floor suite at 1106 Connecticut Ave., with occupancy commencing August 1, 1964, and terminating on election day, November 3. On August 13, they issued a press release announcing the creation of Scientists and Engineers for Johnson-Humphrey, with a grab-bag startup committee of forty-two luminaries from science, engineering, and medicine—among them Wiesner, Kistiakowsky, Buckminster Fuller, Kelly Johnson (designer of the U-2 spy plane), and two celebrities of cardiology, Paul Dudley White and Michael E. DeBakey. The debut announcement stated that the committee "hopes to stimulate the involvement in active politics of scientists and engineers across the country." It endorsed a broad band of liberal Democratic goals, including arms control, support of science and technology, educational opportunity for all, strict enforcement of the Civil Rights Act, and "rejection of extremism under any guise." With that step taken, political amateurs Donald MacArthur and Rodney Nichols, joined by Diana MacArthur (on leave from the Peace Corps), proceeded to orchestrate two communities that are customarily distant from each other in Washington: science and politics. Equipped with an organizational name and an address, they obtained $12,000 for grassroots efforts from the campaign's central office, Citizens for Johnson-Humphrey. The national coordinator for that group was a Washington insider and close adviser of Lyndon Johnson, James H. Rowe Jr., a social acquaintance of Donald and Diana MacArthur. But even as they waded into electioneering and summoned colleagues nationwide to join them, the organizers of Scientists and Engineers for Johnson-Humphrey narrowed the focus of their campaign. They were guided by the advice of a professional campaign strategist, David Garth, whose services were enlisted by Donald MacArthur upon the recommendation of the Democratic campaign professionals.

TARGET: GOLDWATER

Despite the package of Democratic Party issues listed in the kickoff announcement, the guidelines for the campaign specified that the prime topic was to be Johnson versus Goldwater. Goldwater was to be depicted, by the leading figures of science and medicine, as unsuitable for the nuclear-age presidency, unthinkable for managing the dangerous standoff between the United States and the Soviet Union. Scientists who created the bomb would be the prime witnesses against him. The bomb was the central issue: other issues were allowed but must be secondary. The organization was to serve as a nonpartisan haven for Republicans opposed to Goldwater as well as for traditional Democrats and the politically unaffiliated. They were united in opposition to Goldwater's nuclear stance; on social and economic issues, differences existed—but why bring them up? Along with the defeat of Goldwater, more money for science was a common goal of the diverse membership. But the topic of science support looked too self-serving and received only minor attention during the campaign. Scientists and Engineers for Johnson-Humphrey arose as an "anti" campaign inspired by the nuclear rattlings of a particular candidate, and far less so by affection for Lyndon Johnson. It was a political freak, from its birth to its method of finance and its commitment to disband on election day.

In a widely distributed booklet, *The Alternative Is Frightening,* the new organization described itself as dissociated from the political system: "Since we are fully *bi-partisan* and *self-supporting* [original italics], membership implies no permanent political affiliation." Apart from the small startup fund provided by the national campaign organization, Scientists and Engineers for Johnson-Humphrey was to be self-financing and thus independent of the Democratic party organization. However, through Donald and Diana MacArthur, these election campaigners held privileged access to the White House. Five weeks before election day, President Johnson met with a group of prominent scientists, engineers, and physicians invited to the White House by Donald MacArthur. MacArthur's telegraphed invitation stated that the group "will express to the President our conviction that the continuance of enlightened policies of this and previous administrations is essential for future welfare of nation." In a rare departure from the nuclear emphasis, the invitation added, "Means for strengthening national programs in science, technology, and health will be discussed."

News of the Washington mobilization quickly spread throughout the country, stimulating cash contributions and the establishment of local chapters of Scientists and Engineers for Johnson-Humphrey. In a hectic, exhilarating campaign that reached into all but two or three states, the organization enrolled more than 50,000 scientist and engineer members, raised some $500,000, and wrote and ran more than 100 newspaper advertisements and 3,000 spot radio announcements. With its members aroused by their common aversion to the Goldwater candidacy, academic decorum took a campaign holiday. In a letter to colleagues and former students, twenty-five faculty members of the Harvard Chemistry Department denounced Goldwater and his running mate, Congressman William Miller, of New York, as unfit for the presidency. Describing themselves as "conservative through liberal, Republican, independent and Democratic," the Harvard chemists declared: "We are convinced that our country would be presented with the clear prospect of disaster in the domain of foreign relations, and grave setbacks in economic, social, technological and political progress at home, under an administration led by these men."

In a widely broadcast radio roundtable, a team of prominent figures in science and medicine gravely expressed their fears of the Republican candidate. Somberly introducing his colleagues, moderator Herbert York, a nuclear-weapons designer, said, "During the Eisenhower administration, I was director of Defense Research and Engineering. Here with me are men from science, engineering and medicine." York's manner suggested the performance of an unpleasant but necessary task.

Pointing out that the broadcast participants included Republicans and Democrats, York observed that "we scientists and engineers are supposed to represent the so-called non-political community in America. Usually, professors, scientists, physicians, engineers do not take very active roles in political campaigns. . . . But this time, we're involved in grass-roots political activity, because this time it's different." York declared nuclear responsibility as the theme of the discussion, noting that "we've helped develop the power that could destroy mankind. We have worked to build this power to insure our national security, and national security in every sense is our deepest concern."

The radio show, hurriedly assembled, seemed to go off the track when the first speaker introduced by York, America's beloved children's doctor, Benjamin Spock, addressed his own concern of the moment, government support of education. "President Johnson has backed education to the hilt," Spock declared, asserting that Goldwater "voted against aid to elementary education, aid to vocational education, aid to college education, aid to medical and dental students."[2]

The radio roundtable quickly returned to the nuclear issue with the introduction of George Kistiakowsky, of Harvard, a key scientific leader in building the bomb during World War II. With a Russian accent and precise command of English, Kistiakowsky was an imposing radio performer. "George," said moderator York, "you and I worked very hard and faithfully for President Eisenhower during his administration. Can you tell us why so many Republicans are involved in behalf of President Johnson in this campaign?"

2. With Spock's pronouncement, according to popular newspaper columnist Inez Robb, "all hope oozed away from the Republican candidate. . . . Millions of American mothers and grandmothers in the United States would as soon question Dr. Spock as they would holy writ." Quoted in Theodore H. White, *The Making of the President 1964* (Atheneum, 1965), p. 352.

Kistiakowsky responded that Goldwater's nuclear positions "would produce a great discontinuity, a critical break in policies successfully prosecuted by Presidents of both parties during the last 30 years. . . . he is outside the mainstream of responsible American thinking and is clearly unqualified to be trusted with the great powers of the Presidency."

The pounding of Goldwater by the creators of the bomb and the managers of national security went on. Cataloging major increases in U.S. military capabilities, Admiral W.F. Raborn, introduced as the mastermind of the Polaris submarine missile system, said Goldwater's proposals for a further military buildup "don't make sense." Pointing out that "I know both the good Senator and President Johnson personally," the admiral counseled that Goldwater is "just not smart enough to be the President of the United States"—to which York appended, "I'm afraid I feel the same way." Nobel laureate Harold Urey, also a scientific alumnus of the Manhattan Project, said he perceived Goldwater as "a blustery, threatening man, who talks often without thinking, shoots from the hip, as they say. This frightens me [and] I fear it might frighten the USSR. And if they become frightened, I think their reaction would be to build up an aggressive group in the USSR, which is exactly what we don't want. We would like to get along with these people."

Turning to Jerome Wiesner, whom he introduced as having "worked very closely with Eisenhower, Kennedy and Johnson," York asked, "What are your observations of the way President Johnson understands and takes into account the role of science and engineering and technology in the modern world?" Recalling Johnson's assumption of the presidency "in those sad days last fall" when Kennedy was assassinated, Wiesner extolled "his clear, almost intuitive understanding of the great problems of security and peace, and of the opportunity science has created to build a better society here at home." Goldwater, Wiesner said, opposed arms control "and he's even said that he expects that there will be a nuclear war." The broadcast participants continued their denunciations of Goldwater. "I've heard some say that Goldwater is bold," Kistiakowsky stated, "but to me, his views are simply rash and primitive." Noting that Goldwater opposed the nuclear test-ban treaty, Kistiakowsky added, "My former boss, President Eisenhower, supported the treaty . . . as a first and limited but very important step toward reducing the possibility of nuclear war. The choice which Senator Goldwater advocated was hollow and destructive." In clear, direct language, without innuendo or subtlety, the makers of the bomb, joined by a leading military man and America's revered pediatrician, savaged Goldwater beyond political repair.

The Goldwater campaign initially followed the brain-trust model, announcing the appointment of a Goldwater task force on space, science, and the atom. But outwitted and outgunned by the scientists' surprisingly aggressive campaign for Johnson, it responded with a copycat organization, Scientists and Engineers for Goldwater, a feeble effort that made no mark on the campaign. Denounced by the superstars of science and medicine, Goldwater was indelibly tarred as an irresponsible nuclear cowboy. "My candidate had been branded a bomb-dropper," said Denison Kitchel, Goldwater's campaign chief and long-time confidante, "and I couldn't figure out how to lick it. And the advertising people, people who could sell anything, toothpaste or soap or automobiles—when it came to a political question like this, they couldn't offer anything either."[3] Scientists thus contributed to the avalanche that buried Goldwater and kept Johnson in the White House, by more than 61 percent of the popular vote.

RETURN OF AN ANCIENT ISSUE

In their public pronouncements, the rival party organizations in the 1964 presidential campaign were indistinguishable in support of government support of basic research as essential to national security and well-being. But they split along an old fault line in American politics: the issue of the proper role of government in promoting industrial technology and innovation, a division dating back to Alexander Hamilton's advocacy of government support for industrial development and Thomas Jefferson's agrarian preferences. As noted previously, with his focus on basic research, Vannevar Bush, in *Science, The Endless Frontier*, discreetly skirted the politically volatile issue of direct government assistance for industrial research by merely nodding to "research clinics" for business firms as "certainly worthy of further study" (see chapter 3).

Starting in 1961, the Kennedy administration, in a characteristically interventionist gambit, sought to create a civilian industrial technology program, aimed at pumping research funds into nonmilitary industry. Wiesner and other scientists high in the administration, and later in the 1964 presidential campaign, were the principal architects of Kennedy's industrial-technology plan. Congressional Republicans, joined by conservative Democrats, rejected it as unneeded, wasteful, and inappropriate for government. Now the 1964 Democratic campaign, in a statement drafted

3. Ibid.

with the assistance of Scientists and Engineers for Johnson-Humphrey, endorsed the program, calling for the establishment of university-based "industrial clinics" to "serve the plurality of industrial needs in different regions of the United States." Scientists and Engineers for Goldwater-Miller countered that "government should confine its major research activities to projects which private industry cannot be reasonably expected to undertake." Thirty years later, virtually the same ideological dialogue, conducted along the same party lines, resumed between President Bill Clinton and resurgent Republicans led by Newt Gingrich.

CHEERS, AND MISGIVINGS

Scientists and Engineers for Johnson-Humphrey won rave notices from Democratic campaign professionals. After the election, the organization's impact was summed up by David Garth, the political professional who counseled the scientists' campaign: "By the time we were through, any guy in Pittsburgh in a T-shirt with a can of beer in his hand knew that the smartest people in this country considered Goldwater unfit." The adulation was seconded by the campaign-chronicling Theodore H. White. Scientists and Engineers for Johnson-Humphrey "operated so effectively," he reported, "as to lead many of the slide-rule thinkers to wonder whether they might not permanently enter politics and change them—a problem to be considered in future campaigns."[4] However, it was evident that the scientists' unprecedented political romp left serious misgivings in some of them. Even among scientists alarmed by Goldwater's nuclear rhetoric, science's turn to overt partisan politics was troublesome and unacceptable, despite the campaign's repeated avowals of political purity. The concern was reflected in a little-noticed effort during the 1964 campaign by scientists seeking to reconcile organized electoral participation with nonpartisanship. They formed a politically neutral organization, the Scientists Committee for Information. Chaired by Edward L. Tatum, a Nobel laureate at the Rockefeller Institute, the committee offered itself as a resource for providing "impartial and accurate information" on scientific issues arising during the campaign. In the clamor of the Johnson-Goldwater campaign, the offer of untainted information attracted little attention.

After its political debut in 1964, science demobilized and never again returned to national politics on a significant scale. Here and there, politi-

4. Ibid.

cal efforts sprouted, in behalf of one of the rare congressional candidates with professional scientific credentials, or for a politically threatened legislator who had been especially supportive of science. After the Johnson-Goldwater contest, science's reversion to its apolitical tradition in national elections can be attributed, in part, to the absence of a serious candidate with the fearsome qualities of Barry Goldwater. But another factor was at work, too: misgivings among scientists about the propriety of science engaging in partisan politics. Was it right to entangle science, an enterprise dedicated to truth-seeking, in the messy business of politics? And would partisan political involvement undermine the sciences' ability to maintain independence while prospering on government funds?

Skeptics might say that, given the Cold War financial underpinnings of major stretches of American science, both concerns were based in idealistic misperceptions, or self-delusion, about the true relationship between science and politics. The concerns, nonetheless, were strongly felt and were in fact based on accurate perceptions of changes in the growth patterns in government support of science during the 1960s. The nonmilitary sector, in which science was jealously managed by civilian scientists, was growing rapidly, both in dollars and as a proportion of the nation's research activities. In 1960, when federal support for research and development stood at $7.5 billion, the Defense Department received $5.7 billion, 76 percent of the total. By 1968, when federal support of R&D had approximately doubled, to $15.9 billion, the Pentagon's share had also grown, to $7.7 billion; but in percentage terms, it had declined sharply, to 48 percent of the total. Nearly quadrupling during those years were the budgets of the federal government's two major civilian financiers of academic science: the National Science Foundation, whose funding rose from $75 million to $284 million, and the Department of Health, Education and Welfare (home of the National Institutes of Health), whose budget rose from $320 million to $1.2 billion.[5] The rapid growth of the officially civilian NASA, in Cold War competition with the Soviets, helped produce the near balance in government spending on civilian and military research in 1968. Apart from space, civilian research still trailed the military by far, but the trends were favorable for increased funding. And, except for the singular political extravaganza of 1964, spending had increased without science demonstrating political strength, either on big national issues or the narrow, but heartfelt, issue of money for research. Washington was increasingly attentive to the needs of

5. *Indicators 1976* (NSF 77-1), p. 227.

science, even before science established or reinforced its capital-city out-posts to campaign for more.

Though inspired by the alarming nature of the Goldwater candidacy, the venture of scientists into electoral politics remained troubling even among the organizers of Scientists and Engineers for Johnson-Humphrey. In an interview with me in 1965, Jerome Wiesner said, "I certainly oppose, very much, the continuation of the organization in any form." Wiesner, who had returned to MIT after serving briefly in the Johnson White House, added, "I think it would be wrong to set up an organization to be a lobby for scientists and engineers. You have a competition with all the other orga-nizations, including the AAAS [American Association for the Advancement of Science] and various other organizations. Secondly, it couldn't be a very effective organization, just by its very composition." Referring to the Johnson-Humphrey organization, Wiesner emphasized, "It was bipartisan, deliberately bipartisan."

As the 1968 presidential campaign approached, doubts about the wis-dom of science again going political were restated by Philip Handler, a prominent figure in science and government affairs who chaired the Duke University School of Medicine Department of Biochemistry. In 1964, while serving as vice chair of the National Science Board and as a member of the President's Science Advisory Committee, Handler headed the North Caro-lina chapter of Scientists and Engineers for Johnson-Humphrey. Like many other scientists in the 1964 campaign, Handler bridged science and politics. Four years later, he was appointed chair of the National Science Board and was elected president of the National Academy of Sciences. In 1968, as the Democratic party split over the Vietnam War, Handler expressed support for the mainline candidacy of Vice President Hubert Humphrey, who faced the insurgent candidacy of Senator Eugene McCarthy in primary elections for the Democratic presidential nomination. In the spring of 1968, Handler was inclined toward another go for scientists in politics. As he later ac-knowledged, in describing his initial response to an approach by a member of Humphrey's staff, "I happily agreed to his invitation to be among a small group of scientists, physicians, and engineers who would organize to sup-port Mr. Humphrey." A few weeks later, however, Handler reversed course, taking himself out of politics and urging the scientific community to follow his example.

Explaining his turnabout in a letter to the Humphrey staff, Handler warned that "the organization of partisan groups of scientists supporting individual candidates for high political office threatens to generate serious rifts in the scientific community, 'dividing the house' as it were, whereas the issues that separate them are entirely external to science itself and indeed to the application of scientific solutions to the problems of our nation." Handler added that if scientists organized and joined in partisan politics, "it is inevitable that national attitudes and federal support for science must also come to involve political considerations. Appointments of scientists to administrative posts in science-using agencies and appropriations for federal support of science will surely be influenced by the political activities of those concerned." He noted, too, that, as chair of the board presiding over the National Science Foundation, "it would be particularly inappropriate for me to be associated with the formation of Scientists, Engineers, and Physicians for any candidate. The National Science Foundation," he asserted, "is essentially non-political. It would be a disservice to the Nation for me to jeopardize, in any way, the future of this agency by personally engaging in partisan politics on the national scene."[6]

Both camps of the 1968 presidential campaign—Humphrey versus Nixon—recruited and advertised lists of supportive scientists and associated professionals. However, these efforts, along the old showcase style, never came close to the scale and vigor of the anti-Goldwater campaign—though not for lack of interest on the part of Donald MacArthur, the organizer of the scientists' 1964 political debut.

ANOTHER TRY AT POLITICS

Following Johnson's landslide election in 1964, MacArthur was appointed to a senior research post at the Pentagon. As deputy director of research and engineering, he still kept watch on political sentiments in the scientific community. The topic was of increasing concern to Uncle Lyndon as opposition to the Vietnam War grew on university campuses. In the fall of 1967, Johnson, or possibly an aide, asked MacArthur to assess a report in *Science* that Johnson's 1964 scientific supporters had turned against him because of the Vietnam War. MacArthur responded with a candidly pessimistic memo to the president, dated November 1, 1967, four months prior to Johnson's unexpected announcement that he would not run for reelection.[7]

The *Science* article, MacArthur advised the president, "is a fair represen-

---

6. *Science,* July 12, 1968.
7. MacArthur's response and other correspondence between him and the White House were in the trove of his personal papers that his widow, Diana MacArthur, kindly made available to me for this book.

tation of the mood of the scientific community. In fact, based on many conversations over the last couple of months, the 'defection' may be somewhat greater than the article implies, especially in the academic community." Vietnam was *the* source of disaffection, MacArthur told Johnson, obscuring approval of "what you have done on the domestic front for education, civil rights, war on poverty, health and transportation." MacArthur then offered a shrewd dissection of the ideological composition of the "community"—distinguishing among scientists, engineers, and medical researchers:

> Scientists, particularly in the academic world, are the most critical. They have "defected" in large numbers and tend to focus on Vietnam related to issues such as domestic spending constraints. Engineers tend to be more conservative, and generally would tend to support the Administration, even with increased escalation in Vietnam. They are not too concerned about the domestic and international implications of Vietnam policies. The medical research community is quite mixed; some, who are sensitive to foreign affairs matters, are quite critical; others are apathetic; many are happy with federal funding for health research and are not concerned with Vietnam at all. Because of Vietnam concerns, it would probably not be possible *today* [original italics] to form a scientific and engineering political coalition with as broad a base as we did in 1964.

THE "THREE MOST INFLUENTIAL" SCIENTISTS

Proceeding to political tactics, MacArthur urged Johnson to "enlist the support of the three most influential leaders in the scientific community"—Detlev Bronk, president of Rockefeller University; Wiesner, recently appointed provost of MIT, and Kistiakowsky, of Harvard—by inviting them "to an informal meeting to discuss the Vietnam issue. They recognize you have a tough problem. Let them discuss their anxieties, their fears, and their ideas about Vietnam." MacArthur also advised Johnson to commission Ithiel de Sola Pool, professor of political science at MIT, to "conduct a private opinion poll of the scientific, engineering and medical community across the country" to obtain "a more precise reading, on a more comprehensive scale, of those aspects of the administration's policies that the scientists and engineers across the country dislike." De Sola Pool, he assured the president, "is completely trustworthy and has worked very successfully for the Department of Defense in Vietnam, and is an expert in opinion polls." Johnson did not act on MacArthur's recommended meeting with the three pillars of American science, or on the suggested poll. It is even doubtful that MacArthur's memo reached the beleaguered president.

On January 15, 1968, MacArthur sent Johnson a follow-up memo, based, he wrote, on a conversation with Wiesner: "He has made it clear to me, and I gathered that he wished that I would inform you, that *he is a continuing supporter of the Johnson administration*" [original italics]. MacArthur wrote that Wiesner was "concerned that his name may be incorrectly associated" with scientists backing Senator Eugene McCarthy's challenge to Johnson in the Democratic presidential primary in Massachusetts. He again urged Johnson to meet with Bronk, Wiesner and Kistiakowsky, stating "it should be possible for a third party to arrange to have them request the meeting," and assuring Johnson that "these three men, in my opinion, would be discreet about such a meeting."

A note by W. Marvin Watson, special assistant to the president, merely acknowledged receipt of MacArthur's renewed urging for Johnson to reach out to the three scientific leaders. Three weeks later, in a letter to Watson, MacArthur again appealed for Johnson to meet "with the three 'statesmen' of the scientific community if he wants to keep open the option of retaining their support this year." He noted that Wiesner had recently returned from Moscow, where he had discussed arms-control issues and Vietnam with scientists whom Aleksei Kosygin, the Soviet president, "calls upon for advice." Johnson, MacArthur suggested, "could ask Wiesner to talk to him on what he thought the attitude of the Russians was on these issues." A few days later, Watson responded to MacArthur with a "Dear Don" note concerning the proposed meeting with Wiesner: "We appreciate very much your interest in suggesting this but it just isn't feasible to work out anything at this time."

The political mobilization of science occurred in special circumstances and was disbanded as quickly as it arose. But it added to an accumulation of ill will that cost science dearly in the presidency of Richard Nixon. The experience left an enduring impression on the politics of science, affecting how scientists deal with Washington in their quest for money and influence—and how Washington responds.

CHAPTER 11

Nixon Banishes the Scientists

The distinguishing characteristic of the scientist as a participant in political life stems from a fundamental ambiguity in the scientist's psychological make-up. At the same time that he appreciates the need for him to participate in political life, the scientist is often repelled by the requirements for success in politics. The appeal to passion, the skillful political maneuver, and the risk of public disfavor are highly repulsive to most scientists. Yet their sense of social responsibility, their desire to accomplish certain political goals, and even the desire for public honor draw scientists into political life. In short, the scientist wants to be in and out of politics at the same time.

—Robert Gilpin (*American Scientists and Nuclear Weapons Policy*)

THE 1964 mobilization of scientists was not repeated in the 1968 presidential campaign, when Richard Nixon was elected, or ever again. For Nixon and company, however, grievances persisted over the lopsided presence of scientists in support of the Democratic cause. Nixon had ample reason to believe that scientists disliked him, and, after several conciliatory efforts on his part, he did not conceal his dislike for them. A prickly, distrustful relationship festered between Nixon and the policy-related scientists in and around his administration; ultimately, it led to an abrupt disruption in the structure for linking science and government. Institutional repairs were made a few years after Nixon resigned; but the trauma suffered by the politicians of science at the hands of Richard Nixon fundamentally reordered the relationship between presidents and their science advisers. After Nixon, the scientists who served in the White House harbored no noble delusions about loyalty to values that transcend politics and presidents. After Nixon, humbler political behavior prevailed in the senior ranks of science politics.

Several streams of resentment contributed to Nixon's animus

toward scientists, including the highly visible role of Jerry Wiesner in the Kennedy administration, and, after Wiesner's return to MIT, his prominence in the 1964 anti-Goldwater mobilization. Following his full-time White House service, which started with Kennedy and extended into the early months of the Johnson administration, Wiesner reverted to the role of the commuting policy scientist as a member of the President's Science Advisory Committee (PSAC) serving the Johnson White House. The Washington rumor mill told of overt, pro-Democratic scheming at official PSAC sessions during the 1968 presidential campaign.[1]

THE WHITE HOUSE SCIENCE POST

Following his election, Nixon and his dedicated collaborators on their long march back from political oblivion faced the question of whether to fill the job of presidential science and technology adviser. To do so would mean retaining the supporting Office of Science and Technology (OST), home base of the adviser's staff, housed adjacent to the White House, in the Old Executive Office Building—precious, prestigious space in the capital's power structure. If custom prevailed, appointment of a presidential science adviser would assure continuation of the President's Science Advisory Committee (PSAC), established a decade earlier by Eisenhower, with roots going back to the Truman administration. The science question was a minor item among the cosmic issues that confront a new presidential administration, but it was of critical importance to the leadership classes of American science. The science adviser, backed by the Office of Science and Technology and the President's Science Advisory Committee, was their direct link to political power. A continuing scientific presence at the White House had evolved slowly, and with difficulty, after World War II; now that it seemed to be firmly established through service in the Eisenhower, Kennedy, and

---

1. Confirmation of partisan politicking in the inner sanctums of government science policy was naturally elusive. An allegation of such political activity was contained in a 1971 MIT doctoral dissertation based on interviews with scientists in the upper echelons of science advice in Washington. During the 1968 presidential election campaign, according to this account, a PSAC panel meeting "was converted into a working session of Scientists and Engineers for Humphrey-Muskie, to the chagrin of at least one panel member who was a Nixon supporter. He viewed with distaste the sight of his colleagues 'arranging calling and canvass activities at the expense of the legitimate responsibilities of PSAC.'" The dissertation adds, "Other panel members, when questioned about this, either stated that they had not attended the meeting or could not remember such an activity occurring, but no outright denials were issued." Anne Hessing Cahn, *Eggheads and Warheads: Scientists and the ABM* (MIT Center for International Studies, Science and Public Policy Program, 1971).

Johnson administrations, the leaders of science were accustomed to it. After some indecision, the new Nixon administration chose continuity and announced a distinguished, though ultimately disastrous, choice for the senior science position in the U.S. government: Lee A. DuBridge, a physicist who was a great figure of the postwar science establishment. During World War II, DuBridge headed the MIT Radiation Laboratory. As the American center for radar research and development, the "Rad Lab," managed by MIT, did more to win the war than the Hiroshima and Nagasaki atomic bombs, which conspicuously punctuated its end. From 1946 to 1969, while serving as president of the California Institute of Technology, DuBridge personified the new breed of postwar science statesmen, commuting to Washington to advise the highest officials of government, in both Democratic and Republican administrations. He was a member of the General Advisory Committee of the Atomic Energy Commission, a uniquely influential body in the formative postwar years of the nuclear-weapons and the nuclear-power industries. During the Eisenhower administration, DuBridge chaired the Science Advisory Committee in the Office of Defense Mobilization, a precursor of the President's Science Advisory Committee; in that role, he was de facto science adviser to the president. He advised the military services on weapons development, and, among other advisory positions, he was a charter member of the National Science Board, the governing body of the newly launched National Science Foundation, serving from 1950 to 1954 and from 1958 to 1964. At sixty-eight, a dignified, internationally honored great figure of science and higher education when he was summoned back to the White House in 1969, DuBridge experienced eighteen troubled months as Richard Nixon's special assistant for science and technology. Evidently astute in academic politics, but tone deaf to national politics, DuBridge was the misfit of the Nixon White House. His missteps with Nixon's political staff were many and irritating for the hard-bitten political types who, for the first time, were confronted by a strange species that had evolved during and after World War II: the Washington scientist in the high circles where governing and politicking were intertwined. Finally, DuBridge was abruptly pushed out, amid derisive comments within Nixon's political circle.

A STRUGGLE OVER NSF

At the beginning of Nixon's presidency, and the beginning of DuBridge's service as Nixon's science adviser, the quest for a new director for the National Science Foundation swelled into a noxious episode that publicly embarrassed the fledgling administration. The NSF directorship was normally situated below the threshold of public attention. Awarding its money on the basis of competitive peer review, NSF dispensed no political pork and, with very rare exceptions, was exempted from pressures to provide jobs for political loyalists. Though rooted in political Washington, NSF was robed in a scientific purity that fended off the political roughnecks. Among scientists, NSF was a revered institution, the embodiment, radically reshaped though it was, of Vannevar Bush's grand design for reconciling government money and scientific independence. By coincidence, the NSF directorship had become vacant in 1969, the opening year of the Nixon presidency, when Director Leland Haworth completed the statutory six-year term. The recruitment system, guided by advice from NSF's board and DuBridge's Office of Science and Technology, put forth a capable candidate: Franklin Long, a professor of chemistry at Cornell University with extensive experience in Washington.

Like many scientists, prior to Nixon's arrival in the White House, Long had served without evident political strain under both Republican and Democratic presidents. During the Eisenhower administration, Long held several medium-level advisory posts. In 1961, he reached the pinnacle of advisory committees when Kennedy appointed him to the President's Science Advisory Committee. The following year, Kennedy appointed him assistant director of the newly established Arms Control and Disarmament Agency. ACDA was created by the president in response to the scientists and others who pleaded that the cause of arms control needed a base of its own in the capital as a counterweight to the weapons-proliferating Pentagon and its industrial suppliers. In the arms-control post, and after returning to Cornell in 1963, Long was an outspoken advocate of nuclear restraint and patient efforts to devise arms-control agreements with the Soviets. In accord with those views, he was on record as opposing the Nixon administration's commitment to an antiballistic missile (ABM) program, regarding it as a destabilizing factor in the East-West nuclear standoff. Long clearly possessed a Democratic pedigree on the politically volatile issue of arms control. But in harmony with the nonpartisan tradition of the NSF directorship, which was remote from defense-related issues, the Nixon administration approved his selection. If inner-circle members thought about it at all, they may have anticipated kudos for making an excellent choice, without regard to political issues.

But then White House legislative strategists warned that the announcement of Long's nomination would coincide with Nixon's push for congressional approval of the ABM program. Fears arose that the capital's fine sifters of political clues would interpret Long's appointment as signaling half-hearted dedication by the White House to the ABM goal. Asked to declare his support for the ABM program, or at least wait quietly for the NSF appointment until Congress acted on the ABM, Long refused; he also declined a suggestion that he quietly withdraw on grounds of "personal" reasons. The National Science Board, traditionally a Milquetoast body, publicly denounced the fledgling Nixon administration for interposing political considerations into what the board regarded as protected, sacred territory, the National Science Foundation. Tarred in the press as antiscience—especially unpleasant for a politician who felt unjustly despised by academics—Nixon quickly reversed course and attempted to mollify the scientific establishment. In a meeting with members of the National Science Board and the National Academy of Sciences, Nixon confessed that he had erred in the Long affair, and personally invited Long to come aboard, after all, as director of the National Science Foundation. Long, however, declined.[2] A renewed search, for a politically unencumbered candidate, resulted in the appointment of William D. McElroy, a scientist at Johns Hopkins University, as the next NSF director. The choice indicated an absence of political dogmatism in the Nixon circle: McElroy had served as a White House adviser throughout the Johnson administration.

THE MARS EPISODE

Not just the Long affair but a succession of conflicts between politics and scientific judgment undermined DuBridge's tenure in the Nixon White House and soured Nixon's relations with science. An intimate, revealing vignette was provided in a memoir by John Ehrlichman, the president's chief for domestic affairs and one of Nixon's closest confidantes. Nixon, like all modern presidents, was committed to reducing government spending, yet, as Ehrlichman relates, the National Aeronautics and Space Council, chaired by Vice President Spiro Agnew, was about to recommend "a very costly manned mission to the planet Mars in 1981."[3]

---

2. The Long affair, with references to its extensive news coverage, is discussed in Milton Lomask, *A Minor Miracle: An Informal History of the National Science Foundation* (Washington, D.C.: National Science Foundation, 76-18), pp. 221–23.

3. A manned mission to Mars is a perennial dream of the space bureaucracy and a nightmare for politicians. It is justifiably feared, and rejected, by politics as a runaway budget buster, despite the siren song of wondrous economies via new, cost-cutting technologies. The leading postwar advocate of a manned roundtrip to Mars was Wernher von Braun, designer of the Nazi V-2 rocket. His book, *The Mars Project,* initially published in Germany in 1952, was reissued in 1991 by the University of Illinois Press, with an approving introduction by Thomas O. Paine, head of NASA from 1968 to 1970. Par for the course in space rhetoric, Paine hopefully declared that "the 500th anniversary of

Efforts at "dissuading" DuBridge from supporting the proposal were un-successful, though "it seemed obvious to me," Ehrlichman related, "that Agnew and DuBridge owed it to the President not to include a proposal our budget couldn't pay for": "A Mars space shot would be popular with many people. If the committee [i.e., the Space Council] proposed it and Nixon had to say no, he would be criticized as the President who kept us from finding life on Mars. On the other hand," reasoned Ehrlichman, the adept political tactician, "if the committee didn't recommend it, we avoided the problem altogether." The difficulty facing the White House staff was deemed serious by Ehrlichman, but in condescending fashion, he absolved DuBridge of responsibility: "DuBridge was perhaps to be forgiven for failing to understand such a political argument, but I saw no excuse for Agnew's insistence that the Mars shot be recommended." Backed by Nixon, Ehr-lichman confronted the vice president: "It is your job, with Lee DuBridge's help, to make absolutely certain that the Mars trip is not in there." When the budget appeared, the Mars trip was not in there.[4]

SUPERSONIC POLITICS

Other incidents added to the distaste of Nixon and his loyalists for what they increasingly came to regard as an anti-Nixon Washington science ca-bal. One of the most galling for the president involved Richard L. Garwin, an IBM physicist appointed to the President's Science Advisory Committee by Kennedy in 1961. In scientific circles Garwin was esteemed for his bril-liance and excellent judgment; numerous government agencies coveted his advice. Following the nonpolitical tradition of science at the White House level, Nixon reappointed Garwin to PSAC in 1969, though Garwin, too, was an outspoken opponent of the Nixon-endorsed antiballistic missile pro-gram. But unlike the directorship of the NSF, which required Senate con-firmation, Garwin's PSAC appointment was at presidential discretion, to a publicly inconspicuous advisory body, and passed without notice. As a member of PSAC under Nixon, Garwin chaired a panel that studied another politically contentious project strongly backed by the president, the su-personic transport (SST), which faced serious congressional resistance on grounds of cost, economic viability, and fears of sonic boom and strato-

Columbus's discovery of the new world will see that world setting sail for other new worlds across the ocean of space."
4. John Ehrlichman, *Witness to Power: The Nixon Years* (Simon & Schuster, 1982; Pocket Books edition), p. 123.

spheric pollution. Opponents picturesquely denounced the SST as a tax-subsidized chariot of the rich. Garwin had no difficulty parsing his public and private roles in the raging SST controversy. Testifying to a House Appropriations Subcommittee in April 1970, Garwin acknowledged his PSAC membership. "But I emphasize," he stated, "that I am speaking now as an individual and not as a representative of any group or person." Thus presenting himself as citizen Garwin, the longtime presidential science adviser strongly advised against government assistance for the presidentially supported supersonic transport:

> I would terminate the Government's direct or indirect support of the SST program if I have the option. When the conditions are ripe for a commercial program, U.S. industry and finance will rise to the occasion. Government support before that time seems to result in great pressures to continue an uneconomic program, in a warping of the environmental protection regulations to suit these machines and not the people, and may well lead to an increase in all air fares if the airlines and passengers are expected to bear some or part of the cost of procurement or operation of the SST.[5]

Garwin suggested that the White House had withheld unfavorable information about the SST's costs and environmental effects, and that, because of the SST's high operating expenses, the "airlines do not want an SST per se, they want one only if another airline is also to have one, either a Concorde [the Anglo-French SST] or a U.S. SST." Under questioning at the Congressional hearing, Garwin said the gist of his testimony had previously appeared in news reports in *Aviation Week,* which, he noted, favored the SST. He indicated that he was merely restating publicly available information. In March 1971, both the House and Senate rejected Nixon's request for $134 million for proceeding with the SST, a project on which the government had already spent $840 million. For the jobs and accompanying political support it would create, and for its appeal to Nixon's zest for American high-tech supremacy, the SST ranked high in the administration's priorities. The White House angrily denounced the termination votes as "a severe blow not only to the tens of thousands of workers affected but also to the United States' continued leadership in the aerospace industry."[6]

5. Hearings, House Appropriations Subcommittee for the Department of Transportation and Related Agencies, 91st Cong., 2d sess., April 15–17, 1970, pp. 980–94.
6. *Congress and the Nation,* vol. 3, 1969–1972 (Congressional Quarterly, 1973), p. 168.

Garwin's public opposition to an embattled major program of the administration reinforced the Nixonian perception of scientists as perfidious, as abusers of their privileged status within the president's own house. Even a mainstay of the science establishment, former MIT president James R. Killian Jr. (whom Eisenhower summoned to the White House in 1957 as the first full-time presidential science adviser), regarded Garwin's performance with distaste and expressed, in his memoir of science and politics, understanding for Nixon and company's sense of betrayal:

> During the Nixon Administration, a PSAC panel submitted a report critical of the SST. Later, relations with the Nixon White House were damaged beyond repair by a member of PSAC, who testified against the SST without resigning his PSAC membership. While I believed him when he insisted that he had not drawn on any PSAC classified material in preparing his testimony and I respected his conclusions and his right to them, I still cannot defend this act, but I can understand Nixon's resulting skeptical view of his science advisers.[7]

Though Killian did not identify the "member of PSAC" by name, Garwin's role in the SST episode was public knowledge. Insisting that he had not revealed confidential information to Congress, Garwin argued that in advising government, scientists owed their loyalty to truth, not to politics, and that the nation would benefit if politicians recognized and encouraged that higher loyalty.[8] In politics, however, the highest loyalties are to person, party, and program, usually in that order.[9]

EXIT DUBRIDGE

DuBridge's days in the White House were running out. In May 1970, Nixon announced a shakeup of senior officials. DuBridge was out as science

---

7. James R. Killian Jr., *Sputnik, Scientists and Eisenhower: A Memoir of the First Special Assistant to the President for Science and Technology* (Cambridge: MIT Press, 1977), p. 23.

8. Richard L. Garwin, "Scientists and Public Policy, Help or Hinderance?" address to the American Physical Society Forum on Physics and Society, 1976.

9. Among his many honors, Garwin has twice received the Public Service Award of the Federation of American Scientists, in 1971 for his role in the SST episode and in 1997 for his careerlong participation in public affairs. The citation accompanying the second award notes that in 1971, FAS honored Garwin "for his unique contribution toward the defeat of the Supersonic Transport, which required, besides his skills, the courage to defy the Nixon Administration by testifying before Congress." The citation also states that "if Dick [Garwin] says 2 + 2 = 5, even Nobel Prize winners recalculate before replying." *FAS Public Interest Report*, January/February 1998.

adviser, while Under Secretary of State Elliot Richardson, number two to Secretary of State William Rogers, was shifted to a new job, Secretary of Health, Education, and Welfare. Apparently, as part of the change, DuBridge was assigned some duty, perhaps an advisory role, at the State Department, though the publicly announced change made no mention of it. In a final jab at DuBridge, Ehrlichman wrote in his memoir, "At Richardson's swearing in, William Rogers leaned over to me and muttered, 'Some trade: I give Elliot Richardson and get Lee DuBridge!' "[10]

A New Adviser for Nixon

After ruminating on whether to appoint another science and technology adviser, Nixon agreed to give it a try. The choice this time was a fast-rising scientist-administrator at Bell Labs, Edward E. David Jr., age forty-five. The sixth in a succession of full-time presidential science advisers, David was the first to come from industry; he was not part of the university-based science-policy "in-crowd" that came of age during World War II and dominated Washington science advice for over two decades. Aware via the grapevine of the downward course of DuBridge's tenure, David knew that Nixon's staff believed DuBridge "was running a renegade operation in the White House."[11] David told me that prior to accepting the offer, he discussed the job, "sitting around a table" in the White House with Peter Flannigan, a senior White House aide; Ehrlichman; and Henry Kissinger, Nixon's assistant for national security affairs. Kissinger, David recalled, was mainly concerned about the antiballistic missile program, a high-priority goal for the president, "but there were a lot of other issues he was concerned about."

"They didn't present any menu," David related. "They just said, 'We need somebody to come in here to make sure that we have an effective operation, and that's part of the White House operation.' And I said, 'Well, I'm not coming down here to disestablish science and technology in the United States.' " They replied, David recalled, that " 'we couldn't do it with Lee [DuBridge] there, so you are now the guy we want to work with, and we'll have to look at each individual issue that's in front of us, and you will have to contribute to that.' " David signed on.

Nixon seethed with anger about scientists, accusing them of ingratitude, David recalled to me, an account corroborated by Hugh Loweth, a

10. Ehrlichman., op. cit., p. 81.
11. Interview with author, July 1, 1998.

career civil servant who handled science issues in the Office of Management and Budget. David was nominally a Republican, but personally apolitical. Even after serving in the Nixon White House for nearly two years, he retained a hopeful innocence about the relationship between science and politics. In a conversation in 1972, David explained to me: "I look on science and scientists as the antidote to politics. Science is the technique for establishing reality. In all these arguments about pollution, energy, drugs, product safety—some group has to stand up for reality. That's what science is all about."[12] David said he noted the puzzlement and then the mounting anger of Nixon and company over the continuing presence of Kennedy- and Johnson-era science advisers in the Nixon administration's science councils. As we have seen, from the earliest times of postwar science advising for the White House, appointees had passed from one administration to the next, without attention paid to party affiliations, by the scientists or the administration. But the tolerance of scientists as apolitical creatures declined as the Nixon White House got to know them better. "'Get all those Democrats out of there,'" David says he was told by Nixon's political henchmen. The matter was stated more emphatically by John Ehrlichman, according to OMB's Loweth: "Those bastards," he recalled Ehrlichman saying, "we've got to cut them back."[13] David said he protested. "Basically, I stood up and said, 'You shouldn't fire them. That would be a big event in the scientific community, it would turn everybody off, and you gain nothing.' That was a fight I won, but there was a strong adversarial feeling."[14]

Nixon, like presidents before and after him, wondered why the government's ever-rising expenditures for research weren't producing the spectacular economic payoffs promised by scientists in their appeals for federal support for R&D. In June 1971, in a conversation captured by the White House taping system, Nixon rambled at length on this topic, seasoning his views on research with derisive remarks about his science advisers, who were not present. He proclaimed admiration for Edwin Land, the Polaroid camera pioneer who developed photography systems for the U-2 spy plane and orbiting spy satellites. In a lengthy monologue, Nixon told Ehrlichman, George Shultz, and others that he wanted to see Land's innovative spirit

> infused throughout this whole government, in everything. But it isn't go-
> ing to happen unless you do something other than what we've been do-

---

12. Quoted in Daniel S. Greenberg, "David and Indifference," *Saturday Review of Science*, September 30, 1972.
13. Interview with author, March 15, 1999.
14. Interview with author, July 1, 1998.

ing, like, for example, in the scientific field. . . . Ed David, just like his predecessor before him, DuBridge, will argue, I'm sure, the way to do it is just to give another half million to the National Science Foundation. That isn't going to do a goddamn bit of good. . . . There must be half a dozen places where there are nuts running around. We think they're nuts, but they have great ideas, where Presidential support is needed. One thing that occurs to me is this. . . . The attitude of those in the [science] establishment may be too goddamn conservative. . . . I want [Edward] David and the National Science Board to—I want that bunch to shape up.[15]

Proceeding with his rant of disapproval about the scientists in his service, Nixon declared:

I am not satisfied. . . . The scientists that are good people running a school of engineering or being a dean of MIT or Caltech . . . wonderful guys. But they don't know a goddamn thing. And David, I think is a fine guy. . . . I think he's the first to say he's a practical man, he's no scientist. But he's damn good [at] looking it over. What you got to get is these brilliant guys, a genius. Take Bill Lear [developer of the Lear Jet aircraft]. Lear's a genius. He's nuts as hell. Drive you crazy. That little Lear Jet is a fine airplane. It made a helluva lot of money as long as people could afford it. . . . A guy like [Edwin] Land is the kind of guy who appeals to me. I want people around. I don't want the dumb ones. When I say the dumb ones, they're not dumb. They're perfectly smart, but they're men who always come up with the routine, quantitative answer, but with no quality or brilliance.[16]

In 1971, Nixon briefly considered the creation of a major federal program of economy-boosting "technological initiatives," headed during its brief, embryonic existence by the jobless director of the defeated SST program, William Magruder, reporting directly to the president. In political-science circles, the technology program was seen as an affront to the bypassed White House Office of Science and Technology. In the budget office of the White House, it was regarded with alarm as Magruder worked up a list of project proposals that exceeded $1 billion. Hugh Loweth recalled to

15. National Archives and Records Administration, Nixon Presidential Materials Project, 513-4, June 7, 1971. (Transcribed by author.)
16. Ibid.

me his instructions "from the highest level" at OMB, not otherwise identified: "I was told, 'Work with this, keep an eye on it, make sure it doesn't go anywhere.' "[17] Within a few months, the Magruder operation fizzled out and was gone. The animosity toward the scientists festered on in the White House. In a conversation with Nixon in June 1971, Ehrlichman reported that David had raised questions about a political directive to lavish money on California, vital for victory in next year's election:

Ehrlichman: I wrote Ed [David] a memo, based on our last conversation on the subject. He came up to me at the staff meeting this morning and said, "I got your memo and I'm just caught flat-footed. I think I have to talk to the President about this." I said, "Well, I sent you a memo right out of my notes of my conversation with the President, and that's the way it is." And he said, "I'm going to ask for an appointment with the President." So, that's just the way we left it.

Nixon: Like DuBridge, he wants to keep the money for [inaudible].

Ehrlichman: He wants to tell you their side of the story, and—

Nixon: You know how I feel. Talk to him about their side of the story. Let's find out. . . . I want the money spent, and he knows that. And why the hell do we have—. Don't let me hear any argument. Their only argument is that we're going to lose the support of the scientific community. We don't have the support of the scientific community. We will never have their support.[18]

OUSTER FROM THE WHITE HOUSE

By the end of his first term, Nixon had had enough of what he and his inner political circle regarded as vipers in the White House. Reelected by a landslide in 1972, Nixon planned his response. He banished the lot of them from the White House and also disposed of the director of the National Institutes of Health, Robert Marston, a holdover from the Johnson administration who had expressed doubts about the scientific wisdom of Nixon's war on cancer. In an executive order issued on January 26, 1973, the president terminated the position of special assistant to the president for science and technology and the White House Office of Science and Technology;

17. Interview with author, March 15, 1999.
18. Op. cit., Nixon Presidential Materials Project, 516-11, June 10, 1971.

with them, the President's Science Advisory Committee lost its home base and disappeared, too. Nixon thus eliminated the scientific community's cherished place in the presidency, where, in one form or another, it had formally existed since Eisenhower's days, and, prior to that, starting in Truman's presidency, in the nearby Office of Defense Mobilization. For scientific advice, when needed, Nixon said, he would call upon the director of NSF, a small agency in no way suited to dictate, or even suggest, budgets or policy for defense, space, health, and other sectors of federal research. The role of presidential science adviser—serving from a distance and only upon request—passed to NSF Director H. Guyford Stever. However, measured in budget growth, federal research agencies and programs continued to prosper, because not even the aggrieved, vengeance-minded Nixon could separate modern America from its dependence on science and technology.

Federal appropriations for research in universities, a principle locale of Nixonian ire, rose from $1.5 billion in fiscal 1968, the year of his inauguration, to $2 billion in 1974, the year of his resignation. True, in purchasing power during those high-inflation years, federal support declined. But the loss was more than compensated by large increases in research spending by state and local governments, by universities putting their own money into research, and private philanthropy. The reckoning can appear puzzling, since NSF, which keeps the numbers, has most recently calculated purchasing power for that stretch of years in 1992 dollars. By that measure, total support for academic science rose from $7.8 billion in 1968 to $8.1 billion in 1974.[19] It was during those years, too, that Nixon and Congress collaborated on designing and enacting the National Cancer Act, which rapidly expanded support for the biomedical sciences. And environmental regulation, with a major research component, was firmly established during the Nixon presidency with the amalgamation of scattered government activities into the newly created Environmental Protection Agency. Acrimonious personal relations between Nixon and the scientific leadership did not impede the growth and progress of the great national scientific enterprise. Federal research funds continued to pour into MIT—headed by Jerry Wiesner, reviled by Nixon and his old gang—despite Nixon's irate directives for financial punishment against that institution. The hated Wiesner was enshrined on the infamous "enemies list" of the Nixon White House.[20]

19. *Indicators 1998* (NSB-98-1), pp. A-197, 198.

20. The 200-member list was drawn mainly from politics, organized labor, the news media, and Hollywood, but the scientific community received a few places on what came to be regarded as an honor roll. In addition to Wiesner, the enemies list included Mat-

BACK TO THE WHITE HOUSE

Science had become too valuable to national well-being, and too skilled in proclaiming its importance and alleging neglect, for a mere president to crimp its support. Nixon's ouster of scientists from the White House seared the scientific psyche and further vindicated the warnings expressed by Academy President Philip Handler and others who feared the consequences of political engagement by scientists. With that lesson understood, the return of science to the White House became the overriding political objective of the scientific leaders and their friends in Congress. Following Nixon's resignation in 1974, sympathetic signs from President Gerald Ford heartened the restoration movement. In 1976, a bipartisan coalition, led by Republican Vice President Nelson Rockefeller and Senator Edward Kennedy, restored science to the presidency through legislation creating the White House Office of Science and Technology Policy. The legislation specified that the OSTP director would serve as the president's science and technology adviser; it also authorized creation of a successor to the vaunted PSAC—to be called the President's Committee on Science and Technology. The White House scientific presence abolished by Nixon in 1973 had been created by executive order during the Kennedy administration. The newly established successor, though similar in role and structure, gained stature as the offspring of a law passed by a Democratic Congress and signed by a Republican president, Gerald Ford. For science, bipartisan comity was obviously more productive than partisan political combat.

As the 1980 presidential election approached, the prospect of Ronald Reagan as the Republican nominee set off alarms in liberal academic and scientific circles, particularly among those familiar with Reagan's gubernatorial bashing of the University of California. Talk of a campaign revival then stirred among scientific alumni of the 1964 election. But the spirit was lacking. Addressing the annual spring meeting of the National Academy of Sciences, Academy President Philip Handler emphatically urged scientists to refrain from creating "Scientists and Engineers for Whomever"—a mocking title that signified disdain for scientific politicking. Acknowledging his own participation in the 1964 scientists' campaign for Johnson-Humphrey, Handler informed his fellow academicians that he had "awakened to the great undesirability of any such organization. I consider it a potential disas-

---

thew Meselson, professor of biology at Harvard, and Jeremy Stone, director of the Federation of American Scientists. Ironically, the list also included Edwin Land—for whom Nixon had expressed deep admiration.

ter thus to split the scientific community with respect to an issue which is essentially external to the scientific endeavor itself."[21]

The Politically Tamed Scientists

Handler's newfound distaste for scientific involvement in conventional politics harmonized with prevailing sentiments among the leadership and the rank and file. Science was focusing its political senses on the special interests of science and developing its own methods for engaging in politics to support those interests. And the methods didn't employ the low-efficiency crudities of doorbell ringing and money-raising at election time. More important, they did not entail favoring any particular candidate, at the unavoidable risk of antagonizing another, who might win—as did Richard Nixon in 1968, with serious effects on major interests of the scientific enterprise. The Nixon experience figured large in science's dismissal of ballot-box politics and the practice of conscience politics, à la Richard Garwin and the Supersonic Transport. Team play became the holy writ of scientists summoned to the White House. By abolishing the White House science office, Richard Nixon taught the leaders of science a punishing lesson: this president, and presumably other presidents, too, would not tolerate their intrusions into political territory. The scientists now understood that when summoned into service at the highest levels of government, where politics and administration are intertwined, they must serve the cause of politics—rather than what they perceive to be the higher truths and values of science. Advocacy of money for science was expected and acceptable—if not too brashly done or in violation of White House designs to restrain spending[22]—but expansionism beyond the boundaries of science was not. In describing their roles in speeches to their scientist colleagues and to journalists, the post-Nixon presidential science advisers emphasized that they were not emissaries from science to politics, posted to the White House to represent the scientific community; rather, they worked only for the president.

21. "In Brief," *SGR*, June 1, 1980.
22. Biomedical research is a permissible exception, manifested in an annual *pas de deux* of Congress and the favored National Institutes of Health. In their annual appearance before the Congressional Appropriations Committees, the leaders of NIH dutifully state the White House budget proposal for NIH—which customarily calls for a small increase, in expectation of a large increase by Congress. Following this official presentation, the legislators invite the NIH officials to give their "professional" judgment of NIH's financial needs. Under that dispensation, they state the need for a great deal more than the amount sought by the president. Though presumably still subject to discipline by their ultimate superior, the president, they thus support higher spending, under the banner of scientific judgment.

Frank Press, who served as Jimmy Carter's science and technology adviser, explained to me that "if you just go in and say, 'We need more money for science. Period,' you know what's going to happen. You become the representative of the science community, just as they had a representative of the Jewish community, or a representative of the black community and a representative of veterans' affairs in the Executive Office of the President. I didn't want to do that. I just wanted to be a member of the team."[23] George A. Keyworth described himself as "a guest" in the White House of Ronald Reagan. D. Allan Bromley, President Bush's science adviser, likened public divergence from the president to "a leap off the nearest cliff." Bromley explained that C. Everett Koop, the outspoken surgeon general who openly differed with the Reagan administration on AIDS policy, and thereby gained public stature, was a different case: "The Surgeon General is sufficiently removed from the White House to have substantially more freedom with respect to off-the-cuff remarks."[24]

These protestations did not dissuade the heads of universities and scientific societies from tacitly regarding the presidential science adviser as *their* representative in the White House; nor did they discourage the adviser from trying to attend to needs of science, in the cause of strengthening a national asset. The declarations of scientific fealty to politics were intended to counter the suspicion among White House staff that the presidential assistant for science and technology was different from other presidential assistants, that the science aide was bound by loyalties that were disconnected from conventional politics. Thus, shortly before the 1988 presidential election, a privately convened commission of scientists and political friends of science, volunteering science advice for the next administration, noted, "In the past, some members of the S&T [science and technology] community have erroneously expected the Assistant [to the President for Science and Technology] to be their spokesperson. There have also been occasions when the Science Adviser has been viewed within government as a special pleader for science. The performance and effectiveness of the Assistant must challenge and transcend that misperception."[25]

However, over the post-Nixon decades, despite their earnest manifestations of presidential fealty, the White House scientists were still regarded

23. Interview with author, May 14, 1998.
24. D. Allan Bromley, *The President's Scientists* (New Haven, Conn.: Yale University Press, 1994), p. 26.
25. *Science & Technology and the President* (Carnegie Commission on Science, Technology, and Government, 1988), p. 10.

as a breed apart by the political operatives at the core of the presidency. Domestic politics, economics, and national security were at home in the White House—presidential necessities, recognized by all. Not so science. Reflecting both amusement and pain, John Gibbons, who served for five years as President Clinton's assistant for science and technology, recalled to me his long-running struggles for staff positions in a White House that adopted lean staffing as a politically advantageous sign of frugality: "These people in the White House typically don't think of science and technology and analysis as being that important to politics. They just don't get it. Many of them just don't get it":

> It's been that way, I think, since before I went there. There's a running feeling within the White House that the science crowd is much bigger than they ought to be. A lot of bitching and moaning about we've got all these people, and the Domestic Policy Council or the Economic Policy Council doesn't have that kind of resources.[26]

THE SCIENCES' OWN SPECIAL MEANS

Dependent as it was on government money, science did not entrust its fortunes to political goodwill or the ability of the presidential science adviser of the moment to make its case in the budget councils. Rather, it developed its own special means for influencing the public and politics. Other professions raised campaign money for their political friends or smoothed the political waters by donating to both sides, using political action committees or other devices allowed by law. For example, from January 1, 1995, to June 30, 1996, the American Medical Association donated $1.6 million to parties and candidates. A similar amount was donated by the National Education Association. The American Institute of Certified Public Accountants provided $1 million, while the American Dental Association contributed $860,000.[27] Law firms gave nearly $40 million in campaign contributions between January 1997 and June 1998, according to the Center for Responsive Politics, which also recorded $26.7 million by organizations of retirees and $19.5 million by physicians and other health profes-

---

26. Interview with author, December 6, 1998.
27. "In Political Money Game, The Year of Big Loopholes," *New York Times*, December 26, 1996.

sionals.[28] For the 2000 congressional election campaigns, the U.S. Chamber of Commerce—a major business lobby in Washington—budgeted $8 million, to be spread among chosen candidates of both parties, thirty-five to forty of them in the House, ten to twelve in the Senate.[29]

Nowhere on the lists of money-giving political action committees are the scientific counterparts of these organizations and interest groups, such as the American Association for the Advancement of Science, the Association of American Medical Colleges, the American Chemical Society, the American Physical Society, or the Federation of American Societies for Experimental Biology. These organizations, collectively numbering hundreds of thousands of members, work diligently to promote government spending on science, but never by exercising their legal right to venture into elective politics. The political forays of scientists that began with the 1960 Kennedy campaign peaked in 1964 and then virtually disappeared. Savoring the fruits of bipartisanship, scientists discontinued all but token quadrennial forays into elective politics. Only minor activities, usually of a local nature, persisted. At the presidential-campaign level, the descendants of the activist efforts of the 1960s have limited themselves to letterhead efforts. In 1992, the sixty-four-member, big-name Council of Scientists and Engineers for Clinton-Gore proclaimed its existence about a month before election day, but otherwise did nothing public. Similarly late in the 1996 campaign, a group of twenty-four, cochaired by former astronaut Sally Ride, announced the formation of "Scientists and Engineers for Clinton-Gore." Five days before the election, the Clinton-Gore General Committee issued a press release stating that five hundred scientists and engineers, including twelve Nobel laureates, had endorsed the ticket. The closing lines of the press release summarize the special nature of science and elective politics: "The endorsements were made by the scientists and engineers in their individual capacities and are not endorsements of the organizations for which they work." In the 2000 presidential campaign, scientists collectively went through another episode of firing blanks. On this occasion, again a few days before the election, 57 Nobel laureates joined some 750 other scientists in announcing their support for the Democratic ticket. Attention was sought through an announcement to the press and a telephone press conference—

28. "America's Business Lobby: Who Speaks for Main Street?" *The Economist,* June 26, 1999.
29. "Special Interests: The Chamber's Business of Politics," *Washington Post,* January 27, 2000.

sparsely attended—with Nobelists Harold Varmus and Murray Gell-Mann. In the clamorous finale of the bitter campaign, the late-arriving savants went unnoticed. For political ineffectiveness, it would be difficult to surpass their performance. The intent, to sway public opinion, was undermined by the scientists' customary ambivalence toward political involvement.

Here and there, scientists dabbled in elective politics. But these were minor, sporadic efforts. Through its existing organizations, and with the creation of others, science pursued its political goals by adopting and polishing a variety of other means for managing its dependence on Washington.

CHAPTER 12

The Sciences' Way of Politicking

With the possible exception of veterans, farmers, and college students, there is no group that squeals more loudly over a reduction of federal subsidies than scientists. They are the quintessential special interest group, and in effect, they make the oil industry look like a piker. I'm sure that, like all the others, they feel they are doing God's work, but that's why federal spending is about to cross the one trillion mark.

> —Edwin L. Dale Jr., Assistant Director for Public Affairs,
> Office of Management and Budget, January 18, 1985

Of the 3,759 lobbying firms registered in Washington, D.C., more than 800 list "science" as an . . . activity, according to House of Representatives lobbyist registration records.

> —*The Scientist*, October 26, 1998

AN ENTERPRISE dependent on uninterrupted billions of dollars in government money cannot disregard politics, even if it stands aloof from participation in elective politics—that is, raising money and votes for candidates and parties. Before its trauma in the Nixon White House, but especially afterward, science diligently cultivated other means of advancing its political interests in Washington. Building on the themes sounded by Vannevar Bush in his 1945 plan for peacetime government support of research, the methods emphasized warnings of national danger and decline if generous support was not forthcoming. This approach led to the scare tactics of the "shortfall" alarms and the countless inflated assessments of Soviet scientific prowess—succeeded, after the USSR collapsed, by alarms of economic misfortunes if government science budgets did not grow. The science advocates, as shown earlier, would sometimes enrich their litany with recollections of bygone golden ages of government finance of research.

The campaign in behalf of science ranged from honors bestowed upon

politicians by scientific societies for their wisdom and foresight in supporting science, to inventories of the local economic impact of research money
from Washington. These were well-established tactics, utilized by the
countless interest groups that seek favor in Washington. However, in its
style of politicking, science differed from virtually all the other lobbies in
one important respect: it remained absent from the rolls of cash donors to
political parties and candidates. Like other citizens, scientists participated
in the political system, sometimes collectively but customarily with dis-
claimers of institutional involvement. Scientists employed nonelective tactics, refining and expanding their chosen methods into standard techniques for relations with politics, government, and the general public. A
strong base of government support for research was assured by the scientific
accomplishments of World War II, the technological content of Cold War
rivalry, and the health and economic expectations of the American people.
But wallflowers do not thrive in the competition for government funds.
Confident of its value to society, and relishing prosperity, along with the
rest of America, science was not content to acquiesce in minimal support.
It went after the money.

VARIETIES OF LOBBYING

The pursuit of federal money for research falls into two basic categories:
quests by individual universities for money to fund buildings and research
programs, and broadly based endeavors aimed at raising the total amount
of money available for a major sector of research—such as the medical sciences, a big project such as a particle accelerator, or for science in general.

We start with the pursuit of money by individual universities. In the
aggregate, universities and their lobbyists have developed this activity into
a major Washington industry. By one knowledgeable accounting, the funds
annually produced by this branch of lobbying rose from $16.5 million in
1980 to $327.8 million in 1996, for a grand total of $5.1 billion during those
years.[1] Since then, a couple of billion more have been added to the total.
Effective, but least visible for enriching money-seeking universities, are the
Washington lobbyists-for-hire who serve academe like any customer who
pays their fees. Rates of pay for their services vary. The minimum for a blue-
chip firm, which usually means a staff roster of well-connected, senior
alumni of Capitol Hill and the White House, is approximately $20,000 per

---

1. James D. Savage, *Funding Science in America: Congress, Universities, and the Politics of the
Academic Pork Barrel* (Cambridge University Press, 1999), p. 3.

month, plus expenses, with one year's payment required in advance. The leading firm for scientific and academic lobbying is Cassidy & Associates, which emerged from a partnership cofounded in 1975 by Gerald S. J. Cassidy, an attorney who previously served as general counsel of the Senate Committee on Nutrition and as executive director and general counsel of the Reform Commission of the Democratic National Committee—excellent preparation for connecting to Washington politics at many levels. In fees for its services, Cassidy's firm "earned a total of $2.5 million from some two dozen colleges and universities during the first half of 1997," including $260,000 from Tufts University and $338,000 from Boston University.[2] Tufts paid the Cassidy firm $3,162,056 for lobbying services between 1984 and 1993, a Tufts official testified to the House Science, Space and Technology Committee in September 1993. By 1998, the Cassidy firm was tops in lobbying receipts in Washington, with a grand total of $19.9 million in fees from its many clients in various sectors of the economy, including academe. Among them, again, was Boston University, with lobbying fees having risen to $760,000.[3] (In 1999, the Cassidy firm was acquired for a reported $70 million to $80 million by Shandwick, a public-relations company owned by the Interpublic Group, a New York–based international advertising company.) Hitting its lobbying stride in the early 1980s, the Cassidy firm repaid the fees of its university clients manyfold in money that it helped extract from the U.S. Congress for delivery to its clients by agencies of government. These acquisitions include $32 million from the U.S. Department of Agriculture for a nutrition research center at Tufts University and $7.5 million for a new library at Boston University, among other special deliveries from Washington for that institution. Other big hauls included millions for a chemistry center at Columbia University and a research laboratory at Catholic University, in the District of Columbia.

THE ACADEMIC PORK BARREL

The prized objective of the mercenary branch of the lobbying trade is an "earmark" in a congressional appropriations bill—words that translate into money for a specific institution or project. Derided in the press and by rule-abiding scientists as "pork barrel" appropriations, earmarks are often stealthily written into appropriations bills during hurried, sometimes wearying all-night deliberations at the end of a congressional session. The uni-

2. William Horne, "When Higher Ed Lobbies," *University Business*, July/August 1998.
3. Lobbying data from Center for Responsive Politics, Washington, D.C.

versity seeking to tap into the U.S. Treasury feels certain that it is pursuing a worthy goal, even if, as is usually the case in earmarking circumstances, it has failed to win approval from panels of researchers appointed by government research agencies to bring expertise and objectivity to the money-granting process. The quest for earmarked money can range from mere hundreds of thousands of dollars for a research program; millions for a laboratory building or a mega-machine of science; to scores of millions, over many years, for an entire research facility. With or without a hired lobbyist serving as orchestrator of the event, the ultimate perpetrator in an earmark operation is most likely a member of Congress who is strategically situated on the right committee to do good for a hungering institution back home. But if the vagaries of committee membership fail to provide such a benefactor, horse-trading with a well-situated congressional colleague can accomplish the deed. Earmarking, regardless of the purpose, is ingrained in the give-and-take of the legislative process. It helps keep Congress moving.

In October 1998, late with its work and eager to get off to the election campaign, the 105th Congress hurriedly combined all pending money legislation into a $500 billion-plus Omnibus Appropriations bill, covering nearly four thousand densely printed pages. In the light of day, the bill was found to be loaded with a plenitude of pork, possibly a record-breaking quantity, though counting is difficult in the dimly lit chambers of earmark politics. A review by Senator John McCain (R-Ariz.) cited several thousand appropriations that he described as "unauthorized" or outside "the normal competitive award process."[4] The grand total of earmarks was later tabulated at $528 million, en route to $797 million in 1999.[5] The wads of money for specific institutions included "$250,000 for Urban Research and Learning, Loyola College, Chicago," and for projects such as "$1 million for peanut quality research in Georgia." In the tradition of pork-barrel appropriations, McCain pointed out, the earmarks had not been debated or even made available for scrutiny prior to passage: "They were simply added, behind closed doors, to this massive, non-amendable omnibus bill." McCain's laments found no favor among his many earmarking colleagues, who are regarded by their electors as benefactors, not villains, when they deliver a library or laboratory to the hometown campus. McCain's anti-earmark

4. "McCain Objects to 'Pork Barrel' Items in Omnibus Appropriations Bill," press release from Senator John McCain, October 21, 1998.
5. "Pork-Barrel Spending on Academe Reaches a Record $797-Million: Surplus and an 11th-Hour Budget Spur 51 Percent Rise in Earmarks by Congress," *Chronicle of Higher Education,* July 23, 1999.

campaign was turned against him during his unsuccessful run for the Republican presidential nomination in 2000. Several breast-cancer research projects were among the earmarks he had identified and voted against as evasions of the scientific review system. On the basis of that vote, the George W. Bush campaign denounced McCain as opposed to breast-cancer research. Though absurd, the inflammatory charge caused McCain to devote precious campaign time to explaining the intricacies of peer review and congressional pork.

The research-related earmarks not only elude congressional examination, but, by definition, they also bypass professional peer review, the system sanctified by scientific tradition as the *sine qua non* for optimal allocation of research resources. The review process varies among federal research agencies and private foundations. But basically it is a blue-ribbon jury system in which panels of researchers evaluate and rank research proposals. Aimed at achieving objective assessment by disinterested experts, peer review is often assailed as intrinsically biased against novelty and innovation because, the critics contend, it relies on people who constitute the status quo of science. Paraphrasing Churchill on democracy, some of the strongest defenders of peer review limply respond that it is the worst possible system, except for all others. As might be expected, the "haves" of federal academic research funding strongly favor peer review and are generally opposed to earmarks. Lesser institutions, however, angrily complain that peer review inevitably assures that the rich get richer while others are excluded. Inequity is inherent to the system, they insist, and justifies alternative means of getting at the money—specifically, earmarking. Despite repeated denunciations as unclean, earmarked money is irresistible for many universities, including some that also compete successfully for peer-reviewed funds.[6] Though the trend is consistently upward, we should keep in mind that in any year, at least so far, the earmarks are a small portion of the many billions, depending on what's counted, appropriated for academic research via aboveboard routes.[7] In 2000, the official count for all academic research appropriations was over $15 billion, of which alleged earmarks constituted a small share. But the earmarks going to universities are nonetheless sub-

6. According to an analysis of the murky finances of earmarks, "The top ten state recipients of federal research funds also obtained more than a third of all earmarks. Earmarking helps the rich states get richer." James Savage, *The Distribution of Academic Earmarks in the Federal Government's Appropriations Bills, FY 1980–1989,* Working Paper 89-5, Institute of Governmental Studies, University of California, Berkeley.

7. Op. cit., *Chronicle of Higher Education,* July 23, 1999.

stantial in the scarcity economy of research funding. The earmark process is galling to institutions that feel penalized for complying with the rules, even if the rules favor their success.

The practice outrages the officials of the established system to the point of evoking extravagant recriminations—especially from program managers in federal agencies. When their budgets are hijacked to finance earmarks, decision-making authority over research projects passes to the political budget raiders on Capitol Hill. The right order of things is upset, with far-reaching undesirable consequences, they contend. In 1994, Martha Krebs, the director of energy research at the Department of Energy, told a congressional hearing that earmarks "may also inadvertently discourage young scientists from pursuing research careers because they believe it is not an honest or open process."[8] This may be so, but as with many provocative speculations and assertions in the politics of science, supportive evidence is lacking.

With earmarking publicly condemned in leading academic circles as unclean, pork victories are not among the triumphs that are customarily trumpeted by university chiefs as evidence of their fund-raising prowess. Most universities and academic leaders discreetly shun public recognition of their earmarking quests and triumphs. Not so the contentious John Silber during his 1971–96 reign as the expansionist president of Boston University, and afterward as its chancellor. Silber openly acknowledged his satisfied patronage of the Cassidy lobbying firm and went before Congress to denounce the federal system of research grants and contracts as rigged in behalf of a handful of elite universities. In 1987, when the issue of academic pork flared briefly in Congress, Silber indignantly testified that two years earlier, "the 20 top universities received more than half—a full 55.56 percent—of all federal R&D dollars allocated to universities." In his thunderous fashion, he declared: "This narrow channeling of a huge percentage of federal research support to only a tiny handful of schools is relentlessly promoted by the schools that benefit from it and by their organizational representatives, such as the Association of American Universities"—the Washington-based lobby for so-called research universities.[9] Contending that the "haves" are awarded huge sums of government research money

8. House Committee on Science, Space, and Technology, *Academic Earmarks—Part III: Hearings before the Committee on Science, Space, and Technology,* 103d Congress, 2d session (no. 174), p. 11.
9. House Committee on Science, Space, and Technology, *The University Research Facilities Revitalization Act: Hearings on HR 1905,* 100th Cong., 1st sess., June 25, 1987.

without peer review, Silber tweaked the anti-earmark camp with detailed listings of eternal federal support for research programs at elite universities and in government laboratories. "There are seven national laboratories that are funded by non-peer review at $2 billion a year at MIT, Caltech, Chicago, California, Columbia, Johns Hopkins and Harvard," Silber testified. "There are 19 federal funded research and development centers in this country with $6.3 billion that is done through earmarking, not through peer review."[10]

The laboratories and programs cited in Silber's denunciation included huge research enterprises managed for the federal government by universities, such as NASA's Jet Propulsion Laboratory, at the California Institute of Technology; the Argonne National Laboratory, under the wing of the University of Chicago ever since its founding as an offshoot of that university's important role in the World War II Manhattan Project; the U.S. Navy's Applied Physics Laboratory, ostensibly an academic department of Johns Hopkins University, which has run the facility for the Navy since World War II; and the Los Alamos National Laboratory, managed by the University of California since 1943. Though paying lip service to peer review, the government agencies sponsoring these large and complex research establishments prefer to avoid the disruptions that accompany changes of management. And the managers of the facilities are pleased to be spared the horrendous burden of documenting a proposal to continue what they have been doing for the U.S. government. In the absence of publicly visible blatant incompetence, the big management contracts are routinely renewed without competition.[11]

The Exempt Academy of Sciences

A strong scent of hypocrisy is sometimes detectable when prestigious institutions confront the prickly issue of unrestricted competition for choice federal projects versus politically ordained delivery of the money.

---

10. Op. cit., *Academic Earmarks—Part III*, p. 347.

11. A rare termination of a management contract for a major federal research facility occurred in 1998, when the Department of Energy abruptly ousted Associated Universities, Inc. (a consortium of twenty-four universities) as the contractor for the Brookhaven National Laboratory in Long Island, N.Y. The precipitating circumstance was a radioactive leak in a research reactor that, though harmless, created alarm in the surrounding community. Senator Alphonse D'Amato (R-N.Y.), facing an election, which he lost, berated the Department of Energy and the laboratory as a menace to Long Island's health, whereupon DOE, which had known of the leak for several years, fired the contractor and opened a competition for new management.

No organization can match the pious declarations in behalf of competition issued by the venerable National Academy of Sciences, which exists primarily on government grants and contracts; in its 1998 fiscal year, the academy collected revenues totaling $221.2 million, of which $153.4 million was provided by federal agencies.[12] A 1995 report by the academy's Committee on Criteria for Federal Support of Research and Development extols peer-reviewed competition for federal research money: "Because competition for funding is vital to maintain the high quality of FS&T [federal science and technology] programs, competitive merit review, especially that involving external reviewers, should be the preferred way to make awards."[13] Nonetheless, on January 19, 1993, the day before George Bush's term as president ended, he signed, at the academy's request, an executive order essentially exempting the academy from the rigors of the competition that the academy deems "vital to maintain the high quality of FS&T programs." The midnight presidential order authorized noncompetitive contract awards upon determination that "the Academy, because of its unique qualifications, is the only source that can provide the measure of expertise, independence, objectivity, and audience acceptance necessary to meet the department or agency's program requirements. . . . "[14] President Bush's 1993 eve-of-departure order reaffirmed, and adopted the language of, a 1984 memorandum from the Office of Management and Budget that initially shielded the academy from competition. In the hierarchy of government decrees, however, an executive order carries more swat than a mere memo from OMB.

To crack the system, Silber unabashedly declared, his university bought assistance in Washington—that is, it hired Cassidy to obtain earmarked money. Cassidy's staff was sprinkled with former senior aides to congressional leaders, other insiders seasoned in the ways of Washington, and even a few ex–university presidents. James D. Savage, an academic chronicler of the earmarking phenomenon, lists among Cassidy lobbyists Frank Rose and Elvis J. Stahr Jr., former presidents of the University of Alabama and the University of Indiana, respectively; General Paul X. Kelley, former Marine Corps commandant; Jody Powell, White House press secretary in the Carter administration; and Sheila Tate, a press aide for President Bush.

The links between those serving in the government and alumni of gov-

---

12. Budget data are from IRS Form 990, which nonprofit organizations are required to make available to the public upon request.

13. *Allocating Federal Funds for Science and Technology* (Washington, D.C.: National Academy Press, 1995), p. 25.

14. Executive Order 12832, January 19, 1993.

ernment service are close, cooperative, and usually nonpartisan. Incumbent representatives can look forward to the high income of the lobbying trade after they leave Capitol Hill. After fourteen terms in Congress, Chairman Don Fuqua (D-Fla.) of the House Science and Space Committee voluntarily stepped down in 1986 to become president and general manager of the Aerospace Industries Association, at a salary of $202,021—about two and a half times his congressional pay. In 1997, upon completion of ten terms in the House, Representative Robert Walker (R-Pa.) retired from Congress and his chair of the House Science Committee. Walker, an arch Republican and close friend and political compatriot of Speaker Newt Gingrich, moved directly from Capitol Hill to the presidency of the Wexler Group, a lobbying firm headed by Anne Wexler, long prominent in Democratic Party circles. Congressional opponents of earmarking have urged their colleagues to refrain from the practice. But as was pointed out in 1985 by Representative Fuqua, "These Senators and Congressmen don't just think these things up. They come from the universities."[15] In the congressional culture, satisfying such requests is known as constituent service. It's the great tool of incumbency and reelection.

LOBBYING ON THEIR OWN

While many institutions rely upon for-hire lobbyists to navigate their way to money in Washington, others employ the do-it-yourself method, with the assistance of supportive legislators, who thereby cultivate a favorable image among grateful constituents. In 1994, at one of the very occasional congressional inquiries into academic and scientific pork, the Olympian record of the Oregon Health Sciences University was spread on the public record: "well over $100 million," from fiscal years 1983 to 1995, according to a steadfast opponent of earmarking, the late Representative George E. Brown Jr. (D-California), chair of the House Science, Space, and Technology Committee. Stating that his fortunate institution did not employ a lobbyist, Joseph D. Bloom, dean of the Oregon medical school, explained, "We discussed our needs with all Members of Congress in our delegation." There was no need for him to add that the discussants included Senator Mark O. Hatfield (D-Oregon), chair of the Committee on Appropriations. Dean Bloom was unapologetic. The university was the only health

---

15. Interview with author, January 22, 1985; in "Q&A With Rep. Don Fuqua: Science Programs Are 'Going to Take Their Lumps,'" *SGR*, February 1, 1985.

sciences center in Oregon, he said; it needed the money, found no other way to get it, and therefore took the political route.[16]

In addition to the earmarking mercenaries and their congressional enablers, the nation's capital is also the home base of well-staffed scientific and professional societies that, along with individual university representatives, diligently hover over research-related issues. Circumscribed by restrictions on lobbying by tax-exempt organizations, they modestly describe their role as monitoring of Washington affairs for the benefit of their home institutions. They usually acknowledge a bit of allowable lobbying, within the legal limits for nonprofit institutions, though what's allowable is far from clear in the tortuous legislation governing lobbying.[17]

But their activities go beyond passive observation and reporting. On the overt level, the Washington-based representatives of scientific interests provide a ready pool of witnesses, researchers, and ghost writers for Congress's annual procession of hearings on appropriations and policies for science and higher education. More muscular activities in support of science also occupy these outposts of science in the nation's capital. In 1996, the Federation of American Societies for Experimental Biology (FASEB), which regards itself as the Washington voice of researchers in the life sciences, budgeted $1.5 million for a three-year educational campaign in behalf of increased appropriations for the National Institutes of Health, the grant lifeline for nearly half of FASEB's membership, which then numbered about 45,000.[18] While continuing to cultivate the old-timers on Capitol Hill, FASEB said it would also focus on newly elected members of Congress, "to gain their support during the appropriations process." For all lobbies, not just science, educating the changing cast of legislators is a never-ending process. To provide professional savvy for this effort, FASEB employed a

16. *Academic Earmarks—Part III*, op. cit., pp. 121, 123.

17. The opacity of the Lobbying Disclosure Act is evident in a letter from an official of the University of Tulsa contesting a press report that the university spent $80,000 on lobbying activities, but reported only $30,855 in lobbying expenditures to the Internal Revenue Service. After summarizing the provisions of the lobbying and disclosure law, he concluded: "We agree that this structure gives a strange picture to anyone attempting to make sense of the act's complex legal reporting requirements." Roy A. Ruffner, vice president for business and finance, University of Tulsa, letter to the *Chronicle of Higher Education*, December 11, 1998.

18. FASEB, headquartered a couple of miles up the road from the Bethesda, Md., campus of NIH, is an umbrella organization of scientific associations that had grown by 1999 to fourteen member societies and five associate societies, with unduplicated membership totaling over 66,000. FASEB reports that of the $9.8 billion in outside grants awarded by NIH in 1998, FASEB members received $5.7 billion. Howard Garrison et al., *A Profile of the Members of FASEB Societies: NIH Awards, Degrees, and Institutional Affiliations* (Federation of American Societies for Experimental Biology, 1999).

major Washington lobbying firm, Van Scoyoc Associates, Inc. The FASEB account there was the prime responsibility of Vice President Michael A. Stephens, who, until the Republican takeover of the House in 1995, was a senior Democratic staff member on the House appropriations subcommittee that provides money for the National Institutes of Health. From his twenty-one years of service on the subcommittee, Stephens was a widely acknowledged master of the appropriations process and the intricacies of NIH money and politics.

HONOR THY BENEFACTORS

Over the years, FASEB has bestowed its Public Service Award on key congressional supporters of NIH, including House Speaker "Tip" O'Neill, Senators Nancy Kassebaum, Lowell Weicker, Mark Hatfield, Arlen Specter, and Tom Harkin, and Representatives Nancy Pelosi, William Natcher, and John Porter. The political gap between the health sciences and all the other sciences is evident in FASEB's choice of legislators for its honors. Not among them was Representative George Brown, "Mr. Science" to NSF constituents. Brown's congressional career was largely spent on the House Science Committee, which does not encompass NIH and medical research in its jurisdiction. Unconnected to biomedical politics, Brown publicly questioned NIH's high priority in federal research spending and its emphasis on a high-technology curative strategy, to the neglect of preventive measures based on life-style changes. The managers of biomedical research politics in Washington responded by ignoring Mr. Science.

Congress's great figures of biomedical budget growth are commemorated on the NIH campus in Bethesda, Maryland, with buildings named after them. The honorees are chosen mainly from the ranks of appropriations committee chairs who provided great servings of money for NIH. On Capitol Hill, as in the military, rank hath its privileges, and the appropriations chairs are renowned for exercising theirs. The tabulations of pork scholar James Savage show that the appropriations chairs accounted for 61 percent of the $3.8 billion in academic earmarks received by seventy-three universities and colleges between 1980 and 1996.[19]

NIH's named buildings recognize the good works of Senators Warren Magnuson, Lister Hill, Lowell Weicker, Lawton Chiles, and Mark Hatfield, and Representatives John Fogarty, William Natcher, Silvio Conte, and

19. Savage, *Funding Science in America*, p. 139.

Claude D. Pepper (who was also a strong NIH backer during prior service in the Senate). In 1998, budget growth fueled a new construction surge on the NIH campus, thus providing new buildings for honoring a later crop of congressional supporters, including the Louis Stokes Laboratories for the Cleveland, Ohio, congressman who had announced plans to retire at the end of the session; and the Dale and Betty Bumpers Vaccine Research Facility in tribute to the tireless advocacy of children's health issues by Senator Dale Bumpers (also on the way to retirement) and his wife. The designations are usually written into NIH appropriations bills, but it may be assumed that NIH management is asked for a nod on these matters—though Congress is at liberty to honor its own as it chooses.[20]

In contrast to the unremembered thousands who have also held congressional seats, the memory of supporters of medical research is enshrined on the buildings, signposts, and stationery of NIH. The process does not encourage legislators to probe into the difficult but important questions of NIH's research priorities or its record of success in choosing among competing proposals for improving the health of the American people. Hope and gullible adulation, rather than informed inquiry, permeate Congress's dealings with NIH.

With annual dues of $55,000 per institution, the Washington-based Association of American Universities (AAU) watches over the governmental concerns of what are referred to as research universities—universities that rank high or are gaining substantially in receipt of federal research funds. The AAU now numbers fifty-nine American universities, plus Canada's McGill University and the University of Toronto, at 10 percent of the American fee. The AAU embodies an elite that includes Harvard, MIT, Stanford, the University of Chicago, and the University of California, Berkeley, but now and then it admits an up-and-coming institution not commonly regarded as high-ranking in the major leagues of academic research. Many universities seek to join, drawn by the cachet of AAU membership signifying major-league status in academic research; but, guarding its elite image, the AAU is prudently stingy with new memberships, letting years go by before admitting another school. Reflecting the widening recognition of research as an activity both virtuous and economically important, admission to the AAU can bring rejoicing beyond the confines of academe. In 1989, when the State University of New York at Buffalo gained admission,

---

20. The biomedical enterprise is merely one among numerous federal dependencies that are plastered with the names of supportive politicians, ranging from presidentially named aircraft carriers to federal office buildings.

raising the AAU's membership to fifty-seven, the *New York Times* editorially cheered, noting that Buffalo was the first public institution in New York or New England admitted to the AAU. "It's an honor worth special notice," the *Times* stated.[21] The AAU depends upon the collective reputation of its member institutions, rather than mass numbers, for performing its work in Washington. For this purpose, it employs a staff of eighteen or so that keeps a close watch on federal legislation, regulations, and budgets that affect academe and, especially, research. The pay for heading this pint-size operation exceeds anything on the U.S. government scale (short of the presidency, which was raised from $200,000 to $400,000 per year in 2001). The 1996 remuneration of the AAU president consisted of a salary of $276,846, benefits and deferred compensation of $31,984, an expense account and other allowances of $9,063, and an automobile.[22] For many years, the AAU president lived gratis in an AAU-owned town house on a fashionable stretch of Washington's Massachusetts Avenue known as Embassy Row. The building, according to the AAU, was donated to the association by Johns Hopkins University, which had received it as a bequest. In explanation of the presidential housing assistance, the AAU annually intimated on its federal tax return that its president was allowed no choice in this matter, stating that he resides there "as a condition of his employment," noting that "various activities directly related to the interest of the association are engaged in at the residence." However, following chilly glares from the Internal Revenue Service, the residence was sold in 1997, for $815,000. The proceeds went into the AAU endowment, and the AAU president was left to forage in the Washington housing market.

WASHINGTON WAGES

The affluent presence in Washington of science, interwoven with higher education, is also evident in the compensation of chief executives of other organizations that work for science in the capital city. Bruce Alberts, the president of the National Academy of Sciences, received a salary of $339,247 plus $39,158 in benefits in 1998. Unopposed, Alberts was reelected to a second six-year term in 1998. His predecessor, Frank Press, held the job for twelve years. An academy-owned residence in the Watergate Apartment complex once went with that position, at no cost to the presidential occupant. But the president is now required to pay half of the con-

21. "A Rockefeller Legacy in Buffalo," *New York Times*, February 25, 1989.
22. Data from IRS Form 990.

dominium fee—which cost him $16,920 in 1998. Jordan Cohen, the head of the Association of American Medical Colleges, which represents the nation's 125 allopathic, or mainstream, medical schools, was paid $327,667, plus $109,919 in benefits in 1996. Cohen was in his sixth year as head of the association in the year 2000; his predecessor held the job for eight years. In 1998, Richard Nicholson, the Executive Officer of the American Association for the Advancement of Science, received a salary of $331,002 and benefits of $27,500—about quadruple the remuneration he received in 1988, when he left the National Science Foundation for the AAAS job. In 1982, John Crum was appointed Executive Director of the American Chemical Society (ACS) and was still serving in that position in 2001. In 1996, Crum received a salary of $574,073, plus benefits of $34,900; in 1997, Crum received $600,000 in pay and $36,510 in benefits.

Over the past few years, the ACS, like many other professional societies, has expanded its support for increased federal research budgets. In August 1998, as appropriations bills were moving toward completion on Capitol Hill, the ACS held its Fourth Annual ACS Contact Congress Week. To support the Federal Research Investment Act, a bill favored by the ACS, "Each local section [of ACS members] received a packet of background information about the bill, sample letters and addresses of their senators."[23] These are standard lobbying tools, long employed by labor unions, business groups, and industry, but relatively new among research lobbies. Having joined the herd, the ACS then proceeded to move ahead with the fast-changing technology of lobbying. In 1999, as appropriations bills for science encountered budget-cutting snags on Capitol Hill, the ACS deployed for the first time a new weapon for saturation lobbying: sophisticated e-mail technology. As described in the ACS journal *Chemical & Engineering News:*

> The e-mail message that went out to about 60,000 ACS members last week asks them to go to a web site . . . where they can identify their legislators simply by entering their zip code. From there, the web site provides a predrafted message and will send either a personalized e-mail or a letter from chemist constituents to their representatives in Congress.[24]

In its "News of the Week" section in the same issue, the chemistry journal stated, "During the next several weeks, Congress will direct spending to-

---

23. *The Capitol Connection,* August 1998, monthly newsletter of the ACS Office of Legislative and Government Affairs.

24. "R&D Funding Crisis Prompts First ACS Global E-mail Alert," *Chemical & Engineering News,* September 20, 1999.

ward areas that its constituents indicate are most important. And it isn't necessarily looking good for science." Added an ACS legislative official: "As scientists, we cannot believe that the inherent value of our research is recognized by Congress anymore. We have to clearly articulate the link between research and the quality of life we now enjoy."[25]

TEAMED UP FOR LOBBYING

In harmony with the federal budget cycle, many Washington-based science organizations coalesce annually for mass lobbying efforts in behalf of federal money for research. Preeminent among these seasonal alliances is the Ad Hoc Group for Medical Research Funding, which has perennially risen each budget season since 1982. The Ad Hoc Group is based at the Association of American Medical Colleges, and comprises, along with the AAMC's 125 medical schools, some 250 professional societies, universities, and other organizations whose members are financially linked in some fashion to the National Institutes of Health. The Ad Hoc Group's chief product is a proposed budget for NIH, detailing the increases deemed necessary in the coming fiscal year. Though unofficial, the Ad Hoc budget establishes a target for legislators who support health research. NIH is an agency of the executive branch of government. But, in terms of practical politics, it was long ago captured by Congress and made a special charge of the legislative branch, and that is where its policies and budgets are determined, while the White House looks on helplessly. Presidential science advisers all tell the same story. "There's not much you can do about NIH," D. Allan Bromley, White House science adviser in the Bush administration, candidly acknowledged to me. "It really reflects the fact that every member of Congress knows that sooner or later they're going to be on a stainless steel gurney with an M.D. looking at them, and their view is it doesn't pay to make M.D.'s real unhappy." Bromley added, "You simply cannot control that, because that's a very personal relationship that Congress has with NIH."[26] Hugh Loweth, who served in the Office of Management and Budget, and its predecessor, confirmed to me—with a mixture of frustration and professional admiration—that biomedical politics eluded budget control. Not even the powerful OMB could wrest it away from Congress, Loweth acknowledged.[27] It is an open secret in Washington that the NIH bureaucracy

---

25. Ibid.
26. Interview with author, October 7, 1998.
27. Interview with author, March 15, 1999.

works closely with the Ad Hoc Group in formulating the NIH budget, irrespective of preferences at the White House. In defensive response to its exclusion from biomedical-research spending, the White House annually proposes a small budget increase for NIH, in realistic expectation of a big budget increase on Capitol Hill. In 1998, for example, the White House asked for an 8 percent increase—quite generous, given tight curbs on federal spending; Congress came through just a few millions short of the 15 percent increase proposed by the Ad Hoc Group for Medical Research Funding; in 1999, the White House proposed a 2 percent increase for NIH; Congress voted an increase of nearly 15 percent.

The Ad Hoc Group does not silently suffer political inattention to its budget preferences. In March 1999, the chairman of the Ad Hoc Group, Richard Knapp, who is a vice president of the Association of American Medical Colleges, chastised President Clinton in a letter released to the press. The members of his organization, nationally numbering more than three hundred institutions, Knapp pointed out, "are profoundly disappointed that medical research is not listed on the Democratic Agenda for 1999." Knapp reminded Clinton that he had endorsed medical research in his recent State of the Union Address. "Yet, less than two months later," he chided the president, "it appears that medical research has been abandoned and the National Institutes of Health does not even merit a mention among the Democratic priorities."[28] The admonitory letter, with its hyperbolic accusation of abandonment, was a piece of the annual charade of biomedical politics. The Washington-based employees of the lobbies posture and grandstand as the White House "lowballs" the budget, and Congress, almost inevitably, delivers a respectable, sometimes whopping, increase.

Like teammates exuberantly exchanging congratulations after a great game, the lobbies backslap each other for budget work well done. In 1999, the Council of Scientific Society Presidents presented its CSSP Leadership Award to the president of the medical-research lobby Research!America, Mary Woolley, "for demonstrating outstanding leadership in support of fundamental research." In that same year, Research!America honored the Ad Hoc Group for Medical Research with its Advocacy Award for medical research. In acknowledging the award, president Jordan Cohen of the Association of American Medical Colleges—the core organization of the Ad

28. Richard M. Knapp, chair, The Ad Hoc Group for Medical Research Funding, letter to President Clinton, March 11, 1999.

Hoc Group—said, "The AAMC and the Ad Hoc Group have enjoyed many successful collaborations with Research!America on the advocacy front."[29]

For some universities, membership in these Washington organizations, whether broadly based or narrowly focused, is insufficient for representing their interests. In addition to their various association memberships, scores of universities maintain their own Washington offices—mini-embassies of academe. Those so represented generally rank high in receipt of federal funds for research, training, and related facilities, as shown in NSF tabulations of the government money awarded for these purposes in fiscal 1997: the University of Washington, $321 million; the Massachusetts Institute of Technology, $311 million; the University of Michigan, $296 million; Harvard University, $223 million; and the nine campuses of the University of California, over $1 billion.[30] In 1999, the upwardly striving University of Florida announced the appointment of its first Washington-based lobbyist, a veteran of eighteen years' service with the American Academy of Pediatrics and the American Dental Association. A press report stated, "University officials estimate that the new Washington office will cost up to $350,000 annually."[31]

BATTLEFIELD COMMUNIQUES

In dispatches to their superiors back home, it is common for the lobbyists to describe the perils that science faces in Washington and to report their accomplishments in overcoming them. In the lobbying trade, the term for successful performance is a droll borrowing from the witch doctor's craft: "rainmaking." Who accomplishes what in this business is difficult to determine, since many ingredients, from a variety of sources, go into Washington policymaking, regulations, budget decisions, and acts of Congress signed into law by the president. From the fog of battle come many reports of heroism. When James Rowe, Harvard's vice president for government, community, and public affairs, retired in 1998, the *Harvard Gazette* reported: "As a lobbyist for Harvard and higher education in general, Rowe was instrumental in counteracting efforts to reduce federal funding for research and student aid brought on by the change in party control of Congress. Funding levels are now up across the University . . . and Harvard is in

29. Association of American Medical Colleges, press release, March 14, 2000.
30. *Indicators 2000*, p. A-315.
31. "Lobbyist Watch," *Chronicle of Higher Education*, May 14, 1999.

the forefront of a variety of successful legislative coalitions." From another source comes a variation, which states that in tandem with his Washington counterpart from MIT, Harvard's Rowe played a central role in establishing the Science Coalition, a grand alliance of 370 institutions "created by eighteen major research universities, mostly private ones, with their senior government relations and public affairs officers taking the lead."[32]

The difficulty of maintaining academic purity while drawing government largess is suggested in correspondence that was not intended for public view.[33] In 1983, in its customary opposition to pork-barrel depredations on federal R&D budgets, the exclusive Association of American Universities urged elected officials, university administrators, and scientists "to refrain from actions that would make scientific decisions a test of political influence rather than a judgment on the quality of the work to be done." The statement, reflecting the interests of the "haves" of academic research, was prompted by a pork-spending blitz on Capitol Hill. The earmarked bills were regarded by most AAU members as a diversion of money that rightly belonged to the elite of academic research—that is, themselves, though, paradoxically, as noted before, some elite institutions were on the earmark trail, too. These included Columbia University, a member of the AAU, for which the Cassidy lobbying firm had just obtained millions for a chemistry building. MIT President Paul E. Gray endorsed the AAU's anti-earmark declaration in a letter to an inquiring alumnus who sought assurance that MIT was making good use of its congressional connections. President Gray responded with a trenchant analysis of the difficult politics of pork:

> we must proceed with caution and considerable restraint in moving
> through purely political channels to develop support for scientific pro-
> grams at individual universities. If this becomes the established mode of
> operation, it will be a bloody free-for-all and the devil will take the hind-
> most. The competition will not be limited to the [then] fifty premier re-
> search institutions which belong to the AAU, and it is, perhaps, those in-
> stitutions which have the most to lose if funding of science comes to
> operate in a way analogous to the funding of river and harbor improve-
> ments.[34]

32. Constance Ewing Cook, *Lobbying for Higher Education: How Colleges and Universities In-fluence Federal Policy*, Vanderbilt University Press, 1998, p. 149.
33. "Seeking Goodies on Capitol Hill—MIT Style," *SGR*, September 1, 1986.
34. Ibid.

MIT would indeed have a great deal to lose from a pork-barrel romp of the have-nots. According to data compiled by NSF, in 1983, MIT ranked second (behind Johns Hopkins) in expenditure of federal funds for research in universities. Of the $200,349,000 that MIT spent for research in that year, federal agencies provided $162,801,000. Having described the practicality of virtue, President Gray then turned to the politics of MIT's extensive financial dependence on Washington, noting the high-ranking positions of three members of Congress from Massachusetts—two Democrats and a Republican, all faithful supporters of MIT: House Speaker "Tip" O'Neill and Representative Edward P. Boland, chair of the Appropriations Subcommittee for NSF and NASA, and Representative Silvio O. Conte, Ranking Republican on the Appropriations Committee. "Each of these three individuals has been unfailingly helpful to us in matters related both to MIT in the narrow sense and to the research universities in the broader interests of education and research," Gray wrote, noting that "the Speaker hosted a Congressional breakfast for the Massachusetts [congressional] delegation to meet Dave Saxon [president of the MIT Corporation], and we had an excellent opportunity there to discuss MIT's interests with eight members of the delegation, including the three mentioned above." Gray did not elaborate on the "narrow sense," nor did he mention specific projects for which political assistance might have been sought, and none has come to light. Thus, the letter, though suggestive, is not incompatible with MIT's public endorsement of peer review and stated opposition to earmarks and political pork. Cynics would say that, like royalty, MIT instinctively expects deference and radiates an intimidating superiority that, if only subtly, subverts objective peer review. MIT and its elite colleagues respond that their success in peer-reviewed competition for federal research money simply reflects their superior quality.[35]

Greed, however, easily overrides piety. Between 1980 and 1996, fifty-one AAU member universities collected $1.47 billion in earmarked funds— over 28 percent of all earmarked money for academe, according to James

---

35. In 1990, in a surprising peer-reviewed competition, MIT lost an important, government-financed facility that it had managed for many years, the Magnet Research Center. The winner was Florida State University, which was initially considered to have a poor chance of replacing MIT when the operating contract, with the National Science Foundation, came up for renewal. NSF Director Erich Bloch upheld the award to Florida, citing its enthusiasm and ambitious plans for running the facility. Explaining his decision to me, Bloch said the facility had become a "third-rate lab" under MIT's management, and that MIT's claims of valuable experience in running the lab did not impress him. Interview with author, June 8, 1998.

Savage's tabulations. As he notes in his book on academic pork, "Some of these funds were obtained by the truly elite schools, which, no matter how small the amount involved, compromised the principled nature of the AAU's fight against earmarking."[36] The 1980–96 recipients and amounts cited by Savage included the University of Pittsburgh, $151 million; Iowa State University, $142 million; University of Florida, $87 million; University of Rochester, $73 million; University of Maryland, College Park, $67 million; and University of Nebraska, $67 million. Savage lists the figures as "apparent academic earmarks," since some institutions reject the pejorative designation, insisting they did nothing wrong. By 1987, the AAU faction opposed to earmarks recognized a lost cause and quieted its opposition; in 1993, the AAU dropped the issue as hopelessly divisive.

The political promotion of science, via science's apolitical tactics, sprawls across the public arena. For over two decades, the American Association for the Advancement of Science, numbering some 140,000 members, has annually orchestrated the preparation of a detailed analysis of the president's budget for research activities in the coming fiscal year; joining in the exercise are twenty other scientific and technical organizations. The findings and related commentary are presented at a gathering that in recent times has attracted about 500 attendees, mainly from universities and other federal dependencies throughout the country, to an annual two- or three-day meeting in Washington. Speakers usually include the president's assistant for science and technology; senior officials of NSF, NIH, and other federal research agencies; and congressional members notably favorable to science. In the early days of these annual gatherings, the programs were devoted to reporting the status and trends of federal support for research. But in later years, and especially since deficit-reduction took hold in domestic politics, attendees have been exhorted to beat the drums, in Washington and back home, for higher science budgets. Washington gatherings of this type are increasingly frequent and well attended by the vice presidents for research, government affairs officers, or similarly titled officials from universities and other research institutions. Also in the audience are the science attachés and counselors from embassies in Washington, collecting information about American science policy and budgets to relay to their home ministries. Among nations deeply engaged in science, or aspiring to be, international comparisons—particularly with the budget-bountiful Americans—are useful weapons in their own science politics. Meetings of this type are also popular among scientific societies devoted to a single disci-

36. Savage, *Funding Science in America*, p. 69.

pline. In April 1997, the AAAS and the Princeton University Materials Institute discovered themselves unwittingly and simultaneously checked into the same downtown Washington hotel, with several of the same government officials on their respective programs to discuss policy and finance. The two-day Princeton meeting, with an attendance fee of $190 per head, drew about 200; the AAAS meeting, three days at $234 per head, drew 525. In a makeshift act of cooperation, the AAAS and the Princeton organizers combined several of their sessions. In attendance fees, travel, lodging, meals, and other costs, the two meetings probably cost the American scientific enterprise a minimum of $1 million, plus the incalculable loss of services to the attendees' institutions during their time away from their home offices and duties.

IN SERVICE TO CONSTITUENTS

Even without the lobbyists' prods, politicians, local and national, cater to the interests of constituents who value a flourishing scientific enterprise. For the congressional delegation from New Mexico, the overriding task in Washington is the preservation of the two great federal laboratories—the Los Alamos National Laboratory and the Sandia National Laboratories, both financed by the Department of Energy—that bring over $2 billion a year into their otherwise impoverished state. At a signal, the proponents and protectors of science spending can inspire the dispatch of countless e-mails and faxes to the White House or any congressional office. And they have, as demonstrated by the effective counterattack that researchers and their political friends mounted against the budget-cutting goals of the 1995 "Republican Revolution" (to be examined later in detail). The barrages are directed not only at Congress. The White House, teeming with staff and schemes, is not of one mind on financial priorities for science. Accordingly, the friends of science on the presidential staff also stimulate mass appeals from the ranks of science for use in their internal struggles for generous budgets for research. Thus, having repeatedly urged scientists to badger politics for more money for science, John Gibbons, President Clinton's assistant for science and technology, appreciatively noted in 1998 that "a blizzard of letters from scientists and students from all parts of the country enveloped the White House urging increased government support for science."[37] The appeals, he said, contributed to generous treatment for research in an otherwise sparse budget season.

37. *APS News,* March 1998.

In 1995, as budget-cutting war whoops emanated from the new Republican majorities in Congress, the AAAS hurriedly called a meeting of scientific societies to discuss the crisis. Among the speakers was William G. Wells Jr., a George Washington University professor who also served part-time in the Clinton administration's Office of Science and Technology Policy. For the anxious audience, Wells described a possible range of political action, and cited—descriptively rather than approvingly—the example of the anti-abortion Christian Coalition: "With only 1.6 million members but a budget of $25 million (an average of $15 per member) and the leadership of an astute Executive Director, Ralph Reed, the Coalition has become one of the most potent political forces in the nation—with easy access to political powers at the national and state levels. By contrast, and for the most part, the S&T [science and technology] worlds are not even on politicians' radar screens." No mention was made of the political adventure Science & Engineers for Johnson-Humphrey that had occurred thirty-one years earlier. Given the ahistorical psyche of the scientific enterprise, it is doubtful that the younger members of the audience had any awareness of it. The audience of scientists showed no interest in emulating the tactics of the Christian Coalition, or in exploring any other type of ballot-box activism. Deliberately shunning elective politics, it pursued other methods. We will now go on to examine one of them: missionary work among the masses to convey the importance of science and to warn of its perilous neglect.

CHAPTER **13**

The Public Understanding
of Science

There's always wan encouragin' thing about th' sad scientific facts
that come out ivry week in th' pa-apers. They're usually not thrue.
— Finley Peter Dunne ("On the Descent of Man,"
Mr. Dooley on Making a Will)

Rampant scientific illiteracy in the general public is, in my opinion,
one major cause of the current lack of opportunities for scientists.
. . . A public that is ignorant of science, and of how science is done,
is not going to support scientific research enthusiastically.
— Alan Hale, director, Southwest Institute for Space Research,
"Shattered Hopes and Dreams: The Dim Prospect for Careers in
Science," *Chronicle of Higher Education* (December 5, 1997)

THE MONEY-SEEKING methods of science ex-
amined thus far focus on the Congress and the White House. But for its
financial progress, science also assigns a high priority to another target: the
public. Evangelical work with the masses is a thriving enterprise aimed at
elevating what the trade refers to as "the public understanding of science."
If public enlightenment were the sole motive for these activities, we could
pass them by with an approving salute as worthy, unselfish public service—
which they are, in part; the endeavors in PUS, as it unfortunately abbrevi-
ates, would be of no relevance to our exploration of the politics of science.
The goal of enlightenment, however, has a political element to it—namely,
the conviction that the public understanding of science is essential for public support of science. The ensuing efforts warrant our attention because of
the ample government resources they command and because PUS manifests
the cargo-cult mentality in science: Like the post–World War II Pacific is-
landers who faithfully tended abandoned airstrips and piers in hopes of
shipments of goods again coming over the horizon, scientists anguish over,
and promote, the public understanding of science as indispensable to pub-

lic financing of their work. Like Vannevar Bush worship, the assumed connection between public understanding of science and public support of science does not stand up to examination, as congenial as the connection might be to democratic values. Nonetheless, the delusional association pervades the politics of science and generates voodoo assertions, questionable behavior, and career opportunities. PUS is a sacred ancillary endeavor of the scientific enterprise, rarely ever subjected to external criticism, though internally rent by sectarian quarrels over technique and resources.

Over many decades, a consistent finding of the PUS movement is that public understanding of science does not improve. A leading researcher in this field reported in 1991: "The 1990 estimate of the level of scientific literacy in the United States shows little improvement over the result of previous studies in 1979, 1985, and 1988."[1] Extending the study of PUS to fourteen nations, the same researcher reported in 1999 that "not more than one in 10 adults in the 14 countries were well-informed [about science], or scientifically literate."[2] In 2000, reporting on its biennial survey of the public understanding of science, the National Science Board concluded that "Science literacy in the United States (and in other countries) is fairly low," adding that "most Americans have little comprehension of the nature of scientific inquiry."[3]

Among those who speak for science, many dangers are attributed to deficiencies in the public's understanding of science. Science, democracy, and prosperity are said to be at risk, though, mysteriously, all have spread robustly despite the dearth of public understanding. But presented in these menacing terms, the threat has spawned an enterprise, distinct from conventional schooling. Careers are spent promoting the public understanding of science through the press, television, films, and museums. As part of this effort, the major scientific societies annually honor journalists with medals and cash awards for delivering good news about science to the general public. In reaction to the self-serving selectivity of these awards, the National Association of Science Writers (NASW) established its own awards,

> to provide recognition—without subsidy from any professional or commercial interest—for investigative or interpretive reporting about the sci-

1. Jon D. Miller, *The Public Understanding of Science & Technology in the United States 1990: A Report to the National Science Foundation,* p. 17.
2. Jon D. Miller, *Public Understanding of Science and Technology in OECD Countries: A Comparative Analysis,* paper to OECD Symposium on Public Understanding of Science, Tokyo, November 5, 1996, p. 18.
3. *Indicators 2000,* pp. 8–9.

ences and their impact for good or bad. NASW especially wants to encourage the kind of critical, probing article that would not receive an
award from an interest group.[4]

Academic respectability for the public-understanding movement is certified
by a quarterly international scholarly journal, *Public Understanding of Science,* edited at Cornell University and published jointly by the U.K. Institute
of Physics and The Science Museum, London. "Understanding" is variously
defined by the specialists in this field, but they agree that the public level
of understanding is less than desirable and often deplorable. The public-
understanding movement enters into the politics of science on the back of
a seemingly sensible but fallacious conviction—namely, that public understanding is an indispensable ingredient of public support of science. But
whatever is meant by public understanding of science, no evidence is offered, because none exists, of a consistent relationship, negative or positive,
between public understanding of the whole or parts of science and the provision of public money for research.

UNDERSTANDING AND MONEY

Consider the following: in 1998, the U.S. Department of Energy provided approximately $680 million for high-energy physics research—an ar-
cane field of science, opaque to the general public and even to scientists in
other disciplines, and acknowledged by its practitioners as remote from useful applications. In the same year, the National Cancer Institute spent about
$500 million on breast-cancer research, a highly politicized and publicized
disease of justifiably extensive concern. A relationship between these sums
and public understanding or concern, no matter how defined, is nowhere
visible. The unfortunate, nondemocratic truth is that science in the United
States, and other nations, too, prospers in a state of disengagement from
public understanding of the substance of science, the relative priorities
among fields of science, and the peculiarities of science politics. The scientific leadership does not seek to encourage public participation in the politics of science. Rather, it seeks public support for more money for science,
without public interference in the use of the money.[5] On rare occasions,

4. National Association of Science Writers, announcement, Science-in-Society Journalism
Awards, 1999.
5. Taking a skeptical view of the promotion of the public understanding of science, Jerry
Ravetz, a British sociologist and historian of science, scoffs that the more appropriate ti-
tle would be the "public understanding of the wonders of science." J. Ravetz, "Less
Than the Sum of Its Parts," book review, *Social Studies of Science,* April 1999.

often in matters concerning medical research, the public does become obstreperous. In 1998, after various patients' lobbies clamored for more money for research on *their* disease, and more influence over its use at NIH, NIH Director Harold Varmus shrewdly blunted their ardor by creating the Council of Public Representatives, serving as adviser to the director, for which he selected the members, the agenda, and a twice-a-year meeting schedule. Creation of the council was recommended by the Institute of Medicine, an arm of the National Academy of Sciences, institutions knowledgeable about the difficulties of maintaining professional authority over science in a democratic society.

The improvement of public understanding is indisputably a desirable goal, in science, as in constitutional law, economics, international relations, urban design, and on down a long list of topics and fields of knowledge in which public understanding is regrettably deficient. But no other sector of society can match the scientific enterprise in the perception of perils linked to poor understanding of its domain by the public. And no other sector comes close to the scientific enterprise in receipt of federal and philanthropic money to spread its message. Bountiful budget years do not soften the alarms. Thus, the head of communications and public liaison for the National Institutes of Health expressed concern in 1998, a year in which the NIH budget reached a historic high, that public support is based "on a partial—and only partial—recognition of the link between research and better health. Consequently," she warned, "it may not be reliable over time."[6] But public support of health research has long been, and continues to be, a durable element of our culture and politics. The same is true of other fields of science.

While serving as director of the National Science Foundation, Neal Lane, later the president's assistant for science and technology, often told scientific audiences that the public cannot be expected to support science if it does not understand science, which is both sensible-sounding and faithful to democratic belief in the value of an informed public, but nowhere evident in the record of money appropriated, or denied, for the various fields of science. Under the banner of what he called "civic science," Lane urged all scientists to undertake missionary work in behalf of their profession. By doing so, Lane told an audience of scientists in 1997, researchers

6. Anne Thomas, "Public Support for Medical Research—How Deep, How Enduring?" *Academic Medicine*, journal of the Association of American Medical Colleges, February 1998.

"can also favorably impact the long-term support for science."[7] On an earlier occasion, Lane acknowledged to me, however, that evidence is lacking for a link between public understanding and political support, as manifested in appropriations.[8]

The assumption of a direct link between public understanding and public support of science is as deeply accepted in and around the scientific community as the law of gravity. "Here's science dependent as never before on public funds," the late Carl Sagan argued, "and so continuing science depends on public support. And how's the public going to support it if they don't understand it?"[9] Writing in *Nature*, an essayist declared, "Although the capacity to convey to society a compelling vision of the whole of science may not be necessary in the day-to-day progress of investigation, it is crucial in maintaining cultural, political and financial support for science."[10] The understanding-support thesis spans the natural, physical, and social sciences. An article by the editor of the American Psychological Society's *Observer* stated, "Increasingly, the general public's awareness of psychological science has implications for a number of critical issues, from research funding (where public support can have a favorable influence) to the use of psychological science in society."[11] The thesis extends to the friends of science on Capitol Hill, where Chairman James Sensenbrenner (R-Wisconsin) of the House Science Committee declared, "Communicating science is, I believe, critical to ensuring continued public support for science."[12] Responding to an article that discussed the state of public understanding of science, a letter to *Physics Today* (published by the American Institute of Physics) argued that the level of understanding is deplorable and "Any new rationale for Federal support must remedy this situation. If the general public is to find basic research attractive, it will need an appreciation of the sense of wonder and serendipity that drives humans to learn more about this world."[13]

7. Neal Lane, "Science: Stepchild or Superstar," address to the American Association for the Advancement of Science, February 14, 1997.

8. Interview with author, November 7, 1996, in "Post-Election '96: Q&A with NSF Director Neal Lane," *SGR*, November 15, 1996.

9. "The Final Frontier: All Sagan Wants to Do Is Understand the Universe. All He Needs Is Time," *Washington Post*, May 30, 1996.

10. Mott T. Greene, "What Cannot Be Said in Science," *Nature*, August 14, 1997.

11. Elizabeth Ruksznis, "Giving Psychology Away," *Observer*, January 1999, p. 1.

12. Quoted in *Washington Fax*, May 28, 1998.

13. Charles F. Keller, letter, *Physics Today*, August 1998. That observation brought an unusual response from the authors of the original article: "Scientists ought not to assume," they cautioned, "that increased science literacy on the public's part would be accompanied by an increase in support for research; in fact, the converse could well be

THE LOSS OF THE COLD WAR

An awkward fact for science is that during and after the Cold War, and
to this day, public and private money for science has been provided in immense and, overall, steeply rising quantities, despite the lamented deficiencies in the public understanding of science. True, there have been a few
financial dips along the way, but over the years money for science has
soared, with the federal share of R&D rising from $2.5 billion in 1955 to
$76 billion in 1999.[14] Declines did occur, but they were concentrated in
defense research—not unreasonable, given the collapse of the Soviet Union
in 1991 and increased emphasis on nondefense research. In 1985, national
defense consumed 67.5 percent of federal spending for research and development; in the year 2000, defense and civilian spending for R&D shared
the budget 50-50.[15] In the mythical constructions of the shamans of science
politics, however, the ineradicable lack of public understanding of science
has been compounded by the end of the Cold War. Representative George
E. Brown Jr. (D-California) emphatically declared in 1998: "The end of the
Cold War disrupted the link between science and a clear justification for
its support, and has meant shrinking budgets for some areas of research."[16]
Plans to establish a science-policy research center in Washington were announced in 1998 by the vice provost of Columbia University, Michael M.
Crow, in a "Dear Colleague" letter: "The end of the Cold War signaled the
loss of a comprehensive national mission for science and technology. We
now lack an overarching rationale for S&T [science and technology] that
can stimulate and justify public support across a great breadth of S&T pur-
suits." Asked, "Do you miss the Cold War, at least as a funding edge?" Nobelist Leon Lederman replied, in part, "As soon as it was over they didn't
need science. We're fighting that presumption now. It's a tough job. You
have to educate." Lederman added, "That's one reason we wanted a television show"—a bizarre, government-financed escapade described in the
next chapter.[17]

the case." Roger A. Pielke Jr. and Bradford Byerly Jr., "Beyond Basic and Applied," *Physics Today*, August 1998. We might note here that as the public learned more about nuclear power and the biological effects of radiation, it turned against nuclear power.

14. *Federal R&D Funding by Budget Function: Fiscal Years 1998–2000* (Washington, D.C.: National Science Foundation, NSF 00-303, 1999), pp. 11–12.

15. Ibid., p. 12.

16. George E. Brown Jr., "Defining Values for Research and Technology," *Chronicle of
Higher Education,* July 10, 1998.

17. "A Conversation with Dr. Leon Lederman," *New York Times,* July 14, 1998.

Worn but still serviceable, the Vannevar Bush card was played in 1999 by Jerome Friedman, president of the American Physical Society: "With the end of the Cold War, the social contract between science and society embodied in Vannevar Bush's ground-breaking report, *Science, The Endless Frontier,* has begun to erode. . . . We must transmit the message that the support of science and technology is an investment that is critical for the future of the nation, and that an appropriate portion of the federal budget should go into both basic and applied research."[18] Imbued in the scientific enterprise, in all its many sectors, the litany of public ignorance and public neglect has become a persistent, solemnly repeated mantra. "The Cold War has ended, and public interest in and support of science have waned correspondingly," states a report in 1996 by the advisory committee to the National Science Foundation's Directorate for Education and Human Resources. The report, by a panel of educators, added that "America has produced a significant share of the world's great scientists while most of its population is virtually illiterate in science."[19]

The predominant collective line, in defiance of fact, is that federal support of science wilted with the end of Cold War, and its revival is impeded by public ignorance. On rare occasions, however, the factual baselessness and illogicality of these assertions is acknowledged in the senior echelons of science. Thus, in 1998, the president of Grove City College, John H. Moore, a former deputy director of the National Science Foundation, mused on the public understanding of science in his capacity as president of Sigma Xi, a national society of some 80,000 scientists in more than five hundred chapters in universities and government and industrial research institutions: "Scientists are naturally concerned that ignorance of scientific concepts and processes lessens public support for research funding. Without the stimulus of a perceived serious threat such as existed during the Cold War, poor public understanding might make it harder to support funding for research and development," Moore observed. But, he pointed out, "In fact, federal funds for basic research in total have risen, albeit slowly, since 1989, and federal support for academic basic research actually increased slightly faster (3.1 percent per year, after inflation) in the post–Cold War period than in 1970–89 (2.6 percent per year)." The totality of federal spending on research and development had decreased since the end of the

18. Jerome Friedman, "Meeting the Challenges of the 21st Century," *APS News,* March 1999.
19. *Shaping the Future: New Expectations for Undergraduate Education in Science, Mathematics, Engineering and Technology* (NSF 96-139), p. iii.

Cold War, Moore explained, "mostly as the result of reductions in defense spending."[20] Moore candidly stated: "Whether any of these changes relate to public understanding of science is far from clear."[21] Moore, we might note, is an economist.

WARNINGS OF NATIONAL DECLINE

The realities of federal spending on research in the 1990s warrant skepticism toward the frequent warnings that, without the underlying rationale of Cold War necessity, public ignorance and hostility jeopardize the support and progress of science, which, in turn, threatens national well-being. Through the final years of the twentieth century, and into the new millennium, financial support and scientific activity continued to grow in robust unison. Nonetheless, the public was steadily barraged with seemingly informed but vacuous reports of national decline attributable to deficiencies in support of research. "While Washington is starting to wake up," an editorial in *U.S. News & World Report* declared in 1999, "it has not yet reversed a slippage of 26 percent, relative to GDP [gross domestic product], in federal research and development between 1990 and 1997."[22]

From whence the figure 26 percent? From a report, *The New Challenge to America's Prosperity*, published by a Washington lobby for federal research money, the Council on Competitiveness, an industry-led alliance that includes major academic research universities. Embodying research by Professors Michael E. Porter, of Harvard Business School, and Scott Stern, of the MIT Sloan School, the council report dourly emphasized the seemingly alarming fact that in recent years, a decline had occurred in the percentage of U.S. gross domestic product devoted to research and development—from a peak of 2.74 percent in the mid-1980s, to an average of 2.5 percent during the past decade. Based on what they call the Innovation Index—a compos-

---

20. Delving into the thicket of government statistics, we find that total federal R&D spending actually *increased*, in current dollars, since the end of the Cold War. According to the National Science Foundation, in 1991, when the Soviet Union collapsed, the federal R&D total stood at $65.9 billion; in 1999, it rose to $76.8 billion. In constant dollars pegged to 1992, the federal R&D total was virtually unchanged, from $67.8 billion in 1991 to $67 billion in 1999, but the civilian component rose from $27.3 billion to $31.8 billion. *Federal R&D Funding by Budget Function: Fiscal Years 1998–2000*, p. 12.

21. John H. Moore, "Public Understanding of Science," *American Scientist*, November–December 1998, p. 498.

22. David Gergen, "No Time for Complacency: The U.S. Economy Leads the World, but Its Foundations Are Rusting," *U.S. News & World Report*, March 29, 1999, p. 116.

ite of research spending, education, and other factors—Porter and Stern concluded that the U.S. "may be living off historical assets that are not being renewed." In contrast, Denmark and Finland were cited for "major gains in innovative capacity since the mid-1980s, joining Sweden in establishing a region of world class innovation."[23] The small, socially homogeneous, efficient three nations have long been conscripted for polemical service by critics of the vast and untidy continental giant of North America, but the relevance of their policies and methods to the infinitely more diverse United States is open to question. We might keep in mind that the combined populations of Denmark, Finland, and Sweden, 19.2 million (in 1996), and their combined gross domestic product, $400 billion, were dwarfed by California's population of 32 million and gross state product of $962 billion. Moreover, though convenient for sowing economic anxiety, the GDP yardstick is nonsensical as a relative measure of national research activities.

In their statistical selectivity, GDP alarmists customarily neglect to acknowledge that total spending for research and development in the United States—government and private—rose from $151 billion to over $220 billion between 1990 and 1998, and continued to grow into the new century at a robust pace; that U.S. R&D spending exceeded that of all other major industrial nations combined, and that U.S. nonmilitary R&D expenditures as a percentage of gross domestic product were, and remain, roughly the same as that of other industrialized countries—a bit ahead of some, a bit behind others, but, in any case, vastly larger in the amounts spent than any other.[24] Nonetheless, up to and throughout the final decade of the last century, edgy messages suggesting a parlous state of American science, leading to dangerous industrial and economic consequences, routinely emanated from the organizations that manage the politics and public relations of the national scientific enterprise. From these seemingly authoritative sources, the message of menace seeped into the popular press for transmission to the public. In the case of the alleged R&D/GDP crisis, the Council on Competitiveness replayed the warning in its newsletter, which cited the end of the Cold War as the harbinger of new perils for the American economy:

23. *The New Challenge to America's Prosperity: Findings from the Innovation Index* (Washington, D.C.: Council on Competitiveness, 1999), p. 7.
24. "R&D Exceeds Expectations Again, Growing Faster Than the U.S. Economy during Last Three Years," *Data Brief* (NSF-97-328), November 5, 1997 (Washington, D.C.: National Science Foundation.)

In addition to declining federal investment in basic R&D, the reasons for weakening U.S. innovative capacity include shortages in the scientific and technical workforce; a private sector that is not fully compensating for federal R&D cutbacks; and a legal and regulatory environment that inflicts substantially unnecessary costs on industry.[25]

THREATS FROM ABROAD

Medical research is the grist for especially brazen claims that poor public understanding leads to neglect of the financial needs of science and missed opportunities for improvements in the prevention and treatment of disease. Fundamental research in immunology, central to the study of cancer and other diseases, proceeds in many countries not as a nationalistic endeavor, but as an openly published, international collaborative enterprise for the benefit of humanity. To cast research of this type in terms of a nationalistic horse race is misleading, if not grotesque. Nevertheless, "U.S. Dominant in Immunology Research, But Not in Some Research Specialties," stated the headline on a press release from the National Academy of Sciences in 1999. The text noted that the American dominance in this field of research "could be affected by several factors that could curtail the nation's ability to capitalize on leadership in immunology." Cited as one factor was that "much of U.S. dominance in immunology results from the work of non-citizens who, at any of several stages in their career, have come to this country because of an attractive, well-funded environment in the life sciences in general and in immunology in particular." The press release was derived from one of a series of "benchmarking" studies aimed at assuring that the United States is in the lead, or on par with other nations, in all important fields of research. The study itself reported that between 1981 and 1997, American researchers produced 63.39 percent of the world's "high-impact" papers in immunology; England was listed as runner-up, with 7.47 percent.[26]

TRANSLATING SCIENCE

Recognizing, and feeding, the public interest in medical advances, the press routinely mines major medical journals for hopeful developments,

---

25. *Challenges: Competing Through Innovation*, winter 1999, newsletter of the Council on Competitiveness, Washington, D.C.

26. National Academy of Sciences, press release, April 7, 1999, announcing publication of an academy report, *International Benchmarking of U.S. Immunology Research* (Washington, D.C.: National Academy Press, 2000); immunology data, pp. 3–16.

even if of slight or unknown therapeutic potential. The ultimate product is essentially a skilled translation—from medicalese into lay language, no easy feat, given the complexities of contemporary scientific research. The process, however, puts science writing, and, in turn, the public, at the mercy of an assortment of manipulators, as some science writers themselves acknowledge. In a candid series of articles on the mechanics of science news, David Shaw, a staff writer who covers the news media for the *Los Angeles Times,* observed:

> For the most part, the major medical journals set the journalistic agenda in mainstream press coverage of medical news. They have what amounts to "a stranglehold over information about biomedical research," in the words of Natalie Angier, a medical writer for the *New York Times.* That often means that mainstream news organizations—and, more important, the public—are potential victims of the growing pursuit of publicity, individual and institutional acclaim, research grants and commercial profiteering that often drive the announcement of medical breakthroughs in the journals.[27]

In a symbiotic relationship between science and the science press, popularizers of medical research frequently employ a set piece that declares substantial grounds for hope against a so-far intractable disease while cautioning against undue optimism. The scientifically untutored public can only be left befuddled by the seemingly contradictory news. The minimum effect is to inform the public that science is at work on its problems and merits support. These bait-and-switch events in medical news commonly arouse little notice, except among desperate patients and those who personally care about them. Far greater than usual attention, however, was attracted by an appalling episode that occurred in May 1998 when the customarily prudent *New York Times* created an impression of imminent victory in the so-called war on cancer. On the front page, under the headline "A Cautious Awe Greets Drugs That Eradicate Tumors in Mice," with accompanying lines stating "Hope in the Lab, A Special Report," the *Times* described research conducted by Dr. Judah Folkman of Harvard Medical School and Children's Hospital in Boston. Folkman's research, pursuing a method for cutting off the blood supply to tumors, had previously received considerable attention, in the professional and popular press, including the

---

27. David Shaw, "Medical Journals Exercise Clout in News Coverage," *Los Angeles Times,* February 14, 2000.

Times. On these earlier occasions, the reports were cautious about the thera- peutic potential, which was yet to be demonstrated and later proved to be elusive. Caution was tempered with exultation, however, on this latest oc- casion, in which Nobel laureate James Watson, of double-helix renown, was directly quoted as declaring: "Judah is going to cure cancer in two years." The enticing, but regrettably false prophecy, later denied by Watson as a misunderstood dinner conversation with the *Times* reporter, was accompa- nied by the requisite warning against optimism: "From bitter experience, most cancer researchers have learned to be leery of what one called 'that four letter word' cure."[28] Under extensive criticism for raising unrealistic hopes, the *Times* two days later deflated the optimistic report with another front-page story, headlined: "In Excitement Over Cancer Drugs, A Caution Over Premature Hopes."[29]

The juxtaposition of extravagant hopes and pro forma caution was ex- treme in this case, but the tactic, in less blatant expression, was not rare in the permissive atmosphere of journalism dedicated to the public under- standing of science. In 1999, the *Times* published a lay-language version of a research article initially published in the *Journal of the National Cancer Institute,* a publication written by and for scientists and physicians, but closely monitored for journalistic pickings. The cancer journal reported that a protein that originates in cancerous prostates and is used as a diagnostic tool might be utilized to combat prostate cancer. The *New York Times* head- lined its report of that finding: "Marker for Cancer of Prostate May Fight It." The accompanying *Times* article signaled high importance for this finding, noting that the report in the cancer journal was "published with unusual speed, as an 'accelerated discovery,'" because the prostate protein "may ac- tually be used by the body to fight cancer." The *Times* then proceeded to a restrained assessment by the chair of a urology department in a Texas medical school, who cautioned, "But it is sort of hard to say whether this is going to translate into anything of benefit to individual patients right now." The editor of the cancer journal exhibited even greater caution con- cerning the report in the journal, telling the *Times,* "It is an unanticipated effect, and its medical application is unknowable."[30]

28. *New York Times,* May 3, 1998.

29. Op. cit., May 5, 1998. The furor over the cancer-research episode was aptly summa- rized by editor Howard Lewis, in the spring/summer 1998 issue of *Science Writers,* the newsletter of the National Association of Science Writers: "The most talked about sci- ence news story in years appeared in the top left, off-lead position on the front page of *The New York Times* on Sunday May 3, with the peculiar property of containing no news at all."

30. *New York Times,* October 6, 1999.

Excited press reports of scientific-medical progress, accompanied by cautions against premature optimism, are as predictable as the major causes of death on the nearby obituary pages. In January 2000, under the headline "As Common as Dirt, Bacteria May Yield Powerful Cancer Drug," a front-page article in the *Wall Street Journal* reported the development of a new class of drugs that "can attack tumors unresponsive to Taxol [a drug widely prescribed for breast cancer patients and as a preventive for patients considered at high risk], suggesting that they may also be effective against tumors of the colon and prostate." Several paragraphs on, readers were informed:

> Developers of the new drugs are cautious about their prospects, however, and concerned about unfairly raising the hopes of cancer patients. "Most experimental drugs crash," warns Ernest Hamel, a senior investigator at the National Cancer Institute's Frederick Cancer Research and Development Center, who is familiar with the drugs. Though enthusiastic, researchers at Bristol-Myers and Novartis warn that the new drugs could produce toxicity levels in people not yet seen in animal studies. Scientists say they won't know until later this year whether the drugs will be safe, and efficacy trials won't be completed for several years after that.[31]

In February 2000, the Associated Press reported: "A vaccine-like treatment wiped out or shrank tumors in some patients whose kidney cancer had spread elsewhere in their bodies, researchers say." The good news was tempered with a triple dose of caution in the same article, which noted that the favorable results were derived from "a preliminary study of only 17 patients"; that a vaccine specialist who "called the report encouraging" also "stressed that it must be confirmed by other researchers with more patients"; and that another specialist "noted that cancers that spread from the kidney could sometimes shrink on their own, which could exaggerate the effect of therapy."[32]

MAY CURE, BUT MAY NOT

The announcements of medical hope coupled with caution have led to what might be called "may" journalism, of which there are many exam-

---

31. *Wall Street Journal*, January 27, 2000.
32. "Tumors Reduced in Study," Associated Press report, *New York Times*, February 29, 2000.

ples, such as: "Worm Gene May Offer Key to Aging Process" (*New York Times,* May 13, 1999); "New Drug From Pharmacia May Fight Resistant AIDS Strain" (*Wall Street Journal,* June 24, 1999); "Hot-shot Proteins: The Cell's Chaperons May Provide Novel Cures for a Number of Diseases" (*The Economist,* April 18, 1998); "Gene May Promise New Route to Potent Vaccines" (*Science,* May 7, 1999). Scientific institutions feed the process: "Weizmann Institute Discovery May One Day Contribute to the Development of More Efficient Methods Against Antibiotics-Resistant Bacteria" (press release from the American Committee for the Weizmann Institute of Science, July 1, 1999, directing attention to a scientific report from the Institute in the July 1 *Nature*); "'Knockout' Mouse May One Day Lead to Major Understanding of Human Kidney Disorder" (press release from the National Institutes of Health, August 30, 1999, noting an article in *Nature Medicine* based on a research project supported by NIH).

Even with the de rigueur cautionary qualifiers, the excited, formulaic reports of wondrous medical breakthroughs sometimes run so far beyond clinical reality that confessional correctives become necessary. Gene therapy, a mainstay of medical miracle reports for at least a decade, crashed under the weight of its own extravagant press notices in 1999 when an eighteen-year-old patient at the University of Pennsylvania died after receiving injection of a "corrective" gene for a rare liver disorder. "Delivery Shortfall: Gene Therapy, Touted as a Breakthrough, Bogs Down in Detail," was the headline on the *Wall Street Journal* report, which quoted a researcher as saying: "This has been an overhyped area that has failed to reach its promise for very obvious technical reasons."[33] The *New York Times* reported that a government inquiry into the death "comes amid growing concern that some researchers and companies have not been entirely forthcoming with information about the technology's harmful side effects, as well as patient deaths from causes other than gene therapy."[34]

In the cause of public understanding of science, the translation of research findings works best for medical developments, which can be formulated in understandable terms of discovery versus disease, leading to hope, qualified by caution, even if the fine scientific details are arcane. The nonmedical branches of science are more likely to suffer loss in translation. No matter. The urge within the press to relay news of scientific progress to the public is not deterred by translational barriers, even if insurmountable, as

33. *Wall Street Journal,* October 27, 1999.
34. "A Death Puts Gene Therapy Under Increasing Scrutiny: Treatment May Have Hurt Other Patients," *New York Times,* November 4, 1999.

demonstrated by the following excerpts from an article in the *New York Times* derived from a report by two cosmologists in *Physical Review Letters,* the premier research publication of physics:

> In their paper, they showed that a strange kind of energy named quintessence, which has been posited to permeate the universe, could develop into a repulsive force, when it would accelerate the cosmic expansion. The second part involves the application of an advanced theory called superstring theory, which portrays elementary particles not as points but as wriggling, incredibly tiny 10-dimensional strings. . . . In superstring theory, different vibrations of the strings in 10 dimensions represent particles that carry all the known forces of the universe, including gravity. But string theorists have long wondered what to do with the extra six dimensions that we do not perceive in our four-dimensional universe. If they do not see them, where are they?[35]

Where, one might ask, was the elementary good sense that would recognize the folly of publishing a pottage of gibberish in a misguided attempt to keep the public abreast of the latest in science?

News of progress in science, even if incomprehensible to laypeople, serves the politics of science, and, accordingly, good news of science gushes forth, and is uncritically amplified by a compliant press, with contrite correctives when the gap between hope and reality can no longer be ignored. Readers have good reason to be confused, a condition that should be attributed to the politics of science and the gullibility of the press rather than poor public understanding of science. Reviewing a book about gene therapy in 1999, a writer from the Harvard School of Public Health observed in *Science:*

> The tremendous enthusiasm of early investigators in the field was rapidly communicated to the lay press, who touted gene therapy as the answer to many previously untreatable diseases from cancer to heart disease and AIDS. This exuberant optimism only increased the frustration and disappointment as one major human gene-therapy after another failed to demonstrate any clinical efficacy.[36]

---

35. "Theorists Ponder a Cosmic Boost From Far, Far Away," *New York Times,* February 15, 2000.

36. Jeffrey M. Leiden, "Gene Therapy Enters Adolescence," book review, *Science,* August 20, 1999.

On the endless frontier, "never say never" is a familiar maxim. Scientists are ever hopeful of therapeutic progress, and science journalism tags along. In March 2000, under the headline "Hint of Success in Gene Therapy Study," the *New York Times* reported: "Gene therapy, a technique long on promise and so far very short on fulfillment, may be achieving a glimmer of success in a treatment for hemophilia B, a disease in which the blood does not clot properly." The report of hopeful findings was based on favorable results in two of three patients enrolled in a trial.[37]

GOOD NEWS VERSUS REALITY

If optimistic press reports, even with their customary escape clauses, reflected reality in cancer research and treatment, the scourge would be gone. Unfortunately, the messages of scientific and medical success conveyed to the public—by scientists and the political promoters of science, via a compliant science press—are not confirmed by the casualty lists from the so-called war on cancer. Survival rates and quality of life for patients have increased for many types of cancer, though the pace of progress has, overall, been agonizingly slow. However, because of the growth and aging of the American population into the cancer-prone elderly years, the total number of deaths attributed to cancer rose from approximately 359,000 in 1974 to nearly 565,000 in 1998, followed by an estimated slight decline, to 563,000 in 1999.[38] The reported improvement in five-year survival rates for cancer is questioned by some researchers, who contend that earlier diagnosis creates the illusion of longer survival, but is not reflected in cancer mortality.[39] Such doubts, however, are rarely echoed in the good-news-seeking press.

The politics of science dictates that any good news about cancer must be emphasized and, if need be, manufactured, to keep up public spirits and support. The press collaborates, though in occasional fits of professional conscience, it balks and questions the contrived optimism that shades the news of cancer and so much else in the scientific enterprise. The public appreciates the necessity for research, and supports it. But the insecurities, and opportunities, that gave rise to the public-understanding industry continue to thrive on visions of a benighted public blocking the way to scien-

---

37. *New York Times*, March 2, 2000.
38. Data from *Cancer Facts and Figures,* annual series, American Cancer Society.
39. H. Gilbert et al., "Are Increasing Survival Rates Evidence of Success Against Cancer?" *JAMA,* June 14, 2000.

tific progress. The good-news excesses of the medical sciences continue to raise misgivings within the profession, but with limited corrective effects. Observing that "most patients who have cancer still die of cancer," a January 2000 *Lancet* editorial warned, "The end of cancer cannot be said to be in sight." Unwarranted optimism might endanger charitable contributions, the editorial cautioned, arguing that "maintenance of public confidence is crucial for fundraising. Such confidence will be shattered when the public starts to see the gap between what is being said and what is being achieved."[40] But not even the supposed threat to fundraising can restrain the manufacture of good news. The scientific enterprise proceeds on the assumption that the public must be heavily dosed with wondrous reports for the public to support science. Add the machinations of individual scientists pursuing money and glory, and the mixture is set for misleading the public. The perils for science journalism were described by two *Washington Post* reporters recounting their investigation of the death of the gene-therapy patient at the University of Pennsylvania.

> One lesson that came out of our reporting, especially for Rick [Weiss], who has covered science for 15 years and become friendly with many scientists, including [James] Wilson [director of the university gene-research institute where the patient died], was that there are real downsides to growing so familiar with sources that it becomes difficult to remain sufficiently skeptical of what they tell you. . . . And none of us want to live our working lives in constant suspicion that we're being lied to. But at a time when so much rides on success for scientists—from fame to financial windfalls—it seems more important than ever that we all maintain a higher level of skepticism than ever, and ask the hard questions that in the past might have seemed impertinent.[41]

The level of trust implicit in that description is less prevalent in press coverage of conventional politics, in which self-serving prevarication is routine, and recognized as such by the press. By the admission of science journalists, the science press tends to be in uncritical harmony with the people it writes about.

Greater public understanding of science merits backing as a worthy goal. Our concern, however, is the political and polemical misbehavior of

40. "Overoptimism about Cancer," *The Lancet,* January 15, 2000.
41. Deborah Nelson and Rick Weiss, "How We Uncovered the Hidden Fatality in a Clinical Trial," *ScienceWriters,* spring 2000.

scientific leaders and spokespeople, as manifested in their representations of poor understanding, neglect, and hostility by a public that is actually supportive and appreciative of science. Science's own misperceptions of underappreciation and poor treatment in the general society are reinforced by doting science journalists who faithfully echo the paranoid fears and alarms of the scientific leadership and its publicists.

The devil theory of deficient public understanding continually generates a substantial body of overwrought literature, urgent exhortations, and a generous flow of government and philanthropic money devoted to correctives. The public understanding of science is a missionary cause, as well as a vocational opportunity for the promoters of understanding. The ineffectiveness of their ever-increasing efforts would seem to be certified by their continued alarms about the state of public understanding of science. No matter how great the efforts, the level of understanding is depicted as deplorably low, if not lower than before. The remedial campaign continues on many fronts, including pleadings by the leaders of science for the rank and file of researchers to join in the mission of elevating the public's understanding of science, lest the financial bottom drop out of research. Again, I emphasize that the desirability of a better-informed public is not in question. However, the movement's depiction of financial history, public sentiment, and political reality borders on hallucination; its claims of neglect are so far-fetched as to invite wonder about motivation and trustworthiness on other matters.

Health research has been bountifully supported for decades through government funding of the National Institutes of Health. The sharply upward slope of appropriations—from $7 billion in 1989 to $17.9 billion in 2000—reflects Congress's unwavering, as well as uncritical, support of NIH. A large volume of polling evidence consistently reflects public enthusiasm for the health sciences. Nonetheless, a doleful insecurity, detached from the reality of the postwar years, pervades the public statements of the leaders of the great and favored NIH. Rooting diligently, they find reasons to fear for the financial future of the munificently supported NIH. The eccentrically titled "Research!America" NIH lobby annually commissions public opinion surveys that, in the accommodating fashion of commercial polling firms, produce findings that confirm the preconceptions of the clients who purchase the polls. In reports on opinion surveys in individual states, a consistently uncomplicated leitmotif emerges from Research!America's inquiries into the public mind: medical research is threatened by public ignorance and misunderstandings that lead to financial neglect. In 1999, pollsters for Research!America found that Coloradans strongly support medical research, but only 5 percent of the respondents in that state could identify NIH as the fount of support, whereas 56 percent knew of NASA's role in financing space research and exploration.[42] NASA's lead on the fame scale was to be expected, given that the NASA logo is emblazoned on rockets, spaceships, and space suits that have received prime-time attention during forty years of space extravaganzas—including the moon landings, the *Challenger* catastrophe, and countless televised displays of astronauts weightlessly tumbling in space. NIH, in contrast, stages no life-imperiling blastoffs or photo sessions from distant regions of the universe. Apart from occasional public-relations carnivals, usually connected with peddling of a new drug or, increasingly, the claimed sighting of a disease-related gene, the health sciences embody the reticent cultures of academe and medicine. NASA is a creature of the brash world of aerospace and big-league, high-tech industrial promotion, publicity, and sales pitches. Little wonder, then, that the horn-blasting NASA trumps the reserved, scholarly NIH in public awareness. The relevant question is: does it matter? Not a bit, it appears, by the measure of money.

NIH's pale public image may be a blow to institutional pride, but poor public recognition of NIH's role has apparently been without harmful effect on its financial and political fortunes. Between 1998 and 2000, the budget of the highly publicized space agency was stuck at approximately $13.5 billion per year; during those same years, the annual budget of the poorly recognized National Institutes of Health rose from $13.5 billion to $17.9 billion. From these figures it might be concluded that invisibility is golden and that government spending on research rises with obscurity.

A typically dour conclusion about NIH's poor name recognition was drawn in 1996 by a senior executive of NIH discussing Research!America's gloomy findings at a melancholy convocation in Washington titled "Science in Crisis at the Millennium." "If we don't have a [scientifically] literate populace, we're in a lot of trouble in the coming decades," said Wendy Baldwin, director of the NIH Office of Extramural Research (which is responsible for providing NIH money to universities, hospitals, and other research institutions outside of NIH). Strong support in the past does not assure the future, Baldwin warned as she urged scientists to educate the public about the nature and importance of their work and the government agency that finances it. Noting low name recognition of NIH, Baldwin allowed that among scientists, "there is a natural reluctance to feel that you are lobbying

---

42. *Colorado Residents Speak Out on Medical Research,* public opinion survey for Research!America, Alexandria, Va., spring 1999.

for your grant or your laboratory. I can certainly understand that." But, she added, "We need the scientific community to talk about where science comes from. . . . You can help people understand what that basic process is in a way that I think would be very constructive for the NIH. . . . This is a crisis session. I have to talk about a crisis," Baldwin continued. "A potential crisis for the NIH is the lack of a clear linkage in people's minds between their desired goal for medical research and the agency that supports it."[43] We might recall that in 1996, the NIH budget stood at $12 billion; by 1999, it had risen to $15.6 billion, and next year to $17.9 billion, and then to over $20 billion, without a molecule of evidence of a commensurate increase in the public understanding of science or any indication of wobbling in public and political sentiments for even greater support.

The campaign to promote the public understanding of science is a robust offshoot of the scientific enterprise, distinct from conventional schooling in science. Though overlapping with school-based learning, the movement lacks the continuity and structure of schooling; it attempts to deliver a smattering of science to the public on the fly, mainly through press, TV, films, and museum displays.[44]

The National Science Foundation includes among its efforts for the public understanding of science a program titled Informal Science Education, or ISE, for which annual expenditures of $46 million were budgeted in 1999 and 2000, with the same amount requested for 2001. In the words of a head-spinning NSF solicitation for proposals to spend government money in behalf of the public understanding of science, ISE "supports proj-

43. From proceedings of "Science in Crisis at the Millennium," an international symposium, September 19, 1996, sponsored by the Center for the History of Recent Science, George Washington University, Washington, D.C.

44. The cultural and educational value of science museums for the scientifically aware visitor is not in doubt. To see, perhaps even touch, the real articles from the history of science is thrilling as well as informative. But the value for children invites uncomfortable and therefore rarely asked questions, given the pandemonium that often reigns in museums on days crowded with school-age, or younger, visitors. Martin Harwit, former director of the National Air and Space Museum, states that "the typical attention span of a visitor on his feet was four minutes." Martin Harwit, *An Exhibit Denied: Lobbying the History of Enola Gay* (Springer-Verlag, New York, 1996), p. 293. A study of visitors to the Smithsonian's "Science in American Life" exhibition found that "A video called Night at the Recombinant Opera was viewed by 11.4 percent of visitors who spent an average of 2.16 minutes there, yet none of the visitors interviewed in the Exit Survey said that it conveyed the message of the exhibition, and less than one percent cited it as being most informative or most interesting." That honor went to a video titled Garbage and Landfills. *An Assessment of the "Science in American Life Exhibition" at the National Museum of American History* (Smithsonian Institution, Institutional Studies Office, 1995), p. 12.

ects in which learning is voluntary and self-directed, life-long and motivated by intrinsic interests, curiosity, exploration, manipulation, fantasy,
task completion and social interaction." The declared goal of ISE is:

> to enrich the quality of life by improving the scientific and technologi-
> cal literacy of children and adults so they are informed about the impli-
> cations of SMT [science, mathematics, and technology] in their everyday
> lives; are motivated to pursue further experiences in these areas; and are
> aided in making informed responsible decisions about related policy is-
> sues having societal implications.[45]

Like much else in science, the public-understanding movement has been
globalized, and, around the world, employs rhetoric and tactics that would
be at home in the United States. In a guest editorial in 1999 in *Science,* a
member of the Japanese Council for Science and Technology made a familiar declaration: "If the public loses interest in science or does not understand the importance of research, it will become difficult for scientists to
obtain financial support." To preempt this danger, the editorial continued:

> Japan's Science and Technology Agency this year started a 3-year cam-
> paign to promote better public understanding of the progress of science
> and technology. It includes science festivals for young people, a robot
> olympics, introduction of advanced technologies through video libraries,
> construction of a new science museum (Science World), and so on. Sci-
> ence education for the general public is not easy, however. We have to
> study tactics and strategies to make science education an integral part of
> every stage of life, from children's primary education to lifelong learning
> for adults.[46]

From various locations in and around science, in the United States and
elsewhere, these and similar efforts in behalf of the public understanding
of science are supported by a continuous procession of declarations warning of dangers to science attributable—so it is said—to public ignorance.
Thus, Nobel laureate Arthur Kornberg, presenting his view of the matter
in 1998—ironically, a budget-bountiful year—declared:

---

45. "Informal Science Education Program," solicitation for proposals for fiscal year 2000
(Washington, D.C.: National Science Foundation).
46. Hiroo Imura, "Science Education for the Public," *Science,* June 11, 1999.

The first problem is the rising tide of public fear, distrust and rejection of science. . . . As a result of an uninformed or misinformed public, we have a second problem, the lack of adequate financial support for basic science, a poverty worsened by severe pressures to engage in targeted research such as the treatment of a particular disease or the development of technologies to improve the economy.[47]

Anything goes in asserting the existence and dangers of deficient public understanding of science and the effectiveness of particular solutions. In 1999, writing in the *New York Times,* Bill Nye, the impresario of a popular TV science show, "Bill Nye the Science Guy," stated, "Research shows that about half of what each of us learns about science, we learn through informal education. The more each of us knows about science, the better decisions we can make as voters, taxpayers and neighbors. That means that good science museums are not amenities, but vital to our future."[48]

Research shows? My inquiry to Nye for the research he referred to brought the reply that he had heard of such research, but could not identify it; check with the head of the Informal Science Education program at the National Science Foundation, Hyman Field, Nye suggested to me in a telephone conversation. Asked about the research to which Nye referred, Field told me that he did not know of any, adding that if such research existed he would almost certainly be aware of it. "I have no idea where he got that," Field said. "People obviously learn informally, but I'm not familiar with that," the NSF official remarked in reference to Nye's assertion that "research shows."[49]

New Alarms

On March 23, 1998, the National Science Foundation hosted a four-hour meeting at its headquarters to introduce and discuss a melange of misinformation and anxieties incorporated into a 174-page report by Jim Hartz, a former TV science journalist, and Rick Chappell, a former astronaut serving as associate director for science at NASA's Marshall Space Flight Center. Titled *Worlds Apart: How the Distance Between Science and Journalism Threat-*

47. Arthur Kornberg, "Better Living through Basic Science," *Stanford MD,* summer 1998.
48. Bill Nye, "The Marks of a Good Exhibit? Few Words, Flying Sparks," *New York Times,* April 21, 1999.
49. Author's telephone conversations with Nye and Field, April 22, 1999.

ens America's Future,[50] the publication, and the "research" it incorporated, emanated from outside the scientific enterprise but pandered to science's grievances of poor understanding and news-media neglect. The publisher was the First Amendment Center (based at Vanderbilt University, though not part of it) through the beneficence of the Freedom Forum (formerly the Gannett Foundation). The message was one of anguish and despair, of the variety streaming for decades from the missionaries of science laboring in the cause of the public understanding of science. Though fantastical in its garbling of statistics and history, the publication was ideologically correct in its representation of science friendless and sinking, and therefore rated the hospitality of the prestigious National Science Foundation.

The claim to notice of *Worlds Apart* was a survey of several thousand scientists, engineers, and journalists who indicated their degree of agreement or disagreement with brief statements about the quality, adequacy and other matters concerning press and television reporting of scientific and technological activities. The survey data occupied 10 pages of the 174-page report. The balance was devoted to woeful commentary, by the authors, luminaries of science, journalists and others, on deficiencies in the public understanding of science and the pernicious consequences that would inevitably ensue in the absence of ameliorative efforts by the press, TV, and scientists.

The surveyed scientists and engineers tended toward negative assessments of science journalism while the journalists were more positive, though not enthusiastic about their profession's performance. Oddly, given the title *Worlds Apart,* the two groups were in approximate harmony on many issues. Thus, in response to the statement "Most science reporters give a positive view of scientists, engineers and those in related positions," 51 percent of the journalists and 60 percent of the scientists chose "agree somewhat." Some of the questions were of a murky nature such as: "Most scientists could care less if the public knows about their work." In response, "disagree somewhat" was reported for 43 percent of the journalists and 40 percent of the scientists, while 23 percent of the journalists and 9 percent of the scientists opted for "neither agree nor disagree." In accompaniment to these opaque quantifications, coauthors Hartz and Chappell wrote in their report that over the past 50 years, public and private financing had created "a scientific enterprise that is the envy of the world. But," they continued, "the scientific establishment says that, through complacency, bud-

---

50. Jim Hartz and Rick Chappell, *Worlds Apart: How the Distance Between Science and Journalism Threatens America's Future* (Nashville, Tenn.: First Amendment Center, 1997).

get cuts and plain misunderstanding, it is all in jeopardy"—particularly
basic research, which they described as "the first casualty of this scientific
belt-tightening." "At the risk of seeming unduly alarmist," they stated, "we
must agree. No, the great citadel will not disappear tomorrow. It's the kind
of edifice that will crumble slowly from neglect. Hardly anyone will miss
it until it's gone."[51]

How can misfortune stealthily befall a national asset that is indispensable to America's well-being and envied by the world? The authors explain:
"With a small natural constituency, no spare cash, feeble organization and
little experience in the rough-and-tumble of Washington politics, science
is justifiably worried that it is playing a losing game. At the same time, it
is beginning to understand that a big part of the problem is an inability to
get its message across to the public." Coupling cause and effect, *Worlds
Apart* concludes that "support for science and technology in this country
has dwindled—in part, it appears, because of media inattention."

Why are the media inattentive? Because scientists are poor at explaining science to journalists, Hartz and Chappell state. What accounts for the
explanatory ineptitude of scientists? *Worlds Apart* answers:

> Because science in America came of age during the Cold War in a cli-
> mate of urgent support and ardent secrecy, scientists have grown used to
> funding that comes without question. They are unaccustomed to ex-
> plaining their work to the public.

That passage invites examination: Even in the grimmest days of the Cold
War, the great majority of scientific research, including projects financed
by the Department of Defense, was exempt from government secrecy regulations. Secrecy did indeed exist in the nuclear-weapons laboratories and
in several large, specialized laboratories managed by MIT and other universities under contract to the Defense Department. As a result of student and
faculty protests, many of those were eventually spun off as inappropriate
for academic involvement. At the insistence of academe and the science
establishment, and with the concurrence of the Pentagon's research managers, secrecy rarely ever got a foothold in on-campus university research.
All research sponsored by the National Institutes of Health and the National Science Foundation—the government's largest supporters of basic

---

51. Disclosure: In support of their thesis, Hartz and Chappell quote widely and selectively,
including snippets of writings by this author on budget fluctuations that dovetail with
their prophecies of doom.

research—has traditionally been reported in open, publicly available literature. NASA, from its founding in 1958, took pride in performing in public.

Proceeding with its worried depiction of the faltering state of American science, *Worlds Apart* asserted that "less than 9 percent of all basic research is federally funded. Most is financed by universities, whose funding also is declining." However, according to the National Science Foundation, the official fount of research statistics, "The Federal Government provides the majority of funds for basic research"—58 percent of all expenditures for basic research in 1996.[52] And research financed by universities has increased, rather than declined. Between 1987 and 1996, universities, in the aggregate, doubled their own spending on research, from $2.1 billion to $4.1 billion, according to NSF.[53] Proceeding with their portrait of American scientific decline, the *Worlds Apart* authors invoked the authority of a Nobel laureate, Douglas D. Osheroff of Stanford University, who, in 1996, joined five other newly named Nobel recipients in warnings of danger to the nation's scientific strength. Hartz and Chappell quoted Osheroff as saying that "almost all American industry has gotten out of the business of basic research, with, perhaps, the exception of the biological sciences and biotechnology areas." In fact, industry spends substantial sums on basic research suited to its needs: $6.1 billion in 1995, $6.6 billion in 1996, and $7.2 billion in 1997.[54] The "perhaps" is not warranted in citing the biological sciences and biotechnology as exceptions to the alleged paucity of basic research in industry; they rank high, but industry also supports basic research in electronics, materials, chemistry, and other disciplines.

The Money Is There

With a sense of holy mission overriding fealty to facts, the crusaders in behalf of the public understanding of science have blazed a path to the U.S. Treasury, philanthropic strongholds, and scientific associations. Under the headline "Scientists Seek a New Movie Role: Hero Not Villain," a 1998 report in the *New York Times* described some of the efforts:

> The Alfred P. Sloan Foundation has spent $2 million on a program to encourage more thoughtful treatment of science. . . . To influence the next

52. *National Patterns of R&D Resources: 1996* (NSF 96-333), p. 5.
53. *Academic Research and Development Expenditures: Fiscal Year 1996* (NSF 98-304), p. 29.
54. *Industrial Research and Development Facts* (Washington, D.C.: Industrial Research Institute, November 1997).

generation of film makers, the foundation . . . also offers prizes of up to
$25,000 to students at six film schools who make movies about science
or engineering. . . . A group of scientists affiliated with the American Association for the Advancement of Science has been trying to sell the networks on a science drama. And the American Institute of Engineers, a
group that aims to improve the image of its profession, is hoping to interest networks in creating an annual black-tie awards show for technology and a series called "L.A. Engineer."[55]

The *Times* account observed: "More than just a desire to feel appreciated,
however, is behind such efforts. A better image of scientists and engineers
could lead more people into those fields and to greater public support for
projects ranging from space exploration to particle accelerators."

Upon the public's very real educational deficiencies in science, the PUS
promoters have fabricated specters of hostility to science and science under
siege. No matter that—except for occasional turbulence attributable to
general economic conditions—the appropriations record for half a century
shows strength and durability in political support of scientific research. Or
that over many years opinion surveys have consistently found that the
American public is favorably disposed toward, if not enamored of, science
and committed to its support. The evidence of favorable public attitudes
has been compiled within the house of science and is easily and publicly
available. But because it conflicts with the ignorance-hostility construct of
the crusaders for the public understanding of science, it receives relatively
little notice, and often is ignored in favor of frightening tales of danger to
science. On the basis of periodic opinion surveys that it has commissioned
since the 1950s, the National Science Board, the policymaking body of the
National Science Foundation, reports:

> Science and technology have become integral components of the Ameri-
> can culture. Over 85 percent of Americans believe that the world is bet-
> ter off due to science, and this level of general support has continued
> over the last four decades. . . . Nearly 80 percent of Americans agree that
> the Federal Government should support basic scientific research that ad-

---

55. *New York Times*, December 1, 1998. Author's disclosure-reminder: Support for this book
was provided by the Sloan Foundation, which maintained a hands-off stance throughout the process of research, writing, and publication, and showed no interest, if it was
at all aware, in my jaundiced views on promoting the public understanding of science.

vances the frontiers of knowledge even when it does not provide any immediate benefits.[56]

The outbursts against the teaching of evolution in Kansas and a few other states are deplorable, but, in fact, are negligible blips on science education and the great American scientific enterprise. The anti-evolutionists are, however, godsends for the missionaries of the public understanding of science, providing them the pretext for another surge of doom-mongering. Such was the case in 1999 when the Kansas Board of Education undermined the teaching of evolution in the state's public schools by removing the topic from statewide assessment examinations. Deploring the action of the Kansas board, a letter writer in *Nature* magazine stated, "Despite overwhelming acceptance of the material benefits that science has brought, Americans in general remain deeply ignorant of its basic principles. If such ignorance persists, it will prove devastating to the future of our democracy whose citizens will increasingly be called upon to exercise judgment on the complex social issues that advances in science ultimately bring."[57] Following public outcries, the Kansas foray into evolutionary denial was short-lived. In August 2000, three conservative members of the board were defeated in the Republican primary. In February 2001, the newly constituted board essentially restored evolution to the curriculum, though with a pro forma nod of recognition to fundamentalist sensitivities.

A RARE CRITIQUE OF PUS

Few outsiders devote critical attention to the earnest workers in the holy cause of the public understanding of science or the substantial sums they attract in pursuit of the ever-unattainable goal. A sage nonscientist, did, however, on one occasion dissect this matter with an analysis that merits preservation. It was done by Franklin Raines, an attorney, who was then director of the Office of Management and Budget. The setting was a characteristically gloom-filled Washington meeting on science policy, held April 29–30, 1998, by the American Association for the Advancement of Science. In a question period, a member of the audience asked Raines: "How can we get meaningful public input in the absence of, I won't say an informed public . . . but a public which is unable to deal with the information in its

56. *Indicators* 1998, p. 7-4.
57. Paul M. Grant, letter, *Nature*, August 26, 1999.

hands? Is this a problem which can, in fact, be solved?" Addressing the audience, predominantly scientists, Raines replied:

> I daresay, if I went through this audience and quizzed you on the nature of legislating in Washington, D.C., that most of you would come up pretty well short of a fundamental understanding of the process. But I wouldn't blame you for that, because I think you're doing other things. And, by the same token, I don't think you should aspire to the average citizen understanding the fundamentals of the scientific process. Indeed, the last time I was reading science philosophy, there's not that much agreement within the scientific community about the fundamentals of the scientific process, and whether it's the "Eureka!" approach or the culmination of small advances that gets synthesized [in scientific discoveries]. I don't think that's really the issue. The public is never going to understand high-energy physics. And that's okay. There are other people who are supposed to do that. . . . A significant number of people . . . don't know whether the earth revolves around the sun. Twenty-percent don't know who their Congressman is.
>
> I don't stay up late at night saying that's the end of the world. People are spending their lives raising their kids, going to work, and they've got a lot of problems. What we need to be concerned about is what their intermediaries, the people who are acting on their behalf, don't know. So, I'd be more concerned if I were you that the average Congressman doesn't know about the scientific process than I would that their average constituent doesn't know. And by the same token, if I were working on your behalf to increase science funding, I would be concerned that all of you may not know enough about where decisions are made and where they're influenced than I would about other things.[58]

Another audience member pursued the topic: "My intent is not to focus on knowledge of esoteric details of science, but on the fundamental nature of scientific inference [and] understanding that hypotheses must be verifiable; it must be possible to tell when a hypothesis is false. This is what is truly lacking, not only in the general public, but also in a great number of our legislators, as well. And perhaps even in some of the scientific community, who don't know how to deal with that problem."

Raines replied that "that has to be fundamentally dealt with at the elementary and secondary [school] level. If we can do nothing else in teaching

58. Transcribed by author from AAAS tape recording.

science in elementary and secondary, it is to have an understanding of the scientific method." But, he emphasized, "that is not something you're going to deal with through the popular press."

The leaders and the rank and file of science should be embarrassed by many of the antics performed under the banner of promoting the public understanding of science. But, misleadingly depicted as a holy cause linked to the productivity—if not the survival—of science, the promotion of the public understanding of science possesses immunity to sensible assessment from within the scientific community. At times, however, the nonsense factor exceeds toleration by even staunch loyalists of science. Thus, a dissent was presented several years ago by a famously outspoken pillar of the research community, Maxine Singer, president of the Carnegie Institution of Washington and one of the few women members of the National Academy of Sciences (elected for her cancer research at NIH). Speaking in 1996 to the annual Science and Technology Policy Colloquium of the American Association for the Advancement of Science, Singer observed:

> Public information about science is now, to a large extent, in the hands of institutional public-relations departments, the science-policy establishment, that is yourselves [the policy functionaries in the audience], and the media. We need a more direct line. We need to show that we [working scientists] are real, actually quite ordinary people. . . . If we get a direct line, we will probably have to clean up our act. Too often these days, when scientists are given an opportunity to speak about their work, they are more interested in advancing the cause of their next grant, or their company's financial status, than in conveying information to the public. . . . There is too much hype. Every gene that is discovered will lead to a cure for cancer. Maybe, but not for a long time. Even the Superconducting Super Collider was said to have important implications for improving human health.[59]

Even as Singer urged scientists to take back the crusade for the public understanding of science, an eminent colleague labored on that task.

59. Maxine Singer, "In Quotes: Harsh Words on Overselling Science," *SGR*, May 1, 1996.

CHAPTER 14

The TV Solution

I am fully convinced on the basis of my own experience . . . that
science can be understood by non-scientists. Further, there is no
valid reason that concerned researchers should not be capable of
communicating in a way that the non-scientist citizen can
understand.

—Frederick A. King, director,
Yerkes Primate Research Center of Emory University
(in the American Psychological Society *Observer*, March 1993)

LEON M. LEDERMAN, who shared the 1988 No-
bel Prize in physics, had long been concerned with deficiencies in public
understanding of science and the federal government's financial support of
science. The two are connected, he insisted, in harmony with the scientific
community's beliefs and fears of a linkage. As director of the Fermi National
Accelerator Laboratory from 1979 to 1989, Lederman was an inspirational
scientific leader and institution builder, adept in particle physics and in the
politics that provided hundreds of millions of dollars in federal money for
operating the Illinois laboratory and modernizing its equipment. He was
the prime mover of the ill-fated plan to build the colossal Superconducting
Super Collider (SSC), fifty-four miles around, as a successor to Fermi's four-
mile-circumference accelerator, the Tevatron. During Lederman's tenure
at Fermi, and following his retirement from the directorship, he worked
to invigorate science education in the public schools of Illinois. Lederman's educational activities drew wide praise and encouragement to expand his efforts. His concerns about poor public understanding of science,
and the consequences for science, were intensified by Congress's decision
in 1993 to terminate financial support for the SSC. The political ax fell after some $2 billion had been expended on design and construction, leav-
ing many physicists jobless and with an enduring trauma of abandonment
and harsh feelings toward politicians. While some scientists welcomed

the removal of the financially ravenous SSC from the federal science budget, the loss was seen by Lederman and others as another warning sign of public and political ignorance of and hostility to science. Reflecting on the SSC debacle, Lederman expressed concern about "the increasingly alarming antiscience, antirational mood that seems to emanate from so many unexpected sources."[1] Lederman declared that "scientists must rededicate themselves to a massive effort at raising the scientific literacy of the public. Only when citizens have reasonable scientific savvy," he asserted, "will their Congressional servant vote correctly"—meaning in favor of his preferences. Along with many of his colleagues, Lederman believed that the end of the Cold War had reduced political motivations for supporting science and choked off funds for the SSC. For a corrective, he advocated intensified efforts to elevate the public understanding of science.[2]

In accord with his faith in the political value of scientific understanding, Lederman asserted that the cause of science would benefit from a prime-time, major network television science drama series that would be the "*L.A. Law* and *NYPD Blue* of science and scientists." Distinguished colleagues agreed, Lederman was pleased to find, including Harold Varmus, the Nobel laureate director of NIH, and Neal Lane, director of NSF. The strategy, Lederman explained to me, was to "teach science in the course of entertaining"[3]—a dubious method of instruction, given the attentiveness required to master scientific facts and principles and the absence of a study-hall atmosphere in the typical living room or den. Such difficulties, however, have not deterred crusaders for the public understanding of science.[4]

1. Leon Lederman, *Physics Today,* open letter to colleagues who opposed the SSC, March 1994.
2. Lederman's chimerical analysis of the SSC's demise is of Nobel caliber. The legislators who terminated the SSC spared the government from a financial debacle that started with cost estimates of $4 billion and then swiftly ascended to vague estimates of $12 billion or more, garlanded with contrived assurances of foreign cost-sharing that no other country ever promised or delivered. The project arrived in Congress wrapped in wishful thinking, deception, and half-truths. After the realities were exposed, the SSC withered away. That an elevation in public understanding of science might have saved the venture is doubtful. As we shall later observe in detail, the SSC was opposed by many scientific professionals with scientific savvy far exceeding that of the nonscientific citizenry.
3. Telephone conversation with author, June 4, 1996.
4. Perhaps because it is not self-evident, "Science Is Fun" is the motto of a leading science educator, Professor Bassam Shakhashiri, founder of the Institute of Chemistry Education at the University of Wisconsin and head of science and engineering education at the National Science Foundation from 1985 to 1990. In the tradition of Michael Faraday's famous Christmastime science lectures for the public at London's Royal Institution in the nineteenth century, Shakhashiri, in a T-shirt imprinted with the motto, annually presents banging and popping science demonstrations at Christmas holiday season, in Washington and elsewhere. They are well attended by appreciative audi-

PRIME-TIME AMBITIONS, AND MONEY

Lederman's faith, hope, and fears led to the conception of "The Dean," a proposed TV drama about a fictional laboratory director grappling with dilemmas and conflicts that, fortunately, have never afflicted a real-life counterpart. Though no more vapid or banal than customary pop-dramatic fare on TV, "The Dean" miscarried at an early stage of development and never came close to production, to the unalloyed benefit of public regard for science. But before moving on to the plot lines of "The Dean," we will observe a surefooted Leon Lederman on the trail of money to bring "The Dean" into American homes. Though money for research is ceaselessly reported to be scarce, he had no difficulty acquiring the relatively minor sums he sought for elevating the public understanding of science via TV drama.

A friendly, wisecracking guy with an unpretentious manner, Lederman was seasoned in fund-raising and easily navigated his way through grantland. The Nobel halo helped. Kary Mullis, a 1993 Nobel recipient, has observed that "once you have been given that accolade, no door in the world will fail to open for you at least once."[5] The starting point in Lederman's quest was the acquisition of a base camp for seeking money, because the bankrolling foundations, government and private, are wholesalers. Their modus operandi calls for putting their grants into the safekeeping of local organizations—universities, scholarly societies, etc.—which then parcel out the funds to the winning applicants, who need the money to do the work. In this instance, Lederman easily teamed up with the American Association for the Advancement of Science, where he had served as president in 1991 and still retained a connection that he listed on his honor-filled resume as "special assistant to the director." From the AAAS went forth an application in 1994 to the National Science Foundation for $49,500 for a "Planning Grant for a 'Prime-Time' TV Science Drama." The application stated that preliminary discussions had been held with Lawrence Tisch, head of CBS, and Dan Burke, a director and former CEO of ABC. The two TV executives had requested "a full presentation," NSF was informed, and the money was sought to hire a writer to draft a sample script for the show and to cover travel expenses. The sponsorship of the application was lustrous, the purpose accorded with NSF's mandate to spread scientific enlight-

---

ences of children and parents, but the actual contribution to the understanding of science invites skepticism. Slumping enrollments in science courses suggest that, for many students, science is not fun.

5. Kary Mullis, *Dancing Naked in the Mind Field* (New York: Pantheon Books, 1998), p. 211.

enment, and the amount requested was an infinitesimal splinter of NSF's nearly $3 billion budget at that time. NSF bought in. Shortly afterward, the Department of Energy provided a matching sum, which, for administrative simplicity, was routed through NSF to the AAAS, bringing the total of government support to just under $100,000. Another $50,000 was contributed by the Garfield Foundation, of Philadelphia, a philanthropy established by Eugene Garfield, founder of the Institute for Scientific Information (a computerized retrieval system for much of the world's scientific literature).

For managing the government money, the AAAS received a 10 percent share in overhead payments—a modest cut, as such things go in the peculiarities of the grant economy. The AAAS's involvement dovetailed with the organization's traditional goals and ongoing activities. In 1946, when the AAAS was nearing its 100th birthday, it adopted a new constitution, which included a commitment to an "increase in the public understanding and appreciation of the importance and promise of the methods of science in human progress." Throughout the postwar years, the AAAS steadily expanded these activities. In 1998, the AAAS budget totaled $48 million in membership fees, advertising, and other revenues, plus $12 million in grants from outside organizations. From this money, the AAAS spent $1.3 million of its own funds and $2.5 million in grant receipts for its Education and Human Resources Directorate, home base for the association's promotion of the public understanding of science. In addition, $100,000 was allotted for public lectures and displays at the AAAS annual meeting "that promote public understanding of science."[6] An AAAS spokesperson explained that efforts to promote the public understanding of science permeate many other association activities that are not primarily identified with that goal. Lederman's TV project was situated in friendly territory.

Listed on the TV grant application as "principal investigator" was Gerald Wheeler, director of Public Understanding of Science and Technology at the AAAS; Lederman was identified as "co-principal investigator"—investigator being the term that research-supporting agencies customarily apply to all recipients of their money, whether or not they investigate anything.

INTIMATIONS OF COLOSSAL RATINGS

The application to NSF was not modest in its forecasts of the audience for "The Dean." A TV blockbuster was in the making, the Wheeler-Lederman application strongly suggested in an analysis of the market:

6. Memo to author from AAAS News and Information Office, April 2, 1999.

The proliferation of cable channels has meant that more specialized audiences have become the rule, not the exception. As a result, the traditional networks are in the process of redefining the nature of their programming and their audience. CBS, in particular, has decided to aim its forthcoming programming at an older audience with a higher income. The same may be said of HBO. They are after an audience that watches NFL football and *Masterpiece Theater*. This is precisely the type of audience that will find 'The Dean' appealing.[7]

The stewards of the public's money at the National Science Foundation did not gag on the assertion that the Wheeler-Lederman science drama would attract an audience previously unknown in television, and never yet found: a hybrid mass drawn from viewers of major league football and public television's imports of medium-brow costume dramas. But lest they conclude that the proposed TV series was aimed only at football fans and the staid PBS audience, already served by *Nova* and various odds and ends of so-called science programming, the application asserted that the anticipated audience was even greater: it also encompassed "the 30+ million viewers captive to the sitcom-dominated prime time offerings. There is little question that this audience is 'underserved' in the learning aspect of how science is done," the application added. "The Dean" was thus presented to NSF as a magnet for an audience of unprecedented size and composition, one that had eluded the strategists of commercial television, increasingly desperate though they were to retain, let alone build, their fragmenting and dwindling audiences. Hinting at an eventual bidding war for a hot TV property, the application optimistically asserted, "Which one of the three major networks, CBS, ABC, or NBC will be the partner will be determined at the end of this planning grant."

With nearly $150,000 behind the project, preparation of a script was undertaken by Adrian Malone, producer of several successful TV science programs, including the *Ascent of Man* and *Cosmos*. Lederman and Wheeler provided assistance on a pro bono basis. Luster was added to the project with the appointment of an advisory committee that included Michael Bishop, a Nobel laureate at the University of California, San Francisco; Linda Wilson, president of Radcliffe College; several other senior academics; and a few TV professionals. Advisory committees are standard fixtures in the science business. They can be useful founts of assistance, but even

---

7. AAAS grant application to NSF for "The Dean."

if their advice is not heeded, or even sought (which it need not be), the right names add plausibility and political heft to a project.

Enter "The Dean"

From this mobilization of scholarly and broadcasting talent came a script outline for "The Dean," a TV drama in which the central figure, John Kyrian, is described as "a charismatic powerhouse of Persian-American extraction."[8] Among other attributes, he is "built like a barrel—short, powerful, explosive, scheming and infinitely compassionate." The script states that Dean Kyrian's "grandparents were rug merchants," without explaining the relevance of this vocational ancestry, with its pejorative overtones of unsavory business practices. Kyrian is employed as head of the GRALE Institute—acronym for General Research at the Leading Edge—described as "a new and extremely powerful research venue that combines the scientific and engineering creativity of a Bell Laboratories with the pedagogical passion of an MIT." The GRALE Institute is financed by "a clique of the most powerful corporate moguls in the nation—known as the Gates Group." The Gates in this instance is not Microsoft billionaire Bill, but Adrian Gates, "a black man of about 40" who is "one of the wealthiest and most influential men in the world." For Gates and his colleagues, the script explains, GRALE "will be an engine of discoveries, inventions and minds that can change the world and in the process reveal the beauty and order of the emerging world view. The initiative to create GRALE is anchored in the Gates Group's conviction that America's strength, as well as corporate profits, depends critically on the creativity of its scientists and that it is from well nurtured interdisciplinary teams that creativity soars to unexpected heights."

The Dean and His Agenda

Kyrian's past, the script outline continues, includes "a woman who haunts him," as well as a legacy "of faith turned to dogma, of love turned to hate, and of a Holy War." Bearing that emotional weight, the Dean confronts a crowded, hair-raising agenda at work. "Each week," the outline states, "he must wrestle with issues that range from the social implications of new types of genetic engineering research to the unexpected double-edged megapower of information technologies to the intrigue of securing

8. Details of the script outline are from a copy filed with the National Science Foundation and provided to me by NSF, along with other materials related to the TV project.

top secret military contracts." The Dean is depicted as a match for his daunting tasks: "He can feel comfortable at a luncheon of english [sic] professors, and yet also trade ideas about new DNA sampling techniques in a back stairwell." The Dean's versatility, the script explains, "will be symbolized by the desk in his office—twenty feet long and four feet wide, it is covered with up to 40 files, neatly arranged. The Dean spends half an hour each day circling his desk, thinking about each issue, and how they relate to each other." One of these issues concerns a GRALE researcher whose "self-experimentation into his own sleeping brain . . . has landed him on a slippery slope toward madness and suicide." In another episode, Dean Kyrian and his colleagues confront the possibility that "scientists working in a little corner of a place like the GRALE Institute could realize a set of circumstances in which they would literally create another universe . . . or . . . [original ellipsis] seed the destruction of this one." After grappling with the choices, Dean Kyrian asks, "Do we buy a ticket?"

The scientific staff at the GRALE Institute includes the "statuesque and graceful" Melissa Gebbe, who "can virtually singlehandedly design and build a massive accelerator"—a talent lacking in the real-life drama of the ill-fated Superconducting Super Collider, for which the design and construction workforce numbered thousands. Another member of the GRALE staff is described as "a haughty Brit" who "dresses with nauseating precision" and "professes to care about the world, but abuses those closest to him." Also employed at GRALE is Emily Grimble, "a matriarch of science," who belatedly receives the Nobel Prize for research "previously glossed over by a generation of predominantly male scientists." Grimble "speaks simply and with the natural poetry of her Highland Scottish roots."

Another member of the GRALE staff is Andrus Potemkin, formerly "a top-notch Russian physicist," whose "passion is to put matter together in ways never before achieved to see what new behavior matter is capable of." Potemkin also takes things apart, the script writers add, noting that "His fascination in the stuff of the world is reflected in his habit of crushing objects in his bear-like hands." Described as "sexist in both mind and action," he is a "man of appetite and heart. In another time, he would have led a Cossack charge." Potemkin's daughter, Misha, "an easy-going, quick-witted woman of about 20," is "a hardworking apprentice of Dr. Melissa Gebbe." Misha is notable for "her habit of asking the most simple and powerful questions about the world, questions that catalyze others to rethink long-held beliefs. Misha's questions are as simple as any child's and as profound as any philosopher's."

"Also central to the show," the TV outline stated, "is the department known as Cy-Phi, short for cypher-cyber-philosophy":

> It is a place with information and computational technology beyond the Pentagon. It is a realization of the extreme visions of the information revolution. The department is headed by Thadeus Polk, known as "the Colonel," a no-nonsense pragmatist who used to run the nation's war gaming and simulation program. Underneath him is a group of young can-do cybernauts who can come through on faculty members' wildest requests for data (such as the entire DNA code for a human being), simulations (such as the ability to feel the surfaces of molecules with your fingers), and projections of what specific discoveries or breakthroughs (such as the ability to extend the average human lifetime by 10 or 20 years) might mean for individuals, corporations, ecosystems and the globe.

The authors of this government-financed effort to improve the public understanding of science described the underlying strategy of their assemblage of characters and plots as follows:

> A prime motivation for the show—designed to have the highest level of dramatic appeal—is to share some real science with the audience. We would like to communicate such scientific qualities as skepticism, curiosity and passion. We want to portray science as a body of knowledge, always tentative at the edges, and scientists as a group which spans the range of human strengths and weaknesses. Our science will push the envelope, but it will always be possible, often plausible. We believe these qualities can be conveyed without compromising the entertainment; on the contrary, we believe the gentle learning component will generate an enthusiastic and loyal audience.

ASSESSMENT OF THE ADVISERS

Asked for its opinions of the script, the advisory committee that Lederman and colleagues had brought into the TV project offered responses that diplomatically commenced with expressions of warm approval but concluded with blunt expressions of disapproval and puzzlement. Linda Wilson, president of Radcliffe College, wrote to Lederman, "This is an engrossing set of stories," adding, "I think it could be quite appealing visually.

It would be exciting entertainment and, in my view, would compete well with *NYPD* and *ER*. One of its advantages over *ER*," Wilson continued, "might be that it would be engrossing but not involve such rapid changes of scene." Even so, the Radcliffe president said, "I don't think it would be as good as *Masterpiece Theatre*, but I think it would be much better than most of what is on television now." However, while recognizing audience appeal in the "cataclysmic nature" of the plot line, Wilson cautioned that "I do worry that if it doesn't get tamed fairly soon, the 'Frankenstein' character of the scientific content could begin to do more harm than good for science and scientists."

Walter Massey, a former NSF director who was president of Morehouse College, a predominantly black institution, described the TV outline as "marvelous." He added, however, "I watch very little television. I have never seen *ER, Chicago HOPE,* or any of the other programs on which this is modeled." Massey interspersed praise with reservations: "The idea of having Mr. Gates being black is imaginative, and I like it very much, but I notice there are no black scientists among the very brilliant group who are central to the innovative, intellectual guts of the program. The characters reinforce the image (true or not) that everyone involved in scientific careers is brilliant beyond the pale of most ordinary people. I had thought that one of the messages we wanted to convey is that science is a welcoming community where the major breakthroughs require an extraordinary brilliance and commitment, but that there is room for people of above-average intelligence and commitment who are not necessarily in the genius category."[9]

In her comments on the script, Alice S. Huang, the dean for science at New York University, also commenced with praise, describing the plot lines as "very gripping," "wonderful reading," and "imaginative." "However, I have some reservations," she explained. While the personal relations among the GRALE scientists "can be totally fabricated," Huang wrote, "the science has to remain believable and solid." She went on to assert that in the script, the science was neither, pointing out that the plot's claimed "ability to feel the surface of molecules with your fingers" was far-fetched. Huang also noted that "in presenting the scientist, it is important to underplay the destructive, evil role that scientists can play. Could the Colonel be

9. Massey thus echoed the nonelitist sentiments expressed in 1970 by the late Senator Roman L. Hruska, (R-Nebraska). In defending a Supreme Court nominee who was described as "mediocre," Hruska argued that "there are a lot of mediocre judges and people and lawyers. They are entitled to a little representation, aren't they, and a little chance? We can't have all Brandeises, Frankfurters and Cardozos."

less militaristic?" she inquired, referring to the head of the Cy-Phi department. Huang concluded, "science is very international and I like all the different Brits and Americans, but if you walk into any university these days there are many Orientals. Will they be in the background?"

The GRALE script was rated "fantastic" by Warren M. Washington, an administrator at the National Center for Atmospheric Research. But he relayed to Lederman a note of concern from a senior scientist whose opinion merited attention. In a conversation with Neal Lane, director of the National Science Foundation, Washington wrote, "I brought up the prime time project. His only concern was the portrayal of scientists as real people may tarnish our image with the public. I disagreed in that scientists will probably be shown in mostly a positive light, however, there will be some 'bad guys,' too."

The script was delivered to several senior TV executives, who warmly thanked Dr. Lederman. Though it was no more inane than many TV-drama successes, the story of the GRALE Institute and its extraordinary staff and their trailblazing research was never deployed in the cause of improving the public understanding of science. Lederman told me that after the scripts were delivered, the network executives indicated no further interest in his project to use televised drama to elevate the public understanding of science. Fortunately so, for science and the public.

Though frustrated in reaching the masses, and aloof from elective politics, the scientific enterprise is nonetheless widely believed to possess backdoor access to political power and influence because of its knowledge and skills. We will now examine the long-ago origins of that persistent but misleading belief.

CHAPTER 15

Science and the Illusion
of Political Power

Scientists have hardly yet begun to realize that they hold in their
own hands a great deal of power that they have hardly used. The
ranks of senior scientists and key administrators of science have now
swelled to the point where I think it will not be long before some of
the good ones begin to enter politics rather more forcibly.
                    —Derek J. de Solla Price, *Little Science, Big Science* (1963)

VOGUISH THEORIES about scientists and politi-
cal power flourished after World War II, sowing misperceptions that have
long survived. Today, scientists possess no power beyond the confines of
science, and only limited or no power over scientific matters where their
preferences conflict with "real" politics. It will be useful, first, to trace and
understand the belief that scientists possess political power, supposedly a
special kind obtained through a monopoly of knowledge that makes them
indispensable to our scientifically untutored political leaders.

THE NEWCOMERS IN WASHINGTON

A few years after World War II, the place of scientists in politics
and governance became the object of contentious scholarly and political
interest. The attention arose from the wartime accomplishments of science
and technology and the directly ensuing involvement of previously cloistered academics in nuclear policy, including military and diplomatic issues
in dealings with the Soviet Union. President Truman appointed J. Robert
Oppenheimer, the scientific impresario of the wartime bomb project, to
chair what was then the most influential assemblage of scientists in Washington, the General Advisory Committee (GAC) of the newly established
Atomic Energy Commission. Like many other high-level scientists, then
and today, Oppenheimer held his important government post while also

fully employed elsewhere, in his case as director of the Institute for Advanced Study at Princeton. The committee, as its title indicated, was advisory. Decision-making authority ultimately belonged to the president. But at the beginning of the nuclear age, the workings and creations of science were indeed a mystery to politics; as experienced guides in strange territory, scientists commanded attention and possessed the authority of success.[1]

Fundamental issues of nuclear policy came before the GAC, including whether to divert resources from continued production of the fission bombs of World War II to development of the far more powerful hydrogen bomb. The technical issues became bundled with judgmental matters of conciliation and cooperation versus superior armaments in dealing with the Soviet Union. Also on the AEC committee were other distinguished wartime researchers, including I. I. Rabi, of Columbia University; Enrico Fermi, of the University of Chicago; and Lee A. DuBridge, president of the California Institute of Technology. With others, they linked academic science to the highest levels of government, sectors of society that rarely touched during all of the nation's history prior to World War II. Trust between the senior science advisers and their government was severely strained by the horrific charges of security violations against Oppenheimer in 1953. However, locked in their relationship by mutual need, the joined sectors of science and government survived that trauma and the onslaughts of the House Un-American Activities Committee and Senator Joseph McCarthy, though in battered condition. After a faulty start under an indifferent Truman, Rabi, DuBridge and James Killian, of MIT, inaugurated modern presidential science advice during the Eisenhower administration, laying the foundation for what bumpily evolved into the White House Office of Science and Technology Policy, headed by a presidential assistant for science and technology. Scientists were clearly established in the vicinity of political power. Politically and journalistically, they became interesting, drawing attention and spawning expansive theories of a new kind of power on the Washington scene.

---

1. Even twenty-five years into the nuclear age, President Richard Nixon cringed publicly before the mysteries of science. Nixon, in awarding medals to a group of scientists in 1971, humbly said of the accompanying citations: "I have read them and I want you to know that I do not understand them, but I want you to know, too, that because I do not understand them, I realize how enormously important their contributions are to this nation. That, to me, is the nature of science to the unsophisticated people." Quoted in Daniel S. Greenberg, "David and Indifference," *Saturday Review of Science*, September 30, 1972. A similar presidential confession regarding economics, foreign affairs, military strategy, or even child-raising would be unthinkable.

INSIDERS AND OUTSIDERS

In the early postwar years, the wartime scientific leaders instantly became Washington insiders. Other scientists sought to affect policy from the outside, thus adding bulk and visibility, if not influence, to the scientific presence in Washington. Leo Szilard, the refugee Hungarian physicist who helped enlist Albert Einstein to alert President Roosevelt to the potential of building the atom bomb, petitioned Truman against use of the bomb and then single-mindedly devoted himself to a lonely, futile campaign for international control of nuclear weapons and disarmament.[2]

The scientific insiders traveled a unique path to assigned places of influence. Unlike other sectors of society that occupied seats at the council tables—labor, agriculture, industry, and so on—science arrived by invitation rather than by the exercise of political muscle. The invitations arose from the politicians' realization that they didn't understand the military wonders that science had wrought, and they needed help—more and more help as the Cold War deepened and the United States became involved in the Korean War.

THE FUTURE IN THEIR BONES?

The presence of the scientific insiders evoked hopes, fears, and provocative, flamboyant commentary. Looking back on the debate over his "Two Cultures" lecture, C. P. Snow declared that scientists "have the future in their bones" and, citing this alleged attribute, argued that politics and society in general had not gone far enough in admitting scientists to the high councils. "It is the traditional culture, to an extent remarkably little diminished by the emergence of the scientific one, which manages the western world," Snow concluded unhappily.[3] However, President Dwight Eisenhower declared an opposite concern about the role of scientists in

---

2. Szilard's plight as a freelance thinker and policy proponent is poignantly described by his biographer, William Lanouette, who observes that, by the early 1960s, "Szilard had begun to realize his limits as a humorist and 'outsider' in Washington—a serious and self-important city that squanders laughter and lives by cliques. . . . He was still a professor of biophysics from the University of Chicago. Not a consultant to the Arms Control and Disarmament Agency (ACDA). Not a member of the President's Science Advisory Committee (PSAC). Not a fellow at a local think tank or a consultant to a congressional committee. As he discovered during his first months in the capital, Washington is a city where what you do is often less important than where you do it." William Lanouette, with Bela Szilard, *Genius in the Shadows: A Biography of Leo Szilard, the Man Behind the Bomb* (Charles Scribner's Sons, 1992), pp. 446, 448.
3. C. P. Snow, *The Two Cultures and a Second Look* (New York: Mentor Books, 1964), p. 17.

Cold War America. In January 1961, in a presidential valedictory that became memorable because of his admonition against the "military-industrial complex," Eisenhower also expressed another caution, one that surprised and dismayed his devoted circle of science advisers: "Yet, in holding scientific research and discovery in respect, as we should," the departing president warned, "we must also be alert to the equal and opposite danger that public policy could itself become the captive of a scientific-technological elite."[4]

In 1965, Eisenhower's warning was echoed by Don K. Price of Harvard, the dean of science-policy scholars, formerly a science specialist at the federal Bureau of the Budget, where he helped draft legislation creating the Atomic Energy Commission and the National Science Foundation. From his unusual experience as a Washington science-policy insider and academic observer of science politics, Price stated that "we can no longer take it for granted that scientists will be 'on tap but not on top.'"[5] Moreover, Price wrote, "The fear that the new powers created by science may be beyond the control of constitutional processes, and that scientists may become a new governing clique of secret advisers, has begun to seem plausible."[6] Extravagant assessments and boundless forecasts of the political influence of scientists were common in that period, based on the belief that arcane scientific knowledge would inevitably transmute into political power. In "The Rise of an Apolitical Elite," an article published in 1964, Robert C. Wood, professor of political science at MIT, wrote that "the late 1950s marked the emergence of American scientists as genuine political influentials." The scientist, he glowingly asserted:

> is a good deal more than another expert performing tricks of virtuosity
> at the command of politicians, bureaucrats, or soldiers. He is instead a
> member of a still small and untutored elite which has entered an inhos-

4. Eisenhower's remark, overshadowed by the accompanying and widely quoted caution against the "military-industrial complex," was directed at "the rising power of military science," according to an account of a conversation with the president by his special assistant for science and technology, George B. Kistiakowsky. George B. Kistiakowsky, *A Scientist at the White House: The Private Diary of President Eisenhower's Special Assistant for Science and Technology* (Harvard University Press, 1976) p. 425.

5. Don K. Price, *The Scientific Estate* (Cambridge: The Belknap Press of Harvard University Press, 1965), p. 19.

6. Ibid., p. 57. Price proceeded to downgrade that fear as less than plausible, arguing that "without legal power in their own right, and no assignments except those that the President wishes to give them, this danger that professional experts will exceed their staff roles, and take over decisions that ought to be judged in the light of more general political considerations, is minimized" (p. 255).

pitable political system but which possesses such valuable assets that it bids fair to displace entrenched skill groups in certain parts of the system and to establish an over-all new equilibrium in the competition for power among the professions.[7]

The awe in academe was repackaged in mass-market publications. *The Scientist,* a Life Science Library book published in 1964 by Time, stated:

> Never has society lionized a more creative, or more unpredictable, breed of hero. Intellectually, the scientist is likely to have more in common with the philosopher or the scholar than with the traditional man of action. But the overwhelming triumph of technology has drawn him increasingly into board meetings and councils of state. It is a reasonable assumption that in the decades ahead he will come to wield more power than any elite class has ever done in the past—more than the feudal lords of the Middle Ages, the merchant princes of the Renaissance or the tycoons of the Industrial Revolution.[8]

While those awestruck sentiments continued to circulate, in academic circles and in the popular realm, scientific influence in national affairs, particularly in defense policy, began an irreversible decline. The turning point may have been a little-remembered clash during the Vietnam War between civilian scientists and the military over the so-called McNamara Line, a 1966 proposal backed by Defense Secretary Robert S. McNamara to seal South Vietnam's borders against northern invaders with a high-tech barrier of minefields and sensors backed by heavy firepower. Originally titled "An Air Supported Anti-Infiltration Barrier," the scheme enlisted the services of some of the leading alumni of the World War II science effort, including George B. Kistiakowsky, Jerome Wiesner, and J. R. Zacharias, of Harvard. Though partially completed and eventually put into operation at a total cost of over $3 billion, the project received only lukewarm cooperation from the air force and army, which derided the concept as a reversion to Maginot Line thinking.

Disillusioned with the spreading war, Kistiakowsky publicly resigned from the project's advisory group in 1968, followed by resignations of many

---

7. Robert C. Wood, "The Rise of an Apolitical Elite," in *Scientists and National Policy Making,* ed. Robert Gilpin and Christopher Wright (New York: Columbia University Press, 1964), pp. 41 and 44.

8. *The Scientist,* Life Science Library (New York: Time, Inc., 1964), p. 36.

other members. The military chieftains, resentful of the civilians' persistent badgering for arms control, did not rue their departure. "By the late 1960s," according to a perceptive analysis, "the military could increasingly draw upon technical expertise from within, making the potential scientific contribution [of the part-time academic advisers] much less valuable. . . . With less need for outside scientific advice . . . the military today remains content to chart its own path in this area. The McNamara Line was in many ways the last, and the greatest, attempt by civilian scientist advisors to play such a direct role in defense policymaking."[9]

A few years later, as we have seen, President Richard Nixon, bitterly believing that his science advisers were disloyal to him and his administration, swept science out of the White House, asserting that their onboard services were not needed. Thus, at the central juncture of science and politics, politics asserted its primacy. When science advisers were restored to the White House three years later, they performed as politically tame servants of politics, and continue to do so to this day. Never again would science be perceived, as it was in Nixon's time, as running "a renegade operation in the White House"—science adviser Edward E. David's description of how the scientists were viewed by Nixon and his crew. At lower levels, too, the Washington scientists observed political discipline. Advocacy of money for science was expected and acceptable, if not too brashly done or in violation of White House designs to restrain spending.[10]

However, expansionism beyond the boundaries of science was not permissible, unless sanctioned by the political chieftains. In describing their roles at the center of political power, the post-Nixon presidential science advisers emphasized that they were not emissaries from science to politics, that they were not posted to the White House to channel money to science or to expand the political influence of the scientific community. Rather, they worked only for the president, serving his needs, not those of their scientific colleagues. A rogue operation by the president's servants of science was unthinkable, the stuff of science fiction. In the shorthand terminology of the scholars of science and government, the scientists summoned to service in Washington were granted wide latitude in setting "policy for science," and far less in employing "science for policy."

9. Christopher P. Twomey, "The Vietnam War and the End to Civilian Scientist Advisors in Defense Policy," *Breakthroughs*, spring 2000, published by the Securities Studies Program, MIT; a longer version also appeared in *Minerva*, autumn 1999.

10. Biomedical research was, and remains, the exception, as noted in chapter 11, footnote 22.

Out of Politics

After the blow that Nixon inflicted on science politics by abolishing the White House science office, the arguments, uncertainties, and misunderstandings about the political roles and potency of scientists faded away, though vestiges survive in scholarly circles.[11] The lockstep discipline, loyalty, and subordination of presidential scientists in the service of politics has become so familiar, and seems so natural, that it is not widely appreciated, despite its contrast with Snow's prescription for science power in the throne room and Eisenhower's fears of scientific usurpation of political authority.

The syndrome of science as servant extends beyond the special circumstances of advisory duty in the White House. At the dawn of the new millennium, scientists show remarkably little disposition toward participation in politics, individually or organizationally, covertly or otherwise. Except for a small scattering of individuals, today's scientists are absent from politics and public affairs, both elective and behind-the-scenes. The long-feared political imperialism of science has never mobilized, let alone gone on the march. Minor forays occur, such as science's long-running and sometimes unintentionally comic quest for influence in the State Department, to be explored later. In appointive posts, however, scientists perform as discreet servants of politics. In elective politics, they participate as individual voters, shunning organized efforts under the banner of science. As previously described here, unlike other professional organizations—those of physicians, lawyers, and teachers, for example—the scientists' professional societies and associations deliberately abstain from rounding up votes or pumping money into politics. Other professions raise campaign money for their political friends or smooth the political waters by donating to both sides, using political action committees or other devices prescribed by law. But not the scientists.

In exercising their appointive powers, politicians generally confine scientists to a narrow band of offices. Politics feels no impulse, necessity, or effective pressure to grant scientists anything beyond limited influence at the seats of power. This grant of influence is mainly confined to keeping

11. Analyses of their role in politics tend to fall into two camps, one contending that they possess excessive power, the other that they are mere pawns in the service of increasingly undemocratic politics. The former approach is evident in Frank Fisher's *Technology and the Politics of Expertise* (Newbury Park, Calif.: Sage Publications, 1990); the latter in Chandra Mukerji's *A Fragile Power: Scientists and the State* (Princeton: Princeton University Press, 1989).

the scientific enterprise expertly staffed and smoothly functioning in tempo with political requirements. The scientists to whom these responsibilities are delegated are not welcome to range beyond the institutional boundaries of science and technology. In rare instances, scientists are appointed to head major government organizations that are not predominantly concerned with science and technology. William Perry, a Ph.D. mathematician and former professor of engineering at Stanford University, served as secretary of defense in the Clinton administration; chemist John Deutch, of MIT, headed the Central Intelligence Agency for a brief spell under Clinton. John H. Sununu, a Ph.D. engineer and former university professor, served as governor of New Hampshire for six years and then as White House chief of staff for the elder George Bush. But they were unusual in the general run of government leadership. Perhaps just as often, appointees without scientific or technical backgrounds are named to head highly technical agencies of government. James Webb, a lawyer seasoned in government administration and international affairs, headed NASA from 1961 to 1968, the buildup to the moon landing, when the politics of space were as challenging as the technology of space. The two secretaries of energy appointed by President Clinton, Hazel R. O'Leary and Bill Richardson, did not come out of science or technology. Allowing for infrequent exceptions, scientists are not on top; they have never been there, nor, in retrospect, was there ever a realistic prospect of an ascent to power. Even the invited "on tap" role, as high-level advisers, has diminished to the point where some scientific leaders, asserting that their professional skills are needed by but ignored by politics, complain of exclusion from influential places. However, apart from such occasional expressions of distress, the politicians of science remain preoccupied with matters distant from the reins of power, with the exceptions of obtaining abundant money for science and wide latitude in its use. Strangely enough, scientists possess little power, or even presence, in the governing councils of a society that is increasingly based and dependent upon their works. Irresponsible private control and manipulation of those works for financial profit is the worrisome development at the interface of science and society in the new millennium.

Fear not for behind-the-scenes manipulation of politics by scheming scientists. They're not there. The extreme rarity of scientists in elective office is a durable and little-noted phenomenon of politics. Proceeding with our explorations of the politics of science, we will examine a few rare specimens of scientists in political office, and look at the reasons why there aren't more.

CHAPTER 16

The Political Few

> Would it not be refreshing to see a scientist take his or her place in a
> governor's office (after all, a wrestler did it) or have more scientists
> on the floor of the House or the Senate?
>
> —M.R.C. Greenwood, presidential address to the American
> Association for the Advancement of Science (January 1999)

A SEARCH for scientists in ballot-box politics, as candidates or as supporters of office-seeking friends of science, returns sparse results—so sparse as to invite wonder, given the high educational levels of scientists and their profession's dependence on political support. In special circumstances, a few exceptions have occurred since the one-time political engagement of science in national politics in 1964. But their rarity suggests an incompatibility between the profession of science and the practice of politics, an immunological resistance to politics in the body scientific.

THE POLITICAL PLIGHT OF "MR. SCIENCE"

One of these exceptions took place in 1992, when an especially difficult reelection contest confronted Representative George E. Brown Jr., a research enthusiast who chaired the House Science, Technology, and Space Committee. From his personal interest in science, Brown filled a role which few others aspired to on Capitol Hill, earning him the honorific "Mr. Science" and numerous awards from scientific organizations for his devoted labors in behalf of science during thirty-six years in the House. Brown's service, however, was not routinely reciprocated by its beneficiaries in the scientific community. He often joshed that a continuous procession of scientists brought their political problems to him, but few ever showed a helpful interest in the first concern of an elected official: reelection. Brown regularly appealed to a list of scientists for campaign money, with some success. But, by and large, science remained passively on the sidelines while its honored congressional benefactor struggled for political survival. Brown, a promoter of civil rights and unflinching liberal from the start of his political career, lived a precarious political existence in a Southern California district heavy with military retirees, religious fundamentalists, and conservative businesspeople. Just prior to his death in 1999, when he was bound for his nineteenth House election campaign, the *Almanac of American Politics* observed, "Few members in modern history have held onto competitive districts with as many tough races as Brown."[1] He regularly won reelection, but sometimes just barely.

Brown was especially worried about the 1992 election. Redistricting, on the basis of the 1990 census, had cost him some of his longtime supporters, and Brown, then seventy-two, faced a young opponent with good public recognition, Dick Rutan, copilot of the 1986 nonstop round-the-world *Voyager* flight. Responding to that threatening circumstance, Nobel laureate Leon Lederman and some thirty other scientists hurriedly organized "Friends of George Brown," contributing $40,000 to his campaign fund. "The fact that so many of our nation's best and brightest scientists want George Brown reelected," Lederman stated, "is a testament to Chairman Brown's stature within the scientific community." Lederman's support may also have been a personal testament to his concern for the congressional fate of his brainchild, the Superconducting Super Collider, which was partially under the jurisdiction of Brown's House committee. The SSC was the object of a freewheeling inquiry by the committee's investigations and oversight subcommittee, chaired by Representative Howard Wolpe, who, a few months earlier, had battered the National Science Foundation for its alarmist "shortfall" reports on the supply of scientific manpower. Under inquiries by Wolpe and others in Congress, political support for the SSC was crumbling. In any case, the $40,000 in campaign money from Lederman and his colleagues was welcome, though it was a sliver of the $907,227 spent by Brown to keep his seat. Brown won by a comfortable 79,780 to 69,251, but in prior elections, and later, too, he had close calls. Scientists again came to his aid in the 1994 election, which Brown won by 2,629 votes out of a total of 115,147 ballots cast. But that was the end of organized efforts by scientists in behalf of "Mr. Science" (though, on an individual basis, a handful continued to contribute to his reelection campaigns). The political difficulties that afflicted Brown, and science, intensified after 1994, but without a revival of the Friends of George Brown. In 1996, Brown's winning margin fell to a mere 996 votes; in 1998, against a weak candidate,

1. *Almanac of American Politics 2000* (Washington, D.C., 1999), p. 287.

he won by a hefty 16,000 votes. Brown was bound for another reelection run in 2000, but following heart surgery, he died on July 16, 1999, at age 79, in his eighteenth term in the House.

On September 27, 1999, some 250 chieftains and foot soldiers of national science politics gathered in the auditorium of the American Association for the Advancement of Science for an affectionate memorial service for Brown titled "Remembering Mr. Science: A Tribute to George E. Brown Jr., from the Science and Engineering Community." The sentiment was strong and genuine, but most striking was the political myopia of the mourners for their departed congressional benefactor. Speaking for the host organization, Albert Teich, head of the AAAS Directorate for Science and Policy Programs, hailed Brown for his "enormous influence" on science and technology policy, and declared his loss a grievous one for science and the nation. Lachrymose tributes in a similar style followed: "The nation has lost one of its most important statesmen for science and civil rights," declared Neal Lane, President Clinton's assistant for science and technology. "He was a giant of a man," Lane said. Bruce Alberts, president of the National Academy of Sciences, said, "George became our conscience"—a reference to Brown's persistent badgering for science to be attentive to its social and economic consequences. Representative Rush Holt (D-N.J.), one of the very few scientists in Congress, described Brown as "a wise and sagacious man," adding, "No one had a better understanding of the role and promise of science." Congressman Holt pointed out that throughout Brown's long congressional career, he faced uphill battles to retain his seat. That was the only reference to the difficult political underpinnings of the late George Brown's many years of good works in behalf of science—and it came from a fellow congressman.

My search of Federal Election Commission (FEC) listings of individual campaign contributions to Representative George Brown in 1997 and 1998 failed to show the name of any of the bereaved speakers at his memorial service. A few recognizable names from the scientific community were listed among the 316 entries for personal contributions above $200 up to the legal maximum of $1,000, and undoubtedly there were unrecognized others, too. Contributions to Brown might also have been made in some fashion, perhaps by a spouse, that wouldn't reflect a scientific connection. But if the political career of Mr. Science had depended on financial assistance from the scientists who revered him, it would have been an abbreviated one. George Brown did a great deal for science, but science—typical of its aloofness from the monetary essence of politics—did very little for George Brown. FEC data for the 1998 campaign show $174,000 contributed to

Brown by business organizations and $210,000 by labor organizations. Through political action committees or individual contributions, thirty-two major organizations were identified by the FEC as "Top Contributors" to Brown's campaign. Among them were the American Federation of Teachers, Planned Parenthood, Lockheed Martin, the Teamsters Union, the Association of Trial Lawyers of America, and the American Nurses Association. No science organization was on the list.

RATING THE CONGRESS

At the presidential-campaign level, the scientist descendants of the activist efforts of the 1964 Scientists and Engineers for Johnson-Humphrey continued to limit themselves to letterhead efforts and other minimal political involvements, if any at all. In the 1996 congressional elections, the first after Gingrich and company took control of Congress, a group of scientists perpetrated a wondrously bumbling attempt to identify the friends of science in the House—and, by implication, thereby discern and target the unfriendly officials. The effort can be traced to the Council of Scientific Society Presidents, a Washington-based association of heads of some thirty scientific and professional organizations, who periodically assembled to discuss policy topics. The council, like many such bodies, was generally satisfied to talk to itself. But now it sought to reach out into politics.

In compliance with restrictions on political activities by nonprofit organizations, council members created a political offshoot, Science Watch, Inc., which produced a "Science ScoreBoard" [sic] that purported to rate House members for their support of science in the 104th Congress. Just as performance statistics permeate sports, congressional vote counts are part of politics, regularly tallied by interest groups on sliding scales based on ideology and particular issues. The founding members of Science Watch were a distinguished cross section of seasoned science politicians, starting with its chair, Roland Schmitt, president-elect of the Council of Scientific Society Presidents, former senior vice president and chief scientist of General Electric, former president of Rensselaer Polytechnic Institute, and member of the National Science Board from 1982 to 1994, a stretch that included six years as chair of the board. Serving as CEO of Science Watch was Martin Apple, executive officer of the Council of Scientific Societies and hands-on manager of the Science Watch enterprise.[2]

2. Among other founding members of Science Watch were D. Allan Bromley, White House science adviser in the Bush administration; Erich Bloch, former NSF director; James Duderstadt, a former chair of the National Science Board; Maxine Singer, presi-

The Science ScoreBoard of House members' support of science was released by Science Watch on September 18, 1996, in ample time for circulat-
ing the ratings prior to election day, November 3. On the basis of thirty
items that had come to a vote in the preceding eighteen months, the Score-
Board concluded that "Democrats in the House (at 72 percent average) supported science on these indicator votes about twice as frequently as the Republicans (35 percent average)." Inexplicably low on the list of supporters
was the widely worshipped, cash-producing champion of medical research,
the chair of the House Appropriations subcommittee for NIH, Representative John Porter (R-Ill.), a proponent of doubling the NIH budget in five
years. By the ScoreBoard's tally, Porter's pro-science score was only 33 percent in 1995 and 45 percent in 1996. Representative George Brown, who
surrendered the chair of the Science Committee when the Republicans took
control of Congress in 1995, was rated 89 and 100 percent for the two years
of voting. His successor as chair, Representative Robert Walker, came in low,
at 37 and 45 percent in votes rated favorable to science. The unavoidable
inference, that Democrats were better friends of science than Republicans,
induced an antipolitics warning reminiscent of the morning-after misgivings of the 1964 scientists' campaign against Barry Goldwater. It came from
Cornelius J. Pings, the president of the Association of American Universities, the Washington-based voice of big-league academic research. Pings
warned that the ScoreBoard's rating of congressional representatives "is a
serious mistake and may anger friends in Congress who have been among
the best friends of scientific research." Science Committee Chair Walker,
who counted himself among those best friends, condemned the ScoreBoard
as an attempt to "politicize science." Admitting some failings, the managers
of the ScoreBoard blamed their disputed ratings on faulty research by a graduate student and part-time assistance. Another ScoreBoard was promised
for the 1998 election, but it was not produced.[3]

Here and there, scientists dabbled in local elective politics. But these
were minor, sporadic efforts. After the 1964 anti-Goldwater campaign, science never again returned collectively to politics.[4]

---

dent of the Carnegie Institution of Washington; Leon Lederman and fellow Nobelists
Kenneth Wilson, F. Sherwood Rowland, Herbert Simon, and Gertrude Elion.

3. "R&D Ratings for Congress Called Misleading, Divisive," *SGR*, October 1, 1996.

4. Following the 1995 change of party control in Congress, I published an article in the
MIT *Technology Review* (February–March 1996, "Scientists Must Join the Fray") urging
scientists to recognize that the budget-cutting plans of the Republican congressional
majorities would, if enacted, severely reduce federal support for research. With characteristically clouded journalistic foresight, I argued that political action, rather than
mere petitions for kindness, was the only route to salvation for science. The article

Missing from Politics

Here we must make it clear that we are discussing the practitioners of the so-called hard sciences, the disciplines that receive the lion's share of federal money for research, and, accordingly, are deeply involved in the politics of science. Their scarcity in organized politics may seem understandable. Given a normal share of political diversity and interests among scientists, all might favor a candidate or party on science-related matters, but differ on other issues. There is also the propriety factor, as expressed by Academy President Philip Handler, a biochemist, after the 1964 political mobilization of scientists, when he warned science against partisan entanglements. Then, too, there has been an absence of a starkly frightening candidate, à la Goldwater, to provide the glue of an "anti" campaign. Nonetheless, the scarcity of physicists, chemists, biologists, and mathematicians in politics is a striking fact of American political life, and all the more so, given their plentiful numbers and the dependence of science upon public finance and political support. Few of these scientists show up in the counts of candidates, officeholders, or campaign activists. Many follow politics closely and talk about it a good deal, as spectators. They don't play the game.

Doctorates in education, political science, economics and the various social sciences are fairly plentiful on Capitol Hill. Not so the Ph.D.'s of the so-called hard sciences. In 1998, a record was set with the election or reelection of four of them to the House, which numbers 435 members, thus giving the hard-science contingent a .9 percent share in that chamber. The Senate continued without even one Ph.D. scientist in its ranks, which have included scarcely any in prior times. A recent exception was Harrison Schmitt, a NASA scientist-astronaut, with a Harvard Ph.D. in geology, who visited the moon's surface in 1972 on the final Apollo flight. Schmitt's public recognition helped him win the Republican Senate nomination and election in New Mexico in 1976. After an undistinguished term, he was defeated for reelection in 1982 and disappeared from elective politics.

Precise counts in the state legislatures, the farm teams of national politics, are obscured by the bunching habits of the occupational tabulators, who combine in one number scientists and engineers and, mysteriously, architects, though these are different species, vocationally and politically. Even so, the combined numbers of the three professions are minuscule. In the fifty state legislatures, 1.4 percent of 7,424 elected representatives were

---

evoked no interest—a frequent, deserved fate of journalistic prophecy and prescriptions. Science continued to abstain from ballot-box politics, and came out of the supposed crisis with budgets plumper than ever.

in the category "Engineer/Scientist/Architect" in 1995.[5] Lawyers, the traditional occupational leaders in politics, have lost ground in recent years, but still were the dominant profession, at 15.5 percent of the legislative membership. The high percentage of lawyers in American political life was drawn from a professional pool of active attorneys that numbered 1,000,440 in 1999; the very low percentage of scientists and engineers came from an active pool that was smaller, 654,900 in 1997, but not so small as to explain the huge disparity.[6]

The second leading professional category in the state legislatures, at 14 percent, was "Full-Time Legislator," a relatively new designation that reflects the evolution of state office holding from a low-paid, part-time avocation to year-round, professional status. "Business Owners" constituted 12.3 percent, while "Business: Executive Manager" accounted for 5.4 percent. "Medical" was the professional designation for 2.5 percent of legislators, nearly double the percentage for "Engineer/Scientist/Architect." Some definitional confusion is evident in the occupational categories. But, by any measure, a scarcity of scientists is a durable reality of state-level politics, and, in turn, congressional politics. According to the National Conference of State Legislatures, over half of congressional freshmen previously served in state legislatures.[7]

In the U.S. Congress, lawyers are proportionately even more plentiful than in the state legislatures, filling 39.5 percent of the House seats in 1997, and 53 percent in the Senate.[8] In recent years, physicians have enlarged their presence in Congress, rising from five members in the House in 1991 to twelve in 1997, and from none in the Senate in 1991 to two in 1997, small numbers but significantly more than the number of scientists in the U.S. House and Senate. Doctoral-level scientists in the United States constitute a small proportion of the workforce; nonetheless, in their totality, they add up to a lot of people. But they're as scarce in politics as they are in witchcraft.

In exploring the politics of science, and the manner in which science makes its way in politics, it is necessary to search for the origins of the scar-

---

5. *State Legislators' Occupations: 1993 and 1995,* National Conference of State Legislatures, March 1996.

6. Data from American Bar Association, "Legal Education Statistics, Membership Rankings by States," and *SESTAT: A Tool for Studying Scientists and Engineers in the United States* (NSF 99-337), table B-11, p. 7.

7. *State Legislators' Occupations: 1993 and 1995,* quoting research by Michael Berkman.

8. Norman J. Ornstein, Thomas E. Mann, and Michael J. Malbin, *Vital Statistics on Congress: 1997–1998* (Congressional Quarterly, 1998).

city. The training regime and work style of the laboratory sciences, in contrast to those of law, business, and other professions, are unfavorable, even hostile, to the development of political interests, skills, and advancement. Perhaps at the intake points of the various professions, psychologically based self-selection influences are at work. Lawyers are expected to make the best of a bad case; scientists are expected to reject a faulty hypothesis. Lawyers and politicians are not renowned for meticulous adherence to the truth. On the other hand, the historically enshrined ethos of science, though not infrequently violated, is bound up with truthfulness, precision, objectivity, and other pristine qualities. In notices in scientific journals, scientists routinely fess up to errors, even trivial errors, in previously published papers.

The beginner striving to make a mark in science must commit to a secular monasticism, first as a graduate student, rarely less than a five-year enlistment in the sciences; then, with rare exception, as a postdoctoral fellow, for two to three years, often more, in a relatively low-paid, subordinate role; and, finally, assuming competence and good fortune, a probationary research job in academe, industry, or government. At that stage, the newly hired fledgling scientist is at least thirty, perhaps forty years of age.[9] Gregarious personalities flourish in science, as elsewhere, but the opportunities for sociability are constrained by the long hours and solitary or small-group format of a scientific apprenticeship and early career. For those embarked on this career odyssey, incentives as well as opportunities are nil for getting around the community and becoming known, engaging in public activities, and developing a political persona. But that is what many young lawyers and businesspeople do on their career tracks, to their economic benefit and political potential.[10]

9. Lengthy as it has always been, the training phase in science has been growing in recent times. An upward shift in age of full-fledged professional entry into the life sciences, and probably in other science fields, too, was noted in a 1998 report by the National Research Council: Compared with students in the 1960s and 1970s, it states, "Today's life scientist will start graduate school when slightly older and take more than two years longer to obtain the Ph.D. degree. Today's life science Ph.D. recipient will be an average of 32 years old. . . . It is not unusual for a trainee to spend 5 years— some more than 5 years—as a postdoctoral fellow. As a consequence of that long preparation, the average life scientist is likely to be 35–40 years old before obtaining his or her first permanent job." *Trends in the Early Careers of Life Scientists* (Washington, D.C.: National Academy Press, 1998), p. 2.

10. Modern politics also shows increasing favor toward other professions that provide public exposure: acting, hosting talk-radio shows, and televised wrestling. Actor Ronald Reagan made it to the top, as no scientist has since polymath Thomas Jefferson; engineer Herbert Hoover is, perhaps, an exception. In celebrity-conscious America, wide recognition of scientists is a rarity. As a letter-writer to the *New York Times* (March 11,

In commenting on the political and social qualities of members of their profession, several prominent scientists, in good standing in their respective professional communities, show no affinity for C. P. Snow's assertion that scientists "have the future in their bones," that prophetic powers of political value reside in scientists and should be recognized by politicians. In fact, from these scientists come harsh assessments of scientists that would be regarded as offensive, even sacrilegious, if stated by politicians, the lay press, or other nonscientific sources; but coming from scientists with excellent credentials, they're shrugged off as crankiness in the scientific family. Thus, in 1998, Edward O. Wilson, the Harvard zoologist and social theorist of *Sociobiology* renown, wrote of successful scientists:

> They learn what they need to know, often remaining poorly informed about the rest of the world, including most of science for that matter, in order to move speedily to some part of the frontier of science where discoveries are made. There they spread out like foragers on a picket line, each alone or in small groups probing a carefully chosen, narrow sector. . . . They know the first rule of the professional game book: Make an important discovery, and you are a successful scientist in the true, elitist sense in a profession where elitism is practiced without shame. . . .
> When a scientist begins to sort out knowledge in order to sift for meaning, and especially when he carries that knowledge outside the circle of discoverers, he is classified as a scholar in the humanities. . . . A fundamental difference thus exists in the natural sciences between process and product. The difference explains why so many accomplished scientists are narrow, foolish people, and why so many wise scholars in the field are considered weak scientists.[11]

Addressing the performance of universities in the education of scientists, another honored figure of contemporary science, Maxine F. Singer, president of the Carnegie Institution of Washington, spoke in a similar vein, also in 1998. Singer warned that "the specialized demands of contemporary science leave little time, and sometimes even less motivation, to provide gifted young people with the requisite *liberal* [original italics] education."

2000) lamented, "alas, most citizens can barely name a living scientist along with his or her accomplishments."

11. Edward O. Wilson, "Scientists, Scholars, Knaves and Fools," *American Scientist*, January–February 1998, p. 7.

Singer, the recipient of the 1999 Vannevar Bush Award "for lifetime contributions to science and engineering," lamented that:

> too many young scientists have no concept of the history of their own fields, let alone the history and literature of the nation and the world or of the fact that the 'liberal' in liberal education has nothing whatever to do with politics. Too many of them glean from their mentors a narrow view of the roles that they, as scientists, can play in our society.[12]

These critical views of scientists by scientists command attention because they provide what the lawyers nicely term "admissions against interest." From outside the family of science comes an observation that also merits attention, though many scientists would surely dismiss it as ignorant ramblings. In *Science: The Glorious Entertainment,* Jacques Barzun, the distinguished cultural historian, observed that the methods and machines of science assure attainments that can obscure the otherwise mediocre qualities of their users:

> The chances are that "the scientist," from the high school teacher of science to the head of a research institute, is a person of but average capacity. It is one of the great advantages of scientific method, as Bacon long ago pointed out, that it can raise ordinary ability above what might be expected of it: science is the democratic technique par excellence. It calls for virtues which can be learned—patience, thoroughness, accuracy. It tests what it does by conventional means—numbers and instruments; it guards against error by the communal sense of sight. . . .
> Hence with care and industry a man of normal endowments can be a satisfactory scientist. Vision, intuition, genius are not excluded but neither are they required. The average performer in science may never distinguish himself, or he may do so but once in his life; he is none the less useful and deserves the name of scientist. Intelligence and will power equal to his would make only a negligible artist or philosopher, useless not to say harmful, except perhaps as a teacher.[13]

---

12. Maxine F. Singer, address at the presidential inauguration of David Baltimore, March 9, 1998, at the California Institute of Technology, in *Engineering & Science,* no. 1 (1998, California Institute of Technology).

13. Jacques Barzun, *Science: The Glorious Entertainment* (New York: Harper & Row, 1964), p. 75.

For scientists, the imperatives of work and the scientific culture are disadvantageous for getting started and advancing in politics. Original publication in well-recognized, peer-reviewed journals is the *sole* propellant for success in the basic sciences; with all sciences cluttered with ever-expanding rosters of narrowly focused specialty journals, not any journal, even a peer-reviewed journal, will do. And mercy on the scientist who seeks to maintain professional standing within the community while energetically performing for the general public. The experience of the late Carl Sagan suggests that the profession regards that dual track with reservation.

THE SIN OF CELEBRITY

Sagan was a tenured professor of astronomy and director of the Laboratory for Planetary Studies at Cornell University. His curriculum vitae recorded a productive career in research, listing over 350 scientific papers and articles in astronomy journals, appointments to many NASA advisory committees, scientific participation in the Mariner, Viking, and Voyager interplanetary missions, and three medals from NASA as well as major awards from scientific societies. Sagan was known to the public as the creator of the 1980 public-television series *Cosmos,* which drew audiences estimated at over 500 million in some sixty countries, said to be the largest ever for a science-related show. Sagan's book version of *Cosmos* was on the *New York Times* best-seller list for seventy weeks; a later book, *The Dragons of Eden,* was awarded the Pulitzer Prize. Sagan was widely honored, in the United States and abroad, but the greatest scientific honor that could be bestowed by his own peers eluded him: election to the National Academy of Sciences.

In the pecking order of science, academy membership is the highest honor within the American scientific community, surpassed internationally only by the Nobel Prize. Since its founding in 1863, the academy has proceeded without written criteria for election to its hallowed ranks. However, Philip M. Boffey explains in his unsurpassed 1975 study of the academy, *The Brain Bank of America,* the "chief criterion has traditionally been excellence in original scientific research." (Boffey notes, too, an old saying of scientists about the academy: "It's nothing to belong, but it's hell not to.")[14] Sagan was repeatedly nominated for election to the academy, "a self-perpetuating society," as it describes itself, which means election is by the previously elected. With a membership numbering about 1,850 in recent years, the academy replenishes its ranks with the annual election of some

---

14. Philip M. Boffey, *The Brain Bank of America* (New York: McGraw-Hill, 1975), pp. 19, 21.

sixty new academicians. Informed opinions divide on whether scientists of lesser scientific excellence than Sagan have been elected to the academy. The basis for his exclusion is known only within the academy, which, with the reticence of exclusive clubs, will not discuss the matter. Amends of a sort were made in December 1993, shortly after the academy chose as its president Bruce Alberts, a molecular biologist with an unrestrained passion for improving science education and the public understanding of science. The academy president cannot dictate the election of members, which is decided in a complex system of balloting that annually distributes the new places among twenty-five disciplinary tribes of the natural, physical, mathematical, and social sciences. However, six months after Alberts became academy president, nonmember Sagan was named the recipient of the academy's Public Welfare Medal, the institution's highest honor short of election. "In the public's view," Alberts said, "Carl Sagan's name may be associated more with science than that of any other living scientist."[15] Three annual elections to membership in the academy took place between the presentation of the award and Sagan's death in 1996, without the members voting him into their select ranks. The whispering was that Sagan's election was blocked by academy members resentful of his celebrity. Following Sagan's death, NASA administrator Daniel Goldin, who is not an academy member, publicly berated the academy for its failure to elect Sagan. Appearing on a radio talk show, Goldin stated, "I think it is shameful that Sagan was not admitted into the National Academy of Sciences." Asked whether posthumous membership might make amends, Goldin responded: "I think the academy ought to search its soul and think about such an award to Dr. Sagan. . . . The problem I think he had is that there was this connotation that if you popularize science, you're not a scientist."[16]

The academy's bylaws do not provide for posthumous election. And Sagan had already been awarded the academy's highest medal. The tradition- and rule-bound academy could do no more. But the elders of science now sought other ways to honor the late Carl Sagan. The National Science Foundation posthumously awarded him its Distinguished Public Service Award, which it described as "NSF's highest honor given to a private citizen for contributions to the agency's activities in science and education." As described in two recent biographies of Sagan, in his extraordinary

15. "In Brief," *SGR*, December 1, 1993.
16. Goldin made his remarks on January 21, 1997, on the nationally syndicated Derek McGinty radio talk show, originating in Washington; his comments were reported in "Goldin Criticizes Academy for Failure to Elect Sagan," *SGR*, February 1, 1997.

odyssey through science and celebrity, his manner did not endear him to professional colleagues: he was difficult and demanding and could be treacherous in personal relations, he coveted the spotlight, and his egotism grated on many.[17] These are recognized as common qualities in successful politicians, and they are not unknown in the ranks of successful scientists honored by their peers. The Sagan tale is complex, but it suggests the difficulties of straddling science and celebrity. At a minimum, it invites attention to the absence of scientist-celebrities in America today. Name one.

Science, The Political Yawn

On those rare occasions when scientists seek elective office, they don't find the electorate interested in science as a political issue or clamoring for scientist-politicians to devote their skills to the application of science to public problems. In the politically myopic world of science, however, a contrary impression of science as a popular political issue is projected and possibly even believed. A month or so prior to the 1998 congressional elections, Research!America, a Washington lobby for medical research, headlined its newsletter with "Medical Research Will Play Key Role in 1998 Elections." The forecast was based on opinion surveys in New York, Oklahoma, Tennessee, and Missouri, in which potential voters were asked: "If a candidate is a strong supporter of federal spending for medical research, would that make you more or less likely to vote for that candidate?"[18] Approximately 70 percent in each state opted for "more likely"—not surprising, given the seductive though vague nature of the question. In the 1998 election, few candidates referred at all to medical research. Except for lobbies of the afflicted, organized into pressure groups in Washington, medical research is an issue that the public entrusts to the care of distant powers in Washington. It was only late in his presidency that Bill Clinton acted on the fact that the public ranks medical research among the good works that it expects of politicians. He proposed, and in his speeches highlighted, substantial budget increases for the National Institutes of Health. In the 2000 presidential election, both major candidates picked up the theme and, with variations, pledged to double the NIH budget. However, the towering issues in that election were social security, tax cuts, education, patients' rights, and pharmaceutical drug benefits. NIH was a small sideshow. The support, ob-

17. Keay Davidson, *Carl Sagan: A Life* (New York: John Wiley & Sons, 1999); William Poundstone, *Carl Sagan: A Life in the Cosmos* (New York: Henry Holt, 1999).

18. *Membership Matters*, newsletter of Research!America, September 1998.

jectives, and management of research—ceaselessly important to the politicians and lobbyists of science—are of scant concern to the great mass of American voters. The rate of budget growth and the distribution of funds among the scientific disciplines cannot compete for public attention with the bread-and-butter concerns of post–Cold War America. The public is not hostile to science. Rather, busy with other concerns, it entrusts the care and feeding of science to others, even if unsure about who they are and what they are doing.

NOVEL CANDIDATES

Novelty makes news. Accordingly, the national press was fascinated by one among the thirty-six gubernatorial elections in 1998: that of Minnesota, in which a celebrity professional wrestler, Jesse Ventura, won office. The oddity of a wrestler-candidate attracted attention. Scientists are not as scarce as professional wrestlers in state and national politics. Nonetheless, their rarity in American elective politics was evident in the news-media attention that accompanied a congressional campaign and election in New Jersey in 1998. The Democratic candidate in the state's 12th Congressional District, Rush Holt, was not a public celebrity, nor did he possess the TV renown and earthy appeal of wrestler-candidate Jesse Ventura. However, the general press and professional scientific journals deemed Holt newsworthy because he was an extremely uncommon type among office-seekers: a Ph.D. physicist, a real scientist who, prior to running for office, had served as assistant director of a major research facility, the Princeton Plasma Physics Laboratory. Holt's transition from science to politics was not as abrupt or as unusual as it might seem; he possessed a political ancestry. His father, Rush Dew Holt, served as a U.S. senator from West Virginia from 1935 to 1941, following six terms in the state legislature. The son was only six years old when his father died, but Holt says he grew up in a political atmosphere. His mother was secretary of state in West Virginia, and, Holt told me, "In the seventh grade, I had my own subscription to the *Washington Post*."[19]

Holt also had experienced Washington as a congressional fellow of the American Physical Society, serving on the staff of a member of the House of Representatives in 1988–89. Nonetheless, scientist Holt was one of a kind among the 40 freshmen elected to the House of Representatives in 1998, as well as a rarity among the 435 members of the House and 100 members

19. Conversation with author, March 13, 2000.

of the Senate. "At Last, A Politician Who Knows Quantum Mechanics," was the *New York Times* headline on a lengthy, friendly postelection interview with Holt.[20] The science press, more attentive to the minutiae of science and politics, reported extensively on the primary and election campaigns of one of science's own, while noting, postelection, that Representative-elect Holt would find some scientific companionship in the House that had previously elicited little attention: Representative Vernon Ehlers, a Michigan Republican reelected to a third term, who also possessed a Ph.D. in physics; Representative Roscoe Bartlett (R-Md.), first elected in 1992, who holds a doctorate in physiology and formerly taught at the University of Maryland and Loma Linda University School of Medicine, and Representative John Olver (D-Mass.), first elected in 1990, a Ph.D. chemist who formerly taught at the University of Massachusetts-Amherst. The previous inattention to this scientific trio was perhaps attributable to the vagaries of news coverage and their choosing not to use their professional identification for campaign fund-raising; the rediscovery of the three House scientists, after Holt's election, may have been due to the inflammation of science politics by Republican budget-cutting proposals.[21]

Why aren't more scientists in politics? Holt told me, "They don't get the culture"—meaning, he explained, that, by the standards of science, they regard politics as a grimy endeavor.

SCIENCE'S OWN HOMETOWN SUCCESS

Science headlined the news of Holt's election with "Democrats Match GOP in Sending a Physicist to Washington," a reference to Representative Ehlers's prior arrival in the House.[22] In an expression of hometown chauvinism, the accompanying article reported that "researchers and science lobbyists hope that Holt's victory will provide a sorely needed boost to the scientific expertise of the nation's legislative branch, which contains only a handful of scientists and engineers." Holt's candidacy stirred political passion within science, producing money for his campaign from scientists, near and far, apparently eager to support an office-seeking scientist. The

---

20. *New York Times,* November 24, 1998.

21. The our-gang interest in scientist-politicians, as well as novelty-is-news, was evident in a 1998 article in *Science* (the journal of the American Association for the Advancement of Science), "Scientists Step onto Political Stage," reporting that the prime ministers of Poland and Bulgaria and the president of Romania were full-fledged scientists or engineers (*Science,* July 17, 1998, p. 325).

22. *Science,* November 13, 1998, p. 1234.

surge of contributions could indicate a latent political spirit within science that rarely finds an opportunity to support one of its own for political office. Generalizations are out of order. With his family background in politics and experience in Washington, Holt was not a laboratory drudge suddenly running for office. On the other hand, it is a safe assumption that at least a few similarly attractive, politically savvy potential candidates are submerged in the amply populated, politically underrepresented scientific community. In all, Holt raised $885,377, a lofty amount for any House candidate, but especially for a first-time hopeful. The House average for campaign expenditures that year was $675,000. Eighty-eight percent of Holt's campaign money—$769,087—was provided through 1,025 individual contributions, for which the allowed maximum is $1,000. Data collected by the Federal Election Commission show that hundreds of those contributors identified themselves by university addresses or resided in university towns. Focusing on the conjunction of Holt as scientist-legislator, a *New York Times* interviewer observed that he had received campaign contributions from fourteen Nobel laureates, as well as many other scientists, and inquired whether Holt would stake out science as his special area of legislative interest. No novice in politics, Holt dismissed that possibility, pointing out that "science was not much of a factor in the campaign." Noting that "issues of science did not seem to move most voters," Holt said that "people cared more about health care, Social Security, education—issues that they felt affected their daily lives, and I tried to address those."[23] In 2000, Holt won a bid for reelection in a hard-fought campaign against a previous occupant of his seat who had dropped out for a run for the Senate—unsuccessfully so. Scientists around the country again contributed heavily to Holt, but as in his first run, Holt didn't play the science card. He and his opponent duked it out over the standard bread-and-butter issues of new millennium politics.

In dismissing science as a vote-catching issue, Holt reflected a political reality that has never penetrated the scientific enterprise: American voters are not interested in what the scientific community regards as its life and death needs—ever-increasing volumes of government money for research and limited restraints on its use (preferably none at all). Science does not resonate as a political issue. In 1982, space hero John Glenn, the senator from Ohio, commenced a nationwide campaign for the 1984 Democratic presidential nomination. Glenn, the biggest vote getter in Ohio state his-

---

23. *New York Times,* November 24, 1998.

tory, cast himself as a champion of science and accused the Reagan administration of creating an "R&D crisis in America." Booked to speak to many
scientific audiences during his presidential run, Glenn pandered to the
crowds with such surefire lines as, "Decisions about support for research
on energy, space and health should not be made only by accountants and
lawyers."[24] Glenn failed to win a single delegate in the Democratic pri-
maries, thus confirming a durable fact of American politics: science is not
a vote-winning issue.

As an economic and cultural force, science is woven into modern American society. But in the political marketplace, it doesn't sell. Perhaps it
could, but, as we have seen, scientists, with their aversion to connecting
their profession to elective politics, avoid partisan appeals. With few exceptions, they maintain a safe distance from the fundamentals of politics:
money raising, candidate endorsements, and mobilization of votes to elect
supporters and defeat antagonists. In the capital city, science voluntarily
inhabits a ghetto, walled off from politics.

24. "Glenn Sees Paydirt in Championing Science," *SGR*, March 15, 1982.

CHAPTER 17

The Scientific Ghetto

Science has seldom been strong politically. Even after WWII, when we had produced radar and nuclear weapons, and after Sputnik, when we were frightened by the specter of being surpassed by the Soviet Union, the scientific community has not been a strong political force. Contrast the political clout of the R&D community with that of the agricultural community. There are over 5 million working scientists and engineers in the U.S., under 3 million farm workers. The U.S. government spends about $70B per year on R&D, only about $17B in government payments to farms. So, by objective measures, the R&D community is bigger and the federal government has a bigger stake in it than in agriculture. But by any measure, the farm community is orders of magnitude more influential politically.

—Roland Schmitt, president, Rensselaer Polytechnic Institute (1991)

POLITICAL WASHINGTON is a metropolis of distinct communities, each bound by particular concerns: foreign affairs, defense, health care, housing, agriculture, senior citizens, and science, too, among others. Science is a profoundly powerful force in human affairs; it is an indispensable ingredient of national power and individual well-being, as evidenced by strivings among nations worldwide for scientific capability. However, the capital's science leaders, managers, and supporting cast of lobbyists and other functionaries are an insular, inconspicuous community in the capital city, where vibrant politics is the principal business. Virtually all these communities, science included, defend and advance their interests from headquarters in or close to Washington. Of the many national organizations that are headquartered elsewhere, some (like the Chicago-based American Medical Association and American Bar Association) also maintain offices in Washington. In a distinctive respect, however, the science community, intertwined with higher education, sits apart from its neighbors: the others participate in politics by raising and giving money—the indispensable lifeblood of politics—to politicians and parties; they also supply rhetorical support and work at voter mobilization, which are welcome, too, but money comes first. As we have seen, science, for sound reasons of its own, renounced that style of politics after one long-ago venture, its 1964 presidential campaign against Barry Goldwater. And that exception was selflessly focused on Goldwater as a trigger-happy politician, unfit for the presidency. The scientist-campaigners deliberately refrained from emphasizing the permanent interest of the scientific community, a growing supply of government money for research. In the political city, science uniquely practices apolitical, nonpartisan politics.

A Caste Apart

The scientists are different in other ways, too. Political rank and social circles demarcate them from the rest of Washington. Because of the administrative dispersal of science throughout the federal government, science falls short of a critical mass; though concentrated in a few departments and agencies, science is everywhere but headquartered nowhere. There is no Pentagon of science, no Foggy Bottom as a metaphor for the federal presence in science. Science does not hold cabinet status, à la defense, housing, transportation, education, agriculture, and veterans affairs. In other countries, including France, Great Britain, Germany and Japan, major segments of government activities in science and technology are bundled into cabinet-level ministries, often in combination with the government's industrial or educational functions. In the U.S. government, there is no departmental equivalent of the foreign ministries with jurisdiction over science or science and technology. This absence, however, is not rued by the great majority of the leaders of American science. Most of them steadfastly prefer a plurality of research-supporting agencies rather than a single superagency for science that would concentrate money and power, but also concentrate risks of ill treatment in a government science monopoly. Members of Congress prefer the fragmentation, too, since power on Capitol Hill comes with committee jurisdiction over executive branch agencies. The all-powerful congressional chairs who rule over segments of the federal research enterprise do not favor an amalgamation that would deprive them of their jurisdiction. If Vannevar Bush's proposal for an all-in-one, government-financed research foundation had been adopted, even with so-called mission agencies functioning in parallel, science and government in the United States might have evolved in a more centralized fashion, and science might have achieved greater visibility and political strength in Washington. But while revering the memory of Bush, scientists also prefer the benefits of a pluralism that provides multiple streams of government money, both for basic and applied research, flowing into universities and government and industrial laboratories. Pluralism created a scattering of science and technology agencies. Though large in the aggregate, they are dispersed throughout the government and among innumerable nongovernmental organizations of science—and so is their potential for political influence.[1]

LABELS VERSUS REALITY

The dispersion of science is accentuated by the diversity of roles among government research agencies. Their responsibilities in supporting research are not neatly compartmentalized; whatever the nameplates attached to the agencies, many of them overlap in function and support similar research. Only one government agency, the National Science Foundation, holds a legislative charter to nourish basic and applied science, without reference to utilitarian goals. Off and on, however, to appease politicians who demand to know what the American people are getting for their science expenditures, the managers of NSF insist that, in the long run, the work they support is extremely practical.[2]

1. The presumed benefits of multiple research-supporting government agencies has long held doctrinal status in science politics. But doubt on this topic was briefly expressed in a 1999 report issued by the National Academy of Sciences. After noting post–Cold War fluctuations in science funding, the report states: "Finally, what about the argument that having diversified agency support is preferable to being dependent on a single major source of support because it is less vulnerable to sudden budget changes? This analysis provides little support for that hypothesis." Michael McGeary and Stephen A. Merrill, "Recent Trends in Federal Spending on Scientific and Engineering Research: Impacts on Research Fields and Graduate Training," in *Securing America's Industrial Strength*, Washington, D.C.: National Academy Press, 1999.

2. The choreographers of NSF's public image chronically dither between political demands for visible economic benefits and NSF's founding tradition of support for long-term, nondirected research initiated by scientists. The tension between the two shows up in an official NSF declaration of methods and goals: "Among the many research and education frontiers that NSF's programs address are areas of clear strategic importance to the nation. The foundation invests a major portion of its resources in these strategic areas, which are organized and focused around specific national objectives identified by the President's National Science and Technology Council (NSTC) and the Foundation's own planning process. It is important to note, however, that the fundamental nature, the quality and the educational impact of the work supported in these strategic areas does not differ from those of other activities supported by the Foundation." *NSF in a Changing World: The National Science Foundation's Strategic Plan* (NSF 95-24, 1995), p. 25.

Other government agencies support science as a tool for doing their practical work. In the politics of science, NASA, the Department of Energy, NIH, and others are "mission-oriented" agencies. In practice, however, the distinction between feeding and using science is blurred. Incessant pounding by the leaders of science and their lobbying organizations has imbued politics with deep respect, and high expectations, for basic research. All the major federal agencies that support research provide money for basic research. Thus science, unlike most other activities sponsored by government, exists in many parts of the federal establishment; to its satisfaction, it has no headquarters, no single home of its own.

CONNECTED AT THE WHITE HOUSE, LOOSELY

The central junction of the entire system is, ostensibly, the president's science and technology adviser and supporting staff in the White House Office of Science and Technology Policy; closely associated with them are the outside scientists and technologists serving on the President's Committee of Advisors for Science and Technology, and the high-ranking insiders of the National Science and Technology Council (consisting of most of the president's cabinet and heads of agencies with major research programs). As a construction of intricately linked staffs and committees, the advisory apparatus is a landmark in the history of science and government, a restless hub of panels, committees, and meetings and a beehive of report production. But the sprawling government-supported research enterprise eludes tight control by the complex structure at the center, and even responds slowly to efforts to achieve governmentwide uniformity on relatively simple matters of research administration. In 1992, the Senate Appropriations subcommittee for both NSF and the White House science office declared the need for a uniform definition of scientific misconduct, requesting delivery within one year. As often in these matters, nothing happened; the issue dropped from sight when the Republicans won Congress in 1994, took control of all committees, and discarded the Democratic agenda of unfinished business. The misconduct issue, however, lingered on. In April 1996, the White House National Science and Technology Council established a panel to develop a governmentwide definition of scientific misconduct and to establish uniform procedures for handling misconduct cases. Proposed guidelines emerged from the White House system in October 1999—three and a half years later. Why the prolonged gestation? All interested parties— in academe, government research agencies, and anywhere else—were invited to express their views, which were then digested, regurgitated, and recirculated for further comment.[3] The center for science-policymaking in the U.S. government does not dictate; it tries to manage, but with a light touch. In power-conscious Washington, it is correctly seen as a small, unaggressive power.

Another example: For decades, the White House science complex, heavy with advisers and staff members drawn from academe, has urged the Pentagon to provide more money for the university-based science programs that in large and small measure ultimately contribute to the development of new weapons and military systems. During the Reagan administration, NSF Director Erich Bloch publicly berated the Defense Department for taking a "free ride" on basic research—all to no avail: from 1993 to 1999, the Pentagon reduced its support of basic research by 25 percent.[4] Dependence on science is acknowledged by the Defense Department. But facing budget constraints, other defense needs were deemed more important. In this matter, as in others concerning research, the Defense Department, controlling approximately half of all federal spending for research and development, possesses a political mass that enables it to go its own way. For different reasons, the same spirit of independence prevails at the other great source of government money for research, the National Institutes of Health. As the mecca of medical hope, NIH is a political possession of the U.S. Congress, with only a loose connection to the presumed orchestrators of research downtown at the White House.

No Central Command

Anarchism would be a misnomer for the organizational state of science in Washington; lightly orchestrated pluralism is the appropriate term. Working closely with the money masters in the Office of Management and Budget, the White House advisory complex scripts cooperative harmony for big multiagency programs in information technology, global climate studies, and several fields less grand in scope. But also in the picture are the Congress, a variety of lobbies directly or distantly concerned with research, the executive branch bureaucracies that finance and manage research, and

3. "Research Misconduct? A New Definition and New Procedures for Federal Research Agencies," fact sheet, Office of Science and Technology Policy, October 14, 1999.
4. *Research and Development,* AAAS Report XXIII, Fiscal Year 1999 (Washington, D.C.: American Association for the Advancement of Science, 1998).

the organizations that perform it. Who's in charge? No one. Lacking a center, deliberately distant from elective politics, and no longer regarded with awe as the keeper of arcane knowledge, science is a political outsider in Washington. And, though respectful of the men and women who speak for science in the capital, politicians know it's an outsider.

In the administration of the elder George Bush, presidential science and technology adviser D. Allan Bromley served with a title boosted up a notch from that of his predecessors—from special assistant to the president, low on the White House totem pole, to assistant to the president, higher. Bromley, as he noted with pride in his memoir of office, attended cabinet meetings, though not as a member of the cabinet.[5] But title inflation fools no one in power- and status-conscious Washington. As the highest ranking scientist in government, the presidential science adviser rates high with professional colleagues. However, in the broad and deep waters of Washington politics, the adviser is a small fish. Because science is outside the mainstream of politics, the presidential science adviser is regarded as something of an oddity by devoutly political colleagues in the presidential circle. A taste of the culture clash is conveyed in a minor memoir of the Bush administration, in which a junior political flunky describes the morning staff meetings in the Bush White House after the resignation of the formidable Chief of Staff John Sununu:

> Suddenly people who had been silent in the Sununu years would start
> talking and never stop. Minor White House aides were dominating the
> meeting while the genuinely powerful ones . . . would sit in silence. Sci-
> ence Advisor D. Allan Bromley, universally considered the Official White
> House Bore, would talk for five minutes about how the General Services
> Administration was determined to move the National Science Founda-
> tion [from downtown Washington] to a new building in Northern Vir-
> ginia and how this was a disaster for the president as the scientific
> community would take the move out of D.C. as evidence that the ad-
> ministration was not serious about science.[6]

5. D. Allan Bromley, *The President's Scientists: Reminiscences of a White House Science Advisor* (New Haven, Conn.: Yale University Press, 1994), p. 30.

6. John Podhoretz, *Hell of a Ride: Backstage at the White House Follies 1989–1993* (New York: Simon & Schuster, 1993), p. 63. That abbreviated account of NSF's real estate problems is based in reality. The Secret Service, which shared an office building with NSF two blocks from the White House, had asserted its political clout and commandeered the entire building. The NSF brass and staff wished for another downtown site, to retain their proximity to the White House science office, the National Academy of Sciences, Capitol Hill, and downtown amenities. The issue became entangled in a Maryland-Virginia pork-barrel competition for NSF and its 1,000-member payroll, with

The absence of a secretary of science position in the U.S. government poses protocol problems on the American side when national science chiefs confer. The United States makes do with the president's assistant for science and technology, or the director of the NSF—respected positions among scientists in the United States and abroad, but of no great stature in political Washington.

SOCIAL CIRCLES

Reflecting their separation from political Washington, the elders of science gather in their own social center, the Cosmos Club. Founded in 1878 by John Wesley Powell, the pioneering geologist-explorer, and other leading scientists of the day, the club is dedicated to "The advancement of its members in science, literature, and art." Since 1952, the club has occupied what it describes as "a grand city mansion, in the style of French royalty," on Massachusetts Avenue, in downtown Washington. The Cosmos is Washington's scholarly club, as distinguished from the Metropolitan Club, noted for big-league lawyers, lobbyists, and other moneyed members. According to an ancient joke, the Cosmos is for people with brains and no money; the Metropolitan, the other way around.

Two clubs on Capitol Hill are the watering holes for politics: the National Democratic Club and the National Republican Club. However, dividing their time between Washington and political home bases, beset by the need to be hospitable to endless streams of visiting constituents, and tied to the erratic and heavy schedules of congressional committee meetings, caucuses, and late floor sessions, elected politicians lead harried lives incompatible with clubbiness. They tend to favor restaurants, particularly the "power steak houses" such as The Palm, Morton's, The Capital Grille, and Sam and Harry's, where gaping tourists are sure to spot carnivorous political celebrities.

The Cosmos Club is not for scientists only. But in the club directory, about one-third of the approximately 3,000 members list a scientific profession; physicians, engineers, lawyers, and humanities scholars constitute most of the balance, with elected officeholders extremely rare to nonexistent over many years. In Washington's social institutions, scientists and politicians do not often rub shoulders.

---

the voteless District of Columbia reduced to bystander status. NSF naturally sought help from the senior scientist in the U.S. government, the president's assistant for science and technology. Virginia ultimately prevailed, and NSF relocated to a soulless suburb, Ballston, in Northern Virginia.

A Rare Invitation

The scientists' remoteness from the political culture of the capital is evident in an episode experienced by Neal Lane while he was director of NSF. Lane, a physicist, came to the NSF directorship in 1993 from Rice University, where he was provost. Like all heads of science agencies in Washington, Lane received many invitations to address academic and scientific audiences interested in a leader's report on how their professional issues were faring in the capital. In 1996, Lane received an unusual invitation: to address the Rotary Club of Arlington, Virginia, the suburban county site of NSF's headquarters, across the Potomac River from Washington. Rotary, Kiwanis, Lions, Elks, and other community-based clubs are basic local stops in conventional politics, settings for luncheon and dinner talks in which politicians and others who thrive on public exposure make themselves known to local business and community leaders. But for Lane, as would be the case for many of his scientific colleagues, a rendezvous of science and a community club was a novelty. Lane later enthused that he valued the opportunity because of his perceptions of a chasm between science and the society from which it draws support. He regarded the invitation as so important that, to prepare for the address, he published an article in the *American Scientist* (the journal of the Sigma Xi national scientific society) inviting scientists to recommend ideas and material for his forthcoming address to the Rotarians and also to reach out themselves to their communities. The growth and well-being of science, he argued, is hampered by its traditional insularity. "It may be time," Lane wrote, "to expand the professional responsibilities of science to include informing fellow citizens about science, the linkage between research and education, and the complex relationship among science, technology and social progress."[7] Addressing the Rotary Club a month after the article was published, Lane candidly explained, "I must confess that I considered today's meeting such an important event that I wrote an editorial for the magazine *American Scientist* that I entitled the 'Arlington Rotary Club.' " In his talk and in the magazine article, Lane emphasized the importance of scientists making themselves and their work better known and understandable to the public.[8] He acknowledged a need for broadening the customary efforts to promote the public understanding of science, going beyond science museums, TV, and other news-media productions, to personal contacts between science and the public, particularly

---

7. Neal Lane, "The Arlington Rotary Club," *American Scientist,* May–June 1996, p. 208.
8. Neal Lane, untitled address to the Arlington (Va.) Rotary Club, July 25, 1996.

the influential public. Lane was playing the science brand of politics, relying on education, information, and persuasion. The stance he adopted is traditional among scientists. Raising money and mobilizing votes is not.

Strong belief in the importance of science may be seen in scientists' efforts to promote its appreciation and understanding. That motive is powerful, arising from the deep regard that scientists feel for their work and their faith in its value for society. But as we are on a political exploration, let it be noted, again, that science's intense, and ever-growing, interest in public attitudes toward science also arises from its insecurities about the continuity and volume of public support and the maintenance of scientific sovereignty over the territory of science. The metropolis of science is embedded in a larger society, from which it draws indispensable support while striving to maintain self-governance and, at times, exert influence on the larger realm. This brings us to an important region of science politics, the border between science and government.

CHAPTER 18

Connecting to Politics

A Prince, therefore, always ought to take counsel, but at such times and seasons only as he himself pleases, and not when it pleases others; nay, he should discourage everyone from obtruding advice on matters on which it is not sought.

—Machiavelli, *The Prince*

THE BORDER between science and government is attentively guarded by each party—kept passable, but only lightly traveled. The border is the site of flare-ups when intrusions occur, which is not often; each side is aware of and usually respects the other's sensitivities. The relationship, however, is conducted primarily on terms dictated by politics, which controls the money, though in deference to science, home rule prevails on most internal matters of the science community. In basic research, scientists pick their topics and scientists determine who gets most of the money; the exception is politically controlled pork spending on science, a noisily debated but actually small portion of the total. Science enjoys a great grant of sovereignty, but it is not absolute. Fundamental policy issues arise in which science has no choice but to defer to politics. The glib formulation "on tap or on top" has no real meaning and, appropriately, has close to disappeared from policy dialogue. Scientists are never on top. For example, long-standing congressional restrictions on federal support for research on intentionally aborted embryos and other aspects of reproductive biology are disliked; but they are grudgingly acquiesced in by the scientific enterprise as politically untouchable because of the feared ballot-box power of the religious fundamentalist right. In 1999, over the protests of the nation's major scientific societies, the Clinton White House put into effect a congressional mandate providing public access to research data produced at government expense. As a concession to scientific fears of troublesome intrusions by litigants and cranks, the terms of access were narrowed consider-

ably, but not enough to allay the concerns raised by the scientific organizations. Cordiality prevails between scientists and the politicians who run
government, reflecting their unalterable need for each other. But, as demonstrated in a continuing string of episodes, politicians jealously reserve
their primacy in dealing with scientists, as Harry Truman did in rejecting Vannevar Bush's design for the postwar support of science through a
government-financed, independent foundation. Richard Nixon asserted
dominance in the science-government relationship by abruptly abolishing
the White House Office of Science and Technology, without consultation
with his scientists, who were shocked and appalled by their ouster. The succession of winning episodes for politics further defined the relationship between science and government, and, in the process, dampened the fires of
political activism and initiative among the leadership and rank and file of
science. We can learn much from a collision between science and politics
that occurred during the Kennedy administration, which was otherwise exceptional for its harmonious relationship between the president and his
scientists.

POLICY DIFFERENCES

Frank Press, President Carter's science and technology adviser, related
to me a discussion he had with Jerome Wiesner, President Kennedy's science and technology adviser, that reveals much about the science politics
of the Kennedy era. "Wiesner had the advantage that he and Kennedy were
close, were good friends before [Kennedy's election]," Press recalled to me.
In contrast, Press had no prior relationship with Carter, and he arrived in
a White House staffed with several old cronies of the president he served.
"And yet, Jerry [Wiesner] resigned his position—this was before Kennedy
was shot—and handed in his resignation, because he had lost influence to
the other presidential assistants, and the president was not following any
of his advice. This is what Jerry told me," Press said.[1] Wiesner, ranked by
Press and others as the most influential of presidential science and technology advisers, was particularly chagrined by the loss of two major battles in
the White House. The most critical concerned Kennedy's concession to the
hardliners who demanded an acceleration of underground nuclear testing
as the price for their support of the 1963 treaty with the Soviets banning
tests in the atmosphere. For Wiesner and other scientists in the arms-

---

1. Interview with author, May 14, 1998.

control camp, the refusal to ban all tests was a disheartening setback in their crusade to discourage nuclear proliferation and reduce the risk of nuclear war. The other lost battle for Wiesner concerned his opposition to rising demands for an accelerated space program focused on a manned round-trip to the moon. Back at MIT, after briefly delaying his departure from the White House to assist in the post-assassination transition, Wiesner described that controversy to me in an interview in 1965. By then, the Apollo moon-landing program, proposed by the late president in 1961, had evolved into a heavily financed national commitment. Wiesner recalled that "my position, which was the Kennedy position when he became president, was that we shouldn't drive as hard as we're driving now [i.e., in 1965] in the lunar program." Late in 1960, between Kennedy's election and inauguration, Wiesner chaired a transition team on space. The team, he recalled to me, recommended to Kennedy that "we ought to set a fast but not a desperate pace to get to the moon."[2]

Consensus had developed within the Kennedy administration for a moon landing, but the timetable and, equally important, the technical strategy for getting there, remained unsettled. "Our recommendation," Wiesner recalled, "was that we proceed with the big booster and with earth satellite experiments and rendezvous experiments directed toward a program that might lead to the moon in '72 or '73"—a restrained pace, given that the first landing occurred in 1969. The preference for earth-related experiments reflected a desire to reap benefits from Apollo other than a round-trip to the moon, as spectacular as that would be, both as a pioneering feat and for besting the Soviets. Many scientists considered the moon program a political stunt, admittedly with challenging engineering problems but lacking scientific content. NASA, however, was a technical organization entwined in both Cold War and domestic politics, as evidenced by Kennedy's appointment of a politically astute director as its chief, James Webb, an attorney who had served as director of the Bureau of the Budget for Harry Truman and later as undersecretary of state, before going on to corporate

---

2. The report was a foretaste of academic science's critical attitude toward space priorities for the next forty years. Recommending more scientific research in space, it questioned the high priority accorded the manned MERCURY program: "Indeed, by having placed the highest national priority on the MERCURY program, we have strengthened the popular belief that man in space is the most important aim of our non-military space effort. The manner in which this program has been publicized in the press has further crystallized such belief." "Report to the President-Elect of the Ad Hoc Committee on Space," January 10, 1961, in *Exploring the Unknown: Selected Documents in the History of the U.S. Civil Space Program*, vol. 1, "Organizing for Exploration," ed. John M. Logsdon (NASA History Office, 1995), p. 416.

success with Kerr-McGee oil. Seeking minimal complexity, NASA favored a direct flight to lunar orbit, followed by a descent to the surface of the moon—the method ultimately employed. "*Life* magazine and others were putting a lot of pressure on us for not racing harder," Wiesner pointed out in our discussion. But time for arguing the space issue within the White House was cut short by an extraneous, world-shaking event—the ill-fated Bay of Pigs invasion on April 17, 1961, by American-backed Cuban émigrés seeking to overthrow the Castro regime. The folly of that episode devastated the fledgling Kennedy administration, politically and psychologically. On May 25, Kennedy announced a decision to proceed with the moon landing. The timing, Wiesner said, "was affected by the Bay of Pigs, although it was not something that was brought in and invented as a way of taking the public's mind off the Bay of Pigs. Although, I'm sure," Wiesner added, "that the president faced the decision and moved faster than he might have if it hadn't been for that." Describing his own position, Wiesner said he regarded the moon program as

> essentially a political problem. You could do it fast, if you wanted to spend enough money. But one shouldn't do it in the name of science, because you couldn't justify it as a scientific venture. And if people said to me, "Here's $5 billion to spend for science," I would certainly not put it into the space program, although I would probably put something in. We had sort of an agreement: Kennedy wouldn't call it science, and as far as I was concerned, if it was his political judgment that we had to do it, I would support it.[3]

STAR WARS

Other episodes demonstrated politics' resistance and, at times, indifference to unsought or politically unpalatable advice from scientists, notwithstanding C. P. Snow's hopeful confidence in their powers of foresight and the benefits they could bring to politics. A telling case is provided by President Reagan's sudden and, even to many of his closest associates, surprising commitment in March 1983 to potentially the greatest technological undertaking of all time, the Strategic Defense Initiative. If carried to completion in the distant mists of technological possibilities, Star Wars, as it came to be known, would ultimately cost hundreds of billions of dollars.

3. Interview with author, 1965.

The costs for the first six years were estimated at $33 billion, thus, on an inflation-adjusted basis, putting SDI roughly on a par with the four-year-long World War II Manhattan Project.[4] But high-tech megaproject estimates invariably are understated. That SDI would cost more was never doubted.[5]

Beyond the budgetary burden that it posed in a era of politically enforced austerity elsewhere in the federal government, SDI threatened the survival of the antiballistic missile treaty and other laboriously negotiated, and fragile, arms-control agreements with the Soviets. Our concern, however, is not with the strategic implications of missile defense, a matter in which the partisan certitudes, on all sides, lack firm grounding. We want to look at the conflict that ensued on the border between science and politics when scientists opposed to SDI, including scientists serving high in the Reagan administration, attempted to carry their views across the line. In examining Star Wars, we might recall the juxtaposition of scientists "on top" versus "on tap" in the making of great state decisions with scientific or technological components—which, in our time, involves many great state decisions, from missile defense to global warming. In Star Wars, as it turns out, a solitary figure, the venerable Edward Teller, "father of the H-bomb," by popular legend, was neither on top nor on tap. He was better situated: inside—deep inside—the White House. And the regulars who had been appointed to provide scientific advice for the president of the United States were outside, unheeded, and impotent. In this instance, politics excluded the official advisory system and chose instead to rely on one member, Teller, a politicized scientist who inflamed the Reagan administration's hard-line tendencies. The scientists who were on tap chose not to challenge what they knew was bad advice. A decade earlier, a scientific adviser in the Nixon White House, Richard Garwin, spoke the truth, as he saw it, concerning the pros and cons of building a supersonic transport. In doing so, he helped bring Nixon's political wrath down upon the White House science advisory structure. In the Reagan administration, his science advisers looked on appalled as the Teller-inspired Star Wars program received a presidential blessing—and billions of dollars. Political fealty took precedence over scientific integrity.

<hr/>

4. The Manhattan Project costs, through 1945, "totaled $1.9 billion in then-year dollars ($21.6 billion in 1996 dollars)," according to *Atomic Audit: The Costs and Consequences of U.S. Nuclear Weapons Since 1940*, ed. Stephen I. Schwartz (Washington, D.C.: Brookings Institution Press, 1998), p. 58. The six-year estimate of $33 billion for SDI is from *Ballistic Missile Defense Technologies* (Office of Technology Assessment, 1985), p. 29.

5. The regularity of modest initial estimates followed by runaway costs inspired the quip that the mega-R&D projects pass through two cost-accounting phases: too early to tell, and too late to turn back.

Teller and SDI

A candid account of Star Wars decision making at the presidential level was given to me by D. Allan Bromley, who served on the White House Science Council throughout the Reagan administration and then as the elder President Bush's assistant for science and technology. The council was created as a successor to the famed President's Science Advisory Committee when Congress and President Ford undid Richard Nixon's abolition of science advice at the White House. The resurrected council—with comings and goings, the membership ranged around fifteen—embodied the concept of scientists on tap to serve politics. Bromley was a major figure of long endurance in the relationship between science and government. His career was divided between two locales: Yale University, where he was the founder and full-time director of the Wright Nuclear Structure Laboratory, and Washington, where, on a commuting basis, he filled many positions over several decades of advisory service to federal agencies and also held high office in major scientific societies. Among other positions, he was president of the American Association for the Advancement of Science and served on the National Science Board. Unlike the many scientists who commuted to advisory duty in Washington, Bromley was not aloof from partisan politics. While serving on the White House Science Council during the Reagan administration, Bromley became acquainted with Vice President George Bush. In 1987, Yale alumnus Bush accepted Bromley's invitation to speak at the dedication of a new accelerator at Bromley's laboratory. Recalling Bush's visit on that occasion, Bromley notes in a memoir that "as one of the very few Republican members of the Yale faculty, I volunteered to be of as much assistance as I could during his continuing election campaign." Bush didn't take him up on that offer, but, as Bromley notes, "Shortly *after* [original italics] the election campaign in November 1988, he reminded me of that promise." And then came the summons to serve as Bush's assistant for science and technology.[6]

Looking back on the Reagan years, Bromley told me,

> I think the White House Science Council was a damn good group of people, but they were not used effectively at all. And what happened frequently was that, after we would discuss something, and agree that it was not a particularly good idea, Ed Teller [a member of the council] would trot across and walk into the President's office, and say, "Ron,

---

6. Bromley, op. cit., p. 15.

you should hear about this," and give his own personal view of what happened, even though he was in the minority.[7]

Asked whether George (Jay) Keyworth, Reagan's special assistant for science and technology at the time, was privy to the president's Star Wars announcement, Bromley replied, "Jay came late in the game. There's no question."

"LACK OF TRUST"

I asked Bromley whether the members of the White House Science Council were consulted about the decision to proceed with Star Wars. "Council was not consulted, not until after the fact," Bromley replied, noting that the Star Wars decision "did not go through any of the normal channels." Referring to the exclusion of the White House Science Council from the decision, Bromley recalled that "a lot of people on the council felt that in some sense that this was really a measure of the lack of connection, lack of trust that we were facing." Bromley explained that he had personal reasons to be suspicious of Teller's claims for the X-ray laser, touted as the needed breakthrough for destroying hostile missiles in space: "The X-ray laser was hyped as far as I know from the very beginning," Bromley recalled. "Actually, the guy who was given the job of building an X-ray laser happened to be one of my graduate students, so I had a fairly close and good communication channel. That was one of those areas where Ed Teller really hoped to make Livermore a key player," Bromley said, referring to the Lawrence Livermore National Laboratory, founded in 1952, after an insistent lobbying drive by Teller, as a rival to the much older Los Alamos National Laboratory. Bromley said he doubted "there ever was a chance" that the X-ray laser "would live up to its publicity." But even with these grounds for doubt, the members of the White House Science Council were impotent to affect the president's commitment to missile defense. Were Teller's claims for the X-ray laser subjected to independent review? "Not really," Bromley replied, "because it was highly classified and it was being run in one of the major weapons laboratories [Livermore]. There was very little external review. We in the White House Science Council got a few rather superficial presentations on it, but we were in no position to raise the really key questions that would come from a detailed technical examination." When I

7. Interview with author, October 7, 1998.

asked Bromley about the critical reviews of Star Wars produced by the American Physical Society (among several nongovernmental scientific organizations), he replied: "It had no influence on events because there's nothing more useless than advice that is not wanted. And so, nobody got asked for this particular study and so nobody paid that much attention to it."[8]

A Tongue-Lashing for Scientists

For years, SDI persisted as a source of boundary-line conflict between science and politics. In 1985, amid continuing controversy over the technical feasibility and political effects of missile defense, George P. Shultz, secretary of state in the Reagan administration, publicly rebuked scientists for meddling in politics. Nationwide, some 2,300 university researchers were doing the unthinkable, pledging they would not apply for or accept the bountiful funds that the Strategic Defense Initiative Organization wished to infuse into academic research.[9] This so-called Lysistrata tactic drew derisive responses from SDI officials, who reported over 3,000 applications for funds from university scientists willing to do business with the missile-defense program. But the scientific opposition, carried to the extreme of refusing money, rankled the Reagan administration; like other presidents, Reagan wished to be liked and supported by his scientists. Shultz carried his ire about resistance to SDI into sacrosanct scientific territory, delivering his remarks to a surprised dinner audience in the high temple of science, the National Academy of Sciences. His words stung, because politicians invited to that setting usually spoke respectfully to the paragons of the American scientific enterprise. The sainted John F. Kennedy, it is true, had demarcated the boundary between science and politics in an address to the academicians in 1963, one month before his death, stating: "Scientists alone can establish the objectives of their research, but society, in extending support to science, must take account of its own needs." The science establishment of the time had no difficulty swallowing that balanced formulation. In politely referring to the source of support for science, the revered Kennedy asserted political supremacy but also acknowledged a realm of scientific sovereignty. Moreover, Kennedy's remarks were directed at the perennial conflict between basic and utilitarian research, and only by a stretched inference extended to the issue of scientists intruding into predominantly political issues. In contrast, the message from Secretary of State Shultz car-

8. Bromley, interview, op. cit.
9. "2300 in Star Wars Boycott," SGR, November 1, 1985.

ried a sharp edge, and, unlike Kennedy's gentle treatment of an old issue, was explicitly related to the ongoing border conflict between science and politics over the political wisdom of the expanding missile-defense program. Shunning the issue of technical feasibility, Shultz, in condescending fashion, seemed to resurrect Eisenhower's fears of the "scientific-technological elite" invading politics: "Scientists should not expect their words to have special authority in non-scientific areas where they are, in fact, laymen," Shultz lectured the scientists. Noting the opposition to Star Wars and Reagan's arms buildup, Shultz added that "the core issues in dispute here are really not technical, but political and moral."[10] The academicians had not expected a harsh message from their after-dinner speaker. Shultz arrived at the academy lectern with a reputation as an understanding friend of science from far back. In 1970–72, as director of the Office of Management and Budget, he fought for science against the budget-cutting enthusiasts of the Nixon administration. A Ph.D. economist and former dean of the Graduate School of Business at the University of Chicago, Shultz was an academic rarity in the Reagan cabinet. But now, the Reagan White House was infuriated by scientists' intrusion into politics. In admonishing his academy audience, Shultz defended the border.

AVOIDING THE CONFLICT

Many veterans in the arms-control camp of the scientific community feared SDI as a threat to East-West nuclear stability and as a drain on government money for civilian causes they favored, including university science. They urged the National Academy of Sciences to apply its skills and prestige to a technical analysis of missile defense, confident that the study would confirm their doubts about feasibility and thus put the academy's respected imprimatur on opposition to the multibillion-dollar project. The academy, however, did not venture over the border between science and politics. Sound reasons compelled that decision, according to Frank Press, who was elected president of the academy in 1981, following his service as President Jimmy Carter's special assistant for science and technology. The Reagan administration, Press said, would not cooperate with an academy review of SDI: "If you don't get an official request for a study, you're not going to get access. You cannot do an SDI study without going into all of the classified stuff to see what they know, where they're at, what the Russians know,

10. "Secretary of State Assails Scientists in Political Roles," *SGR*, March 15, 1985.

come to understand the vulnerabilities, the Russian countermeasures. And that's all classified." Press added that "for us to undertake a study without access would be ridiculous."[11]

Press said that he looked into obtaining congressional support for an SDI study, without success. But he recalled, too, that "something else happened that made it very difficult for me. A petition circulated among members of the academy—a large number of them objected to SDI." Signed by over half of the members, the petition undermined the academy's credibility as an independent analyst of SDI's feasibility, Press contended. The academy, the nation's most prestigious scientific institution, embodying the elite of American science, thus was a silent bystander in the debate over SDI. With an immense store of expertise in its membership, the academy could have worked from the outside to produce a credible critique based on openly published physics, as well as information gleaned from the buzzing grapevine of the garrulous community of physicists. Though Livermore guarded its alleged secrets, the leaders of American physics—many opposed to SDI—possessed a very good understanding of the scientific realities behind Livermore's inflated claims concerning the X-ray laser and other wondrous breakthroughs. Other organizations, with lesser resources than the academy, mobilized the leaders of physics to tackle SDI from the outside. But not the academy.

On other issues, particularly the financial needs of science, the academy frequently initiated studies, for which it used both its endowed funds and money raised from government agencies and philanthropic sources. For conducting these studies, government research agencies, sharing an incestuous interest with the academy in bigger budgets for science, were pleased to cooperate by providing money and data.[12] Star Wars presented the dilemma of a government program veiled in military secrecy that the government declined to lift for independent examination. The difficulties of conducting such an examination were thus great, but not insurmount-

---

11. Interview with author, May 14, 1998.
12. Studies conducted by the academy generally cost at least several hundred thousand dollars and sometimes exceed $1 million. With meetings spread out over a year or two, sometimes more, the studies are usually assigned to part-time ad hoc committees of a dozen or more specialists, supported by full-time staff members at academy headquarters. The spending is mainly for staff salaries and travel and lodging expenses for committee members, mostly from universities, research organizations, and industry throughout the country. Though reimbursed for expenses, the committee members serve without compensation, unless—in rare cases—the study schedule requires large blocks of time away from normal employment. The academy lives on studies, mainly for federal agencies, from which it derived $153 million of revenues totaling $221 million in 1998.

able. In 1984, the Union of Concerned Scientists, a nonprofit alliance of researchers focused on arms control, environmental protection, and other heartfelt policy issues of science, published *The Fallacy of Star Wars*, a 293-page negative critique of the technical feasibility and strategic implications of the antimissile program.[13] The contributors included members of the National Academy of Sciences with long service as senior government advisers on strategic weaponry, among them Richard Garwin, of IBM; Hans Bethe, of Cornell University, a Nobel laureate and alumnus of the Manhattan Project; Henry Kendall, another Nobel recipient, and Victor Weisskopf, both physicists at MIT. Addressing the vaunted X-ray laser and other SDI technologies, the authors dismissed them as technically impractical, easily defeated by decoys and other countermeasures, and worthless, at huge expense, for protecting the United States against a missile attack. Though also proceeding without access to classified information, the American Physical Society critically examined the antimissile program in an openly published study co-chaired by two internationally recognized physicists, Nicolass Bloembergen, a Nobel laureate at Harvard, and Kumar Patel, of Bell Labs.[14] The Council on Economic Priorities (motto: "We furnish the facts that fuel the corporate conscience") assailed SDI as a financially gluttonous boon for the defense industry that would undermine the ABM treaty and lessen national security. Contributing to the council's critique were two alumni of the President's Science Advisory Committee in prior administrations, the ubiquitous Richard Garwin, of IBM, and Jack Ruina, of MIT, formerly a senior Pentagon research official. In a preface to the council's report, Paul Warnke, the chief arms-control negotiator in the Carter administration, argued that SDI "is not an acceptable alternative to arms control. It will drive both sides to seek security in unilateral action, rather than negotiations."[15]

CHALLENGES TO SDI

Congress's own research agency, the Office of Technology Assessment (OTA), burrowed into SDI, producing two reports, in response to requests from the House Armed Services Committee and the Senate Foreign Rela-

---

13. Union of Concerned Scientists, *The Fallacy of Star Wars* (New York: Vintage Books, 1984).

14. "Report to the American Physical Society of the Study Group on the Science and Technology of Directed Energy Weapons," in *Reviews of Modern Physics* 59, no. 3 (part 2), July 1987.

15. *The Strategic Defense Initiative: Costs, Contractors & Consequences* (New York: Council on Economic Priorities, 1985).

tions Committee. In doing so, the scientifically oriented OTA crossed into sensitive political territory and incurred liabilities that contributed to its demise a decade later when Republicans won control of both the House and Senate for the first time in forty years. Given its congressional sponsorship, it is likely that the legislative research agency was allowed access to classified information that was unavailable to the academy and others; preferential treatment for OTA is suggested in a foreword acknowledging the assistance of government agencies. But more than any other subject examined by OTA during its twenty-two years of operations, SDI—a prime objective of the Reagan White House and congressional Republicans—strained politicians' tolerance of independent scientific scrutiny of politically sensitive issues. As required by its founding statute and a hovering, evenly balanced board of congressional Democratic and Republican overseers, OTA approached the Star Wars study in an evenhanded manner, appointing an advisory panel that included declared advocates, opponents, and the uncommitted on the various aspects of the SDI controversy. To the chagrin of missile-defense supporters, however, the ensuing two reports from OTA were studded with critical technical observations of the feasibility of missile defense.

Under the research and writing procedures that had evolved at OTA, the full-time staff was responsible to its congressional overseers and drew guidance from part-time advisory panels appointed to assist with specific studies. But the OTA staff wrote the actual reports; and though the written product was theoretically subject to higher review, the editorial assembly line usually hurried along, under deadline pressure, with scant time for substantive changes. In analyzing Star Wars, the OTA skeptically pointed out, for example, that "the immense battle management system, including 10 million or more lines of software code, would have to function reliably the first time it is tested under full battle conditions." Combined with other technical uncertainties, OTA implied, missile defense might carry a degree of unacceptable risk to national security.[16] Missile-defense advocates gagged on the critical items, contending that OTA—founded by Democrats in 1972 and heavily staffed with liberal-leaning young academics, many from the sciences—had produced a partisan report. While the OTA missile-defense study was in progress, General Daniel Graham, a Star Wars supporter, re-

16. *Ballistic Missile Defense Technologies* (Office of Technology Assessment, 1985), p. 215. In tandem with that OTA report, another, *Anti-Satellite Weapons, Countermeasures, and Arms Control,* was published in a single volume, *Strategic Defenses* (Princeton: Princeton University Press, 1986).

signed from the OTA advisory committee, accusing the OTA director of press leaks "to advance your personal point of view."[17]

The director of OTA was John Gibbons, a physicist, ardent environmentalist, and confrere of Al Gore during Gore's ascent from congressman to senator to vice president; both came from a Tennessee background. For fourteen years, Gibbons served as an apolitical servant of Congress in the nonpartisan OTA directorship. In 1992, President-elect Bill Clinton named Gibbons to the government's top science post, assistant to the president for science and technology. When Gibbons moved to the White House job, he took several senior OTA staff members with him, reinforcing the not-unreasonable impression of political affinity between OTA and the Democratic side of politics. Though helpless in their minority status during Gibbons's long reign as head of OTA, congressional Republicans sensed a Democratic flavor in the supposedly nonpartisan OTA throughout the 1980s and halfway through the 1990s. Resentments accumulated and festered over those many years; retribution arrived in 1995 with new Republican majorities in both houses of Congress.

OTA was, in some respects, the congressional counterpart of the White House Office of Science and Technology—abolished by Nixon, as we have seen, because he perceived it as disloyal to presidential causes and disrespectful of the boundary between science and politics. Though working for different branches of government, OTA and the White House science and technology office were similarly situated on the science side of the border between science and politics. As a research agency for Congress, OTA was staffed with a broad array of skills, but with a tilt toward science; of 115 staff professionals, 35 held doctorates in the so-called hard sciences, including OTA's physicist director, John Gibbons. In 1995, the newly empowered congressional Republicans settled the score with OTA, abolishing the agency as ill-suited to congressional needs and tainted with a Democratic pedigree. Among the sins cited were OTA's criticisms of the Strategic Defense Initiative.

DEFENDING THE LINE FOR REAGAN

On watchful alert in the 1980s at the boundary between science and politics was George (Jay) Keyworth, who served as President Reagan's first science and technology adviser. At the time of his appointment, Keyworth was unfamiliar with Washington, unlike the eight previous presidential science assistants, dating back to 1957, when Eisenhower made the position

17. "OTA: Past Its Shaky Start," *SGR*, March 15, 1985.

a full-time job. Age forty-two when he was appointed, Keyworth had spent the previous fifteen years in basic physics research at the Los Alamos National Laboratory, in New Mexico. It was upon the recommendation of Reagan's trusted scientific wizard and old friend Edward Teller that Jay Keyworth was selected, after bigger names shied away from the uncertain role of science counselor to the antigovernment Ronald Reagan. Unlike previous advisers, who assumed and never doubted that science deserved a seat in the high councils, Keyworth arrived with and sustained a modest view of his place in the presidential scheme of things. "I am a guest in the president's house," he often said. Keyworth took part in the many White House discussions that preceded Reagan's announcement of SDI. However, he was not in the select group who knew Reagan's public endorsement of SDI was imminent. In that respect, according to a published account, Keyworth was in an elite company of outsiders, which included Secretary of State George Shultz and Secretary of Defense Caspar Weinberger. When Keyworth was alerted to the forthcoming SDI announcement by Robert McFarlane, Reagan's national security adviser, he reportedly expressed astonishment, declaring, "There are so many considerations we have not thought through here."[18] Nonetheless, Keyworth performed loyally for his president, stridently advocating the SDI program and publicly assailing its detractors. So loyally, in fact, that "At one White House meeting," it was reported, "Shultz wheeled on Jay Keyworth for encouraging the president on his utopian notion. 'You're a lunatic,' he bellowed at Keyworth."[19] Did Shultz actually utter those words? Years later, Keyworth confirmed the encounter with Shultz, explaining to me, "I think he really meant that President Reagan was a lunatic, and he wasn't going to call President Reagan a lunatic." The secretary of state, Keyworth explained, was technologically behind the times, and "needed to understand what amounts to the nearest thing we had to a secret weapon."[20]

ASSAILING THE OPPOSITION

Keyworth took the lead in confronting scientific opposition to SDI. In an interview with me in 1985, Keyworth denounced the attempts to organize an academic boycott of Star Wars research as "demagoguery":

18. Quoted by Hedrick Smith in *The Power Game: How Washington Works* (New York: Random House, 1988), p. 611, from an interview with McFarlane.
19. Op. cit., p. 614.
20. Interview with author, July 8, 1998.

What I am particularly talking about is the position that the scientific
community has taken publicly, in particular the Union of Concerned Scientists, which I do not think reflects well upon the objectivity of the scientific profession. Were it not for the fact that our public has seen this
in the past, I think it would seriously—and perhaps has, to some extent—injure the credibility of the scientific profession.[21]

Keyworth continued: "Look at the correlation of people who led Scientists
and Engineers for Mondale and opposition to SDI," he said, referring to a
last-minute letterhead campaign for the 1984 Democratic presidential candidate. "The two are so completely intertwined that I'd have grave doubts
about whether many of those gentlemen would even have gone out on the
political trail had it not been for their monomaniacal dedication to at-
tacking SDI and the change it encompassed."

As "a guest in the president's house," Keyworth steadfastly defended
SDI, technically and politically, even after he returned to private life in
1987. However, a decade later in a tape-recorded interview with me, he reflected on differences between his old laboratory, Los Alamos, and its great
rival, Livermore, home of the X-ray laser. Suddenly, he exclaimed: "You
know, Los Alamos, with all its imperfections, Los Alamos doesn't lie; Livermore lies."

"Tell me a lie that Livermore has told, a big lie," I replied.

Keyworth demurred, but I pressed, and he continued: "This is a painful
process," he said. "The whole argument for so-called third-generation nuclear weapons, directed-energy nuclear weapons whose radiated energy
could be focused into a directed-energy weapon and used, for instance, as
an SDI entity, was a pack of lies, unadulterated lies." Pointing out that he
had worked on the X-ray laser as a researcher, Keyworth described it as "a
perfectly feasible entity." But, he added, "to turn it into a practical tool
stems from religion, not science. It stems from some kind of profound commitment to solve a problem with a nuclear weapon; to give a nuclear
weapon, which is basically an evil device, a friendly face, I think."[22] Keyworth's moral ruminations came many years after he performed stalwart
duty for politics, at the border between science and politics.

In conflicts between the two, politics triumphs over science. But we
should not conclude that science is in helpless subservience to politics. Just
as servants can influence their masters, science, over many decades, has

21. "Q&A, Part 2: Keyworth Blasts SDI Critics as 'Demagogues,'" *SGR*, November 15, 1985.
22. Keyworth, op. cit.

developed and refined techniques for influencing politics. We previously looked at the apolitical lobbying methods of science, ranging from fax barrages upon Capitol Hill to promotion of the public understanding of science. We will now study a frequently employed instrument of persuasion in the political armory of science: reports.

Politicking by Report

One of the chief problems a modern society has to face is how to provide an outlet for the intellectual's restless energy and yet deny him power. How to make and keep him a paper tiger.

—Eric Hoffer (in Calvin Tomkins,
Eric Hoffer: An American Odyssey, 1969)

Granted that work (and especially paper-work) is . . . elastic in its demands on time, it is manifest that there need be little or no relationship between the work to be done and the size of the staff to which it may be assigned. A lack of real activity does not, of necessity, result in leisure. A lack of occupation is not necessarily revealed by a manifest idleness. The thing to be done swells in importance and complexity in a direct ratio with the time to be spent.

—C. Northcote Parkinson,
Parkinson's Law or the Pursuit of Progress (1961)

FROM NIXON on, extending to this day, scientists at high levels in Washington have been politically neutered. Nonetheless, they remain restless, concerned, as ever, primarily about money for science, but also, though to a far lesser extent, about their opportunities for participation in politics and policies that involve science and technology. For assuring a generous supply of government money for research, the institutions of science developed a formidable lobbying enterprise, though, among Washington's many lobbies, it is distinctive for stopping short of all but minor involvement in elective politics. These truncated lobbying methods of science evolved in tandem with a technique that has not received sufficient recognition, one that has been refined to high art by the scientists: politicking by report.

Starting in 1945 with Vannevar Bush's *Science, The Endless Fron-*

tier, the institutions of science politics have tirelessly issued streams of reports, falling into two categories, both in mounting quantities: one focused on the eternal need for more money for science; the other on policy and politics involving science. The congressionally compiled *Bibliography of Studies and Reports on Science Policy and Related Topics, 1945–1985* listed 221 pages of report titles, totaling over a couple of thousand in all. Many were related to routine congressional hearings and minor organizational matters. But included, too, were scores of money-seeking arguments for science and policy manifestoes, from the National Academy of Sciences, the American Association for the Advancement of Science, the American Council on Education, the National Science Board, the Organization for Economic Cooperation and Development, and others.[1] In the years following the period spanned by the congressional bibliography, the production of both types of reports accelerated, fueled, in part, by the ingestion of past reports and their reformulation into new reports, many battening on the ever-expanding quantities of statistical information in NSF's biennial *Science & Engineering Indicators*. In 1993, the National Academy of Sciences issued *Science, Technology, and the Federal Government: National Goals for a New Era*, arguing for Washington to finance U.S. preeminence or, at a minimum, parity in all important scientific disciplines. In the same year, the philanthropically financed Carnegie Commission on Science, Technology, and Government produced *Science, Technology, and Government for a Changing World*, which recommended (among many other things) higher status for science advice in the federal establishment. In 1996, the Council on Competitiveness, an industry-academic alliance, published *Endless Frontier, Limited Resources*, calling for more money for research and closer cooperation among academe, government, and industry. In 1997, the National Science Board, the policymaking body of the National Science Foundation, issued *Government Funding of Scientific Research*, which coyly observed, "We conclude that changed circumstances in recent years do not reduce the desirability of continued government funding of scientific research."

HIDDEN AGENDAS?

When committees are created to produce reports, they are customarily depicted as search parties assigned to ferret out information and compose

---

1. House of Representatives, Task Force on Science Policy, Committee on Science and Technology, *Bibliography of Studies and Reports on Science Policy and Related Topics, 1945–1985*, 99th Congress, 2d session, Serial HH, December 1986.

recommendations. However, the role of reports as declarations of pre-ordained positions or as diversionary operations serving the actual power center is well known, though rarely discussed publicly. An exception to the discreet silence occurred in 1992, when Lewis Branscomb, a Washington science-policy veteran on the Harvard faculty, spoke out at a meeting of the Commission on the Future of the National Science Foundation, which itself was at work on a report, one that we will later study in detail. Noting that "I've seen lots of commissions in Washington," and that on some of them "there is a hidden agenda that's already built in concrete in the commissions," Branscomb declared: "Most presidential commissions are there to lay hands on something, or to make it look like something is being thought about, when in fact the locus of power is somewhere else and the real decision's going to be made some other place." Apparently drawing upon personal experience, Branscomb warned that because of a hurried schedule for the NSF commission, the "staff will have to write this report. Then we'll find ourselves in a position, at the last minute, of trying to change paragraph three on page six. And it isn't going to be our work."[2]

Science-policy reports generally originate in or near the government sector of the scientific enterprise, and their readership is concentrated in that area. As the official literature on the fiscal state of science, they help shape science's own view of its place in the political realm. In addition, with good luck in the uncertain processes of general news coverage, they can also infuse the public atmosphere with the sciences' customary message of governmental neglect of science, even when government support has been bountiful. Expressions of satisfaction with the status quo rarely appear in the report genre. The general press usually ignores the report literature as too narrowly focused for the public at large, leaving the scientific community talking to itself about the reports, at professional meetings or in editorials and letters in *Science* and other hometown publications of science. For example, in 1999, the National Academy of Sciences issued a typically pessimistic report about the flow of federal money for science. With the money at flood stage just then, the report teemed with anxieties about keeping the money at a high level. Titled *Securing America's Industrial Strength*, the academy report went largely unnoticed in the lay press, but not so in science's own chambers of literary echoes. *The Scientist*, a privately published newspaper for the trade, granted space to an official of the academy, who, taking off on the theme of the report, warned that the nation's eco-

---

2. National Science Board, Commission on the Future of the National Science Foundation, September 17, 1992, transcript, p. 62.

nomic success "raises a troubling red flag. If our economic prosperity has been built on our scientific and technological prowess," he asserted, "we may be putting that advantage at risk."[3]

Occasionally, however, one of these generally dour studies receives notice in a major newspaper or news weekly, thus conveying the message of neglect to the public at large. In the boiler rooms of report production, such occasions bring rejoicing. We earlier saw an instance of this echo phenomenon when *U.S. News & World Report,* citing a report from the Council on Competitiveness, editorialized, with obvious concern, about "a slippage of 26 percent, relative to GDP [gross domestic product] in federal research and development between 1990 and 1997."[4] Within the report industry, such mentions are carefully and appreciatively collected and circulated internally in compendiums of news clippings as measures of influence and success. Rejecting campaign money and votes to influence politics, and avoiding the "rogue" tactics that enraged Richard Nixon, scientists utilize reports as a complementary political weapon. Attempted persuasion via reports is an accessible choice. Moreover, it harmonizes with the scientists' work style: meeting around a table, evaluating data, developing conclusions, publishing findings, and counting up evidence of impact, in this instance, press clippings about the reports.

Over many years, an infrastructure evolved in Washington to support and expand this adjunct to the main goal of science politics: money raising. The case for what the scientists sought was embodied in reports embellished by the names of senior figures drawn from research, higher education, and high-tech industry, plus, now and then, a few recruits from major-league real politics, usually retirees. From the pool of participants in report production, a few individuals became renowned—"he's a good chairman," it would be said of the stars of the committee system, followed by accolades for developing an appropriate agenda, curtailing irrelevant discussion, meeting invariably difficult deadlines, and other managerial skills attendant to committee life. In Washington's folklore of committees, for instance, Robert Galvin, former CEO of Motorola, Inc., was recognized as a brisk, efficient chairman. Accordingly, he drew major committee chair assignments, among them a 1995 review of organizational sclerosis and managerial ineptitude in the U.S. Department of Energy. The recommendations

---

3. Stephen Merrill, "Keeping America's Economy on Track," *The Scientist,* August 30, 1999.
4. David Gergen, "No Time for Complacency: The U.S. Economy Leads the World, but Its Foundations Are Rusting," *U.S. News & World Report,* March 29, 1999, p. 116.

in the Galvin committee report, for a major reorganization of the DOE laboratories, were virtually all ignored—a frequent outcome of committee
work—unsurprising given the Galvin report's own acknowledgment:

> There have been many studies of the Department of Energy Labora-
> tories. As one reads these reports, one recognizes that the items which
> were recommended in previous reports are for the most part recom-
> mended in most subsequent reports. . . . However, the Department and
> the Congress should recognize there has been little fundamental im-
> provement as a function of past studies. In fact, the cost-benefit relation-
> ship of the Department/Laboratory operation has continued to degrade.[5]

MILLION-DOLLAR PRODUCTIONS

Committee members, usually serving part-time, are heavily dependent
on the services of the offstage, hands-on workers in the report business—
full-time employees, or part-time hires, of the Washington-based institutions of science policy. So, here, too, the able performers in committee land
become known and sought after. Report production, Washington science-
policy style, is financially expensive, customarily costing a minimum of several hundred thousand dollars per report, rising to the million-dollar range,
and sometimes beyond. In this literary genre, a relationship between cost
and product—measured in intellectual quality, difficulty of assemblage, societal value, or mere number of pages—is neither present nor required.
Science-policy reports are wholly subsidized in preparation and production,
published in small editions of perhaps a few thousand copies, and generally
distributed without charge, or at reasonable cost. Report literature exists
in an economy of its own, detached from the cruel business strictures of
conventional publishing as well as from serious critical scrutiny for intrinsic
merit. Internal review as a guardian of quality is piously proclaimed by
many report-producing organizations, such as the National Academy of Sciences, but the opportunities for back-scratching in that process are abundant; prepublication review by untethered outsiders is rare, while postpubli-
cation review on the order of independent book reviews is practically
nonexistent. By and large, the science-policy report industry produces a predictably tendentious product that keeps the workers busy and the committee members hurrying to and from meetings. Nonetheless, they are impor-

---

5. U.S. Department of Energy, *Alternative Futures for the Department of Energy National Laboratories* (DOE Energy Advisory Board, February 1995), p. 54.

tant in the politics of science: to the extent that the world beyond the scientific enterprise is aware of the financial state of science, much of its understanding comes from products of the report industry that seep into the popular press. And, almost invariably, the report industry issues tales of danger to national well-being from financial neglect of research.

EXPENSIVE, BUT THE MONEY IS THERE

From the scores of billions of dollars that the federal government annually spends on research, and the many millions provided by private philanthropy, it has never been difficult to obtain the relatively small funds needed for the report industry. In and out of science, reports are the expected work product of the committees, lobbies, agencies, and think tanks stationed in the nation's capital. "This project was supported by the National Science Foundation, the U.S. Department of Energy and the Kellogg Endowment Fund of the National Academy of Sciences"—such are the credits, not atypical, on a 1995 report from the National Academy of Sciences titled *Reshaping the Graduate Education of Scientists and Engineers.* Another, *Capitalizing on Investments in Science and Technology,* published in 1999, notes support from the Alfred P. Sloan Foundation and the National Institutes of Health, as well as from the academy's own funds, some of which can be traced back to the U.S. Treasury.

Over the years, the science wing of the report industry developed a ritualistic format for its products and their public delivery. Press releases, telephone calls, and, later on, faxes and e-mail notices would announce that an important report is to be released. The report would be delivered to politics and the press in invitational unveilings at the National Academy of Sciences, the American Association for the Advancement of Science, the National Press Club, or, with good connections to a friendly legislator, a congressional hearing. Recognizing the reality that much is written but little is read in official Washington, the standard report format consists of a press release summarizing the report, and within the report, an "executive summary" providing a somewhat lengthier distillation of the contents. The themes and thrusts of each report are generally prescribed by the sponsoring organization, which then bestows authority upon the committee chair who selects the members or is influential in the selection process. The chair is eponymously identified with the report, hence the famous Bush report in 1945; or, in 1995, the so-called Press report, after Frank Press, former president of the National Academy of Sciences, who chaired an academy committee that produced one of the more durable, though little-known to the public, science-policy documents of our time, *Allocating Federal Funds for Science and Technology.*[6] An examination of the genesis and production of the Press report carries us deeper into the workings of the politics of science.

THE PRESS REPORT

U.S. Senator Tom Harkin (D-Iowa), a devoted supporter of NIH, initiated the Press report, but if he hadn't, it may be assumed that it would have been produced anyway: the time was ripe. In the 1990s, deficit-cutting dominated domestic politics, and fears of wholesale reductions in government spending flourished in science as in other sectors financed by Washington. The senator was fearful for the future of NIH. Growing up with a deaf brother, in a family too familiar with the ravages of cancer, Harkin had long been a champion of medical research. The report he sought was a welcome opportunity for the leaders of the scientific enterprise, who utilized the invitation to appeal for money for all the sciences, not just the politically and financially favored medical sciences. Until the Democrats lost control of Congress in 1995, Harkin chaired the Appropriations Subcommittee for NIH; afterward, he remained strategically situated on the subcommittee as the ranking Democrat, concerned as ever about increasing the flow of money for NIH, a goal shared across party lines. In the report accompanying the 1995 money bill for NIH, Harkin allocated $750,000 to "commission a study by the National Academy of Sciences and the Institute of Medicine," the health-policy arm of the academy, to examine whether the federal "research budget is designed to meet new national security concerns, military, economic, and health, that confront our nation in a post-cold war world." Harkin's Senate report specifically expressed concern "that medical research is not at its optimal level of priority and support relative to its importance to national security." Aware of the nimble tactics that can produce answers unrelated to questions, the staff of the Senate Appropriations Committee later instructed the academy that the "study should not conclude that the answer to the problem is just to increase funding for federal research and development. The study *must* [original italics] focus on shifting the balance within existing levels of funding." The staff also asked, "Should a process be established to measure the quality of federally funded science (for both its extramural and intramural programs)?"—a touchy

6. *Allocating Federal Funds for Science and Technology* (Washington, D.C.: National Academy Press, 1995).

question, given its built-in implication that quality measurement was lacking.[7]

Chairman Frank Press and the committee working with him interpreted the charges from Harkin and the staff in their own fashion, and, with scant reference to medical research or quality measurement, emphasized the topics of their concern, principally the totality and future of federal support for research in universities. The product of their efforts was unveiled in November 1995 at a briefing at the National Academy of Sciences well attended by the science press and science lobbyists; prior to the briefing at the academy, Press personally discussed his report with members of Congress involved in the policy and money aspects of research.

The Press report recommended stricter bookkeeping to account for federal R&D spending, through adoption of a "comprehensive FS&T [federal science & technology] budget." In harmony with previous reports by the academy, it also endorsed U.S. superiority or parity in all important fields of research. The report argued that federal spending on science was actually lower than it appears because government statistics distort the sums by including humdrum weapons testing that the Pentagon lists as part of its research and development activities. The proposed comprehensive budget, the report explained, would provide a clarity unavailable in the scattering of science and technology funds among the budgets of numerous federal agencies. The focus under the proposed budgeting scheme would be on activities that added to scientific and technological knowledge, excluding the many other activities encompassed under the commonly used heading "research and development." Reflecting its origins in the National Academy of Sciences, an organization dominated by university-based scientists, the Press report also recommended that federal research funding "generally favor academic institutions because of their flexibility and inherent quality control, and because they directly link research to education and training in science and engineering." Eleven of the fifteen committee members who served to the end of the study either worked for universities or were otherwise closely associated with academe; the Press committee included no representation from federal laboratories, academe's main competitors for federal research money. Press had spent a large part of his career at MIT. Though Senator Harkin specified $750,000 for what became the Press report, that sum apparently was insufficient; the published report also acknowledged additional financial support: $50,000 from the Department of

7. "NAS Policy Study Told It Can't Prescribe More Money," *SGR*, January 15, 1995.

Defense, $66,000 from the National Science Foundation, and $88,000 from the academy itself, for a total of $954,000—of which all but about $10,000 was expended.[8] How this amount of money was consumed may be difficult for outsiders to understand, but it is evident that money is both abundant and swiftly spent when legislators and scientists unite for report politics. Like ice cream at a teenage pajama party, the money goes fast. Over one-third, $363,198, went to overhead, or indirect costs, at the academy—about average for government research projects in universities and other nonprofit organizations. A financial summary of the project includes $170,655.35 for salaries, $9,800 for "commissioned papers," $13,758 for "employee domestic travel," $49,508 for "committee domestic travel," $4,007 for expenses for a meeting at Woods Hole, Mass., $36.56 "for books and periodicals," $5,022.76 for "postage and delivery," and $2,326.05 for "overtime."

The report itself was not a multivolume compendium; between its shiny blue covers were seven prefatory pages and a series of sections totaling ninety-seven pages. Of these, twenty-seven pages constituted the body of the report and the recommendations; the balance was devoted to endnotes and several separate "supplements," mainly filled with background statements borrowed from the conventional wisdom of science and government relations (for example, "Linking federally funded research and development to the education of scientists and engineers has powerfully enhanced both"). The committee that produced the report started with eighteen members, and finished with fifteen still on board; in all, it held four meetings, for a total of ten days of meeting time. The academy, as is its custom, paid the participants' travel and lodging costs—at modest government-prescribed expense levels—but they received no pay. Six staff members at the academy were listed on the report, several of whom were credited for producing background papers. The report states that one of the background papers, attributed to Robert M. Cook-Deegan, a senior program officer on the academy staff, "reviews some major reports on U.S. federal science policy relevant to the committee's tasks"—thus acknowledging a subdivision of the report industry: report writers reporting on prior reports.[9]

8. Financial data from the communications office of the National Academy of Sciences, February 1 and October 5, 2000, in response to my inquiry.
9. In 1997, the Science Policy Research Division of the Congressional Research Service, part of the Library of Congress, published summaries of ten science policy reports published since 1991. An introduction to this report on reports explained: "They were selected from among a large number of reports of merit based upon one or more of the following criteria: they are recognized as influential reports, express a range of views, were done by leaders in the field, focus on one or more subjects to be covered, or repre-

Following its publication, the Press report, *Allocating Federal Funds for Science and Technology*, was brushed off by President Clinton's science and technology adviser, John Gibbons, who politely said that the topics addressed are "certainly worthy of a lot of different studies." Gibbons, however, said he preferred to rely on the various branches of the White House science-advisory apparatus to achieve Press's goals of budget clarity and pre-eminence for American science. The American Physical Society, with many members employed in government laboratories, criticized the recommended preference for university-based research.[10] For several years afterward, Press proselytized for the "comprehensive" presidential budget for science and technology. Three years later, in 1998, though no visible change had occurred in government budgeting accounts, Press remained optimistic about his proposal, saying, "I think it's moving in that direction."[11] One year later, partial victory was declared when the Clinton White House, extending its media-savvy techniques to the obscurities of research funding, declared the creation of the "21st Century Research Fund." Apart from the trendy, forward-looking title, the fund was little different from the governmentwide research compilations annually produced by the Office of Management and Budget for thirty-five years. But in politicking by report, success, if any, comes in small measures and is hailed on arrival, as it was in 1999 in yet another report from the National Academy of Sciences. Recalling the budget-design recommendation in Frank Press's 1995 report, the academy noted:

> This year, the $38.1 billion dollar 21st Century Research Fund is the centerpiece of the President's R&D investment strategy, and grows by 3 percent in FY 2000. The 21st Century Research Fund is similar in concept to an integrated FS&T budget with the inclusion of DOD basic and applied research, although the two budgets differ somewhat across all agencies in terms of the level of funding and the activities funded.[12]

---

sent views of current policymakers. The ten reports are not exhaustive in range, and although they cover a number of policy viewpoints, may not reflect all perspectives." An appendix to the congressional report listed over a dozen "policy studies currently underway in the S&T [science and technology] policy community." *Analysis of Ten Selected Science and Technology Policy Studies*, William C. Boesman, coordinator (Congressional Research Service, September 4, 1997).

10. "Frank Press Pushes on With His Science-Policy Plan," *SGR*, April 1, 1996.
11. Interview with author, May 14, 1998.
12. Committee on Science, Technology, and Public Policy, National Academy of Sciences, "Observations on the President's FY 2000 Federal Science and Technology Budget," in *Research and Development FY 2000* (American Association for the Advancement of Science, 1999), p. 53.

Now that we have some familiarity with the procedures and products of the report industry, we will move to an examination of politicking by report by an extraordinary assemblage of scientists and their supporters seeking places of influence high in the federal government—namely, the State Department.

CHAPTER 20

Science to the State
Department: You Need Us

You can't hurry love.
No, you just have to wait.
　　　　　　　　　　—The Supremes

MONEY IS the primary concern of science in its relations
with politics and government. But for decades, extending back at least
to Vannevar Bush's proposal for creation of a Science Advisory Board to
counsel the federal government, scientists also lectured, sermonized, and
pleaded that government needed them for policymaking on issues beyond
the scientific arena. C. P. Snow's mystical assertion about the scientists' fu-
turistic capabilities was scarcely ever mentioned; very likely it was unknown
to many scientists. But, carried on through report politics, the message was
essentially the same: government needed scientists to apply their analytical
techniques and knowledge to trans-scientific issues—problems and responsibilities that include important scientific and technical components, such
as arms control, environmental policy, health care, and high-tech industrial
development. Minimal involvement, at low staff levels, was valuable but
not sufficient, the scientists insisted. They wanted to be in on the policy
deliberations and decision making at high levels, necessarily by invitation;
the temperament of scientists, and their avoidance of ballot-box engagement, ruled out attempts to get there by political means.

THE CARNEGIE COMMISSION

In the late 1980s and early 1990s, the quest for participation
resulted in a series of reports by an extraordinary mobilization for the conduct of politics by report, the Carnegie Commission on Science, Technology, and Government, an assemblage of influential figures dedicated to
expanding the presence and influence of science in government. David
Hamburg, the president of the philanthropic Carnegie Corporation, had

experienced Washington as president of the Institute of Medicine, the medical wing of the National Academy of Sciences, from 1975 to 1979. With many of his colleagues, he believed that "the government was not using science well."[1] Upon Hamburg's recommendation, the Commission on Science, Technology, and Government was established in 1988 as a satellite of the Carnegie Corporation, which eventually provided approximately $8 million for nineteen reports produced by the commission over the following five years. That's a bargain rate, on a price-per-report basis, as such literature is customarily priced; and even more so, considering that, unlike the National Academy of Sciences, which prides itself on paying only the expenses of the distinguished figures summoned to service on its committees, the Carnegie Commission paid its members consulting fees of $500 per day, plus expenses. Participants included leading members of the scientific community, among them former presidential science advisers Jerome B. Wiesner, who served President Kennedy, and H. Guyford Stever, who worked for President Ford; chief executives of high-tech business and industry, such as Norman R. Augustine, of what was then the Martin Marietta Corporation, and William J. Perry, mathematician and former engineering professor at Stanford University, who later served as secretary of defense in the Clinton administration. The Carnegie Commission was also graced by two Nobel laureates, Robert M. Solow, of MIT, and Joshua Lederberg, of Rockefeller University. Lederberg cochaired the commission with a venerable figure of science politics, William T. Golden, a successful Wall Street operator involved in science politics ever since President Truman sought his counsel on the organization of science advice for the White House. From Wall Street, Golden devoted considerable time, and some of his fortune, to scientific affairs, serving for many years as treasurer of the American Association for the Advancement of Science and as president of the New York Academy of Sciences, among other positions. In the Washington science-policy set, Bill Golden was revered as the grand old man of science policy, as well as a generous financial contributor to science and other good causes through the Golden Family Foundation, which reported assets of $49 million in 1997. In 1991, the National Science Board honored Golden with a unique citation for "Sustained and Exemplary Contributions to Science Policy."[2]

1. Author's interview with David Z. Robinson, executive director of the Carnegie Commission, June 29, 1998.
2. Golden, never modest about his early postwar role in science-policy affairs, wrote in 1988, "My recommendation . . . 'for the appointment of an outstanding scientific leader as Scientific Advisor to the President,' was promptly approved by President Tru-

As members or advisers, the Carnegie Commission included former Presidents Ford and Carter; former House Majority Whip John Brademas, president of New York University, who played a major role in establishing federal aid to public education and the arts during his long congressional career; and former Attorney General Dick Thornburgh, a past governor of Pennsylvania with a long record of interest in fostering research for economic development. The commission thus embodied a rare presence of real politicians, albeit *hors de combat,* for a body focused on a topic that had never rated prime time in national politics. The executive director of the Carnegie Commission, David Z. Robinson, had served nearly thirty years earlier on Wiesner's science staff in the Kennedy White House prior to joining the Carnegie Corporation, where he was vice president and treasurer when the Commission on Science, Technology, and Government was established.

ADVICE TO THE NEXT PRESIDENT

A few weeks before election day in 1988, the commission issued its first report, an admittedly hurried document urging whoever won the White House to appoint an assistant to the president for science and technology (as mentioned earlier, this was an upgrade from the traditional title of "special assistant," a level lower in the White House staff hierarchy). More than bureaucratic nomenclature was involved. The Carnegie Commission report reflected new concerns about the vitality of the White House Office of Science and Technology Policy (OSTP) and the position of presidential science adviser. Both had fallen into decrepitude in the final years of the Reagan administration, raising fears that the White House science outpost, a little over a decade after President Ford restored it from Nixonian banishment, might sink into insignificance, or even disappear. Following science adviser George Keyworth's departure from the Reagan administration in 1985, the

---

man." William T. Golden, "Then and Now: Personal Reflections," in *Science and Technology Advice to the President, Congress, and Judiciary,* ed. William T. Golden (Pergamon Press, 1988), p. 5. Bruce L. R. Smith, a historian of science policy, describes the matter somewhat differently, noting that Golden, convinced of the need for "an effective science advisory apparatus at the White House level," recommended "the creation of both a full-time science adviser post and a part-time advisory committee. President Truman accepted the recommendation in part. He created a science adviser and an advisory committee within the Office of Defense Mobilization (ODM) under the direction of General Lucius D. Clay. . . . President Truman did not in practice make much use of the ODM science advisory committee." Smith adds, "Science advisers began to play a useful role in the first term of the Eisenhower presidency." Bruce L. R. Smith, *The Advisers: Scientists in the Policy Process* (Washington, D.C.: Brookings, 1992), p. 163.

supporting staff in the Office of Science and Technology Policy had trickled down to a few loyal hands. Viewing that decline, Carnegie President David Hamburg, his scientific colleagues, and the political friends of science feared for the survival of science at the presidential level and the support and, especially, the wise utilization of science and technology by the U.S. government. Hence, the creation of the Carnegie Commission, the selection of White House science advice as its first subject, and the commission's recommendation for elevating the rank of the scientist at the president's elbow: "The significance and pervasiveness of S&T [science and technology] in Presidential decisionmaking and the increased complexity of technological issues justify this status and the need for direct access to the President," the commission stated in its first report, *Science & Technology and the President.*[3]

Proceeding with its recipe for the next presidential administration, the commission declared, "It is essential that officials inside the government perceive that the Assistant [for science and technology] has direct access to the President, is effective and has a close relationship with the White House senior staff." But what if, in reality, the science adviser did not possess a close relationship with the president and the senior staff? That possibility (often the case between presidents and their science advisers) posed no problem for the leaders of science and their political colleagues: "The perception may be as important as the reality," the Carnegie Commission stated, in a burst of magical thinking: "If government officials believe that the President understands the importance of S&T to his policy and decisionmaking and that he relies on his Assistant, their cooperation will be forthcoming."[4] The tone of the report might strike the uninitiated as indiscreetly directive for addressing the next president of the United States. But the strategists of science policy tend not to be timid about the necessity of others adopting their advice. Continuing with its exercise in unsolicited advice for the next president, the Carnegie Commission declared that it "stands ready to help the President and his Assistant for Science and Technology during and following the transition period." There is no evidence that George Bush ever accepted the offer, during or following his transition into the presidency, or that he, or his associates, were even aware of the Carnegie Commission. But, coincidentally or not, Bush did elevate the position of presidential science and technology adviser from special assistant to

---

3. *Science & Technology and the President* (Carnegie Commission on Science, Technology, and Government, 1988).
4. Ibid., p. 13.

just plain assistant to the president. Whether the change in title mattered, substantively or perceptually, is doubtful. George Bush was inaugurated on January 20, 1989, and apparently did not feel an urgent, immediate necessity for a science adviser at his elbow. His choice for the position, D. Allan Bromley, reports that President Bush first notified him of his selection on April 21, 1989, three months after Bush's inauguration; Bromley served on a consulting basis until his Senate confirmation in August.[5] The lack of a full-time presidential science adviser during the crucial formative months of a new presidential administration does not indicate that high importance was attached to the position. The Carnegie Commission made known its displeasure with the delay.

Noting, with concern, the slippage in the appointment timetable, the Carnegie Commission—in a second report on presidential science advice, issued with an eye on the 1992 presidential election—strongly recommended that the adviser should be on board on the first day of the presidential term. We don't know whether Bill Clinton was responding to that suggestion, but on January 20, 1993, the first day of his administration, John Gibbons was at work as the president's assistant for science and technology, the earliest filling of that position since its shaky beginnings under President Harry Truman in 1950.

Bygone Influence

The scientists' persistent quest for political influence, without the rigors of participation in conventional politics, invites a question: Weren't they already influential at high levels? Initially, yes, for perhaps two decades after World War II, but then, as we have seen, their influence receded.

In 1994, Bromley, recalling a conversation with one of the postwar pioneers of science in Washington, observed that in those early days, politics was baffled by science; politicians failed to understand why Sputnik remained in orbit, Bromley wrote, because "Newton's laws had not yet penetrated Washington."[6] C. P. Snow, the evangelist of scientists in politics, eloquently argued that politics would benefit from—indeed, needed—the professional knowledge and foresight of scientists. However, after the atom and space became familiar topics in Washington, futurology and facility with the laws of physics lost cachet in governing circles. As for President Eisenhower's valedictory fear that public policy might "become the captive

5. Bromley, op. cit., p. 18.
6. Bromley, ibid., p. 3.

of a scientific-technological elite," the danger turned out to be the opposite: public policy was increasingly detached from the scientific-technological elite. Despite the abundance of scientists in Washington, many with impressive titles, little more than nodding recognition was accorded science in many important parts of government, especially so in the State Department.

FOGGY BOTTOM BLUES

Throughout the latter half of the twentieth century, the State Department repeatedly acknowledged that it suffered from a deficiency of scientific and technical expertise; during most of that time, however, it maintained an armor-plated imperviousness to doing anything significant about it. The recognition of its backwardness in matters of science did not originate in the State Department. It came from scientists, with an often-repeated message to the managers of foreign affairs: You need us to help you understand and respond to the scientific revolution and its impact on global affairs. In 1999, after an actual reduction of the already modest scientific capabilities at the State Department, anguished appeals from the scientific leadership brought guarded promises of a turnabout from Secretary of State Madeleine Albright. But overall, state and science is a tale of an unfulfilled fifty-year quest by science, conducted via report politics, for respect in Foggy Bottom. Our interest is not in the making of foreign policy, but in border conflict, between scientists seeking to extend their influence into politics and politicians mainly ignoring them, but when pushed to it, resisting them, very effectively.[7]

The need seems clear for bringing scientific and technical understanding into foreign policy and diplomacy. From nuclear power to international property rights for scientific data, collaboration in space, ocean-fisheries management, disease surveillance, environmental safety, and arms control, the State Department is frequently in negotiations, or crises, that involve the products and processes of science and technology. Nevertheless, as re-

---

7. In following this saga, it is advisable to apply some skepticism to the assurances of benefits that science insists it can bring to the making and management of foreign policy. The claims are difficult to evaluate, because the State Department has kept its would-be scientific benefactors at a distance, rarely giving them an opportunity to perform. However, some sympathy is in order for a State Department bureaucracy assailed by outsiders who, though untutored in foreign affairs, demand positions of influence in its upper echelons.

vealed in a string of episodes dating back decades, a scientific capability has never taken hold at the State Department, either through the appointment of full-time staff members with scientific credentials or the use of part-time advisory services; the Pentagon, the White House, and other parts of government are well-supplied with scientists in both categories. However, with intermittent exceptions of no long duration, the State Department has persisted in a benighted indifference to things scientific, sometimes to the astonishment and dismay of scientists who cross its path. Wolfgang K. H. Panofsky, a Stanford University physicist long active on the Washington advisory circuit in arms control, reported an episode that is both disturbing and amusing. In 1958, as a member of a technical working group in Geneva on an agreement on nuclear-test detection methods, Panofsky found himself in disagreement with the head of the Soviet delegation on the inclusion of ionospheric radar, which can detect tests in outer space as well as missile trajectories; the dispute threatened the progress of the negotiations. After proposing that "we simply should agree to disagree on that point so work could go forward," Panofsky related, "I then cabled the State Department for instructions to permit me to 'agree to disagree.' A reply cable said, 'What is an ionospheric radar?' I cabled back, 'Please check with the President's Science Advisor.' I received a cable back, 'The cognizant person . . . in the President's Science Advisor's office is in Geneva negotiating as part of the [Technical Working Group] team.' So," Panofsky concluded, "we went full circle and ended up making up our own instructions."[8]

In 1986, the State Department asked the National Institutes of Health to investigate reports of a new Soviet ploy in the cat-and-mouse espionage bouts in and around the U.S. Embassy in Moscow. The embassy staff was concerned about the possible health hazards of a mysterious substance, called "spy dust" by the Americans, newly discovered on the embassy premises. Upon investigating, without detecting any hazard, a senior NIH official privately exclaimed to me: "The level of scientific understanding at the State Department is so abysmally low that it is difficult to believe."[9]

But it is to be believed. The State Department's unremitting resistance to scientific enlightenment was recorded in anguished detail in 1992 in *Science and Technology in U.S. International Affairs,* by the Carnegie Commission on Science, Technology, and Government. The Carnegie report asked:

8. Wolfgang K. H. Panofsky, "Memories of Casting a Wide *Nyet* at Geneva Talks," letter, *Physics Today,* August 1998.

9. "In Brief," *SGR,* May 1, 1986.

"What has been the government's capacity to anticipate the scientific needs of foreign policy, plan reliable programs and budget agreements, conduct imaginative and constructive negotiations, and gain a sure grasp of technical data?"

The Carnegie Commission's answer: Despite a series of studies, over many years, reporting the lack of scientific capacity in the management of foreign affairs, "it becomes clear there is a long history of frustrated aspirations" for establishing scientific competence in the Department. Specifically cited was a 1949 study, commissioned by the State Department and chaired by Lloyd Berkner, a former naval aviator and physicist with extensive experience in research and administration in the academic sector and in defense. The Berkner report noted that the State Department was deeply involved with scientific and technical issues that were being "handled at various points without adequate scientific evaluation." Management of these issues, the report stated, "requires top policy consideration and the aid of professional scientific judgment."

Looking back on that advice, the Carnegie study concluded that "The depth and prescience of the Berkner recommendations were not recognized. Few follow-up steps were taken"—none sufficient to bring mid-twentieth century science into the service of foreign policy. The situation at the State Department in 1950–51 was summarized by William T. Golden, who was then making the rounds of government agencies in response to President Truman's interest in appointing a White House scientific adviser. At the State Department, Golden encountered the response to the Berkner recommendations in the persons of two newly named officials, Dr. Herman A. Spoehr and Walter M. Rudolph. In a memorandum to his files, Golden noted:

> Dr. Spoehr is the newly appointed Science Adviser to the Under Secretary of State, the position recommended in [the] Berkner report. . . . Mr. Rudolph is attached to Dr. Spoehr's office, having in recent years headed the predecessor unit in the State Department as an adjunct to his original duties in the Cartel Section of State. He is an economist, not a scientist. Dr. Spoehr is a biochemist, a little over 65 years of age, with no previous experience in government. He was, for many years, with the Stanford University branch of the Carnegie Institution.[10]

10. William T. Golden, *Impacts of the Early Cold War on the Formulation of U.S. Science Policy: Selected Memoranda of William T. Golden, October 1950–April 1951*, ed. William A. Blanpied (Washington, D.C.: American Association for the Advancement of Science, 1995), p. 7.

Golden's memorandum added that he was told of ambitious plans to establish a network of science attachés at American embassies around the world. With various appointees along the way, science at the State Department remained inconspicuously situated at the level of adviser to an under secretary and then faded away. Warner R. Schilling, a political scientist, observed in 1962:

> Deprived of any jurisdiction in the atomic energy field, the Office [of Science Adviser] was moribund within four years of its birth. The number of overseas science attachés administered by the Office went from a peak of eleven in 1952 to zero at the end of 1955, and the Office itself languished without a scientist from February, 1954, to January, 1958.[11]

The shock of Sputnik reopened the doors to science in the State Department. In 1958, the year after the pioneering Soviet space feat, Wallace Brode, former director of the National Bureau of Standards, was appointed science adviser to Secretary of State John Foster Dulles, and then continued to serve under Dulles's successor, Christian Herter, until 1960. Brode and state were a poor match. President Eisenhower's science adviser, George B. Kistiakowsky, noted in his diary for August 6, 1959, "Wallace Brode for lunch at the White House Mess. He was full of complaints that he is being bypassed in the State Department and is not sufficiently recognized in the Federal Council [for Science and Technology, an appendage of Kistiakowsky's office]." Kistiakowsky wrote that Brode "Would like to become assistant secretary and 'enlisted' my help in that effort."[12] On November 21, 1959, following a meeting with Secretary Herter, Kistiakowsky wrote: "Herter spoke very explicitly and stated that as far as he was concerned, Brode was not useful, that he could never get advice from him on scientific problems and that Brode was only building up his own office."[13] On June 9, 1960, Kistiakowsky recorded that Herter had requested Brode's resignation.[14] Two successors with scientific credentials, Walter Whitman and Rag-

---

11. Warner R. Schilling, "Scientists, Foreign Policy, and Politics," in *Scientists and National Policy Making*, ed. Robert Gilpin and Christopher Wright (New York: Columbia University Press, 1964), a revised version of a paper published by Schilling in the *American Political Science Review*, June 1962.

12. George B. Kistiakowsky, *A Scientist at the White House: The Private Diary of President Eisenhower's Special Assistant for Science and Technology* (Cambridge: Harvard University Press, 1976), pp. 32, 33.

13. Ibid., p. 170.

14. Ibid., p. 349.

nar Rollefson, maintained the scientific presence for the next few years, but it wasn't until 1965 that, for the first time, science appeared to be taking root in the State Department—under the guidance of a nonscientist career diplomat, Herman Pollack. Unlike his scientifically credentialed predecessors, Pollack understood Foggy Bottom and how to spoon-feed scientific information to his scientifically untutored superiors. During Pollack's tenure, which lasted a decade, the State Department posted science attachés or science counselors at a dozen major embassies, plus a few minor ones, and several international organizations around the world. Over a span of months in 1973 and 1974, the role of science in foreign affairs appeared to gain further recognition with the establishment of the Bureau of Oceans and International Environmental and Scientific Affairs (OES), created by amalgamating scattered activities within the State Department. When Pollack retired in 1974, the State Department's relations with science swiftly nosedived. Pollack's successor, heading the newly established OES, was Dixy Lee Ray, former chair of the Atomic Energy Commission. Ray stormed out after six months, declaring she was consistently ignored by Secretary of State Henry Kissinger, and returned home to win election as governor of the state of Washington. Kissinger took the opportunity to install a nonscientist in the office, Frederick Irving, a career diplomat serving as ambassador to Iceland, who lacked Pollack's touch. The old sense of neglect of science at the State Department revived and festered among leaders of the scientific community. In 1975, twenty-five years after the Berkner report, the issue of science and foreign policy was again examined, this time in a study assigned by State Department officials to a retired career diplomat of great distinction, Robert D. Murphy, whom Franklin Roosevelt had entrusted with sensitive diplomatic missions during World War II. Concluding that the department needed to go much further in developing its scientific capabilities, Murphy recommended broadening the position of Under Secretary for Economic Affairs to Under Secretary for Economic and Scientific Affairs. The recommendation was ignored, as were most others in the Murphy report. Though science appeared to be more prominent than ever in the State Department's budget and hierarchical structure, the Murphy report concluded, it didn't amount to much in its actual operations. That's where matters stood when Jimmy Carter was elected president in 1976.

The first Carter appointee to head the State Department science office was another nonscientist, Patsy Mink, a former member of the House, fresh from an unsuccessful run for the 1976 Democratic Senate nomination in Hawaii. Reported as uninterested and unhappy in the job, Mink abruptly quit after a year—the seventh in a succession of full-fledged or acting appointees in the science position during the preceding four years. After that poor start at the outset of the Carter administration, the signs then brightened with the appointment of a rapidly rising star of diplomacy as head of the Bureau of Oceans and International Environmental and Scientific Affairs, Thomas R. Pickering (who later served under Clinton as ambassador to Russia and as Under Secretary of State for Political Affairs). Within the Foreign Service, Pickering's appointment to OES signaled high-level recognition of science and thus a promising line of career opportunity. The Pickering reign at OES, from 1978 to 1981, enlarged the network of scientific specialists at U.S. embassies around the world and brought scientific and technical considerations, as never before, into the State Department's policymaking processes. But, like an organ transplant, science at the State Department always had to reckon with incompatibility and rejection.

In 1979, an attempt was made on the House floor to cut $3 million from the OES Bureau's $6 million budget and reduce the staff from 138 to 69. A congressional supporter of the reductions said he had heard that during his tenure as secretary of state in the Nixon administration, Henry Kissinger regarded the science-related bureau "as where the Department of State places its incompetents." Another congressman explained, "It is a little like the trust department of banks in past years, where people whose careers held little promise were assigned."[15]

Congress legislated on the issue of state and science in 1979, enacting an appropriations provision, Title V, "Science, Technology, and American Diplomacy," that gave the State Department "primary responsibility" for all of the government's international activities involving science and technology. The mandate, however, was not accompanied by what the State Department regarded as adequate funds. But in any case, the department was not especially interested in the task. The Carnegie Commission report noted that the State Department fell short even in the legislative requirement to describe and analyze the issues of science and international affairs in an annual report to Congress. The neglect in that arcane corner of foreign policy did not cause distress on Capitol Hill. "In truth," the Carnegie report glumly states, "most of the Congress knows and cares little about the subject and most of the past Title V reporting is, indeed, largely a retrospective catalog of activities." In 1981, Pickering was appointed ambassador to Nigeria, and science at the State Department again went into decline.

Carrying its review to the early 1990s, the Carnegie Commission report noted a dearth of scientific competence in the American diplomatic service

15. "State Science Office Survives Budget Attack," *SGR*, August 15, 1979.

in contrast to the staffing practices of other industrialized nations. France, Germany, and the United Kingdom maintained a combined total of thirty-four science and technology specialists at their embassies in Washington, while the United States posted two at its embassy in Paris, one in Bonn, and one in London. The report did not point out that the imbalance in postings attested to foreign recognition of American superiority in most fields of science and technology. Collecting research papers from scientific and technical meetings and sending them home and keeping in touch with American scientists, engineers and industrial managers were prime duties for those U.S.-based scientist-diplomats.[16]

GLOOMY PROSPECTS

In unusually vivid language for the science-report genre, the 1992 Carnegie Commission report on *Science and Technology in U.S. International Affairs* noted "the deeply ingrained cynicism, perhaps hopelessness, voiced in some quarters about State's 'growth potential' in science and technology."

Nonetheless, the report hopefully renewed the recommendations for a strong scientific presence in the State Department, starting with the creation of a new senior post: science and technology counselor to the secretary and deputy secretary. The report observed that the suggested position "has been considered briefly in the distant past, and even implemented sporadically, but because of the generally low priority accorded by state to science, the idea was rarely taken seriously." Nor was the Carnegie Commission's resurrection of the idea in 1992 taken seriously. In this instance, as on similar past occasions, the State Department soberly accepted the indictment, expressed gratitude bordering on repentance, and pledged sympathetic consideration of the recommendations for improvement.[17] Again,

16. Whether the harvest of papers benefited their home countries is a separate matter. During the 1980s, I asked a Washington-based French science attaché about the use made of the research papers he avidly picked up at meetings. They were shipped to Paris, he explained. But then, with a wink, he added that collecting mattered for scorekeeping in the bureaucratic game, and he doubted that much use, if any, was made of the papers.

17. The Carnegie Commission's 1992 portrayal of science in the State Department and strong recommendations for corrective measures were promptly endorsed by George Shultz, secretary of state under Reagan. Shultz, who served as an adviser to the Carnegie study, stated, "We have a race between the creators of new knowledge and the statesmen," leaving no doubt who was ahead. John C. Whitehead, deputy secretary of state under Reagan, declared: "State, alone of all the mission agencies [of government], lacks a ready ability to call upon America's enormous intellectual resources in science and technology." The two former statesmen, quoted in a press release accompanying publication of the Carnegie report, did not discuss their tolerance of the situation they now deplored while they were running the U.S. State Department a few years earlier.

keep in mind that our interest in this long-running misalliance is not in determining the validity of the scientists' remonstrations, but in observing the futility and the ineffectiveness of their earnest efforts to enter political territory where, clearly, they were not wanted.

In 1992, as in the past, the State Department did little in response to the criticisms that it endorsed, not even simple, cost-free, easily accomplished steps toward raising its scientific competence. For example, as late as 2000, the entrance examination for selection of foreign service officers, the career corps of the State Department, tested knowledge of many subjects, but not among them any related to science or technology. The State Department advised candidates that the examination would range over English composition, western civilization, U.S. history, U.S. political systems, comparative politics and geography, principles of economics, international trade, and several other topics, but none related to science or technology. In 1997, the department quietly terminated the special career path, or "cone," as it is called, that it had established for specialists in science and technology, of whom it never had very many. Cones signified areas of specialization in which foreign service officers could expect to spend most or all of their careers. The remaining categories were in administrative and consular services, economic and political assignments, and duty with the U.S. Information Agency. For staffing purposes and career progress in the State Department, science and technology were granted no more recognition than, say, woodcarving or culinary arts.

SCIENTISTS NOT WELCOMED

At times it appeared as though the State Department not only was inhospitable to the entry of scientists and technologists, but was determined to oust the few who had joined its ranks. As federal spending was restrained by the early 1990s deficit-reduction measures and then the 1995 Republican Revolution, the State Department reduced the activities it deemed least important. As a first step, it eliminated or downgraded the posts of science and technology counselors and attachés at many major U.S. embassies, including those in New Delhi, London, Paris, and Bonn. The science-related duties were added to the responsibilities of other embassy personnel—few, if any, trained in science or technology—who were already burdened with traditional duties in the financially pinched State Department; in any bureaucracy, a secondary duty is a candidate for neglected duty. But here we must observe that, in reality, the symbolic effects of these personnel changes and policies may have been more biting than the actual effects on the monitoring of foreign research activities and the furtherance of international scientific collaboration, the major duties of the science and technology counselors and attachés. The overseas scientists of the State Department were not generally held in high regard by scientists or diplomats, American as well as those in the countries where they were posted. Without an established career path of its own for scientific staff members, the State Department relied heavily on borrowed staff from government research agencies, a recruiting tactic fraught with the pitfalls of internecine Machiavellian strife and maneuvers. When approached for a borrowing, agencies have been known to grasp the opportunity to unload deadwood or, in some instances, to accept an attractive foreign assignment as an early parting gift for a staff member bound for retirement in two or three years, and therefore not especially concerned with performance ratings. Organizations are not inclined to lend out their star performers for lengthy service in other bureaucracies. In journalistic travels, I got the impression that the abilities of the science counselors varied widely, as did their integration into the work patterns of their respective embassies. Some privately said they were treated as outsiders by the traditional embassy staff and rarely, if ever, worked with the ambassador or the deputy chief of mission, a coveted sign of recognition in diplomatic service. Much of their time was occupied with setting up appointments, ceremonial proceedings, and sightseeing tours for visiting chieftains of American science (often accompanied by their spouses).

No Help at the White House

Through succeeding presidential administrations, scientists campaigning for science in the State Department naturally sought help from the government's highest-ranking scientist, the president's assistant for science and technology. But the presidential science advisers possessed no influence over the State Department. D. Allan Bromley, President George Bush's science adviser, recalled his frustrations in dealing with the State Department, particularly in seeking the department's support for international cost-sharing of expensive research facilities, an urgent issue for science as the megamachines of science strained national budgets. "All [presidential] science advisers have failed miserably in dealing with the State Department," Bromley told me. "Maybe someday state will establish an American desk," he caustically remarked in describing his frustrated efforts. "I tried personal contact with the Secretary [of State]. I went over and talked to [Secretary] Jim Baker. And I talked to—thank God for [Deputy Secretary and later Secretary of State] Larry Eagleburger. He was a bright light in the whole thing. The problem there was that the State Department really didn't believe that science and technology were an important part of foreign relations."[18] After leaving the White House, John Gibbons spoke despairingly of his relations with the State Department during his five years as President Clinton's science adviser:

> They are driven. They are deeply possessed of the traditional sort of high
> stiff collar international diplomacy. They go to Tufts and Georgetown.
> They don't know science. They will speak favorably toward it, some of
> them, but it simply does not pervade the present bunch, from [former
> Secretary of State Warren] Christopher onward, who said, "Yeah, we've
> got to have stronger science in the State Department." If you look at our
> embassies overseas, our science advisers, our science counselors are peo-
> ple who are on one year's leave from Los Alamos [National Laboratory].
> They're not professionals, in that sense. They're learning on the job.[19]

From his experiences with the State Department as presidential science adviser in the Reagan administration, George Keyworth observed that "technology issues were not high on their value system. To them, wars were won by negotiation." Keyworth described the State Department as "atechnical, not antitechnical," adding that "oftentimes in old institutions, technology is not considered a high priority. At the Pentagon, it always has been," he said, "because we were rewarded by technology."[20]

ENVIRONMENTAL SUCCESS

Early in the Clinton administration, Secretary of State Warren Christopher embraced environmentalism as a prime goal of American foreign policy, directing the remaining embassy-based science counselors and attachés and the nonscientists who had inherited science duties to give priority to environmental matters: global change, protection of endangered species on land and sea, air and water pollution, and so forth. The secretary's commitment reflected Vice President Al Gore's passionate environmentalism. Declaring herself an environmentalist, too, Christopher's successor, Madeleine K. Albright, announced that "the State Department is changing the way we do business." Despite the budgetary constraints that had crimped

18. "News Notes," *SGR*, November 15, 1994.
19. Interview with author, December 6, 1998.
20. Interview with author, July 8, 1998.

the science positions in the embassies, Albright announced the creation of "regional environmental hubs" at U.S. embassies in Costa Rica, Uzbekistan, Ethiopia, Nepal, Jordan, and Thailand; she also declared the elevation of environmental cooperation as "an important part of our relationships with countries like Japan, India, Brazil, and China." Since many scientists, including leaders of science in Washington, were in the vanguard of the environmental movement, the Christopher-Albright commitment to environmentalism represented a victory for scientists in policymaking. But it was paid for by further reductions in the scientific presence in the department. The hierarchical ups and downs and personnel shifts within obscure sectors of the State Department did not rate the attention of the general press, but they were grimly noted by the leaders of the scientific community and their friends in Congress.

In 1997, citing the need to economize, the State Department eliminated the position of deputy assistant secretary for science, technology, and health, the highest science-related position within the department's home for science, the Bureau of Oceans and International Environmental and Scientific Affairs (OES). The termination of that job continued an erosion that had quietly been in progress for some time, including the reassignment of several staff members from work on international scientific issues to environmental duties without a fuss arising. However, science officials and their friends in Congress reacted with indignation to the elimination of the office of the deputy assistant for scientific matters. "We always thought state should pay *more* attention to science," said E. William Colglazier, executive director of the National Research Council, the operating arm of the National Academy of Sciences. "They're going in the wrong direction, downgrading the role of science," he told me, adding that "Environment is important, but science is important, too." Timothy Wirth, a former senator serving as under secretary for global affairs at the State Department, offered an imaginative perspective on the shrinkage in science-related positions under his jurisdiction. Wirth explained that the department "had shifted the responsibility for science to a higher level . . . and redistributed, not eliminated, the science and technology functions."[21]

A New Study

As the scientists' protests continued, with echoes of support from Capitol Hill, Secretary of State Albright publicly expressed concern about scien-

21. "In Brief," *SGR*, September 15, 1997.

tific deficiencies in her department—a matter that had not previously engaged her interest in visible fashion. Science had effectively wielded its embarrassment weapon, leaving the secretary with the choice of acting in a positive-seeming manner or appearing indifferent to the public-spirited concerns of leading figures of science. The secretary declared herself in sympathy with the scientists, saying she shared their distress about the condition of scientific competence in her department. Notwithstanding the many unfilled prescriptions for remedying the venerable problem, Albright announced that she had commissioned a new study to recommend how the State Department might strengthen its scientific and technical capabilities. The study would be conducted, she said, by the National Academy of Sciences, a deft choice that suggested contrition and a determination at last to strengthen the department in an important area after decades of neglect. As a source of agitation for infusing science into the making of foreign policy, the academy was not a dispassionate adviser. It could not be expected to conclude that the dearth of science at the State Department was no great impediment to the conduct of foreign policy; nor could the academy be expected to consider the possibility that the grousing scientists tended to exaggerate the benefits they could bring to Foggy Bottom. The secretary thus could be credited with courageous willingness to face shame by seeking advice from a harsh critic. As the elite institution of American science, renowned for providing expert, impartial advice to federal departments and agencies, the academy possessed credibility. Turning to the academy for advice demonstrated the State Department's determination to obtain a solution to its chronic neglect of science. Among the critics of the State Department, good manners now dictated a respectful silence while the academy worked on its assignment; when it was done, the State Department surely deserved a respite from criticism to ponder the recommendations and try, best as it could, to put them into effect. And thus began another episode in the department's half-century of seemingly earnest, but rarely productive, efforts to bring scientific understanding into the management of international affairs. Though as backward as ever in dealing with the complexities of science, technology, and international relations, the State Department had declared good intentions, moved swiftly to obtain sound advice, and thus was granted a ceasefire by the indignant scientists.

In May 1998, a member of Secretary Albright's inner circle, the counselor of the department, Wendy R. Sherman, sent a formal request for a study to Bruce Alberts, president of the National Academy of Sciences. "As you know," she wrote, "the State Department takes its responsibilities in the area of ST&H [science, technology and health] very seriously." Alberts was on record as holding the opposite opinion, having previously protested the neglect of science at the State Department to Under Secretary Wirth, apparently with the good effect of Wirth prodding Albright to commission the study. Counselor Sherman's letter of request stated that Secretary Albright invited the academy to join the department in a collaborative study of "the contributions that ST&H can make to foreign policy, and how the Department might better carry out its responsibilities to that end, within resource constraints."[22]

We have seen that academy studies come at a stiff financial price. The State Department was willing to be advised about its scientific failings, but in its straitened condition, did not choose to pay for remedial counseling. As so often happens in report politics, scientific style, angels appeared. William T. Golden, the Wall Street financier who remained deep in science politics ever since studying presidential science advice for Harry Truman, came forward with a donation of $275,000 from the Golden Family Foundation. An additional $25,000 was provided by the Carnegie Corporation. The State Department itself provided no financial support for the study it now requested, nor did the academy dip into its own resources, as it does on occasion for financing studies.[23]

In June 1998, about a month after the State Department sought the academy's assistance, but before the academy study was under way, an announcement from the State Department indicated a preemptive move concerning its faulty management of science and international affairs: the department would soon appoint a "science adviser," a "distinguished person," to "work with scientific issues at the State Department and to develop a scientific policy."[24] The intention was announced by Melinda Kibble, the assistant secretary in charge of the Bureau of Oceans and International Environmental and Scientific Affairs, the long-criticized center of scientific neglect in the foreign-policy establishment. The State Department hoped to make the appointment during the summer of 1998, Kibble announced, a hope that was finally fulfilled—three years later.

---

22. *Plus ça change, plus c'est la même chose:* Forty-eight years earlier, in addressing the subject of science in the State Department, Lloyd Berkner and his colleagues asked, "How can the potentialities of scientific progress be integrated into the formulation of foreign policy, and the administration of foreign relations, so that the maximum advantage of scientific progress and development can be acquired by all peoples?" Quoted in *Science and Technology in U.S. International Affairs* (Carnegie Commission on Science, Technology, and Government, 1992), p. 32.
23. Financial information concerning the study was provided, at my request, by the academy's News Office.
24. "State Department to Hire Science Adviser," *Nature,* June 18, 1998.

Meanwhile, the academy quickly responded to the State Department's request for assistance, appointing a seventeen-member study committee, chaired by Robert Frosch, a scientist-technologist with unrivaled experience in the management of major research endeavors and in Washington science politics. In a long career, Frosch had served as assistant secretary of the navy for research and development (from 1966 to 1973) and administrator of NASA (from 1977 to 1981). In 1982, Frosch became vice president of General Motors Research Laboratories, a post he held for eleven years. At the time Frosch accepted the academy committee assignment, he was a senior research fellow at the Center for Science and International Affairs at Harvard's Kennedy School of Government. Among the members of the committee were:

David Hamburg, recently retired from the presidency of the Carnegie Corporation, parent of the commission that assailed the State Department in 1992

Robert White, former president of the National Academy of Engineering

Roland Schmitt, former GE vice president for research, former president of Rensselaer Polytechnic Institute, and former chairman of the National Science Board

Philip Smith, in business as a consultant on the Washington end of science and technology issues, following long service as the chief assistant of Frank Press during Press's nearly four years as Jimmy Carter's science adviser and twelve years as president of the National Academy of Sciences

With these and others of similar distinction, the academy fielded an estimable committee. In the crucial roles of staff members for the committee were two scientists who had experienced the interplay of science and diplomacy firsthand: John Boright, the academy's executive director for international affairs, formerly posted at the U.S. Embassy in Paris; and Glenn E. Schweitzer, a former science attaché in the Moscow Embassy.

URGENT RECOMMENDATIONS FOR REFORM

Under Frosch, known as a martinet chairman, the committee moved quickly, in comparison to the customary pace of many of these bodies. In September 1998, four months after the announcement of its appointment, the committee issued an "interim report" specifying "immediate and practical steps" to remedy some of the most serious deficiencies in the State Department's capacity for dealing with science-related issues.[25] Frosch later said the interim report was prepared at the request of the State Department, though, in keeping with tradition, the department did virtually nothing in response to the recommendations. Conveying a sense of urgency, the interim report called for promptly establishing a scientific presence at key points throughout the department, starting with the secretary's designation of an under secretary of state to ensure proper attention to science-related matters. Under secretaries, of which there are only six in the State Department, are at the third level of the hierarchy, immediately below the deputy secretary of state. There is also a need, the interim report stated, for "receptors in dozens of offices throughout the Department capable of identifying valid sources of relevant [scientific] advice and of absorbing such advice." Though the interim report was necessarily the product of hurried deliberations, and only nine pages in length, the Frosch committee devoted several of those pages to portraying the State Department as an unrelieved wasteland of scientific neglect and ignorance:

> The Department has little appreciation of the existence, significance, and implications of many of the hundreds of collaborative arrangements between the Department of Defense and researchers in the former Soviet Union and other important countries. The Department has not addressed the international dimensions of the alternative U.S. energy policies that must take into account a variety of technologies being developed throughout the country. . . . In addition, only because of the last-minute intervention of the scientific community did the Department recognize the importance of access by researchers to data bases that were the subject of draft legislation and international negotiations with regard to intellectual property rights.[26]

The report noted that some senior State Department officials felt that, within the Foreign Service, recognition of the place of scientific issues in international affairs was "at a low level, perhaps comparable to the level of acceptance of the field of economics as a central aspect of foreign policy 15 years ago. However, there is a difference," the Frosch interim report asserted: recognition of the importance of economics had long been on the upswing, while attention to science and health in Foggy Bottom "comes

---

25. "Improving the Use of Science, Technology, and Health Expertise in U.S. Foreign Policy: A Preliminary Report" (National Academy of Sciences, 1998).
26. Ibid.

and goes." Mindful of the budget difficulties that the State Department had cited in explaining its neglect of science, the Frosch committee said that "up to $500,000," for about a dozen new positions and related costs, would suffice for implementing the interim recommendations, a sum it described as "modest given the stakes involved." Having issued the interim report in September 1998, the Frosch committee said that its final report would be released in September 1999. But, even before the committee delivered its final recommendations, it could not contain its fears of scientific recidivism by the managers of foreign policy. Expressing doubt about reforms taking root at the State Department, the Frosch committee said it would consider ways to "institutionalize" a working relationship between science and foreign policy, "even if future leaders of the Department have less of a personal interest in this topic than the current leaders." It might seem presumptuous for an inconspicuous advisory committee to attempt to superimpose its preferences on future secretaries of state, assuming it could succeed with that strategy. But, repeatedly frustrated by indifference in Foggy Bottom, the leaders of science were determined to maximize their opportunity.

Not all were optimistic, however. D. Allan Bromley, who had futilely grappled with science and state while serving as President Bush's assistant for science and technology, was frankly skeptical that the academy study would have any effect in Foggy Bottom. Though not a member of the Frosch committee, Bromley knew of its work from the science-policy grapevine. Discussing it with me in October 1998, Bromley said a State Department official had confided to him that the proposed science adviser in the State Department would hold GS-15 rank—top of the government's general salary schedule, but below the select ranks of the federal senior executive service. Bromley said he relayed the information to William Golden, the financier of the academy study, telling him, "You'll be damned lucky if you get a bachelor's degree for this. . . . Bill [Golden] was appropriately shaken by this," Bromley told me, "and he says, 'I've got to do something.' When I saw him on Monday, he had talked to Albright again, and pointed out that this was not adequate, this was not what he had in mind. She sort of patted him on the head and said she would look into this, but the fact of the matter is," Bromley concluded, "they do not really want this."[27]

Though nothing tangible occurred in response to the interim recommendations that the Frosch committee produced at the request of the State Department, reaffirmations of good intentions continued to emanate from

---

27. Interview with author, October 7, 1998.

Foggy Bottom. In April 1999, Frank E. Loy, the newly appointed successor to Timothy Wirth as under secretary of state for global affairs, declared his commitment to raising the level of scientific expertise within the department. As a first step, he said, to be taken even before the scheduled September 1999 delivery of the Frosch committee's final report, the State Department was seeking a science adviser—a quest, it should be recalled, initially announced fifteen months earlier, with the stated expectation of filling the position within a few months. The science adviser, it was explained, would have "dotted line" reporting authority to the secretary of state—a pathway second only to solid-line reporting authority in administrative cartography at the department. Loy also announced plans for a series of roundtable discussions between scientists and State Department officials.

The final report of the Frosch committee, "The Pervasive Role of Science, Technology, and Health in Foreign Policy: Imperatives for the State Department,"[28] was released at the National Academy of Sciences on October 7, 1999, eighteen months after it was requested by the secretary of state. The report provided fresh details on the pallid condition of scientific competence in the department—for example, "The number of Science Counselor positions in [U.S.] embassies and missions has been reduced from 22 in the mid-1980s to 10, and whereas almost all of the 22 had strong technical backgrounds, few of the 10 current incumbents have such backgrounds." The report stated that "issues involving science and technology have moved to the forefront of the international diplomatic agenda," but the department still lacked suitable staff for dealing with them. As examples, it described foreign policy issues with "significant STH [science, technology and health] content," among them "U.S. Sanctions on Russian Scientific Institutions," "Removal of Uranium from Kazakhstan," "Global Climate Change," and "Arsenic in Drinking Wells in Bangladesh." The report recommended the upgrading of scientific competence throughout the foreign-policy establishment, starting with the appointment of a "highly qualified STH Senior Advisor to the Secretary" and extending to in-service science courses for foreign service officers. The report, however, candidly acknowledged that, apart from bringing the tale up to date, it was retelling an old story:

> A number of conclusions and recommendations in this report were also
> set forth in earlier studies. Some were accepted and implemented by the
> Department for a period of time (e.g., technically trained Science Coun-

---

28. "The Pervasive Role of Science, Technology, and Health in Foreign Policy: Imperatives for the State Department" (Washington, D.C.: National Academy Press, 1999).

selors at key embassies, an advisory committee on science and technology), but then the Department changed its approach. Others have been rejected altogether (e.g., organizational restructuring of the Department). Thus, the report may at times seem repetitious of previous efforts. The committee believes, however, that even if suggestions similar to its own recommendations have been rejected in the past, they should be raised again because of the rapid technological changes underway throughout the world, which call for new directions in the formulation and implementation of foreign policy.[29]

Chairman Frosch said Secretary of State Albright had "expressed interest in the report" and that Academy President Bruce Alberts had asked to meet with her, but a date had not yet been arranged because of the Secretary's crowded schedule. Asked what he thought the outcome would be, Frosch said, "We can be as cynical as anybody else." But, he emphasized, "We have had an expression of interest from the secretary."

It cannot be said that the State Department remained immobilized on the issue following release of the academy's critical findings and hopeful recommendations on the department's treatment of science. A few days later, the State Department announced that it had engaged John Gibbons, President Clinton's former adviser for science and technology, to provide counsel on implementing the recommendations. For this purpose, the department announced, Gibbons would serve one day a week as a consultant. In December 1999, Under Secretary Frank Loy briefed the President's Committee of Advisors for Science and Technology on the State Department's response to the Frosch recommendations. That he had little progress to report was noted by several members of the presidential advisory committee, among them David Hamburg, the former Carnegie Corporation president, who had served on the Frosch committee. Loy insisted that, in difficult circumstances, the department was sincerely attempting to improve its scientific capabilities. Referring to congressional sentiments on the side of science, the under secretary complimented the political prowess of science: "The scientific community has more sway on Capitol Hill than the foreign affairs community." Even so, science remained an outsider when the State Department entered the new millennium. In February 2000, a little over four months after delivery of the Frosch report to the State Department, Secretary Albright addressed the annual meeting of the American Associa-

29. Ibid.

tion for the Advancement of Science. Acknowledging that the "State Department's science capabilities have not been as substantial as they should be," Albright said she was awaiting "the final report of a Departmental Task Force on Strengthening Science at State." But one step was assured, she said: "I will appoint a Science Advisor as soon as possible, who will be located within the Under Secretariat for Global Affairs."[30]

In May 2000, Secretary Albright announced plans to upgrade the department's scientific capabilities. As a first step, she said, she would appoint a science and technology adviser to "lead a department-wide effort to ensure that science, technology and health issues are properly integrated into our foreign policy."[31] A search for the adviser was under way, State Department officials said, but they pointed out that recruiting was difficult with just a few months remaining in the presidential term. In September 2000, with just four months in office remaining for the Clinton administration, the State Department swore in a science and technology adviser to the secretary of state: Norman P. Neureiter, a Ph.D. chemist, age 68, a retired industrial executive with extensive international experience and prior service at NSF, the White House science office, and the State Department. The longevity of his appointment was uncertain, given the imminence of inauguration day and the selection of a new secretary of state. But the strategy was clear: to get someone on board in Foggy Bottom and hope for the best.

Neureiter was among the State Department officials who, at least initially, survived the change of cast when Colin Powell succeeded Albright as secretary of state. In February 2001, Neureiter reported progress in establishing scientific and technical competence in the department: five scientists on temporary loan from NASA, plus an unspecified number from NSF, would be posted to the department; the American Institute of Physics had established a fellowship for a scientist to serve at state, and a competitive contract had been awarded to the American Association for the Advancement of Science to provide scientific and technical training for Foreign Service officers. These were hopeful steps, though of modest expense to the cash-strapped department and, given the disadvantages of borrowed staff, far short of creating a robust presence of science and technology. But, viewed against the long history of neglect, the trend was favorable.

The saga of state and science illuminates the limited power of science in public affairs. Pending the outcome of the latest installment in the long

30. Secretary of State Madeleine Albright, "Remarks at American Association for the Advancement of Science," Washington, D.C., February 21, 2000.
31. Albright, "Policy Statements on Science & Technology and Diplomacy," May 12, 2000.

campaign to bring science to Foggy Bottom, only the chronically gullible can accept that the managers of the U.S. Department of State are durably concerned about its deficiencies in scientific expertise, or ever had been. In response to nagging and embarrassment, the department intermittently adopted remedial measures, but none took hold to become integral to the conduct of international relations. In the most political city, science is deliberately and thoroughly apolitical, for good reasons of its own, as recounted earlier. Irrespective of the wisdom or necessity of that choice, science remains apolitical, aloof from the system of money, votes, and the ensuing influence that undergirds American politics. As a consequence, science is relegated, in pursuing its goals, to relying on the respect and goodwill that American society generally bestows upon science. Like other weaklings in difficult situations, science can employ the weapon of embarrassment against those who fail to satisfy its wants, financial and political. Additionally, it regularly invokes the broad national interest as a justification for attention to its concerns. But curiously, as the long-lived scientific alumni of World War II and the early postwar years fade from the Washington scene, social passions and political concerns have diminished in the great American scientific enterprise. We move on to look at that phenomenon.

CHAPTER 21

From Social and Political Passion to Grubbing for Money

Much of my academic training discouraged meaningful involvement in the public arena. . . . I was equally dismayed to see that most scientists in the field—many of them government scientists or academics whose work was being discounted by industry lobbyists— kept their distance from policy debates. The general view in academe was that scholars should merely provide information; their scientific objectivity was suspect if they revealed an interest in how the information was used. Many colleges and universities penalized professors during tenure reviews for trying to get involved in policy debates.

> —Carl Safina, lecturer, Yale University School of Forestry
> and Environmental Studies, and director,
> Living Oceans Program, National Audubon Society,
> *Chronicle of Higher Education*, November 6, 1998

The failure of science to produce benefits for the poor in recent decades is due to two factors working in combination: the pure scientists have become more detached from the mundane needs of humanity, and the applied scientists have become more attached to immediate profitability.

> —Freeman Dyson, in *Imagined Worlds*
> (Harvard University Press, 1997)

THE SCIENTIFIC assault on the State Department was the work of the old guard of science politics. Otherwise, in the new millennium, the political and social fires burn low or have gone out in science, while the pursuit of money remains an obsession—a rising, pervasive, organized activity throughout the scientific enterprise. In most years over the past two decades, politics obliged with increasing volumes of money.

But when it hesitated or lagged, universities and other dependencies of government research funds responded quickly and formidably with their own special lobbying forces and techniques. Professionally run and politically potent in their innovative apolitical fashion, the science and higher education lobbies benefit from the obsolete impression that they are provincial innocents in the dangerous wilds of Washington. As we have seen, they are not. Doubts about the high priority that science claims on public resources are assailed as ignorance, as in the denunciations of Congress for balking at the runaway costs of the SSC. Legitimate inquiries are dismissed as hostility to science, and denial of financial growth deemed to guarantee economic misfortune. In the intricate financing of science by government, the assault on government and the public is, ironically, financed by government under the benign guise of promoting the public understanding of science.

Retreat from Arms Issues

The demobilization of science from politics and social engagement is a fact of scientific life that is recognized, and sometimes lamented, in the profession. Reviewing the deep involvement of scientists in arms control from the end of World War II until the mid-1980s, Kurt Gottfried, professor of physics emeritus at Cornell University, observed in 1999 that "the physics community's current engagement with the issue is feeble in comparison with earlier years."[1] The union of science and mammon was described in characteristically blunt terms by Kary Mullis, the eccentric, brazenly outspoken recipient of the 1993 Nobel Prize in chemistry (for his invention of the polymerase chain reaction, the indispensable tool of genetics research):

> Probably the most important scientific development of the twentieth century is that economics replaced curiosity as the driving force behind research. Academic, government, and industrial laboratories need money for salaries for staff: the primary investigator and his technicians, postdocs, graduate students, and secretaries. They need lab space, equipment, travel expenses, overhead payments to the institution, including the salaries and expenses of administrators, financial officers, more secretaries, maintenance of grounds around the institution, security officers, publication costs for scientific reports in scientific journals, librarians,

1. Kurt Gottfried, "Physicists in Politics," *Physics Today,* March 1999.

janitors, and so on. It's expensive, and there's a lot of pressure on a professional scientist to maintain or expand a laboratory domain.[2]

The last large-scale political mobilization of scientists unrelated to money for research occurred in the mid-1980s, when several thousand university scientists vowed to take no part in Ronald Reagan's Star Wars program.[3] The individual opposition to the missile-defense program was accompanied by searching studies and critical public reports by professional scientific societies and scientifically oriented public-interest organizations. Thousands of other scientists, however, sought Star Wars money and took it when they could get it. The issues that concern us here are not the technical feasibility of missile defense, or its strategic merits and liabilities. Rather, we can look back to the Star Wars controversies of the 1980s as the last major eruption of political passion in the community of science—apart from the periodic eruptions exclusively related to money. Overall, the scientific community was gratefully aware that Ronald Reagan had evolved into a pro-science president, committed to a rapid doubling of the NSF budget and construction of the Superconducting Super Collider. After Reagan left office, Star Wars continued to flourish under President Bush, though at a lesser financial pace than originally planned. However, both the scientific leadership and the rank and file of scientists lost interest in this extracurricular political concern and all others. Shedding Teller's fantasies of the X-ray laser, and rechristened as the Ballistic Missile Defense Organization, the former Star Wars enterprise continued at $3 billion to $4 billion per year throughout eight years of the Clinton administration—barely, if at all, noticed or protested by the scientific community.

From the birth of Star Wars, in 1984, to the end of the century, missile defense consumed over $60 billion.[4] The enormous expenditures, which have produced negligible results, were approximately double the sums spent in that time by NSF for research in universities; or, to consider a government research commitment that resonates with the general public, Star

2. Kary Mullis, *Dancing Naked in the Mind Field* (New York: Pantheon Books, 1998), p. 113.

3. It might be objected that the widespread agitation for rapid expansion of AIDS research early in the epidemic provides another example of scientific social involvement. Some scientists indeed were prominently involved in that cause. But the main propulsion for a government-financed response to AIDS came from gay organizations in association with patient groups and sympathetic figures in politics, entertainment, and the arts. Concerned about shortcuts in established scientific methodology, the scientific leadership, in fact, was resistant to demands for accelerated testing of drugs and relaxation of the conventional standards for clinical trials.

4. *Physics Today*, July 1999.

Wars outspent cancer research by at least three to one, without evoking, among scientists or the general public, detectable discussion of research priorities. In 1999, when the Comprehensive Test Ban Treaty came before a hostile Republican-controlled Senate, where it was swiftly rejected, support invoking the knowledge and prestige of science was limited: a petition for approval by thirty-two Nobel laureates, mostly elders of the profession, and low-power supportive statements by several scientific organizations. Otherwise, the scientific enterprise demonstrated no interest and raised no protest over the defeat of what was a holy goal among American scientists for nearly half a century. In July 2000, as a decision approached on deployment of a limited missile-defense system, fifty Nobel laureates expressed their opposition in an open letter to President Clinton sponsored by the Federation of American Scientists. The FAS described the Nobel assemblage as perhaps the largest ever in behalf of a given cause. The appeal received six inches on page A8 of the *New York Times,* but virtually no other notice in the press or support from other scientists or scientific organizations. Leading the petition was one of the surviving leaders of the Manhattan Project, Hans Bethe.

The practice of science is detached from historical understanding: the state of scientific knowledge is what this week's journal says it is; last week's journal is obsolete. And so it is at the intersection of science and public policy, where institutional amnesia easily flourishes. Throughout the early post–World War II years, the American Physical Society—the professional association of many of the guilt-ridden bomb builders of World War II—was deeply engaged in resisting government-imposed secrecy, promoting international collaboration against the chill of the Cold War, working for arms control, and resisting political intrusions on scientific integrity. But as the years went on, the APS receded from politics and turned its attention to lobbying for money. Occasionally, the old spirit of political engagement would revive—it was the APS that rounded up the thirty-two Nobelists in 1999 to support the nuclear test ban. But for the new generation running the American Physical Society, the past involvement of their organization in the great scientific-political issues of wartime and the Cold War era was apparently unknown. In 1999, in commemorating its centennial, the *APS News* stated:

> Until recently, the American Physical Society prided itself on its aloofness from matters of public policy. It saw itself as an organization devoted exclusively to the affairs of pure science. The archival record tells another story, and one of which the Society might equally be proud. Time and again the Society entered the field of politics—with petitions

to Congress, telegrams to news agencies, and well-placed letters—in order to defend the scientific integrity, freedom, and loyalty of its members. During the war years, the APS was responsive to the needs of
national security without losing sight of the long-term goals of international cooperation.[5]

The renewed scientific agitation in the 1990s for admission to the State
Department was a rare venture beyond the professional reservation, inspired and conducted by a small number of scientists and political colleagues, with no involvement of the mass of scientists (or even noticeable
awareness on their part). In the final two decades of the twentieth century,
sparks of social or political concern would occasionally appear within the
scientific community, but they were increasingly rare, brief, and narrowly
focused on matters of special importance to the culture of science.

For example, in the tradition of scientific internationalism, many of
the leaders of American science came to the aid of their dissident Soviet
counterparts during the 1980s, the final decade of the Cold War. American
scientists, joined by European colleagues, attempted to use their prestige
and professional connections to ease the plight of Soviet scientists at home
and to assist emigration and find employment for those who left the USSR.
In 1980, the National Academy of Sciences suspended many of its collaborative research activities with the Soviet Academy of Sciences to protest the
persecution of dissident Soviet scientists. Prominent among them was An-
drei Sakharov, "father" of the Soviet hydrogen bomb, whose odyssey from
bomb building to arms control paralleled the experience of many American
nuclear-weapons scientists. Unaffected by the suspension, however, were
arms-control discussions between members of the two academies—reflecting the deep concerns about nuclear proliferation and war among the
American participants, extending back to World War II. Though Soviet scientists were eager to retain their connections to the world-leading American
scientific community, their government persisted in its crackdown on the
dissidents, sending Sakharov into internal exile in Gorky, a closed city. In
1985, the U.S. National Academy of Sciences moved toward a resumption
of the collaborative ties, without any sign of humanitarian softening by the
Soviets. Three Nobel-laureate members of the academy objected to reports
of a rapprochement between the two elite scientific institutions, asking, in
a letter published in *Science:*

5. "Public Affairs," *APS News,* December 1999, excerpts from an exhibit displayed at the
APS Centennial Meeting.

What then has changed in the past 5 years to explain the about-face from the moral stance of 1980? Have human rights for scientists in the USSR shown improvement? Sakharov is representative of scores of others; his situation has worsened—neither he nor his wife can get the medical attention they request, and she too has been banished to Gorky. Scientific seminars by refusenik scientists are in danger of elimination. The NAS [National Academy of Sciences] Human Rights Committee, in a recent report, sounds angry: "none of our numerous letters and telegrams to the Soviet authorities have been answered. Many new arrests of scientists have come to the attention of the Committee. . . ." If anything has changed, it has been for the worse.[6]

Nearly a year later, the Soviets granted Sakharov's wife an exit visa to obtain medical care in the west, but Sakharov's status remained unchanged. At about the same time, Anatoly Sharansky, another dissident scientist, was released from prison and permitted to leave the Soviet Union. A few days later, the two academies announced a new agreement for reciprocal research visits and other collaborative activities. The Soviets had yielded some, but very little, on human rights. Nonetheless, the U.S. academy, valuing scientific relations over human rights, had entered into another agreement with the oppressors of Sakharov and other scientists. In justification of the renewed ties, the academy stressed the importance of maintaining communications with its influential counterpart in an adversary nation in a tense period. The argument cannot be wholly dismissed, but it should be recalled that throughout the long suspension of scientific relations, the two academies continued to confer on arms-control issues. For the managers of the U.S. academy, the decision to resume scientific relations with the Soviets may have reflected the future in their bones, but it did not indicate a passion for justice in their hearts.

ATTENTION TURNS INWARD

The retreat of scientists from social and political concerns has been a creeping, continuous process, with only occasionally a dramatically revealing event, such as the Sakharov episode. But, as with a slowly receding glacier, the movement is recognizable over time. Scientists constitute a very small part of the American population, and we must allow they are not

---

6. *Science,* May 3, 1985, letter by Christian B. Anfinsen, Johns Hopkins University; Paul J. Flory, Stanford University; and Arno Z. Penzias, Bell Laboratories.

always identifiable as scientists when they become involved with issues out-side their profession. The civil rights and anti–Vietnam War movements were strongly supported by academics; scientists were among them, promi-nent in publicizing the health effects of the massive defoliation program that the United States conducted during the war. Many scientists enlisted in the environmental cause, where their skills could be relevant, but they were swallowed up in what evolved into a mass movement capable of roll-ing on without them. The past suggests that a frightening issue with a nota-bly scientific character is necessary to bring scientists out under the banner of science. For that purpose, nothing has matched the bomb. At the begin-ning of the nuclear age, scientists created the Federation of American Scien-tists and published the *Bulletin of the Atomic Scientists* to campaign for arms control, civilian control of nuclear energy, international scientific coopera-tion, and similar causes dear to the scientific community. Barry Goldwater's nuclear bravado spawned Scientists and Engineers for Johnson-Humphrey in 1964, followed by doubts of propriety among scientists that precluded further large-scale forays into politics. As a mobilizing cause for scientists, the nuclear threat was unique, unmatched in later years by chemical and biological weapons, the idealism of environmentalism and human rights, and Pandora's-box fears of genetic engineering.

No great mass of scientists has coalesced around any of these issues, nor have any of the standing professional organizations of science embraced them with the same gusto, and expenditure of resources, that they devote to the money issues of science. A reconnaissance along the border of science and society finds scientists comfortably established in the scientific ghetto, rarely looking or venturing outward except to politick for money for science and minimal regulation of research. The indices are scattered and perhaps not definitive, multiple bits and pieces here and there, but they all point in a single direction—away from social and political involvement by America's scientists. In this respect, they do not differ from their compatriots outside the scientific enterprise. Voter participation in presidential elections fell to 49 percent in 1996, from a post–World War II peak of 62.8 percent in 1960. Robert D. Putnam's intriguing, though disputed, "Bowling Alone" thesis contends the "joiner" tradition has faded from society, leading to sharp declines in Parent-Teacher Association and labor union memberships, and the titular 40 percent decline in league bowling during the 1980s.[7]

---

7. Robert D. Putnam's "Bowling Alone," originally published as an article in the *Journal of Democracy* in 1995, has been expanded into a book-length study, *Bowling Alone: Civic Disengagement in America* (New York: Simon & Schuster, 2000).

That scientists have been moving with these currents is not surprising. In important respects, however, they differ from others who have been swept along: scientists are the creators and custodians of special knowledge of universal consequence. And for doing their work, scientists are dependent on political support and public money. Yet they are increasingly remote from the public. The efforts that science invests in promoting the public understanding of science are overwhelmingly motivated by the belief that understanding brings money, that public ignorance is a hindrance to science. The aim is to induce the public to like and want science—but to leave science to the scientists.

Signs of Detachment

In tracking science's retreat to the ghetto, let's start with a report of an episode at a gathering of scientists. At the March 1998 meeting of the American Physical Society, in Los Angeles, the program listed a workshop of the APS Committee on the International Freedom of Scientists (CIFS) titled "International Freedom of Scientists: What the Physics Community Can Do and Is Doing." But, as reported in *Science,*

> [the] workshop on human rights had to be canceled when only two of the thousands of physicists at the meeting registered for it. Then a Chinese graduate student in physics destroyed literature at a CIFS booth, enraged by what he said were false depictions of human-rights abuses in his home country. To top it off, an APS official then ordered CIFS representatives to remove the materials that had just been defaced, saying that boldface words like "torture" and "repression" on posters and flyers were too inflammatory. For human-rights activists in the scientific community, the combination of apathy from many scientists, ambivalence from others and hostility from a few has become a familiar experience in recent years. Many organizations have seen scientist interest in human rights slip into a long-term decline after decades of raucous agitation on behalf of Soviet dissidents during the Cold War. . . . although human-rights subcommittees at the AAAS [American Association for the Advancement of Science], the American Chemical Society and the National Academy of Sciences remain active advancing their cause, their parent organizations are increasingly decoupling scientific activities from activism.[8]

8. James Glanz, "Human Rights Fades as a Cause for Scientists," *Science,* October 9, 1998.

Another item, inconclusive by itself but deserving notice, is the steady decline, over the past two decades, in the paid circulation of *The Bulletin of the Atomic Scientists* (as reported annually in the publication, in accordance with postal regulations). In 1975, the *Bulletin* reported a circulation of 18,500; the figure rose slightly over the next decade, reaching 21,467 in 1985. Then the circulation went into a decline, falling to 16,513 in 1990 and down to 6,925 in 1998.[9] No publication has supplanted the *Bulletin* in its self-assigned performance—a bit on the preachy side—as the conscience of science, as well as an intrepid investigator of science-related issues. The performance goes on, but the audience has dwindled.

The opposite is the case with another publication, the century-old MIT *Technology Review*, where the performance was abruptly changed and the audience soared. Owned by the Association of Alumni and Alumnae of the Massachusetts Institute of Technology, the publication is for obvious reasons closely identified with MIT. Prior to 1998, *Technology Review* occupied a special niche as a forum for articles and opinion pieces on the social and political implications of scientific and technological developments. In 1998, virtually all the staff that had presided over the established editorial menu were cast out and the magazine was reformulated as a predominantly gee-whiz, cheerleading chronicle of the latest wonders from R&D and their commercial exploitation; a new banner, "MIT's Magazine of Innovation," now sits above the original title.[10] Circulation rocketed, from 92,000 to 205,000 in less than two years, the *New York Times* reported; it attributed the extraordinary growth to changing "the focus from sometimes Luddite reviews to more upbeat coverage of innovation in technology, science and business." The *Times* added, "The magazine is gambling in its attempt to mix science and the marketplace, two sectors that traditionally keep each other at arm's length."[11]

Membership in the Federation of American Scientists stood at approximately 7,000 in 1975, according to Jeremy Stone, longtime FAS president,

---

9. Mike Moore, editor of the *Bulletin,* cautions against attempting to derive sociopolitical conclusions from the circulation data. The publication, he told me, has "always been a shoestring operation." Scientists were "a big part" of the audience in the 1960s, he said, but, because of its limited resources, the *Bulletin* has not analyzed its current audience. Moore noted that the *Bulletin* "is not popular among scientists. Scientists feel you compromise science if you speak on politics; that you compromise your objectivity." Conversation with author, January 5, 2000.

10. Disclosure: prior to its changeover, I occasionally published articles and reviews in the old *Technology Review.*

11. "MIT Re-engineers Magazine to Attract New Readers and Ads," *New York Times,* July 19, 1999.

who retired in 2000. By the late 1990s, it had fallen to 2,000–3,000, he said, adding that the "hard core" remained from the FAS's early days of activism on nuclear issues. Because of rising mail and promotion costs and competition for similar recruits from a proliferation of other public-interest organizations, Stone told me, the FAS increasingly relied on philanthropic grants. He said that for a promotional mailing, he once attempted to obtain the membership list of the Federation of American Societies for Experimental Biology, but FASEB declined, though it does rent its list to other organizations. "FASEB denied us the list. They were against political action," Stone said.[12] FASEB, however, energetically lobbies in behalf of raising government spending on biomedical research.[13]

New generations of scientists have displayed little interest in the nuclear issues that animated their post–World War II forebears. A possible explanation is that international agreements and the collapse of the Soviet Union have significantly reduced the nuclear menace. But that's debatable, given the nuclear ambitions of Iraq, Iran, North Korea, and other states, uncertain accountability for the huge nuclear arsenal left behind by the Soviet Union, and the nuclear attainments of China, Pakistan, and India. But even without the nuclear threat, scientists could rally to social and political causes, as they once did, if they were so inclined; or, at a minimum, they could seek to keep abreast of issues related to but beyond the professional boundaries of science.

Fewer and fewer, however, appear interested in doing so, as suggested by the sluggish growth, and recent declines, in the membership of the nation's preeminent general scientific society, the American Association for the Advancement of Science. The AAAS is best known as the publisher of the weekly journal *Science,* which accompanies membership and is the main attraction for joining the organization. With a subscription to the journal included, the annual individual membership fee, $112 in 2000, was not prohibitive; many subscribers can legitimately charge the cost to their research grants or institutional funds. In addition to being a coveted site for

12. Telephone conversation with author, October 22, 1998.
13. In a memoir published in 1999, Stone wrote: "No one in Congress or in foundations seemed to care much about how many members we had. It was, really, just an issue of raising revenue. And for this, membership was not very cost-effective. . . . What did seem to matter to the media and Congress was the quantity and quality of names on our letterhead. Accordingly, I worked hard at recruiting famous scientists, especially Nobel Prize winners"—of whom he eventually signed up forty, "about 50 percent of all living U.S. Nobel Prize winners in science and peace." Jeremy Stone, *Every Man Should Try: Adventures of a Public Interest Activist* (New York: Public Affairs Press, 1999), p. 73.

original research papers, *Science* provides extensive news coverage of science and government relations, and also fosters lively discussions of the social implications of scientific research. No other magazine like it is published in the United States. The internationally circulated British journal *Nature* is the only close competitor in the publication of original research and discussions of social and political issues. But, with approximately one-third the *Science* circulation, and only a portion of that in the United States, *Nature* does not cut heavily into the AAAS market.

In addition to its role as a leading scientific publisher, the AAAS is also involved in various activities at the interface of science and society. The AAAS Directorate for Science and Policy Programs includes the Science, Freedom and Law Program, the Science and Human Rights Program, and the Program of Dialogue Between Science and Religion. The directorate also tracks government support of science through the AAAS R&D Budget and Policy Program, and it manages the Center for Science, Technology, and Congress, which aims to enlighten Capitol Hill about research-related matters. The AAAS annually presents a plaque and a $2,500 award for Scientific Freedom and Responsibility, in recognition of good works in the public realm by a scientist or engineer. In recent decades, this broad range of activities, along with the excellent journal *Science,* would seem to ensure a large and growing membership from within the expanding ranks of science, and from beyond, as well, among the many laypeople interested in research. But it hasn't.

In 1980, according to the National Science Foundation, 645,000 scientists and engineers, at all degree levels, were employed in research and development in the United States.[14] By 1995, the number had increased almost fivefold, to 3.2 million.[15] Using generous definitions of training and vocational involvement with science and technology, NSF says that "the size of the S&E [science and engineering] workforce stands at upwards of 6 million people, with a probable ceiling of 8 million."[16] Definitions and numbers are debatable, but by any measure, the professional ranks of science and technology have grown rapidly, in accompaniment to the expanded role of science and technology in national security, the economy, and culture. However, the AAAS has failed to grow with its natural constituency and draws only a minuscule slice of the contemporary scientific com-

14. *Indicators 1980* (NSB 81-1), p. 208.
15. "Employment of Scientists and Engineers Reached 3.2 Million in 1995," *Data Brief* (NSF 98-325).
16. "Counting the S&E Workforce—It's Not Easy," *Issue Brief* (NSF 99-34, May 3, 1999).

munity. The AAAS membership grew rapidly after World War II, rising from 28,725 in 1945 to 98,307 in 1965. After that, growth continued, though sluggishly, reaching 135,851 in 1990. For the decade of the 1990s, the AAAS figures show average annual total membership and the foreign component within the total. The numbers reveal a substantial decline in domestic membership and an accompanying increase in the foreign count, with the total almost unchanged from the beginning to the end of the decade:

	Total	Foreign
1990	135,851	4,965
1991	132,675	5,485
1992	135,300	8,430
1993	140,086	12,422
1994	142,740	15,346
1995	143,460	17,732
1996	141,691	19,318
1997	142,032	21,392
1998	140,971	21,611
1999	136,851	21,230

These figures indicate not only a decade-long stagnation in membership, but also a domestic decline from 130,886 in 1990 to 115,621 in 1999—a period of substantial growth in the American scientific enterprise.[17] Richard S. Nicholson, executive officer of the AAAS and publisher of *Science,* told me foreign members have been increasingly solicited to satisfy advertisers' reach for global markets. He attributed the drop-off in American members to "a lot of little things," including institutional purchase of Internet access that enables scientists to scan papers and job ads in *Science.* There has also been a drop-off in membership among scientists who received bargain-priced subscriptions as graduate students and postdoctoral fellows. Nicholson pointed out, too, that the great majority of AAAS members are Ph.D. holders employed in the physical and life sciences; and estimating that pool at about 250,000—the count varies, as we have seen—said market penetration was fairly strong. As for trends in participation in the AAAS' public-affairs activities, Nicholson said, "It's always been a small fraction of the membership."[18]

17. Data from AAAS Office of Membership and Meetings.
18. Conversation with author, March 16, 2000.

Among the members of the AAAS, participation in the annual election of officers is negligible, as it is in most scientific societies. In the 1999 election for the AAAS presidency, the two candidates received a total of 16,098 votes, a participation rate of under 12 percent. If not for the attraction of the journal *Science,* the AAAS would probably fade away as an anachronism of scant interest to modern scientists. Writing in *Science* in 1999, Stephen Jay Gould, of Harvard, president-elect of the AAAS, deplored the decline of interest in the AAAS annual meeting. The gatherings were notable in past years as a meeting ground of the many fields of science and as a fount of public information. "Unsurprisingly," Gould wrote, "many scientists have become cynical about the AAAS annual meeting—'a good thing' as Martha Stewart likes to say, but not worth attending for any motive of professional learning." Gould stated that "I confess to the cynicism," noting that prior to his election, "I had not attended a AAAS meeting for 20 years, but had to go in my role as president-elect, in 1999." He found it worthy, he said, and urged other scientists to join him in restoring the annual meeting to its previous role as a unifying event in the life of science.[19]

Founded in 1969, the attractively titled Union of Concerned Scientists, based in Cambridge, Mass., is one of the most publicly visible organizations flying the banner of scientific activism. For scientists who wish to be *engagé,* if only with their checkbooks, the Union of Concerned Scientists is there. Arms control, nuclear proliferation, and the antiballistic missile rank high among its concerns, though in terms of distribution of effort, the organization might more appropriately be titled the Union of Concerned Environmentalists. Programs in global resources, energy, and transportation accounted for 51 percent of UCS's $5.6 million in expenditures in 1998; arms control received 14 percent (most of the balance went to fund-raising and administrative costs). In recent years, however, while the pool of scientists has rapidly grown, the UCS has experienced a decline in membership. Financially, the organization thrives on foundation grants and individual donors. According to Executive Director Howard Ris, membership in the mid- to late 1980s ranged from 90,000 to 100,000; in 1999, membership was between 60,000 to 70,000, about one-third of them scientists.[20] The UCS's 1998 financial statement reports that 52 percent of income was provided by foundation grants; 30 percent came from individual donations, ranging from "$100,000+" to $500. For all its good works, the Union of Concerned Scientists, like other organizations rooted in the scientific enterprise, draws

19. Stephen Jay Gould, "Take Another Look," *Science,* October 29, 1999.
20. Conversation with author, July 20, 1999.

relatively little membership or financial support from the great mass of American scientists.

Stability verging on torpor characterizes the internal politics of the major scientific societies. Their chieftains generally hold office for many years, leaving only upon retirement. Measured against high-end remuneration in industry, business, law, sports and entertainment, and on Wall Street, the financial rewards of these politicians of science are relatively low. There are no signing bonuses or stock options, no golden parachutes when they depart from Washington's science associations. But, by the measures of risk and brilliant performance, they can properly be regarded as well-recompensed, even generously so. They occupy comfortable berths. The nonprofit organizations they head encounter no competition; they receive little external scrutiny, journalistic or otherwise, and the bit that occurs is mainly in captive publications of scientific organizations. The nonprofits are not stalked by Wall Street vultures, nor are they vulnerable to blind-side attacks by upstart technologies. Though paid on a par with the presidents and chancellors of middle- to major-size universities, the science-association executives do not have to contend with the strife and stress of campus politics. The heads, almost always men in the major science associations, usually hold office on an appointive basis, though, in some instances, they go through pro forma, single-candidate elections—the way it's done at the National Academy of Sciences.[21] The AAAS is a rarity in holding two-candidate elections. Those who are appointed serve at the pleasure of tame boards. (In the format common among the science associations, the executive head and staff that run the operation are permanent while the elected officers—usually employed full-time elsewhere—hold office for just a few years.) At Ph.D.-granting universities, where burnout is a leading occupational hazard, presidents averaged five years on the job in 1995, and only 26 percent of them held office for more than eleven years, according to the American Council on Education.[22] In contrast, many of the chiefs of Washington's major science organizations hold office for a decade or more.

21. In 1995, Harold Liebowitz, an insurgent, write-in candidate, was elected president of the National Academy of Engineering, sister of the science academy, after charging that the management of the NAE neglected the membership and the interests of working engineers. Personally erratic and fractious in relations with the NAE officers and staff, Liebowitz was removed after one year in office by an overwhelming vote of the NAE membership. His departure was eased with a $687,500 good-bye payment from the academy.

22. *The American College President* (Washington, D.C.: American Council on Education, 1998), pp. 12–13.

Low Visibility in Washington

In harmony with science's turn away from politics and retreat to the ghetto, political Washington is indifferent to, even unaware of, the politics of science—except for the incessant clamor about money, and even that ranks relatively low on the attention scale. The scientific "trade" press, i.e., the research journals such as *Science* and *Nature,* reported the latest episodes of scientists pounding on the door of the State Department. But little or nothing appeared in the general press. And in the metaphysics of political Washington news coverage, nothing has happened until it is recorded in the *New York Times* or the *Washington Post.*

Confined, by choice, to its politically antiseptic ghetto, the scientific enterprise goes remarkably unnoticed in the capital among politicians and political journalists, save for occasional staged, ceremonial events. One occurred in June 2000, when the completed mapping of the human genome was publicly hailed by President Clinton, with the genome impresarios in attendance at a White House ceremony and a TV hookup to British Prime Minister Tony Blair and the UK's genome wizards. Though well-known in scientific circles, the participating scientists were strangers in the broader world of politics and public affairs.

In his published memoirs, Dwight Eisenhower, who inaugurated full-time science advice at the White House in the excited aftermath of Sputnik, paid homage to his scientific aides, James Killian and George Kistiakowsky. "Without such distinguished help," he wrote, "any President in our time would be, to a certain extent, disabled."[23] Eisenhower was exceptional in his strong expression of presidential regard for scientific assistance; no doubt he was grateful. Perhaps, too, he was doing penance for having bruised his scientists with his valedictory warning of the menace of a "scientific-technological elite." The kind words are in a footnote rather than in the main text of the 741-page volume.

Over the past fifty years, the memoirs of other presidents and their principal aides and biographers contain few, if any, references to the key figures and heartfelt issues of science politics, including funding, priorities in research, the pork barrel, peer review, and access to the inner sanctums of politics. In 1988, Hedrick Smith, former Washington bureau chief of the *New York Times,* published a 793-page study of contemporary politics, *The Power Game: How Washington Works* (Random House), which was favorably

---

23. Dwight D. Eisenhower, *Waging Peace: The White House Years: A Personal Account, 1956–1961* (New York: Doubleday, 1965), p. 224.

received in political and academic circles. Apart from passages concerning the then-simmering issue of the Strategic Defense Initiative, the thirty-six-page index contained no references to the people and grist of science politics, government research agencies or federal research officials, or any of the issues that animate the politics and politicians of science. Lyndon Johnson's memoir of his presidency discussed the space program, for which critical decisions regarding the Apollo program had to be made, but otherwise Johnson was silent about science politics, not even mentioning the science adviser who served him during his five years in the White House, Donald Hornig.[24] Richard Nixon's autobiography, published in 1978, four years after he resigned from office, contained no reference in its 1,090 pages to two historic events in the relationship between science and his presidency: Nixon's declaration of the so-called war on cancer and his abolition of the White House Office of Science and Technology and the termination of the position of the special assistant to the president for science and technology. Nixon devoted only a few pages to the Apollo moon landing, which occurred in the first year of his presidency.[25] Well received by critics, *Truman*, the best-seller presidential biography by David McCullough, briefly mentions Vannevar Bush twice in its 992 pages, both times for his role in the development of the atomic bomb. There is no reference at all to the five-year-long political struggle over the postwar organization and control of government support for science, a historic event in the psyche of American science.[26]

Politics appears to possess only a superficial recognition of the origin of the scientific revolution and its continuing impact on economics, warfare, health, and virtually all aspects of life. Though inconclusive in itself, an episode near the end of the twentieth century merits attention. In 1997, on the occasion of its seventy-fifth anniversary, *Foreign Affairs*, the house journal of the American foreign policy establishment, asked its ten regular book reviewers "to assess not the most 'recent' books, but rather the most significant books in their fields published over the last 75 years." In the Military, Scientific, and Technological category, reviewer Eliot A. Cohen (professor of strategic studies at the Paul H. Nitze School of Advanced International Studies, Johns Hopkins University) named the following: *On War*, by Carl von Clausewitz; *Selected Military Writings of Mao Tse-Tung; Makers of*

24. Lyndon Baines Johnson, *The Vantage Point: Perspectives on the Presidency 1963–1969* (New York: Holt, Rinehart and Winston, 1971).

25. Richard Nixon, *The Memoirs of Richard Nixon* (New York: Grosset & Dunlap, 1978).

26. David McCullough, *Truman* (New York: Simon & Schuster, 1992).

Modern Strategy: Military Thought from Machiavelli to Hitler, edited by Edward Mead Earle; *Analysis for Military Decisions,* edited by Edward S. Quade; *The Soldier and the State: The Theory and Politics of Civil-Military Relations,* by Samuel P. Huntington; *The Professional Soldier: A Social and Political Portrait,* by Morris Janowitz; and *Marlborough: His Life and Times,* by Winston S. Churchill.[27]

Our interest is in books that did not make the grade as "most significant" among military, technological, and scientific books of the previous seventy-five years. Not among the chosen were any of the great works of and about science and science-related matters, including: *Cybernetics,* by Norbert Wiener; *The Structure of Scientific Revolutions,* by Thomas Kuhn; *The Making of the Atomic Bomb,* by Richard Rhodes; and the later works of Sigmund Freud. *Silent Spring,* by Rachel Carson, made the list in the category of Economic, Social, and Environmental books. Among the missing was *Science, The Endless Frontier,* an omission that should not be attributed to controversy about its author's role in the postwar development of science in America. Like so much else of great importance to the politicians of science, the legendary work does not register with real politics, if it ever did. Science is voluntarily disengaged from politics, politics is comfortably disengaged from science.

In the *Washington Post,* the hometown newspaper of American politics, the inattention to the politicians of science is quantifiable. A search of the *Post*'s electronic database produces a relatively small harvest of articles containing references to the senior figures of science politics. In 1993, the first year of the Clinton administration, John H. Gibbons, the president's assistant for science and technology, appeared in 25 articles; in 1995, the Gibbons count dropped to 8. Between July 1997 and July 1999, the *Post* published 15 references to Neal H. Lane, who moved during that time from the directorship of NSF to the White House post vacated by Gibbons. Over those two years, the *Post* published 5 articles mentioning Bruce Alberts, President of the National Academy of Sciences. In contrast, it published 437 articles containing the name of Samuel R. (Sandy) Berger, the president's assistant for national security. This numbers exercise reveals nothing about the impact of science on national strength and well-being. But in a capital where visibility is a sinew of politics, the numbers show that politicians of science rank low in visibility. We should recall here the words of a White House science official, William G. Wells Jr., addressing a meeting of scien-

27. "Significant Books of the Last 75 Years," *Foreign Affairs,* September/October 1997.

tists anxious about money following the Republican takeover of Congress in 1995: "for the most part, the S&T [science and technology] worlds are not even on the politicians' radar screens."[28]

Finally, we might note a novel development concerning the highest ranks in the politics of science. In 1996, the Washington Advisory Group, a for-profit consulting organization, was established, renting offices in the downtown headquarters building owned and occupied by the AAAS. In our narrative, we earlier came across many members of the Washington Advisory Group, which lists as its "principals" three former White House Science advisers: Edward E. David Jr. (Nixon); Frank Press (Carter), and D. Allan Bromley (Bush). Also in the Washington Advisory Group: Erich Bloch, former director of the National Science Foundation; Robert Frosch, former administrator of NASA, among other senior government positions; James Wyngaarden, former director of the National Institutes of Health; Robert White, former president of the National Academy of Engineering; Frank H. T. Rhodes, former president of Cornell University and former chair of the National Science Board; Alan Schriesheim, former director of the Argonne National Laboratory, a major facility of the Department of Energy; and Daniel C. Tosteson, former dean of Harvard Medical School. In three years, trading on their intimate knowledge of the workings of the U.S. government, the Washington Advisory Group compiled an impressive list of clients, including: Brown University, the Carnegie Corporation, the Department of Energy, Florida State University, several institutes of the National Institutes of Health, the Electric Power Research Institute, and Ohio State University. Billings rose from $300,000 in the first year to a projected $2.5 million in 2000.[29] Similar assemblages of the leaders of science politics—including all of the aforementioned—could be found throughout the post–World War II decades on pro bono committees in the service of government. From in and around government, nonscientists who rose high in Washington have frequently resurfaced as commercial consultants. Henry Kissinger, statesman turned global consultant, is the preeminent example. Never before, however, had such a high-powered group from science, the blandly titled Washington Advisory Group, coalesced in a profit-seeking business.

28. See chapter 12.
29. *SGR*, August 15, 2000.

CHAPTER 22

The Ethical Erosion
of American Science

University entrepreneurship shifts the ethos of academic scientists toward a private orientation and away from the public interest role that has largely dominated the scientific culture since the middle of the century. . . . Scientists who are tethered to industrial research are far less likely to serve in the role of vox populi. Instead, society is left with advocacy scientists either representing their own commercial interests or losing credibility as independent spokespersons because of their conflicts of interest. The benefits to academia of knowledge entrepreneurship pale against this loss to society.

—Sheldon Krimsky, Tufts University,
in *Issues in Science and Technology* (fall 1999)

. . . the commercial entanglements for science are getting so common and complicated that I think it's time for the scientific community to have guidelines and to define the limits beyond which behavior is not tolerated.

—David Korn, senior vice president,
Association of American Medical Colleges
(quoted in the *New York Times,* November 1, 2000)

DURING THE 1980s and 1990s, the scientific withdrawal from social and political concerns was accompanied by a greater emphasis, by universities and their scientists, on harvesting corporate money from science. Cause and effect? I don't know. But a gold rush spirit flourished and spread on the endless frontier. Federal and local regulations and scientific tradition prescribed scrupulous behavior for academic managers and researchers at the intersection of money and knowledge. But as is often the case when great riches beckon, rules that governed behavior in simpler times were trampled. Since exposed transgressions by the piously upright make news, the public has heard a good deal about scientific falls from grace. My purpose is not simply to chronicle episodes of dubious, even corrupt, behavior in the scientific enterprise, of which many have occurred in recent years. Rather, we will look at a handful of selected cases that reveal the systemic, pervasive invasion of the money ethic in the conduct and presentation of research. In contradiction to an ancient metaphor often invoked in exculpatory fashion by apologists for these developments, the difficulties are not confined to a single wormy apple in the barrel.[1] In its retreat to the ghetto, science repudiated elective politics and social engagement. In its limited external relations, it found a new interest: corporate America, eager to reap the scientific riches created by decades of spending on science by the U.S. government.

THE PHARMACEUTICAL FOLLIES

The relationship between academic scientists and the pharmaceutical industry is of direct consequence to the trusting millions who consume the drugs produced by their collaboration. In the cycles of scientific advances, the life sciences are currently in an extraordinarily productive phase. Their progress is powered by the interaction of discoveries, marvelous new laboratory instruments, the rapid growth of NIH support of academic research, public expectations of medical wonders, and the "pull" of pharmaceutical firms that convert scientific knowledge into drugs. The institutions of discovery and innovation are flush with government money, venture capital, and Midas legends of scientific findings transformed into biotech share options and great personal wealth. The setting is not favorable to the fragile culture of scientific integrity. As with all deviant behavior, the revealed cases of pharmacological misdeeds are an unknown fraction of the total— a small fraction, some contend, though no one knows for certain. For details of such dealings, we need not rely on fringe critics with antiestablishment or unknown motives or questionable credentials. We can go to a respected institution of the biomedical-research enterprise, the *Journal of the American Medical Association*, the world's most widely circulated medical journal.

---

1. Nor will we venture into the many well-publicized cases in recent times of scientific fraud, euphemistically referred to in official discourse as scientific misconduct. Mercenary motives were sometimes involved in these episodes of fabrication, falsification, and plagiarism—the formally proscribed categories of scientific sins. In others, the operative greed was for recognition and glory, which could lead to wealth. But these malefactors were proceeding on their own, rather than in collusion with external partners, and their misdeeds are remote from the politics of science. Hard times in the grant economy may inspire scientific fraud, as some contend, but evidence for this connection is lacking.

Along with its customary fare of medical and scientific articles, *JAMA* devotes considerable attention to the ethical underside of contemporary science. It has ample company in scientific-medical publishing in this respect, but as we must start someplace, we will start with *JAMA*.

In collusion with money-seeking academic researchers, *JAMA* tells us, some pharmaceutical firms, large and small, have misrepresented and inflated scientific data to gain, first, regulatory approval, and then to influence physicians to prescribe their products to an unwitting public. A favored tactic is the duplicate publication of the same body of experimental drug data in multiple journals to create the impression of a substantial base of favorable therapeutic evidence. In 1999, an article in *JAMA* deplored the practice as deliberately misleading, while pointing out that it has persisted, despite prior exposures.[2] Deputy Editor Drummond Rennie noted that questionable uses of duplicate publications were exposed in critical articles published in European medical journals, in 1989 and 1996. These articles cited the unacknowledged reappearance of the same data in a succession of European and American medical publications. Rennie specifically discussed the publication tactics concerning two drugs, fluconazole, an antifungal agent manufactured by Pfizer, Inc., and risperidone, an antipsychotic drug manufactured by Janssen Pharmaceutica NV, Beerse, Belgium. For the manufacturers employing these tactics, Rennie observed, the benefit of multiple publication is "more reprints [of articles], by apparently different and unconnected authors, for company detail representatives [i.e., sales promoters] to press into the hands of physicians, and a bigger dossier to file with the regulatory agencies." However, he declared, for independent researchers seeking to assemble, analyze, and compare accumulated data from separate studies—a process known as meta-analysis—unacknowledged duplicate publications skew the results. Asking, "Why is this happening?" *JAMA*'s deputy editor concluded: "Reviewing these case studies, it is hard not to suspect that this practice, which serves commercial interests so well, is deliberate, and, because it confuses and biases information important to the care of patients, it has to stop."

While condemning the drug manufacturers, Rennie also deplored the complicity of the academic researchers, whose participation was essential for achieving publication of the repetitious articles in scientific journals. "An equal share of the responsibility for these practices must fall on researchers," he wrote, adding that "the rules governing authorship and

2. Drummond Rennie, "Fair Conduct and Fair Reporting of Clinical Trials," *JAMA*, November 10, 1999.

against redundant publication are well known." Rennie noted that the various American and European journals in which the articles were repetitiously published claim adherence to the so-called Vancouver Guidelines of the International Committee of Medical Journal Editors. "These specifically forbid the submission of articles that are being considered for publication, or have already been accepted or published elsewhere." He added, "At the very least, good science practice dictates that there must be accurate cross-referencing of articles that are duplicates." In these, and other cases, he reported, cross-referencing was absent; in some instances of duplicate publication of the same data, the sequence of authors was altered, thus complicating the task of literature searching. The episodes cited by Rennie in 1999 extended back to the 1980s, and would not surprise anyone knowledgeable in the financial relations of academic medical researchers eager for money and pharmaceutical firms seeking regulatory approval and physician acceptance for their drugs.

Mercenary distortions of pharmaceutical research have been repeatedly documented, but they persist. Writing in the British journal *Lancet* in 1999, a group of researchers at an Edinburgh hospital plaintively observed:

> For researchers it is all too tempting to accept large sums of money by joining, or even appearing to run, heavily sponsored [industry] trials; but if the company demands complete control over the selection of sites, the protocol, data collection, analysis, and even the publications, the research design will inevitably meet industry and not public health priorities. . . . Ethics committees should insist on absolute transparency of the amount of involvement by commercial sponsors in trials submitted for their approval, and declare that the approval will be granted only if the results are published, irrespective of the final result.[3]

Ethics committees, however, compete poorly against the wiles and wealth of commercial sponsors of research and the eagerness of many academic scientists to do business with them. The rhetorical devotion to scientific integrity is unalloyed—who can speak against it?—but, in fact, the ethical base has been continually eroding for many years, in many sectors of the scientific enterprise. The mercenary incentives are powerful and inviting, the need for money is great, and the guardianship of values within science is timid and uncertain. A tin trumpet of scientific integrity was sounded in

3. *The Lancet,* June 26, 1999, correspondence.

1997 by a major lobby for science that we have encountered previously in this book, the Association of American Medical Colleges (AAMC). In a publication titled *Developing a Code of Ethics in Research: A Guide for Scientific Societies*, the AAMC declared that

> with over a decade of widely publicized revelations of fraud and other abuses in research, many thoughtful individuals, including those in the profession, have come to believe that greater effort is necessary to ensure that the highest ethical standard is practiced throughout the research community.[4]

But the *Guide* then proceeds to observe that

> in spite of the prevalent view that it is a worthwhile activity, many [scientific] societies are reluctant to develop codes of ethics in research. They are concerned that the process will be time consuming and even pointless if they are not prepared to enforce whatever codes they adopt.

Endorsements of integrity are a popular and painless pastime of science; enforcement is not, for many understandable reasons: it can scare away money, besmirch reputations, and bring on ruinous publicity and litigation. And so, the ethical guide offered to the sciences by the medical school lobby makes the best of a difficult situation, simply noting: "A code has an inherent educational value, whether a society chooses to enforce it or not." I am not aware of any that do. Moreover, we might consider that respect for a code is not enhanced by neglect of enforcement. We continue on, passing over spot episodes of ethical decline, and concentrating on evidence of pandemic disorders.

THE AMA SCANDAL

In 1997, the American Medical Association, the parent organization of *JAMA*—supporter of integrity—was convulsed by a profit-seeking transaction involving the use of its good name to sell health-related consumer goods. In pursuit of what loomed as easy money, the managers of the AMA had entered into an agreement to endorse products of the Sunbeam Corporation, such as thermometers, blood-pressure monitors, and bathroom

---

4. *Developing a Code of Ethics in Research: A Guide for Scientific Societies,* executive summary (Washington, D.C.: Association of American Medical Colleges, 1997).

scales. The arrangement did not provide for the AMA to conduct or in any way seek evaluation of the goods that would bear the imprimatur of the nation's leading medical society and respected publisher of medical research. Sunbeam would get the AMA's logo; the AMA would effortlessly collect royalties. After protests and expressions of disgust by AMA members, the association spent $10 million to settle a breach-of-contract suit brought by its aggrieved, erstwhile partner, Sunbeam, plus legal fees and other costs. As described in the AMA's publication *American Medical News:*

> The Association pulled the plug on a co-marketing agreement with the appliance maker only weeks after it had been announced. The endorsement deal, which paid royalties to the AMA based on sales and required the AMA to do no product testing, triggered an avalanche of criticism and eventually led to the firing or resignation of several top AMA executives. In addition to the money the AMA paid to settle [Sunbeam's breach-of-contract] suit, the AMA paid at least $3.5 million in legal fees and an undisclosed amount for severance packages paid to the departing executives.[5]

The AMA-Sunbeam episode stimulated the ethical juices at *JAMA*'s closest rival, the *New England Journal of Medicine* (NEJM). In marketing its public trust, "the AMA is not alone," declared NEJM's editor, Jerome P. Kassirer, in a joint editorial with his colleague Marcia Angell. Other medical organizations provide product endorsements, they noted, but receive costs—no royalties—in return. "Nonetheless," they asked,

> why should the American Heart Association endorse only Bayer aspirin? And why should the American Cancer Society endorse only SmithKline Beecham's anti-smoking products? These organizations would do well to review the financial benefits of these associations against the potential blemishes to their reputations as keepers of the highest principles.[6]

But Kassirer, champion of the highest principles, was a dispensable anachronism, out of step with the new, reigning importance of money in science. Two years later, a money-tinged dispute concerning scientific purity broke out at the Massachusetts Medical Society, publisher of the august NEJM. As

5. *American Medical News,* January 18, 1999.
6. Jerome P. Kassirer and Marcia Angell, "The High Price of Product Endorsement," *New England Journal of Medicine,* September 4, 1997, p. 700.

a direct result of that dispute, Jerome Kassirer was fired, after eight years as editor of the journal distinguished for its medical-scientific contents, ethical sermonizing, and money-making prowess.[7]

Kassirer was ousted because he opposed the Massachusetts Medical Society's plans to exploit the prestige and name recognition of the *Journal,* its prize property, as a brand name for marketing other publications to physicians as well as to consumers—health advice for the masses being a booming business. In a discreet joint statement, the Massachusetts Medical Society and the deposed editor were harmoniously uncommunicative about their estrangement, attributing it to "honest differences of opinion between Dr. Kassirer and the Medical Society over administrative and publishing issues." Kassirer's valedictory editorial echoed the waffling verbiage: "Because the officers of the Massachusetts Medical Society and I would not resolve our differences over administrative and publishing issues," he cryptically explained, "they decided to seek a new editor-in-chief, and I leave the post in a few days."[8] The unpleasant facts were described in independent accounts of Kassirer's ouster, including a *New York Times* report headlined "Editor Forced to Resign Over Marketing of Medical Journal's Name."

> But other [NEJM] editors said the dispute reflected tensions generated as the [Massachusetts Medical] society, like other traditional non-profit medical organizations, seeks to generate more revenues to expand its influence in an increasingly competitive and political world of health care. . . . In recent years . . . the Massachusetts Medical Society has added other publications for doctors and health newsletters intended for the general public. The society also built a plush headquarters in suburban Waltham and hired more staff members to deal with health and political issues. . . . At stake are huge revenues generated by the journal's publication of findings from largely taxpayer-supported research. Although the Massachusetts Medical Society once published figures on the jour-

7. In 1998, NEJM, with 245,000 subscribers, at $145 per year for physicians, took in $19 million in display advertising. *JAMA,* with fifteen foreign editions, claims an international readership of 750,000; it is priced at $129 per year in the United States and published $21.4 million in display ads in 1998. In the news media, the two journals are perhaps the most widely quoted among the world's thousands of medical and scientific journals, an eminence they competitively pursue with complimentary subscriptions and advance notice of eye-catching articles for journalists. They are not alone in this practice, but, attractive for researchers seeking wide recognition, they are favored places of publication among scientists for the good news of health research welcomed by the general press.

8. Jerome P. Kassirer, "Goodbye, For Now," *New England Journal of Medicine,* August 26, 1999.

nal's finances, it has refused to do so in recent years as its profits have soared to estimates of more than $20 million from $386,540 in 1979.[9]

At the time of Kassirer's departure from NEJM, the editorship was vacant at *JAMA*, where George Lundberg, who had held the position for seventeen years, had been abruptly fired six months earlier. In the NEJM's case, commercial aspirations clearly motivated the head-lopping exercise: the managers of the parent Massachusetts Medical Society wished to exploit the valued NEJM brand to enrich the society; in pursuit of this goal, they removed an uncooperative impediment, Editor Jerome Kassirer. Marketplace considerations were not directly involved in George Lundberg's departure from *JAMA*. But they were present in the background of the long-running rivalry between the two journals for public attention, medical-scientific glory, circulation, and advertising.

Lundberg, recognized over many years for drawing professional and public notice to the journal of the American Medical Association, was deemed by his AMA superiors to have gone editorially overboard by addressing a terminological issue of the moment: whether oral sex constituted "sexual relations"—a key point in President Clinton's impeachment trial. To provide "empirical data," while the trial proceeded, in January 1999, Lundberg hurried into print a report of a survey of 599 Midwest college students, conducted eight years earlier, in which "Only 40% indicated that they would say that they 'had sex' if oral genital contact was the most intimate behavior in which they engaged (60% would not)."[10] Suspicions of grandstanding were raised by the reliance on eight-year-old data and the small number of students surveyed; also, in contrast to the customarily languid pace of medical publication, once the decision to publish was made, the sex survey received the fast-track treatment usually reserved for life-saving therapeutic findings. Lundberg "has threatened the historic tradition and integrity" of *JAMA*, E. Ratcliffe Anderson, executive vice president of the AMA, declared, "by inappropriately and inexcusably interjecting *JAMA* into a major political debate that has nothing to do with science or medicine."[11]

In research and in scientific publishing, tradition and integrity are de-

9. *New York Times*, July 27, 1999.

10. Stephanie A. Sanders and June Machover Reinisch, "Would You Say You 'Had Sex' If . . . ?" *JAMA*, January 20, 1999.

11. "Medical Journal Editor Fired; Study on Defining Sex Is 'Political,' AMA Boss Says," *Washington Post*, January 16, 1999.

votedly celebrated and especially urged upon the young. If ethical anguishing and preachments could elevate standards of practice, they would surely be lofty, for the ceremonial platforms of science resound with appeals to tradition and integrity, the journals of the profession record and deplore misdeeds, and the popular press even occasionally confesses to being misled by the mercenary influences infesting science. The lamentations suggest genuine unease at the erosion of ethical standards in the sciences—but the erosion continues.

Accounts of ethical trimming and neglect of educational responsibilities in hot pursuit of money are a remarkably durable phenomenon in contemporary science. In 1998, a report caustically titled *Enterprise University* was published by the Research Corporation, a respected foundation established in 1912 to promote the transfer of technology from academe to industry. In the words of eyewitness academics, the report describes the economic contamination of science and related higher education.

> "We're adopting a business instead of an education model," says chemist Brian M. Tissue of Virginia Polytechnic Institute and State University. "The rationale is collaborations [with industry] are good because they bring in money. People say we can have better facilities and more students, and it's a win-win situation, but it's not. There *can* [original italics] be benefits, but you're not training students any more; you're bringing them in to work to satisfy a contract. The emphasis shifts from what's best for the student to the bottom line."[12]

Enterprise University also quotes Orville Chapman, a UCLA chemist:

> Virtually every academic in biotechnology is involved in exploiting it commercially. We've lost our credentials as unbiased on such subjects as cloning or the modification of living things, and we seem particularly reluctant to think it through. In particular, there is the question of whether or not someone who has decided to go into the commercial side of things should remain in academia. That has been answered affirmatively many times, but in my mind it remains an issue.[13]

12. *Enterprise University,* in the 1997 annual report of the Research Corporation, Tucson, Arizona.
13. Ibid.

A 1995 survey of scientists in the top fifty university recipients of money from the National Institutes of Health found that over 25 percent of them were in "relationships" with industry, and that industrial money promoted secrecy in their research. "Our data suggest," the authors of the study reported in the *New England Journal of Medicine*, "that investigators with industrial support are at least twice as likely to engage in trade secrecy or to withhold research from colleagues as are investigators without such support." Academic involvement assists the commercial application of scientific knowledge, the authors pointed out, but possibly at the cost of participation in fundamental research and the free circulation of scientific knowledge.[14] The academic-industrial collaborations are justified on the grounds that they assist the transition from scientific knowledge to marketplace product, a process that is hailed as beneficial for public well-being and a major contributor to America's remarkable economic vitality. The ratio of ethical costs to social and economic benefits is difficult to determine. But most notable in the tango of academe and business is the intensity of the corporate money quest by academe and the intensity of its misgivings.

An Ethical Lapse and Apology

Pursuit and ethical anguishing characterize the sciences' dealings with industrial money, because commercial gold is considered both desirable and dangerous. So dangerous, in fact, that in the more righteous sectors of science, the corporate presence is regarded with the gravest concern—akin to finding Typhoid Mary in a preemie nursery. In 2000, a public mea culpa by Editor-in-Chief Marcia Angell and other editors of the *New England Journal of Medicine* reflected their deep fear not only of commercial contamination of science, but even the perception of a possibility of contamination. For scientists reporting their research in NEJM, published disclosure of related financial connections, such as stock holdings in or grant support from a pharmaceutical firm, was deemed sufficient to alert readers to potential conflicts of interest. However, for coping with financial contamination, disclosure was not a universal disinfectant: the NEJM's rules declare that reviews and editorials are different from reports of research because they rely on "selection and interpretation of the literature." Therefore, "the *Journal* expects that authors of such articles will not have any financial interest in

---

14. David Blumenthal et al., "Participation of Life-Science Faculty in Research Relationships with Industry," *New England Journal of Medicine*, December 5, 1996.

a company (or its competitor) that makes a product discussed in the article."[15] In 1999, the *Los Angeles Times* reported that NEJM had deviated from its own purist policy in its continuing series titled Drug Therapy, an authoritative, and commercially influential, review of the uses, efficacy, and risks of drugs. Nine reviews, the newspaper reported, were written by authors who had financial dealings with the manufacturers of the drugs they reviewed. However, NEJM readers were not informed of the authors' financial links to the manufacturers, a step that some journals consider an antidote to conflicts of interest. But even if the financial ties had been disclosed, the NEJM would be in violation of its absolute proscription. In November 1999, the NEJM published a note acknowledging one deviation from the rule: the author of an article published in September, the journal stated, had informed the editors of her consulting work for the manufacturers of the drugs that she discussed in a Drug Therapy article; but, the editors admitted, "we failed to respond in accordance with our conflict-of-interest policy, which would have disqualified her."[16] Following that incident, the editors reviewed Drug Therapy articles extending back to January 1997. In eighteen additional instances, the NEJM editors acknowledged, NEJM had violated its own rule: "The authors had informed us of these financial arrangements [with industry], and the editors in Boston were aware of them and approved them." In the list of companies involved were the elite of the pharmaceutical industry, including Merck, Novartis, Eli Lilly, Glaxo Wellcome, Smith-Kline Beecham, Pfizer, and Roche. No wrongdoing was attributed to the companies or the reviewers; none of the reviews was said to have been influenced by the authors' financial relations with industry. The authors, as the editors pointed out, had abided by the NEJM's rules of the disclosure, but the editors had failed to disqualify them, a lapse that was explained as follows, in a *Wall Street Journal* report:

> Dr. Angell said the growth of corporate support for medical research has made it increasingly difficult to find highly qualified researchers to write the Journal's widely read editorials and reviews. "Sometimes when we've been soliciting editorials, we've had to give up because the first five or six people on the list all had conflicts," she said.[17]

15. The restriction appears in "Information for Authors," in each issue of NEJM, and is stated to be "in accordance with the Uniform Requirements for Manuscripts Submitted to Biomedical Journals." Adherence, however, varies among the journals.
16. Marcia Angell et al., "Disclosure of Authors' Conflicts of Interest: A Follow-up," *New England Journal of Medicine*, February 24, 2000.
17. *Wall Street Journal*, February 24, 2000.

In the ledgers of corruption in America, these and similar episodes would barely rate a footnote, if any notice. However, where ethical sensitivity still survives in science, they are regarded with the deepest concern. Public trust underpins the sovereignty and support of science. There is nothing inherently unwholesome, let alone corrupt, about corporate relations with academic science; the production of knowledge in universities, and its conversion into goods and services by business and industry, is a process ingrained in the economy, culture, and politics of America. Within that process, science built public trust by demonstrating truthfulness, openness, and dedication to public benefit, qualities that fortified it against the money-making imperatives of the market. As we have seen, and will explore further, those qualities are receding.

Protecting Humans in Experiments

Federal regulations for the protection of human volunteers in medical experiments are strict and clear on the central point of informed consent: participants must not be coerced or misled, they must be capable of understanding the risks entailed in the experiments, and the risks must be explained to them in understandable language. The regulations are important in the academic-pharmaceutical nexus because a major portion of clinical drug trials are conducted by academic researchers under contract to manufacturers of drugs. The academics welcome the money and the manufacturers value the academic cachet, which carries weight with the drug-approval authorities at the Food and Drug Administration. Inspired by the horrors of Nazi experimentation on humans, and written into federal regulations that have evolved over many decades, the informed-consent code reposes great trust in the scientific community. For protecting human participants in experiments, scientists are responsible for watching over scientists, through Institutional Review Boards (IRBs). These local committees, largely drawn from university and hospital staffs, must approve all experiments involving human subjects, and animals, too. Nonscientist, public representatives are included on the boards, but scientists are in the majority.

IRB members serve as unpaid volunteers, which signifies low standing for the boards in the well-financed realm of biomedical research. We may assume that if the review boards were considered important, money would be there, as it is for researchers' salaries, graduate stipends, conferences, and travel (and even, as we saw in the disputes over indirect costs of research, for flowers in the presidential campus residence). Repeatedly, the trust invested in the boards has been violated, in countless incidents that demonstrate that among the many who so choose, the regulations are regarded as a nuisance that can safely be ignored. The basis of that confidence is the negligible to nonexistent oversight and enforcement of informed-consent regulations from Washington. For many years, national responsibility for the performance of the local Institutional Review Boards was located deep inside the many-layered bureaucracy of the National Institutes of Health, in the Office for Protection from Research Risks (OPRR) and in a counterpart office at the Food and Drug Administration. In 1999, when the budget of NIH stood at a historic high of $15.6 billion, OPRR operated on a budget of $2.6 million. Its staff numbered twenty-seven—with eight assigned to the OPRR Division of Animal Welfare, fifteen to the Division of Human Subjects Protection, and four to educational and clerical duties.[18] Their responsibilities ostensibly extended to nearly 4,000 research institutions throughout the country, and some 30,000 research projects involving humans and animals. But, in fact, OPRR was primarily a paper-shuffling enterprise. The OPRR staff included only one full-time investigator, one full-time attorney, and one physician serving part-time. In 1999, Gary Ellis, director of OPRR, told me that during the previous nine years, members of his office had conducted a total of thirty-eight inspections of research institutions under its jurisdiction; during one thirteen-month period, he said, no inspections were conducted.[19]

The skimpy budget, and the unavoidably low level of oversight activity, were visibly disproportionate to the scale of experimental activity involving humans and animals. However, no protests were raised by the amply staffed biomedical-research lobbies that patrol Washington. The biomedical-research community was not dismayed by Washington's failure to monitor the protection of human volunteers in scientific experiments. Nor was it unaware of gross inadequacies in the system. In 1996, the General Accounting Office reported that the IRB requirements had "heightened the research community's awareness of ethical conduct standards." But the GAO also noted that the review system was inadequately staffed and financed, pointing out that "in some cases, the sheer number of studies necessitates that IRBs spend only one or two minutes of review per study." The NIH Office for Protection from Research Risks and its counterpart at the Food and Drug Administration were criticized by the GAO for the rarity of their visits to the research centers that experiment on humans and for relying on reports

18. "Report to the Advisory Committee to the Director, NIH from the Office for the Protection from Research Risks Review Board," June 3, 1999.
19. Conversation with author, May 19, 1999.

from the local boards as their only evidence of compliance with the rules. In some instances, the GAO reported, scientists applying for approval of their own projects sat on the review boards.[20]

In 1998, the inspector general of the Department of Health and Human Services raised serious questions about the effectiveness of the Institutional Review Boards. Based on a review of federal records, interviews with members of seventy-five boards, and visits to six academic health centers, the inspector general concluded that many boards were understaffed, overwhelmed with applications, and lacked the appropriate expertise for research projects under review. The prevailing regulations mandated the presence of at least one nonscientist on each board. The inspector general recommended the appointment of more nonscientists as further protection for experimental volunteers. The recommendation was opposed by a senior executive of the Pharmaceutical Research and Manufacturers of America, who warned that the addition of laypeople might cause research to "bog down."[21] The president of the Association of American Medical Colleges, Jordan Cohen, lyrically defended the performance of the review boards:

> Guided by the principles of beneficence, justice, and respect for persons, IRBs weigh the risks posed by research against the benefits that the research may offer to the patient and society. They work *collaboratively* [original italics] with investigators, the vast majority of whom are motivated by altruism.[22]

Cohen added that if the federal government desired better performance by the review boards, it should provide money for their operations—in effect saying that to assure ethical use of the government's research money, the government should pay for oversight.

Long regarded, for good reasons, as a toothless tiger, OPRR astonished the scientific community in 1999 by cracking down hard on a major recipient of NIH research money, the Duke University Medical Center. Accusing Duke of letting four months go by without responding to notification of numerous violations of ethics and safety regulations, the NIH office ordered a suspension of all federally supported research involving humans at the

---

20. *Scientific Research: Continued Vigilance Critical in Protecting Human Subjects* (GAO/HEHS-96-72, 1996).

21. "Medical Research Protections Called Inadequate," *Washington Post*, June 12, 1998.

22. Jordan Cohen, "IRBs: 'In Jeopardy,' or in Need of Support?" *Reporter*, newsletter of the Association of American Medical Colleges, August 1998.

Duke Medical Center; the stoppage extended to some 2,000 projects after Duke voluntarily included research supported by nongovernment sources. No harm was reported to participants in experiments at Duke. The failings were limited to inadequate information provided to volunteers and rubberstamp project approvals by the boards that were supposed to protect their interests. The NIH investigation found that a member of the review board at Duke was also responsible for obtaining money for research at the university—thus putting him in the conflicted role of judging the ethical acceptability of grant-supported projects while foraging for grants. After four days of intense publicity, contrite apologies, and assurances of ethical compliance by Duke officials, NIH lifted the suspension and biomedical research resumed at Duke.[23]

The Duke episode was a bloodless exercise in ethical surveillance and enforcement. Though extensively reported in the professional and popular press, it apparently had no effect on institutional self-monitoring at another great center of biomedical research, the University of Pennsylvania. At Penn, the scientific gold rush left behind a dead body and revelations of indifference to ethical safeguards and deep concessions to the money chase. Like many other universities, Penn sought a place on the new frontiers of genetics research and gene therapy. Ambitions of this kind are often implemented through the recruitment of a scientific leader, an impresario who can bring in money and talent. To get its leader, Penn reached out to a leading academic center of genetics research, the University of Michigan, where it found the man and the money: James M. Wilson, a prominent genetics researcher and academic-corporate entrepreneur. While a professor at Michigan, Wilson founded one of the innumerable startups in the biotech industry, Genovo, Inc., which was fueled with millions from Biogen, Inc., and other well-established pharmaceutical firms. Moving to Penn in 1993 to become head of the university's newly established Institute for Human Gene Therapy, Wilson, according to the *Philadelphia Inquirer,* cut a deal that allowed him to control up to 30 percent of Genovo's stock, a departure from the generally required 5-percent limit in Penn's conflict-of-interest guidelines.[24] It was also agreed that Genovo would provide $21 million for

23. Several months later, Ellis was abruptly removed as head of OPRR. The operation was renamed the Office for Human Research Protections, and Greg Koski, an associate professor at Harvard Medical School, was appointed director. Pledging strict enforcement of conflict-of-interest regulations, Koski stated that financial dealings between researchers and industry "have gotten entirely out of control." (*Washington Fax,* September 7, 2000.)

24. "Penn Reviewing Gene Institute's Ties to Company," *Philadelphia Inquirer,* February 27, 2000.

the university's new institute, which eventually derived about one-quarter of its budget from the company. Wilson agreed not to take a salary from Genovo, but, as holder of more than twenty patents in gene therapy, he was first in line for the jackpot if the institute made good on the great but elusive potential of gene therapy. As the deal with Wilson took shape, officials at Penn viewed with some concern the extensive intertwining of academic research, corporate interests, personal financial rights, and medical treatment. Two special committees were established to review the Wilson enterprise and its relations with Genovo and the university. Apparently, their findings were satisfactory. The Institute for Human Gene Therapy flourished, with a scientific and medical staff rising to nearly 200.

THE FATAL TRIAL

In September 1999, the institute made medical history by causing the first known fatality directly attributed to gene therapy. The victim, Jesse Gelsinger, age eighteen, suffered from a mild form of a hereditary rare liver disorder, ornithine transcarbamylase deficiency, which, in his case, was kept under control by diet and drugs. Gelsinger volunteered to participate in a trial of an experimental therapy for babies afflicted by a fatal form of the disease—the eighteenth patient enrolled in a series of such trials at the institute. Shortly after he was infused with a supposedly therapeutic gene solution, Gelsinger went into a coma and died four days later. After immediately suspending further gene therapy trials at the institute, federal investigators found that Gelsinger had not been informed of toxic reactions in other patients who received the treatment, nor was he told of the deaths of several monkeys treated with the gene solution. None of the negative reactions had been reported to the Food and Drug Administration, as required by government regulations. The *Philadelphia Inquirer* reported that under James Wilson's agreement with the University of Pennsylvania, volunteers for experimental treatment were to be informed of his financial interest in the institute and its experiments. In fulfillment of the disclosure obligation, patients were advised:

> Please be aware that the University of Pennsylvania, Dr. James M. Wilson (the Director of the Institute for Human Gene Therapy), and Genovo, Inc. (a gene therapy company in which Dr. Wilson holds an interest) have a financial interest in a successful outcome from the research involved in this study.[25]

25. Ibid.

The disclosure statement was in the final paragraph of an eleven-page patient-consent form. In May 2000, the university announced that the institute would no longer experiment on humans.

If their ethical senses were outraged by these events, the major institutions of science successfully concealed their distress from public view. Comfortable within the scientific ghetto, deft at raising public expectations and thereby stimulating generous support, the politicians of science are not comfortable with the seamy underside of their glittering enterprise. But they are not moved to do anything effective about it.[26]

In contrast to this incapacity to curb violations of the ethos of science in private pursuit of greed, the scientific enterprise has been extremely effective in mobilizing to enlarge and protect its access to government money. We will now look at several important actions on that front.

26. In October 2000, Jordan J. Cohen, president of the AAMC, gingerly addressed press reports and the public perception of malfeasance in science. After noting the "intrinsic goodness" and "altruistic ideals" of biomedical researchers, Cohen urged two steps "to maintain that all-important [public] trust. . . . The first is to better educate the public about how, with proper safeguards, limited financial incentives in the conduct of clinical research can work to the benefit of everyone. The other is to visibly strengthen those safeguards so that we can, with confidence, assure everyone that our financial conflicts of interest are being managed effectively." ("Trust Us to Make a Difference," Jordan J. Cohen, address to the AAMC annual meeting, October 29, 2000.)

CHAPTER **23**

Post–Cold War Chills

European and, to a lesser extent, Japanese scientists have begun to surpass their American counterparts. In the U.S. the scientific community is beset by a budget squeeze and bureaucratic demands, internal squabbling, harassment by activists, embarrassing cases of fraud, and the growing alienation of Congress. In the last decade of the 20th century, U.S. science, once unassailable, finds itself in a virtual state of siege.

—"Crisis in the Labs," *Time*, August 26, 1991

IN 1992, a presidential election year, the country began to emerge from an economic recession, but anxiety still flourished about the competitive standing of American industry, particularly the high-tech sector. The beginning of the last decade of the twentieth century was a time of introspection and concern for the future in many American institutions, including science, with its inborn insecurities about public understanding and doubts about the durability of government funding for research. The Berlin Wall fell in 1989. In 1991, the Cold War ended with the collapse of the Soviet Union, thus invigorating the fearful belief that, without a national-security rationale, government support for science would decline—catastrophically, some warned. Though the trade balance in advanced-technology products remained positive, the trends were unfavorable, leading to pessimistic assessments of American technological performance and awe of other nations, particularly Japan, depicted as invincible and growing stronger. In mysterious and disconcerting fashion, Japan was weak where America was strongest, in basic scientific research; yet shops around the world offered superior Japanese electronic products that embodied scientific discoveries made outside of Japan, many in the United States. Great Britain retained its traditional place as a power on the frontiers of basic science, but suffered a continuing industrial decline. The "linear model" sanctified by Vannevar Bush, depicting basic science leading to technology, was wobbling under observations that commercially successful high-tech innovations grew out of a complexity of scientific and technical inputs, marketing skills, and economic and cultural conditions. Science, though essential, was not the only ingredient. The scientific discoveries had to be made someplace, but Japan demonstrated that science need not be homegrown to be commercially exploited, thereby challenging the contention of American scientific leaders that a nation's investment in basic research returns an industrial advantage.[1]

Nonetheless, whatever its source, scientific knowledge was a prominent ingredient of technological achievement, and, more so than any other ingredient in the American context, dependent on government money and policies. The issues arising from this dependency dated back at least as far as the closing days of World War II and Vannevar Bush's brief for federal money, and minimal control, in *Science, The Endless Frontier*. Now, nearly half a century later, as the Cold War ended, the role of government in nourishing science and promoting its commercial applications once again came under examination, by government, industry, and, in self-defense, the scientific enterprise itself. Heavy duties fell upon the Washington report industry.

WARNINGS OF DANGER

In 1991, a report by the Council on Competitiveness, a Washington-based alliance of high-tech industrial firms and research universities, concluded that America had fallen dangerously behind in developing and applying wealth-creating technologies.[2] The pessimistic report meshed with the prevailing down cycle in America's mood swings. Many press accounts and reports from academe and the think-tank business extolled the Japanese way, though with little agreement on what it was. Yankee ingenuity, also never uniformly defined, was chauvinistically hailed as a unique source of past wealth creation in America, but now mourned as sickly or departed. It was a time of national doubt, compounded by the continuous provision

---

1. In one of its periodic pronouncements on science policy, the National Science Board left no base uncovered in addressing this issue in 1993: "The country in which a discovery is made has an enormous initial advantage in exploiting such advances in understanding. Furthermore, by maintaining strength in a variety of basic research fields, we will be positioned to benefit from breakthroughs made by investigators in other parts of the world." *In Support of Basic Research* (NSB 93-127), May 14, 1993.

2. *Gaining New Ground: Technology Priorities for America's Future* (Washington, D.C.: Council on Competitiveness, 1991).

of economic diagnoses and prescriptions from many quarters. American high-tech exports actually rose, from $93 billion to $105 billion between 1990 and 1992, an increase of nearly 13 percent; but imports grew at a brisker pace, rising from $59 billion to $71 billion—a gain of over 20 percent.[3] In and around the National Science Foundation, regarded by academic science as its bastion in Washington, old questions were revived about the relevance of NSF's programs to industrial competition in the world's high-tech markets. Vannevar Bush worship, with its historical distortions and idolization of basic research, masked the realities of the government's role in research. NSF was not the only source of government money for basic research in universities; it was one of several sources, providing only some 15 percent of total government support for the basic sciences. And NSF was not confined to basic research; it also supported research and training in engineering and science education, from kindergarten to graduate school and beyond, to the American public through its programs for the public understanding of science. Nonetheless, the image persisted of NSF as a philanthropy dedicated to providing small grants for individual scientists, with minor smatterings of programs in education and engineering. Year by year, the foundation had actually became more involved with activities "downstream" from pure science. To the dismay of many scientists, NSF cautiously, but continuously, expanded its presence in engineering and technology.

During the 1984–90 reign of Director Erich Bloch, NSF inaugurated a series of university-based engineering research centers. Though starting at a low level, and predicated on cost-sharing collaborations with industry, the centers program was viewed by NSF's basic-research clients as a danger to their funding. But by financing these programs in universities, rather than dealing directly with industry, NSF muffled opposition among its academic beneficiaries. In 1990, the NSF engineering directorate was far behind the other disciplinary directorates in budget share—$200 million versus $557 million for the mathematical and physical sciences. But, pushed by political concerns about the relationship between research and economic growth, engineering was gaining in share, with a 20 percent increase proposed by President Bush for fiscal 1993, compared with 16 percent for the mathematical and physical sciences.[4] The NSF strategic plan for fiscal years

3. *Statistical Abstract of the United States, 1994* (Washington, D.C.: U.S. Department of Commerce), p. 820.
4. *Research and Development FY 1993*, AAAS Report XVII (Washington, D.C.: American Association for the Advancement of Science, 1992), pp. 86 and 88.

1989 to 1993 sought to quiet fears that center-based science would consume the money that had traditionally gone to individual scientists, the practitioners of so-called little science; but it also plainly stated that solo scientists did not have a monopoly on NSF's resources.[5]

"A major issue for NSF in its support of research centers and groups," NSF's strategic plan stated, "will be one of balance with the more traditional support of individual investigators—a model that has been enormously successful for NSF and the nation." The NSF strategic plan offered a dubious expression of fealty to little science, stating that support for that sacred obligation "will not diminish in the foreseeable future," to which was added, seemingly as an afterthought, an assurance that "individual awards will remain the dominant recipients of NSF funding." Nonetheless, the NSF strategic plan offered a memory refresher: "Centers are not a new idea for NSF," it pointed out, noting the foundation's support for materials research laboratories, industry-university cooperative research centers and engineering research centers.[6] The scientists' resistance to the centers and to the technology and engineering programs evoked acerbic remarks from Director Erich Bloch in a farewell Senate committee hearing in 1990 upon his departure from NSF. Bloch, it should be recalled, had received marching orders to shake up NSF, to put it in the service of the nation's economic needs, when the Reagan White House appointed him six years earlier. While acknowledging that "The primary mission of NSF is to support basic research and education in science and engineering," Bloch told the senators:

> It is a mission that, today more than ever, ties NSF to the broader needs
> of the nation. And in that respect, NSF should mirror those needs. . . .
> This interpretation may rankle those who view NSF's role as solely to advocate one approach to academic research in only a specific set of fields.
> But NSF is not the captive of individual investigators. NSF supports
> groups and centers, as well. NSF does not focus solely on science; NSF

5. Semantic muddling infested the politics of little science versus center-based science. In several fields—such as atmospheric studies, astronomy, and particle physics—basic research is conducted by teams, ranging in size from a few to hundreds of scientists, and takes place in centers that provide staff support and major equipment. So-called little science—individual or small-group research—can just as well be devoted to industrial problems as to basic research. Nonetheless, in contention over NSF's resources, centers are generally associated with industry and technology, and grants for individual scientists are identified with basic research.

6. *National Science Foundation Long-Range Plan FY 1989–1993* (NSF 88-56).

supports engineering, as well. NSF supports more than research; we are increasingly responsible for math, science and engineering education.[7]

Economic Pressures

It was in this turbulent political milieu that the Bush administration named a new NSF director: Walter Massey, a physicist from the University of Chicago, where he was vice president for research for the university and the Argonne National Laboratory, a multipurpose research center that the university managed for the Department of Energy. At Argonne, which was his main responsibility, Massey became familiar with an increasingly demanding problem in the politics of science: protecting the independence of science while making it socially and commercially beneficial, maybe even profitable. In 1990, when his appointment to NSF was announced, Massey was on leave from the university to study the European Community's programs to link academic research to commercial goals. While his colleagues in the United States fretted as usual about their nation's purported decline in science, Massey obtained another perspective during his six-month tour in Europe. Discussing his findings with me in Paris in December 1990, he observed,

> I'm impressed by the strong degree to which the United States is still respected [in scientific affairs]. We seem to have much more respect abroad for our [research] institutions than some people give ourselves credit for in the United States. We lament a great deal about the status of science, which is seen to be our strength over here. Things are well planned and stable here. But in the U.S., the individual researcher has a great deal of freedom, the universities have a great amount of independence themselves. The National Science Foundation gets a great deal of respect here in Europe. And the quality of science [in the United States] is still seen to be the standard of excellence in science.[8]

As the last decade of the century commenced, the managers of science were confronted by the old question: what are you doing for the country?

7. Senate Committee on Commerce, Science, and Transportation, *The National Science Foundation Director's Views on Science and Technology Policy: Hearing before the Committee on Commerce, Science, and Transportation*, 101st Cong., 2d sess., August 2, 1990, reported in *Science & Government Report*, September 1, 1990.

8. "Q&A with Walter Massey, Nominee to Head NSF," *SGR*, February 1, 1991.

The question was heard even within that great shrine of science, the National Science Foundation, just as the Clinton-Bush presidential campaign approached its finale.

A NEW ROLE FOR NSF?

In August 1992, doubts about the science-technology balance at NSF and other government research agencies were expressed by a committee of the National Science Board, NSF's policymaking body, cochaired by Arden L. Bement Jr., vice president for science and technology at TRW, Inc., and Roland W. Schmitt, president of Rensselaer Polytechnic Institute (RPI). Schmitt bridged academe and industry, having served as a longtime industrial researcher and ultimately as senior vice president for corporate research at General Electric before taking the RPI presidency. Dipping into NSF's voluminous collections of domestic and foreign R&D statistics, the Bement-Schmitt committee pointed out that the U.S. government spent a mere 0.2 percent of its R&D funds on projects of "direct relevance to commercial technology," whereas the figures for Japan were 8 percent and for West Germany 19 percent. As often in the statistics-strewn world of science politics, the numbers dished up by the NSF committee were correct, but their relationship to comparative national economic performance was unclear and disputed, in various directions, by economists, scientists, industrialists, and political ideologues. Despite its seeming concerns about the statistical disparities between the United States and other nations, the Bement-Schmitt committee was wary of reallocating NSF's stretched resources. While urging NSF to consider support for new programs in engineering and management, the committee cautioned: "Any significant changes in this direction would represent a substantial departure from NSF's traditional role, and thus should be given careful examination."[9] For the national press, the cautious recommendation of a committee of the board of the National Science Foundation was beneath the threshold of notice, in any season, not just on the eve of the traditional Labor Day commencement of the home stretch in the presidential campaign. Arcane by its very nature, science policy could not possibly compete for attention in the 1992 presidential campaign with the bread-and-butter, voter-sensitive issues of economic growth, taxes, jobs,

9. *The Competitive Strength of U.S. Industrial Science and Technology: Strategic Issues,* A Report of the National Science Board Committee on Industrial Support for R&D (NSB 92-138, August 1992).

health care, education, and welfare reform, plus Bill Clinton's character blemishes. However, science policy was the compelling issue for the leaders of basic science, their compatriots in industry, and the attendant chorus in the science press. For them, the politics of science was top-of-the-agenda, extraordinarily serious business.[10]

ALARMING PROPHECIES

Financial carnage in science was widely predicted as a consequence of the end of the Cold War. In 1992 and 1993, Edward E. David Jr., who had served as President Nixon's science adviser, issued a horrific forecast in a series of talks to scientific and business groups. As a successful industrial-research consultant, and an active committeeman in his dual membership in the National Academy of Sciences and the National Academy of Engineering, David was conversant with the economics and politics of science. Total national spending on R&D would shrink by 25 to 30 percent over the next decade, David predicted, and the federal laboratory system—which received about one-third of all government R&D spending—would "be treated like excess military bases." Noting lingering anxieties about shortages of scientists and engineers, David observed that "the opposite seems to be in prospect," adding that "the number of out-of-work scientists is still increasing. I know first hand about this trend in New Jersey and California. Downsizings and layoffs are likely to continue," he predicted. In the new science economy, David warned, federal agencies would shift support to contracts for "targeted R&D," at the expense of investigator-initiated basic research, the revered ultimate in scientific independence. David noted that "NSF is already making noises about moving in that direction."[11] The forecast stoked primal fears in the basic-science community, ever uncertain

10. Throughout this book, with a few minor exceptions, I abstain from reliance on anonymous sources, for all the good reasons that this abused technique has drawn opprobrium. But I allow myself here an anonymous indulgence, with solemn assurance of authenticity: during the 1992 presidential campaign and the postelection transition period, scientists, among others, offered policy recommendations for the next administration. Topping the scientists' list were prompt appointment of a White House science adviser and generous support for basic research, low-priority issues for the incoming administration. A Clinton aide assigned to "massage" the scientists—an especially insistent lot about their concerns—confided to me, with eye-rolling exasperation, "It's like talking to mental patients. You have to look like you take them seriously." *Science & Government Report,* December 1, 1992.
11. Edward E. David Jr., "Presentation on Science in the Post Cold War Era," address to the Council of Scientific Society Presidents, Washington, D.C., December 5, 1993.

about the steadfastness of its political support and public understanding of the value and fragility of science.[12]

From politics came similar warnings that the end of the Cold War would painfully reverberate throughout science. The avuncular guardian of science on Capitol Hill, Chairman George Brown of the House Science, Space, and Technology Committee, implored scientists to recognize the new world: "I must warn you that the generous support you enjoy today was part of the fallout of the creation of nuclear weapons, not because of the great contributions of science to a more humane society."[13] Like the thermometer readings of a feverish child, the budget charts of science were closely watched by the science press and academic scientists. The numbers could be read in various ways. The NSF budget actually kept rising, but the growth fell short of the expectations of NSF's managers and university clients—and the latter, at liberty to sound off as they pleased, complained bitterly, in the opinion columns of their professional journals, in the general press, and at Congressional hearings.

THE GRANT ECONOMY

The academic research enterprise was so constructed that no amount more could possibly suffice. The availability of more money would inevitably stir up the money-seeking spirits, stimulating grant applications from researchers within the fields of funding and alerting scientists in adjacent fields to a nearby mother lode of new support. Ironically, more money could lead to poorer success rates for applicants, a process summarized by the Office of Technology Assessment as "increased R&D budgets, mounting proposal submissions, and a declining proportion of proposals funded at most agencies."[14] The research budgets were rising, but scientists could legitimately point out that they had been led to expect greater growth. In 1988, President Reagan proposed, and Congress approved, a commitment to double the NSF budget in five years, from a base of $1.7 billion in fiscal 1988 to $3.5 billion in fiscal 1993. The doubling plan was incorporated into the

---

12. David's gloomy budget prophecies, plausible at the time but never fulfilled, coincidentally matched closely with the spending reductions initially proposed by Newt Gingrich and the resurgent Republicans when they took control of Congress in 1995. David, as ever, an apolitical science booster, had nothing to do with Gingrich and company, and it is doubtful they were aware of his pessimistic forecast.

13. Representative George E. Brown Jr., address to the American Association for the Advancement of Science, February 15, 1991, reported in *SGR*, March 1, 1991.

14. *Proposal Pressure in the 1980s: An Indicator of Stress on the Federal Research System* (Washington, D.C.: Office of Technology Assessment, 1990).

NSF Authorization Act of 1988. Authorizations, however, merely express legislative intent. The next step, indispensable but discretionary, is the appropriation of money. While good intentions existed at the White House and on Capitol Hill, money to meet the NSF's doubling schedule was difficult to extract from the congressional appropriations system. And neither the Reagan administration, nor any other, was inclined to wage all-out political war for NSF, a government agency virtually unknown to the American public. In the peculiarities of congressional committee organization, NSF shared an allocation of money with housing and veterans' programs, both highly popular and backed by politically potent lobbies. In contrast, NSF financed work remote from public view and visible benefits, serving a constituency that demanded money but avoided political engagement. As deficit reduction and antispending politics intensified the competition for funds, NSF proved to be a weak competitor. Year by year, the NSF budget increased, but by 1993, the promised year of doubling, it stood at $2.749 billion—$750 million short of the goal. Because of inflation, the purchasing power available to NSF rose by only $120 million during the promised five-year doubling time. In 1999, six years behind the schedule announced by the Reagan administration, the doubling was finally attained, and surpassed by a bit, when the NSF budget reached $3.672 billion.

In the opening years of the last decade of the century, the scientific ghetto resounded with fears for the financial future of science—in particular, the future of the National Science Foundation. We will now examine NSF's response to these fears, closely observing along the way the elders of science in the workshop of science politics, the committee room.

What Future for the National Science Foundation?

I think it is only fair to say that most pure scientists have themselves been devastatingly ignorant of productive industry, and many still are. . . . Pure scientists have by and large been dimwitted about engineers and applied science. They couldn't get interested. They wouldn't recognize that many of the problems were as intellectually exacting as pure problems, and that many of the solutions were as satisfying and beautiful.

—C. P. Snow, *The Two Cultures and the Scientific Revolution*

IN THE spring of 1992, as NSF Director Massey and his colleagues were barraged with warnings about the changing world, they were confronted by a worrisome phenomenon: the veneration of technology, and the virtual neglect of science, in the presidential primary campaign. Extolling technology as a job creator, candidate Bill Clinton promised it would receive big budgets if he were elected.

The Bush administration, declining in the polls, sniffed the political attractiveness of the technology issue, after long waving it away as best left to the marketplace. Presidential Science Adviser D. Allan Bromley announced the creation of a multi-agency Presidential Advanced Manufacturing Initiative, in which NSF and its engineering programs would play a major part. The aim, Bromley explained, was to help industry adopt robotics, computerization, and other high-tech methods. In the past, Bush and company had denounced such endeavors as "industrial policy," words pronounced with derision. From the sidelines, the scientific leadership noted with concern that Clinton's mentions of science were rare and subordinate to his references to technology. As the beneficiary of wise policies and generous support, science was in good shape, Clinton said, but technology was not, to the detriment of industrial competitiveness, economic growth, and jobs. Consolidating their views in a position paper in September 1992, Clinton and running mate Al Gore argued that success in science was insufficient to assure industrial superiority and international competitiveness:

> Science policy alone does not address these issues. In essence, science
> policy is a supply-push policy in which the government supports science
> education, basic research and some applied R&D that relates to specific
> national missions. During the Cold War, this policy worked well because
> U.S. industry dominated world markets and massive U.S. defense spend-
> ing for high-tech weapons systems provided a big demand for leading
> edge technology. . . . The absence of a coherent technology policy is one
> of the key reasons why America is trailing some of its major competitors
> in translating its strength in basic research into commercial success.[1]

The candidates referred only briefly to basic research, and without mention of NSF, the federal agency historically devoted to financing its costs. "University research accounts for a large part of the federal basic research budget," the Clinton-Gore paper stated, adding:

> Funding for basic university research should continue to be provided for
> a broad range of disciplines, since it is impossible to predict where the
> next breakthrough may come. While maintaining America's leadership
> in basic research, government, universities and industry must all work to-
> gether to take advantage of these new breakthroughs to enhance U.S.
> competitiveness.[2]

Congressional Criticism

Though disturbing, the declarations from the campaign trail merely slighted science, without criticizing it, by concentrating on technology. Of more immediate concern were the declarations of dissatisfaction from NSF's money masters on Capitol Hill. Candidate Clinton could only declare his intentions—which were subject to change upon entering the White House. Members of Congress could act. In the summer of 1992, the Senate Appropriations Subcommittee for NSF presented its own formula for the future of NSF, demanding greater emphasis on applied research and technology.

1. "Technology: The Engine of Economic Growth. A National Technology Policy for
   America," position paper, Clinton-Gore National Campaign Headquarters, September
   21, 1992.
2. Ibid.

In the chair of the subcommittee, Senator Barbara Mikulski (D-Md.), a former social worker in impoverished neighborhoods of Baltimore, declared that NSF was out of touch with the needs of America. The report accompanying the subcommittee's money bill prescribed radical revisions in NSF's priorities and constituencies. While praising NSF for U.S. leadership in basic research, the subcommittee report—a product of Mikulski and her staff—declared that "the new world order requires the Foundation to take a more activist role in transferring the results of basic research from the academic community into the marketplace." The report continued:

> The Committee believes the Foundation will play the key role in making the Nation's academic research infrastructure more accessible to those endeavoring to build America's technology base and improve U.S. economic competitiveness. This role should include: opening up applied research programs to greater participation by nonacademic personnel; making education programs better prepare future scientists and engineers for the needs of industry; and building up day-to-day relationships with other Federal agencies whose missions require cutting edge technology.[3]

The report directed NSF to establish a "working relationship" with the Commerce Department's National Institute of Standards and Technology, the government agency chartered to collaborate with industrial research. The senator's vision conflicted with NSF's proud understanding of its special place in America. The virtue of NSF was its commitment to long-term research and its exemption from demands for quick technological fixes. The senator was directing NSF to shed its heritage and become something other than NSF.

A Place in the "New Order"

In that setting of disappointing budget growth, warnings of worse to come, and political discontent with NSF, Director Massey sent a memorandum to the National Science Board:

> Superpower tensions have declined, and national security based on military strength will no longer be the predominant Federal research and de-

---

3. Report of the Senate Appropriations Subcommittee for Departments of Veterans Affairs and Housing and Urban Development, and Independent Agencies, 102d Cong., 2d sess., July 23, 1992, p. 157.

velopment priority. The U.S. economy now competes in a global arena
where success is increasingly linked to capitalizing on scientific advances
and new technologies. I think it is imperative that NSF determine its
place in this new order.[4]

Doomsday visions arose in the imagination of NSF's academic constituency
as allegations proliferated about NSF's poor match with the needs of America's troubled economy. Particularly apprehensive were the physicists, suffering dethronement from their long reign as the royalty of Cold War science. Physicist-cum-journalist-lobbyist Robert Park, the Washington-based
gadfly for the American Physical Society, monitored events. On August 28,
1992, in his weekly e-mail bulletin, *What's New,* Park dispatched an alarm to
thousands of his scientific kinfolk, making the worst of a clouded situation:

> NSF IS POISED TO TAKE A DRASTIC TURN TOWARD INDUSTRY SUPPORT! It had every ap-
> pearance of a coup. Within the month of August, the Senate Appropria-
> tions Committee, the Director of the National Science Foundation and
> the National Science Board, in strikingly similar language, have called
> for a redefinition of NSF's mission to compensate for industry's failure to
> invest in research. . . . NSF officials and staff from the Senate committee
> insist that there was no coordination; it's all just coincidence. Neverthe-
> less, some of the "new directions for NSF," called for by Walter Massey,
> were taken verbatim from the Senate Report.

In this excited atmosphere, and in swift response to Massey's declaration of the urgent need for NSF to find its place in the post–Cold War world,
NSF's board convened an assemblage of high authority and influence: the
Commission on the Future of the National Science Foundation. Four of its
fifteen members were currently or previously senior executives of leading
high-tech industrial corporations, one member came from politics, and the
rest from academe—an unusual mixture for the university-oriented NSF.
At NSF, where cautious deliberation and incrementalism were the customary style, the commission was both hurriedly created and set on a rocket-
speed schedule. Massey had begun his term as director of NSF in March
1991. Now, eighteen months later, in the midst of the presidential campaign, the commission was created and scheduled to terminate after three
one-day working sessions spaced over seventy-five days. The timetable over-

---

4. Walter E. Massey, memorandum to members of the National Science Board, NSB-92-
   145, August 14, 1992.

lapped with the national political calendar, starting with an inaugural meeting on September 17, 1992—during the height of the presidential campaign—and terminating with the delivery of a report on November 20, a little over two weeks after election day. Named as cochairs were Robert Galvin, former CEO and, at the time, chair of the executive committee of Motorola, and William Danforth, chancellor of Washington University, brother of Senator John C. Danforth (R-Mo.). The commission members included Ian Ross, president emeritus of Bell Laboratories; John Armstrong, IBM vice president for science and technology; Lewis Branscomb, of Harvard University, formerly a chief scientist of IBM; and former congresswoman Lindy Boggs, of Louisiana.[5]

Massey insisted that the creation of the commission was simply part of a routine process to develop a new five-year strategic plan for NSF, as a successor to the expiring 1989–93 plan. The overlap with the election campaign was coincidental, he explained, emphasizing that the commission "is not meant to address short-term considerations. It is in no way a response to current fashion or what other people think the Foundation should do or be."[6] Nonetheless, Massey pushed the board into acting by publicly recommending creation of the commission. "The Board was stunned by the fact that Walter [Massey] did this," according to Charles Brownstein, a veteran NSF staff member who was appointed to the key job of executive secretary of the commission.[7] The external pressures for utilitarian research were mounting on Massey's watch. While proceeding cautiously, Massey sought to move NSF toward closer involvement with industry and socially relevant research. But he needed consensus on how to execute that maneuver while remaining faithful to NSF's traditional role as

5. The commission, created by the board to serve as its adviser, was a characteristically inbred creation of the scientific enterprise. Except for former representative Boggs (who provided political window dressing, though she knew little about NSF and its problems), recruitment did not range beyond NSF's family of grantee universities and high-tech industrial users of basic research. Three of the fifteen-member commission were also members of the board: Ian Ross; Frank Rhodes, president of Cornell University; and Marye Anne Fox, professor of chemistry at the University of Texas, Austin. This trio was thus cast in the role of providing advice as commissioners and receiving it as board members. Others on the commission were Jacqueline Barton, professor of chemistry, Caltech; Peter Eisenberger, director, Princeton Materials Institute, Princeton University; C. Peter Magrath, president, National Association of State Universities and Land-Grant Colleges; Percy Pierre, vice president of research and graduate studies, Michigan State University; Earl Richardson, president, Morgan State University; and Donna Shalala, chancellor, University of Wisconsin, Madison.

6. Commission on the Future of the National Science Foundation, September 17, 1992, transcript, from which all quotations from commission proceedings are taken, unless otherwise indicated.

7. Telephone conversation with author, August 17, 1999.

financier of academic basic research. On only four prior occasions in its forty-two years had the NSF board exercised its statutory authority to appoint "special commissions"—far loftier than "committees" on the organizational scale.[8]

Massey and many of his colleagues favored moving NSF further "downstream" in support of technology and industry. But they wished to proceed in nuanced steps, with respect for NSF's historical role as the patron of academic basic research, and with minimum upset for their traditional academic beneficiaries, who were capable of raising an embarrassing din in the science press and in Congress. Science politics and the academic community would not be kind to Walter Massey or anyone who could be fingered for wrecking what was mythologically depicted as Vannevar Bush's magnificent legacy.

Massey Prescribes the Limits

As is customary among nimble bureaucratic tacticians, Massey created a confining framework of choice by unilaterally declaring "three broad options . . . for the future of the National Science Foundation"—two of them unpalatable, and the third attractive. The logistics of the commission put Massey in command, though, by statute, NSF was legally embodied in the presidentially appointed board that had appointed the commission. Massey was at NSF fulltime; the commissioners, all busily employed elsewhere, commuted to the commission's meetings in Washington, in many instances from far away. In a preparatory paper, Massey stated, "As a first option, the Foundation could revert to its historical roots as a small agency predominantly dedicated to the support of individual investigators and small groups at universities." That would be a poor choice, he said, because it "would almost certainly mean discontinuing the programs that have sought to connect basic research with the user community." Massey's wording scuttled option one. The second option would continue support for academic research plus "marginal and exploratory ventures . . . linking universities and industry." Massey frowned on that option, too, describing it as a likely "path of unstable equilibrium, because the importance of these 'other areas' on the national agenda will require more than token efforts.

8. In contrast to the vaguely titled Commission on the Future of NSF, the earlier commissions were focused on narrowly defined topics: Special Commission for Rubber Research, 1955; Special Commission on Weather Modification, 1963; Special Commission on the Social Sciences, 1968; Commission on Precollege Education in Mathematics, Science and Technology, 1982.

It is likely," he warned, "that other agencies, new or existing, will be more than willing to devote serious efforts to such activities." The "third possibility, one that I prefer," Massey acknowledged, "would build on our traditional mission and exercise new leadership across a broader spectrum of research areas." Massey explained that "it is difficult now to provide a blueprint for NSF under this option," noting that "it is much too soon to provide details on what NSF might look like in the next stage of its evolution."

BUSH WORSHIP

At the opening session, September 17, 1992, Massey urged the commission, "First, do no harm." Invoking holy myth, he declared, "The scientific research enterprise envisioned by Vannevar Bush and supported by NSF has flourished over the past four and a half decades, and has served as a model for the world."[9] Massey continued: "I personally believe that any realistic vision of NSF's future must have, at its core, the longstanding partnership with the nation's academic institutions." Summing up the task that the board had assigned to the commission, Massey stated: "Specifically, it has asked the Commission to recommend whether it is appropriate for NSF to expand its role in fostering links between research and technology."[10]

Cochair Galvin extended reverence for Vannevar Bush into new territory, declaring that Bush, in devising a plan for government support of science, "had the instinct to understand what was the intent" of the nation's founders. Introductory statements completed, the first session of the commission commenced with invited contributions from distinguished figures in the affairs of science, higher education, and government. Cochair Danforth summarized a paper by Frank Press, president of the National Academy of Sciences, who was absent with laryngitis. The paper Press sent in his stead was his 1992 annual address to the members of the academy.[11] Commencing with the requisite homage to Vannevar Bush, Press depicted three stages "in the history of science and technology policy in the United States"—the pre-Bush era, prior to World War II; the entire postwar period, for which, according to Press, Bush "set the stage" in *Science, The Endless*

---

9. In reality, the research enterprise scarcely resembled Bush's vision, differing in most important respects—as described earlier in this book—from the structure Bush recommended in *Science, The Endless Frontier*. Moreover, though NSF is admired around the world, no nation has adopted it as a model.

10. Op. cit., Commission on the Future of the National Science Foundation, pp. 9–10.

11. Frank Press, "Science and Technology for a New Era," presidential address, 129th annual meeting, National Academy of Sciences, April 27, 1992.

Frontier; and, finally, "the post–Vannevar Bush era." Presenting himself and his colleagues as the legatees of Bush, Press offered "new policies for the post–Vannevar Bush era." The recycled paper by the absent academy head posed a difficulty for its reader, Cochair Danforth: "Dr. Press's paper does not mention NSF. One might assume that he believes that its traditional approaches and broad mission are unquestioned."

In Press's view, as summarized by Danforth, NSF's success in producing science had gone unmatched "downstream," where industry had experienced "a real decline in complex but practical matters, such as design and manufacturing." Press, however, would not tinker with NSF in seeking a solution. Rather, he favored a remedy proposed earlier that year by an academy committee. For promoting industrial technology, the committee had regressed to the ill-fated organizational design that Bush proposed to Truman in 1945 for postwar support of basic research: basically, a formula for government money to be expended by private citizens with virtually no accountability to government.[12] Truman rejected the Bush design as incompatible with democratic principles of accountability. But it was back again, its proponents reminiscent of Talleyrand's observation of the French Bourbons: "They have learnt nothing, and forgotten nothing." The academy's plan called for the government to provide a $5-billion investment fund for industrial technology. The money would be controlled by a "quasi-public 'Civilian Technology Corporation'" that would be "managed outside the government by a private board appointed by the President and approved by the Senate." Recognizing the difficulty of obtaining large new sums in a period of government retrenchment, Press suggested that the $5 billion "might be found within a small reallocation from the $23 billion budgeted annually for more than 500 federal laboratories"—a favorite hunting ground for academic partisans seeking government money.

A Voice of Industry

The first in-person witness before the commission, John McTague, vice president for technical affairs at the Ford Motor Co., defended the status quo at NSF. McTague, who had served in the White House science office under Reagan, strongly endorsed NSF's traditional role in financing the training of scientists and engineers: "If you ask people in industry what we need from the National Science Foundation," McTague declared, "the first

---

12. *The Government Role in Civilian Technology: Building a New Alliance* (National Academy Press, 1992).

thing I will say, universally, is people. We need the best scientists and engineers that we can get. We need them both for product and for manufacturing, and for the management of corporate change." In research, McTague
stated, industry wanted NSF to "continue to play a leading role in supporting 'non-obvious research areas' . . . because it is from these areas that the
unexpected comes that gives us such a competitive edge in emerging technologies." McTague said NSF might experiment with methods for establishing closer relations between industry and basic research in universities. But
he emphatically stated: "I do not think NSF should fund industrial research.
I think that would be a mistake to do that in any significant way." Addressing McTague, a commission member, Marye Anne Fox, professor of
chemistry at the University of Texas, Austin, read aloud a passage from the
holy book, *Science, The Endless Frontier:*

> The simplest and most effective way in which the Government can
> strengthen industrial research is to support basic research and to develop
> scientific talent.

"Has anything changed?" Fox asked.

Seated in the NSF boardroom, McTague replied: "I think it should be
engraved on [the] wall over there. I happen to have read that over once
again about four months ago, and an awful lot of what is in there is timeless.
An awful lot of that is timeless."

An attempt to move the discussion toward financial and political reality was made by Lewis Branscomb, a commission member who chaired the
NSF board a decade earlier. Warning that "we can have a seminar here all
day long," Branscomb reminded the commissioners that they would hold
only three one-day meetings before delivering their report at a fourth and
final meeting. Branscomb asked, "How are we going to operate together to
efficiently get a good answer?" Cochair Galvin vaporously replied that:

> we will operate by the submission of presentable materials, such as we
> have had examples here this morning with Frank Press and John
> McTague, and others as we go on. Those will be vivid points for our de-
> liberation. We may solicit such, and others will be volunteered to us. All
> will be welcomed and they will be distilled and presented to us. They
> will be stimulations for us.

Galvin, the reputed whip-cracking chairman, thus cleared the roadway
for the inchoate meanderings that characterized the commission through-

out its short existence. Branscomb pressed on, observing that NSF shouldered responsibilities for science, engineering, and education, but lacked funds to support all three in adequate fashion. In science education, Branscomb continued, NSF worked without help from far richer government agencies that should be sharing the costs, such as the Department of Education. In response to its financial limitations, he observed, NSF had traditionally given budget priority to science, followed by education, with the leftovers consigned to engineering, leaving all three without sufficient support. And that is how they will remain, he warned, if the imbalance persists between NSF's resources and its responsibilities for important national needs. Without realistic prospects for major budget increases, the future of NSF should not be planned in isolation from the other sectors of the scientific enterprise, Branscomb argued, nor should the commission ignore that it was meeting on the eve of a presidential election: "Either it will be a rejuvenated Bush administration or an alternative Clinton administration. I think we have got to come to grips with what the rest of the government has got to look like and be prepared to do."

A NATIONAL POLICY ROLE

Branscomb then extended his argument to the governance of the federal sector of the scientific enterprise, urging an expanded role in science policymaking for the NSF board. He reminded his commission colleagues that under its founding statute, the board was given, as he put it, "a mandate to look at research across the whole government. It has never really done it, because it is politically not practical to have much influence on other agency budgets. But there is every bit of a mandate there for the Director of the Foundation and the Science Board to take a very articulate, open and aggressive attitude toward what the total science and technology program of the government ought to be." Branscomb thus argued for the board to assert itself as the voice of science, a role it had deliberately avoided for four decades—and would continue to shun as politically unwise, and clearly even dangerous, for a small government agency. The major research powers in the U.S. government—defense, health, and space—would not defer to NSF for guidance on how to spend their money. They even resisted herding by the president's assistant for science and technology.

Branscomb sketched his own three alternative futures for NSF. The first would "stick to the narrow conception of our mission," be reconciled to a static budget, and "recognize that the linkages between science and the rest of the economy will not be as healthy as they should be, but nevertheless try to preserve what's best that we have." Stated that way, choice one was out. Branscomb sidetracked the second alternative by introducing it as "one that I hear the academic community telling me they're terrified we're going to include." The feared choice, Branscomb explained, would be a decided turn toward support of applied research, in a misguided attempt to compensate for neglect by government and industry. If the terrorization of academe were not sufficient to banish that proposition, Branscomb assured his colleagues that it would be "an unmitigated disaster." Branscomb progressed to the third alternative, which he described as "feasible but difficult." The goal, he explained, would be "to define the role that we think NSF should play in a properly structured and missioned federal government, working with an industry which I believe is learning its lessons very fast." Branscomb possessed a rare combination of relevant professional experience for addressing the intricate issues of NSF's future in the new era of global high-tech industrial competition. His statement was specifically prepared for the commission, not recycled from a prior engagement. At the completion of Branscomb's presentation, Cochair Galvin thanked him warmly for an "excellent opening stimulating statement." However, Branscomb's vision of a macho role for the NSF board in the politics of science aroused scant interest among the majority of his colleagues.

Others spoke to the commission, among them Harold Shapiro, president of Princeton University, who distributed a paper, "Functions and Resources: The University of the Twenty-First Century," that he had given a year earlier at a symposium at the University of Chicago.[13] In his remarks to the commission, Shapiro ruminated on the role of change: "There is only one thing more common than change itself, and that is comments about change. . . . There is no question that change is part of our lives." Universities, he continued, "are about to begin a journey." Decisions must be made, Shapiro said. "What road to take? What baggage from the past to bring along? What objective to seek? Try to figure out what others will be doing?" The task of the commission was not new, Shapiro pointed out: "No matter what you do, if you take all the years between 1900 and 1990 and put them on a dart board and throw a dart at it, you will find a year in which someone has appointed a commission to deal with the future of higher education and its transition." He did not provide specific recommendations for the future of NSF.

---

13. Harold T. Shapiro, "Functions and Resources: The University of the Twenty-First Century," delivered at the University of Chicago Symposium on "The University of the Twenty-First Century," October 5, 1991.

SCIENTISTS AGAINST CHANGE

As the seventy-five-day life span of the commission ticked away, the deliberations on the future of NSF stimulated support for the status quo from NSF's normally quiescent beneficiaries in universities. For them, the existing NSF was satisfactory, except for the insufficiency of its budget. Closer ties with industry were deemed acceptable—the politics of the time restrained overt opposition—but not at any cost to NSF's traditional priorities. At the second meeting of the commission, on October 16, 1992, Commissioner Percy A. Pierre, vice president of research and graduate studies at Michigan State University, reported the sentiments at his institution (based on "direct meetings and letters"): "The most pervasive finding was that nothing should be done at the expense of basic research; that most people felt that closer university/industry relationships were desirable but should not be done at the expense of basic research."[14] Similar opinions were plentiful in the communications that the commission received in response to its open invitation for members of the public—meaning, in effect, members of the scientific enterprise—to express their views. The commission staff reported receipt of 724 "letters and messages," two-thirds from academe.[15]

The largest bloc of correspondents, 282 of them, was categorized as opposed to change and expressing favor for "NSF to retain its support of basic research and not expand its mission to any significant extent." Only 94 of the respondents, the staff analysis stated, "expressed the opinion that it is important for NSF to broaden its focus and foster closer ties of academia with industry and the national laboratories. These people did not address support of basic research." But "An additional 135 indicated that NSF should continue to support basic research, but expansion of its mission is possible or desirable. There was a considerable range of enthusiasm for expanding the mission, however, running from cautious to exuberant support." Another 213 communications were silent on the crucial issue of "the appropriateness or desirability of expanding the Foundation's mission."[16]

---

14. National Science Board Commission on the Future of the NSF, October 16, 1992, meeting summary.

15. Charles S. Brownstein, "Overview of Letters," memorandum to the NSB Commission on the Future of NSF, November 6, 1992, files of the National Science Board.

16. NSF and its board were acutely sensitive to opinion within the scientific enterprise. At about the midpoint in the commission's seventy-five-day lifespan, the e-mail newsletter of the American Physical Society, *What's New*, reported that the commission's executive secretary, Charles Brownstein, "dismissed the authors [of letters to the commission] as 'self-selected,'" and that NSF Director Massey agreed with Brownstein's appraisal. The *What's New* report was promptly disputed in a memorandum to members of the board, copied to members of the commission, from Marta Cehelsky, execu-

Territorial Protection

Frequent among the communications was a preference for maintaining, if not expanding, the correspondent's existing advantages at NSF and opposition to changes that might be disadvantageous, while those not receiving NSF's money appealed for shares. In NSF's distillation of comments, the American Astronautical Society opposed the redirection of NSF funds "to other activities such as education at the expense of basic research." The Microscopy Society of America agreed that NSF should foster closer relations among academe, industry, and government laboratories, "but not at the expense of basic research." The Council of Independent Colleges urged recognition of "the importance of undergraduate education in re-thinking NSF's mission." The Council on Undergraduate Research complained that the commission's membership did not include "representatives from primarily undergraduate institutions," while the Association for Women in Science urged "explicit steps to ensure that women and underrepresented minorities are included in [NSF's] long range strategy." The American Institute of Steel Construction urged NSF to "focus more attention on applied engineering research." The American Society for Engineering Education recommended an expansion of engineering programs and greater industrial representation on NSF's advisory bodies. The DuPont Company, like other high-tech corporations that benefited from government-financed research in universities, favored continuity for NSF. Summarizing DuPont's views, the commission staff wrote: "NSF [is] an example of government working well and any changes should be carefully considered. . . . current trend is that industry will rely more heavily on universities to conduct basic research." The referred-to trend arose from industry seeking quicker payoffs from the research it financed, and therefore shifting away from investments of corporate money and time in the uncertainties of long-term basic research. Under this form of corporate welfare, risk shifted from the shareholders to the taxpayers. Director Massey reported his personal encounters with concerns for the future of NSF: "In talking with many people," the minutes reported, "he [Massey] found that more was being read into the establishment of the commission than had been intended, causing anxiety and concern about what the process would

---

tive officer of the board, who wrote: "Please be aware that this characterization is inaccurate. As borne out by the transcript of the discussion, the Director exercised scrupulous care to refrain from interpreting the correspondence. " Marta Cehelsky, "Memorandum to the National Science Board," October 21, 1992, Subject: "October 16 Meeting of the NSB Commission on the Future of the National Science Foundation," in files of the National Science Board.

be and the 'real agenda.' "[17] Out there in the community of science, fears flourished of hidden forces working toward concealed goals, to the detriment of fundamental research and scientific independence in academe.

When writing time arrived for the commission's report, the Vannevar Bush nostalgists prevailed in making their case for minimal alterations at NSF. The product of the commission's hurried proceedings was released to the public on November 20, 1992, just a few weeks after Bill Clinton was elected president. Titled "A Foundation for the 21st Century: A Progressive Framework for the National Science Foundation," the report, a mere ten typewritten pages, contained a splatter of observations, assertions, and recommendations. In its totality, it bolstered the fortifications on the science side of the traditional boundary between science and politics. The case for maintaining NSF virtually unchanged as the flagship of academic basic research was strongly stated, rendered more credible by the commission's high-ranking industrial members. The report's opening section directly disputed the politically damaging charge that the basic-research system must share responsibility for the poor performance of American industry:

> Failures in the market place have not been the result of slow transfer of academic science to industry. In fact, American firms have been the first to commercialize virtually all innovative products, but have lost market share to competitors with shorter product cycles, lower costs, and superior quality. . . . Success requires: an enlightened federal science and technology policy that touches all relevant agencies, a determination by industry to reach out for talent and knowledge, and the development of appropriate links. . . . Redirecting the NSF's activities from research and education would have little or no effect on the U.S. competitive position in the near term, but would severely restrict prospects for the long term.[18]

After the strong opening, the commission dribbled dabs of honey for all interests, including Branscomb and his insistent recommendations for a significant role for NSF's board in national science-policy affairs. The language was coy, and required reading between the lines. Nonetheless, the

---

17. NSB Commission on the Future of the NSF, October 16, 1992, meeting summary, NSB files.
18. "A Foundation for the 21st Century: A Progressive Framework for the National Science Foundation," a report of the National Science Board Commission on the Future of the National Science Foundation, November 20, 1992.

concept was present in several passages, including a cautiously written closing paragraph:

> Finally, the Commission returns to the role of the Board in influencing
> science and engineering and technology policy for the Nation. The
> Board and the National Science Foundation are today the lead organiza-
> tions representing the interests of broad science and engineering in the
> United States. The Board must work with its peers in the private and
> public sectors so that the nation might formulate a much needed sci-
> ence and technology roadmap.

Addressing the tension between political demands for utilitarian science
and scientists' desire for professional autonomy, the commission oscillated
between the two:

> In accepting society's support, the scientific community naturally as-
> sumes an obligation to be both responsive to national needs voiced by
> society as well as the intellectual priorities solely initiated by the scien-
> tist or engineer. Concern over technology application and competitive-
> ness sometimes conjures up a choice that budgeting is decided on either
> the criteria to please the scientists or to serve the public. In reality, these
> criteria and interests are congruent.

The commission did not neglect the venerable cause of the public understanding of science. NSF, it stated, "should more aggressively lead in
communicating the 'case' for science and engineering, which deserves a
high priority in the minds of public officials and citizens alike." Invoking
unstated lessons from the "history of science," the commission recommended the dual goals of "first-rate research at many points on the frontiers
of knowledge, identified and defined by the best researchers," and "a balanced allocation of resources in strategic research areas in response to scientific opportunities to meet national goals." The commission thus seemed
to favor a fair division between projects originated by scientists, irrespective
of potential benefits to society, and projects inspired by promising scientific
opportunities to meet national goals. In both cases, however, the commission recommended that the choice-making authority should remain with
scientists, in a process based on the "initiation of proposals by investigators
and selection of those to be funded by merit review carried out by experts.
This method," the commission asserted, "has proved to be the best way

of tapping into the creativity of research scientists and engineers." Many of
the commission's proposals, including a recommendation for larger grants,
would require additional money from a new presidential administration
pledged to reduce the federal deficit. On this matter, as on others, the commission offered two mismatched replies: NSF will need more money to "respond to these challenges," it stated, while conceding "that policies to control spending need the support of the citizenry."

Was the report a deliberate exercise in obfuscation? Or was its amorphous content the outcome of an earnest effort to answer a question that
evoked many confident assertions but little agreement: how to draw prosperity from the restless relationships of science, technology, politics, government, industry, and academe? Having assuaged all parties by endorsing
a bit of everything, the Commission on the Future of NSF disbanded, and
the exegetic phase commenced.

WHAT DID THEY SAY?

Four days after the commission issued its report, Commissioner Lewis
Branscomb expressed reservations in a letter to Board Chairman James J.
Duderstadt.[19] Given the helter-skelter conditions under which the report
was produced, Branscomb wrote, "the consensus we reached is remarkable."
But, he noted, because of the hurried schedule, the members of the commission lacked an opportunity to review the final version prior to publication.
The report, Branscomb asserted, "is so even and the message is so muffled,
the key points are hard to pull out. . . . As best as I can tell, the national
press shared this impression, since they seem to have ignored the report
because they could not discern a story within it."

Branscomb renewed his pleas for the board to take a major role in the
formulation of national science policy and for NSF to encourage closer relations between academe and industry. In a delicately phrased, knowledgeable assurance, he advised the board that professors follow the money: "NSF
should not tell university scientists what to do; it need only put properly
allocated resources in the paths of bright people"—a discreet variant on
the tactic endorsed by Perle Mesta, the celebrated Washington hostess, for
attracting a crowd to a party: "Hang a lamb chop in the window."

Branscomb argued that the board "must not remain passive while enor-

19. Correspondence concerning the Commission on the Future of NSF, from members of
the commission and others, is in the files of the National Science Board.

mous changes are taking place in the U.S. science and technology enterprise, its policies, institutions, and goals." To do so, he grimly prophesied, "leads to disaster." Three weeks later, Branscomb wrote again to Board Chairman Duderstadt, stating that he had not had a response to his earlier letter and describing the commissioners' conclusions as "waffled in the writing of the final report." He also informed Duderstadt that he had sent a copy of his first letter to Sally K. Ride, the former astronaut, who was serving on the transition team of the incoming Clinton administration as chair of the science, space, and technology "cluster."[20]

An Urgent Appeal

Among the commissioners, disputes continued about what they had concluded. Ian Ross, who was both a commissioner and a member of the NSF board, complained to Duderstadt about "some misinterpretation of the report or at least misplacement of emphasis." Though praising the report as "an excellent document," Ross declared:

> The Commission was forced to work to an impossibly short schedule.
> . . . The report represents a consensus that could be reached on those issues that were raised during the Commission meetings. There was, however, no process to develop a comprehensive list of issues and to assign priorities. In all probability there were other important issues that were never raised.

Ross thickened the fog around the report by declaring that the "most urgent attention" should be given to Branscomb's proposal for expanding the board's role in national science policy—a role that few inside or outside NSF wished to assign to the board. In pressing this recommendation, Ross upheld the quixotic tradition in science politics, wherein chieftains of science fire pop guns at distant targets. The commission's report, as we have

---

20. At transition headquarters, NSF affairs registered close to zero among the concerns of president-elect Bill Clinton and his close associates. Ride, who was head of the California Space Institute at the University of California, San Diego, had chaired a small, late-starting organization of Scientists and Engineers for Clinton-Gore during the campaign. The transition group she headed was nominally responsible for a grab-bag of agencies: NASA, NSF, the Federal Communications Commission, and the National Commission on Libraries and Information Services (an obscure advisory group established in 1970). Clinton later appointed Ride to the President's Committee of Advisors for Science and Technology. The fate of Branscomb's letter is lost to history.

seen, mentioned the policymaking goal, among others, but not in a clear or emphatic fashion. As Charles Brownstein, executive secretary of the commission, later commented to me, "NSF is a little dog," and the commission and the board recognized that it couldn't set research policy for the big dogs of defense, space, and medical research.[21] Ross nonetheless urged immediate attention to the policymaking recommendation, but warned that to pursue it, the board must plunge into big-science politics, citing specifically the space station and the Superconducting Super Collider, neither of which belonged to NSF. These multibillion-dollar projects were strongly guarded crown-jewel possessions of NASA and the Department of Energy, respectively, both far wealthier and politically more powerful than little NSF, and not inclined to take their policy orders or even cues from that agency. Moreover, the space station and the SSC were rich in pork-barrel value, which involved political forces and dealings remote from NSF in its role as patron of "little science." To exercise influence in the megaproject league, Ross naively suggested, "The Board may need to augment its membership to include a broader set of talents and experiences. It may need a stronger independent staff and may need access to independent legal counsel, just to mention a few possible consequences." Ross urged immediate, exclusive attention to settling the question of the board's role. "If you agree with these observations," he advised Board Chairman Duderstadt, "I suggest you consider canceling our existing agendas to give first priority to resolving this issue." Chairman Duderstadt ignored the invitation to a dead-end exercise.

IMPROVING A "FINE EXISTING SYSTEM"

Explaining that many people had asked for his opinion of the report, Director Massey said that he and the commission were in harmony, though, as we have seen, in the comments of Commissioners Branscomb and Ross, the commission itself was not in harmony.[22] "The charge to the Commission," Massey stated, "specifically asked for an assessment of the environment for science and technology." His own view, he explained, was "that the environment is changing dramatically, both because of changes in research itself and also because of social, political, and economic factors. These changes, in my opinion, require a rethinking of the policies that have guided NSF since its inception. The commission has concurred in my assess-

21. Telephone conversation with author, August 17, 1999.
22. Walter E. Massey, "Discussion of Key Findings on the Future of NSF," NSF Office of Legislative and Public Affairs, December 1992.

ment," Massey asserted, adding that the ideas it proposed should be explored as possible improvements "to a fine existing system." Massey noted the recommendations for closer ties between science and technology, support of both basic research and "strategic areas that are closely aligned with national priorities, including promising areas of technology," and preservation of the "essential strengths of the current system: merit review, the connections between research and education, the flexibility to pursue new ideas unencumbered by bureaucracy, and the support for research at universities." These methods underpin the greatness of American science, and must be retained, Massey said. In summarizing the recommendations of the commission, the NSF director made no reference to expanding the role of the board in national science affairs, the recommendation deemed so urgent by Ross that he urged Duderstadt to cancel the board's agenda and address it immediately.

In late December 1992, with Inauguration Day for Bill Clinton less than a month away, the board and its staff struggled to compose a response to the diffuse set of recommendations of the commission created by the board to recommend the future of NSF. Publicly congratulating the commission for its advice, Chairman Duderstadt said the board must proceed to chart the future of NSF. This next phase entailed many difficulties, given the anxious watchfulness of NSF's clients in the basic-science community and the emphasis on technology in the campaign addresses of President-elect Clinton and Vice President-elect Gore (who was slated for the role of science and technology "czar," according to widespread, but, as it turned out, mistaken reports).

The board could simply have said, "Thank you" to the commission and blamelessly proceeded to plan the future of NSF without making a written response to the pottage of recommendations. However, the report industry, with staffs in place and eager for work—though often complaining of oppressive workloads and daunting schedules—is genetically programmed to produce and emit documentation. At the staff level of the board, labor commenced on a preface to be attached to the report of the Commission on the Future of NSF. Prepared by a member of the board's staff, and endorsed by Chairman Duderstadt, the initial product of this effort was a bland preface expressing appreciation for the commission's work and even-handedly endorsing the recommendation that NSF retain its traditional values while responding to the challenges of the post–Cold War era. Textual nit-picking commenced immediately, continuing without letup, even during the Christmas holidays.

DRAFT STATEMENT REJECTED

On December 23, 1992, Charles Brownstein, the NSF staff member who had served as executive secretary of the commission, declared the draft of the prefatory statement unacceptable. In a memo to Marta Cehelsky, executive director of the board, and Ray Bye, NSF's director of legislative and public affairs, Brownstein advised: "I suggest that it not be used in its present form as it may raise ill will on procedural grounds in the NSB while adding little value to the commission report." Brownstein generously attributed some of the difficulties to "just a garbled style." Quoting from the draft of the preface, he noted that it credited the commission with " 'correctly' " observing that " 'changes in the world are forcing changes in how we as society view and support science and engineering research.' " However, the statement went too far, he protested, because the board had not yet issued a judgment about the correctness of the commission's report. Brownstein faulted the draft preface for a series of "must statements," including: " 'Public confidence in and support of science and engineering research must be restored.' " The commission "did not particularly deal with" that issue, Brownstein pointed out, while he also cautioned that the use of "must statements . . . could prove contentious and if it does the entire exercise will be undermined." At the conclusion of his critique, Brownstein noted that "Duderstadt had signed off," meaning the board chair had approved the prefatory statement. Brownstein urged reconsideration, stating, "I see no reason to let this go forward without fixing these potential problems."

"PARANOIA" REPORTED

Back in Ann Arbor, in the presidency of the University of Michigan, Duderstadt responded to Brownstein by e-mail at 9:40 A.M. on December 23, rejecting Brownstein's criticisms of the preface Duderstadt had approved for the commission's report. Stating, "I'm not comfortable with the 'suggested revisions,' since your draft really amounts to a total rewrite of the preface," Duderstadt exposed a subdermal sore beneath the smooth surface of Washington's report-writing industry: doubts, and sensitivities, about authorship. Reports are issued in the names of the overscheduled, part-time committee members, who hurry to meetings, sometimes arriving late and leaving early. But the day-to-day workers in these endeavors are the full-time staff members who prepare the agendas and background papers, attend the meetings, and afterward draft the reports that supposedly reflect the nature of the proceedings and the conclusions of its faraway committee members. Wrote Duderstadt:

> While I'm willing to consider modifications to the existing text, the preface must be something originating within the Board rather than the NSF staff. (Here, I probably don't need to remind you that there is already great paranoia among both the Commission and NSB [National Science Board] members about the perception that NSF staff are spindoctoring the report.) Hence, send me your concerns about specific wording in the original draft and I will consider modification. But also please note that the original draft (below) will hold until I modify it myself [appended to Duderstadt's memo was the original draft].[23]

Duderstadt thus openly acknowledged sectarian strife of high intensity, though of minuscule, inconsequential substance. Home-based outside of NSF, Duderstadt and the commissioners appointed to advise his board suspected the presence of an insularity and resistance to change within the NSF headquarters staff. Now here was one of those NSF staff members, Charles Brownstein (who had served as executive secretary of the commission, on detached duty from NSF's directorate for computer science and engineering), proposing a pallid preface to the board's statement concerning the advice it had received from the commission. Veterans of the Washington report industry recognize that introductory passages are vital, even decisive, for shaping opinion: readership and comprehension of these inveterately opaque documents wearily sags with each line. At this stage, the issue was not the report—which was in final form, ambiguities and all—but the kinship between the report of the commission and the preface to be attached to it by the board that had created the commission. Both documents were products of enigmatic prose artistry, and the changes in the preface proposed by Brownstein and resisted by Chairman Duderstadt did not elevate the level of specificity in the dense, omnidirectional wording of either document. Thus, where the commission had, with equanimity, affirmed both NSF's need for more money *and* the importance of government frugality, the preface proposed by Brownstein, and opposed by Duderstadt, described the commission's stance as follows: "The Commission acknowledges the difficulties of responding to new challenges within the

23. James J. Duderstadt to Charles Brownstein, e-mail, December 23, 1992, in file, Future of the National Science Foundation, National Science Board.

present resource base. Never the less [sic] the Commission strongly recommends NSF leadership."

Linking the money issue to the commission's muffled recommendations for the board to assume a major role in national science-policy affairs, the proposed preface stated: "To this end, the commission urges the National Science Board to speak out broadly on an 'integrated' national science and technology policy." Board Chairman Duderstadt rejected that version in favor of the wordage composed by his staff ghost, which described the NSF budget as "inadequate to support even its present responsibilities and programs." On the issue of policymaking, Duderstadt's version declared, "To this end, the Commission urges the National Science Board to view its recommendations in the context of its own responsibility to develop and carry out national science policy for science and engineering research more broadly."[24]

Into the New Year (1993), contention continued over the wording of the board's response to the report of the commission. As always, major league, real politics was moving to its own rhythms, preparing at that time for the inauguration of Bill Clinton and oblivious of the intense textual strife that occupied the board members, managers, ex-commissioners on the future, and anonymous staff specialists of NSF. On January 18, 1993, two days before Inauguration Day, Duderstadt e-mailed yet another version of the preface to Marta Cehelsky. "Here is another try at the statement," he informed her, adding, "We should keep it short and simple to avoid more wordsmithing debates. And we should probably keep it vague with respect to next steps, since this will require more discussion in February."[25] Like a homeopathic nostrum, the intractable preface had been diluted into a solution in which none of the original substance was detectable:

We find that the Commission has performed an outstanding service in discharging its responsibility to stimulate thinking on long-range strategies for the Foundation. Further, we find ourselves in strong agreement with the Commission's strong reaffirmation of the traditional role of the Foundation, namely, the support of fundamental research in science and engineering and the enhancement of science and mathematics education at all levels, while recognizing the challenges and opportunities

24. At this point, it may be recalled that Cervantes attributed Don Quixote's descent into madness to his incessant and credulous readings in the literature of knight-errantry and chivalry. The comparable risks of science-policy readings may warrant attention.
25. James J. Duderstadt, e-mail to Marta Cehelsky, January 18, 1993, files of the National Science Board.

posed by a period of unusual change. The Commission has raised a number of significant issues and recommendations that will deserve broader deliberations by the Board, both concerning its own role and responsibilities as well as NSF policy directions and strategies. . . . We intend to continue the constructive dialog that we have established with all interested parties as we prepare for the inevitable demands that the future will bring.[26]

Cehelsky forwarded copies of this latest draft of the preface to several members of the senior NSF staff. Back from one of them, unsigned, came a copy with a handwritten comment:

> Marta—Hopeless! Too wishy washy—even for the NSB The Board (mostly) agrees with the Report & ought to say so. This is a *"dismissal"* [original italics and quotes] of the recommendations about strategic research, larger awards, [illegible], etc and will be *widely* interpreted as such.[27]

MASSEY'S SURPRISE

The plot, sinuous as it had been, was about to acquire an additional twist that would extend the deliberations for many more months. Recall that Walter Massey initiated the examination of the future of NSF in August 1992, about eighteen months after the Senate confirmed him as director for the statutorily specified six-year term. The tenure was designed by NSF's postwar creators to insulate the frail house of science against the whims and forces of quadrennial presidential politics. Regardless of the starting date of the director's service, a portion would remain after the next presidential election, unless the president took the unthinkable step of discharging the director, which has never happened.

In November 1992, when Clinton was elected, over four years remained of Massey's term. Though appointed by a Republican administration, the customs regarding NSF, plus the politics of science and race, secured his tenure. By background, Massey was a nonpolitical academic research administrator holding a traditionally nonpolitical science job; he was one of the highest-ranking African Americans in the Bush administration, thus

---

26. National Science Board, file on the Commission on the Future of the National Science Foundation.
27. Ibid.

making it awkward, though not impossible, for the newly elected Clinton administration to seek his resignation or oust him. Massey seemed a sure-shot for staying on to navigate NSF into the uncertain future, for which he had sought guidance from a special commission. But by choice, his own future with NSF was short-lived. One week after Bill Clinton's inauguration, and while the board continued to dither over a response to the advice of the commission it had created—at Massey's insistence—Massey announced, to widespread astonishment, that he would leave NSF in March 1993, the second anniversary of his six-year appointment. Beckoning was the number two position in the statewide University of California system, a plum job with better pay and fewer headaches than the directorship of the nerve-racked, politically pecked-at NSF. But the main attraction for Massey was a good shot at the presidency of the University of California, the nation's preeminent system of public higher education. A search was underway to fill the number one position, occupied since the previous fall by Jack Pelta-son, age sixty-eight. As senior vice president, Massey would be well-situated to reach the top, though, as it turned out, he didn't. "This offer came very quickly," Massey explained to douse rumors that he had been ousted by the new administration. "I was approached in January, as a matter of fact. It is something that is just too good for me to turn down. These things come when they come. So, I haven't been planning to leave, and there was nothing in the [White House] transition that prompted this."[28]

As the Clinton administration settled into office, with emphasis on re-forming the health-care system and producing the economic stimuli that Clinton had promised during the campaign, the anxieties and hopes of the NSF registered dimly, if at all, at the White House. From his departure an-nouncement at the end of January 1993 until his resignation officially took effect on April 5, Massey was a lame duck. Named to serve as acting director was Frederick M. Bernthal, an ex–science professor whom President Bush had appointed as deputy director in 1990. From the outset of the Clinton administration, it was understood that Bernthal would not be the next NSF director. Unusual among the administrators of government science, Bern-thal appeared to have a political pedigree because of staff service with Re-publican Senator Howard Baker and appointments by Bush to the State De-partment and the Nuclear Regulatory Commission prior to his appointment to the deputy director job at NSF. That's where Bernthal was that week in January 1993 when Bill Clinton became president, Walter Massey suddenly

---

28. "NSF Director Tells of the Offer He Couldn't Refuse," *SGR*, March 1, 1993.

announced that he was bound for California, and the NSF board continued stewing over the recommendations of the Commission on the Future of NSF.

Meanwhile, the technology theme that Clinton had sounded during the campaign was strongly repeated during the opening phase of his administration. Plans for bigger federal technology programs dominated the Senate confirmation hearing of John H. Gibbons, Clinton's nominee for director of the White House Office of Science and Technology Policy. The administration's emphasis on technology was noted by Senator John Danforth (R-Mo.), whose brother, William Danforth, had cochaired the nearly forgotten Commission on the Future of NSF. "I hope you're not downgrading the role of basic research," Danforth said. Gibbons assured the senator that basic research would be well-supported by the new administration.[29] But, clearly, on the commonly understood spectrum of science and technology, the latter held primacy. One month after Clinton's inauguration, the White House issued a manifesto of technology policy: *Technology for America's Growth: A New Direction to Build Economic Strength*.[30] The remarkable speed of publication in a customarily languid process of multiple drafts, consultations, revisions, and editing reflected the metamorphosis of leftover campaign literature into White House policy.

By the spring of 1993, the Clinton administration was beset by politically crippling turmoil. The health-care reform plan that Clinton promised to deliver in the first hundred days of his presidency was bogged in controversy and repeatedly postponed. The Congress of Clinton's inaugural year, with his own party in majority, rejected his proposals for a $16 billion "economic stimulus" package. The armed services were disrespectfully balking at the commander-in-chief's "don't ask, don't tell" policy for gays in the military. Unnoticed amid these tumultuous events, the NSF board labored on through the winter and into the spring of 1993 to complete the process for which it had sought counsel in the summer of 1992 from the Commission on the Future of NSF. The board's persistence with the task was irrelevant and futile in its remoteness from Washington's continuous procession of fast-changing, prime-time political dramas. In addition, the acting head of NSF, handicapped by his Republican connections, held office on a temporary basis while the new administration sought its own choice. At the dawn of the Clinton presidency, crackling with ideas for a new America, the NSF board and the acting NSF director were, by the normal processes of

29. "Clinton's Science Adviser Sails Through Senate Hearing," *SGR*, February 1, 1993.

30. Office of Science and Technology Policy, 1993.

politics, yesterday's men and women. By the standards of other government agencies, the management of NSF had been rendered politically obsolete by the election results.

Science, however, does not abide by the normal processes of politics. The six-year terms of the members of the National Science Board provided political legitimacy in an administration that had appointed none of them—akin to lifetime judges surviving the presidents who appointed them. Moreover, political coloration was virtually absent from the board, whose members predominantly came from the upper administrative ranks of academe, with a sprinkling of industrial executives, mostly from the new high-tech industries. By political ideology and professional profile, the board appointees of Republicans Bush and Reagan were generally indistinguishable from the appointees of Democrats Carter and Clinton. So, shielded by law, history, and culture from the winds of politics, the NSF board soldiered on with the preparation of a document conceived in the twilight of the Bush administration. Without the political strength that comes with votes and campaign money, paper products are a major weapon in the politics of science—a unique brand of politics.

A Declaration for Basic Research

The final product of the board's exercise in futurology was a wondrously brazen, artfully composed two-page manifesto, "In Support of Basic Research," accompanied by a matching press release headed "NSF Reaffirms Commitment to Basic Research."[31] The board was not obliged to discuss the tortuous odyssey that led to its declaration, and it didn't. The board's statement saluted the Clinton administration as a dedicated supporter of basic research, though the Clinton oratorical record, pre- and post-election, contained virtually nothing to warrant the gesture; its budget allocations held basic research more or less steady while sharply increasing spending for industrial technology. The board, however, deftly linked basic research with Clinton's campaign emphasis on economic growth and government stimulation of industrial technology:

> In the 21st century, our quality of life will depend in large measure on
> the generation of new wealth. Basic research, the underpinning of the
> scientific enterprise, will play a vital role in this process. As stated in a re-

---

31. "In Support of Basic Research" (NSB 93-127), was dated May 14, 1993, but was made public with a June 2 press release (NSF PR 93-50).

cent White House report, ". . . scientific advances are the wellspring of
the technical innovations whose benefits are seen in economic growth,
improved health care and many other areas." [Here, a footnote referred
to the newly issued White House report *Technology for America's Growth:
A New Direction to Build Economic Strength*.] Appropriately, the Administration has made continued world leadership in basic science, mathematics,
and engineering a centerpiece of its strategy to revitalize the nation and
to ensure its well-being. Maintaining this leadership is a special responsibility of the National Science Foundation.[32]

The board anchored its statement in the long-disbanded, now-forgotten Commission on the Future of NSF, declaring that "This statement
responds to the specific Commission recommendations that the Board re-
affirm the role of the National Science Foundation in the support of the
U.S. research system, and that the Board exercise leadership over a broad
range of science and technology issues." The vague reference to board "leadership" was the final product of prolonged wrestling over Lewis Branscomb's urgings for the board to take a major part in the formulation of
national science policy. However, like its predecessors in the long-ago
startup of NSF, the board, forty years later, would not presume to prescribe
policy for the government's bigger and stronger research agencies. Though
often urged on, never in its history had NSF's board asserted claims to that
territory. It was not inclined to veer from that tradition, especially at the
start of a new presidential administration.

The board's rendering of the advice provided by the Commission on
the Future of NSF was selective, in favor of basic research. The commission
had clearly endorsed two goals for NSF: "first-rate research on the frontiers
of knowledge, identified and defined by the best researchers"—which trans-
lates to the traditional role of supporting basic research; and, as the second
goal, "a balanced allocation of resources in strategic research in response
to scientific opportunities to meet national goals"—meaning research
"downstream" from the basic sciences. The board's version reconstructed
the original two-part design of basic research and strategic research into a
focus on basic research, stating:

> The Commission's report noted that research can be undertaken to
> achieve strategic ends and to increase the base of knowledge. Basic re-

32. Ibid.

search is the foundation and essence of both, assuring a deep reservoir
of knowledge and providing choices and flexibility for addressing future
needs. Moreover, in the age of technology, the problem solving approach of basic research helps prepare minds for work in all walks of
life. . . . Assuring the knowledge base appropriate for economic growth,
long term job creation and social well being requires a conscious commitment to strong and consistent long-term support for basic research
and education. Providing requisite support for this process is a matter of
strategic national importance.

The board's declaration, which it described as a response to the recommendations of the Commission on the Future of NSF, omitted a word that
was sprinkled throughout the Commission's report: engineering. In the battle for textual supremacy, basic research was triumphant. Amid the economic anxiety arising from international industrial competition, this was a
remarkable achievement. To outsiders, the outcome might seem even more
remarkable, given that James J. Duderstadt, chair of the board, was an engineer, and the dean of engineering before he was appointed president of the
University of Michigan. In the bastion of basic research, in the government
agency repeatedly extolled as the sacrosanct institutional embodiment of
Vannevar Bush's seminal design, the worshipful endorsement of basic research was a preordained outcome of introspection. Like a Vatican Curia
Romana on the existence of God, it would not produce surprises.

By creating the commission, and thus setting the stage for the wran-
gling that followed, did the board overreact to the vagaries of federal budgeting, congressional demands for practical science, and the campaign rhetoric of candidate Clinton? These were powerful forces in the politics of
science. But hindsight also suggests that the exercise into the future of NSF
was a frightened response to the menacing ghosts that have been sighted
near science ever since Vannevar Bush delivered his ill-fated proposal to
President Truman. The scientific enterprise is inclined, and generously
staffed, to see the worst for itself in real politics. The participants, with their
blinkered view of politics and tendency to equate a minor budget cut with
doom, were genuinely fearful for the future of NSF. They had all heard tales
of the political fragility of basic science, along with worrisome accounts of
its roots in the now-gone Cold War. Though basic research prospered during the Cold War, as did applied research, ancient maxims, echoing the
Bush report, held credence: applied research will drive out basic research,
the sages muttered, even as a new generation of science-policy analysts contended that the basic-applied dichotomy was a fallacy.

Should we conclude that the exercise into the future of NSF was unwarranted and fruitless? No. Lacking a presence in real politics, the managers of science responded to their perception of danger at the border by employing two of the few weapons available to them: meetings and reports. Fearing that politics was en route to diminishing science in favor of industrial technology, they called for help from industrial technologists, who strongly defended basic research as an essential ingredient of industrial superiority. For the cause of science, these were unsurpassable witnesses. The very act of creating the commission mobilized political sentiment in the scientific community and inflamed the paranoid spirits that permanently lurk among the beneficiaries of public support of science.

Looking back in 1999 on the lengthy and argumentative deliberations into the future of NSF, Charles Brownstein, who served as executive secretary of the commission, rated the exercise a success. The many meetings, the community involvement, and the reports of the commission and the board played an educational role for the NSF community, Brownstein concluded. When the issue of NSF's place in the American economy arose later in the 1990s, as it often did, "the foundation was not dealing with it *de novo*," Brownstein pointed out. He also noted that the edge was taken off the technology issue by the clear acknowledgment that NSF supports science *and* technology, though primacy remained with science.

NSF was thus braced for the arrival of the Clinton administration, with its emphasis on technology and seeming indifference to science. At the Department of Energy, the financial mainstay of megaphysics, similar preparations were lacking, and catastrophe lay ahead. We will now look into that and related matters.

CHAPTER 25

Clinton, Atom Smashing, and Space

> Society does not *a priori* owe the scientist, even the good scientist, support any more than it owes support to the artist or the writer or to the musician. Science must seek support from society on grounds other than the science is carried out competently and that it is ready for exploitation.
>
> —Alvin Weinberg, former director of Oak Ridge National Laboratory, in *Reflections on Big Science* (MIT Press, 1966)

THE PHYSICS community, originally welcomed to Washington for its nuclear knowledge, was dethroned from decades of political influence by the end of the Cold War and the parsimonious politics of the 1990s. The atom was in low repute, if not disgrace, associated with bombs, the Chernobyl and Three Mile Island accidents, unmanageable nuclear waste, and mysterious cancer "clusters." In the distribution of federal research money, biomedical science was favored more than ever, though with little effect on the chronic sense of financial insecurity among its practitioners. In other scientific disciplines, health research was enviously regarded as specially blessed and politically propelled by the curative demands of the public, remarkable scientific advances, and a growing output of tantalizing press reports of cures to come. Large and well-financed, the lobbies for NIH feasted on success and narrowly focused their efforts on their own sector of research, rather than seeking to raise financial support for all the sciences.[1]

---

1. By 1999, the NIH budget had galloped so far ahead of the other federal science agencies that NIH Director Varmus reminded Congress that medical research utilizes physics, chemistry, computers, and mathematics—disciplines mainly supported by nonmedical agencies, principally NSF and the Department of Energy.

The High Costs of Physics

To study the innards of the atom, physics had spawned a succession
of research instruments, starting small with the first cyclotrons before
World War II and evolving to the four-mile-around particle accelerator, the
Tevatron, that went into operation in 1983 at the Fermi National Accelerator Laboratory, near Chicago. Particle physics was the purest of pure science.
Over the postwar years, politicians accepted the judgment of physicists and
paid the rising bills. Public understanding of this arcane branch of science
was nil, but the money was kept flowing by a firm alliance of science and
politics. The only political quibbles concerned pork-barrel issues of locale
for the great projects. Peace was achieved by employing a politically sani-
tized, objective selection process, based on site suitability, travel conve-
nience for visiting physicists, electric-power supply, and so forth, judiciously managed by taint-free committees of the National Academy of
Sciences. In 1993, when the technology-minded Clinton administration
took office, it inherited one of the biggest construction projects of all time
and the greatest ever in the history of physics: the Superconducting Super
Collider (SSC), a proton accelerator—atom smasher, in lay language—mer-
iting superlatives in all its dimensions, from its fifty-four-mile underground
circular tunnel, with 10,000 superconducting magnets of cutting-edge design, to its continually rising multibillion-dollar cost. The SSC epitomized
basic research. Ebullient forecasts of serendipitous industrial spin-offs from
the project were contrived for selling the SSC to politics. But it was well
understood, in both science and politics, that practical results were not the
object, or to be expected. The goal was fundamental knowledge, a quest
underwritten, and expensively so, by the U.S. government during the preceding forty years.

Even before Clinton was elected, the SSC nearly foundered in the new
politics of the 1990s on Capitol Hill, losing out in the House in June 1992,
232-181, but salvaged in the Senate with support from the Bush White
House. Runaway costs in a deficit-cutting environment caused that near
disaster. But the costs kept rising. In the next year, when decision time
came, the newly inaugurated Clinton administration abandoned the SSC
to the deficit-cutting wolves on Capitol Hill, thus adding to the perception
of presidential indifference, and political danger, to basic science. Meanwhile, the new president extolled technology as a vital but neglected tool
for invigorating the economy. For understanding the anxious state of the
scientific psyche in the closing decade of the last century, we should keep
in mind that the SSC debacle occurred in 1993, when Democrats controlled

the Congress and the White House. Still to come, a little over a year later, was the "Republican Revolution," led by Newt Gingrich, taking control of Congress with vows to slash federal spending and shrink the federal government.

Launched by Reagan

Following years of planning in the committee rooms and design centers of physics, the SSC was launched in 1986 by politics' leading supporter of scientific megaprojects, President Ronald Reagan, not long after he endorsed the space station and the Strategic Defense Initiative. According to a widely circulated account, reported by columnist George Will and echoed by Nobel physicist Leon Lederman, Reagan, upon being briefed about the choices of circumferential sizes for the next big accelerator, uttered a football metaphor to indicate his preference for the biggest: "Throw deep." Lederman explains that this was taken to mean "Let's do it."[2] The original cost estimate, approximately $4 billion, was softened by assurances from the sponsoring Department of Energy that other nations would contribute perhaps as much as one-half. In fact, no other nation had pledged a penny. But, with the forecasts of foreign money and the costs spread over a decade of design and construction, the SSC estimate did not upset Reagan's commitment to domestic austerity. Planning proceeded and in 1989, the Bush administration inherited the project, for which the chosen site was Waxahachie, Texas, near Dallas. As the project moved from discussions and planning to site preparation and construction, the Bush administration found the cost estimates from DOE inexorably rising. Nurtured on the carefree economics of nuclear weaponry, and habitually slovenly in its spending forecasts, DOE continued to assure the White House that major contributions would be forthcoming from other nations.[3]

In a theatrical ploy to attract foreign money, DOE unilaterally declared the SSC an "international" facility. Meanwhile, the budget forecasts rose far above the original $4 billion, climbing to $8 billion and then to $12 billion, with no assurance of a firm final total. The academic physicists who had initiated and planned the great project pleaded with their colleagues

2. Leon Lederman, with Dick Teresi, *The God Particle* (New York: Houghton Mifflin, 1993), p. 380.

3. Established in 1977, the Department of Energy acquired the facilities, culture and financial guile of its forebear, the Atomic Energy Commission, where, according to an "oft-quoted dictum . . . buildings didn't have to be cheap, they just had to look cheap." *Fermi News*, published by the Fermilab, January 28, 2000.

in Europe and Japan to urge their governments to contribute money. With Texan George Bush unflinchingly committed to the project, his science and technology adviser, D. Allan Bromley, joined the appeal for foreign alms. But foreign money never arrived. Even with an international label attached to the SSC, no realistic basis existed for expecting foreign help for a facility initiated by the United States, designed without foreign participation or consultation, located in the United States at Congressional insistence, and intended as a rival to Europe's successful collaboration in particle physics at CERN, the Center for European Nuclear Research, near Geneva. Bromley recollected to me the concern in the American physics community and in the Bush administration as the costs of the SSC continued to rise:

> People were a little shaken by this, but figured, well, it's all right. We're going to get international contributions. So, the group of high-energy physicists went out saying to people in Japan and Europe, "We have this marvelous new machine. It's going to answer the secrets of the universe. We'd like you to help us pay for it. And you'll all have the chance to use it a bit." So most of these people said, "Screw you. How come you didn't ask us before you started?" It was a good question. . . . And so, I called up some old friends in Japan. It happens that two former presidents of the University of Tokyo happened to be personal friends. They told me point blank that they would fight to the death [against] Japan putting any money into our damned SSC. I talked to some friends in CERN and got the same answer. The Europeans weren't going to put any money into this thing. We hadn't asked them anything [about design or location]. This was our machine and we could damn well pay for it, and lots of luck.[4]

SCIENCE BREAKS RANKS

On spending issues, scientists of different disciplines had previously refrained from internecine combat over shares of the budget, practicing live-and-let-live in their dealings with Washington. But that was before the financially ravenous SSC intersected with a general slowdown in budget growth for research. In 1988, in response to a request from the Senate Budget Committee, the Congressional Budget Office (CBO) undertook a study of "the potential risks and benefits of building the SSC." The CBO's econo-

---

4. Interview with author, October 7, 1998.

mists and budget specialists routinely toted up budget proposals, counted dollars appropriated and spent, and prepared economic forecasts. The CBO possessed no independent scientific capability, but it heard the dialogue of dissent concerning particle physics, including negative appraisals from subdisciplines of physics that feared their budgets would be drained by the SSC. Philip Webre, a CBO economist who was the principal author of the report requested by the Budget Committee, told me that "when word got around that I was studying the SSC, every disgruntled physicist in the world got in touch with me."[5] As a budget and policy analyst, Webre concentrated on measurable matters, noting, for example, that high-energy physics did not have a good record of accuracy in estimating construction costs. Webre cited the Fermi Laboratory's Tevatron: initial estimated cost, $70.5 million; final estimated cost, $174 million. However, assuming the accuracy of the SSC construction estimates, the CBO study also pointed out:

> The SSC would account for between 6 and 7 percent of the entire [federal] basic research budget and 13 percent of the physical sciences for over half a decade, doubling the share of the science budget going to particle physics. Unless the Congress provides for substantial growth in other relevant research agencies, the SSC may well crowd out other basic science research.[6]

In "spin-offs" of computer technology and high-tech instruments, Webre's report stated, the SSC "is no more or less likely to produce an important advance than any other major laboratory." The CBO periodically updated its analyses for each new round of congressional budget deliberations. In 1993, the year of Clinton's inauguration, CBO advised Congress that "the share and absolute amount of federal funds devoted to this project [the SSC] are out of proportion to the likelihood of the SSC's producing usable science or technology in the near future."[7]

In contrast to the CBO's unsentimental calculations, the SSC's promoters extolled the intellectual excitement of working on the frontiers of knowledge, confidently forecasting commercially valuable spin-offs. But by the 1990s, Washington was preoccupied with the political menace of deficit

5. Conversation with author, December 14, 1999.
6. Congressional Budget Office, *Risks and Benefits of Building the Superconducting Super Collider: A Special Study* (Washington, D.C.: U.S. Government Printing Office, 1988), p. 13.
7. Congressional Budget Office, *Reducing the Deficit: Spending and Revenue Options: A Report to the Senate and House Committees on the Budget* (Washington, D.C.: U.S. Government Printing Office, 1993).

spending and was unmoved by these familiar sales arguments. In earlier times, the physicists seeking government funds for particle accelerators would go lyrical, likening their machines to medieval cathedrals and invoking cultural values in support of their designs on the U.S. Treasury. In 1969, Robert R. Wilson, a leading high-energy physicist and later the founding director of the Fermi Laboratory, was asked at a Senate hearing about the military significance of particle physics. Wilson replied:

> Only from a long-range point of view, of a developing technology. Otherwise, it has to do with: Are we good painters, good sculptors, great poets? I mean all the things that we really venerate and honor in our country and are patriotic about. In that sense, this new knowledge has all to do with honor and country but it has nothing to do directly with defending our country, except to make it worth defending.[8]

Nearly twenty-five years later, when the SSC was sinking in politics, the likening of science to painting, poetry, and sculpture would not be a good selling point on Capitol Hill, where the arts struggled to retain the smidgen of money allotted to them in the federal budget.[9]

In 1993, the newly inaugurated Clinton administration and the Democratic Congress, both spouting antideficit pledges, were thus confronted by runaway bills for an esoteric scientific facility. The SSC had been conceived by Ronald Reagan and was under construction in Texas, home state of Former President George Bush, where the Democratic party was rapidly losing its historic majority. Moreover, a new element had crept into the politics of the SSC: public dissent by scientists opposed to the project's ravenous share of research money, of which there was never enough to satisfy all the fields of science. Among them was Professor Philip Anderson, of Princeton University, a solid-state physicist who shared the Nobel Prize in physics in 1977. Anderson publicly charged that DOE officials had lied to Congress about the SSC and that SSC scientists had acquiesced in the mistruths. Testifying to the House Budget Committee in 1991, Anderson expressed doubt about the "intellectual importance" of the SSC, which he described as "liberally funded" while other fields of research were neglected. Ridiculing

---

8. Robert R. Wilson, testimony, Congressional Joint Committee on Atomic Energy, 91st Cong., 1st sess., April 16, 1969.

9. For the central laboratory building at Fermilab, Wilson chose a striking sixteen-story design modeled after the twin-towered cathedral in Beauvais, France. In 1978, in a rare act among administrators of federal research facilities, Wilson resigned in protest against what he regarded as inadequate financial support for the laboratory.

claims of valuable commercial "spin-offs" from high-energy physics, Anderson raised the issue of integrity:

> . . . as the message about the SSC gets diluted in the Department of Energy and in the political rhetoric, one finds false claims that particle physics did everything from MRI [magnetic-resonance imaging] and the computer revolution to the television screen and sliced bread. To me, the saddest sight of all is to see officials of the Department [of Energy] responsible for our energy supply deliberately misleading Congress and the public with these false claims, and to see my particle-physics colleagues, many of whom I admire and respect, sitting by and acquiescing in such claims.[10]

Collectively and individually, other scientists openly shared his reservations. In January 1991, the Council of the American Physical Society, while conceding that the SSC was scientifically meritorious and "should be built in a timely fashion," asserted that "support for individual investigators must have the highest priority." The council argued that other fields of physics should not be drained to finance the SSC.[11]

Congress also heard from Erich Bloch shortly after he stepped down from six years as NSF director. As a private citizen, Bloch was free of the necessity of toeing the White House line. "I find it mind boggling," Bloch bluntly told a House hearing in 1991, "to look in the budget and see a 120 percent increase for the SSC, and in other areas [of research] they go begging. Are we right to give such a high priority to a so-called prestige project like the SSC?" Bloch answered his own question: "No, I don't think so."[12] The SSC's defenders argued that other fields of science would not benefit from cancellation of their project; the money would simply disappear into the labyrinth of federal finance, they predicted—correctly, as it turned out.

The Clinton administration was on record in support of the SSC, but the White House's political energy was invested in health-care reform and other issues; the interest in the SSC was negligible and presidential efforts to save the project were perfunctory. In June 1993, the House again voted to kill the project. Once more, the Senate came to the rescue. But this time,

10. *Establishing Priorities in Science Funding: Hearing before the House Budget Committee*, 102d Cong., 1st sess., July 11, 1991

11. American Physical Society Council, "Statement on Physics Funding and the SSC," January 20, 1991.

12. "Former NSF Head Says SSC Should Be Delayed," *SGR*, July 1, 1991.

the House held firm, repeating its termination vote and thus sinking the SSC in an October finale. At that point, administrative and laboratory buildings had been constructed at the site and fourteen miles of the fifty-four-mile tunnel were completed; expenditures totaled approximately $2 billion, virtually none of it salvageable. Hundreds of scientists and technicians had given up jobs and moved to Texas in the reasonable expectation of spending years, if not their entire careers, working on the great particle accelerator. After the termination, Nobelist Leon Lederman delivered a despairing appraisal of the U.S. Congress: "It's disheartening that a large number of fairly intelligent people could do such a dumb thing."[13] Among the many branches of science, sentiments were divided on the wisdom of proceeding with the SSC in the stormy and uncertain financial circumstances that confronted all the sciences. However, even among some scientists who opposed the SSC, I observed apprehension: for the first time in the long and mutually beneficial relationship between science and government, the White House had abandoned an important basic-research project.

New Grounds for Fear

As the SSC went down, Washington's scientific leaders found additional grounds for concern with the new administration. In this instance, dismay arose from the president's all-out efforts to save a major technological project even more grandiose than the SSC but scientifically without merit. While the SSC foundered on Capitol Hill, the Clinton administration was confronted by the out-of-control costs of another megaproject that President Reagan had launched at the height of the Cold War, in 1984: the space station, a celestial turkey of uncertain purpose and intractably rising costs. With his customary ideological finesse, Reagan christened it *Space Station Freedom*—yet another high-tech challenge, like Star Wars, to the gasping Soviet Union. Behind it stood the NASA bureaucracy, the aerospace industry, and broadly based congressional support linked to the project by widely distributed contracts; in contrast, Texas got the lion's share of SSC spending, leaving other states with crumbs, if any at all, and scant interest in providing more money for the project.

The station was the centerpiece of NASA's primal, unalterable commitment to humans in space. Scientists opposed to the station argued that sophisticated, miniaturized instruments could produce far more data from

---

13. "Proponents of Collider Give Up: Atom Smasher's Image as Budget Profligacy Is Said to Doom It," *Washington Post*, October 21, 1993.

space, at far lower cost, than fragile humans, with their dependence on immensely expensive life-support systems; moreover, when instruments were lost in space, there was no need for national mourning. NASA, however, believed the circus aspects of space attracted public attention and built political support. Without the technological grandeur and human crews of the space station, NASA feared a severe shrinkage of popular and political interest and money for its ambitious goals. NASA planned the station as a manned follow-on to the moon-landing project. The space station provided a justification for another manned NASA megaproject, the Space Shuttle. The fleet of four shuttles, with their heavy hauling capacity, figured in the scheme as the delivery system for the large tonnage of materials and equipment required for the station. Shuttle and station complemented each other, assuring a bright future for NASA well into the twenty-first century, when the next step would be a human expedition to Mars. Widely dispersed contracts and audience interest were the core strategies of space politics. However, repetition took a toll on audience interest. The first flight of the Space Shuttle, in 1981, and a handful of succeeding flights rated prime-time, front-page news coverage. When editors and producers concluded that the public was jaded with weightless tumbling and space walks, NASA's publicists devised a new stunt: a nationwide competition to select a school-teacher for a ride on the Shuttle. With space-age fanfare, the winner, Christa McAuliffe, a New Hampshire teacher selected from among 11,400 applicants, went aboard the ill-fated *Challenger,* for the twenty-fifth flight of the Shuttle, launched on January 28, 1986. When it exploded in flight, the nation grieved and NASA grounded the remaining three shuttles for nearly three years. But the station project proceeded, saved by the contractual money it spread across the American landscape.

As the costs ballooned, NASA, like the SSC entrepreneurs, was compelled to look abroad for financial assistance. NASA was successful in this quest. Far smaller than the giant NASA, the European Space Agency and the even smaller space agencies of Japan and Canada were lured into joining the giant space station project by NASA's warnings that, if they didn't take part, they would fall far behind both the United States and the Soviet Union in space technology and its commercial applications. Space bureaucrats in the other nations successfully argued the case to their political superiors. And it paid off for NASA when doubts about costs and purpose threatened the space station on Capitol Hill. The participation of Europe, Canada, and Japan confirmed the value of the project, NASA officials told Congress. At moments of great budget danger, foreign space officials hurried to the aid of their American space brethren, testifying to Congress that they joined the American-dominated project in good faith; termination, they said, would waste their investment and undermine international confidence in American reliability. The space station survived. But even with foreign participation, the main financial lifeline for the project still ran directly to the U.S. Treasury.

Runaway Costs

Reviewing the cost history of *Space Station Freedom* in 1991, the General Accounting Office reported that the estimates for design, construction and operations had risen from $8 billion in 1984 to $38.3 billion in 1991.[14] NASA's bookkeeping was opaque, deliberately so, it might be suspected. Some budget versions included the substantial costs of equipping the station; others merely stated the empty, pre-equipped price; postconstruction operating costs were vaguely estimated, if at all. Given the technical uncertainties of the unprecedented building project in space, financial exactitude was not to be expected. But, for the penny-pinched researchers in university-based little science, the financially ravenous project loomed as a huge bite into federal R&D funds, a direct threat to their sustenance. Reconfirmation of open-ended costs for the station was provided by the GAO in 1993:

> In May 1991, we testified that NASA's estimate of $30 billion did not include some cost elements attributable to the space station program. First, it did not include at least $10 billion in program cost attributable to the program prior to permanent occupancy [of the station]. Second, it did not include at least $78 billion in funding required after permanent occupancy. When these costs were considered, the space station estimate was at least $118 billion. . . . We noted that some cost elements were still undefined and significant cost growth could occur during hardware development.[15]

In the intricate layout of congressional appropriations, NASA's financial appetite, unlike that of the SSC's, posed a direct threat to other fields of science. The Department of Energy's money for the SSC came through the

---

14. *Space Station: NASA's Search for Design, Cost, and Schedule Stability Continues* (U.S. General Accounting Office, GAO/NSIAD-91-125), March 1991.
15. *Space Station: Information on National Security Applications and Cost* (U.S. General Accounting Office, GAO/NSIAD-93-208), p. 6.

House and Senate energy subcommittees, which tended to generosity for the big, nationally dispersed DOE. NSF, however, was lodged in an appropriations subcommittee that also financed NASA, as well as housing and veterans affairs, all backed by heavy-spending lobbies. Under the zero-sum rules mandated by deficit-reduction politics, the space station could bring budget misery for NSF and its apolitical constituents, as well as for NASA's own basic-science programs. From the abundant ranks of Nobel laureates, yet another came forward, a 1981 laureate in physics, to state his concerns about the space station: Nicolaas Bloembergen, president of the American Physical Society and professor of physics at Harvard. At a House hearing in 1991, Bloembergen lacerated the project, including the claim that microgravity aboard the station would provide unique research opportunities:

> It is the view of the American Physical Society that scientific justification is lacking for a permanently manned space station in Earth orbit. The United States needs a vigorous science program, but such a program can be implemented for the foreseeable future in unmanned satellites and unmanned space probes. In our opinion, the importance of microgravity as a scientific subdiscipline has been vastly exaggerated. Basic research experiments that might benefit from a microgravity environment can be done, and should be done first, on Earth using drop towers or on unmanned space platforms. . . . In our opinion, the only remaining scientific justification for the space station is to study the feasibility of maintaining human life during long space flights. In short, the only reason for putting humans into space is to learn more about how to put more humans into space. . . . It has been asserted that the program will result in important spinoffs for industry and society. It seems likely that any project costing $30 billion or more will produce some spinoffs, but to compete in today's markets we need better robots, not better space suits.[16]

Starting in 1991, Congress put a $2.6 billion annual spending cap on the space station. At one point, the House came within one vote of cutting off money, but the outcome was far less a close call than it appeared. The opportunity to wave the banner of frugality appealed to many members, but, as with many votes in Congress, switch votes were available if needed.

16. House Government Activities and Transportation Subcommittee, *Costs, Justification, and Benefits of NASA's Space Station: Hearing before the Committee on Government Operations*, 102d Cong., 1st sess., May 1, 1991.

Though repeatedly scaled down, or "descoped," in NASAese, to placate horrified budget managers in the White House and Congress, the space station entered the 1990s with sufficient momentum to overcome any resistance, no matter how far out of control its costs. After the one close House vote, the project was never again in serious trouble on Capitol Hill.

When Clinton was elected, the space station was still earthbound—an assemblage of plans, contracts, and hopes. But, politically, it was a *fait accompli* and untouchable. The aerospace industry, concentrated in states rich in congressional seats and electoral votes, was in a post–Cold War recession, with employment down from a peak of 1.3 million in 1989 to 966,000 in 1993.[17] The space station remained the biggest project on the order books. Clinton responded with a new mission and a new name for *Space Station Freedom*. Rechristening it as the *International Space Station,* Clinton brought the once-mighty but impoverished, rapidly decaying Russian space enterprise into the project. However, unlike the Europeans, Canadians, and Japanese, the Russians did not pay their own way for participation in the big American-dominated space project; instead, they were paid to participate. In return for $400 million from NASA, the Russians agreed to take American astronauts aboard their aging *Mir* space station, then in continuous orbit since 1986, to gain experience in the prolonged weightlessness they would encounter aboard the *International Space Station.* The claimed medical and technical benefits of the new Russian-American partnership were arguable, since the space station project had long proceeded without plans involving *Mir*. But the Clinton White House and NASA also claimed an additional benefit: the Russian space specialists drawing pay from the American-financed *Mir* operations would be less inclined to sell their skills to Iraq, Iran, North Korea, and other regimes seeking to develop missile capabilities.

With its pork-barrel prowess reinforced by a foreign-policy justification, the space station possessed unmatchable survival advantages over the SSC. In the closely monitored politics of austerity, each was a standout item, though in volume of dollars, the space station was the unrivaled behemoth, by virtue of its technical requirements, magnified by the great tradition of unrestrained aerospace spending. Expenditures totaled $11.2 billion for the station's design and development between 1985 and 1993—and that was before any "metal was bent," as they say in the aerospace industry.[18] In

17. *Aerospace Facts & Figures: 1994–1995,* Aerospace Industries Association of America, 1994, p. 140.
18. *Space Station: Estimated Total U.S. Funding Requirements* (U.S. General Accounting Office, GAO/NSIAD-95-163, 1995), p. 5.

contrast, when the SSC was terminated, the expenditures totaled about $2 billion.

THE VIEW FROM THE WHITE HOUSE

The *realpolitik* of the two multibillion-dollar projects, from the perspective of the Clinton White House, was described to me in 1998 by John Gibbons, shortly after he stepped down after five years as Bill Clinton's assistant for science and technology. I recalled to Gibbons the skepticism he had expressed about the space station while serving as director of the Congressional Office of Technology Assessment prior to joining the Clinton administration. Gibbons explained his conversion from space-station doubter to supporter, describing a presidential megascience summit that determined the differing fates of the SSC and the space station:

> Well, I saw a different light when I got to the White House. In part because of the job [as presidential science and technology adviser], but in part because of what we did with the station. . . . I remember one day early in 1993 . . . we scheduled a time for me to meet with the President and the Vice President and some other people on the budget, and covering—I guess it was two hours—[the] space station and the Superconducting Super Collider. It was an interesting couple of hours, and I had to lead the discussion on both. On the station, it was clear, first of all, that there was a lot of momentum behind the station, a lot of years of stuff. Secondly, there was a lot of support for it, especially among the [congressional] conservatives. But it was a very expensive device. At the opening, I said, there's no way you can justify this [the space station] just on the basis of science or just on the basis of technology.[19]

Did that reservation give Clinton, Gore, and the others second thoughts about proceeding with the space station? I asked. Gibbons replied:

> No, they understood it. But Clinton openly was concerned about [terminating the] station as yet another massive potential change in regions of the country that were already being heavily impacted by the defense build down. And he was trying to figure out ways. He said, "These folks are headed toward a really rough economic time, not because the mar-

---

19. Interview with author, December 6, 1998.

ketplace is doing it, but because global events are doing it. It's externally imposed on the system." And he tried to devise ways both in [military] base closings and in [the space] station, and other things, to keep as many of these things as he could moving so that he could temper the rate at which they scaled down from government support. I know that weighed heavily on him, and, of course, those are important.

The concentration of space-station contracts in politically significant states, with lesser shares also distributed throughout the country, entered into the decision, Gibbons explained:

> I only realized later those are also political states. It's California, it's Texas, it's Florida, it's the Midwest; in fact, [the space] station is spread out all over the country. The big new idea was to use this as a mechanism to build international big science and technology, and to bring Russia into it rather than justify it on the basis that the "evil empire" is out there. That was the big switch. Also, to so-call downscale [the space station], because it was monstrously out of balance in terms of size. And take the case to Congress and support both the station and the SSC. But to really go all out on the station for this multiplicity of reasons. Form a commission and have them prepare a recommendation to NASA, and that's what Chuck Vest [president of MIT] chaired, and did an excellent job, I think.

Continuing with his recollections of the megascience summit early in 1993, Gibbons explained to me the political calculus that doomed the SSC:

> And in SSC, we decided—I said now, this is good science, it's state-of-the-art science. No problem about that. The problem is that it's not that well connected to people or jobs. It's focused on Texas. People don't understand it, and there are some cost overruns and some real questions on some of the magnet designs. We decided we would support it. I did testify [in Congress] in favor of it as fervently as I could, but it was too little, too late. It was not internationalized. Bush had chosen it to stay a U.S. effort. We got pleas from the high-energy physics community for the president to try to get Japan and some of these other countries involved. It was just too little, too late, and Congress wanted some scalps anyhow. This was one. And we didn't fight for that one as hard as we could have. But you have to limit your fights.

Recalling that Gibbons had told me in 1994 that the SSC "was headed over the waterfall" when Clinton took office, I asked him whether a stronger effort by the administration might have rescued the project. He replied:

> I doubt we could have saved it. There was a fervor of cutting. It took SSC, it took OTA [Congressional Office of Technology Assessment, formerly headed by Gibbons, abolished by the Republican Congress two years after the SSC termination]. Congress was bound and determined and the administration was, too, to cut that deficit. It was horrendous. We were headed toward a $350 billion annual deficit, and that focused the minds early on what we would have to do, because it was the *sine qua non* for turning around the economy, holding down interest rates, encouraging investment. And if we were going to preserve key R&D, we were just going to have to cut everywhere else we could.

The events and decisions described by Gibbons took place in 1993, the opening year of the Clinton presidency, with Democrats in control of Congress. Clinton faced a choice between a scientifically and technologically inconsequential but politically valuable project in space and a unique scientific facility for studying the fundamental components of matter. The president, weighing the relative political factors, opted for space. As the Clinton administration neared the end of its first year in office, the science-policy grapevine buzzed with anxiety and grievances. At Gibbons' recommendation, the White House responded with a hurriedly organized, conciliatory conference, "Forum on Science in the National Interest"—a two-day affair, starting January 31, 1994, that drew some three hundred onlookers and participants to the National Academy of Sciences. Not among them was Bill Clinton, who was yet to bestow a coveted ceremonial gesture on the scientific community. The underlying tension was evident in Vice President Al Gore's remarks to the gathering:

> There are those who have raised concern about this administration's commitment to science, especially fundamental science. Some ask whether we really want an "S" in OSTP [Office of Science and Technology Policy.] Well, we do passionately.[20]

20. Vice President Al Gore, remarks to Forum on Science in the National Interest, February 1, 1994.

Speaking in the temple of basic research, Gore pandered to the audience, declaring that

> you don't have to do a cost-benefit analysis to justify science. Without science—by science I mean an inquiry performed out of curiosity, without the motive of practical benefit, motivated largely by disinterested love of truth—without that, civilization would stagnate.

But Gore offered nothing tangible—that is, promises of additional money or new projects, the tribute usually experienced by the leaders of science when the president or vice president joined them in public ceremonials. In these difficult times, Gore said, administrative efficiencies could free up money for research, and wiser use of money would also result from the elimination of pork-barrel appropriations for universities.

Following Gore's address, NSF Director Neal Lane closed the proceedings by observing to the audience that "some of us were a little nervous about this whole thing—to put it together so quickly, and to ask you on short notice to come, participate with the very little time that was available. We weren't quite sure what would come out. And I'll say," Lane assured the audience, "I'm very impressed." Nonetheless, the congeniality of the gathering, the soothing words from Gore and others high in the Clinton administration, did not alter the imbalance between the scientists' deep belief in the importance of their work and the Clinton administration's obvious preoccupation with other matters. In 1995, with the newly reigning congressional Republicans vowing war on government spending, the politicians of science saw good reasons to be fearful of both ends of Pennsylvania Avenue.

CHAPTER 26

Caught between Clinton
and Congress

> In the big picture the Administration continues to allow short-term
> political objectives to override critical investments in science and
> technology that promise real long-term payoffs for the Nation.
> —Democratic members of the House Science Committee,
> assessment of Clinton's R&D budget (March 15, 1995)

BIOMEDICAL RESEARCHERS proudly con-
sidered themselves an indispensable strength of American health care.
They were the ingenious creators of new cures, and America was indisputably the world leader in medical research. For the medical sciences, the central institution in government was titled the National Institutes of *Health*,
not the National Institutes of Research, or the National Institutes of Medical
Science. With a prudent political touch dating back to the first institute at
NIH, the National Cancer Institute (founded in 1937), virtually all seventeen institutes subsequently established within NIH were named after diseases or body organs: the National Institute of Allergy and Infectious Diseases, the National Institute of Arthritis and Musculoskeletal Diseases, the
National Heart, Lung and Blood Institute, the National Eye Institute, and
so forth. Though NIH laboratories were heavily staffed with doctorates in
science, NIH, from its founding, was always headed by a physician—though,
invariably, one with experience in research. Skeptics groused that, irrespective of the nomenclature, the culture of NIH emphasized long-term, basic
scientific research rather than sharply focused quests for treatment and disease prevention. NIH dismissed the allegation as absurd, and presented itself to the public and politics as a scientific research institution dedicated
to the health of the American people. Moreover, fighting disease was clearly
a dominant personal motivation in the community of NIH scientists.

Given these commitments, institutional and personal, dismay
quickly spread in biomedical policy circles following the arrival of the Clinton administration: NIH and biomedical research were given only a handful

of places, and no leadership role, on the 200-member task force assembled by Hillary Rodham Clinton to produce the administration's ambitious plan to remake the American health-care system.

WHAT ROLE FOR MEDICAL SCIENCE?

In a speech outlining his health-care goals to a joint session of Congress in September 1993, the president made no mention of medical research or the role of improved scientific understanding of disease in protecting the health of the American people. Universal access to medical care and cost containment were the twin pillars of the administration's health-care strategy. In the following months, the Clintons and their health-reform campaigners said virtually nothing about medical research, but when they did, they emphasized preventive research—a sensitive topic at NIH, where the molecular level was the preferred site for studying disease. For decades, advocates of prevention felt left out at NIH, equated with soft-headed faith in the health-giving powers of broccoli and tofu. Now it seemed that the Clintons were championing the long-neglected strategy of prevention. In a widely distributed booklet that was intended to explain the health-reform plan to the general public, the White House stated, "From free coverage of a wide range of preventive services to wellness education and increased research funding, the plan offers unprecedented focus on prevention." The pamphlet nodded to academic health centers, describing them as "the sites of the basic research that ushers in modern medical advances," and assuring them of funding through a share of health-insurance premiums.[1] New cures for old diseases—*the* selling point of NIH and the biomedical-research enterprise that it financed—were thus acknowledged, but merely in passing, in the same way that the administration lauded industrial technology while only nodding to basic research. Intense cost consciousness about health care actually cast doubt on the virtues of research, suggesting that medical innovations were in part responsible for the nation's rising medical bill. "In other industries, technological change is often considered to be a force that reduces costs," the General Accounting Office reported to Congress in 1992—on the eve of Clinton's election—"but in medical care generally and in acute hospitals specifically, the net effect of medical advances has been an increase in costs."[2]

1. *Health Security: The President's Report to the American People* (The White House Domestic Policy Council, October 1993), p. 64.
2. *Hospital Costs: Adoption of Technologies Drives Cost Growth* (U.S. General Accounting Office, GAO/HRD-92-120, September 1992), p. 16.

Vacuum at the Top

NIH was effectively leaderless and shut out of politics for nearly all of 1993, the first year of the Clinton administration. Bernadine Healy, the Bush appointee at the head of NIH, had openly expressed her wish to remain in office in the new administration. However, her reign at NIH had been a tumultuous one, marked by friction with the career staff and clashes with Congress over her management of the issue of scientific misconduct. Moreover, Healy had ventured over the boundary between science and politics. Her hobnobbing with Vice President Quayle inspired reports of political ambitions, and during the 1992 election campaign a meeting she held with Ross Perot was cited as further evidence of political aspirations.[3] Rejecting Healy's request to continue at the head of NIH, the Clinton administration asked her to remain only until a successor was in place. Openly expressing her disappointment, Healy quit NIH in June 1993. It wasn't until November—ten months into Clinton's first term—that Harold Varmus, Nobel laureate from the University of California, at San Francisco, was confirmed by the Senate as director of NIH.

Alarmed by the Clinton administration's seeming indifference to biomedical research, NIH's backers rallied at a strange Senate hearing—held late in 1993, toward the end of Clinton's first year in office, after Congress had adjourned for the year. Organized by Senator Tom Harkin (D-Iowa), a devoted champion of NIH and its works, the hearing was titled "Health Care Reform and Medical Research." Witness after witness extolled the importance of biomedical research and urged funding in order to continue and expand the programs of NIH. A memorable moment in the hearing occurred when the doors to the Senate committee room opened, and staff members rolled in a medical relic: an iron lung, borrowed from the National Museum of Health and Medicine. Pointing to the fearsome-looking apparatus, the director of the museum explained that, thanks to vaccines produced by research, "They're in museums today, instead of hospitals."[4]

---

3. Healy explained that she and Perot merely discussed routine matters of health policy. But Healy had an interest in politics. In 1994, the year after she left NIH, she unsuccessfully ran for the Republican Senate nomination in Ohio, a rare instance of a senior research administrator seeking elective office.

4. "NIH Role in Health Reform Leads to a Bouncy Hearing," *SGR*, December 15, 1993. The archaic iron lung was displayed *sans* patient. Such was not the case in an earlier episode of medical lobbying that has acquired legendary status in the folklore of legislative dramatics. In 1971, at a House hearing on national health insurance, a dialysis machine was brought into the hearing room, and a patient, testifying for the National Association for Patients on Hemodialysis, was attached to the apparatus and dialyzed. A startled committee member was heard to exclaim, "What the f— is going on here?"

In February 1994, early in Clinton's second year in office, the biomedical-research community's dismay with the new administration was heightened by the unexpected intrusion of partisan politics into a traditionally
congenial ceremonial event: a visit of First Lady Hillary Rodham Clinton
to the serene, leafy NIH campus, in Bethesda, Md., ten miles distant from
politically embroiled downtown Washington. Geographically and politically, NIH was a demilitarized zone, in whose behalf congressional Republicans and Democrats labored in harmony in the sacred cause of more money
for research on disease; both parties were united against cancer. A royal visit
to NIH by each reigning first lady had become a postwar custom. On these
occasions, the honored guest, accompanied by an entourage of senior NIH
officials, would tour an apparatus-crammed laboratory or two, express
amazed gratitude at the march of medical progress, pose with sick children
in the renowned NIH Clinical Center, and speak appreciative but politically
bland words to a staff assembly. Mrs. Clinton made the requisite tour but
went beyond the adulatory, head-patting role. This first lady was unique,
the de-facto associate president in the "two-for-the-price-of-one" package
that Bill Clinton had promised the voters. For the NIH staff, overflowing
the largest auditorium on campus and gathered around closed-circuit TVs,
she was of intense interest as both a celebrity and as chief of the president's
health-care reform movement. First Lady Hillary Clinton was different from
her predecessors. And her message was different.

After dispensing rhetorical balm about the marvels she had seen, Mrs.
Clinton went political: "For much of the past decade," she declared—thus
encompassing the Reagan and Bush years—"biomedical research has been
neglected and underfunded and even unappreciated, and the president in-
tends to fix that." Under the Clinton administration, she asserted, the damage had been reversed with generous budgets for NIH. In fact, during the
pre-Clinton decade, the NIH budget had been accorded extraordinarily generous treatment by the usual alliance of White House and Congress, which
together sent the NIH budget soaring from $4.8 billion to $10.3 billion.
Upon taking office, Clinton's budget proposal for NIH was sparse, increasing funds for AIDS research while trimming elsewhere. The president had
proposed a $342 million increase for fiscal year 1994; Congress voted a $631
million increase. The biomedical research community was intimately famil-

---

Observes Richard Rettig, a historian of biomedical politics: "This event was widely publicized afterwards and was believed by many to have been decisive in the decision of
Congress to enact the kidney disease entitlement." Richard A. Rettig, "Origins of Medicare Kidney Disease Entitlement: The Social Security Amendments of 1972," in *Biomedical Politics*, ed. Kathi E. Hanna (Washington, D.C.: National Academy Press, 1991).

iar with the NIH numbers. So was the White House science office, which, I later learned, had not been consulted by the first lady or her staff in preparation for the NIH visit. Continuing her partisan address on the politically neutral NIH campus, Mrs. Clinton advised her audience that the opponents of the Clinton health plan also opposed increased funding for basic biomedical research—which wasn't so.

With the diplomacy of a host confronted by a high-ranking boorish guest, NIH Director Harold Varmus gracefully concluded the proceedings. Varmus warmly praised Mrs. Clinton as "a powerful teacher about health-care reform, a wonderful student of molecular biology and genetics—A's for both." Bidding her farewell, he said, "Next time, bring the spouse."[5]

Outraged reaction from the aggrieved leaders of Republican support for NIH came swiftly. In an open letter to Mrs. Clinton, the four Republican members of the House appropriations subcommittee for NIH, comrades in arms with their Democratic colleagues for the financial growth of biomedical research, plaintively pointed out:

> [W]e led the successful effort last year, along with other members of the House and Senate Appropriations Committees, to reject *the President's proposed cuts in NIH funding for 1994* [original italics]. . . . We agree that the federal government ought to increase its support for this important enterprise. However, by comparison with previous budget requests, President Clinton's budget requests to Congress for NIH funding are quite low and indicate, in our opinion, a lack of vision for the future of medical research.[6]

The justifiably irate Republicans concluded their letter to Mrs. Clinton with an additional shot at the administration's regard for biomedical research. Noting the virtual exclusion of NIH from the Clinton health-reform deliberations—acknowledged by NIH directors under questioning at congressional budget hearings the previous year—the letter asserted, "We believe that biomedical research has been largely ignored in the President's health care reform proposals and encourage you to provide leadership that will result in an enhanced federal commitment to basic biomedical research." One of the signatories, Representative John Porter (R-Illinois), demonstrated his devo-

5. "Mrs. Clinton Assures NIH of Basic-Research Support," *SGR*, March 1, 1994.
6. Letter to Hillary Rodham Clinton, February 22, 1994, by Reps. John Porter, C.W. Bill Young, Henry Bonilla, Helen Delich Bentley; "Republican Backers of NIH Enraged by Hillary's Speech," *SGR*, March 15, 1994.

tion to NIH under political fire in the following year, when Gingrich-led Republicans took control of the House. Porter ascended to the chair of the House subcommittee for NIH funding and persuaded his budget-slashing party not only to exempt NIH but to accelerate its budgets to historic highs, well above the amounts sought by President Clinton.

EMPHASIS ON TECHNOLOGY

For the Washington science-policy community, the signs of political indifference, and perhaps even rejection, continued to accumulate as the Clinton administration sought to infuse its preferences into the workings of the U.S. government. Faithful to his campaign pledges, Clinton stressed industrial technology in his spending priorities for research and development. In his budget for fiscal 1995, Clinton proposed $18.6 billion for civilian applied research and development—an increase of $850 million, or 5 percent; for basic research, the Clinton budget proposed $12.8 billion, an increase of $301 million, or 2 percent. A 4 percent increase proposed for NIH was concentrated on AIDS research, leaving most of the other programs level or in decline. Under Clinton's spending plan, few of the NIH institutes were budgeted for the increase in purchasing power deemed indispensable by the worried Washington lobbies for biomedical research.

MONEY FOR TECHNOLOGY

The president's money proposals matched his campaign promises of greater support for technology intended to be of direct value to industry. The favored location of spending for this purpose was the little-known and, up to that point, sparsely funded Advanced Technology Program (ATP), situated deep inside the Department of Commerce. ATP was managed by an agency within the department, the National Institute of Standards and Technology (NIST), which congressional Democrats (reasserting their traditional *dirigiste* tendencies for government and industry) had fashioned from the old National Bureau of Standards in the closing days of the Reagan administration. The bureau, founded in 1901, was chartered to work with industry—the only government agency with that mandate, it proclaimed with pride. In the workings of American industry and commerce, the venerable Bureau of Standards filled a vital behind-the-scenes role, setting nationwide standards for industrial products and processes and collaborating with industry to establish test criteria for reliability and performance. The Advanced Technology Program established a new role in the recently created

National Institute of Standards and Technology. ATP was to provide government money for research by industrial firms, thus paralleling the National Science Foundation's role in academic research.

Created primarily by Democrats, ATP exemplified the "industrial policy" routinely denounced by Republican politicians as wasteful and counterproductive government intrusions into the allegedly superior workings of free enterprise. But the renamed and functionally expanded NIST, with ATP built in, slipped into law as an appendage to the Omnibus Trade and Competitiveness Act of 1988, which contained tax and trade provisions desired by the Reagan White House. The technology program was designed to serve as a financial angel and marriage broker for high-tech industrial collaborations, bringing firms—even competing firms—together to pool their skills to solve common technical problems. In justification of the program, Democrats pointed out that other countries promoted technology in a collaborative fashion, and thereby gained an advantage over American industry. The focus, ATP's proponents explained, would be on projects of high economic potential that were too risky or expensive to attract private venture capital. Through collaborations, they contended, the research could achieve critical mass and provide shortcuts to innovation, new products, and jobs. As a concession to antitrust considerations, research assisted by ATP was described as "generic" and "pre-competitive," and available to all the participants, presumably without special advantage to any of them.

THE POLITICAL DIFFERENCE

In the context of industry's spending on research—some $62 billion of its own money in 1988, plus another $35 billion from government, mainly for military and space hardware development—ATP was a barely visible sideshow. When it was finally up and running, a few years after enactment into law, it initially supported no more than a few dozen projects, at $2 million to $3 million apiece spread out over several years. However, measured in political terms, ATP constituted a significant shift toward publicly acknowledged, direct federal involvement in commercial research. As the antideficit vise tightened on federal spending, the increase in political affection, and money, for technology created additional anxieties for the friends and practitioners of science in universities and the government's own laboratories.

Throughout the post–World War II period, and with antecedents in prewar research in agriculture and aviation, the U.S. government actually expended a great deal of money on the development of technologies with commercial value. With its carte blanche Cold War mandate, the Pentagon was unconcerned with ideological labels when it came to the support of promising science and technology. Defense agencies had supported research in industry since the end of World War II, without stirring political jibes about "industrial policy" or doleful warnings about the inability of sheltered civil servants to pick winners among high-tech industrial competitors. From computers to the design of automotive gears, from aviation to electronics, material sciences, and systems engineering, the Pentagon functioned as a generous Ministry of Technology, giving money to industrial firms to conduct research aimed at satisfying the military services' requirements. Though paid for by the Department of Defense to meet its needs, militarily motivated research seeped into the civilian economy. However, the crossover from military to civilian purposes was never as great as the Pentagon claimed in citing "spin-off" as a bonus from its lion's share of federal R&D money—nearly 75 percent of the total at the height of the Cold War. The Pentagon's dominant role in financing industrial research drew criticism, but it came mainly from the political left and rested on the argument that military research ran wastefully on open-ended finance and misused money and talent while America's industrial competitors focused their research on the marketplace.

In contrast to the Pentagon, the civilian agencies of government possessed far less explicit authority to put money into industrial laboratories, but again, rhetoric did not match the actual workings of the research economy. Ideological objections to funneling government research money through NIH were nil, because NIH focused on basic research conducted in nonprofit universities and hospitals. But the boundaries between fundamental knowledge and the market were blurred. In a 1995 review titled *Federal Financial Support of Business,* the Congressional Budget Office stated:

> Most of the research funded by NIH involves basic and academic research, but a substantial portion supports applied biomedical research and clinical development, which are of near-term use to firms and doctors in health and related lines of business. Based on previous patterns of research funding, CBO assumes that $3.7 billion of the $11 billion NIH is estimated to spend this year will fall into that category. NIH uses a quarter of the applied research funds, or about $1 billion, for the preclinical and clinical development of specific pharmaceuticals.[7]

7. *Federal Financial Support of Business* (Washington, D.C.: Congressional Budget Office, 1995), p. 24.

Indeed, the NIH money went primarily to academic institutions. But it produced research close to the needs of industry—at no cost to industry.

A quest for clarity or consistency in the government's role in industrial research would encounter many anomalies. The acronym NASA stands for National Aeronautics and Space Administration, but aeronautics—of great commercial importance—was routinely shortchanged by NASA in favor of the glamour of space. Second only to the Pentagon as an industrial benefactor, the Department of Energy financed commercially relevant research in nuclear energy and safety, fossil fuels, and renewable energy sources. Ostensibly, direct aim at commercial goals was generally out of bounds for civilian agencies of government. The Advanced Technology Program, created by congressional Democrats in the waning days of the Reagan administration, represented a major change in policy only because it openly acknowledged a long-existing government role in commercially directed civilian research.

As a lure for companies to participate, the rules called for ATP to provide part of the money for the research conducted by the industrial consortia, with the participating firms providing the balance as evidence of genuine interest. In the few months that it still had in office, the Reagan administration dealt with the unwelcome addition of ATP to the U.S. government, rendering it inoperative by denying it money and staff. The Bush administration was similarly aloof at the outset, providing only $10 million for the program in 1990. But upon being lashed by presidential aspirant Governor Bill Clinton of Arkansas and congressional Democrats for failure to help industry in international competition, the Bush White House cautiously increased the flow of money into ATP. By January 1993, when Clinton was inaugurated, the industrial technology program was running on an annual budget of $67.9 million—trifling compared to NIH's $11 billion and NSF's $3 billion. However, for the ever-anxious basic scientists, fearful of the loss of political support and money for university-based research, the new administration's preferences and declared financial intentions were alarming. Clinton set the industrial programs on a path to extraordinarily rapid growth. Under the Clinton plan, the ATP budget nearly tripled, from the $67.9 million in 1993 to $199 million in 1994, and then to $451 million in 1995. The administration's proposed billion-dollar mark for this once-infinitesimal program was just a year or two off, even as the president preached, and practiced, frugality for many other programs of government. While the technology program in the Department of Commerce soared, NSF and NIH rated only single-digit increases in the carefully watched growth category. In percentage terms, the Advanced Technology Program was the fastest-growing program of a government committed to austerity.

Barbs for Clinton

The eternal financial anxieties of basic science resonated with the bud-get numbers and Clinton's veneration of industrial technology, leading to an open expression of dismay by a leading figure of the Washington science community, Maxine Singer, president of the Carnegie Institution of Wash-ington—long the home base of the late Vannevar Bush. Singer delivered her views in the Carnegie annual report, which was normally devoted to news and commentary about strictly scientific matters. Writing in 1994, the second year of the Clinton administration, Singer declared that she and her colleagues "are concerned that the current national emphasis on tech-nological development is weakening support for fundamental science." Re-ferring to the so-called economic summit that Clinton held in Little Rock between his election and inauguration, Singer noted that "science was one of the few endeavors not represented. Technology was there, but not sci-ence. Meanwhile," she pointed out, "among the large circle of 'Friends of Bill' reported in the media, no scientist appears."[8] In an interview with me in 1995, Singer spoke caustically of Clinton—an unusual departure from the discreet protocol of science in its relations with politics. Noting that Clinton had at last made a visit to the NIH campus, she remarked that NIH Director Harold Varmus "was very pleased that the president came out to NIH not long ago and said all the right things. But," she continued, "there's no indication that there's real substance behind that. I suspect that if you pushed him [Clinton], you would find that he doesn't really have more than the most superficial concept of what and how science contributes to society."[9]

From Clinton's White House to Congress, scientists felt a political chill.

8. Maxine Singer, annual report, Carnegie Institution of Washington, 1992–1993, issued in March 1994.
9. Interview with author, November 22, 1995; "In the Words of the Wise," *SGR*, Decem-ber 1, 1995.

CHAPTER 27

Science versus the Budget Cutters

> The magnitude of the cuts that are looming [in federal funds for research and development] boggles the mind.
>
> —Rep. George E. Brown Jr., address to the annual meeting of the American Association for the Advancement of Science, February 17, 1995

> Do thou live and let all the Governments in the World go to the Devil. Thou cam'st out of thy Mother's Belly without Government, thou hast lived hitherto without Government, and thou may'st be carried to thy long home without Government, when it pleases the Lord. How many People in this World live without Government, yet do well enough and are well look'd upon?
>
> Terez Panza, advice to her husband, Sancho, squire of Don Quixote

IN MAY 1995, when the budget of the National Institutes of Health stood at a record $11.3 billion, NIH Director Harold Varmus delivered a notably pessimistic lecture. The message of the Nobel-laureate scientist-physician echoed widely beyond his immediate audience, the Massachusetts Medical Society. His discussion of NIH's worsening prospects for budget growth was titled "Biomedical Research Enters the Steady State."[1] "Steady state" is a scientific term signifying an unchanging condition. From 1992 to 1993, appropriations for NIH rose by $1.4 billion, to reach a total of $10.3 billion. But from 1993 to 1994, the increase was only $611 million, and from 1994 to 1995, when Varmus spoke, the increase had declined to

---

1. Harold Varmus, "Biomedical Research Enters the Steady State," Shattuck Lecture, Massachusetts Medical Society, May 20, 1995.

$445 million—alarmingly slow growth on the NIH historical chart.[2] Nonetheless, the 1995 budget, about 4 percent above the previous annual budget, was sufficient to keep NIH slightly ahead of inflation, though far below the levels demanded by the core trio of biomedical politics: medical schools, disease lobbies, and the associations of biomedical scientists. Varmus now warned that in forthcoming budgets, even modest increases were doubtful.

In recent years, congressionally initiated budget-balancing laws had slowed the growth in federal spending, but not enough to fend off demands for bigger and faster reductions. In the final decade of the millennium, national politics was shaped by strong recollections of the 1992 presidential election, when Ross Perot, the billionaire maverick, suddenly went from obscurity to national prominence as an independent candidate campaigning against Washington and deficit spending. Without the prior buildup, experience, and political persona considered essential in presidential politics, Perot, the instant candidate, received an astonishing 19.7 million votes, nearly 19 percent of the total cast. Inflamed by Perot, the anti-government spirit—ever present in American politics—intensified against taxation, spending, and Washington. In November 1994, promising a balanced budget by 2000, Republicans won control of both houses of Congress for the first time in forty years. The 104th Congress opened in January 1995, with the victorious Republicans in charge and the newly installed House speaker, Newt Gingrich, certified by the celebrity-hungry media as the new power on the American political landscape. As a manifesto for political change, Gingrich brandished the poll-tested ten-point Contract with America, a clever campaign device pledging swift enactment of conservative economic and social legislation. Buoyed by a Republican majority of twenty-five seats, Gingrich decisively ruled the House, casting aside sacred seniority rules to put his own choices into key committee chairs and tightly controlling the legislative agenda. For the shivering scientific enterprise, chilled by two years of Bill Clinton and the Democratic Congress, the new majority and the new speaker were both puzzling and frightening.

The Self-Styled "Techno-Nut"

Gingrich dominated the political stage with staccato techno-political rhetoric about a new era of prosperity—but only if America were liberated

2. NIH Appropriations History, provided to me by NIH Office of Communications and Liaison. Reminder: as is often the case with R&D statistics, data differ somewhat from official NSF tabulations, but they're roughly similar.

from oppressive taxation and dependence on government. The calcification of the government research enterprise drew Gingrich's fire. A self-described "techno-nut" and computer enthusiast, he was ecstatic about space but derisive about NASA, assailing the space agency as hopelessly bureaucratized and overpriced. "In principle," Gingrich asserted, "a ticket to go into orbit should not be dramatically more expensive than a first class ticket to Australia." In scattershot fashion, Gingrich also indiscriminately attacked virtually everything touched by government, though he waffled on defense. "Our defense spending today is at the lowest share of the economy that it has been at since Pearl Harbor," Gingrich declared in 1995, thus suggesting that the Pentagon had contributed its share to deficit reduction. "We run a deficit," he explained, "because we have become a huge welfare state with massive transfer payments and a big centralized bureaucracy." But, he added, "I don't think we ought to salute waste just because it is in uniform." On the other hand, the Contract with America specifically pledged "restoration of the essential parts of our national security funding to strengthen our national defense and maintain our credibility around the world."[3] Even with those mixed signals, the inclusion of the untouchable Pentagon in his antispending declarations seemed to assure even bleaker days ahead for the nondefense portions of the federal budget. Gingrich's remedies for the ills of America started with a reduction in Washington's share of national wealth. Though he extolled science as the key to prosperity and national power, less for science was implicit in Gingrich's design for shrinking government. The financial danger to science was built into the structure and politics of the federal budget, regardless of Gingrich's love fest with science.

The government's spending on science came from the so-called discretionary sector of the budget, requiring annual dollar decisions and agreement by the White House and Congress on the amounts to be spent. In the final budget submitted by the Bush administration, for fiscal year 1993, discretionary spending continued on a downward track as a proportion of the budget, and was destined for an even smaller share.[4] Nearly 40 percent, or $522 billion, was in the discretionary category. Of this amount, $278 billion was consigned to defense, a category least vulnerable to budget cutting. Another $20 billion was for foreign aid and other international programs, politically unpopular, and therefore reducible, but too small to matter much. The balance in the discretionary account, $224 billion, financed

3. Newt Gingrich, *To Renew America* (New York: HarperCollins, 1995), pp. 192, 89, 184.
4. *Budget of the United States Government, Fiscal Year 1993* (Washington, D.C.: U.S. Government Printing Office, 1992), part 1, p. 25.

a variety of domestic programs, including housing, education, environmental protection, law enforcement, job training, national parks, the judiciary, and science. The biggest chunk of federal spending, some $765 billion, about 60 percent of the whole budget, was nondiscretionary, expended on debt service for past borrowings and so-called entitlement programs, such as Social Security, Medicare for the elderly and disabled, Medicaid for the poor, unemployment and federal retirement benefits, and other items permanently engraved in federal law and not dependent on annual budget agreements by Congress and the White House. The aging of the population into the entitled retirement and disease-prone years guaranteed greater demands on the nondiscretionary programs. For purposes of budget cutting, the civilian discretionary programs were the most accessible. Almost alone among the civilian programs, science stood deliberately aloof from the elective politics that many of the others deemed essential to their well-being in Washington.

AN EASY TARGET

Widely expressed fears that science would become a target of budget-cutting opportunity were grounded in political reality. Science was rhetorically cherished but for decades it had practiced political disarmament, relying on the good sense and goodwill of politics to respond to its appeals for support. Though never flagging in enthusiasm for science, Gingrich contended that private enterprise could conduct research more cheaply and quickly than the creaky U.S. government. "The challenge for us," Gingrich ominously declared, "is to get government and bureaucracy out of the way and put scientists, engineers, entrepreneurs, and adventurers back into the business of exploration and discovery."[5] Who was to pay for it? He didn't say.

In 1995, shortly after becoming speaker, Newt Gingrich, lecturing to a group of science writers, tortuously extracted a previously undiscovered ideological lesson from a long-ago episode of technological history: "The Wright brothers, with a nongovernment experiment," he pontificated, "succeeded while [Samuel] Langley was crashing a steam-catapult aircraft built at the Smithsonian into the Potomac."[6] Omitted from this rendition was the fact the Wright brothers were students of Langley's research papers on aerodynamic principles. But Gingrich's preference was plain: the Wright

5. Gingrich, op. cit., p. 192.
6. "Gingrich on Research Policy: In His Own Words," SGR, March 15, 1995.

brothers were productive free enterprise; the Smithsonian was inept, wasteful government. The task confronting the Republican Revolution, Gingrich explained, was "how do we create a general climate, a general tax code, a general environment where the next thirty potential Edisons have an opportunity to invent the future?" The answer was clear in the battle cries of the Republican Revolution: cut taxes, cut government.

Specific proposals for spending reductions were offered by the House Budget Committee, chaired by a Gingrich disciple holier than the master himself in the antideficit cause, Representative John Kasich (R-Ohio). In March 1995, as deliberations for next year's budget were under way in the House, Kasich's committee issued a list of budget-balancing expenditure reductions, spread over five years, for some seventy federal agencies and programs, with claimed total savings of $176 billion. Agencies and programs nurtured by scientists and technologists to conduct and support science were well represented on the list, which included such items as: "Limit Rate of Growth for the National Science Foundation"; "Abolish Bureau of Mines"; "Abolish Geological Survey"; "Reduce Agricultural Research Service"; "Eliminate Advanced Technology Program"; "Reduce Educational and Cultural Exchange Programs"; "Reduce Spending for the High-Performance Computing Program"; "Reduce the Overhead Rate on Federally Sponsored University Research"; and "Abolish the National Biological Survey."

The list was stunning in its destructive sweep, but also puzzling in its selectivity—a clue to the hurried, haphazard treatment of government research spending in the reform program of the Republican Revolution. Of special interest to academic science was the inattention of Gingrich and company to a large but little-known sinkhole of federal money, Small Business Innovation Research, consuming at that time about $800 million a year. SBIR pandered to American faith in small business as the backbone of the nation's economy. University-based science suffered financially from the SBIR program, because money for SBIR came out of the budgets of government agencies that financed research, including academic research. Starting with set-asides for SBIR of 1 percent, the rates were periodically raised by Congress, reaching 2.5 percent, or approximately $1.1 billion per year, in the late 1990s. Between 1983 and 1998, SBIR made 45,000 awards, totaling $8.4 billion[7]—money clipped from the budgets of NIH, NSF, DOE,

---

7. *Federal Research: Evaluation of Small Business Innovation Research Can Be Strengthened,* U.S. General Accounting Office. GAO/RCED-99-114, June 1999, p. 2.

and other government research agencies, and diverted to backyard inventors and startup firms.

When Congress initially considered the SBIR legislation, the science agencies futilely protested; in sympathy with them, Reagan's science adviser, George A. Keyworth, denounced SBIR spending as "Money down the sewer."[8] But the White House acquiesced to passage of the SBIR in a deal for votes on a defense measure sought by Reagan. For Reagan's budget minders, the set-aside arrangement posed no threat since it merely shifted money from general research accounts to SBIR accounts, with no effect on overall spending levels. Once entrenched in the federal budget, SBIR became unmovable, though expandable. At that level of spending, it might be expected that the Republican Revolution, with its aversion to corporate welfare, would post SBIR on its roster of disposable federal spending. Private venture capital was plentiful and the cost-benefit case for SBIR had never been strong. But, with its ability to spread money through all fifty states, the small-business program was spared by the budget-slashing new majorities in Congress. Wasn't SBIR a form of corporate welfare, no different than the Advanced Technology Program? I asked Rep. Robert Walker (R-Pa.), vice chair of the House Budget Committee and chair of the Science Committee. He replied:

> In a sense, I suppose it has some of that context to it. The fact is, though, that they tend to be relatively small contracts and it does, in fact, have a lot more of the entrepreneurial aspects to it than some of the big corporate subsidy kinds of things that were happening in these other programs. It's something that, in all honesty, we haven't thought a lot about. It's not one that has been up on my radar screen. I'm sure that there have been some abuses there that probably we ought to look at in some context. What we were primarily again concerned about doing was trying to change the direction of so-called R&D money. I happen to believe that the ATP program is not only wrong from the standpoint of the government picking winners and losers, but I think it has a very, very big political context to it.[9]

The small-business levy on government research agencies would remain intact under the Republican budget plan. By themselves, the amounts taken for small-business research were tolerable. But now they added to a threat-

---

8. In Brief, *SGR*, October 1, 1984.
9. "Q&A: Chairman Walker on Republican Science Policy," *SGR*, June 15, 1995.

ening pattern of political indifference to the vulnerabilities of science. The Clinton White House remained fascinated with technology. Gingrich and his ideological warriors stood by their plans. "In any form, this is a prescription for disaster," Harold Varmus declared in forecasting the effect that the Republican budget-reduction program would have on government-supported research.

Contract with America

When Varmus lectured on the dismal future of finance for NIH, Gingrich was in his fifth month as speaker, committed to implementing the gimmicky ten-point Contract with America that called for shrinking the federal role in American life. Among its now-forgotten provisions were a commitment to a constitutional balanced-budget amendment, a line-item veto enabling the president to kill pork-barrel appropriations, and congressional term limits as a presumed safeguard against legislators succumbing to inside-the-beltway contamination.[10] It was in this atmosphere, and in a clinical manner, that Varmus assessed the financial prospects of the biomedical sciences: "It is now possible to make a diagnosis: the research enterprise is making a painful transition from an era of growth to an era of steady-state activity." As described by Varmus, "steady state" would terminate the extraordinary expansion that the biomedical sciences had experienced during the postwar decades, financed by an NIH budget that rose from $1 billion in 1970 to $11.3 billion in 1995. "In the steady state," Varmus explained, "new grants can be funded only when old grants expire, new faculty can be hired only when older faculty retire, and new NIH programs can begin only when other programs are ended." Varmus thus portrayed a constricted future for an enterprise nurtured for decades in

---

10. The credibility of the Contract with America was frayed by disparities between its terms and the practices of its proponents. In 1994, when Gingrich advocated a three-term House limit, he was in his eighth term, as was Representative Bob Livingston, of Louisiana, Gingrich's choice to chair the House Appropriations Committee. Gingrich's closest comrade in arms, Representative Robert Walker, of Pennsylvania, was in his ninth term. The contractors also aimed "to reinforce the central role of families in American life." At the time of signing, the speaker, in his second marriage, was secretly involved in a romantic relationship with a House staff member, twenty-three years his junior, for whom he left his spouse, as revealed in divorce proceedings in 1999. Livingston, the heir-designate to the speakership, resigned from the House when porno-pioneer Larry Flynt threatened to publish details of his private life. Under searing publicity, Gingrich gave up a $4.5-million book deal with Rupert Murdoch, the TV-publishing tycoon, who was fishing in political waters for business favors.

a continuous expansion of grants, professorships, laboratories, research programs, and graduate enrollments.

Though some members of the NIH community nostalgically grieved for a bygone golden age of government support for biomedical research, NIH was actually at a peak of wealth when Varmus delivered his steady-state forecast. Over the decades, more each year had become the natural state for NIH and its clients in university science departments, medical schools, and hospitals throughout the country. However, the prospects existed for even worse than steady state, Varmus warned. The House Budget Committee had proposed a 5-percent reduction for NIH in the coming fiscal year; the Senate Budget Committee, yet to act, reportedly favored a 10 percent reduction—maybe 20 percent, according to rumors that flourished in the excited atmosphere of the Republican congressional takeover. Calculating the long-term losses for science in the publicly stated Republican spending plans for the coming five years, Varmus estimated that "by the year 2000 our spending power would be about 40 percent below current spending levels. In any form," he declared, "this is a prescription for disaster."

Doomsday Averted

But instead of having to cope with calamity, NIH greatly prospered. Not far behind were other research agencies of government, too, with the grand totals of government money for research and development rising from $71 billion in 1994 to nearly $80 billion in 2000. Basic research, widely, but erroneously, regarded as especially vulnerable to political neglect, passed the $18-billion-dollar mark, an increase of 16 percent in purchasing power between 1993 and 2000.[11] Meanwhile, industrial support of research, which is often stimulated by government research spending, soared to new records, reaching an estimated $157 billion in 1999. The scientific metropolis—comprising government, industry, and academe—survived the Republican Revolution and greeted the new century on a historic peak of wealth, productivity, and political appreciation.

Amid the political turbulence and fears felt by scientists, and other beneficiaries of government, a disabling fault in the Gingrich-led Republican Revolution went unobserved: though the triumphant Republicans uttered frightening battle cries for their campaign against government, they lacked a coherent strategy and the unity required for agreeing on goals and means.

---

11. *Research and Development Funding: Fiscal Year 2000,* Congressional Research Service Issue Brief, September 20, 1999.

The Contract with America was closely identified with the House and its ebullient, publicity-savvy speaker, who, during the 1994 election campaign, lined up some 300 Republican House candidates for a contractual signing ceremony on the steps of the Capitol. At the bottom of the ten-point "contract," each affixed his or her signature to a statement that read: "Respecting the judgment of our fellow citizens as we seek their mandate for reform, we hereby pledge our names to this Contract with America."

A comparable ceremony was not held by Senate Republicans, whose longtime leader, Bob Dole, was neither a fire-breathing conservative nor disposed to be number two to upstart Newt Gingrich. Moreover, compared to their party colleagues in the House, the Senate Democrats, though also in minority (47 to 53), were better positioned to resist the Republican tide because of Senate rules favorable to unlimited debate. With 60 votes required for cloture, the Democrats could immobilize the chamber with talk.

But of greater importance for protecting research, the political sides were not crisply drawn on the government's role and financial responsibility. Fifty years after Vannevar Bush delivered his legendary proposal to Harry Truman, science was deeply integrated into the American economy and culture, and strong political support and personal sentiment for even more science were abundant in both parties—irrespective of their commitments to reduce government spending and the bizarre rantings of some of Gingrich's freshman troops in the House. The National Weather Service is not needed, Representative Dick Chrysler (R-Michigan) declared at a hearing of the House Science Committee on September 12, 1995, because, "85 to 90 percent" of newspapers and TV and radio stations "receive their weather information from private sector companies." Informed that the basic weather information originates with the National Weather Service, Chrysler despairingly responded, "I don't know, I don't know."

PORK POWER

When the Republicans took control of the Senate in 1995, Senator Mark O. Hatfield, a moderate Republican from Oregon and a notable pork-barrel provider for medical research in his home state, became chair of the Appropriations Committee. Turning against his party, Hatfield led the defeat of the Contract with America's balanced-budget amendment, a blunt antispending instrument designed to crimp congressional spending authority. Passed by the Gingrich-controlled House, the amendment was considered by the Senate, where proposed reductions for NIH were described by NIH Director Harold Varmus as "devastating." Hatfield assured him, "We are going to fight this prescription for disaster. We may fail, but if we fail, we're going to die with our boots on."[12] The balanced budget amendment failed by one vote in the Senate. (Upon Hatfield's retirement from the Senate in 1996, his congressional colleagues commemorated his service to NIH by assigning his name to a building under construction, thanks to his largess, on the NIH Bethesda, Md., campus: the Mark O. Hatfield Clinical Research Center.)

Serving under Hatfield as chair of the appropriations subcommittee for the NIH budget was Senator Arlen Specter, a moderate Republican from Pennsylvania who harbored far-fetched presidential ambitions for the 1996 election. The seven medical schools in Pennsylvania (two later merged), all heavily dependent on NIH for research and training funds, looked to Specter to keep up the flow of money; he did not disappoint them. In 1999, Specter's congressional colleagues commemorated his service to NIH by prefixing his name to the National Library of Medicine (like the Hatfield center, also on the NIH Bethesda campus).

Among NIH's many Republican friends in the Senate was Connie Mack, of Florida, a member of the NIH appropriations subcommittee chaired by Specter. Before his election to the Senate in 1988, Mack served in the House, where, as a fiscal conservative, he was an ideological ally of the rising Newt Gingrich. In the Senate, Mack became a leading supporter of rapid budget growth for NIH. In this instance, as in many others among congressional supporters of biomedical research, the devotion to NIH originated in personal experience with disease: Mack's father died of esophageal cancer in 1988; Mack was treated for melanoma in 1989, a disease from which his brother had died a decade earlier. Mack's wife was a breast cancer survivor. In 1997, Mack introduced the Biomedical Research Commitment Resolution, which called for doubling the NIH budget in five years. The resolution was nonbinding, but, adopted unanimously, conveyed the mood of the Senate. In the following years, both the House and Senate delivered large increases that set NIH on the doubling schedule.

With the Republican takeover of the House in 1995, an unrestrained enthusiast of medical research, Representative John Porter (R-Ill.), became chair of the House appropriations subcommittee for NIH, the starting point for medical-research appropriations in the long legislative process. As chair, Porter did not merely listen to and appraise the budget appeals of NIH and its supporters: he energetically stimulated support for NIH, inside and out-

12. "Scientists Mobilize to Fight Cuts," *Science,* May 26, 1995.

side Congress. In 1995, Porter conducted a delegation of scientists to meet with Speaker Gingrich to plead for favored treatment for the NIH budget—successfully so, as manifested in a respectable budget increase for NIH at the height of the Republican Revolution and its ongoing rhetoric of budget cuts; even Senator Bob Dole, the Republican majority leader, was talking tough, calling for budget reductions ranging "from Amtrak to zoological studies."[13]

In 1996, when budget cutting again threatened the NIH budget, Porter telephoned ten university presidents and urged them to enlist the members of their boards of trustees in behalf of NIH—a shrewd, efficient move, given the influential figures, local and national, who customarily serve on university boards. Porter also escorted members of his subcommittee on a daylong tour of NIH laboratories, and at his request, NIH Director Varmus brought five fellow Nobel laureates before Porter's subcommittee to describe the promise of biomedical research, but only if the money continued to increase.[14]

NIH was not a hard sell. Faith in the great scientific center of disease fighting was a nonideological, bipartisan verity of Capitol Hill. Political support arose naturally, from fear and hope, but was also cultivated by the NIH management. Orrin Hatch (R-Utah) recalled that he was a standard, anti-Washington, budget-cutting conservative when he was elected to the Senate in 1976. But he, too, joined the NIH contingent on Capitol Hill. "While showering one morning," Hatch told a meeting of cancer specialists in 1985, "I found a lump under my arm. I felt I was going to die." Hatch called the director of the National Cancer Institute, "and he told me to come right out there." The alarming symptom was diagnosed as a harmless fatty deposit, and removed under local anesthetic. Ever since, Hatch declared, he's been a strong supporter of NIH, in tandem with another NIH enthusiast in the House, Representative Henry Waxman, of California, a liberal Democrat. "You have to go pretty far to the left to get to the left of Henry," Hatch said—but on NIH matters, Hatch accomplished the maneuver.[15]

Nonetheless, the antigovernment rhetoric of the 1995 Republican Revolution was frightening in its ferocity, and seemed to apply to all but the Pentagon (and perhaps even it was not immune). NIH's Varmus, and other scientific leaders, found no reason for complacency in the expressions of

---

13. "On Lookout for Clues That Gingrich Is Keen for Science," *SGR*, February 1, 1995.

14. "NIH's Congressional Angel Explains Success," *SGR*, April 1, 1996.

15. Daniel S. Greenberg, "What Ever Happened to the War on Cancer?" *Discover* magazine, March 1986.

good feelings toward science that were mixed in with the budget-cutting declarations of the new regime on Capitol Hill. The din from Congress was contradictory, but still alarming.

By virtue of seniority, the House Science Committee chair went to an old personal friend and political comrade of Gingrich, Representative Robert Walker, of Pennsylvania, whom Gingrich also installed as vice chair of the Budget Committee. A deft parliamentarian and floor tactician, Walker was a dedicated warrior in the Gingrich cause of both science and budget conservatism. "Indeed, as much as anyone, he is the father of the revolution that led to the Republican victory in 1994," according to the authoritative *Almanac of American Politics 1996.*[16] For the worried scientists, Walker seemed to offer reassurance, while Gingrich continued with contradictory rants for science and against government. Walker stood up for science, declaring, "We propose dramatic increases in science spending despite decreases in other areas."[17] Like the speaker, Walker opposed the industrial-research programs favored by the Clinton administration as spurs to product innovation and jobs—though, as we have seen, the small-business research program eluded notice. Not so the others. "Corporate welfare," Walker sneered, arguing that government lacked the ability to pick marketplace winners; worthy commercial research projects would attract private capital. On the other hand, he strongly endorsed government support for university-based basic research. Industry shied away from that kind of science, Walker argued, because it was expensive, uncertain in outcome, and, when openly published—commonly the case in the culture of basic research—available to any competitor.

Walker was the leading warrior in the science-policy sector of the Republican Revolution. But he was not a durable one: though he held an unassailable seat in the Pennsylvania Dutch country (winning reelection with 70 percent of the vote in 1994), one year after the Republicans took control of the House, Walker, at age fifty-three, announced that at the end of the term he would retire—after serving only two years as chair of a committee on which he had long been overshadowed as a minority member. He had no secret reason for leaving Congress, Walker repeatedly assured puzzled journalists and congressional staff members, who assumed he would relish and seek to retain the influence and attention that came with his committee

16. *The Almanac of American Politics 1996* (Washington, D.C.: National Journal, 1995), p. 1168.
17. *Science,* November 18, 1994.

chair and uniquely close relationship with Gingrich. But after twenty years in the House, Walker simply wanted to do something else.

In January 1997, upon retiring from Capitol Hill, Walker, the dedicated fiscal conservative comrade of Newt Gingrich, became president of the Wexler Group, a Washington lobbying firm closely associated with the big-spending Democratic Party. The Wexler Group was headed by Anne Wexler, whose husband, Joseph D. Duffey, served as chair of the National Endowment for the Humanities under President Carter and as director of the United States Information Agency under President Clinton. The Wexler client list included American Airlines, Burger King, General Motors, the states of Alaska and Oregon, Texas A&M University, and the Science Coalition, an assemblage of some 300 organizations, including 70 universities, interested in Washington's relations with science.

Walker's place as chair of the House Science Committee was filled by Representative James Sensenbrenner Jr., of Wisconsin, a strong advocate of government support for basic research. But even with these well-placed, devoted friends of science calling for more government money for research, the budget strategy of the reigning Republicans mandated reductions throughout the civilian sector of the federal establishment.

No Solace in Clinton

Appropriately frightened by the antigovernment war whoops of the triumphant congressional Republicans, the academic and biomedical wings of the scientific enterprise found no comfort in the recognition or budget treatment they had received during the first two years of the Clinton administration—when Democrats still controlled the Congress, prior to the Republican victory in November 1994. True enough, fulfilling the expressed wishes and high hopes of Washington's science politicians, Clinton had not delayed in promptly naming a suitable nominee for *their* post in the White House, the presidential assistant for science and technology, who also served as director of the Office of Science and Technology Policy. At the start of the Carter, Reagan, and Bush administrations, many months elapsed before the dual-hatted science position was filled, often spawning rumors in science-policy circles that it might not be filled at all. On the opening day of the Clinton administration, however, the president's choice was in place, a hopeful sign in the calculations of Washington's science politicians. The job went to a well-known and respected figure in science-and-government affairs, John H. (Jack) Gibbons, director of the Office of

Technology Assessment, Congress's own think tank. Holding a Ph.D. in physics, Gibbons had spent over twenty years at the Oak Ridge National Laboratory, in Tennessee, and had also directed environmental research at the University of Tennessee and the Department of Energy before his appointment to head OTA in 1979. Folksy, yarn-spinning, and versed in the pre-Gingrich cooperative style of legislative operations on Capitol Hill, Gibbons knew the people, the issues, and the clockwork of government and science politics far better than any of his predecessors in Washington's premier science position. The science politicians regarded him as one of their own; the elected politicians and their staff workers of both parties knew him as dependable and trustworthy, invaluable characteristics in their working milieu.

However, like all who served in the White House science post since the dark days of the Nixon administration, Gibbons clearly recognized that he worked for the president, not for the financially insatiable scientific community. Nonetheless, as he explained to me, in his relations with the political core of the Clinton White House, he felt the need to compensate for the seemingly indelible expectation that the presidential science adviser and his office served as unrelenting advocates for greater science spending:

> And I made it a careful, purposeful act that every time we were asked to comment on an agency's science budget, I tried to tell where I thought it could be cut, as well as where it could be expanded, and they weren't used to that. They were used to science coming in and saying, "We want more."[18]

But Varmus's message of doom, preceded and followed by others of a similarly drastic nature, pervaded the scientific enterprise and stimulated a powerful and effective political mobilization and counterattack. Building on the techniques they had fashioned for acquiring public money during the preceding half century, scientists contributed to bringing the Republican Revolution to a standstill and eventual retreat. Five years after Varmus delivered his dour prophecy of steady state and disaster, the NIH budget climbed to $17.9 billion—some 50 percent above its level at the time of the steady-state speech. By that time, Newt Gingrich, creator and commander of the Republican Revolution, was a private citizen, having retired from Congress in 1998 after self-destructing politically. Looking back, Gingrich recalled, "When I became Speaker of the House in 1995, and we began to work toward a balanced budget, we were prepared to cut discretionary

---

18. Interview with author, December 6, 1998.

spending almost everywhere." But in 1999, he urged large increases for science:

> The highest investment priority in Washington should be to double the federal budget for scientific research. No other federal expenditure would create more jobs and wealth or do more to strengthen our world leadership, protect the environment and promote better health and education for all Americans. . . . Doubling the budget of the National Institutes of Health would be a good start. . . .[19]

THE CONVERTS TO SCIENCE

Bill Clinton, too, became a proselyte to science, after being publicly pelted by the Washington science community for neglect of research. With its promise of health and prosperity, its growing economic impact in communities across the nation, and clean image, science had become good politics—extremely good politics. I would conjecture, too, that spending on health research served as relatively inexpensive balm for a political system that neglected health-care reform, leaving some forty-four million Americans without health insurance at the end of the 1990s. President Clinton's conversion to champion of research was symbolized by the choice of a seat mate for Hillary Clinton in the balcony of the U.S. House of Representatives when Clinton, with the burgeoning Lewinsky scandal hanging over his head, delivered the State of the Union address in 1998: at the first lady's side, conscripted for a supporting role in Bill Clinton's resurrection drama, was the director of the National Institutes of Health, Nobel laureate Harold Varmus, renowned among researchers for his scientific achievements and the position he held at NIH, but unknown on the national stage. The TV cameras focused on Varmus and the correspondents identified him by name and title, as the president proposed raising the NIH budget by $1.1 billion, from $13.5 billion to $14.6 billion, nearly an 8 percent increase—among the very largest in an otherwise straitened federal budget. Applause followed. With the lurid Lewinsky allegations dominating the news, image-wise Clinton reached out for respectability by composing an appealing package: the Nobel laureate leader of the government's war on disease, the wronged but loyal spouse, and over a billion dollars more for health research. The outcome in money, after Congress got down to business, was

---

19. Newt Gingrich, "We Must Fund the Scientific Revolution," *Washington Post*, October 18, 1999.

a far larger increase for NIH than even Clinton sought: $2.1 billion, nearly 15 percent, for a grand total of $15.6 billion.

An amazing turnaround had occurred in the politics of science, leading to a new surge of federal money for research, especially the ever-popular medical sciences, but with gains, too, rather than feared reductions, for other fields of science. Gingrich and his revolution never recovered from public opprobrium when budget impasses between congressional Republicans and Bill Clinton closed most civilian agencies of the federal government for six days in November 1995 and then, starting in mid-December, for three straight weeks. The second shutdown was extended in Washington for four additional days by heavy snows. Until the shutdowns, the public may not have fully grasped the intricacies of the federal budget process or appreciated the salutary pervasiveness of the federal government in American life. But tourists in Washington were confronted by locked Smithsonian museums during their Christmas-holiday visit, travelers faced shuttered passport offices, and throughout the nation, the flow of federal payments for businesses and individuals was interrupted. The ensuing resentment landed heavily on the cocky, fast-talking Gingrich and his glib proposals for shrinking the federal establishment, sending his personal standing, and antigovernment designs, plummeting in the polls. Public opinion, and the wants and political powers of the elderly, the education and veterans lobbies, and other federal beneficiaries far bigger and politically stronger than the scientific enterprise contributed to the rapid demolition of the Republican Revolution. But science both benefited from the change of political weather and contributed to it. The high regard in which science is held by the American public helped discredit the plans of the new Republican majorities, and, in the process, protected science against savage budget reductions and set it on a course to unprecedented heights of financial support. The public understanding of science, deemed essential for public support of science by many in the scientific enterprise, registered no improvement from its customarily dismal levels.[20] But a lobbying campaign by scientists, working in tandem with their political friends, contributed to saving science from draconian budget reductions. Science mobilized politically, as it had in 1964 to oppose Goldwater's presidential candidacy. But this time, it mobilized for its own salvation.

20. Each biennial edition of *Science & Engineering Indicators* relates new tales of mass ignorance. The 1998 edition, (pp. 7–8) reported that "only 11 percent of Americans can define the term 'molecule'" and that "despite substantial media attention to deep space probes and pictures from the Hubble Space Telescope, only 48 percent of Americans know that the earth goes around the sun once each year."

CHAPTER 28

The Political Triumph of Science

The National Science Foundation today announced the largest
budget request in Foundation history—a record $4.57 billion for
fiscal 2001. The total 2001 request is 17.3 percent higher than the
current year's budget, and the planned $675-million increase for
2001 is double the largest increase proposed in NSF history. . . . Rita
Colwell, NSF director, said, "Industry CEOs, economists, academic
and scientific leaders, the Council on Competitiveness and many
others are in agreement on the importance of federally supported
fundamental research in the growth and strength of the American
economy."

—NSF press release, February 7, 2000

IN THE reversal of the Republican Revolution, assistance for
science came from many sectors, including a highly visible, especially influential one that had previously been only tangentially concerned with
the politics of science: Fortune 500 high-tech industry. In a full-page advertisement in the *Washington Post* in May 1995, CEOs, former CEOS, and presidents of sixteen major corporations warned against cutting federal science
spending. The proposed reductions, they said, would endanger American
prosperity.[1]

It was not the charity-ball spirit that motivated these executives.
They spoke out of corporate self-interest, aware that Washington paid for
basic research that much of corporate America neglected in its own laboratories in pursuit of quick profits and high ratings on Wall Street. Though
big business and industry traditionally went Republican, and supported the
antispending, tax-cutting provisions of the Contract with America, the cor-

---

1. The signatories were from General Electric, IBM, DuPont, Eastman Kodak, Lockheed
Martin, Motorola, Eli Lilly, Merck, Phillips Petroleum, United Airlines, Bellcore, Bell-
South, Texas Instruments, Chrysler, TRW, and McDonnell Douglas.

porate manifesto emphatically endorsed public finance for particular types
of science in particular locales: basic and applied science in universities,
where the results were accessible to industry and where the specialized
workers needed by industry were trained. The industrialists frankly acknowledged their reliance on government research spending:

> History has shown that it is federally sponsored research that provides
> the truly "patient" capital needed to carry out basic research and create
> an environment for the inspired risk-taking that is essential to technolog-
> ical discovery. . . . We can personally attest that large and small compa-
> nies in America, established and entrepreneurial, all depend on two prod-
> ucts of our research universities: new technologies and well-educated
> scientists and engineers. Technological leadership by its very nature is
> ephemeral. . . . For all these reasons, it is essential that the federal gov-
> ernment continue its traditional role as funder of both basic and applied
> research in the university environment. If we want to keep the Ameri-
> can Dream intact, we need to preserve the partnership that has long sus-
> tained it.[2]

Support for the embattled science agencies came from other quarters,
too, but science contributed heavily to saving itself from the harsh politics
of government retrenchment. Developed over decades, well-financed and
seasoned, the forces and techniques employed by science were formidable,
perhaps all the more so because of the widespread impression that science
suffered from political naivete and helplessness.[3] Against the designs that
the Republican Revolution aimed at its money, science fielded cadres of
experienced Washington-based lobbyists and representatives of universities
and scientific societies. No master plan guided their efforts, which, initially,
were timid and unsure in the face of what the scientists considered incomprehensible political indifference to the immense value of their work for
the nation's well-being. Thus, in June 1995, the Board of the American Association for the Advancement of Science issued a waffling statement that
combined support for congressional efforts to cut federal spending with
pleas for favorable treatment for science, and concluded with a tinny call

2. "A Moment of Truth for America," advertisement, *Washington Post,* May 2, 1995.
3. In his 1999 reincarnation as an advocate of increased government spending on science, Gingrich described scientists as "among the least effective lobbyists" (*Washington
Post,* October 18, 1999), apparently oblivious of their success in lobbying him and his
budget-cutting colleagues into exempting science from spending constraints.

to arms for scientists to fight for their federal money. The AAAS board—a representative slice of the scientific leadership—declared itself "particularly pleased by the acknowledgement by congressional leaders of the key role played by science and technology in improving the nation's economy and quality of life." But then asserting that, under the House-approved spending plan of Budget Chairman Kasich, federal money for nondefense research and development would drop by 34 percent over the next seven years, the statement added:

> The Board urges Congress to exercise great caution in making changes of this magnitude and consequence for the nation's vital research enter-prise. It further encourages the research community to make known its concerns, and to do so with an appreciation of the fundamental unity of the research and education enterprise and an understanding of the importance of congressional concerns about the federal budget.[4]

Alarmed by the ominous budget forecasts, the threatened branches of the scientific enterprise did not need encouragement to make known their concerns. We came across their Washington strongholds earlier in this book, but, as a refresher, the order of battle included the 143,000-member American Association for the Advancement of Science, whose Directorate of Science and Policy Programs had meticulously tracked, analyzed, and issued alarming annual reports about the federal R&D budget since 1976.[5] The AAAS amplified its voice by orchestrating a loose alliance known as the Intersociety Working Group, which consisted of twenty scientific societies, large and small, several with their own lobbying arms. Also in the scientific force were the Association of American Medical Colleges, representing the nation's 125 allopathic medical schools and hundreds of hospitals, scien-tific societies, and health-related organizations; the Federation of American Societies for Experimental Biology, a consortium of scientific associations, with a membership then totaling some 45,000 researchers in fields heavily

4. "Statement of the AAAS Board of Directors," adopted June 24, 1995 (Office of Commu-nications, American Association for the Advancement of Science).

5. Even as Washington's R&D budgets steadily rose, from $20 billion in 1976 to approxi-mately $80 billion in 2000, persistent complaints from the science lobbies led the press and public to believe that the federal government was withdrawing from the support of R&D. Thus, in reporting the concerns of 140 "high-tech bosses" in Silicon Valley, the *Economist* stated that "one of their key complaints is that the federal government's R&D spending over the past 30 years has declined dramatically" ("Liberty.com," Octo-ber 30, 1999, p. 23).

supported by NIH; the Association of American Universities, then consisting of sixty schools that were major recipients of federal research money; the American Chemical Society, with over 150,000 members; and the American Physical Society, with approximately 40,000 members.

The Washington-based forces were backed by nationwide e-mail and fax networks originally developed for routine office and scientific communications, but now readily applied to political alerts and petitions. These communication links extended throughout the scientific community, tying together the most computer-literate and teleconnected population in the world. Years of cultivating friends in politics provided science with sympathetic supporters on Capitol Hill, among members and staff. A continuing supply of science and engineering doctorates was channeled to congressional staffs and federal agencies by fellowship programs conducted by the AAAS in collaboration with other professional societies. Starting with six fellows in 1973, the program was popular among young scientists and valued by lawmakers for the highly educated free help it furnished for their eternally shorthanded staffs. In accord with the Parkinsonian model, legislating and constituent service—the grist of congressional survival and success—are limited in volume only by the availability of staff. By the year 2000, 91 fellows were working in Washington, and the alumni of the program totaled some 1,200. Like others struck by the contagion of Potomac Fever, about one-third of the fellows remained in Washington, many as full-time congressional staff members, rather than return home upon completion of their fellowships. Earlier we encountered one ex-fellow who was elected to the House in 1998, Representative Rush Holt (D-New Jersey), a Ph.D. physicist. The purpose of the fellowship program was to educate scientists in the ways of the government on which science depended for money.[6]

The normal confusion about the ups and downs of money in the politics of science was compounded by turmoil among the reigning Republicans regarding their long-term budget plans. In that atmosphere, the doomsday numbers in public utterances rarely matched. The threat of a 34-percent reduction in science spending over seven years was cited by the board of the AAAS. Representative George Brown, bumped from the chair of the House Science Committee by the Republican congressional takeover in 1995, exceeded the scientists in prophesying the extent of budget reductions: "Total federal funding for research and development is projected to decline by 50 percent or more within five years under the terms of the Re-

6. Data supplied by AAAS Directorate for Science and Policy Programs.

publican Contract with America," Brown warned in March 1995.[7] The captive science press went to work for its sponsors. *Chemical & Engineering News,* the weekly magazine of the American Chemical Society, relayed an off-the-shelf cataclysmic assessment that it cagily attributed to an unnamed "Washington academic lobbyist": "If the Republicans enact their budget plan, they will have destroyed the foundation of scientific research in this country."[8] Taking its cues from the hair-raising alarms of the science lobbies, a sympathetic popular press equated research with economic prosperity and Republican budget reductions with scientific decline and economic misfortune. In an editorial titled "Crippling American Science," the *New York Times* declared:

> The budget plan passed by the House mounts an assault on scientific research, science training and American research universities that are the envy of the world. . . . The magnitude of the House cuts is shocking. Civilian research would fall over five years from about $35 billion to $25 billion, a 35 percent cut after accounting for inflation. . . . Knocking out innovative research can lead to stagnant productivity and growth. By that calculation, the House plan is an irresponsible gamble.[9]

INTO THE POLITICAL FRAY

The defensive reaction to the Republican budget plans spanned the major institutions of science and government, from grant-dependent universities and the professional societies of their faculties to Capitol Hill and the political center of science, the office of the presidential science and technology adviser. Ever since Richard Nixon temporarily banished scientific advice from the White House in 1973, presidential science advisers had discreetly conducted themselves as objective counselors, protecting their credibility in political circles by judiciously refraining from public rows over science spending. However, in the threatening circumstances of the Republican Revolution, the restraints were lifted. In the vanguard of the scientific counterattack was John Gibbons, the president's assistant for science and technology, accompanied by Neal Lane, the director of the National Science

7. "Federal R&D Funding Projected to Decline 50 Percent Under the Republican Contract," press release, Democratic membership, House Science Committee, March 1, 1995.

8. Wil Lepkowski and Janice R. Long, "Republican Budget Reductions Alarm R&D Community," *Chemical & Engineering News,* May 29, 1995.

9. *New York Times,* May 23, 1995.

Foundation, and Harold Varmus of NIH. In happier times, presidential science advisers and the chairs of the House Science Committee were in harmony, sometimes squabbling over programs or dollars, but overall, concurring about the importance of government support for science and the continuing necessity for increasing support. Now, overt animosity replaced amity. Gibbons publicly denounced the Republican plans to abolish the National Biological Service (NBS), an environmental agency cobbled together early in the Clinton administration from various parts of the Department of the Interior. Its original name, the National Biological Survey (a nomenclature match for the U.S. Geological Survey, a venerable sister agency in the department), connoted land survey—a red flag for conservative western Republicans, who denounced the agency as an insidious Washington instrument for expropriating private land holdings. The name was hurriedly changed, though to no avail. Under old and new names, the agency was strongly defended by Gibbons, a staunch environmentalist. The purpose of the Biological Service, he said, is to provide "a national inventory of our natural plant and animal resources." Elimination of the agency, Gibbons argued, "is analogous to book burnings of yesteryear. Since when is ignorance a promising route to deliverance? The NBS isn't a land grab, as its detractors claim. Science doesn't get much purer than that," Gibbons jibed, referring to Republican claims of devotion to pure science.[10]

Republican Robert Walker, chair of the House Science Committee, responded with a letter to President Clinton asserting that "the only 'book burners' with which I am familiar in recent world political history were the Nazi Party fanatics of Hitler's Germany." The congressman declared that the remark attributed to Gibbons was so unbelievably offensive that he checked its accuracy with Gibbons's office, "which did not deny that the statement quoted was accurate." Walker advised Clinton to instruct Gibbons in civility.[11] Such jousting between Congress and the White House is a standard act on the political stage, employing staff ghostwriters who are keen to see their creativity conveyed to the public via the press. However, the exchanges between Gibbons and Walker—copies provided to reporters—were unusually nasty. On the issue of the proper government role in the financing of research, they had moved from disagreement over policy into the realm of personal dislike.

10. John Gibbons, address to AAAS Policy Colloquium, April 12, 1995.
11. "Feuding on Science Policy," *SGR*, October 1, 1995.

SAVING THE SOCIAL SCIENCES

Neal Lane, the director of NSF, had his own ongoing run-ins with Chairman Walker, on the Republican spending plans for research in general and, in particular, on Walker's attempt to reduce, if not altogether eliminate, NSF's support for the social and behavioral sciences. The social-behavioral issue was politically and professionally touchy for NSF—the federal bankroll for excellence in academic research outside the health sciences—and for Director Lane. A physicist, age fifty-four when he was appointed head of NSF in 1993, Lane came after the generation of World War II physicists who implanted their values, including disdain for the social and behavioral sciences, on government science policy for decades. The social and behavioral sciences were the poor relations of federal support for research, arrogantly dismissed as the "soft sciences" by the reigning physicists of postwar science (who regarded themselves, along with chemists, mathematicians, and biologists, as practitioners of the "hard sciences"). Psychology, sociology, anthropology, political science, and economics were peremptorily excluded from Vannevar Bush's grand design for postwar support of research by government. In his 1945 letter of transmittal to President Truman accompanying *Science, The Endless Frontier,* Bush stated that, in commissioning the report, FDR "had in mind the natural sciences, including biology and medicine, and I have so interpreted his questions. Progress in other fields, such as the social sciences and the humanities," Bush conceded, "is likewise important; but the program for science presented in my report warrants immediate attention."[12] It was by no whim of politics, however, that the social and behavioral sciences were excluded from "immediate attention." Bush, the astute science politician, had drafted the letter in which President Roosevelt requested recommendations for the postwar support of science. "Hard" scientists and politicians were wary and disdainful of professors who studied and pronounced on race relations, sex, divorce, poverty, child raising, and crime and punishment. Senator William Proxmire, with his Golden Fleece awards, reaped prime-time attention by ridiculing odd-sounding research projects, many in the social sciences. In 1978, for example, Proxmire assailed NSF for financing a study titled Ethno-Endocrinology of Female Pairs of Western Gulls, denouncing the project as "the gay seagull study."

NSF weathered that one, but in its early days, in the 1950s, the founda-

---

12. Vannevar Bush, *Science, The Endless Frontier,* p. 1.

tion's managers were wary of ideological conservatives who assailed social-science research as a threat to traditional American values. Fearing a political backlash, it wasn't until 1953, two years after NSF began operations, that it cautiously began to explore support of the social sciences. In recognition of the political volatility of the suspect disciplines, Alan Waterman, the founding physicist-director of NSF, assured Congress that NSF "would proceed cautiously in the area of the social sciences and only after serious study."[13] No such assurance was needed for math or physics. By 1958, when the NSF budget totaled $40 million, the research portfolio included only forty-nine grants in the social and behavioral sciences, totaling $725,950. Growth came slowly, but steadily—in part because economics came in under the social-science umbrella, raising NSF's budget for the social, behavioral, and economic sciences in 1980 to $52 million out of a total NSF budget of $685 million. Support for the social and behavioral sciences also flowed from the Pentagon and the National Institutes of Health, but NSF became their principal supporter in university-based fundamental research. During the Reagan administration, ideological objections initially pushed NSF's support down to $32 million, but the budget made a comeback when corporate managers and strategists complained about a falloff in the production of useful social-science data. Opposition, however, persisted within the old ranks of science. As late as 1988, one of the most distinguished figures in the "hard" sciences openly assailed the social and behavioral sciences as pretenders to scientific legitimacy. In a published interview, I. I. Rabi, the 1944 Nobel laureate in physics and science adviser to a string of presidents, brazenly lamented the admission of social-science disciplines to the elite and select National Academy of Sciences:

> What has happened with the Academy is that we've added new divisions in recent years, like sociology and economics, that really have no place there. I think there should be no place in the Academy for activities that aren't connected with the hard sciences, for a very simple reason: The hard sciences are an essential element of our culture and the novel element in our culture for the last few hundred years. Sociology and economics are valuable in themselves, but they're not science in the sense of physical and biological sciences. When the Academy speaks on such subjects, however, it speaks to politicians who feel they are just as

---

13. J. Merton England, *A Patron of Pure Science: The National Science Foundation's Formative Years, 1945–57* (Arlington, Va.: National Science Foundation, 1982), p. 270.

capable of talking about such subjects as are the scientists, maybe more capable.[14]

Rabi's dismissive remarks reeked of ignorance and arrogance, a trait not rare among the aristocrats of physics. Social-science research varies in quality, as does research in the "hard" sciences. The social and behavioral sciences embrace methodological rigor and are as addicted as the natural and physical sciences to the dual hurdles of peer review to get money for research and peer review to publish the results—frequently in *Science* and *Nature*, favored journals for the natural and physical sciences. But reservations toward the social sciences were not limited to the passing generation of scientific barons. In 1993, NIH Director Harold Varmus, who shared the 1989 Nobel Prize in the category of medicine or physiology, told an interviewer from the *New York Times*, "And while I'm trying to learn more about behavioral science, I must say I don't get tremendous intellectual stimulation from most of the things I read."[15] However, while the old sentiments lingered on in some quarters, a new spirit of interdisciplinary solidarity was arising in the leadership of American science as political and financial storm clouds gathered over the scientific enterprise.

In the spring of 1995, as blizzards of budget numbers and cross-party recriminations swirled through Washington, House Science Committee Chairman Walker reiterated his support for basic research, declaring that "the National Science Foundation will continue to grow"—except for the social and behavioral sciences. Asked to explain the exception, Walker, speaking informally at a press briefing, replied in somewhat convoluted language:

> In large part, we think that's an area where the National Science Foundation has largely wandered into those areas in recent years that was kind

14. "Presidential Science Advising and the National Academy of Sciences: An Interview by William T. Golden," in *Science and Technology Advice to the President, Congress, and Judiciary*, ed. William T. Golden (New York: Pergamon Press, 1988), p. 281.

15. *New York Times*, November 23, 1993. Varmus later said that the remark was misinterpreted to suggest a lack of appreciation on his part for the social sciences. Describing himself as "an addict about things that would have to be construed as behavioral and preventive strategies in managing my own health—for diet, exercise, even mood control at a certain level," Varmus, however, added, "I see more definitive, exciting discoveries being made in molecular genetics these days than I do in behavioral sciences." *SGR*, interview, October 1, 1994. With prods from several influential congressional supporters of the social and behavioral sciences, these disciplines gained ground at NIH during Varmus's six years as director.

of a politically correct decision in recent years. And that is a place where
the science budgets can be rescoped. We think that the concentration
ought to be in those areas of the physical sciences.[16]

Under the budget proposal endorsed by Walker, increases for the physical
sciences were to be financed by taking away the entire $110 million budget
of the NSF Directorate for the Social, Behavioral and Economic Sciences.
Counterpunching came immediately from a Washington outpost of the
threatened disciplines, the Consortium of Social Science Associations, an
alliance of thirteen professional societies, twenty-eight affiliated scholarly
groups, and over sixty supporting universities. Founded in 1981, the consortium straightforwardly describes itself as "an advocacy organization for
federal support for the social and behavioral sciences."[17] Like their lobbying
counterparts in the "hard" sciences, the social and behavioral science organizations were versed in the melodramatic phraseology of budget strife.
Elimination of the NSF Directorate for the Social, Behavioral and Economic
Sciences "would decimate a cornerstone of our pursuit of knowledge," declared Howard Silver, executive director of the consortium. The American
Psychological Society, representing some 15,000 academic psychologists,
warned that the budget-cutting plan would be "a tragic error." These ri-
postes were off-the-shelf rhetoric, but they delivered a message to Capitol
Hill: the professors are fighting for their money.

In defense of the social and behavioral sciences, NSF Director Lane, a
gentle-mannered administrator, employed a nonconfrontational approach.
In a letter to Chairman Walker that NSF released to the press—a standard
tactic, on both sides, in the rising budget strife between Congress and the
administration—Lane apologetically put the blame for the threat to the social and behavioral sciences on NSF itself. The difficulty over these disciplines has arisen, he lamented to the chairman, because NSF "has not been
more effective in informing the Congress" about the value of their research
to the nation. "For example," Lane wrote, social and behavioral research
projects financed by NSF "have stimulated important new work that will
advance computer design and understanding of human cognition." Lane
did not need to say, since it was a given of science politics at century's end,
that no American leader would wish to impede the advance of computer
design and understanding of human cognition.

16. "GOP Plan Favors Science, Cuts Heavily Into Technology," *SGR*, May 15, 1995.
17. From *COSSA Washington Update*, the newsletter of the consortium, published 22 times
a year.

It soon became evident that, as the sidekick of Speaker Gingrich, Chairman Walker was preoccupied with grander issues than research: deficit reduction, Medicare finance, welfare reform, education, and other topics that aroused the antigovernment ardor of the new Republican majorities in Congress. Walker had already backed away from his presumably money-saving proposal to bundle a group of federal research agencies into a Department of Science. As the congressional session wore on, he became a half-hearted warrior in the Republican Revolution, soon to leave Congress for a lucrative lobbying job in the private sector. When I spoke to Walker several weeks after he proposed the termination of NSF's support for the social and behavioral sciences, he appeared disengaged from the issue and the turmoil he had created:

> I'm not certain that we understood that we were going to kick up as much fuss as we did over it. Of course, anytime somebody has a stream of government money coming their way, they get to kick up a fuss if they think it's going to be ended. But I viewed it, and I think the others who were also concerned viewed it, as a way of saying to the National Science Foundation that we think your priorities in this area have been misplaced and we want a course correction. I think as a result of what we're doing, we're getting the course correction.[18]

Walker indicated that he was cool, but not opposed, to NSF support of research on social problems such as violence, which he acknowledged as "a legitimate subject of research." By "course correction," Walker explained, he meant integration of NSF's social and behavioral research programs with research in other fields:

> Neal Lane and I just had a conversation this morning, and he makes the point that some of the work they're doing, for instance, in trying to understand the quality revolution [in manufacturing and services], obviously involves some engineering questions, but it also involves some culture questions. It involves some questions about how people are integrated into that, and those are sociological in nature there; that any complete study of the quality revolution probably needs to have the social and economic side woven into it. That's where I think that SBE [the

18. Interview with author, June 7, 1995; "Q&A: Chairman Walker on Republican Science Policy," *SGR*, June 15, 1995.

NSF Directorate for Social, Behavioral and Economic Sciences] is legitimately woven into what NSF is doing.[19]

Walker's gambit against the social and behavioral sciences failed to stop
their financial growth, though perhaps they might have fared even better
without his dank threats. In 1995, when he declared his budget intentions,
the NSF Directorate for the Social, Behavioral and Economic Sciences was
budgeted for $110 million. In 1996, the budget rose to $116 million.[20] By
1999, the budget had risen to $144 million. The money can be tabulated
precisely, but far more difficult to fathom is the crucial question of whether
Walker's financial threats produced intimidating effects on the content of
NSF's social and behavioral projects. None were felt, according to Alan G.
Kraut, executive director of the American Psychological Society (which
keeps a close watch on government social-science programs). Comparing
the response to the threatened reductions in 1995 to those actually carried
out against the social and behavioral sciences by the Reagan administration
in 1981, Kraut told me, "Neal Lane was absolutely great" in opposing
Walker. Kraut also credited NSF Deputy Director Anne Petersen, a psycholo-
gist, with rallying resistance to Walker. Petersen's message to the social-
science organizations, Kraut said, was, "'Give us the ammunition to protest'" the proposed budget reduction. Times had changed, Kraut recalled,
"I didn't have to teach psych 101 to anyone."[21] Howard Silver of the Consortium of Social Science Associations seconded that assessment.

For the social and behavioral sciences, as well as for the historically
favored natural and physical sciences, the Republican Revolution possessed
more bite than a paper tiger, but turned out to be far less destructive than
its rhetoric suggested. The outcome, however, was not foreseeable during
that spring of 1995, a time of fear that justifiably energized the scientific
enterprise.

A SCIENTIFIC RALLY

On June 26, 1995, as the congressional wrecker's ball arced closer to the
budgets of government research agencies, representatives of ninety-eight
scientific societies and higher-education organizations gathered in a downtown Washington hotel for a meeting organized by the AAAS. The gather-

---

19. Ibid.
20. *Congressional Action on Research and Development in the FY 1996 Budget* (Washington,
   D.C.: American Association for the Advancement of Science, 1996), p. 49.
21. Conversation with author, November 17, 1999.

ing was extraordinary, starting with its title: "Unity Under Adversity." If money for research were indeed to become as scarce as the Republicans threatened to make it, the scientific leadership feared that competitive tensions among the scientific disciplines, normally subdued when growth was available for all, might erupt into a free-for-all. The political rejection of the Superconducting Super Collider two years earlier was assisted by scientists who contested the priority of the multibillion-dollar project in sharply worded congressional testimony. While NIH Director Varmus expressed fear of a steady state in the financing of biomedical research, scientists in other disciplines knew that in science politics, disease fighting was an easy sell in comparison to physics, chemistry, and mathematics. Envious glances were being cast at the traditionally favored budget of NIH. Addressing the gathering, which was pervaded by a palpable sense of imminent catastrophe for the nation's scientific enterprise, presidential science adviser Jack Gibbons departed from his customarily folksy lectern manner and spoke heatedly:

> I have been faulted in recent weeks for introducing a partisan note in the debate on science and technology funding. The science adviser to the President has always been apolitical, I've been told, a cheerleader for science who left the world of politics behind and worked for the overall good of the community. That's fine if you're a science adviser with an expanding budget. If your job is to hand out money, then it's very easy to be on good terms with everybody. I do not have that luxury. It is not a pleasant task to go before the Congress and tell them they're making a big mistake—that they are compromising the nation's future for the sake of ideology. . . . But this is my job, and if I must, I will use the harsh rhetoric that focuses attention on science and technology issues.[22]

When Gibbons spoke, virtually nothing was clear or predictable in the cacophonous propaganda battle raging between the White House science wing and congressional science chieftains over the appropriate role of government in their shared area of responsibility. The Republicans boasted of their budget-cutting plans; the House Budget Committee had pinpointed NSF and other research agencies for budget restraints or reductions to compensate for tax reductions. On the other hand, Chairman Walker insisted that basic research in universities would actually receive greater support. Speaker Gingrich extolled both science and severe reductions in federal spending. The Clinton White House said it was working toward deficit re-

22. John H. Gibbons, "The First Rule of Tinkering," address to the Forum on Unity Under Adversity, Washington, D.C., June 26, 1995.

duction while also investing for the nation's future by exempting research and education from the new frugality. Gibbons described to the audience the president's plans for financial growth for research: increases by the year 2002 of $2.5 billion for NIH, $500 million for NSF, and $500 million for basic research at NASA. Amid the gloomy forecasts, his numbers were uniquely hopeful, though meaningless, since Clinton's presidency would end in January 2001. "But none of us," he warned, "will get a full meal if we continue to fight each other for table scraps." As it turned out, the amounts stated by Gibbons were hugely exceeded by the sums appropriated by the Republican Congress, despite its commitment to reduce federal spending. Between 1996 and 2000—two years short of Gibbons's projections—NIH's budget grew by approximately $6 billion; NSF's budget rose by over $2 billion. The NASA budget remained unchanged, but space research flourished with resources freed up by a transition to simpler, less-grandiose space satellites and drastic reductions and economies in the agency's swollen empire of quasi-independent centers.

Gibbons was fifteenth in the select ranks of presidential science advisers that began with Vannevar Bush's service under Franklin Roosevelt during World War II, and included some of the most distinguished figures in the construction of the postwar partnership of science and government: Oliver Buckley, retired president of Bell Labs, who briefly served under Truman; I. I. Rabi, under Truman and Eisenhower; Lee DuBridge, who served both Truman and Nixon; James R. Killian and George Kistiakowsky, successively appointed by Eisenhower as the first full-time presidential science advisers; Jerome Wiesner, who served under Kennedy and briefly under Johnson; Wiesner's successor, Donald Hornig; Edward E. David Jr., in the Nixon administration; Guy Stever, in the Ford administration; Frank Press, under Carter; George (Jay) Keyworth and William Graham, in the Reagan White House; and D. Allan Bromley, science adviser to President Bush. As heir to the tradition of science in service at the highest level of government, Gibbons emphatically declared: "I do not want to be the science adviser on whose watch our future foundered for lack of commitment to the very things that made us great." Gibbons's declaration encapsulated a durable political fact of the science-and-government relationship over the previous fifty years: constant growth—now threatened by the ideological storm raging on Capitol Hill. The AAAS audience, in sympathy with Jack Gibbons, their representative in the White House, responded with strong applause.

Gibbons was followed at the lectern by NSF Director Neal Lane, who emphasized the unity theme, warning that "we must be careful not to give in to our individual instincts to save ourselves at the cost of others." Next came Rita Colwell, the president of the AAAS and president of the University of Maryland Biotechnology Institute. She also cautioned against interdisciplinary scrapping for money: "We must shoot outward from our circle of wagons, rather than inward at each other," Colwell declared.

VICTORY, WITH CASUALTIES

The Republican Revolution did inflict casualties on the roster of government research organizations. The personal and professional suffering of those directly affected, and the loss of valuable scientific and technical capability, were substantial. But by the measure of havoc threatened, compared to damage actually inflicted, the harm was negligible. Proposals to abolish the Departments of Energy, Education, and Commerce came and went without effect. The Bureau of Mines was abolished, but it had been shrinking for many years and was long overdue for termination. Though designated by congressional Republicans as a high-priority target for termination, the newly created National Biological Service survived in diminished form as a division of the Geological Survey. Year after year, House Republicans "zeroed out" the budget of the Advanced Technology Program—reviled as the exemplar of corporate welfare—but it, too, survived, though not on the grand, growth-oriented scale originally envisioned by the early Clinton administration. Rather than the $1 billion a year planned for the end of the decade, ATP received $210 million for the year 2000. From 1991 through 1998, the program provided $1.39 billion in federal funds for 431 projects, while the firms involved paid in $1.4 billion as their share of the costs. Debate continued over the necessity of the program in America's booming high-tech economy, with its abundant pools of private venture capital. But, for our examination of the politics of science, the instructive aspect was the survival of the Advanced Technology Program in fairly robust condition. As with virtually every aspect of the American scientific and technical enterprise, the forces for continuation were more powerful than the forces for termination. And, with rare exception, the forces for growth overcame all resistance. The intrinsic political power of science was evident in the bland summary of science and money issued in December 1999 by a Washington-based bastion of science with an Olympian record of dour prophecy, the AAAS. Shortly after Congress and the president completed work on government science budgets for the year 2000, the AAAS reported:

> Federal support for R&D continues to flourish in the new era of federal
> budget surpluses, at least for the most favored priorities. Although it was

expected that tight statutory caps on discretionary spending would result in a painful FY 2000 budget process of allocating cuts, Congress and
President Clinton, while technically sticking to the caps, obliterated
them in practice and competed to award large increases for discretionary
programs. Most areas of federal support of R&D receive moderate increases in FY 2000, even after a last-minute across-the-board cut in all
discretionary spending, while selected high-priority areas in defense and
health receive substantial increases.[23]

However, the habits of financial panic-mongering—conceived at mid-
century and energetically and expensively nurtured ever since—did not
vanish in the face of incontestable evidence of political enthusiasm for science. "The ink is barely dry on the FY 2000 budget agreement," reported
Washington Fax, a news service aimed at the science-policy community,
"but the political maneuvering already is well underway for the FY 2001
spending battle. At the White House, administration officials, according to
several sources, are working with a draft budget plan that reportedly provides no funding increase for a range of programs, including the National
Institutes of Health and the National Science Foundation."[24] For fiscal 2001,
however, Congress again provided major increases for federal research
agencies, raising their budgets to historic highs. NIH gained $2.7 billion;
NSF went up by over $500 million; research at NASA, DOE, and the Penta-
gon rose, too. Nonetheless, from within the scientific enterprise, the delu-
sionary lamentations of neglect continued. Writing in the *New York Times*
shortly before election day 2000, Caltech president and Nobelist David Baltimore deplored the absence of science-policy discussions in the presidential campaign: "If I were a politician, I would insist that the science budgets
of the National Science Foundation, NASA, the Department of Energy, and
the Department of Defense be strengthened." The NIH budget, he conceded, was "keeping up with the opportunities." A small headline in the
body of the article stated: "The tiny budget for research erodes our global
edge."[25] To arms!

23. *Congressional Action on Research and Development in the FY 2000 Budget* (Washington,
    D.C.: American Association for the Advancement of Science, 1999), p. 1.
24. *Washington Fax,* "Keep Your Eye on the NIH Funding Ball; It's Back in Play," December
    17, 1999.
25. David Baltimore, "Stifling the Source of the Surplus," *New York Times,* October 28,
    2000.

POSTSCRIPT

For the sciences, the paradox of isolation and triumph was starkly illu-
minated in the presidential transition of 2001 and the early days of the
George W. Bush administration. While sitting out the election—except
for the previously described letterhead endorsement of Al Gore—science
asserted its claim of recognition in a preelection manifesto from the National Academy of Sciences. Titled "The Presidential Appointment Process,"
the academy—citing as authority prior Carnegie Commission reports—
proclaimed the necessity of the early installation of scientific and technical advice at the highest level of the incoming administration:

> Before and after the presidential election, the eventual president-elect
> needs advisors with expertise in science and technology (S&T) to advise
> on policy issues and help to locate a candidate for the position of Assis-
> tant to the President for Science and Technology (APST). . . . Soon after
> the election, the APST candidate is needed to help set priorities, plan
> strategy, advise the president-elect and cabinet designees, and find quali-
> fied candidates for key S&T positions.[1]

The election-campaign and transition entourages of George W. Bush
were unattended by scientific expertise. The campaign itself was devoid of
science-related discussions, except for general promises by Bush and Gore
to support science and double the NIH budget.

The president-elect's failure to share the academy's belief in his need
for scientific advice was hopefully attributed in scientific circles to the pressure of the truncated transition period. Once in office, however, George W.
Bush persisted in neglecting the academy's advice. Cabinet officers and
other senior officials were appointed, and priorities and strategies were devised, without the naming of a presidential science adviser or the evident
presence of scientific expertise.

In the opening weeks of the Bush administration, the Executive Office
Building suite of the Office of Science and Technology Policy was staffed
by an idle skeleton crew of civil servants, Clinton's political appointees all
having left by inauguration day. The budget that Bush presented to Congress at the end of February 2001 was composed without scientists on board

---

1. "The Presidential Appointment Process," Committee on Science, Engineeering, and
Public Policy, National Academy of Sciences, 2000.

at the White House to defend and promote the interests of the enterprise. Except for NIH, it was an extremely austere budget, containing the sparsest proposals for science since the terror-filled 1995 Republican Revolution. For NSF, Bush proposed a miserly increase of $56 million—insufficient to keep inflation from gnawing at its $4.5 billion budget. Even so, the new administration upheld the tradition of abundant billions for science. The hereditary feud of Democrats and Republicans over industrial research was manifested in Bush's decision to "suspend" the Advanced Technology Program, pending study of its effectiveness. The science lobbies pouted, complained to their congressional friends, but remained mystified about who, if anyone, at the White House was responsible for their sensitive interests.

The self-ghettoized, apolitical scientific enterprise rated scant notice at the commencement of the new administration.

Epilogue

> There is a tendency for scientists to assume that the social effects of science *must* be beneficial in the long run. This article of faith performs the function of providing a rationale for scientific research, but it is manifestly not a statement of fact. It involves the confusion of truth and social utility which is characteristically found in the non-logical penumbra of science.
> —Robert K. Merton, *Social Theory and Social Structure* (1957)

FROM OUR explorations, we know the following about the politics of the American scientific enterprise:

- The psyche of science is touched, and scientists are often energized, by magical thinking and voodoo misperceptions of plain matters of fact in the political history, financing, and public acceptance of science.

- Many important institutions of science are bureaucratically calcified, financially insecure, and risk-averse.

- An infinity of researchable topics renders science insatiable for money and increasingly indiscriminate in ways to get it.

- Within the metropolis of science, the academic core shuns conventional politics while vigorously employing nonelectoral techniques for obtaining government money, the denial of which it attributes to public and political ignorance and hostility.

These characteristics, all related, bring us to a difficult and essential question: Do the values and behavior of science in America warrant concern? We know that science fulfills its primary purpose, the production of knowledge—which, in complex relations with technology, responds to many needs of society or provides reasonable prospects for doing so. Why wonder, let alone fret, about the pathologies of science and the privileged place it occupies on the American political and social landscape as it performs its work? Despite the centrality of money in the politics of science, research is not a troublesome burden on America's economy. In our explorations, money has served as a measure for tracking the politics of science. But at the end of the last century, research and development, which encompass science, accounted for only about 2.8 percent of a gross domestic product of approximately $9 trillion a year. The United States and several other major industrialized nations spend roughly the same portion of their wealth on R&D. The United States is not staggering under the costs of research, though a contrary, misleading impression arises from contention over government support for science in the politically restrained federal budget. Science is financially bearable and productive. Why, then, worry about science in America?

In search of an answer, we must concentrate on two qualities of modern science: in both method and substance, it is poorly understood by the great majority of nonscientists; and it is increasingly potent in its effects on technology and society. Laypeople possess scarcely any understanding, and much misunderstanding, of what science is doing and can do. The franker apostles of the public-understanding movement concede the impenetrability of science, while insisting that their pop reformulations can bring enlightenment to the untutored. That the masses remain unenlightened, a central tenet of the public-understanding movement, is not attributable to lack of missionary efforts, but to the recondite nature of modern science. We will take a lesson on this point from an outstanding figure of the public-understanding movement, Stephen Jay Gould, of Harvard, a zoologist-geologist, popular author, and recent president of the AAAS.

> We have now reached the point where most technical literature not
> only falls outside the possibility of public comprehension but also (as we
> would all admit in honest moments) outside our own competence in sci-
> entific disciplines far removed from our personal expertise. I trust that
> we all regard this situation as saddening, even though we accept its
> necessity.[1]

If the masses are intellectually walled off from science at the professional level, as scientists convincingly tell us they are, then the tasks of understanding, surveillance, and assuring accountability should, we hope, be sit-

---

1. Stephen Jay Gould, *Science*, October 29, 1999.

uated elsewhere than in the scientific enterprise itself. But where? Auditors monitor banks; Wall Street rides herd on corporate managers; courts perform in open session attended by the press. Who watches over science? Politics has virtually abandoned oversight of science in favor of adulation and a rivers-and-harbors approach to obtaining a share for constituents. The principal exception, unworthy of emulation, is biomedical research associated with abortion, embryos, and related red-flag issues that are under the benighted scrutiny of the fundamentalist religious right. Overall, however, the deference of politicians to the barons of biomedical research is awesome and disturbing in its default on public accountability. The physical sciences stumbled over the Superconducting Super Collider, and thereby lost face with politics. But they are back in favor as the underpinnings of information technology and the wealth-producing Internet and its many business offshoots.

We cannot count on the invisible hand of storybook capitalism for monitoring or for socially beneficial guidance of science. The surviving conscience of academic science resounds with tales of corporate contamination in pursuit of profit, with the eager cooperation of academe. As an influence on the direction, priorities, and work practices of research, the vaunted marketplace is fickle, easily manipulated, and uncertainly linked to the needs of society. We should also recall that the ideology of basic science anchors the economic case for government support on the reluctance of private companies to finance research whose results will be made available to all, including competing firms. Industry unsentimentally abides by the imperatives of moneymaking—investing in science for profit, not to reinforce scientific independence, truthfulness, freedom of inquiry, professional collegiality, material public benefit, or cultural enrichment. For a long stretch in the late 1980s and early 1990s, industry retreated, without apology, from the support of basic research, in its own laboratories and in universities, because of disappointing financial returns. It came back when science was reevaluated as a good way to make money, in part by drawing more and more professors into trading academic independence for consulting fees and stock options. The press, with some exceptions, serves as a chorus of worshipful approval for science and technology. It sometimes shows repentance for its toady relationship with science by acknowledging, for example, previously celebrated "cures" that failed to cure. The mea culpas have improved but the journalistic performance has not. Under the banner of democratic participation, but mainly for stimulating popular support for money for research, the scientific enterprise is ostentatiously devoted to improving the public understanding of science. However, the many well-financed programs for that purpose are on a fool's errand, beneficial for the earnest functionaries they employ, but fundamentally ineffective. As its budgets and efforts expand, the PUS industry unfailingly reports that the understanding it works to elevate remains alarmingly low. Laypeople are in the dark and scientists know little about science beyond their own patch.

Responsibility Declined

Among the learned professions and various vocations, science alone has enshrined the principle that its practitioners are not responsible for the consequences of their acts. For our lesson on this matter, we take the words of a pioneering figure of scientific counsel to politics, Sir Solly Zuckerman (1904–93), a distinguished biologist, senior adviser to successive British governments during and after World War II, and prolific author on science and politics. Writing in 1970, Sir Solly noted, with seeming aloofness, the creation in Britain of the (now-long-gone) Society for Social Responsibility in Science—"the latest of a number of efforts to engage the social conscience of scientists," he pointed out. "As I have observed," Sir Solly explained, "scientists have to choose which way they salve their social consciences." But, indicating a condescending tolerance on his part, he went on to suggest the futility of their efforts:

> What needs to be borne in mind at all times . . . is that we cannot invest science with any inherent moral direction. That is imparted by the way science is used. . . . The element of the unknown in government increases with every step we are now taking to apply the fruits of science. If the basis of power is being changed, it is less by some governing body, however formed; and more and more by a process of applying scientific knowledge without any real possibility of determining its final consequences.[2]

The matter was stated another way by Tom Lehrer, the professor-balladeer, in his sardonic lyrics about Hitler's pioneering missile designer:

> "Once the rockets are up, who cares where they come down? That's not my department," says Wernher von Braun.

2. Sir Solly Zuckerman, *Beyond the Ivory Tower: The Frontiers of Public and Private Science* (New York: Taplinger, 1971), Pages 6, 7.

The tandem difficulties of understanding science and attempting to foresee its social consequences are inherently daunting, even for scientifically informed individuals who are politically alert and concerned. However, the difficulties are compounded by the dominant, and rising, commercial portion in the totality spent on science, and the academic sciences' continuing, boundless appetite for money, though government support for research has substantially increased. Here I reemphasize a paradoxical point that is not sufficiently recognized: While academe, presumably a publicly oriented, socially responsible enterprise, remains the intellectual core and the training ground of science, profit-seeking industry, not government, is the dominant source of money for research and development in America. True, the federal government provides well over half the money spent on research in universities. Nonetheless, industry is the giant on the national scene—rapidly, steadily growing over the past decade—while federal research spending has increased at a lesser pace. Industry now finances over 65 percent of the R&D in America. And, with the great wealth at its command, industry radiates its profit-seeking values to the other sectors of research.

Ravenous, as always, for money, academic science increasingly embraces marketplace values, with embarrassed apologies for departures from conflicting, cherished academic values, but with little restraint. The process is encouraged by government policies and spending priorities that smooth the path for academics and their institutions to make money from science by allowing them to receive patents and collect royalties from their government-financed research. Academic ties with industry, nourished with industrial money, naturally flourish in this supportive legal framework. Starting with hero worship in the business and scientific press, our culture celebrates the entrepreneurial academic, the professor who profitably straddles campus and corporation—as a startup pioneer in biotech or informatics, backed by venture capital, or as a richly rewarded consultant. With codes of conduct, universities attempt to reconcile marketplace values with their traditions of openness, collegiality, and devotion to academic duty, especially responsibility to students. But codes of conduct fare poorly at the juncture of knowledge and money. The neglect of students by commercially engaged professors is a widely lamented, but persistent, fact of modern higher education.

At present, the share of industrial research money spent in universities is a relatively small part of academe's total research expenditures, the balance coming from federal and state governments, endowments, tuition, personal gifts, and philanthropic foundations. But industrial money is especially attractive because it is so-called new money—a fresh vein of ore in heavily worked territories. In the United States, few universities have sat out the gold rush. For a handful of universities, the financial gains have been substantial, inspiring them, and less-successful institutions, to go for more. But, overall, the irony of academe's dealings with industry is so much ignominy and hypocrisy, for so little lucre; so much neglect, even betrayal, of principle and tradition, for minor gains. Count all the money paying for science in universities, and the portion from industry has leveled off at about 7 percent, with much of the money concentrated in a small number of schools. The concentration is also true of royalties from patented research findings licensed to industry, including much research financed by the U.S. government. The industrial research money going into academe is only one manifestation of corporate power on campus. Electronic and molecular millionaires, later joined by Internet millionaires, are the new celebrities, and glittering role models, for today's students. Campus-based laboratories not only draw industrial money but they also serve as home base and a resource for academics who take the initiative in seeking to turn knowledge into a product. Science without profit seeking continually recedes in the twenty-first century. How different it was not long ago: In 1955, Edward R. Murrow asked Jonas Salk, inventor of the polio vaccine, "Who holds the patent on this vaccine?" Salk replied, "Well, the people, I would say. There is no patent. Could you patent the sun?"[3] The modern-day entrepreneurs of science are backed by venture capital and guided by university offices of technology transfer and patent counsel. By the year 2000, over one thousand human genes had been patented and more gene patents were being applied for, while ethicists and scientists debated the propriety of staking claims to the fundamental biological material of human existence. Success stories from the scientific marketplace have stimulated universities to more determined pursuit of industrial support, more ardent declarations of piety, and sleazier behavior.

The Neglected Public Interest

Who minds the interests of the scientifically untutored public when science is crisscrossed with private deals and sugarplum visions of gargantuan wealth? We are familiar and comfortable with the powerful role of personal glory—manifested in acclaim by professional colleagues—as moti-

---

3. Richard Carter, *Breakthrough: The Saga of Jonas Salk* (New York: Trident Press, 1966), p. 283.

vation for achievement in science. As a medal-giving enterprise, science is perhaps exceeded only by nursery school graduations and the military services. But in science, status and glory have been joined, if not surpassed, by money as a motivating force, often to the neglect and abuse of traditional, and desirable, values of science. Number among the fading values of science the protection of the public, as revealed in numerous episodes of dangerous drugs coming to market and violations of candor and humanity in medical experiments with human subjects. Reports of declines in professional collegiality, honesty, and openness are commonplace in scientific journals, as are reports of misuse of public funds by individual scientists and their institutions. "Whistle-blowing" brings some misdeeds to public attention but, especially at the core of the tight-knit scientific enterprise, the practice is not conducive to career advancement.

Deviations from upright behavior are not new to science. The scientific enterprise, however, seeks political and popular trust, sovereignty, and public money on the basis of its claims of self-enforced purity. But more slippages from the ideal occur as science becomes bigger, richer, more insular in its detachment from politics, more powerful in its effects on society, more money-minded, while continuously pushed by government and lured by industry into commercial deals that conflict with traditional values and societal responsibilities. Though the venerable standards of right behavior in science are rhetorically honored, perhaps more so than ever, their power in the life of science has substantially diminished. Piety competes poorly with economics.

How do we know of these failures in science? In large part, from introspections at estimable institutions within the metropolis of science, which, whatever its failings, retains a strong reserve of ethical sensitivity and rectitude. Much of the evidence of ethical erosion in science has been revealed by dismayed scientists, and concerns tradeoffs between scientific independence and integrity, on the one hand, and, on the other, money. Decades of factual trimming by scientific leaders in their relations with government helped undermine the foundations of integrity. When anything goes in methods employed to panic the public and Congress into boosting the budget, lucrative deals in the commercial marketplace become a tempting, easy next step, even on terms that offend the fundamental precepts of scientific integrity. In the annals of science and politics, count as historic events of ethical consequence the Cold War red scares and other false alarms of foreign scientific superiority, the manufactured Ph.D. "shortages," the careless creation of surplus labor pools of scientists, the annual recurrences of financial "crises," the spurious announcements of imminent disease cures, the deliberate underpricing of megaprojects, the claims of popular hostility to science, and the public-understanding scam. All of these, with the special exception of the politically self-destructed Super Collider, passed the pragmatic test: they worked. In the journals of research and in the popular press, the good news of science today is increasingly accompanied by plaintive reports of dubious deals and casual betrayals of society's faith in the practitioners of science; in some instances, astonishing reports.

In this lamentable genre, I assign a high mark to a report that encapsulates the eroding ethical state of the American scientific enterprise. In bland prose, two Harvard academics related a farcical cameo of academic corruption in a letter to *Issues in Science and Technology,* a journal cosponsored by the National Academy of Sciences and the Center for the Study of Science and Society, at the University of Texas, at Dallas:

> At the Massachusetts Institute of Technology (MIT), an undergraduate was unable to complete a homework assignment that was closely related to work he was doing for a company because he had signed a nondisclosure agreement that prohibited him from discussing his work. Interestingly, the company that employed the student was owned by an MIT faculty member, and the instructor of the class owned a competing firm. In the end, the instructor of the course was accused of using his homework as a form of corporate espionage, and the student was given another assignment.[4]

The squalid dealings are deplorable on many grounds. However, the authors of the letter confined themselves to warning that restraints on open discussion could "result in scientists with an incomplete knowledge base, a less than adequate repertoire of research skills, a greater tendency to engage in secrecy in the future, and ultimately in the slowing of scientific advance." The dangers to science are evident. But so are the dangers to society, when apprentices in the arcane business of science are steeped in sleazy practices by their mentors.

Though better known and more successful than most in melding science, education, and business, MIT has ample company in the intense pursuit of industrial money, pious avowals of scientific and academic integrity,

4. Eric G. Campbell and David Blumenthal, Institute for Health Policy, Harvard Medical School, Massachusetts General Hospital, letter, *Issues in Science and Technology,* fall 1999. The episode they describe was previously reported in the *Wall Street Journal,* June 24, 1999: "MIT Students, Lured to New Tech Firms, Get Caught in a Bind: They Work for Professors Who May Also Oversee Their Academic Careers."

and profitable tolerance of behavior that invites the worst in the lexicon of corruption.

A Few Modest Prescriptions

After these hundreds of pages of descriptions and diagnoses, we arrive at a point where it is fair to ask what should be done, what can be done, and how, to make a better public servant of America's great scientific enterprise? Given the sciences' insulation from politics, the economic heft of industry, and the deep entrenchment of the scientific institutions at the core, few grounds exist for optimism about the prospects for beneficial change. Though the academic-government system is bureaucratically calcified, risk-averse, and unreceptive to innovation, its enormous wealth finances enough productivity to give credence to the battle cry of the status quo: "If it ain't broke, don't fix it." Look at the outpouring of discoveries and new technologies, and their bewilderingly rapid entry into the economy and culture. Surely, the new millennium brings in a golden age of science that surpasses the multiple golden ages in the last half of the last century. Why change anything?

My answer is that science is too powerful, too potent in its effects on society, and too arcane to be entrusted to the expanding alliance between a profession that has retreated into a ghetto and the commercial sector, with their shared focus on making money. While this relationship flourishes, a deadening complacency has settled over the institutions that should be protecting and advancing the public interest in science: the research agencies of the executive branch of government, Congress, the press, and, within science, leaders who should be stewards of scientific tradition, rather than apologists for its neglect. Science finds advantage and claims virtue in its detachment and aloofness from politics. But politics is the medium through which a society decides upon and implements its values and its choices. That the political system frequently goes awry and fails to work to its full potential of beneficial effects is a reason for involvement, not withdrawal. And this is especially so for an enterprise that draws heavily on the public purse and radiates powerful effects in all directions and on all things—while denying responsibility for the consequences of its work.

In its retreat into political isolation, science cannot detach itself from relations with the outside world. But increasingly, these relations are with industry seeking profits from academe's scientific strength and prestige, distressingly often to the detriment of scientific integrity and public well-being. The sciences' introspective agonizing over their falls from grace has continued long enough to sustain the expectation that few, if any, correctives will come from within. With rare exceptions, the public is satisfied to leave science to the scientists. Politicians put hands on science mainly to get a share for their voters. More satisfied than dissatisfied with things as they are, particularly the sudden gusher of money from federal surpluses at the turn of the century, none of the professional sectors concerned with science are inclined to push for change on their own. But coming from several directions, small impulses for change can reverberate through the various sectors with energizing effects beyond their original strength. The goal should be more involvement of science with politics, rather than less, because more would benefit society by opening science to public view and controversy. More involvement with politics would surely be uncomfortable for science, because it would threaten the reigning combination of support without scrutiny or responsibility. But it would be beneficial for society in its dependence on science, and possibly even helpful for science itself. The aim is to dislodge science from its comfortable ghetto and move it into the rough waters of the political mainstream.

The press, on its own, if it chooses, can make the transition from cheerleaders of science to independent observers. The symbiosis of science and science writing is evident in the uncritical journalistic mining of scientific and medical journals, the gullible acceptance of the sciences' hollow complaints of financial neglect, and, in general, the rote willingness to pass along to the public any pronouncement bearing the imprimatur of science, no matter how self-serving or foolish. On these and related matters, science writers themselves are critical and contrite about the performance of their profession, but the failings persist. The journalistic trumpeting of medical cures on the basis of wisps of evidence, even though accompanied by sober cautions against optimism, deserves to be severely throttled back, in recognition of an unfortunate reality: though news is sold around the clock, major advances in medicine come along infrequently. A prime, neglected topic for continuous journalistic scrutiny are the shrill Washington lobbies for science, heavily subsidized in roundabout fashion by federal funds through nonprofit tax exemptions. The public-understanding-of-science movement also merits an examination of its large expenditures versus unrealistic goals and meager accomplishments.

Uncritical congressional pandering to the financial demands of science will continue as long as the leaders of science are exempted from serious questioning about scientific priorities and choices. A skeptical science press, unawed by its subject, can encourage congressional initiative in assessing the spending choices of a government scientific bureaucracy that functions with little or no oversight, by politics or the press. A wondrous transformation is not to be expected in political dealings with science; a recommendation should not be confused with optimism. But continuous nudges, here and there, by the press could help transform congressional hearings on science from love fests to probing legislative inquiries.

No single disinfectant can cope with the corporate contamination of academic scientific integrity, especially when the recipients are willing, even eager, to be contaminated. But do not discount the power of public exposure of ethical failures in an institution that boasts of adherence to lofty ethical standards. Like crawly creatures that scurry from sunlight when the rock is lifted, the malfeasants of science do not relish exposure; and they are a gross embarrassment to their honorable colleagues.

WIDENING THE PATH TO POLITICS

The dearth of scientists in elective public office is in large part explained by the monastic nature of scientific training and career progress. But it also comes from a scientific culture that derides politics as unclean and debased, ethically distant from the ideals of science. For inspirational purposes, the concept of the role model is central to the culture of science, but in elective politics, role models with scientific credentials are few. The professional societies of science should advance beyond clichés and act on the recognition that participation in the nation's political life is a virtuous activity, good for the nation and good for science—and well worth the support of scientists. The fellowship programs that bring scientists and engineers to staff positions in Congress and elsewhere in Washington are useful but insufficient. Politics would benefit from more office-holding scientists; science would benefit, too. With that understanding as a starting point, the scientific enterprise should extend help to scientists who dare a plunge into politics. Physicians, lawyers, and schoolteachers apply collective strength to politics through political action committees and other organized political efforts. Why not scientists? As we saw, latent scientific support for scientists in politics was brought forth by scientists rallying to finance the congressional candidacy of physicist Rush Holt in 1998 and 2000. In modern America, participation in elective politics is measured in money and efforts to mobilize votes—activities (with rare, local exceptions) shunned by science ever since its one-time, 1964 venture into big-league politics. Antiseptic aloofness from elective politics contributes to the marginalized role of scientists in public affairs, as evidenced by their frustrations with the State Department and the compartmentalized presence of scientists in the White

House. With the prestige and glamour of presidential staff appointments, the White House scientists serve the presidency. But no one in the know in political Washington is fooled. The president's scientists are peripheral to the political structure of the presidency because science has made itself peripheral to politics.

No amount of sermonizing, here or elsewhere, or acknowledgment of the desirability of scientists in elective politics, can send a flood of mathematicians, physicists, and biochemists into seeking elective office. The laboratory is a poor launching pad for politics. However, the prevailing antipolitical culture of science encourages science to stick to the ghetto, and perhaps even to strengthen its walls. In the year 2000, over half a million holders of doctorates in the natural and physical sciences and in engineering were employed in the United States. Only four were members of Congress.

The isolation of science from politics is furthered by traditions that have become entombed in bureaucratic concrete. Consider a small but revealing item, the anachronistic title of the venerable National Science Foundation, an organization whose historic and spiritual significance for science transcends its money-giving capacity. NSF long ago acquired responsibilities beyond science, expanding into engineering and elementary and high school science education. However, the mandarins of academic basic research scramble to the ramparts at the hint of a title expansion that would accurately reflect the work of NSF. Their friends in Congress, with little interest in this obscure sectarian strife, find it simplest to leave the name unchanged. Meanwhile, the managers and beneficiaries of NSF express puzzlement and disappointment over the failure of politics to provide NSF with funds that match its expanded responsibilities. On good grounds, they contend that the foundation's entire budget, over $4.5 billion in 2001, could be well spent in any one of the three sectors: science, engineering, or education. By monopolizing the title, the scientists assert a symbolic claim over NSF, but at the cost of truth in labeling and the potential for broadening public and political recognition and the financial fortunes of the foundation.

In the senior echelons of academic science, political vision is blurred by reverence for basic research and outdated anxieties over its political support. As we observed in examining the proceedings of the Commission on the Future of NSF, the self-designated legatees of Vannevar Bush ominously chant that applied research drives out basic research. But through good times and bad, both the White House and Congress have strongly supported basic research, even during those periodic bouts of political infatuation with technology. For purposes of prodding science out of its isolation and broadening political and popular support for science, wonders might be achieved through an even more expansive name change: why not make it the National Science, Engineering, and Humanities Foundation, with perhaps a nonscientist at its head? The chieftains of science will gag on that proposal as a denial of their place in the sun. Congressional barons, sensitive about maintaining their jurisdictions, will resist loss of authority. The long-deprived humanists will probably fear a trick by the politically suave scientists and their political compatriots. But let's not file away that suggestion in hopes someday of a more favorable environment for reshaping the science wing of the U.S. government. A first step would be to recognize the beneficial potential of housing science and the humanities under the roof of a single government source of financial support. Nothing is certain in these matters, but the merger might contribute to the intellectual enrichment of both the sciences and the humanities. We might recognize, too, that separate bankrolls do not advance the goal of bringing together the two cultures.

Another beneficial step would be removal of the physical sciences from the chronically dysfunctional Department of Energy, and their resettlement into an independent agency or the well-run NSF. As for NIH, with an annual budget that exceeds $20 billion and continues to rise, the problem is bureaucratic elephantiasis in a government agency that holds a near-monopoly on finance for the biomedical sciences. A breakup of NIH into several separate government philanthropies for the medical sciences would introduce the vigor of competition into a sector that constantly flagellates itself for scientific conservatism and operational sloth—without correcting either.

All these suggested changes would contribute to opening the politics of science to public view and—horror of horrors—political scrutiny and contention. The object isn't more money or less money, though more could conceivably result from bringing science into the political mainstream. The object is to encourage science to bear its responsibilities in a new millennium dominated by the works of science. For over fifty years, the political instincts and talents of science have been heavily focused on a single goal: more money. The struggle is won. Politics and the public manifest the holiness of converts. Now it is time for the people and institutions of science to justify that confidence by stepping out into the unruly world of politics.

Appendix

Table 1

Support for Academic R&D, by Sector: 1953–98

Year	Total	Federal Government	State/Local Government	Industry	Academic Institutions	All Other Sources
			Millions of Current Dollars			
1953	273	149	40	21	37	27
1954	301	165	45	24	40	29
1955	342	191	50	27	42	32
1956	391	221	57	32	46	36
1957	433	242	64	37	51	40
1958	491	280	72	39	56	45
1959	586	356	81	40	61	50
1960	705	453	90	40	67	55
1961	834	557	101	40	75	62
1962	993	687	112	41	84	70
1963	1,178	839	125	41	96	78
1964	1,375	995	138	41	114	88
1965	1,595	1,167	150	42	136	101
1966	1,818	1,335	160	45	165	114
1967	2,035	1,491	168	52	200	126
1968	2,187	1,586	185	58	221	139
1969	2,280	1,624	208	61	233	155
1970	2,418	1,686	237	66	259	171
1971	2,565	1,760	262	72	290	182
1972	2,757	1,890	282	79	312	195
1973	2,953	2,009	302	90	343	211
1974	3,216	2,160	320	104	393	239
1975	3,570	2,400	348	118	432	272
1976	3,899	2,619	369	131	480	300
1977	4,346	2,893	394	155	569	337
1978	4,996	3,329	443	182	679	364
1979	5,715	3,848	482	215	785	386
1980	6,455	4,335	519	264	920	419
1981	7,085	4,670	581	314	1,058	463
1982	7,603	4,879	621	363	1,207	534
1983	8,251	5,210	658	432	1,357	595
1984	9,154	5,748	721	518	1,514	654
1985	10,308	6,388	834	630	1,743	713
1986	11,540	7,028	969	745	2,019	780
1987	12,807	7,768	1,065	831	2,262	882
1988	14,219	8,592	1,165	934	2,527	1,003
1989	15,631	9,314	1,274	1,062	2,852	1,131
1990	16,935	9,935	1,399	1,167	3,186	1,249
1991	18,201	10,662	1,482	1,243	3,457	1,358
1992	19,383	11,523	1,524	1,321	3,568	1,448
1993	20,499	12,311	1,550	1,388	3,719	1,533
1994	21,626	13,009	1,611	1,448	3,960	1,598
1995	22,647	13,604	1,741	1,539	4,139	1,624
1996	23,720	14,180	1,839	1,655	4,375	1,672
1997	25,001	14,849	1,940	1,773	4,686	1,754
1998	26,343	15,558	2,070	1,896	4,979	1,840

Table 1 *continued*

Year	Total	Source of Support				
		Federal Government	State/Local Government	Industry	Academic Institutions	All Other Sources
		Millions of Constant 1992 Dollars				
1953	1,350	738	196	102	181	134
1954	1,475	806	218	115	194	142
1955	1,649	921	241	130	203	154
1956	1,821	1,029	263	147	214	168
1957	1,952	1,089	289	165	230	180
1958	2,162	1,233	317	172	244	196
1959	2,553	1,549	351	172	266	216
1960	3,028	1,945	387	172	288	236
1961	3,541	2,364	427	170	316	263
1962	4,163	2,880	470	170	352	292
1963	4,884	3,476	518	168	398	323
1964	5,615	4,065	562	165	464	359
1965	6,388	4,675	599	166	545	403
1966	7,082	5,201	623	175	641	442
1967	7,682	5,627	634	194	753	474
1968	7,912	5,738	668	208	798	501
1969	7,878	5,610	719	209	805	536
1970	7,931	5,530	778	215	848	561
1971	8,001	5,488	817	225	903	568
1972	8,250	5,655	844	236	932	582
1973	8,365	5,690	854	254	972	596
1974	8,358	5,615	832	270	1,020	621
1975	8,481	5,702	827	280	1,025	646
1976	8,751	5,879	828	294	1,077	672
1977	9,163	6,098	831	326	1,199	709
1978	9,816	6,541	871	357	1,334	714
1979	10,347	6,967	872	388	1,421	698
1980	10,699	7,185	859	437	1,524	695
1981	10,733	7,074	880	476	1,602	701
1982	10,834	6,952	885	517	1,719	760
1983	11,278	7,121	899	590	1,854	813
1984	12,057	7,570	950	682	1,994	861
1985	13,126	8,134	1,061	802	2,220	908
1986	14,321	8,721	1,203	925	2,505	968
1987	15,419	9,352	1,282	1,000	2,723	1,061
1988	16,516	9,980	1,353	1,084	2,935	1,165
1989	17,422	10,381	1,419	1,183	3,178	1,261
1990	18,093	10,614	1,494	1,246	3,404	1,334
1991	18,702	10,956	1,522	1,277	3,552	1,395
1992	19,383	11,523	1,524	1,321	3,568	1,448
1993	19,972	11,994	1,510	1,352	3,623	1,493
1994	20,579	12,379	1,533	1,378	3,768	1,521
1995	21,065	12,654	1,619	1,431	3,850	1,511
1996	21,656	12,946	1,679	1,511	3,994	1,526
1997	22,408	13,309	1,739	1,589	4,200	1,572
1998	23,374	13,805	1,837	1,682	4,418	1,632

NOTES: Data for 1998 are preliminary, and data for all years are reported on a calendar year basis rather than an academic year basis. Data in subsequent appendix tables are reported on an academic year basis and therefore differ from those reported in this table.

SOURCE: National Science Foundation, Division of Science Resources Studies (NSF/SRS), *National Patterns of R&D Resources* (Arlington, VA: biennial series).

Table 2

International R&D Expenditures and R&D as a Percentage of GDP: 1981–98

Year	United States	Japan[a]	Germany[b]	France	United Kingdom	Italy	Canada
	Total R&D Expenditures in Billions of Constant 1992 U.S. Dollars[c]						
1981	109.5	NA	23.4	16.6	17.3	6.9	5.3
1982	115.2	36.9	24.2	17.7	NA	7.1	5.7
1983	123.1	40.0	24.7	18.3	16.9	7.6	5.8
1984	134.8	43.5	25.5	19.5	NA	8.3	6.3
1985	146.1	48.3	28.3	20.3	18.4	9.6	6.9
1986	149.3	49.0	29.1	20.6	19.3	9.9	7.2
1987	152.0	52.5	31.3	21.5	19.7	10.7	7.2
1988	155.5	56.6	32.4	22.5	20.3	11.4	7.4
1989	158.2	62.0	33.7	23.9	20.9	12.0	7.6
1990	162.4	67.3	34.1	25.4	21.3	12.8	8.0
1991	165.3	68.8	36.6	25.7	19.6	12.4	8.1
1992	165.2	69.2	36.8	26.4	20.6	12.3	8.3
1993	161.2	67.4	35.5	25.8	20.7	11.2	8.8
1994	160.7	66.4	35.5	25.2	20.7	10.8	9.1
1995	170.4	73.6	36.6	25.7	20.1	10.7	9.7
1996	179.4	77.9	36.4	25.4	20.4	11.0	9.9
1997	189.4	80.9	37.6	25.0	20.3	11.9	10.3
1998	201.6	NA	38.6	NA	NA	12.3	10.6
	R&D Expenditures as a Percentage of GDP						
1981	2.32	NA	2.43	1.97	2.37	0.88	1.25
1982	2.49	2.22	2.52	2.06	NA	0.91	1.40
1983	2.56	2.35	2.52	2.11	2.19	0.95	1.37
1984	2.62	2.43	2.51	2.21	NA	1.01	1.41
1985	2.74	2.58	2.72	2.25	2.23	1.13	1.45
1986	2.72	2.55	2.73	2.23	2.25	1.13	1.49
1987	2.69	2.62	2.88	2.27	2.19	1.19	1.44
1988	2.65	2.66	2.86	2.28	2.14	1.22	1.39
1989	2.61	2.77	2.87	2.33	2.15	1.24	1.39
1990	2.65	2.85	2.75	2.41	2.18	1.30	1.47
1991	2.72	2.82	2.61	2.41	2.11	1.24	1.53
1992	2.65	2.76	2.48	2.42	2.13	1.20	1.54
1993	2.52	2.68	2.42	2.45	2.15	1.14	1.60
1994	2.43	2.63	2.32	2.38	2.11	1.06	1.60
1995	2.52	2.77	2.31	2.34	2.02	1.01	1.58
1996	2.57	2.83	2.30	2.32	1.95	1.02	1.60
1997	2.60	2.92	2.31	2.23	1.87	1.08	1.60
1998	2.67	NA	2.33	NA	NA	1.11	1.60

NA = not available

[a] Due to changes in methodology, data on Japanese R&D in 1996 and later years may not be consistent with data in earlier years.

[b] German data before 1991 are for West Germany only.

[c] Conversions of foreign currencies to U.S. dollars are calculated with purchasing power parity exchange rates. Constant 1992 dollars are based on U.S. GDP implicit price deflators.

SOURCES: National Science Foundation, Division of Science Resources Studies (NSF/SRS), *National Patterns of R&D Resources: 1998*, NSF 99-335, by Steven Payson (Arlington, VA: 1999); and Organization for Economic Co-operation and Development, Main Science and Technology Indicators database (Paris: April 1999).

Science & Engineering Indicators—2000

Table 3

Percentage of World's Scientific and Technical Articles in a Set of Major International Journals, by Country: 1986–97

Science and Engineering

Region/Country	Percent of Articles Published In: 1986–88	1989–91	1992–94	1995–97	Region/Country	Percent of Articles Published In: 1986–88	1989–91	1992–94	1995–97
World	100.0	100.0	100.0	100.0	Singapore	0.1	0.1	0.2	0.2
United States	38.2	37.5	35.8	33.6	Thailand	0.1	0.1	0.1	0.1
Japan	7.1	7.5	8.1	8.5	Malaysia	0.0	0.0	0.1	0.1
United Kingdom	8.1	7.6	7.7	7.7	Pakistan	0.0	0.0	0.1	0.0
Germany	6.4	6.4	6.5	6.8	Philippines	0.0	0.0	0.0	0.0
France	4.5	4.5	4.9	5.1	Bangladesh	0.0	0.0	0.0	0.0
Canada	4.6	4.5	4.4	4.1	Other Asia	0.1	0.1	0.1	0.1
Russia	NA	NA	3.9	3.4	New Zealand	0.4	0.4	0.4	0.4
Italy	2.3	2.6	2.8	3.2	Former USSR, total	6.8	6.5	4.9	4.3
Australia	2.2	2.1	2.2	2.3	Ukraine	NA	NA	0.5	0.5
Netherlands	1.8	2.0	2.1	2.1	Belarus	NA	NA	0.1	0.1
Sweden	1.6	1.6	1.6	1.6	Uzbekistan	NA	NA	0.1	0.1
Denmark	0.8	0.7	0.8	0.8	Estonia	NA	NA	0.0	0.0
Finland	0.6	0.6	0.7	0.7	Latvia	NA	NA	0.0	0.0
Norway	0.5	0.5	0.5	0.5	Lithuania	NA	NA	0.0	0.0
Switzerland	1.2	1.2	1.3	1.3	Armenia	NA	NA	0.0	0.0
Belgium	0.8	0.8	0.8	0.9	Other former USSR	NA	NA	0.2	0.1
Austria	0.5	0.5	0.6	0.6	Brazil	0.4	0.5	0.6	0.7
Ireland	0.2	0.2	0.2	0.2	Argentina	0.3	0.3	0.3	0.4
Spain	1.1	1.3	1.8	2.0	Mexico	0.2	0.2	0.3	0.3
Greece	0.3	0.3	0.3	0.4	Chile	0.1	0.2	0.1	0.2
Turkey	0.1	0.1	0.2	0.4	Venezuela	0.1	0.1	0.1	0.1
Portugal	0.1	0.1	0.1	0.2	Colombia	0.0	0.0	0.0	0.0
Yugoslavia	0.2	0.3	0.2	0.1	Cuba	0.0	0.0	0.0	0.0
Croatia	NA	NA	0.1	0.1	Other C. and S. America	0.1	0.1	0.1	0.1
Slovenia	NA	NA	0.1	0.1	Israel	1.1	1.0	1.0	1.0

Poland	0.9	0.8	0.7	0.8
Czechoslovakia	0.6	0.6	0.6	NA
Czech Republic	NA	NA	0.4	0.4
Slovakia	NA	NA	0.2	0.2
Hungary	0.4	0.4	0.3	0.3
Bulgaria	0.2	0.2	0.2	0.2
Romania	0.1	0.1	0.1	0.1
Other Europe	0.0	0.0	0.0	0.1
India	2.0	1.9	1.8	1.7
China	0.7	1.0	1.2	1.5
Taiwan	0.2	0.4	0.7	0.9
South Korea	0.1	0.2	0.4	0.8
Hong Kong	0.1	0.2	0.2	0.3
Saudi Arabia	0.1	0.1	0.1	0.1
Iran	0.0	0.0	0.0	0.1
Jordan	0.0	0.0	0.0	0.0
Kuwait	0.1	0.1	0.0	0.0
Other Near East	0.1	0.1	0.1	0.1
South Africa	0.6	0.5	0.4	0.4
Egypt	0.2	0.3	0.2	0.2
Nigeria	0.2	0.2	0.1	0.1
Kenya	0.1	0.1	0.1	0.1
Morocco	0.0	0.0	0.0	0.0
Algeria	0.0	0.0	0.0	0.0
Tunisia	0.0	0.0	0.0	0.0
Other Africa	0.2	0.2	0.2	0.2

NA = not applicable

NOTES: Article counts are based on fractional assignments; for example, an article with two authors from different countries is counted as one-half article to each country. Former USSR is the combination of the former republics, and their "1992–94" averages refer to 1993–94 only; the same is true for these averages for Croatia, Slovenia, and Bosnia and Macedonia (included in other Europe). For Czech Republic and Slovakia, "1992–94" refers to 1994 only. German data are combined for all years. Details do not add to World averages because of the various bases for the 1992–94 country averages.

SOURCES: Institute for Scientific Information, Science Citation Index and Social Science Citation Index; CHI Research, Inc., Science Indicators database; and National Science Foundation, Division of Science Resources Studies (NSF/SRS), special tabulation.

Science & Engineering Indicators—2000

Table 4

Federal Obligations for Academic R&D, by Agency: 1970–99

Year	All Agencies	National Institutes of Health[a]	National Science Foundation	Department of Defense	National Aeronautics & Space Administration	Department of Energy[b]	Department of Agriculture	All Other Agencies
				Millions of Current Dollars				
1970	1,476	518	228	216	131	100	65	217
1971	1,645	603	267	211	134	94	72	264
1972	1,904	756	362	217	119	85	87	277
1973	1,917	826	374	204	111	83	94	224
1974	2,214	1,108	389	197	99	94	95	232
1975	2,411	1,154	435	203	108	132	108	272
1976	2,552	1,263	437	240	119	145	120	228
1977	2,905	1,399	511	273	118	188	140	276
1978	3,375	1,588	537	383	127	240	186	313
1979	3,889	1,880	617	438	139	260	200	355
1980	4,263	2,012	685	495	158	285	216	412
1981	4,466	2,101	702	573	171	300	243	376
1982	4,605	2,140	715	664	186	277	255	369
1983	4,966	2,392	783	724	189	297	275	306
1984	5,547	2,715	880	830	204	321	261	335
1985	6,340	3,158	1,002	940	237	357	293	352
1986	6,559	3,243	992	1,098	254	345	274	355
1987	7,337	3,903	1,096	1,017	294	386	280	361
1988	7,828	4,199	1,143	1,071	338	406	305	366
1989	8,672	4,565	1,254	1,189	434	454	328	449
1990	9,138	4,779	1,321	1,213	471	500	348	505
1991	10,169	5,521	1,436	1,152	534	621	386	520
1992	10,271	5,064	1,540	1,403	586	640	438	600
1993	11,208	5,848	1,562	1,616	614	583	433	553
1994	11,797	6,191	1,680	1,703	641	565	439	577
1995	11,928	6,271	1,734	1,589	708	594	435	597
1996	11,980	6,620	1,740	1,447	665	601	376	531
1997	12,561	7,057	1,819	1,345	719	583	441	597
1998 (est.)	13,273	7,509	1,908	1,394	719	584	454	705
1999 (est.)	14,171	8,188	2,150	1,373	719	598	403	739

Millions of Constant 1992 Dollars[c]

Year							
1970	4,930	1,730	762	723	438	335	216	726
1971	5,226	1,917	847	670	426	298	228	839
1972	5,774	2,293	1,099	657	361	256	265	841
1973	5,568	2,399	1,088	592	324	240	274	652
1974	5,998	3,001	1,055	535	268	255	257	628
1975	5,923	2,834	1,068	500	265	324	266	667
1976	5,846	2,893	1,000	551	272	332	274	523
1977	6,186	2,979	1,088	582	250	401	298	588
1978	6,712	3,157	1,068	762	253	477	371	623
1979	7,143	3,454	1,133	805	255	478	367	652
1980	7,192	3,394	1,155	836	266	481	365	695
1981	6,858	3,226	1,078	880	263	461	373	577
1982	6,606	3,069	1,025	952	266	397	366	530
1983	6,809	3,279	1,074	993	260	407	377	420
1984	7,322	3,584	1,162	1,096	269	423	345	443
1985	8,089	4,029	1,278	1,199	303	456	374	450
1986	8,137	4,023	1,230	1,362	315	428	339	440
1987	8,848	4,707	1,322	1,226	354	466	337	435
1988	9,122	4,893	1,333	1,248	394	473	355	426
1989	9,696	5,104	1,402	1,329	485	507	367	502
1990	9,809	5,130	1,418	1,303	505	537	374	542
1991	10,467	5,683	1,478	1,186	549	639	397	535
1992	10,271	5,064	1,540	1,403	586	640	438	600
1993	10,920	5,697	1,522	1,574	598	568	422	539
1994	11,222	5,890	1,598	1,620	610	537	417	549
1995	11,080	5,825	1,610	1,476	658	552	404	554
1996	10,915	6,032	1,585	1,318	605	548	343	484
1997	11,232	6,311	1,627	1,202	643	522	394	534
1998 (est.)	11,729	6,635	1,686	1,232	635	516	401	623
1999 (est.)	12,361	7,142	1,875	1,198	627	521	352	645

NOTE: Percentages may not total 100 because of rounding.

[a] Data for the National Institutes of Health include the Alcohol, Drug Abuse, and Mental Health Administration.

[b] Data for 1970 to 1973 are for the Atomic Energy Commission; data for 1974 to 1976 are for the Energy Research and Development Administration; data for 1977 and thereafter are for the U.S. Department of Energy.

[c] See appendix table 2-1 for gross domestic product implicit price deflators used to convert current dollars to constant 1992 dollars.

SOURCES: National Science Foundation, Division of Science Resources Studies (NSF/SRS), Federal Funds for Research and Development; Fiscal Years 1997, 1998, and 1999, Detailed Statistical Tables, Vol. 47, NSF 99-333 (Arlington, VA: 1999); and NSF, annual series.

Science & Engineering Indicators—2000

Table 5

Federal R&D Budget Authority, by Budget Function: Fiscal Years 1980–2000

Year	Total	National Defense	Total Nondefense	Health	Space Research and Technology	General Science	Energy	Natural Resources and Environment	Transportation	Agriculture	Education, Training, Employment and Social Services	International Affairs	Veterans Benefits and Services	Commerce and Housing Credit	Community and Regional Development	Administration of Justice	Income Security	General Government
								Millions of Current Dollars										
1980	29,739	14,946	14,793	3,694	2,738	1,233	3,603	999	887	585	468	125	126	101	119	45	47	22
1981	33,735	18,413	15,322	3,871	3,111	1,340	3,501	1,061	869	659	298	160	143	106	104	34	43	22
1982	36,115	22,070	14,045	3,869	2,584	1,359	3,012	965	791	693	228	165	139	104	63	31	32	10
1983	38,768	24,936	13,832	4,298	2,134	1,502	2,578	952	876	745	189	177	157	107	44	37	32	6
1984	44,214	29,287	14,927	4,779	2,300	1,676	2,581	963	1,040	762	200	192	218	110	46	24	26	8
1985	49,887	33,698	16,189	5,418	2,725	1,862	2,389	1,059	1,030	836	220	210	193	114	50	47	21	17
1986	53,249	36,926	16,323	5,565	2,894	1,873	2,286	1,062	917	815	248	211	183	111	88	41	14	14
1987	57,069	39,152	17,917	6,556	3,398	2,042	2,053	1,133	908	822	267	223	215	110	99	49	25	17
1988	59,106	40,099	19,007	7,076	3,683	2,160	2,126	1,160	896	882	285	224	195	122	108	51	23	17
1989	62,115	40,665	21,450	7,773	4,555	2,373	2,419	1,255	1,064	907	347	279	212	128	74	45	27	15
1990	63,781	39,925	23,856	8,308	5,765	2,410	2,726	1,386	1,045	950	374	375	216	140	67	44	33	17
1991	65,898	39,328	26,570	9,226	6,511	2,635	2,953	1,582	1,231	1,052	433	378	219	178	88	51	30	4
1992	68,398	40,083	28,315	10,055	6,744	2,659	3,153	1,688	1,523	1,155	365	371	245	192	95	51	37	4
1993	69,884	41,249	28,635	10,280	6,988	2,691	2,677	1,802	1,703	1,152	348	382	250	220	57	49	36	1
1994	68,331	37,764	30,567	10,993	7,414	2,712	2,873	1,865	1,888	1,193	373	254	265	380	68	46	45	0
1995	68,791	37,204	31,587	11,407	7,916	2,794	2,844	1,988	1,833	1,194	369	287	257	525	70	59	43	1
1996	69,049	37,801	31,248	11,867	7,844	2,846	2,521	1,802	1,795	1,176	331	252	259	432	50	56	16	2
1997	71,653	39,591	32,062	12,670	7,844	2,944	2,372	1,886	1,785	1,203	373	190	267	409	48	59	9	2
1998	73,569	39,823	33,746	13,576	8,198	4,360	948	1,855	1,833	1,249	444	163	587	398	42	72	18	2
1999	76,886	40,387	36,499	15,479	8,239	4,739	1,164	1,928	1,731	1,352	457	165	674	401	49	82	37	2
2000	75,415	37,710	37,704	15,824	8,422	4,951	1,348	1,944	1,840	1,522	491	115	663	448	51	59	24	2

Millions of Constant 1992 Dollars

Year																		
1980	50,167	25,213	24,954	6,231	4,619	2,080	6,078	1,685	1,496	987	789	211	213	170	201	76	79	37
1981	51,804	28,275	23,529	5,944	4,777	2,058	5,376	1,629	1,334	1,012	458	246	220	163	160	52	66	34
1982	51,800	31,655	20,145	5,549	3,706	1,949	4,320	1,384	1,135	994	327	237	199	149	90	44	46	14
1983	53,151	34,187	18,964	5,893	2,926	2,059	3,534	1,305	1,201	1,021	259	243	215	147	60	51	44	8
1984	58,361	38,658	19,703	6,308	3,036	2,212	3,407	1,271	1,373	1,006	264	253	288	145	61	32	34	11
1985	63,656	42,999	20,657	6,913	3,477	2,376	3,048	1,351	1,314	1,067	281	268	246	145	64	60	27	22
1986	66,066	45,814	20,252	6,904	3,591	2,324	2,836	1,318	1,138	1,011	308	262	227	138	109	51	17	17
1987	68,816	47,211	21,605	7,905	4,097	2,462	2,476	1,366	1,095	991	322	269	259	133	119	59	30	20
1988	68,880	46,730	22,150	8,246	4,292	2,517	2,478	1,352	1,044	1,028	332	261	227	142	126	59	27	20
1989	69,449	45,466	23,983	8,691	5,093	2,653	2,705	1,403	1,190	1,014	388	312	237	143	83	50	30	17
1990	68,471	42,861	25,610	8,919	6,189	2,587	2,926	1,488	1,122	1,020	402	403	232	150	72	47	35	18
1991	67,831	40,482	27,349	9,497	6,702	2,712	3,040	1,628	1,267	1,083	446	389	225	183	91	52	31	4
1992	68,398	40,083	28,315	10,055	6,744	2,659	3,153	1,688	1,523	1,155	365	371	245	192	95	51	37	4
1993	68,087	40,188	27,898	10,016	6,808	2,622	2,608	1,756	1,659	1,122	339	372	244	214	56	48	35	1
1994	65,003	35,925	29,078	10,458	7,053	2,580	2,733	1,774	1,796	1,135	355	242	252	361	65	44	43	0
1995	63,902	34,560	29,342	10,596	7,353	2,595	2,642	1,847	1,703	1,109	343	267	239	488	65	55	40	1
1996	62,909	34,440	28,469	10,812	7,146	2,593	2,296	1,642	1,635	1,071	302	230	236	393	46	51	15	2
1997	64,073	35,403	28,670	11,330	7,014	2,633	2,121	1,687	1,596	1,076	334	170	239	365	43	53	8	2
1998	65,007	35,189	29,818	11,996	7,244	3,853	838	1,639	1,620	1,104	392	144	519	352	37	64	16	2
1999	67,067	35,230	31,838	13,502	7,187	4,134	1,015	1,682	1,510	1,179	399	144	588	350	43	72	32	2
2000	64,496	32,250	32,245	13,533	7,203	4,234	1,153	1,663	1,573	1,302	420	98	567	383	44	50	21	2

NOTES: Data for 1980–98 are actual budget authority. Data for 1999 and 2000 are preliminary based on the FY 2000 budget. Beginning in FY 1988, a number of Department of Energy programs were reclassified from energy to general science.

SOURCE: National Science Foundation, Division of Science Resources Studies (NSF/SRS), *Federal R&D Funding by Budget Function: Fiscal Years 1998–2000* (Arlington, VA: forthcoming).

Science & Engineering Indicators—2000

Table 6

Federal Obligations for Basic Research: FY 1970–99 (Millions of Current Dollars)

Year	Total, All Agencies	USDA	DOC	DoD	Education	DOE	HHS	DOI	Justice	DOT	Treasury	Veterans Affairs	EPA	AID	NASA	NSF	NRC	Smithsonian Inst.	Tenn. Valley Authority	All Other Agencies
1970	1,926	116	18	317	NA	NA	NA	39	0	0	0	5	5	NA	358	245	NA	18	0	NA
1971	1,980	118	16	322	NA	NA	NA	42	0	0	0	3	6	NA	327	273	NA	15	0	NA
1972	2,187	137	8	329	NA	NA	NA	43	0	1	0	3	6	NA	332	368	NA	21	0	NA
1973	2,232	143	7	307	NA	NA	NA	49	2	0	0	3	9	NA	350	392	NA	24	0	NA
1974	2,388	146	8	303	NA	NA	NA	49	2	0	0	4	10	NA	306	415	0	25	0	NA
1975	2,588	154	8	300	NA	NA	NA	55	9	0	0	4	17	NA	309	486	0	25	0	NA
1976	2,767	171	11	327	NA	NA	NA	54	5	0	0	9	14	NA	293	524	0	26	0	NA
1977	3,259	204	12	373	NA	389	NA	64	5	0	0	9	8	NA	414	625	0	30	4	NA
1978	3,699	243	12	410	NA	441	NA	66	15	0	0	9	6	NA	480	678	0	35	4	NA
1979	4,193	256	12	472	21	463	NA	73	8	0	0	10	10	NA	513	733	0	37	4	NA
1980	4,674	276	16	540	18	523	1,763	72	10	0	2	14	14	0	559	815	0	41	5	NA
1981	5,041	314	16	604	21	586	1,900	81	5	1	2	15	11	0	531	897	0	45	5	NA
1982	5,482	331	17	687	14	642	2,145	76	3	1	2	13	33	0	536	916	0	52	5	NA
1983	6,260	362	19	786	14	768	2,475	103	4	1	4	14	22	4	617	999	0	56	6	NA
1984	7,067	393	21	848	12	830	2,815	126	5	3	4	16	30	3	755	1,132	0	64	5	NA
1985	7,819	445	23	861	15	943	3,233	138	4	1	4	15	39	2	751	1,262	0	71	6	NA
1986	8,153	433	27	924	5	960	3,339	133	5	1	5	15	38	4	917	1,275	0	63	7	NA
1987	8,942	446	26	908	3	1,069	3,828	135	8	5	5	17	31	3	1,014	1,371	0	72	4	5
1988	9,474	481	31	877	4	1,185	4,081	127	8	5	5	17	27	3	1,113	1,433	0	75	3	4
1989	10,602	485	29	948	4	1,411	4,388	189	7	0	3	17	51	3	1,417	1,563	0	80	4	4
1990	11,286	519	31	948	5	1,505	4,649	205	9	0	3	16	74	5	1,637	1,586	0	84	5	4
1991	12,171	558	34	994	9	1,687	5,050	229	6	0	4	16	91	6	1,706	1,676	0	98	2	5
1992	12,490	595	35	1,099	8	1,736	5,059	231	5	1	4	16	110	6	1,738	1,742	0	98	2	6
1993	13,399	616	37	1,268	5	1,755	5,697	230	5	2	7	13	89	8	1,800	1,744	0	102	10	11
1994	13,524	606	40	1,201	6	1,603	5,884	83	6	3	0	14	101	8	1,964	1,871	0	124	9	6
1995	13,877	595	39	1,248	6	1,634	6,061	55	8	47	0	12	70	2	1,978	1,973	0	124	9	14
1996	14,464	550	38	1,138	4	1,930	6,505	56	13	38	0	13	52	2	1,981	2,007	0	127	0	12
1997	14,942	590	39	1,023	3	1,971	6,852	56	12	38	0	14	51	2	2,095	2,057	0	130	0	12
1998	15,862	598	41	1,016	5	2,077	7,361	57	19	59	0	14	57	1	2,246	2,165	0	134	0	11
1999	16,914	609	43	1,106	8	2,227	7,977	66	26	56	0	16	57	1	2,127	2,442	0	142	0	11

NA = not applicable, due to the agency in question not existing, or not having the same definition, in prior years; USDA = U.S. Department of Agriculture; NASA = National Aeronautics and Space Administration; NSF = National Science Foundation; NRC = National Research Council; AID = Agency for International Development; DOC = Department of Commerce; DOD = Department of Defense; DOE = Department of Energy; HHS = Health and Human Services; DOI = Department of the Interior; DOT = Department of Transportation; EPA = Environmental Protection Agency.

SOURCES: National Science Foundation, Division of Science Resources Studies (NSF/SRS), *Federal Funds for Research and Development, Fiscal Years 1997, 1998, and 1999*, NSF 99-333, Project Officer, Ronald L. Meeks (Arlington, VA: 1999); and NSF/SRS, *Federal Funds Survey, Detailed Historical Tables, Fiscal Years 1951–99*, NSF 99-347, Project Officer, Ronald L. Meeks (Arlington, VA: 1999).

Science & Engineering Indicators—2000

Table 7

Federal Obligations for Basic Research: FY 1970–99 (Millions of Constant 1992 Dollars)

Year	Total, All Agencies	USDA	DOC	DoD	Education	DOE	HHS	DOI	Justice	DOT	Treasury	Veterans Affairs	EPA	AID	NASA	NSF	NRC	Smithsonian Inst.	Tenn. Valley Authority	All Other Agencies
1970	6,435	387	61	1,059	NA	NA	NA	132	0	1	0	18	18	NA	1,195	818	NA	61	0	NA
1971	6,292	376	50	1,024	NA	NA	NA	133	0	1	0	10	19	NA	1,040	866	NA	48	0	NA
1972	6,633	416	24	997	NA	NA	NA	131	0	2	0	10	19	NA	1,006	1,115	NA	65	0	NA
1973	6,485	415	19	891	NA	NA	NA	142	6	0	0	9	26	NA	1,018	1,140	NA	70	0	NA
1974	6,469	395	21	821	NA	NA	NA	132	6	1	0	10	26	NA	829	1,125	NA	67	0	NA
1975	6,358	379	20	737	NA	NA	NA	135	23	0	0	10	43	NA	760	1,194	0	61	0	NA
1976	6,340	393	25	749	NA	NA	NA	124	10	0	0	20	31	NA	672	1,200	0	59	0	NA
1977	6,938	435	26	795	NA	829	NA	135	11	0	0	19	18	NA	881	1,330	0	63	8	NA
1978	7,356	483	23	816	NA	876	NA	131	29	0	0	18	12	NA	954	1,349	0	69	8	NA
1979	7,701	471	22	866	38	850	NA	133	15	0	0	17	19	0	942	1,347	0	68	8	NA
1980	7,885	465	27	912	30	882	2,973	121	16	0	3	24	23	0	943	1,375	0	69	8	NA
1981	7,742	482	25	928	32	900	NA	124	7	2	4	23	16	0	816	1,377	0	69	7	NA
1982	7,862	474	24	985	20	921	2,726	110	4	1	3	19	47	0	768	1,314	0	75	7	NA
1983	8,583	496	26	1,077	19	1,053	2,940	141	5	1	5	19	30	6	846	1,370	0	77	7	NA
1984	9,329	518	27	1,119	16	1,096	3,267	166	6	5	5	21	39	4	996	1,495	0	84	8	NA
1985	9,977	568	30	1,099	19	1,203	3,591	176	5	1	6	20	49	2	958	1,610	0	91	7	NA
1986	10,115	537	33	1,146	6	1,191	4,011	165	7	1	6	18	48	5	1,137	1,582	0	79	9	NA
1987	10,783	538	31	1,095	4	1,289	4,616	163	10	0	6	20	37	4	1,223	1,653	0	87	5	6
1988	11,041	561	36	1,022	5	1,381	4,756	148	9	0	6	20	31	3	1,297	1,670	0	87	3	5
1989	11,854	542	32	1,060	4	1,578	4,906	211	8	0	3	19	57	3	1,584	1,748	0	89	3	4
1990	12,116	557	33	1,018	5	1,616	4,991	220	10	0	3	17	79	5	1,757	1,703	0	90	5	4
1991	12,528	574	35	1,023	9	1,736	5,198	236	6	0	4	16	94	6	1,756	1,725	0	101	2	5
1992	12,490	595	35	1,099	8	1,736	5,059	231	5	1	4	16	110	6	1,738	1,742	0	98	2	6
1993	13,054	600	36	1,235	5	1,710	5,550	224	5	2	7	13	87	8	1,754	1,699	0	99	10	11
1994	12,865	577	38	1,142	5	1,525	5,597	79	6	3	0	14	96	2	1,868	1,780	0	118	8	6
1995	12,891	553	37	1,160	5	1,518	5,630	51	8	44	0	12	65	2	1,837	1,833	0	115	8	13
1996	13,178	501	34	1,037	3	1,758	5,926	51	11	35	0	11	47	2	1,805	1,829	0	116	8	11
1997	13,362	528	35	915	3	1,762	6,127	50	11	34	0	12	46	0	1,873	1,839	0	116	0	11
1998	14,016	528	36	897	5	1,836	6,504	50	16	52	0	12	50	1	1,984	1,913	0	118	0	10
1999	14,754	531	37	965	7	1,942	6,958	58	23	49	0	14	50	1	1,855	2,130	0	124	0	10

NA = not applicable, due to the agency in question not existing, or not having the same definition, in prior years; USDA = U.S. Department of Agriculture; NASA = National Aeronautics and Space Administration; NSF = National Science Foundation; NRC = National Research Council; AID = Agency for International Development; DOC = Department of Commerce; DOD = Department of Defense; DOE = Department of Energy; HHS = Health and Human Services; DOI = Department of the Interior; DOT = Department of Transportation; EPA = Environmental Protection Agency.

SOURCES: National Science Foundation, Division of Science Resources Studies (NSF/SRS), *Federal Funds for Research and Development: Fiscal Years 1997, 1998, and 1999*, NSF 99-333, Project Officer, Ronald L. Meeks (Arlington, VA: 1999); and National Science Foundation, Division of Science Resources Studies, *Federal Funds Survey, Detailed Historical Tables, Fiscal Years 1951–99*, NSF 99-347, Project Officer, Ronald L. Meeks (Arlington, VA: 1999).

Science & Engineering Indicators—2000

Table 8

Responses to and Mean Scores on the Attitude Toward Organized Science Scale, by Selected Characteristics: 1983–99 (Selected Years)

	1983	1985	1988	1990	1992	1995	1997	1999
	Percent of Public							
Agree that "science and technology are making our lives healthier, easier, and more comfortable"	84	86	87	84	85	86	89	90
Agree that "the benefits of science are greater than any harmful effects"	57	68	76	72	73	72	75	75
Disagree that "science makes our way of life change too fast"	50	53	59	60	63	60	61	57
Disagree that "we depend too much on science and not enough on faith"	43	39	43	44	45	44	48	46

SOURCES: National Science Foundation, Division of Science Resource Studies (NSF/SRS), *NSF Survey of Public Attitudes Toward and Understanding of Science and Technology, 1999* (and earlier years). For a complete set of data from the survey, see J.D. Miller and L. Kimmel, *Public Attitudes Toward Science and Technology, 1979–1999, Integrated Codebook* (Chicago: International Center for the Advancement of Scientific Literacy, Chicago Academy of Sciences, 1999); and unpublished tabulations.

Science & Engineering Indicators—2000

Glossary of Abbreviations and Acronyms

AAAS	American Association for the Advancement of Science
AAMC	Association of American Medical Colleges
AAU	Association of American Universities
ABM	Antiballistic Missile
ACDA	Arms Control and Disarmament Agency
ACS	American Chemical Society
APS	American Physical Society
ARPA	Advanced Research Projects Agency
AUTM	Association of University Technology Managers
CIFS	Committee on the International Freedom of Scientists
CBO	Congressional Budget Office
COSSA	Consortium of Social Science Associations
DARPA	Defense Advanced Research Projects Agency
DOE	Department of Energy
EPSCoR	Experimental Program to Stimulate Cooperative Research
FASEB	Federation of American Societies for Experimental Biology
FEC	Federal Election Commission
FS&T	Federal Science and Technology
FAS	Federation of American Scientists
FY	Fiscal Year
GAC	General Advisory Committee, of Atomic Energy Commission
GAO	General Accounting Office
GDP	Gross Domestic Product
GRALE	General Research at the Leading Edge, Institute for
HHS	Health and Human Services, Department of
IRB	Institutional Review Board
ISE	Informal Science Education
MIT	Massachusetts Institute of Technology
NAE	National Academy of Engineering
NAS	National Academy of Sciences
NASA	National Aeronautics and Space Administration

NASW	National Association of Science Writers
NBS	National Bureau of Standards
NBS	National Biological Service (formerly National Biological Survey)
NIH	National Institutes of Health
NIST	National Institute of Standards and Technology
NRF	National Research Foundation
NSB	National Science Board
NS&E	National Science and Engineering
NSF	National Science Foundation
NSTC	National Science and Technology Council
OECD	Organization for Economic Cooperation and Development
OES	Oceans and International Environmental and Scientific Affairs, Bureau of, State Department
OMB	Office of Management and Budget
OPRR	Office for Protection from Research Risks
OSTP	Office of Science and Technology Policy
OTA	Office of Technology Assessment
PCAST	President's Committee of Advisors for Science and Technology
PRA	Policy Research and Analysis, Division of, NSF
PSAC	President's Science Advisory Committee
PUS	Public Understanding of Science
SBIR	Small Business Innovation Research
SGR	*Science & Government Report*
SRS	Science Resources Studies, Division of, NSF
SSC	Superconducting Super Collider
SST	Supersonic Transport
ST&H	Science, Technology and Health
STIA	Scientific, Technological, and International Affairs, Directorate of, NSF
UCS	Union of Concerned Scientists

Bibliography

Aerospace Facts & Figures: 1994–1995. Washington, D.C.: Aerospace Industries Association of America, 1994.

American Association for the Advancement of Science. *AAAS Report XVII: Research and Development FY 1993*. Washington, D.C.: American Association for the Advancement of Science, Intersociety Working Group, 1992.

———. *AAAS Report XXIII: Research and Development FY 1999*. Washington, D.C.: American Association for the Advancement of Science, Intersociety Working Group, 1998.

———. *AAAS Report XXIV: Research and Development FY 2000*. Washington, D.C.: American Association for the Advancement of Science, Intersociety Working Group, 1999.

———. *AAAS Science and Technology Policy Yearbook 1997*. Albert H. Teich et al., eds. Washington, DC: Committee on Science, Engineering, and Policy, American Association for the Advancement of Science, 1997.

———. *Campaign Update*. Washington, D.C.: American Association for the Advancement of Science, 1997.

———. *Congressional Action on Research and Development in the FY 1996 Budget*. Washington, D.C.: American Association for the Advancement of Science, 1996.

———. *Congressional Action on Research and Development in the FY 2000 Budget*. Kei Koizumi et al. Washington, D.C.: American Association for the Advancement of Science, 1999.

American Council on Education. *The American College President, 1998*. Washington, D.C.:

American Physical Society. *Their Most Productive Years*. Prepared by Roman Czujko, Daniel Kleppner, and Stuart Rice. Washington, D.C.: Distributed by the American Physical Society, Office of Public Affairs, 1990.

———. "Report to the American Physical Society of the Study Group on the Science and Technology of Directed Energy Weapons." *Review of Modern Physics* 59, no. 3, part 2 (July 1987).

———. "Statement on Physics Funding and the SSC." *APS Council*, January 20, 1991.

Anfinsen, Christian B., et al. Letter to the editor. *Science*, May 3, 1985.

Angell, Marcia, et al. "Disclosure of Authors' Conflicts of Interest: A Follow-up." *New England Journal of Medicine,* February 24, 2000.

Association of American Medical Colleges. "Developing a Code of Ethics in Research: A Guide for Scientific Societies." Executive summary, 1997.

———. "Educating Medical Students: Assessing Change in Medical Education (1992)." *The Road to Implementation* (ACME-TRI report with supplements). Academic Medicine Supplement vol. 68, no. 6, June 1993.

Association of University Technology Licensing Managers. *AUTM Licensing Survey: Fiscal 1996.* Norwalk, Conn.: AUTM, 1997.

Baltimore, David, "Research Endangered." *Technology Review,* May/June 1990.

Barfield, Claude E., ed. *Science for the 21st Century: The Bush Report Revisited.* Washington, D.C.: AEI Press, 1997.

Barone, Michael, et al. *Almanac of American Politics 1996.* Washington, D.C.: National Journal, 1995.

———. *Almanac of American Politics 2000.* Washington, D.C.: National Journal, 1999.

Barzun, Jacques. *Science: The Glorious Entertainment.* New York: Harper & Row, 1964.

Blanpied, William A. "Inventing U.S. Science Policy." *Physics Today,* February 1998.

Blumenthal, David, et al. "Participation of Life-Science Faculty in Research Relationships with Industry." *New England Journal of Medicine,* December 5, 1996.

Boffey, Philip M. *The Brain Bank of America.* New York: McGraw-Hill, 1975.

Bromley, D. Allan. *The President's Scientists: Reminiscences of a White House Science Advisor.* New Haven, Conn.: Yale University Press, 1994.

Brown, George E., Jr. "Defining Values for Research and Technology." *Chronicle of Higher Education,* July 10, 1998.

Brown, Kenneth. *Downsizing Science: Will the United States Pay a Price?* Washington, D.C.: AEI Press, 1998.

Bush, Vannevar. *Science, The Endless Frontier.* 40th anniversary edition. Washington, D.C.: National Science Foundation, 1990.

———. *Pieces of the Action.* New York: William Morrow & Co., 1970.

Cahn, Anne Hessing. "Eggheads and Warheads: Scientists and the ABM." Ph.D. diss., MIT Center for International Studies, Science and Public Policy Program, 1971.

Carnegie Commission on Science, Technology, and Government. *Science and Technology and the President.* New York: Carnegie Commission, 1988.

———. *Science and Technology in U.S. International Affairs.* New York: Carnegie Commission, 1992.

Carter, Richard. *Breakthrough: The Saga of Jonas Salk.* New York: Trident Press, 1966.

Clinton, Bill. *Health Security: The President's Report to the American People*. Domestic Policy Council, 1993.

———. *A Vision of Change for America, 1993*. Report accompanying address to joint session of Congress. Washington, D.C.: U.S. Government Printing Office, February 17, 1993.

Cohen, Jordan. "IRBs: 'In Jeopardy,' or in Need of Support?" *Reporter* (newsletter of Association of American Medical Colleges), August 1998.

Congressional Budget Office. *Federal Financial Support of Business*. Washington, D.C.: Congressional Budget Office, 1995.

———. *Reducing the Deficit: Spending and Revenue Options: A Report to the Senate and House Committees on the Budget*. Washington, D.C.: Congressional Budget Office, 1993.

———. *Risks and Benefits of Building the Superconducting Super Collider: A Special Study*. Washington, D.C.: Congressional Budget Office, 1988.

Congressional Research Service. *Analysis of Ten Selected Science and Technology Policy Studies*. William C. Boesman, coordinator, 1997.

———. *Research and Development Funding: Fiscal Year 2000*. Issue brief, 1999.

Cook, Constance Ewing. *Lobbying for Higher Education: How Colleges and Universities Influence Federal Policy*. Nashville: Vanderbilt University Press, 1998.

Council on Competitiveness. *Challenges: Competing Through Innovation*. Newsletter, winter 1999.

———. *The New Challenge to America's Prosperity: Findings from the Innovation Index*. Washington, D.C.: Council on Competitiveness, 1999.

———. *Gaining New Ground: Technology Priorities for America's Future*. Washington, D.C.: Council on Competitiveness, 1991.

David, Edward E., Jr. "The Federal Support of Mathematics." *Scientific American*, May 1985.

Davidson, Keay. *Carl Sagan: A Life*. New York: John Wiley & Sons, 1999.

Department of Commerce. *Statistical Abstract of the United States*. Washington, D.C.: Government Printing Office, 1994.

Department of Energy Advisory Board. *Alternative Futures for the Department of Energy National Laboratories*. Washington, D.C.: Department of Energy, 1995.

Dyson, Freeman. *Imagined Worlds*. Cambridge: Harvard University Press, 1997.

Ehrlichman, John. *Witness to Power: The Nixon Years*. New York: Simon & Schuster, 1982.

Eisenhower, Dwight D. *Waging Peace: The White House Years: A Personal Account, 1956–1961*. New York: Doubleday, 1965.

England, J. Merton. *A Patron of Pure Science: The National Science Foundation's Formative Years, 1945–57*. Washington, D.C.: National Science Foundation, 1982.

Enterprise University. Tucson, Ariz.: Research Corporation, 1997.

Fisher, Frank. *Technology and the Politics of Expertise.* Newbury Park, Calif.: Sage Publications, 1990.

Friedman, Jerome. "Meeting the Challenges of the 21st Century." *APS News,* March 1999.

Gardner, Marjorie. "How Does Ivan's and Yelena's Education Compare with Johnny's and Helen's?" *CHEMTECH,* August 1988.

Garrison, Howard, et al. *A Profile of the Members of FASEB Societies: NIH Awards, Degrees, and Institutional Affiliations.* Federation of American Societies for Experimental Biology, 1999.

Geiger, Roger, and Irwin Feller. "The Dispersion of Academic Research in the 1980s." *Journal of Higher Education,* May/June 1995.

General Accounting Office. *Department of Energy: Contract Reform Is Progressing, But Full Implementation Will Take Years* (GAO/RCED-97-18). Washington, D.C.: General Accounting Office, 1997.

———. *Department of Energy: Funding and Workforce Reduced, but Spending Remains Stable* (GAO/RCED-97-96). Washington, D.C.: General Accounting Office, 1997.

———. *Department of Energy: Uncertain Progress in Implementing National Laboratory Reforms* (GAO/RCED-98-197). Washington, D.C.: General Accounting Office, 1998.

———. *Federal R&D Laboratories, Letter Report to Rep. John Kasich, Chairman, House Budget Committee* (GAO/RCED/NSIAD-96-78R). Washington, D.C.: General Accounting Office, 1996.

———. *Federal Research: Evaluation of Small Business Innovation Research Can Be Strengthened* (GAO/RCED-99-114). Washington, D.C.: General Accounting Office, 1999.

———. *Hospital Costs: Adoption of Technologies Drives Cost Growth* (GAO/HRD-92-120). Washington, D.C.: General Accounting Office, 1992.

———. *Scientific Research: Continued Vigilance Critical in Protecting Human Subjects* (GAO/HEHS-96-72). Washington, D.C.: General Accounting Office, 1996.

———. *Space Station: Estimated Total U.S. Funding Requirements* (GAO/NSIAD-95-163). Washington, D.C.: General Accounting Office, 1995.

———. *Space Station: Information on National Security Applications and Cost* (GAO/NSIAD-93-208). Washington, D.C.: General Accounting Office, 1993.

———. *Space Station: NASA's Search for Design, Cost, and Schedule Stability Continues* (GAO/NSIAD-91-125). Washington, D.C.: General Accounting Office, 1991.

George Washington University Center for the History of Recent Science. "Science in Crisis at the Millennium." Conference, September 19, 1996 (unpublished transcript).

Gergen, David. "No Time for Complacency: The U.S. Economy Leads the World, but Its Foundations Are Rusting." *U.S. News & World Report,* March 29, 1999.

Gilbert, H., et al. "Are Increasing Survival Rates Evidence of Success Against Cancer?" *JAMA*, June 14, 2000.

Gilpin, Robert. *American Scientists and Nuclear Weapons Policy*. Princeton, N.J.: Princeton University Press, 1962.

Gilpin, Robert, and Christopher Wright, eds. *Scientists and National Policy Making*. New York: Columbia University Press, 1964.

Gingrich, Newt. *To Renew America*. New York: HarperCollins, 1995.

Glanz, James. "Human Rights Fades as a Cause for Scientists." *Science*, October 9, 1998.

Golden, William T. *Impacts of the Early Cold War on the Formulation of U.S. Science Policy: Selected Memoranda of William T. Golden, October 1950–April 1951*. Edited by William A. Blanpied. Washington, D.C.: American Association for the Advancement of Science, 1995.

———. "Then and Now: Personal Reflections." In *Science and Technology Advice to the President, Congress, and Judiciary*, ed. William T. Golden. New York: Pergamon Press, 1988.

Gottfried, Kurt. "Physicists in Politics." *Physics Today*, March 1999.

Gould, Stephen Jay. "Take Another Look." *Science*, October 29, 1999.

Graham, Loren R. *What Have We Learned About Science and Technology from the Russian Experience?* Stanford, Calif.: Stanford University Press, 1998.

Greenberg, Daniel S. "David and Indifference." *Saturday Review of Science*, September 30, 1972.

———. *The Politics of Pure Science*. New York: New American Library, 1967. Reprint, University of Chicago Press, 1999.

———. "Scientists Must Join the Fray." *Technology Review*, February–March, 1996.

———. "Venture into Politics: Scientists and Engineers in the Election Campaign." *Science*, December 11, 18, 1964.

———. "What Ever Happened to the War on Cancer?" *Discover Magazine*, March 1986.

Greene, Mott T. "What Cannot Be Said in Science." *Nature*, August 14, 1997.

Hart, David M. *Forged Consensus: Science, Technology, and Economic Policy in the United States, 1921–1953*. Princeton, N.J.: Princeton University Press, 1998.

Hartung, William D., et al. *The Strategic Defense Initiative: Costs, Contractors and Consequences*. New York: Council on Economic Priorities, 1985.

Hartz, Jim, and Rick Chappell. *Worlds Apart: How the Distance Between Science and Journalism Threatens America's Future*. Nashville, Tenn.: First Amendment Center, 1997.

Hirsch, Eric. *State Legislators' Occupations: 1993 and 1995*. Denver, Colo.: National Conference of State Legislators, 1996.

Horne, William. "When Higher Ed Lobbies." *University Business*, July/August 1998.

House, Peter W., and Roger D. Shull. *The Practice of Policy Analysis: Forty Years of Art and Technology*. Washington, D.C.: The Compass Press, 1991.

Imura, Hiroo. "Science Education for the Public." *Science,* June 11, 1999.

Industrial Research Institute. *Industrial Research and Development Facts, 1997.* Washington, D.C.: Industrial Research Institute, 1997.

Jankowski, John E. "Statistical Data and Their Impact on University Research Efforts: Trends and Patterns of Academic R&D Expenditures." Paper delivered at Conference on Performance Measurements for Research and Development in Universities and Colleges, sponsored by the International Quality and Productivity Center, Washington, D.C., May 18–19, 1998.

Johnson, Lyndon Baines. *The Vantage Point: Perspectives on the Presidency 1963–1969.* New York: Holt, Rinehart and Winston, 1971.

Kassirer, Jerome P. "Goodbye, For Now." *New England Journal of Medicine,* August 26, 1999.

Kassirer, Jerome P., and Marcia Angell. "The High Price of Product Endorsement." *New England Journal of Medicine,* September 4, 1997.

Kennedy, Donald. *Academic Duty.* Cambridge: Harvard University Press, 1997.

Kevles, Daniel J. *The Physicists: The History of a Scientific Community in Modern America.* New York: Alfred A. Knopf, 1978.

Killian, James R., Jr. *Sputnik, Scientists and Eisenhower: A Memoir of the First Special Assistant to the President for Science and Technology.* Cambridge: MIT Press, 1977.

King, Jonathan. "The Loss of David Baltimore and the Role of the Dingell Hearings." *MIT Faculty Newsletter,* November 1989.

Kistiakowsky, George B. *A Scientist at the White House: The Private Diary of President Eisenhower's Special Assistant for Science and Technology.* Cambridge: Harvard University Press, 1976.

Lane, Neal, "The Arlington Rotary Club." *American Scientist,* May–June 1996.

Lanouette, William, with Bela Szilard. *Genius in the Shadows: A Biography of Leo Szilard, the Man Behind the Bomb.* New York: Charles Scribner's Sons, 1992.

Lederman, Leon. "The Privilege and Obligation of Being a Scientist." *Physics Today,* April 1991.

Lederman, Leon, with Dick Teresi. *The God Particle.* New York: Houghton Mifflin, 1993.

Leiden, Jeffrey. "Gene Therapy Enters Adolescence." Review of *The Development of Human Gene Therapy,* ed. by Theodore Friedman. *Science,* August 20, 1999.

Lomask, Milton. *A Minor Miracle: An Informal History of the National Science Foundation* (NSF 76-18). Washington, D.C.: National Science Foundation, 1976.

Lubell, Michael S. "Inside the Beltway." *APS News,* August/September 1998.

Margenau, Henry, David Bergamini, and the editors of *Life. The Scientist.* Life Science Library. New York: Time, Inc., 1964.

Massy, William F., and Charles A. Goldman. *The Production and Utilization of Science and Engineering Doctorates in the United States.* Stanford, Calif.: Stanford Institute for Higher Education Research, 1995.

McCullough, David. *Truman.* New York: Simon & Schuster, 1992.

Merrill, Stephen. "Keeping America's Economy on Track." *The Scientist,* August 30, 1999.

Miller, Jon D. *Public Understanding of Science and Technology in OECD Countries: A Comparative Analysis.* Paper presented at the OECD Symposium on Public Understanding of Science, Tokyo, November 5, 1996.

———. *The Public Understanding of Science and Technology in the United States 1990: A Report to the National Science Foundation, Public Opinion Laboratory.* DeKalb: Northern Illinois University, 1991.

Moore, John H. "Public Understanding of Science." *American Scientist,* November–December 1998.

Morrison, Philip, and Phylis Morrison. "100 or So Books That Shaped a Century of Science." *The Scientist,* November–December 1999.

Mowery, David C. "The Bush Report After Fifty Years—Blueprint or Relic?" In *Science for the 21st Century: The Bush Report Revisited,* ed. Claude Barfield. Washington, D.C.: AEI Press, 1997.

Mukerji, Chandra. *A Fragile Power: Scientists and the State.* Princeton, N.J.: Princeton University Press, 1989.

Mullis, Kary. *Dancing Naked in the Mind Field.* New York: Pantheon Books, 1998.

National Academy of Sciences. *Allocating Federal Funds for Science and Technology.* Washington, D.C.: National Academy Press, 1995.

———. *Forecasting Demand and Supply of Doctoral Scientists and Engineers: Report of a Workshop on Methodology* (Office of Scientific and Engineering Personnel). Washington, D.C.: National Academy Press, 2000.

———. *The Government Role in Civilian Technology: Building a New Alliance.* Washington, D.C.: National Academy Press, 1992.

———. *Harnessing Science and Technology for America's Economic Future: National and Regional Priorities.* Washington, D.C.: National Academy Press, 1999.

———. *Improving the Use of Science, Technology, and Health Expertise in US Foreign Policy: A Preliminary Report, 1998.* National Research Council Committee on the Science, Technology, and Health Aspects of the Foreign Policy Agenda of the United States (Robert A. Frosch, chairman).

———. *International Benchmarking of U.S. Immunology Research.* Washington, D.C.: National Academy Press, 2000.

———. *Observations on the President's Fiscal Year 2000 Federal Science and Technology Budget.* Washington, D.C.: National Academy Press, 1999. Also in Research and Development FY 2000, AAAS, 1999.

———. *The Pervasive Role of Science, Technology, and Health in Foreign Policy: Imperatives for the State Department.* Washington, D.C.: National Academy Press, 1999.

———. "The Presidential Appointment Process," National Academy of Sciences, 2000.

———. *Reshaping the Graduate Education of Scientists and Engineers.* Washington, D.C.: National Academy Press, 1995.

———. *Scientific Opportunities and Public Needs: Improving Priority Setting and Public Input at the National Institutes of Health.* Washington, D.C.: National Academy Press, 1998.

———. *Securing America's Industrial Strength.* Washington, D.C.: National Academy Press, 1999.

———. *Trends in the Early Careers of Life Scientists.* Washington, D.C.: National Academy Press, 1998.

National Aeronautics and Space Administration. *Exploring the Unknown: Selected Documents in the History of the U.S. Civil Space Program,* vols. 1–3, ed. John M. Logsdon. Washington, D.C.: U.S. Government Printing Office, 1995, 1996, 1998.

National Institutes of Health. *Report to the Advisory Committee to the Director, NIH, from the Office for the Protection from Research Risks Review Board,* Bethesda, Md.: Office for Protection from Research Risks, National Institutes of Health, 1999.

National Science Board. Commission on the Future of the National Science Foundation, proceedings, 1992. (Unpublished transcript, in NSB files.)

———. *The Competitive Strength of U.S. Industrial Science and Technology: Strategic Issues,* report of the NSB Committee on Industrial Support for R&D (NSB 92-138). Washington, D.C.: National Science Foundation, 1992.

———. *Environmental Science and Engineering for the 21st Century: The Role of the National Science Foundation, 1999* (NSB 99-140). Washington, D.C.: National Science Foundation, 2000.

———. *A Foundation for the 21st Century: A Progressive Framework for the National Science Foundation.* Washington, D.C.: National Science Foundation, November 20, 1992.

———. *Government Funding of Scientific Research, A Working Paper of the National Science Board* (NSB 97-186). Washington, D.C.: U.S. Government Printing Office, 1997.

———. *In Support of Basic Research* (NSB 93-127). Washington, D.C.: U.S. Government Printing Office, 1993.

———. *Science Indicators 1972* (NSB 73-1). Washington, D.C.: U.S. Government Printing Office, 1972.

———. *Science Indicators 1976* (NSB 77-1). Washington, D.C.: U.S. Government Printing Office, 1976.

———. *Science Indicators, 1980* (NSB 81-1). Washington, D.C.: U.S. Government Printing Office, 1980.

———. *Science Indicators: The 1985 Report* (NSB 85-1). Washington, D.C.: U.S. Government Printing Office, 1985.

———. *Science & Engineering Indicators, 1991* (NSB-91-1). Washington, D.C.: U.S. Government Printing Office, 1991.

———. *Science & Engineering Indicators, 1998* (NSB-98-1). Washington, D.C.: U.S. Government Printing Office, 1998.

———. *Science & Engineering Indicators 2000,* vols. 1 and 2 (NSB-00-1). Washington, D.C.: U.S. Government Printing Office, 2000.

National Science Foundation. *Data Brief, 1997* (NSF 97-305).

———. *Data Brief, 1997* (NSF 97-328).

———. *Data Brief, 1998* (NSF 98-325).

———. *Directory of Federal Research and Development Installations for the Year Ending June 30, 1969* (NSF 70-23).

———. *Federal R&D Funding by Budget Function: Fiscal Years 1998–2000* (NSF 00-303), 1999.

———. *Federal Support to Universities, Colleges, and Selected Non-Profit Institutions, Fiscal Year 1978* (NSF 80-312).

———. *Infrastructure: The Capital Requirements for Academic Research, Division of Policy Research and Analysis* (PRA Report 87-3), 1987.

———. *International Science and Technology Data Update 1986* (NSF 86-307).

———. *Issue Brief, Counting the S&E Workforce—It's Not Easy* (NSF 99-34), 1999.

———. *Issue Brief, How Has the Field Mix of Academic R&D Changed?* (NSF 99-309), 1999.

———. *NSF in a Changing World: The National Science Foundation's Strategic Plan* (NSF 95-24), 1995.

———. *National Patterns of R&D Resources, 1996* (NSF 96-333).

———. *National Patterns of R&D Resources, 1998* (NSF-99-335).

———. *National Science Foundation Long-Range Plan FY 1989–1993* (NSF 88-56), 1988.

———. *Retention of the Best Science and Engineering Graduates in Science and Engineering* (NSF 99-321), 1999.

———. *Science & Engineering Degrees, 1966–1995* (NSF 97-335).

———. *Science and Engineering Doctorate Awards: 1997* (NSF 99-323).

———. *Shaping the Future: New Expectations for Undergraduate Education in Science, Mathematics, Engineering and Technology* (NSF 96-139), 1996.

———. *The State of Academic Science and Engineering* (NSF 90-35), NSF Division of Policy Research and Analysis, 1989.

Nelson, Deborah, and Rick Weiss. "How We Uncovered the Hidden Fatality in a Clinical Trial." *ScienceWriters* (National Association of Science Writers), spring 2000.

New York Academy of Sciences. *The Crisis Facing American Science: A Preliminary Report on the Effect of Decreased Federal Support of Scientific Research and Education.* Conference proceedings, 1968.

Nixon, Richard M. *The Memoirs of Richard Nixon.* New York: Grosset & Dunlap, 1978.

Nye, Bill. "The Marks of a Good Exhibit? Few Words, Flying Sparks." *New York Times,* April 21, 1999.

Office of Management and Budget. *Budget of the United States Government. Fiscal Year 1993.* Washington, D.C.: U.S. Government Printing Office, 1993.

Office of Science and Technology Policy, Executive Office of the President. *Research Misconduct: A New Definition and New Procedures for Federal Research Agencies.* Fact sheet, 1999 (informationostp.eop.gov).

———. *Technology for America's Growth: A New Direction to Build Economic Strength.* White House paper, 1993.

Office of Technology Assessment, U.S. Congress. *Anti-Satellite Weapons, Countermeasures, and Arms Control,* 1985. Reprinted as *Strategic Defenses* (Princeton, N.J.: Princeton University Press, 1986).

———. *Ballistic Missile Defense Technologies,* 1985.

———. *Demographic Trends and the Scientific and Engineering Work Force: A Technical Memorandum,* 1985.

———. *Proposal Pressure in the 1980s: An Indicator of Stress on the Federal Research System.* Daryl E. Chubin, staff paper, 1990.

Ornstein, Norman J., et al. *Vital Statistics on Congress: 1997–1998.* Congressional Quarterly, 1998.

"Overoptimism about Cancer." Unsigned editorial. *The Lancet,* January 15, 2000.

Paine, Thomas O. *The Mars Project.* Urbana: University of Illinois Press, 1991.

Panofsky, Wolfgang K. H. "Memories of Casting a Wide *Nyet* at Geneva Talks." Letter to the editor. *Physics Today,* August 1988.

Parkinson, C. Northcote. *Parkinson's Law or the Pursuit of Progress,* London: John Murray, 1961 edition.

Pielke, Roger A., Jr., and Bradford Byerly Jr. "Terminology and Science Literacy Issues Extend the Debate on Revamping Science's Relation to Society." Letter to the editor. *Physics Today,* August 1998.

Podhoretz, John. *Hell of a Ride: Backstage at the White House Follies 1989–1993.* New York: Simon & Schuster, 1993.

Poundstone, William. *Carl Sagan: A Life in the Cosmos.* New York: Henry Holt, 1999.

Press, Frank. "Growing Up in the Golden Age of Science." *Annual Review of Earth and Planetary Sciences,* 1995.

Price, Don K. *The Scientific Estate.* Cambridge: Harvard University Press, Belknap Press, 1965.

Price, Derek J. de Solla. *Little Science, Big Science.* New York: Columbia University Press, 1963.

Putnam, Robert D. *Bowling Alone: Civic Disengagement in America*. New York: Simon & Schuster, 2000.

Rennie, Drummond. "Fair Conduct and Fair Reporting of Clinical Trials." *JAMA*, November 10, 1999.

Rosenberg, Leon. "Research Is in Ruins." *New York Times*, September 2, 1990.

Ruksznis, Elizabeth. "Giving Psychology Away." *Observer* (American Psychological Society), January 1999.

Sanders, Stephanie A., and June Machover Reinisch. "Would You Say You 'Had Sex' If. . . ?" *JAMA*, January 20, 1999.

Savage, James D. *Funding Science in America: Congress, Universities, and the Politics of the Academic Pork Barrel*. Cambridge: Cambridge University Press, 1999.

Schilling, Warner R. "Scientists, Foreign Policy, and Politics." In *Scientists and National Policy Making*, ed. Robert Gilpin and Christopher Wright. New York: Columbia University Press, 1964. Revision of a paper by Schilling in *American Political Science Review*, June 1962.

Schwartz, Stephen I., ed. *Atomic Audit: The Costs and Consequences of U.S. Nuclear Weapons Since 1940*. Washington, D.C.: Brookings Institution Press, 1998.

Sigma Xi Forum. *Vannevar Bush II—Science for the 21st Century: Why Should Federal Dollars Be Spent to Support Scientific Research?* Sigma Xi, 1995.

"Significant Books of the Last 75 Years." *Foreign Affairs*, September/October 1997.

Singer, Maxine (president). *Annual Report*. Carnegie Institution of Washington, 1994.

———. Address at Inauguration of David Baltimore as President of the California Institute of Technology, in *Engineering & Science*, no. 1, 1998.

Smith, Bruce L. R. *The Advisers: Scientists in the Policy Process*. Washington, D.C.: Brookings, 1992.

Smith, Hedrick. *The Power Game: How Washington Works*. New York: Random House, 1988.

Snow, C. P. *The Two Cultures and a Second Look*. New York: Mentor Books, 1964.

Stent, Gunther H. *The Coming of the Golden Age: A View of the End of Progress*. Garden City, N.Y.: Natural History Press, 1969.

Stockman, David A. *The Triumph of Politics*. New York: Harper & Row, 1986.

Stokes, Donald E. *Pasteur's Quadrant: Basic Science and Technological Innovation*. Washington, D.C.: Brookings Institution Press, 1997.

Stone, Jeremy. *Every Man Should Try: Adventures of a Public Interest Activist*. New York: Public Affairs Press, 1999, p. 73.

Thomas, Anne. "Public Support for Medical Research—How Deep, How Enduring?" *Academic Medicine*, February 1998.

Tomkins, Calvin. *Eric Hoffer: An American Odyssey*. New York: Dutton, 1969.

Union of Concerned Scientists. *The Fallacy of Star Wars*. New York: Vintage Books, 1984.

U.S. House. *Authorization for NSF*. Report No. 95-993, June 1, 1978.

U.S. House Appropriations Committee. Subcommittee for Department of Transportation and Related Agencies. *Appropriations for Fiscal 1971: Hearing*. 91st Cong., 2d sess., April 15–17, 1970.

U.S. House Budget Committee. *Establishing Priorities in Science Funding: Hearing*. 102d Cong., 1st sess. July 11, 1991.

U.S. House Energy and Commerce Committee, Subcommittee on Oversight and Investigations. *Financial Responsibility at Universities: Hearings*. 102d Cong., 1st sess. March 13 and May 9, 1991.

U.S. House Foreign Affairs Committee, Subcommittee on Europe and the Middle East. *United States-Soviet Scientific Exchanges: Hearing*. 99th Cong., 2d sess. July 31, 1986.

U.S. House Government Operations Committee. *Costs, Justification, and Benefits of NASA's Space Station: Hearing*. 102d Cong., 1st sess. May 1, 1991.

U.S. House Science Committee. *Restructuring the Federal Science Establishment: Hearings*. 104th Cong., 1st sess. June 28, 1995.

———. *Unlocking Our Future: Toward A New National Science Policy*. Report to Congress by the House Committee on Science. 105th Cong., 2d sess. September 24, 1998.

U.S. House Science, Space, and Technology Committee. *Academic Earmarks: Hearings*. 103d Cong., 2d sess. Part 3, 1994.

———. *1988 NSF Authorization: Hearings*. 100th Cong., 1st sess. February 1 and 25 and March 11 and 24, 1987.

———. *Report of the Task Force on the Health of Research*. 102d Cong., 2d sess. July 1992.

———. *University Research Facilities Revitalization Act: Hearings*. 100th Cong., 1st sess. June 25, 1987.

U.S. House Science, Space, and Technology Committee. Subcommittee on Investigations and Oversight. *Projecting Science and Engineering Personnel Requirements for the 1990s: How Good Are the Numbers? Hearings*. 102d Cong., 2d sess. April 8, 1992.

U.S. House Science and Technology Committee. *Bibliography of Studies and Reports on Science Policy and Related Topics, 1945–1985*. 99th Cong., 2d sess. Task Force on Science Policy, 1986.

———. *Scientists and Engineers: Supply and Demand: Hearings*. 99th Cong., 1st sess. July 9–11 and 23–25, 1985.

U.S. Senate Appropriations Committee, Subcommittee for the Departments of Veterans Affairs and Housing and Urban Development. *Appropriations for Fiscal 1993*. Report, 102d Cong., 2d sess., July 23, 1992.

U.S. Senate Committee on Commerce, Science, and Transportation. *National Science Foundation Director's Views on Science and Technology Policy: Hearing*. 101st Cong., 2d sess. August 2, 1990.

Vaughn, John C., and Robert C. Rosenzweig. "Heading Off a Ph.D. Shortage." *Issues in Science and Technology*, winter 1990–91.

White, Robert M. "Science, Engineering, and the Sorcerer's Apprentice." Address to annual meeting, National Academy of Engineering, October 2, 1990.

White, Theodore H. *The Making of the President 1964*. New York: Atheneum, 1965.

Wilson, Edward O. "Scientists, Scholars, Knaves and Fools." *American Scientist*, January–February 1998.

Wilson, Robert R. Testimony before the Congressional Joint Committee on Atomic Energy. 91st Cong., 1st sess. April 16, 1969.

Wood, Robert C. "The Rise of an Apolitical Elite." In *Scientists and National Policy Making*, ed. Robert Gilpin and Christopher Wright. New York: Columbia University Press, 1964.

Zachary, G. Pascal. *Endless Frontier: Vannevar Bush, Engineer of the American Century*. New York: The Free Press, 1997.

Zuckerman, Sir Solly. *Beyond the Ivory Tower: The Frontiers of Public and Private Science*. New York: Taplinger Publishing Co. 1971.

American Physical Society: anti-budget cuts lobbying efforts, 448; history of political activism, 333–34; on merits of SSC, 409; report on NSF commission, 385n16; SDI study, 288; trend away from social involvement and, 337
American Psychological Society, 454
Andelin, John, 136–37
Anderson, E. Ratcliffe, 355
Anderson, Philip, 408–10
Angell, Marcia, 353–54, 357, 358
Annals of Improbable Research, 10
antiballistic missile (ABM) program, 167. *See also* Strategic Defense Initiative (SDI)
Apollo, 98
Apple, Martin, 255
Applied Physics Laboratory, 189
appropriations: constituents' interests and, 203; definition, 70n9; earmark process. *See* earmarks
Argonne National Laboratory, 189
Arms Control and Disarmament Agency (ACDA), 167
Armstrong, John, 378
ARPA (Advanced Research Projects Agency), 31
Associated Universities, Inc., 189
Association of American Medical Colleges (AAMC): anti-budget cuts lobbying efforts, 447; call for ethics guide, 352; president's salary, 196; report on resistance to change, 28–29; territorial protection activities, 37
Association of American Universities (AAU): anti-budget cuts lobbying efforts, 448; earmarked funds collection, 201–2; earmarking opposition, 200; federal research support to members, 188–89; indirect costs reduction opposition, 82–83; status and presence in Washington, 194–95
Association of University Technology Managers, 16

Atkinson, Richard C., 122
Atomic Energy Commission (AEC), 48, 49, 244–45
atom smasher. *See* Superconducting Super Collider (SSC)
ATP. *See* Advanced Technology Program
Auden, W.H., 25
Augustine, Norman R., 306
Aylesworth, Kevin, 128

Baker, James, 318
Baldwin, Wendy, 223
Ballistic Missile Defense Organization, 332
ballot-box politics. *See* elective politics and science
Baltimore, David, 62, 71, 460
Barrie, Joel L., 137
Bartlett, Roscoe: block to NSF name change, 34–35; novelty of "science-candidates," 266
Barzun, Jacques, 261
basic vs. applied science argument: Vannevar Bush and, 45–46, 46n5; distinction between, 4n1; federal obligations for basic research (1970–99), 488 table 6, 489 table 7; industry's reluctance to finance basic research, 465; military funding of applied, 426; military funding of basic, 48–49, 50–51; NSF board's basic research reaffirmation, 400–401; senate hearing on basic research need, 421, 421–22n5. *See also* technology and applied research support
Bayh-Dole Act (1980), 15
Bay of Pigs, 281
behavioral sciences. *See* social and behavioral sciences
Bement, Arden L., Jr., 370
Berger, Samuel R., 346
Berkner, Lloyd, 312, 322
Bernthal, Frederick M., 130, 131, 397
Bethe, Hans, 288